Nathalie Pré...

Fourth Edition

TORONTO
FUN
PLACES

The family-tested guide to
year-round fun in the GTA
and Southern Ontario

Word
— of —
Mouth
Production

This book is dedicated
to my husband and partner in crime.

Published by Word-of-Mouth Production
299 Booth Avenue
Toronto, Ontario, M4M 2M7, Canada
Tel.: (416) 462-0670   Fax: (416) 462-0682
mail@torontofunplaces.com

www.torontofunplaces.com

Writing and photos: **Nathalie Prézeau**
Illustrations: **Johanne Pepin**
Research: **Isabelle Boucher, Cristina Bregar**
Proofreading: **Kerstin McCutcheon**
Design and layout: **Publisher Friendly Inc.** (416) 553-3817
Printing: **Marquis Book Printing Inc.** (418) 246-5666

Library and Archives Canada Cataloguing in Publication

Prézeau, Nathalie, 1960 –
Toronto Fun Places: the family-tested guide to year-round fun
in the GTA and Southern Ontario – Fourth Edition

Includes index.
ISBN 978-0-9684432-4-8
Third edition published in 2004
Second edition published in 2001
First edition published in 1999 under title:
Toronto: the family-tested guide to fun places

1. Family recreation – Ontario – Toronto Region – Guidebooks.
2. Toronto Region (Ont.) – Guidebooks. I. Title.

FC3097.18.P74 2008   917.13'541045   C2008-900748-4

A word from the author

I started the research for **Toronto Fun Places** in 1995 with my 2-year-old. The little blond guy who graced the pages of my previous editions is now 14 years old and 5 foot 10, but I can still bribe him into joining a family outing as long as I promise an all-you-can-eat buffet along the road. My youngest, the 10-year-old, will go anywhere as long as she can bring a friend. So, here I am, with a fourth edition.

The previous edition was already 480 pages thick so I had to drop three chapters (Charity, Getaways and The Totally Arbitrary Section) in order to make room for new material. All is not lost. These chapters will find their way on to my website **www.torontofunplaces.com**, along with top 10 suggestions, photo galleries, book reviews and many additions.

In this new edition, I have grouped all the water activities (including the beaches) under a new **Water Fun** chapter. The **Machines** and **Museums** chapters now include sub-categories. All the parades have their own section in the **Amusement Corner** chapter.

I'm especially proud of the new **What's Around The Subway Stations** chapter, in which I describe anything interesting (for an adult with kids) within a 10-minute walk of every TTC subway station. That should help you go green or save on the parking fees! I've also created an inspiring **Urban Strolls** colour section which fully illustrates how vibrant Toronto has become. It is the perfect tool to play a tourist in your own city or to pose as a savvy guide to visitors.

It is always a pleasure to search, find and share the excitement with you.

Sincerely,

Nathalie Prézeau

TABLE OF CONTENTS

WHAT'S AROUND THE SUBWAY STATIONS

URBAN STROLLS

About the TTC

- FUN PLACES bearing the bus symbol offer TTC public transportation (subway, bus or streetcar) in their vicinity. Those without might still be reached by another local public transportation system.

- Check your Yellow Pages for a subway map and a map showing the major TTC surface routes, with their numbers. You will need the route number to find out the itinerary and schedule through the TTC automatic telephone system or on their web site **www.ttc.ca.**

- To find out about the TTC access to a FUN PLACE, call TTC infoline **(416) 393-4636** (press "0" to reach someone in person from 8 am to 6 pm).

CALENDAR OF EVENTS

JANUARY
New Year's Day Polar Bear Dip 359
  On New Year's Day
Monster Jam (Rogers Centre) 336
  One weekend in mid-January

FEBRUARY
Model Railroad Club 220
  Usually last 3 Sundays of February

MARCH
Bugfeast (Wings of Paradise) 69
  During the March Break
Flapjack Olympics (Mountsberg) 149
  One day during Maple Syrup Days
Maple Syrup Festival (Bronte Creek) 309
  March weekends and March Break
MARCH BREAK LISTING 156
March Through Time (Fort York) 379
  March Break
Spring Fling (Rogers Centre) 336
  March Break
St. Patrick's Day Parade 38
  Sunday closest to March 17
Ultimate Children's Party (Hamilton) 212
  One weekend in March
Warkworth Maple Syrup Festival 152
  2nd weekend in March
Wizard World 33
  Weekends before and after
  March Break weekdays

MARCH-APRIL
All About Pets Show 60
  Usually Easter weekend
Beaches Lions Club Easter Parade 39
  Easter Sunday
EASTER LISTING 157
Easter Procession in Little Italy 40
  Easter Friday
Maple Syrup Time 146-153
  Weekends and March Break
  weekdays, may start early March
  and last until mid-April depending
  on when Easter falls
Sweet Water Season (Crawford) 388
  In March and April

APRIL
Float your fanny down the Ganny 229
  Usually 1st Saturday in April
  or following Easter
Hot Docs 94
  10 consecutive days in April
Sprockets Film Festival 94
  10 consecutive days from mid-April

Vaisakhi Celebration 100
  Usually in April
Four Winds Kite Festival 211
  Last weekend in May
  or 1st weekend in April

MAY
Aberfoyle Junction 222
  Usually first 2 weekends in May
Carassauga 102
  Last weekend of May
Doors Open 114
  Usually during the month of May
Fiddlers' Contest (Black Creek) 383
  Victoria Day
Forsythia Festival 128
  1st Sunday of May
Lilac Celebration (Burlington) 282
  Usually on the last 2 weekends
  of May
VICTORIA DAY LISTING 158
Wings & Wheels Heritage Festival 209
  Last Saturday of May

JUNE
Battle of Black Creek 383
  Father's Day weekend
  (3rd weekend in June)
Battle of Stoney Creek 389
  Usually 1st weekend in June
Canadian Int'l Military Tattoo 24
  Usually 2nd weekend in June
Fly Fest (Hamilton) 212
  Father's Day weekend
  (including 3rd Sunday in June)
London Children's Festival 240
  5 consecutive days including 1st
  or 2nd weekend in June
Markham Village Music Festival 385
  Usually on the 3rd weekend in June
Oakville Waterfront Festival 29
  Always on the weekend one full
  week before Canada Day
Pride Parade 36
  Last Sunday in June
Spadina Strawberry Festival 381
  3rd or last Sunday in June
**Streetsville Bread and Honey Festival
(Mississauga)** 329
  Usually on 1st weekend of June
Woofstock 54
  Usually 1st weekend in June

JUNE-JULY
Dusk Dance 82
  Several evenings in a row,
  end of June, early July

JULY

Canada Day at Black Creek 383
Canada Day
Canada Day at Downsview Park 293
Canada Day
CANADA DAY LISTING 159-160
Carabram 102
Usually on the weekend
after Canada Day
CHIN Picnic 33
Canada Day weekend
Chinguacousy Canada Day 297
Canada Day
Cobourg Waterfront Festival 415
Canada Day weekend
Collingwood Elvis Festival 24
4 days, end of July
Family Fishing Weekend 345
Usually on 2nd weekend in July
Junior Caribana 37
Usually 2 Saturdays prior to
Caribana Parade
Richmond Hill Live Steamers 221
Usually the weekend
after Canada Day
Shakespeare Under the Stars 148
Usually on the mid-July Friday
and Saturday
Strawberry Festival (Downey's Farm) 133
Canada Day
Strawberry Festival (Watson Farms) 129
Canada Day
Strawberry Social (Scarborough) 291
Canada Day
Sunfest 51
Usually 2nd weekend in July
The Fringe 110
12 consecutive days including
1st week in July
Toronto Ribfest 160
Canada Day weekend
Wakestock (Toronto Islands) 400
One weekend in July
Warkworth Western Festival 24
Usually 1st weekend in July
Today's Parent Kidsummer 28
Daily in July and August

AUGUST

Art Naturally Festival (Scarborough) 281
Usually on weekend following
Simcoe Day
Brantford Elvis Festival 24
Usually on the weekend before
Labour Day
Canadian International Air Show 19
Last weekend of August or
1st weekend in September

Caribana Parade 37
Saturday of 1st weekend in August
CNE at Exhibition Place 32
Mid-August to Labour Day
Fergus Scottish Festival 24
Normally around the 2nd weekend
in August
Kingston Sheep Dog Trials 24
Usually 2nd weekend in August
London Balloon Festival 24, 51
Normally on the 1st weekend
in August
Sandcastle Festival 24, 415
Usually 1st weekend in August
SIMCOE DAY LISTING 158
Summer Festival (Brampton) 297
Simcoe Day
Toronto Buskerfest 107
On the weekend before Labour Day
Tugfest (Parry Sound) 317
One weekend in August

AUGUST-SEPTEMBER

Markham Fair 24
Last weekend of August or
1st weekend in September

SEPTEMBER

Anne of Green Gables Day 390
Usually on the 3rd Sunday
in September
Auto Classic Car Show (Markham) 385
On Sunday after Labour Day
weekend
Cabbagetown Arts & Crafts Sale 128
Weekend after Labour Day
**Children's Powwow at Dufferin
Grove 289**
3rd or 4th Saturday of September
Fiesta del Sol 51
Labour Day weekend
Industrial Alliance Kitefest 210
Usually mid-September weekend
**Memories of Summer Fireworks Display
(Wasaga) 420**
Sunday during Labour Day
weekend
Monarch Weekend (Presqu'ile P. P.) 310
Labour Day weekend
**Musical Illumination at
Sharon Temple 122**
1st Friday of September
Pioneer Festival (Black Creek) 383
2nd or 3rd weekend of September
Port Perry Fair 30
On Labour Day weekend
Powwow (Sainte Marie) 394
A weekend in September

Queen West Art Crawl 87
One weekend in September
Richmond Hill Live Steamers 221
Usually weekend after Labour Day
Riverdale Farm Fall Festival 128
Weekend after Labour Day
Six Nations Annual Fall Fair 98
Weekend following Labour Day
Soap Box Derby 215
Mid-September Saturday
Teddy Bear Run 224
On a Sunday mid-September
Wonders of the Earth 273
2nd weekend after Labour Day
Word On The Street 91
Last Sunday of September

SEPTEMBER-OCTOBER
Blessing of the Animals 119
One day end of September
or early October
Fall Harvest Season (Mountsberg) 298
End of September to end of October
Nuit blanche 108
Last Saturday in September or
1st in October (2008: October 4)
Toronto French Book Fair 91
One weekend between end of
September and mid-October

OCTOBER
Apple Festival (Watson Farms) 129
Weekend before Thanksgiving
Boo at the Zoo 59
2 weekends in October
Fall Colours (ski lift ride) 387
Thanksgiving weekend
Fire Prevention Week 213
2nd week of October
Ghosts of the Garrison (Fort York) 379
A few nights in October
Halloween Haunt (Wonderland) 21
Mid-October, Fridays to Sundays
and October 31
Halloween Haunted Car Barn 226
Some nights in October
HALLOWEEN LISTING 163-164
Haunted Adventures at
Chappell Farms 144
Usually every night of the last week
in October
Haunted Mazes Nights at Hanes
Corn Farm 139
Every night in October
Howling Hootenanny (Black Creek) 383
Usually the weekend prior to
Halloween

Lantern Tours (Stoney Creek) 389
In October
Magic Hill Haunted Adventure 164
Fridays, Saturdays and Sundays
in October
October Night of Dread Parade
at Dufferin Grove 289
Around October 31
Oktoberfest Thanksgiving Parade 41
Thanksgiving Monday
Pumpkinfest Parade 42
2nd last Saturday in October
Pumpkinland (Whittamore's Farm) 129
Weekends from end of September
to Halloween
Screamfest 65
3 weekends in October
Screemers 33
13 consecutive nights ending
October 31
THANKSGIVING LISTING 162
Aberfoyle Junction 222
Usually the 3 weekends following
Thanksgiving
Diwali (Hindu Festival of lights) 100
Falls on a new moon day in the
month of October or November
(2008: October 28)

NOVEMBER
Canadian Aboriginal Festival 97
Usually starts last Friday in
November, to Sunday
Christmas Train Show 219
Usually one weekend
end of November
Markham's Santa Claus Parade 385
Last Saturday in November
Oakville Santa Claus Parade 43
3rd Saturday of November
Parade of Lights (Milton) 386
One night in November
Royal Winter Fair 126
10 consecutive days usually
including the 1st week of November
Swedish Christmas Festival 25
Normally last or 2nd last weekend
in November
Toronto Santa Claus Parade 43
3rd Sunday in November
CHRISTMAS TRADITIONS 165-184
ChristmasTown (Mountsberg) 298
Weekends from end of November
to right before Christmas
Lunch with Santa (Downey's Farm) 133
On weekends from late November
to before Christmas

NOVEMBER-DECEMBER

Mennonite Christmas Festival 25
On last weekend in November
or 1st in December
Pioneer Christmas 177
From mid-November to December 31
Twelve Trees of Christmas 171
Usually mid-November
to early December
Walk to Bethlehem 175, 386
4 consecutive evenings end of
November or early December
Niagara's Winter Festival of Lights 184
Mid-November to mid-January
Ross Petty Productions 180
Late November to early January

DECEMBER

**Breakfast with Santa at
Casa Loma** 120, 167
3 Sundays prior to Christmas
**Breakfast with Santa
at Arcadian Court** 167
3 weekends prior to Christmas
**Brunch with Santa at Wings of
Paradise** 69
One weekend, mid-December
Carolling in the Park (Toronto) 318
On the 2nd Tuesday
before Christmas
Cavalcade of lights 170
The 4 Saturdays prior to Christmas
Chanukah Carnival 236
One day during the 8-day Jewish
Holiday in December
Christmas by Lamplight 177
At least 3 Saturday evenings
in December
Christmas Treat Walk 59
Boxing Day (December 26)
Crèche Exhibit/St. James Cathedral 173
Daily, early December to
December 22
Footprints of Christmas 175
1st weekend in December
Howl'n Hikes (Bronte Creek) 309
December 31, early evening
Kensington Festival of Lights 183
December 21 at around 5:30 pm
Lakeshore Santa Claus Parade 43
1st Saturday of December
**New Year's Eve Hoopla
at Mountsberg** 298
New Year's Eve, 6 pm to 9 pm
**New Year's Eve Countdown
at Toronto Zoo** 185
New Year's Eve at 9 pm

New Year's Countdown (CN Tower) 170
New Year's Eve at 12 pm
**New Year's Eve Countdown at Nathan
Phillips Square** 185
New Year's Eve at 12 pm
NEW YEAR'S EVE LISTING 185
Santa Train (Tottenham) 225
Normally the first 2 weekends
in December
**Sharing Our Traditions
at Spadina Museum** 381
3 Sundays in December
Sing-Along Messiah 182
At 2 pm on the Sunday before
Christmas
The Christmas Story 172
Usually the 3 weekends before
Christmas, Friday and Saturday
evenings
The Night Before Christmas 175
On December 24
The Nutcracker 181
Throughout December
Victorian Christmas 176
1st Sunday of December
**Winter Festival at Humber
Arboretum** 294
Usually 1st Saturday in December

DECEMBER-JANUARY

Burlington Festival of Lights 166
From early December
to early January
**Mystery in Paradise
at Wings of Paradise** 69
During the Christmas Break
**Village Lantern Tours at Markham
Museum** 385
Many days around Christmas
until early February

WARNING!

Most of the attractions
in this guide are closed
on the following dates:
December 24, 25, 26, 31
and January 1.

Always call ahead
to find out if they're open
on these dates.

_____

_____

_____

_____

_____

_____

_____

_____

_____

_____

Call your friends and go to a fun place together.

Name	Phone	E-mail

PARENT RESOURCES

EVENT CALENDARS

I suggest you browse through the event calendars of these websites to find the one that better suits your style. You can then check it from time to time to see what's going on. When an attraction catches your attention, look for it in this guide (**Toronto Fun Places**) for my description, photos, tips and nearby attractions. If it is not included, send me an e-mail to let me know. I could add it to my list of places to visit for the next edition or to my website.

www.toronto4kids.com
www.kiddingaroundtoronto.com
www.lifewithkids.ca
www.cityparent.ca
www.theparentlink.ca
www.helpwevegotkids.com
www.torontolife.com
www.toronto.com
www.torontopubliclibrary.ca

HELP
www.parenthelpline.ca
1-888-603-9100
This service is the parents' arm of the great **Kids Help Phone**. It is a national, bilingual telephone and on-line service you can turn to for confidential support from trained counsellors. Talking helps!

Parent Bookstore
www.parentbookstore.com
(416) 537-8334
201 Harbord St., Toronto (just east of Bathurst St, south of Bloor St.).
The only bookstore focusing on books aiming to help parents do a better job. They offer thousands of titles but their main asset is the expertise of their staff.

CABIN FEVER
www.canadiansitter.ca
A website you can subscribe to in order to have access to hundreds of names of babysitters in your area. You need to subscribe to access the phone numbers on the list. You can subscribe for three months for $40, or pay $80 for a full year access to their network.
www.mumnet.ca
A network of support and friendship through weekly meetings including exercise, discussion and childcare.
www.momsinthecity.com
Grown-up outings with the babies (and accompanying childcare service): luncheons, gallery tours, neighbourhood walks, art classes and more.

GETAWAYS
www.campsearch.com
Includes camps from 32 countries.
www.hotelfun4kids.com
About family travel in Canada, US and around the world.

WEB MAGAZINES
www.todaysparent.ca
The source on parenting.
www.yummymummyclub.ca
Mag for mothers looking for adult stimulation... as well as parenting tips.
www.savvymom.ca
Newsletter including articles with tips on home and family life.

REFERENCES
www.cinemaclock.com
It is my favourite movie listing. They do listings for all major cities in Canada. Go to Toronto, then search by movie or by theatre (they specify when the presentation is for parents and babies).
www.toronto.ca/ttc
416-393-4636
The place to get information on the TTC routes and schedule. Call this number to find out how to get to an attraction from your place.

General tips about
Amusement Corner:

- Always check height requirements before waiting in line! Most
amusement parks are really strict
about these and no, fluffing your
kid's hair over her head won't do.
- Be ready to spend a lot on all
the extra costs in most amusement
parks: The cost of food in their snack
bars can be double what you would
expect. There's always a popular
attraction with its cost not included
in the admission fee.
- In most cases, if you intend on
visiting a specific attraction more
than twice during the season, consider a season pass.

AMUSEMENT
CORNER

See the **Chinese Lantern Festival** at **Ontario Place** on p. 18.

ONTARIO PLACE

In the first place

Ontario Place is an excellent waterpark as well as theme park. The numerous rides offer adrenaline rushes for young and old. It is also entertaining, with Imax movies and musical shows on different stages. Finally, it is like a conservation area, with paddle boats, large green spaces and the surrounding lake.

For those who have never visited it, Ontario Place's architecture is an attraction in itself. Children enjoy watching people from the bridges linking the huge white pods built atop the water. You'll find the Imax theatre in the sphere attached to the white structure.

Riding one of the paddle boats from Bob's Boat Yard (included with the Play-All-Day pass) is a great way to admire it all. The Play-All-Day pass actually gives visitors unlimited access to all the rides, including the regular Cinesphere screenings (somewhat hard on young eardrums by the way).

Kids like to take control so younger children will love the Mini Bumper Boats (3 years+, 49" max.), while the older ones will want to ride on the bigger boats (48"+), now located on the western side of Ontario Place.

The battery-powered go-karts at the east end were replaced by the Power Wheels Cars, with cars zooming around a specially-designed track. Expect a long line-up. A few other rides located in this section will thrill the younger kids.

At the western end, the O.P. Driving School (for drivers 5-12 years old) comes

with real traffic lights! The smile on their faces...

We really were excited by the Atom Blaster, located a bit further. There, parents become the favourite target for foam balls launched by air cannons. The less combative kids prefer to feed the balls into a huge cannon which eventually will blow them to the ceiling in a spectacular blast. Microkids offers similar fun on a lower scale, for preschoolers.

The H_2O Generation Station is an impressive structure composed of towers linked by tunnels. Some transparent ones are way up high!

In this area is the Wilderness Adventure Ride (42"+): A raft ride through canyons that features animated characters with a final 50-foot drop. The Megamaze is a multi-level labyrinth consisting of 7 mazes with optical illusions, puzzling for younger children. The F/X Adventure Theatre includes a 30-seat motion simulator taking you on a ride.

The Super Slide, next to the Festival Stage by the waterpark, is the perfect way to kill time before the next show, which we always choose to see later in the day when the kids need a rest.

At the time of print, the **Chinese Lantern Festival** was planned for 2008.

TIPS (fun for 2 years +)

• More on **Ontario Place** waterpark on page 430.
• Ground admission is the cheapest way to visit if you just intend on accompanying a young child to the waterpark and to the kiddie rides. It allows you to watch shows on outdoor stages or even the **Canadian International Air Show** and the fireworks. You can always upgrade your ground admission to a Play-All-Day pass on the site if you change your mind.
• A footbridge connects the western tip of Ontario Place to the West entrance. It's a good shortcut back to the parking lot at the west end. There usually is a water shuttle linking both ends of the park. It offers a quick access to the East entrance.
• If you go on the Wilderness Adventure Ride, bring a garbage bag to cover yourself if you want to stay dry!
• Ontario Place offers a few major firework displays. Expect at least one on **Victoria Day** weekend, one on **Canada Day**, and others during the week before or after **Canada Day**. Call for exact dates.
• During the **March Break**, you can see movies at the **Cinesphere** and maybe, like us, see swans on the icy lake! Check the schedule on their website. Free parking.
• There's a free shuttle bus running from **Union Subway Station** during **Ontario Place** operating hours (except for weekdays in June).

Check **www.chineselanternfestival.ca** to see if it will remain in the following years. It is a separate ticketed event (and they will charge the full parking price even if you only plan on attending after the rides are closed), but it truly creates a magical ambience in the western part of Ontario Place, especially when the water is reflecting the lights.

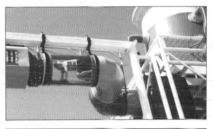

Ontario Place (416) 314-9900 www.ontarioplace.com	**D-3** **Downtown** Toronto 10-min.

Schedule: Open weekends in May and on Victoria Day. Open daily from the first weekend in June until Labour Day, then weekends in September. Attractions open 10 am to 8 pm in July and August. ATTENTION: Shorter hours in June and in the fall!

Admission: Play-All-Day includes the ground admission. It is $33.50/6-64 years, $17.75/seniors and 4-5 years, FREE for children 3 and under (prices vary during CNE). Ground admission alone is $17.75/6-64 years, $11.75/seniors and 4-5 years. If you plan on going more than once ask about their season pass. Parking costs: $12/daytime (reaches $20 after 4:30 pm during special events or CNE).

Directions: 955 Lake Shore Blvd., Toronto (on the waterfront between Strachan Ave. and Dufferin St.).

NEARBY ATTRACTIONS
Harbourfront Centre (10-min.) ...... p. 25
Historic Fort York (5-min.) .... p. 379

CANADA'S WONDERLAND

Do your kids measure up?

Children measuring less than 40 inches tall can access about 40% of the rides and attractions. When they reach 44", two-thirds of the rides become accessible to them. As soon as they're 48" tall, they're allowed on over 80% of Wonderland's 69 attractions and roller coasters.

When my son hit 54", all of a sudden he could go on all the gut-wrenching rides: Drop Zone, Psyclone, Cliffhanger and the likes.

Children's rides

The Candy Factory is a great playground where kids can use up lots of energy. Near it are two areas for children 8 years and under. If your children are comfortable with the Taxi Jam roller coaster in Kidzville (probably too much for children 3 years and under) you might want them to try the Ghoster Coaster (46"+, or 40"+ with an adult) in Hanna-Barbera Land.

Our other favourite rides in these sections include the Frequent Flyers' hot air balloons, the turning cups of the Flavourator and the bumper cars of the Rugrats Toonpike.

Nickelodeon Central is for the very young. Its rides, and most of the other rides in Kidzville and Hanna-Barbera

Land are pretty tame and seem too short to endure long line-ups.

The Zoom Zone features more exciting rides for young thrill-seekers. There's Silver Streak, the long suspended coaster, Blast Off where kids rise and drop on a rocket ship, and Jumpin' Jet, flying riders through looping spins.

In the Medieval Faire is the Speed City Raceway (cars run on 9 hp engines), for riders (58", or 40"+ with an adult).

We love the gorgeous animals on the large Antique Carousel (46"+, or any age with an adult) in the Grande World Exposition of 1890. On the way out, young and old watch with fascination the "crazies" who leap from the top of the Xtreme Sky Flyer tower (48"+), the one you jump off with a bungee cord; a show in itself!

Now, it was my own son with his life hanging by one thread! "You have to try it!" he exclaimed after his jump. Yeah, sure!

Shows

Throughout the summer, there's a host of international festivals going on the various interior and exterior stages.

Aquatic shows are available at Arthur's Baye and professionals dive daily from atop the mountain waterfall.

The Playhouse Theatre in Kidzville usually runs an excellent little musical show several times a day. The theatre is covered and provides welcome shade in the midst of summer.

Furthermore, there's the Paramount Action FX Theatre (46"+), a motion simulator with seats that move in sync with the action on the screen. (There's motionless seating for kids 44" and under.)

More big rides

Our first choice is the Thunder Run, going through the mountain (40"+). It puts you in good spirits for the day! Further on, you're sure to get wet (if you haven't covered yourself with a garbage bag) at the White Water Canyon and the Timberwolf Falls (both 46"+)!

From Splash Works, we can hear the cries (of hysteria, I presume) of thrill-seekers riding at full speed on the Mighty Canadian Minebuster (48"+) and those (of horror, I suspect) of the SkyRider passengers, tracing loops with their feet hanging in the air. For roller coaster fans, there are many other options including the new Tomb Raider in which you are hung under a hang-glider-like structure. A few are accessible to children of 44"+.

TIPS (fun for 3 years +)

• More on **Canada's Wonderland** waterpark on p. 433.

• Canada's Wonderland will please children of all ages but for children measuring under 44", I recommend sticking to **Ontario Place** (p. 12) for a while.

• Consult the table with height requirement on their website (under **Rides & Attractions**). I saw several children crying their hearts out after a long wait for a ride, as they were finding out they weren't tall enough. Since my last edition in 2004, they've readjusted the height requirements, in some cases going from a 40" min. to 46"!

Photo: Courtesy of R.Giddings

• For some years now, we've been able to save $15 off the admission when buying it from one of the sponsors' stores. They change every year, check their website to find out about the current sponsors.

• The best way to enjoy the Wonderland experience is to arrive at opening time and go straight to your favourite ride! Then, spend some time studying the map and schedule of shows, available at the entrance, to plan your day.

• There is a fireworks displays on Sunday of **Victoria Day** weekend at 10:30 pm (no more fireworks on Canada Day).

• They now offer **Halloween Haunt** in October when the park is converted into a "dark playground". It includes nine mazes, a staff of 300 monsters and many regular rides. Not recommended for kids under 12 and better NOT wear costumes (for security reasons). Costs around $27.

• Closest campground is **Yogi Bear's Jellystone Park**, (905) 775-1377, **www.jellystonetoronto.com**. Also check the **Plan a visit** section on Wonderland's website for a list of accommodations offering packages.

Need anything else with that? Every year usually brings a new attraction. For 2008, they promise the Behemoth (Canada's tallest, fastest roller coaster).

Canada's Wonderland • Vaughan (905) 832-7000 www.canadaswonderland.com	C-3 **North** of Toronto 40-min.

Schedule: Open on weekends starting the first Sunday in May right through to Thanksgiving and daily from Victoria Day to Labour Day. Open from 10 am to 10 pm in the summer (closes at 8 pm in Spring and Fall). Also open from mid-October, Friday to Sunday + October 31, 7 pm to midnight for Halloween.

Admission: (taxes not included) approx. $51/7 to 59 years (48"+), $27/3 to 6 years and seniors, FREE for 2 years and under. If you consider going more than once, ask about their season pass! Parking is around $8.

Directions: 9580 Jane St., Vaughan. Take Hwy 401, then Hwy 400 North. Exit Rutherford Rd. (exit #33) eastbound.

NEARBY ATTRACTIONS

PLAYDIUM MISSISSAUGA

Jump-start into adolescence

In awe, my son proceeds into a cold-coloured corridor which leads him under an interstellar-like canopy with noisy machines scattered around. Then, his eye is caught by sculptures reaching towards a black ceiling with coloured dots; luminous floor drawings dance to background music.

I am so terrible at the video games that I keep "dying" within 60 seconds. It's another story for my son and his buddies! They spend a long time competing against each other in the Indy 500 race cars.

The place includes over 200 games. Many are physically fun to ride (and the demos shown on their screens are often entertaining enough for little ones so you won't have to spend a penny): motorcycle, surf, seadoo, cross-country biking, flight simulator.

Last time I visited, my 10-year-old companions were really interested in a soccer game (with ball attached) and basketball.

In the summer, there is a minigolf and a 1.2 km go-kart track awaiting outside. We opted for the latter. Go-kart riders need to be 52"+ and 11 years old (they'll ask you your date of birth!). They also offer seasonal rides.

Last but not least, there's a whole section of games redeeming coupons which can be exchanged for trinkets. Don't grind your teeth, it comes with the territory. I think kids enjoy the machines counting the tickets as much as the games themselves.

Playdium now includes an indoor Sports Dome (accessible from a corridor near the food area). This section offers four bowling lanes, many batting cages and some more games, which you can use with your Play Card.

TIPS (fun for 5 years +)
• Call before you go. All or part of Playdium may be closed for a private function.
• Beware, the noise level is very high!
• Don't hesitate to ask the attendants how the games work. If you have had troubles with a game, they might even credit it for you.
• You may buy snacks and decent fast food on the premises.

NEARBY ATTRACTIONS
Square One (2-min.) .... p. 168
Pearson Int'l Airport (15-min.) ...... p. 206

Playdium Mississauga
• Mississauga
(905) 273-9000
www.playdium.com

D-3
West
of Toronto
35-min.

 Schedule: Open year-round, Monday to Thursday, 12 noon to 11 pm; Friday, 12 noon to 1 am; Saturday, 10 am to 1 am and Sunday, 10 am to 11 pm. Outdoor attractions usually open from Victoria Day to Thanksgiving weekend.

 Admission: On a pay-as-you-play basis debited from your Play Card. Family Power Pack offers 160 credits for $22.50 instead of $25 (min. 3 family members). The average game costs 4-6 credits. Go-kart is $4/lap; $20/8 laps; $3.50/minigolf; $3/per seasonal ride.

Directions: 99 Rathburn Rd., Mississauga (just south of Hwy 403 and west of Hurontario).

DAVE & BUSTER'S

For big... and small kids

What is this place exactly? Isn't it for adults? Can kids go? Is it big? Is it fun? Is it a restaurant? All of the above, and a little bit more.

Some of you might have heard about this entertainment complex... at the office. It is actually a popular corporate outing and primarily an adult establishment. But their arcade section is such a "natural" fit for kids that they have come up with a house policy to suit all ages.

Basically, guests under 19 years old (the legal drinking age) must be accompanied by a parent or a guardian 25 years or older. One guardian can accompany no more than three young guests.

Entering this establishment feels like entering a casino. A large portion of the complex hosts a posh restaurant with bars and pool tables (as well as an amazing indoor golf simulator you can rent by the hour). All the action for kids (small and big) takes place in what they call the Midway section.

From your children's perspective, passing its threshold will be like entering Alibaba's den. There are some 250 games, all competing for your attention so expect noise!

A huge counter bar greets you at the entrance. Around the bar area are retro black-lacquered booths lined with red vinyl. We grabbed one and it became our meeting point for the next three hours.

A third of the floor, to the left, is covered with games rewarding players with coupons they can exchange for trinkets or something fancy (remember, it's an adult place).

To the right, one finds all the virtual games technology can exploit. When we visited there were riding games (race cars, 18-wheelers, motorcycles, planes, tanks, helicopters), sports games (surfing, snowboarding, skiing, skating, football, basketball, hockey, golf, bowling, horse racing), hunting games (alien, dinosaurs... even turkeys!). The works!

TIPS (fun for 5 years +)

• When we visited, it was not busy at all so we had the chance to play on the funny horse-race track (against a wall to the left) where the winner gets 50 coupons. Since it was only our family playing, one of us was sure to win!

• The Midway section offers an affordable kids' menu and edible adult food.

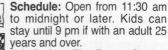

Dave & Buster's
• Vaughan
(905) 760-7600
www.daveandbusters.com

C-3
North
of Toronto
35-min.

 Schedule: Open from 11:30 am to midnight or later. Kids can stay until 9 pm if with an adult 25 years and over.

Admission: The Power Card is $2 and you put the amount of money you want to spend on it.

Directions: 120 Interchange Way, Vaughan. Take Hwy 400 North. Turn east on Rutherford, then south on Jane St. and west on Interchange.

NEARBY ATTRACTIONS

ABOUT FESTIVALS AND FAIRS

Fair trade

Demolition derby, tractor pulls, horse shows, midway, petting zoo, home crafts, live entertainment, candied apples, roasted corn...

Small town fairs are a great excuse to do a road trip to the countryside with the kids. Since most of them include midways, hot dogs and ice cream, they're always a success with kids 10 years and younger.

The **Ontario Association of Agricultural Societies** describes more than 230 yearly Ontario fairs on its website (most of them happening in August and September).

For a good idea of what to expect at an agricultural fair, read my account of **Port Perry Fair** (p. 31). Check **Six Nations Annual Fall Fair** (p. 100) to see what to expect from a powwow.

You'll find many festivals described in this edition of **Toronto Fun Places** but there are so many festivals I haven't had time to check that were on my wish list of attractions to add to this guide!

I'm sure kids would love to do a monster truck ride at **Markham Fair** (in September, www.markhamfair.ca), to watch real rodeo at the **Warkworth Western Weekend** (in July, www.warkworthwesternweekend.com), to admire sandcastles at the annual **Sandcastle Festival** in Cobourg (in August, www.cobourgtourism.ca). I know my daughter would be in heaven if I took her to see the working dogs at the **Kingston Sheep Dog Trials** (in August, www.cityofkingston.ca).

When a festival has its own website, it's a sign of its maturity. I bet these would be really entertaining: **The Fergus Scottish Festival & Highland Games**, with pipe band and highland dancing (in August, www.fergusscottishfestival.com); the **Canadian Int'l Military Tattoo** with military bands and display in Hamilton (in June, www.canadianmilitarytattoo.com); the **Collingwood Elvis Festival** (in July, www.collingwoodelvisfestival.com) or the **Brantford Elvis Festival** (in August, www.memphismotion.com) and the **London Balloon Festival** (in August, www.londonballoonfestival.com).

Wouldn't be surprised if they found their way into the fifth edition!

TIPS (fun for 5 years +)

• Don't forget your bathing suits when visiting a new festival during the summer. You never know what awaits you!
• Exploring is part of the fun of a small road trip. I usually prefer to let the kids have snacks at the fair or festival but lunch or dinner somewhere else. Most small towns have a pretty main street with character and a family restaurant on it.

About festivals

www.ontario-fairs.com
You can browse through the fairs alphabetically, by district or by date (click on **Fairs** from the home page).

www.festivalsandevents ontario.ca
You can download the great 125-page booklet **Festivals and Events in Ontario** from this website or call Ontario Tourism at 1-800-ONTARIO (1-800-668-2746) to get a copy.

HARBOURFRONT CENTRE

Harbourfun

Harbourfront Centre sits on the edge of the water. Its waterfront terrace with panoramic views of Lake Ontario on one

side and CN Tower on the other, the long promenade along the pier with its many choices of harbour cruises, and most of all, the large and small events taking place year-round, explain the site's huge popularity.

For the inquisitive mind, the **Craft Studio** allows visitors to watch artists in action as they are crafting glass, metal, ceramics or textiles. Children are generally impressed by the glassblower's prowess with the large red ball coming out of the oven's belly, and its patient transformation into a shapely vase with handles.

TIPS (fun for 5 years +)
• Read **Stroll around Harbourfront** for more waterfront fun on p. 26.
• Check **www.paddletoronto.com** for information about canoe and kayak rentals to paddle on Lake Ontario.
• See **Kajama** (tall ship) on p. 227.
• More superb **Natrel Rink** on p. 358.
• The **Lakeside EATS** terrace is great during the warmer days and on cold days after skating. The restaurant's menu at the counter is affordable. During the summer, there's also the **Splash** patio between the pond and the lake, serving food and alcohol.
• Check their calendar for the **Swedish** and **Mennonite Christmas Festivals**.

There is the Harbourfront Centre for adults, with its ambitious roster of dance, music and theatre festivals, conferences and visual arts exhibits. At all times you can view at no cost an eclectic selection of art works in the Main Gallery, along the main building's corridors and at nearby **Power Plant**.

Then there is the Harbourfront Centre for children. The **Milk Festival** and **Music with Bites** are not offered anymore but Harbourfront has created a new **HarbourKids** programme which will offer great activities three times a year (probably in October, December and May). We were there during the first one in 2007. Kids explored the inside of a huge inflated sculpture, they created sculptures to be displayed, they did a short film... In May 2008, **HarbourKids** promises to be even more exhilarating.

During the summer weekends, visitors will sample different cultures at the market, the **World Cafe**, with world music as a bonus on the big outdoor stage.

Harbourfront Centre (416) 973-4000 www. harbourfrontcentre.com	D-3 Downtown Toronto 5-min.

 Schedule: Open year-round with variable opening and closing hours depending on the events. Check their calendar.
Admission: FREE ground admission.
Directions: 235 Queen's Quay West (west of York St.), Toronto.

NEARBY ATTRACTIONS

(1) Pier 4 Storehouse

(2) HtO Park

(3) Toronto Music Garden

(4) Along Queen's Quay

(5) By Queen's Quay Terminal

STROLL AROUND HARBOURFRONT

Urban waterfront

Harbourfront Centre is at the heart of the waterfront action. Walk 10 minutes east and west of it along Queen's Quay and you'll find plenty enough to spend the whole day.

If you want to have a bite by the water, walk across the passageway linking **Harbourfront** to the western pier and around the building towards the lake and you'll find the outdoor snack bar of the **Pier 4 Storehouse** (1). Beware of the seagulls, they love their French fries!

The menu inside the nautical-themed restaurant is another affair. It is more expensive but offers a children's section. It provides a great harbour view and is packed with fun memorabilia (**www.pier4.ca**).

The nearby **Radisson Hotel** has a patio with outdoor pool overlooking the lake from its fifth floor. You can pay around $15/person for a day pass to use it (249 Queens Quay West, look up **Radisson Hotel Admiral Toronto-Harbourfront** on www.radisson.com).

At the street level in the same building, there's an in-line skate and bicycle rental shop (**www.wheelexcitement.ca**).

Two minutes further west, you'll notice the umbrellas of **Ht0** (2), the large sand patch coined an "urban beach". It feels like a beach, which is cool because of the **CN Tower** in the background but you won't be able to swim in the lake at this level.

The next block, at the foot of Lower Spadina, hosts the lovely **Toronto Music Garden** (3), (see p. 275). A few blocks more, and there's **Little Norway Park** (see p. 284) facing the Western Channel and the airport.

You'll see it all from the lake if you catch a ride in one of the boats anchored at Harbourfront, such as the **Kajama** (see p. 227).

For a description of another stroll up Spadina, leading to the **CN Tower** and surroundings, read **Think Big! Stroll** on p. 466.

Queens Quay Terminal is the gorgeous shopping centre just east of Harbourfront (**www.queensquay.sites.toronto.com**). It includes restaurants such as **Il Fornello** but fancy chinese cuisine **Pearl Harbourfront** is the one offering the best lakefront view (**www.pearlharbourfront.ca**).

At the south-west corner of York and Queens Quay, look carefully at your feet. You'll see a school of brass fish set in the cement (4).

If you walk toward the lake from the south-east corner, you'll get a great view of **Queen's Quay Terminal** (5), then you'll see the intriguing 6-metre ball-shaped sculpture *Sundial Folly* (6) by the boardwalk, with nooks and crannies to explore.

Keep going east to reach **Harbourfront Square Park**, adjacent to the Ferry Terminal serving **Toronto Islands** (see p. 398).

At the foot of Bay Street is the **Queens Quay Station**, one of the stops of 509 Harbourfront-Bathurst

Streetcar (read about it under **Union Station** on p. 451). Just north of it on Bay is the **Waterpark Promenade** where you'll find a food court on the second level, simply lovely with skylights and a huge sort of boat skeleton hanging in the air (7). In the next building to the north, you can admire a great carved wall featuring surprising details (8). Further north is **Air Canada Centre** (see p. 337), also featuring carvings on its outdoor walls.

(6) Near Queen's Quay Terminal

One block east of Bay on Queens Quay is a giant sculpture called *Beetween the Eyes* (9) which is hard to resist for kids!

Captain John's sea food restaurant in a boat (10) is quite impressive when you look up at it, standing at the foot of Yonge Street.

When you look down, you see metal letters on the sidewalk running to the west, listing names of cities and distances reminding us it is the "longest street in the world".

(7) Waterpark Promenade

(8) By Waterpark Promenade

Further east, kids will be able to walk without danger on an out-of-use train track. On the way, you'll pass the **Redpath Sugar Museum** (96 Queens Quay, **www.redpathsugar. com**). It is small and normally only open on weekdays but worth the visit if you have a chance. That's where I learned about the Ontario sugar beet industry!

The whale mural (11) on the Redpath building is a waterfront landmark not to be missed.

Finally, a good way to end the stroll is to grab snacks at **Loblaws** market on the other side of the street and go upstairs to eat it by the windows (12).

This stroll is roughly 1.5 km long.

(9) Along Queen's Quay

(10) Captain John's on the lake

(11) Along Queen's Quay

(12) Upstairs at Loblaws

TODAY'S PARENT KIDSUMMER

One treat a day

On a Kidsummer day, one might get the "inside scoop" on how ice cream is really made, create a claymation short film or have a behind-the-scenes look in television or radio studios.

For the past 21 years, Kidsummer's mission has been to give children access to fun events during the summer months.

Under the auspices of Canadian magazine *Today's Parent*, the yearly summer-long event provides a myriad of activities all across the Greater Toronto Area and beyond.

Its biggest focus is on offering free children's admission to specific attractions. Accompanying adults usually pay regular admission fees, yet it can represent great savings for a family, especially with big league attractions such

as **Ontario Science Centre**, **Toronto Zoo**, **Reptilia** or **Casa Loma**.

Of course, the roster of activities vary from one year to the next but they always rely on sure values. Over 75% of the attractions offered in Kidsummer 2007 are described in this guide. In order to choose a Kidsummer activity, check their calendar, then look up the attraction in this guide!

Kidsummer also offers the opportunity for exceptional activities you might not have the chance to do normally. In 2007, kids could become restoration experts at the **Elgin and Winter Garden Theatres**, they could watch the sun through the large telescope of **Night Sky Tours**, they could watch a live firefighting demonstration at the **Toronto Fire Services** training station.

The year I participated with my family, drop in activities were offered at the **Orthopaedic and Arthritic Hospital**. It turned out to be interactive, fun and educational. My son ended up with a cast!

For many years now, Kidsummer has started and ended at **Ontario Place** where we could get a two-for-one special on the cost of admission. A tradition?

TIPS (fun for 3 years +)

• Kidsummer is under *Today's Parent* administration. You will find the Kidsummer calendar and pre-registration information in their magazine's July issue.
• Approximately one third of the activities require pre-registration due to a limited capacity. Pre-registration costs $10/child but it is valid for the pre-registration to three activities. In 2007, pre-registration gave access to a wacky show from **Dufflebag Theatre**, a dog and bird show with the **Wonderful World of Circus**, cooking classes at **Loblaws**, to name a few.

Today's Parent Kidsummer
1-866-363-5437 (hotline)
www.kidsummer.com

   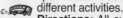

Schedule: July 1 to August 31 (hours vary for different events). Pre-registration starts mid-June.
Admission: Most events are FREE for children 12 years and under but some adult fees might apply. Pre-registration fees to specific activities is $10 for three different activities.
Directions: All over the Greater Toronto Area and beyond.

OAKVILLE WATERFRONT F

Photos: Courtesy of Oakville Waterfront Festival

As good as it gets

Coronation Park during the Oakville Waterfront Festival is my kind of walkabout! The crowd, big without reaching Toronto's proportions, spreads comfortably over the huge waterfront site. The event is extremely well organized, down to the free shuttle buses from the free parking lots at Oakville and Bronte Go Stations.

It takes us fifteen minutes to ride the shuttle bus from **Oakville Go Station** to **Coronation Park**. We get to see how the whole town is celebrating.

Not long after we pass the gates at **Coronation Park**, we come across children involved in a collective clay creation. Next door, others are making big soap bubbles. Further, tents are bursting with activities of cookie decoration, mask making, play dough creation and more.

Children get their share of cardio on the inflatable structures and burn yet more energy at the two playgrounds. Our kids are thrilled to cool down in the great splash pad.

Animal and family shows are the norm at this festival. We saw a parrot show. (In 2007, they had an interactive circus show.)

Past the sponsors' tents, a dynamic

band galvanizes the audience at the big Waterfront Stage which will host a roster of great shows throughout the Festival. There's also the Theme Park with kiddie rides and major big rides and skateboard competitions.

Activities vary each year but you can always count on more to the Oakville Festival than a family can handle in a day. To summarize: This is as good as it gets!

TIPS (fun for 2 years +)

• More on **Coronation Park**'s playground and splash pad on p. 426. Don't forget bathing suits, sunscreen and bottles of water.

• The festival offers one fireworks display on the Satuday at around 10:30 pm.

NEARBY ATTRACTIONS
Shell Park (5-min.) .... p. 357

Oakville Waterfront Festival	D-2 West of Toronto 35-min.

Oakville Waterfront Festival
· Oakville
(905) 847-1216 (hotline)
(905) 847-7975
www.oakvillefestival.com

 Schedule: Always on the weekends that is a full week before Canada Day; Friday, 5 pm to 11 pm; Saturday 9 am to 11 pm and Sunday, 9 am to 5 pm. (2008: June 20-22).

Admission: Around \$15/person at the gate, FREE/3 years and under. (Buy online to save! \$13/person or \$11/person when buying for five or more before the event). Extra fees for rides.

Directions: Coronation Park, Oakville. From QEW West, take exit #118/Trafalgar Rd. southbound. Turn west on Cross Ave. to Oakville GO Station. Take the free shuttle bus to Coronation Park. (Note that Bronte Go Station also offers a free shuttle bus.)

T PERRY FAIR

Family rodeo

Where else could your child try "mutton" rodeo, pig catching, egg throwing or wheelbarrow racing?

After watching the whole Family Rodeo with excitement, my daughter promised to participate next year. This fair was in its 154th year when we attended the event so it is fair to assume it will keep going.

"Sophie needs her mom right now!" announces the caller as a little girl is quickly thrown off her sheep. An eager boy climbs on a new sheep, determined to beat the 57-foot record achieved by the previous participant. He's dismounted in the flash of an eye.

Two lines form for the Egg Throwing Contest and (raw) eggs start flying. They keep bouncing, a testimony to their healthy shells.

Moms and dads line up for the Wheelbarrow Race. Their young partners have to ride in the wheelbarrow to and from a post where a heavy sandbag has to be loaded. The trick is for the child to be young enough to be light, and old enough not to be traumatized by the speed!

There was even a "Frying Pan Throwing Contest" for the moms.

Later, we learned how ropes and hay bails are made during demonstrations, and how cars are destroyed during a demolition derby!

There were acrobatic motorcycle shows in the air, tap dancing and music in the barn, midway, food, horse rides and more.

The Junior Fair Building showcased the best "anything" made by local kids: best "rock concert" (with characters made out of rocks), best "ugly cupcake", best "odd-shaped veggie", etc.

TIPS (fun for 5 years +)

• We took a break from the fair in the middle of the day, intending to return after a swim. When we visited, **Palmer Beach** by Water Street in Port Perry was declared unfit for swimming so we opted for the heated outdoor pool at **Birdseye Aquatic Facility** (by the water, past the **Port Perry Marina**). Call (905) 982-0830 for more information.

• The **Boardwalk Café** by the marina offers a nice view of **Scugog Lake**. Queen and Water Streets in Port Perry are lovely, with lots of small restaurants and gift shops.

NEARBY ATTRACTIONS
See Northwood Exotic Ranch in the tips section on p. 64.

Port Perry Fair   C-4
• Port Perry   **East**
(905) 985-0962   **of Toronto**
www.portperryfair.com   **60-min.**

Schedule: Labour Day weekend, normally opens Saturday evening until 11 pm, then Sunday, 9:30 am to 11 pm and Monday, 9:30 am to 4:30 pm.

Admission: $8/14 years +, $4/5-13 years, FREE for 4 years and under. Parking is $3.

Directions: From Hwy 401, take exit #412 (Thickson Rd) North then turn east on Winchester, north on Simcoe Street (Road #2), then west on Reach Street. The Fair is on the south side.

WINTERCITY FESTIVAL

Photo: Courtesy of the City of Toronto

All fired up

The WinterCity Festival has turned into a high-profile urban and tourist event, in the spirit of Montreal's successful Festival des Lumières. Hence the Winterlicious part involving prix fixe menus in numerous restaurants throughout the city. Time to get a babysitter!

There's a line-up of activities and restaurants to enjoy during the WinterCity Festival, but what I'm looking forward to is the outdoor performances by international companies we've been treated to for the last four years.

In 2008, we could admire towering fire sculptures burning for hours. A few years ago, the opening ceremony was a spectacular affair involving thrilling percussion and showers of fireworks from **City Hall**. Another show featured a giant human mobile 35 metres in the air.

Artists have come from France, Italy, Netherlands and the UK to entertain us with their European tradition of street performance pushed to the limit. You can always expect them to fully exploit the surroundings to create a unique ambience. The overall effect usually is mysteri-ous and original, not your typical family show!

Nathan Phillips Square is the perfect setting for this kind of show which almost invariably incorporates fire in the performance and some means to raise the action above our head. In 2008, a 15-member theatre company performed on high stilts amidst the crowd.

The Festival also includes skating parties accompanied by a DJ at the **Nathan Phillips**' rink and some interactive fun. In 2008, visitors were invited to bring their lonely mitten to join others in the Lost Mitten Project. Cute isn't it?

Every year is different but the spirit remains the same.

TIPS (fun for 5 years +)
• More on **Nathan Phillips Square** on p. 358.
• More on what's around **Dundas**, **Queen** and **King Subway Stations** on p. 450 (including restaurants).

NEARBY ATTRACTIONS
Hockey Hall of Fame (10-min.walk) p. 346

WinterCity Festival	D-3
(416) 338-0338	**Downtown**
www.	**Toronto**
toronto.ca/special_events	**5-min.**

 Schedule: Usually starts on a Friday evening and goes on for 14 days. Check their website for exact dates.
Admission: FREE.
Directions: The majority of the action usually takes place in Nathan Phillips Square. The Winterlicious includes over 130 restaurants throughout the city.

THE CNE... AND BEYOND

Midway stop

With the large rides located close to the Princes Gate, and the younger children's section, the Kids' Midway, located on the site's opposite side by Dufferin Gates, CNE is indeed a children's paradise!

There is a great variety of rides at the Kids' Midway: a merry-go-round, a Ferris wheel, a small and medium-sized roller coaster, the bumble bee, flying helicopter and planes, jeep and construction trucks that went round and round, tossing submarines, shaking strawberries and more. Most of these rides are for children 42" or less. In this area, there are also games of dexterity for an additional cost, where children are guaranteed a prize. That's all they ask for!

The midway closer to the Princes Gate is for bigger kids and adults. Many require a minimum height of 48".

Activities at Kids' World, located by the Kids' Midway, are of another kind, but equally entertaining. Among them, expect a great petting zoo (no more elephant rides). If it is offered this year, don't miss

the original Backyard Circus Show, very interactive for young children. When we visited, it ended with a parade of huge puppets held by the parents themselves!

It usually features a booth with a science theme, packed with widgets to touch and experiments to observe.

To this, add the Super Dogs performances, a big favourite, where dogs compete on an obstacle course.

The Farm exhibits (usually held in the Automotive Building) feature more animals and antique farm equipment. In the Children's Area, they have daily demonstrations such as goat milking, rope making or sheep shearing.

There's more action in the Direct Energy Centre (formerly National Trade Building), closer to Strachan Avenue. Hall B features an International Stage on which are presented performances throughout the CNE. Heritage Court is the place to check out flowers and vegetables entered in a competition.

You can also watch the **Air Show** (which always takes place on the Labour Day weekend) from the grounds of **Exhibition Place**.

Also at Exhibition Place

More events take place at Exhibition Place throughout the year starting with the **Medieval Times** show mixing dinner with chivalry (see p. 377).

Every **Halloween** brings back **Screemers**. It consists of six different attractions plus unlimited rides. Expect a haunted house and a haunted castle with monsters in every corner, a 3-D maze, a black hole, a maniac maze and an executioner theatre... This event is not recommended for visitors under 10 years old.

The same people who are responsible for **Screemers** have created a new **March Break** event for the whole family called **Wizard World**. This one is intended for children 2 to 12 years old. Expect a magical Wizard's Castle, a 3-D maze with dragons, fairies and dwarves, crafts and interactive play area, mechanical rides and inflated bouncing structures. There's also a laser tag game, magic, reptile and stage shows and more.

The **CHIN Picnic** returns every year. Organized by the multicultural radio broadcaster, this free event includes non-stop multicultural community shows, rides, circus, petting zoo, World food kiosks and Bazaar booths.

TIPS (fun for 2 years +)
• It could cost you approximately $17 to park your car on the **Exhibition Place** site during main events. Try neighbourhood parking on Fleet Street, east of Strachan Avenue.
• During the CNE, express trains transport you free of charge across the site. Take advantage of this service as it easily takes 20 minutes to walk from one side to the other.
• There used to be fireworks displays every night during the CNE but they were not offered in 2007. At the time of print, it could not be confirmed if they will be offered in 2008. Check their website closer to Labour Day.

NEARBY ATTRACTIONS

Canadian National Exhibition (CNE)
(416) 393-6300
www.theex.com

D-3
Downtown
Toronto
10-min.

Schedule: Open daily from mid-August to Labour Day Monday, 10 am to 10 pm (gates close at 10 pm but the big midway closes at midnight). Closes earlier on Labour Day.
Admission: Admission only is $14/adults, $10/seniors and children 3-13 years old, $42/family of 4. Ride pass is $31 (or pay-per-unit). Check the website for specials.
Directions: Exhibition Place, Toronto. Take Lake Shore Blvd. and turn north on Strachan Ave. Princes Gate entrance is on the west side.

CHIN Picnic
(416) 531-9991
www.chinradio.com

Schedule: During Canada Day weekend.
Admission: FREE (extra cost for rides).
Directions: Around the Bandshell Park, in the south-west part of Exhibition Place.

Wizard World
(416) 585-9263
www.wizardworld.ca

 Schedule: On weekends before and after the March Break and on March Break weekdays, 10 am to 5 pm.
Admission: $8/person plus the cost of rides ($15/All-Day wrist band).
Directions: In the Better Living Centre by Ontario Dr. at Exhibition Place.

Screemers
(416) 979-3327
www.screemers.ca

 Schedule: Open for 13 consecutive nights ending October 31, 7 to 11 pm (closes at midnight of Friday and Saturday).
Admission: Around $28/person plus tax. Check their website for a discount coupon.
Directions: In the Horticultural Building by Saskatchewan Rd. at Exhibition Place.

CENTREVILLE AMUSEMENT PARK

Old fashioned way

Did you know that an amusement park existed in 1800 at the very same place today's airport sits?

Maybe it's not by chance that Centreville has the charm of a turn-of-the-century village. It is a small-scale amusement park. With its 24 small rides, Centreville is perfect for young families!

Our small group really loved the beautiful carousel, a feast for the eyes! It includes ostriches, zebras, lions, pigs, cats, giraffes, as well as the traditional horses. The animals are laid out in three rows and turn rapidly as they go up and down to the sound of lively music.

The little ones are fascinated by the train that travels through a long tunnel, by the antique cars set on tracks which they drive "themselves" and by the Swan Ride on the pond. They're also pretty excited by the Bumble Bee Ride at the entrance.

Older children appreciate the bumper boats and cars, the Lake Monster Coaster and the train of the Haunted Barrel ride.

TIPS (fun for 2 years +)

• A reader wrote to me with a good tip! If you arrive at opening time and there's a line-up at the entrance, don't buy your tickets there. Enter the park (there's no admission fee), there are more ticket booths inside with no line-ups.
• There are snack bars inside the amusement park.
• More on **Toronto Ferry** terminal and **Toronto Islands** on p. 398.

NEARBY ATTRACTIONS
Stroll around Harbourfront .... p. 26

Those who like heights will want to try the Sky Ride cable car or the Ferris wheel. Don't hesitate to try the Saugeen Lumber Co. Log Flume Ride, even with the smaller kamikazes.

There's a small farm in the far end of the site and a wading pool right in the middle. Note that there are a bigger wading pool and a great splash pad a few minutes from the amusement park, on the other side of the bridge leading to the south shore. A perfect spot for a picnic.

Bring the bathing suits!

Centreville Amusement Park
(416) 203-0405
www.centreisland.ca

D-3
Toronto
Islands
15-min.

Schedule: Open weekends in May and September and daily from Victoria Day to Labour Day, weather permitting. Open from 10:30 am to 8 pm during July and August. Closes between 5 pm and 7 pm the rest of the season.
Admission: The All-Day-Ride Pass is around $28/visitors over 48", $20/48" and under, $86/family of 4.Tickets for each ride can be bought individually.
Directions: Directly accessible by Centreville Ferry line, then a 10-min. walk from Centre Island dock.

FANTASY FAIR

Photo: Courtesy of K.McCutcheon

Footloose at the Fair

On the verge of panic, I alerted the Woodbine Centre security guards. I was searching for my young fugitive, lost in Fantasy Fair. I eventually saw him as he was getting expelled from the little train he had illegally hopped on without a passport bracelet on his wrist.

The 150-shop **Woodbine Centre** includes two levels linked by several escalators. It is connected to a huge parking area by large, easily opened doors so I recommend being extra careful if you go there on a busy day. Having said this, the place is very pleasant.

Thanks to skylights and bay windows, Fantasy Fair is bathed in natural light. The fair offers nine rides, a giant playground over three storeys high and an arcade section. It doesn't sound like much, but it is plenty for children 8 years and under.

Among other things, there's a magnificent Antique Carousel, Bumper Boats (must be under 54"), red and white airplanes that give young pilots a surprisingly realistic feeling (36" to under 54"), Ship's Ahoy spinning ride (under 36" must be with paying adult) and Spinners (min. 36" and under 54" must be with paying adult).

The train running through the park is a youngster's favourite attraction. Avoid the Ferris wheel if the waiting line is long (the ride is slow).

The Smash'n Dash bumper car ride is for drivers min. 54" and passengers min. 36".

The Playvillage is 5,500 sq. ft. with climber, many long slides and a dynamic section with interactive foam shooters!

TIPS (fun for 2 years +)
• See **Woodbine Centre** on page 168.
• On busy days, bring snacks to pass the time while waiting, instead of planning a sit-down meal. The wait for each ride can be as long as 20 minutes. (A reader told me there were no line-ups on a PA day in December!)
• You can visit Santa too when visiting before Christmas.
• There's **Rainbow Cinemas Woodbine** in the lower level of the mall, (416-213-9048, **www.rainbowcinemas.ca**).

NEARBY ATTRACTIONS
Playdium Mississauga (20-min.) ... p. 22
Pearson Int'l Airport (10-min.) ..... p. 206

Fantasy Fair
• Etobicoke
(416) 674-5437
or (416) 674-5200
www.fantasyfair.ca

D-3
N-W
of downtown
30-min.

    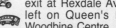

Schedule: Open Monday to Thursday, 12 noon to 7 pm; Friday to Sunday, 11 am to 7 pm. Open from 12 noon to 6 pm on Holidays.

Admission: Around $13.50/for child under 36", $16.75/36" to under 54", $14.50/visitor over 54", $51.50/pass for a family of 4, $3.50/ride or 10 rides for $33.

Directions: Woodbine Centre, Etobicoke. Take Hwy 427 North, exit at Rexdale Ave. East, turn left on Queen's Place Dr. At Woodbine Centre, park between The Bay and Sears.

PRIDE PARADE

You can explain as much, or as little, as you want about the colour-full drag queens, kids won't be traumatized. Remember they all know it's John Travolta dressed as a woman in Hairspray.

The "Men-who-like-to-be-naked" float is a bit trickier, depending on your take on nudity. And you have to know that chances are you'll see a few... eh, members of this association walking naked.

What did you expect?

The least we can say is that this is not your typical family event. But the Pride Week has included a Family Corner in its line-up of activities for a few years now so I had to check it out!

OK, I admit this is not for everyone, but the event certainly has gone a long way since the days when floats and streets were overflowing with participants dressed in drag or S & M outfits and Church Street

was infused with a riotous celebration.

Some lament this evolution. Others consider it a statement to the efficiency of the gay lobbying to forward their cause.

Otherwise, a great ambience rules on Yonge Street while the crowd awaits. Some have brought huge balls that we push over our heads , like at a concert. Many carry water guns to spray the people on the street and on the floats. Most participants in the floats will respond in kind or throw freebies at us.

Anybody with access to roof-tops is out, throwing confetti at us. Some of the floats are really colour-ful, with a Caribana feel to them. I was moved by the floats of support groups created over the years to address the gay issue: kids for their gay parents, parents for their gay kids. So many stories behind it all.

Later, go to Church Street to get a free rainbow flag. Amidst the merchants' booths (selling anything in the colour of rainbows, funky wings or crowns with ribbons), expect scantily-clad painted guys promoting big corporations exploiting the hype. A Kodak moment for many passers-by!

TIPS (fun for 5 years +)

• The **Family Pride** is offered on the last weekend of Pride Week in the school-yard at the corner of Church and Alexander. It features free activities, interactive little shows, playground and is a great source of information.

• The younger the child, the more likely they are to see it just as any other fun parade. Still, I was told by some parents that their pre-teens were really uncomfortable with the whole thing.

NEARBY ATTRACTIONS
Around Bay Subway Station .... p. 441
Allan Gardens (10-min walk.) ...... p. 251

Pride Parade (416) 927-7433 www.pridetoronto.com	D-3 **Downtown** Toronto 10-min.

 Schedule: The parade is on the last Sunday of Pride Week (usually the last Sunday in June) at 2 pm.
Admission: FREE.
Directions: The parade starts at Church and Bloor, goes west on Bloor, south-bound on Yonge, then east on Gerrard. It ends at Church.

CARIBANA PARADE

Irresistible!

We are mesmerized by the explosion of colourful spandex, tulle, lace, sparkles, fringes and pompoms, in what has to be Toronto's hottest street celebration and North America's largest such festival.

When the large float finally reaches us (we heard its loud music from blocks away)

everybody is consumed by an irresistible euphoria. Lost in the engaging rhythms of calypso, the crowd joins the contagious lead of tireless street dancers. A baby claps enthusiastically while a young girl throws in the occasional whistle blow, perched atop her father's shoulders.

Adorable little girls walk in the procession, adjusting accessories and pink leotards too big for them, while some kids catch their breath on a float before jumping again. When we reach the parade's finish point (at Dowling Avenue and Lake Shore Boulevard), some 3.5 km away from Exhibition Place, at around 1:30 pm, we are right on time to see it arriving.

The north side of Lake Shore Boulevard was not crowded as most spectators favour the south side and its line-up of food stands. At no time did we feel overwhelmed by large crowds.

Many pedestrian access points open up during the parade to allow easy passage from the north and south sides of the boulevard.

TIPS (fun for 5 years +)

• Bring the fun up a notch and equip your youngsters with their own whistle.
• Remember to bring bottles of water, hats and sunscreen on sunny days.
• Rain or shine, Caribana takes place. I've attended the celebrations under a torrential downpour and admired participants' determination to continue.
• Be warned, music from the floats can be deafeningly loud to young ears.
• Caribana is notorious for starting later than scheduled, and there can be up to 30 minutes between floats.
• The best way to catch sight of the many fabulous costumes (and snap a few pictures), is at **Exhibition Place**. At 3 pm, dancers are still there waiting for their turn in the procession.
• There is a **Junior Caribana** celebration for children 4 to 16 years old. It usually happens two Saturdays prior to Caribana at 12 noon at Jane/Finch corner.

NEARBY ATTRACTIONS

Caribana Parade
www.caribanatoronto.com

D-3
Downtown
Toronto
5-min.

Schedule: Usually the Saturday of the first weekend in August, from 10 am. Check their website closer to August.
Admission: FREE ($20 for premium seating at Exhibition Place's Stadium).
Directions: Starting point at Exhibition Place (at the corner of Strachan Ave. and Lake Shore Blvd.). Runs westbound along Lake Shore Blvd. up around Dowling Ave.

St. Patrick's Day Parade

Green power

This has to be the easiest parade a family could attend, with subway stations, and enough room on the sidewalk all along its circuit.

The appeal of any parade is the anticipation. What surprise is awaiting us around the corner?

Bands can be majestic (especially the bagpipers playing and walking in perfect sync). Floats can be interesting and often funny with original details.

At the St. Patrick's Day Parade, we saw a "castle" with beautifully costumed lords. There was another one with barbarians feasting at the king's court. This float was followed by peasants pushing their wheelbarrows filled with straw. The parade ended with St. Patrick "himself" waving at us from inside a glass box, not unlike… the Pope himself.

The real appeal of the parade for children is the music from bands and floats. They create ambience and are a reason to wave flags and shake it!

The interaction with the parade's marchers also contributes a lot to the fun of the experience: A clown on a wacky bicycle, two walkers on stilts and a teasing leprechaun, dressed in green with the trademark hat, throwing chocolate coins to the crowd.

Right after the parade, marchers reunite at the **Arcadian Court** (401 Bay Street, 4th floor, in the Hudson Bay building at the south-east corner of Bay and Queen) for a beer and some dynamic Celtic music. Anyone can attend; it gives you a chance to have a closer look at Miss St. Patrick and some of the costumed marchers.

When we left, children were starting to flood the dance floor to skillfully try a few Celtic dance steps.

TIPS (fun for 5 years +)
• This is no Santa Claus Parade. Don't go expecting elaborate floats.
• The parade started at noon, at the corner of Bloor and St. George Streets. When we got to the intersection of Yonge and Queen Streets at 1:45 pm, the parade was already there, and went on until 3 pm.

NEARBY ATTRACTIONS

St. Patrick's Day Parade	D-3 Downtown Toronto 10-min.
(416) 487-1566 www.topatrick.com	

Schedule: If March 17 falls on a Friday, Saturday or Sunday, the parade takes place the Sunday of that weekend, from noon to 3 pm. Otherwise, the parade is on the preceding Sunday.

Admission: FREE.

Directions: Goes from Bloor St. (at Devonshire) eastbound, southbound on Yonge St. then west on Queen St. The parade ends at Nathan Phillips Square.

BEACHES EASTER PARADE

An Easter celebration

There could hardly be a better setting for a successful Easter parade: The Beaches, with its quaint, pleasant architecture, discreet storefront signs, wide sidewalks, and above all, community spirit. With the support of costumed volunteers, pastel-coloured balloons, vehicles decorated by enthusiastic amateurs, and with the participation of clubs and organizations of all kinds, the Beaches take on the atmosphere of a joyous celebration.

Of course, we're not talking about Stations of the Cross and resurrection... but rather about the Easter Bunny and coloured eggs. The Beaches Lions Club House has been organizing this parade for over thirty years. More modest than the Santa Claus Parade, it features majorettes, small marching bands, amateur gymnasts from the area, as well as Mounties and fire trucks.

Certain store owners and organizations create ambitious mini-floats. When we were there, we saw a pick-up truck topped by a giant Easter hat, a "steamboat", a travelling garden, a tractor pulling a multicoloured cart full of clowns, and even a tractor-trailer with costumed children.

Among those parading, there are children on decorated bicycles, boy scouts, preschoolers from local daycare centres riding in decorated wagons, clowns and mascots (Star Wars characters, when we were visiting; Darth Vader delighted many children!).

To sum up, it appeals to the community because the whole community participates! Encouraged by the Lions, a few people wear beautiful hats they made themselves, and some children hold on to their stuffed bunnies.

Don't be scared off by the small crowds gathering at either end of the course. In between, I found lots of room on Queen Street East, even close to **Kew Gardens**. I recommend that you stay close to **Kew Gardens** or the park located close to Glen Manor Drive.

TIPS (fun for 3 years +)
• More than one hour before the parade, a long stretch of Queen Street is closed to motor vehicles and the Queen streetcar line ends at Woodbine.
• For a religious event, see the **Good Friday Procession** on p. 180.
• More about the **Beach Neighbourhood** and restaurants on pp. 402-03.

Beaches Lions Club Easter Parade
(416) 693-5466
www.beacheslions.com

D-3
East of downtown
20-min.

Schedule: Easter Sunday at 2 pm, rain or shine.
Admission: FREE.
Directions: On Queen St. East, begins near Victoria Park and ends at Woodbine St.

GOOD FRIDAY PROCESSION

On a Good Friday

My daughter is given the image of a saint as we wait for the procession to come our way. I had not seen these in years! It adds to the retro feeling I get when I see the people pass in front of us, accompanied by the solemn music of a sombre band. It seems like we're back in the 50's.

Here, we're back in time, before the Easter Bunny became commonplace. I guess it's time for me to explain to my kids what Easter is all about!

Every year, the parish of **St. Francis of Assisi** organizes the mile-long march re-enacting the fourteen Stations of the Cross. It has been a tradition for ages.

Different religious associations take part in the procession. Followers walk behind banners held high. Many of these are beautiful pieces of craftsmanship that must see the daylight only on this specific occasion. The procession quietly proceeds with the display of banners, Jesus and Virgin Mary statues. Crosses are held on small floats, followed by a few shepherds and apostles in long robes.

The most impressive station is obviously the one featuring an exhausted Jesus bearing his cross, surrounded by Roman soldiers. My wide-eyed 5-year-old has to be reminded this is a re-enactment!

How we got from there to the Easter Bunny will be a hard one to explain...

TIPS (fun for 6 years +)
• It's a 5-minute walk from Queen Street East to **St. Francis of Assisi Church**.

NEARBY ATTRACTIONS	
MOCCA (5-min.)	p. 87
High Park (15-min.)	p. 286

Good Friday Procession
(416) 536-8195
www.stfrancis.ca

D-3
Downtown
Toronto
20-min.

Schedule: On Easter Friday, at 3 pm.
Admission: FREE.
Directions: Starting point at St. Francis of Assisi Church at the corner of Mansfield Ave. and Grace St. The procession runs along Grace southbound, turns west on Dundas, goes north on Montrose, then east on College, south on Manning then back to the church.

OKTOBERFEST PARADE

Yodoheleeetee!

There is a great ambience on the street as we wait for the Oktoberfest Parade to start. The crowd is keen; everyone likely got up at the crack of dawn so as not to miss a minute of what must be Canada's earliest parade!

The event, also known as the Thanksgiving Parade, begins in Waterloo at 8:30 am and runs a five-kilometre stretch along King Street. It ends in Kitchener at approximately 10 am. Coming from Toronto, we decide to catch the parade at the end of its journey in Kitchener.

We easily find affordable parking on a public lot. It is 9 am and the crowd keeps pouring in. East of St. Francis Street (where King Street narrows and becomes prettier), there is still plenty of room on the sidewalks. By the Kitchener City Hall, kids burn off some energy jumping on an inflatable structure, while others warm up inside.

By 9:30 am, we find a spot at the corner of Ontario Street next to a family clad in the traditional feathered Bavarian hats. A few minutes later, forty policemen on motorcycles appear in a roar, blasting

sirens and all, followed by the first band, from Michigan.

Composed of around 20 bands and 30 floats (varies from one year to the next), the hour-and-a-half parade boasts a line-up of public officials: mayors, judges, Miss Oktoberfest, the mascot Onkel Hans, as well as members of various German clubs, outfitted in Tyrolian shorts and low-cut dresses. Some really catch children's attention as they flip their whips in the air and yodel. So do the dancers, holding their partners by the waist, feet up in the air and spinning fast.

The floats, although modest, were fun to watch. There was a huge bear drumming on a turtle, a 2-storey-high inflated clown, a 40-foot inflated lion and a big turkey. Shoppers Drug Mart's trademark giant bear was so huge it had to be pulled down to slip under traffic lights.

After the parade, we take in a number of street entertainers at the Wilkommen Platz, downtown Kitchener.

TIPS (fun for 4 years +)

• No wonder Oktoberfest is so strong in that region. In 1873, Kitchener, with a population of 3,000, was still called Berlin!
• The Oktoberfest-Thanksgiving Parade is broadcast live on CTV.
• Call or check the website to find out more about the Oktoberfest program.

Oktoberfest Thanksgiving Parade	D-1 West of Toronto 70-min.

· Kitchener / Waterloo
1-888-294-4267
www.oktoberfest.ca

Schedule: Held on the Thanksgiving Monday, starting at 8:30 am.
Admission: FREE.
Directions: From Hwy 401 West, exit #278/Hwy 8 northbound. Follow King St. to downtown. The Parade runs southbound from Waterloo to Kitchener along King St.

NEARBY ATTRACTIONS
Children's Museum (same place) p. 238

PUMPKINFEST PARADE

It's their party

Families and friends line up their lawn chairs on their front yards in anticipation of the parade. Kids drink hot chocolate from little stands here and there. All these local private parties going on make you want to live in this town.

Waterford takes great pride in its festival. After the parade, we strolled around and admired the Victorian beauties on Main Street and pretty houses on the side streets, many of them decorated for the occasion.

The parade itself is a charming collective effort of the residents and the local business community.

We saw horses, fire trucks complete with their Dalmatian mascot, tractors with the biggest wheels ever and a funky float from the local paintball company. The local music store's float was a big hit with its impersonators of famous singers.

On the cute side: llamas, a dog kennel parading puppies, a clown on tractor with a beaver puppet...

The rest of the day was not enough time to explore everything. There was the 12-row-tall pumpkin tower to admire, not too far from the giant-pumpkin display. Further, a small midway and a great 2-storey-high antique shop filled with enough small trinkets to interest my 10-year-old.

The Pumpkin Express tractors could take us to the other attractions along a circuit: "scary" haunted house, indoor inflated bouncing structures, outdoor stage with food court and the **Van-Go Adventure Farm**.

TIPS (fun for 5 years +)

• There are admission fees to the **Van-Go Adventure Farm**. More on this farm on p. 143.

• The countryside around Waterford is lovely but leave early to get there, the event is popular and you don't want to get caught in local traffic while the parade goes on. There might be lots of walking from the parking lots. Bring a stroller.

• On our way back, we stopped for ribs at **Moose Winooski's** in Brantford (30 mins. from Waterford). We loved the self-serve peanut barrels with peanut shells all over the stool section's floor, and all the fun objects to look at (in Waterford, take Thomson West, follow RR-9, turn right on Hwy 24, leading onto Rest Acres Rd/CR-24, take Hwy 403 towards Hamilton, then exit at Hwy 24/Cambridge (King George Rd.), the restaurant is at 45 King George Rd., **www.moosewinooskis.com**).

Pumpkinfest Parade	E-2
• Waterford	S-W
(519) 443-7492	of Toronto
www.pumpkinfest.com	90-min.

 Schedule: The parade usually starts at 12:30 pm on the second last Saturday in October.

 Admission: Parade is FREE, small fees apply to some activities in Waterford and parking.

 Directions: From Hwy 403 southbound, take exit Rest Acres Road (Hwy 24 South), go southbound then turn east on Thompson Street, and follow signs for parking. (I recommend you check their website closer to the date of the festival for the latest news regarding the parking lots.)

TORONTO SANTA CLAUS PARADE

For over 100 years

Kids are on grown-ups' laps, shoulders or in their arms, on stairways, windowsills or walls. Kids are everywhere, in small clusters in the foreground or packed 2 or 3 rows deep. Among this gigantic brood, brave adults tackle this event with a smile, initiating their little ones to the Santa Claus Parade.

1:30 pm – We settle at the corner of

TIPS (fun for 3 years +)
• To obtain a vantage point suitable for children, it's best to arrive at a chosen spot at least an hour before the parade passes by.
• During the parade, postmen normally collect children's letters to Santa. Write to: **Santa Claus, North Pole, H0H 0H0**, and bring it to the parade just in case!
• If you don't want to brave the traffic, the lack of parking and the cold, you'd better stay home and watch the parade (usually on Global TV at around 4 pm) on the day of the parade.
• If you'd like to see a less-crowded parade, you can turn to Oakville's (since 1948, normally on the third Saturday of November at 9 am, check **www.oakvillesantaclausparade.ca**) or Etobicoke's (since 1991, usually on the first Saturday of December at 10 am, check **www.lakeshoresantaclausparade.com**).
• Check **What's around the subway stations** on pp. 437-54 for suggestions of attractions and restaurants along the parade's route.

Yonge and Front. At the other end, the parade had begun an hour earlier. We've arrived in time to find a small but comfortable patch of sidewalk, but the rows are filling in all around us. We recognize seasoned members of the crowd by their gear: They're fully equipped with snacks, drinks, blankets, chairs, strollers, backpacks, toys and stuffed animals.

1:45 pm – Mothers distribute Smarties to occupy their little elves. The number of grown-ups returning to their stations with coffee in hand is multiplying. Security guards are starting to push feet back on the sidewalk. Are these drums we're hearing? The excitement is rising...

2:30 pm – Children squirm on their parent's shoulders. On the other side of the street, I see two grandparents grinning widely, warmly clothed and seated on their lawn chairs, delighted to mingle with the youngsters.

2:15 pm – The growing clamour is announcing the arrival of the parade. For an hour, we'll be seeing wonders: two dozen marching bands with majorettes, more than 1,000 costumed volunteers and about twenty floats, with Santa's sleigh as the highlight.

In the past years, we've admired Captain Hook's huge crocodile leaping towards the crowd, a rabbit-magician that pulled a... man out of his hat, a dog-robot, a teddy bear picnic, a king with his dragon... and it's been going on for over 100 years!

Santa Claus Parade www. thesantaclausparade.com	D-3 **Downtown** **Toronto** 10 to 30-min.

 Schedule: The parade is held on the 3rd Sunday of November and now begins at 12:30 pm.
 Admission: FREE.
 **Directions:** Starts at Christie and Bloor West and ends at Front and Church (the route usually runs along Queen's Park, University Ave., Queen, Yonge and Front St. but it is better to call to confirm the route).

NEARBY ATTRACTIONS
Royal Ontario Museum (1-min.)   p. 244
Bata Shoe Museum (1-min.) .... p. 243

BEACH FAIRWAY GOLF RANGE

In a hole...

There aren't that many places where one can play minigolf in downtown Toronto! Actually, this is the one.

Beach Fairway minigolf is really cute with its 18 holes layered along a gentle slope.

Minigolf places are often designed with a theme but very seldom do they simply focus on offering a lovely setting amidst the trees, (like a miniature golf course, come to think of it).

I visited the place on the occasion of a birthday party my daughter was invited to. The small gazebo was put to good use for the gifts and cake. After the game, the kids were introduced to the pleasure of driving with a club, with the help of a few parents. They had a blast cheering for each other.

I saw some parents practising their shots while their kids played a game of minigolf. Everybody was winning!

TIPS (fun for 5 years +)

• There's a McDonald's restaurant just south of the golf range.
• Another minigolf in town is the one at Polson Pier (formerly The Docks, p. 352). The other minigolfs I have seen outside an amusement park are **Bathgate Golf Centre** in Mississauga including a driving range (600 Eglinton Avenue, off Cawthra; open 9 am to 9 pm; $3/adults and $2/children, 905-890-0156) and the very pretty one on 9th Line in Stouffville (**www.timbercreekgolf.ca**), including 37 holes with waterfall, jumping castle, slides, gemstone mining area and more.

NEARBY ATTRACTIONS
The Beach (15-min.) .... p. 402

Beach Fairway Golf Range
(416) 686-4101
www.beachfairway.com

D-3
East
of downtown
15-min.

Schedule: Open mid-March to early November, weather permitting, from 8 am until dusk.

Admission: $6.50/adults, $5.50/13-17 years and seniors, $4.50/12 years and under. Second round is half price. Small basket of 45 balls costs $6.50.

Directions: Located between Danforth and Gerrard, on the east side of Victoria Park.

BOWLERAMA

one another. It's a challenge to have little busy bodies try on bowling shoes! The ones my little lad put on didn't close properly, while his friend's were simply too large. Not to worry, it didn't hold anyone back from the game.

We registered. Up to six players can play on one lane. After a somewhat chaotic first round, we finally understood the key procedures, and were better able to focus on our delighted kids. They understood the idea: With three balls, you try to knock down five pins.

Of course, many other aspects of the game will elude them, such as respecting the line between two alleys, not running after the ball, waiting their turn... etc. Besides, little kingpins are different from adults. It was great to see their faces as they watched their ball roll towards its goal. Will it hit… or not? Well, it's hard to miss when you're bumper bowling!

Little kingpin

Young hands drop the balls more often than they manage to throw them. The tiny bowler stamps his feet, jumps up and down and huddles with anticipation. Adults' mute prayers and crossed fingers change to cries of joy, as the ball miraculously knocks down one of the five pins! A young champion is born, amidst the excitement of Bowlerama.

The day we visited, our group consisted of seven adults, three preschoolers and two babies. It was our first family bowling experience. Excitement was in the air as pins and balls rolled down 60 shining lanes, knocking noisily against

---

TIPS (fun for 5 years +)
• Thorncliffe and Bathurst Bowleramas don't belong to the same owners (check www.thorncliffebowlerama.com and www.bathurstbowlerama.com).
• All Bowleramas offer glow-in-the-dark bowling, called Cosmic Bowling.
• When calling to reserve, mention you'll be bowling with children in order to get an alley lined with bumpers. Make sure you reserve a 5-pin lane, with the smaller balls.
• If you are in a Bowlerama which charges by the hour, accompany children to the washroom before registering! If you play beyond your allotted time, you'll be charged an additional hour.
• As a souvenir, you can ask for a printout of your scores.
• Another big bowling alley in the GTA is **Lucky Strike Lanes** at **Vaughan Mills** mall in Vaughan (905-760-9931, **www.bowluckystrike.com**).

Bowlerama
(416) 968-2695 (hot line)
www.bowlerama.com

Schedule: Varies by location. Some are open 7 days a week, 24hrs a day. Call to confirm
Admission: Varies by location. Around $27/per hour or $4.40/ per person per game ($1/children and $3/adults for shoe rental). Bowling shoes are mandatory.
Directions:
Bowlerama Newtonbrook: 5837 Yonge St. North, North York, (416) 222-4657.
Bowlerama Rexdale: 115 Rexdale Blvd., Etobicoke, (416) 743-8388.
Bowlerama West: 5429 Dundas West, Etobicoke, (416) 239-3536.
Bowlerama Barrie: 320 Bayfield St., Barrie (705) 739-2269.
Bowlerama Royale: 2086 Dundas St. East, London, (519) 452-0052.
Bowlerama Stoney Creek: 121 Hwy 8, Stoney Creek, (905) 662-2058.
Bathurst Bowlerama: 2788 Bathurst St., North York, (416) 782-1841.
Thorncliffe Bowlerama: 45 Overlea Blvd., Toronto, (416) 421-2211.

LASER QUEST

Tag!

On our way back in the car from Laser Quest, my friend and I can't get a word in edgewise. Our three boys aged 7 to 9 are still beaming from their first experience with the laser game that even their mothers thoroughly enjoyed. Aerobic exercise has never been more fun!

Our little warriors are rehashing the game to its last detail, score cards in hand. It lists who they tagged, who tagged them, how many shots they fired and how they ranked in the group of sixteen.

At the front desk, each player was invited to choose a nickname. Being a pacifist at heart, I went for "Positive". The kids chose (what else!) Pokemon names. On our second tour, the names get funnier. One of the fathers becomes "Save Me" and my friend, at other times a refined woman with excellent manners, picks the misleading name of "Tralala" and turns into an aggressive amazon ranking third at the end of the game.

In the science-fiction airlock where we put on our equipment, our ranger briefs us on the few rules and we enter the vast two-level maze of walls riddled with large holes. Except for splats of paint lit by black light, we're in the dark and the fog, with loud music matching the pounding of our hearts! I lose the kids in a flash and find them afterwards, teaming up against the adults, from the highest lookout in the room.

The laser beams reach as far as we want them to, amazingly bright and precise. Whenever one hits the flashing lights on our equipment, we are neutralized for 5 long seconds, preventing us from tagging our adversaries.

After 25 minutes of playing, our laser device indicates "Game over" and we follow the arrows on the floor to find our way out of the maze. Laser Quest is exactly what it claims to be: A 21st century combination of two old-fashioned games, tag and hide & seek.

TIPS (fun for 6 years +)

• You may call ahead to reserve. Most players play twice, but there should be half an hour between the two games. The kids will be red-faced and thirsty after the first one.

• We played solo (each on our own). Larger groups play in teams, in which case each team's equipment bears a different colour of lights, and players can't neutralize a player on their own team.

Laser Quest
www.laserquest.com

Schedule: In general, they are at least open Tuesday to Thursday, 5 to 9 pm, Friday, 5 to 11 pm, Saturday, noon to 11 pm, Sunday, noon to 6 pm. Many are open on Mondays and several have longer hours. They offer extended hours during **March Break**. Call to confirm.

Admission: $8/per game.

Directions:
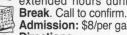
Brampton: 241 Clarence St., (905) 456-9999.
Kitchener: 45 Water St. South, (519) 579-9999.
London: 149 Carling St., (519) 660-6000.
Mississauga: 1224 Dundas St. East, (905) 272-8000.
Richmond Hill: 9625 Yonge St., (905) 883-6000.
Toronto East: 1980 Eglinton Ave. East, (416) 285-1333.

PUTTING EDGE

They'll be glowing with joy!

Walking through the dark place is like being on the set of a children's production. Tall houses in funny shapes seem to lean over the players. Every detail covered with glow-in-the-dark paint contrasts with the darkness of all that wasn't painted. The greens are... black and we are golfing in the dark. Rocks are bright red and yellow. Trees are green and turquoise, with a whole forest glowing in the background.

On the first green, when one of my enthusiastic 7-year-old partners hits his ball and made it fly to the third hole (bouncing on its way off four different vertical props), I realized that watching over them would be quite a challenge!

As we left the forest, we entered an aquatic zone where a whole green takes the shape of a shark. The colour theme switched to blues and pinks. Fish shapes were cut out in the walls and schools of fish were painted on the murals. There was even a treasure glimmering in the middle of a green.

We eventually climbed stairs and reached a level with a space theme and a nice twist, taking the ball back to the first floor through a vertical labyrinth against the wall. My little sportsman insisted on doing it repeatedly when nobody else was playing.

From the flowers painted on the ground and the psychedelic whale hanging from the ceiling to the fluorescent balls and clubs, the attention to detail made this outing a real success.

TIPS (fun for 6 years +)
• Each Putting Edge offers different murals and themes so it is fun visiting different ones.
• You don't have to pay if you just prefer to accompany your children, keeping an eye on them so they won't step into other people's games.
• A maximum of four players per group is permitted. It is suggested you allow faster groups to play through.
• The whole game took us forty minutes to play.

Putting Edge
www.puttingedge.com

Schedule: In general, they are at least open Monday to Thursday, 2 to 9 pm; Friday, noon to midnight; Saturday, 10 am to midnight; Sunday, 10 am to 8 pm. Some have longer hours.

Admission: Around $9/adults, $8/seniors and students, $7/5-6 years, FREE/4 years and under (with paying adult).

Directions:
Barrie: 34 Commerce Park Dr., (705) 737-2229.
Burlington: 1250 Brant St., (905) 315-9155.
Richmond Hill: 9625 Yonge St., (905) 508-8222.
Vaughan: 60 Interchange Way, (905) 761-3343.
Whitby: 75 Consumer Dr., Unit 4, (905) 430-3206.

SANTA'S VILLAGE

Santa in short sleeves

The beard and smile are authentic. Mrs. Claus stands close by. Holiday melodies accompany birds singing. Reindeer rest in their pen. Children are having their picture taken in a sleigh. Others are sucking on candy canes while waiting to sit on the friendly old man's lap.

When summer arrives, Santa trades in his heavy suit for a red vest and short-sleeved shirt. Cooled off by a few fans, he greets children in his village in Bracebridge, in the Muskoka region.

The roller coaster hidden behind the trees by the entrance was the most exciting ride for young thrill-seekers and myself. Rudolph adorns its front car. The coaster goes around the track twice only (which allows children who don't enjoy the ride to get off quickly but disappoints the others). You might want to save this ride for last.

I suggest you start by feeding the deer inside their pen and then hop on the small train circling the Village. It gives a good overview of the activities on the site.

Santa awaits the kids inside his cottage, along with Mrs. Claus (children can hop on her lap too). It's time to takeout the camera, if the white beard doesn't scare your little elves! All children get a notepad from Santa. You can purchase a picture if you don't have your camera.

A path leads to the ride area. All the rides are included in the one-day pass. Enjoy the Ferris wheel with cabins shaped like Christmas tree decorations, a carousel, small planes, pedal boats and floating swans. Don't miss the ride on Santa's Summer Sleigh (the big boat).

This area also offers the Jumpin' Star ride. It gives a great view of the Village from up high before it drops. Any child accompanied by an adult can try it.

Later, you can go to Elves Island, the playground area linked to Santa's Village by a narrow strip of land. An enormous array of nets allows kids to climb way up high. Behind the nets, an ingenious labyrinth made out of nets and tubes presents a challenge to little adventurers. In fact, it can bewilder a child of 3 years or less. I had to rescue my little one who was walking behind her brother and lost his tracks.

There's an inflated, bouncing chamber shaped like Santa's head. To calm down, you can visit the farm or see a musical show for children by the deer pen.

Kids can hop from the wading pool topped with giant candy canes spraying water to the spray pad with spraying rings.

Before leaving, we had an ice cream by the exit. To top it all off, we went to the gift shop to choose a little toy. The shop is surprisingly large and it offers a tremendous amount of trinkets priced at $5 on average. You can easily spend half an hour there to check everything out. Indeed, Santa does things well!

Photo: Courtesy of K.McCutcheon

Photo: Courtesy of Santa's Village

Sportsland

Sportsland is beside Santa's Village and is managed by the same organization. It is an area designed with older kids in mind. The place has less character than the Village, but is well adapted to its clientele. Expect noisy video games, a laser tag room, a go-kart track, a miniature golf course and a batting cage.

My pre-preteen tremendously enjoyed a go-kart ride along with his Dad (no minimum height for the passenger). Two laser-gun fights helped reinforce their male bonding even more.

TIPS (fun for 2 years +)

• I know Santa's Village is far from Toronto, but it's so well designed that I never regretted driving back and forth on the same day. To create excitement, ask your little copilots to watch for Santa signs lining the road. Don't worry about the way back. They'll have played so hard all day they'll be sleeping like logs in no time.

• The Village itself is fun for children 8 years and under. Sportsworld is fine for kids 5 years and over.

• Even during busy weekends, there's hardly a 10-minute wait for attractions. On weekdays, you rarely wait!

• If it's not windy, bring insect repellent. The Muskoka region is paradise for mosquitoes!

• In the past years, they've offered a small **Christmas** event offering cookie decorating, crafts, storytime with elves, face painting, hot chocolate, for a small fee (around $2). Call to check if they will run it this year.

• **Santa's Whispering Pines Campground** is located across the road from the Village. It usually offers an attractive package (including 2 nights camping and 2 days family admission to Santa's Village) for approx. $125. You can reach the campground at (705) 645-5682, **www.muskokacamping.com**.

• There are many snack bars on the premises.

Santa's Village & Sportsland
• **Bracebridge**
(705) 645-2512
www.santasvillage.ca

A-3
North
of Toronto
2 1/4 hrs

Schedule: Open daily mid-June to Labour Day, plus the following weekend, from 10 am to 6 pm. Sportsland closes at 9 pm (except on Sundays when it closes at 6 pm).

Admission: (taxes not included) The Village: around $25/5 years and up, $20/ children 2 to 4 years old and seniors, FREE for children under 2. Sportsland is a pay-as-you-play zone.

Directions: Take Hwy 400 North, continue on Hwy 11. Take exit #4 (Muskoka Rd./Hwy 118 West). Turn left on Santa's Village Rd., at the first light after the bridge in Bracebridge.

NEARBY ATTRACTIONS
High Falls (20-min.) .... p. 272
Muskoka Wildlife (20-min.) .... p. 74

STORYBOOK GARDENS

The whole story

Millions of dollars have been injected into the place. Ambitious new playgrounds, gorgeous spray pad, different characters, more vegetation. Add a new path which turns into an ice skating trail in the winter and you get a clue to another major change: The attraction is now open year-round.

For more than 40 years now, the StoryBook Gardens have been one of London's feature attractions. With a collection of farm and exotic animals, living in cages and paddocks, it could almost qualify as a small zoo but as its name indicates, its primary mission is to display within gardens, various decorative sets inspired by children's fairy tales.

A Cheshire Cat greeted us at the entrance, smiling through a screen of smoke coming from a well. Humpty Dumpty awaited us to our left. To our right, we entered through the mouth of a large whale to see the treasure she had swallowed.

Many animals were missing when we visited, due to the renovations. It gave us more time to admire the seven harbour seals playing in the large pool. We got pretty close to them so we could enjoy their frolicking.

A bit further, two otters were swimming to and fro their small pond.

Deeper into the park, the kids tried the climbing rocks but the immense red spider web was even more challenging. It connected three poles, each offering anchorage for children to climb up. Don't try this barefoot! There was a 3-storey-high slide, a large wooden structure and an impressive pirate ship, a treehouse and a maze.

After all that playing, the Slippery's Great Escape was most welcome: A large colourful spray pad with water cannons, bucket dumps and sprays of all sorts. Kids all ages had a blast.

After they'd cooled down, we watched a little show put together by the young staff, a (free and funny) interactive adaptation of *Hansel & Gretel*.

Kids always like to watch the large carp and ducks from the covered bridge overlooking the pond. The renovations continue. This pond is being rejuvenated. I predict it will become the cutest little nook.

Outside of the attraction's gate, a miniature steam train with its railroad track stretching over one kilometre, adds to the fun. So does the carousel by the water.

TIPS (fun for 2 years +)

• You can catch the bicycle trail bordering the **Thames River** directly from StoryBook Gardens' parking lot. It runs amidst pretty scenery and will lead you to the University in 12 km.

• Within half an hour walk to your right on that trail, you'll find a lovely café under the trees by the water.

• In the winter, the refrigerated path can hold ice for a fun skating experience through the gardens, weather permitting. Animal exhibits are open. During the **March Break**, expect crafts, and small shows.

• Check their website for special events during **Halloween** and on **New Year's Eve**.

• Check www.londontourism.ca for their section **Where to stay**. We took a room at the **Hilton** to spend one night in the area. It allowed us to wind down completely. What a perfect little getaway!

• The **Fanshawe Conservation Area** on the northeast edge of London includes a campground. Call 1-866-668-2267.

• The attraction's snack bars are conveniently located by the water games.

• The cute restaurants and cafés in London are found along Richmond Street by **Victoria Park** in London.

• You could combine your outing with a visit to the local waterpark **Wally World** in **East Park**, east of Highbury Avenue, on Hamilton Road. Admission cost is reduced after 4 pm. For information, call (519) 451-2950, www.eastparkgolf.com. **East Park** also includes go-karts, batting, 36 holes of minigolf, indoor rock climbing, bumper cars and a kids' jungle gym.

• The **London Balloon Festival** (the largest hot air balloon festival in English Canada) always takes place during the Simcoe Day weekend in **Harris Park**, check www.londonballoonfestival.com.

• **Victoria Park**, downtown London, hosts two free musical events: **Sunfest**, a four-day festival usually held around the second weekend in July (call to confirm) and the **Fiesta del Sol**, always on Labour Day weekend. Check www.sunfest.on.ca or call (519) 672-1522.

NEARBY ATTRACTIONS

StoryBook Gardens	E-1
• London	S-W
(519) 661-5770	of Toronto
www.storybook.london.ca	2 1/2 hrs

 Schedule: Open year-round. May, June and after Labour Day until April; Friday to Sunday, 10 am to 5 pm. From June 1 to Labour Day, open daily 10 am to 6 pm.

 Admission: $7.50/adults, $5/2-17 years, FREE under 2. Train or carousel ride is $1.25. During winter (skating): $3.50/adults, $3/students, $2/2-10 years, FREE under 2, $10/family of 4.

 Directions: Take Hwy 401 West, exit # 183 to Hwy 402 westbound. Turn north at Colonel Talbot Rd. Stay on that road until it ends at the entrance to Springbank Park. StoryBook is in the park.

General tips about
Animals:

- A great free outing to do with kids is a visit to a big box pet store. Don't underestimate these! Some are amazing, with rabbits, snakes, hamsters, fish, dogs, cats, ferrets, parrots and so on.

Menagerie Pet Shop is a really cute one located at 549 Parliament, near the **Riverdale Farm** (**www. menageriepetshop.com**).

ANIMALS

See **Reptilia** on p. 61.

WOOFSTOCK

Humans allowed

They come in all kinds, with assorted masters: pocket dogs with funny hairdos, fabulous royal poodles, good old golden retrievers with kids attached. Dog owners really are in their element at this festival.

This event has grown so much over the last years, it now includes some 200 exhibitors and vendors competing at every corner for the attention of dog owners. Dogs (not kids!) get free cookies, samples, and gifts.

The event is obviously for dog owners but frustrated dog lovers like me (who can't have one because of an allergic family member) will enjoy the display of breeds… and masters' reactions.

Last summer, I thought it was hilarious to observe the disapproving looks of the masters of "better behaved" dogs as they watched other owners let their "bad" dogs frolic in the large fountain. (The weather was so hot I personally envied the canines myself!)

In one of the booths, a portrait artist is painting a dog. A street artist has drawn wolves in the middle of the street. Booths are selling dog fashions.

Who knew there were so many products catering to dogs: summer camps, "neckties" for dogs, organic cookies, pet cuisine express, exclusive pet photographers, pet plan insurance, posh pet furniture, dog paddling adventure… the list goes on.

With my dog-lover of a daughter, we camped by the catwalk (is that what you call it when it is for dogs?) across the park by the **Flatiron Building**'s mural, to see great dogs parade with their masters.

TIPS (fun for 5 years +)

• All dogs must be on a leash.
• This event is the perfect place to go if you'd like to get a dog and are wondering what breed to choose. I think you'll see them all amongst the visitors!
• Read **European Flair Stroll** on p. 476 for a description of things to see in this area.

Woofstock
(416) 410-1310
www.woofstock.ca

D-3
Downtown
Toronto
10-min.

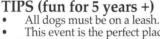
Schedule: Usually the first weekend in June, from 10 am to 6 pm.
Admission: FREE.

Directions: Around St. Lawrence Market. Runs along Front and Wellington Streets, from Jarvis to Scott Streets, overflowing on Church and Market Streets, south of Front.

RIVERDALE FARM

Fieldmouse in the city

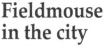

At Riverdale Farm, there are cows of all types, goats, sheep and large pigs. There are hens, roosters, geese and large turkeys. All this in the heart of the city!

Personally, what brings me back to Riverdale Farm is its turn-of-the-century atmosphere and the beautiful flowery and softly steeped setting.

A path brings us to a lower level and a natural pond, our favourite spot. There, a small house sits with mesh-covered

windows, around which my kids like to imagine they're in a prison. During the summer, the pond is covered by natural algae that hides the fish and makes the ducks seem like they are gliding on a green carpet.

The cattle paddock by the farm's entrance, with its huge hairy cows, welcomes visitors. On the other side of the gates, the horse paddock and the Francey Barn await you. That's where you might get a chance to see demonstrations such as ice cream making, horse grooming and cow or goat milking. In the barn you'll find sheep, goats and donkeys. In late spring, you might have the chance to glimpse a cute newborn.

There's also the pig and poultry barn and further down, another pond beautifully surrounded by flowers. Make sure you drop by the Meeting House right in front. It offers children a play area with miniature farm animals and machines, and, usually, craft material for a make-and-take activity.

TIPS (fun for 2 years +)

• There's a wading pool in the park adjacent to the farm.
• More on **Riverdale Farm Fall Festival** on p. 128.
• I like to consult **www.friendsofriverdalefarm.com** to learn more about special events at the farm during **Halloween** and **Christmas**. There are more demonstrations during the **March Break**.
• Their birthday parties are fully booked almost a year in advance.
• There are drop-in sessions at Riverdale Farm Meeting House. Check their website for the schedule (select **FUN Guide** and **Toronto & East York District**).
• In Simpson House is the Farm Kitchen, selling beverages and snacks (open 10 am to 3 pm, closed Mondays).

Riverdale Farm (416) 392-6794 www.toronto.ca/parks	D-3 **Downtown** Toronto 15-min.

 Schedule: Open year-round, from 9 am to 5 pm.
 Admission: FREE (street parking only).
 Directions: 201 Winchester St., Toronto. From Parliament St., go north of Carlton St., turn eastbound on Winchester; from Gerrard St. E., go north on Sumach to Winchester.

NEARBY ATTRACTIONS

TORONTO HUMANE SOCIETY

Beware... you'll melt.

I hear the kids' belly laughs as they watch kittens climb their way up the large cage. Meanwhile, my daughter and a big red cat are in their own world, quietly staring at each other. During our visit, over 300 cats, among other animals, are available for adoption.

When my daughter was six and started lobbying for a dog or a cat, I informed her that her dad was unfortunately highly allergic to them. She explained to me how this was not a problem, he could get another house and she wouldn't mind visiting him on the weekends.

Visiting the Toronto Humane Society seemed like a nice alternative. She was old enough to understand that we would leave the place empty-handed.

By the entrance, we admired a lovely

sculpture adorning a red brick wall, next to memory plates commemorating the lives of beloved pets (including Henry the squirrel!).

Once inside, we went up the stairs on our left, to the cats' floor. They really come in all colours, shapes, ages and state! Little signs by the cages give some narrative on the animal's background. Certain cases are heart-breaking, like the thin cat found sick, with no ears or tail, or the big male given away after 12 years because of an allergic grandchild. "I am a very handsome guy, who deserves to live the rest of my days in a loving home." reads the sign.

If anything, a visit to the Society is the best way to help kids understand the emotional responsibility that comes with wanting an animal.

A very good thing to know about the Toronto Humane Society, entirely funded by charitable donations, is that it has one of the lowest rates of euthanasia in North America. No animal is killed because "it's been there long enough". Only the severely ill or extremely aggressive are put down.

The first floor includes large sections for dogs and others for small mammals (rabbits, hamsters, chinchillas, etc), birds and reptiles.

TIPS (fun for 8 years +)

• Don't expect to pet the animals. It could transfer germs from one sick animal to another healthy one.
• Anyone can buy a memory plate to put on the Toronto Humane Society's brick wall. It could be a great way to ease the pain from the loss of a family pet while helping the society keep up the good work with the donation.
• My daughter would have loved to volunteer but one needs to be at least 18 years old to do so.
• Check the **Adopt a Pet** section on their website to see the photos of the animals currently available for adoption.

NEARBY ATTRACTIONS

Toronto Humane Society
(416) 392-2273
www.
torontohumanesociety.com

D-3
Downtown
Toronto
10-min.

 Schedule: Open year-round for adoption, 11 am to 7 pm.
Admission: Visit is FREE, donations accepted for adoption.
 Directions: 11 River Street, Toronto. Just north of Queen East, west of the Don Valley.

Toronto Zoo

Kid-friendly all year long

Sometimes, we adults tackle an itinerary through the zoo as if it were a shopping list. We just have to see all 5,000 animals between lunch and naptime. Orang-utan? Been there! Giraffes? Done that! Hippo?... "Darn! We missed the hippo!" And while we stand there, confounded in the midst of such a tragedy, we miss the sounds of our young explorers laughing in front of a small otter's cage.

It would take more than eight hours to tour all the trails shown on the zoo's map. How many of us have ever reached the Grizzly Bear den located more than a one-hour walk from the admission gate? (The Zoomobile is actually the way to go!)

The zoo fascinates each child in a different way. It seems logical to adapt the visit according to their interest of the moment. The Visitor's Guide handed out at the admission gate is packed with useful information and includes a map, which will help you locate your child's favourite animals.

Discovery Zone

Splash Island is so much fun that it could become the main reason we go to the zoo, with the animals as a bonus! It is located within the Zellers Discovery Zone.

The spray pad is simply gorgeous. The giant animals seem to be popping out of the water. Kids run from the lake to the wetlands, the river (with water slides), and back to the ocean with whales and polar bear. All of these generously sprayed us when we least expected it.

Kids Zoo's entrance is located near the water games. It is jam-packed with things to do and animals to see. There's a two-storey "tree" from which you'll get a view of all the action: the cute prairie dogs we can observe from viewing domes, the

sand digging for bones, many small animals to look at, giant egg or turtle shells to get into...

Another favourite: the Waterside Theatre with daily encounters with animals. We've seen birds of prey, skunks, wild cats, and fun ferrets running through tunnels held by the kids.

You can try a camel ride for $6 (daily May to October and weekends). They take place not too far from Splash Island.

Around the corner, beside the Australasia Pavilion, don't miss the free-flying birds in the Lorikeet Feeding Aviary. They brushed our hair with their wings! Past the pavilion is another neat attraction: the Aussie Walkabout. It is a fenced section where we're allowed to walk on a path, amidst dozens of kangaroos (unfortunately, you can't expect them to come really close and it is closed during the off-season).

Interactive zoo

There's more to the Toronto Zoo than just walking and spying on animals. At the entrance, take a few seconds to check out the day's schedule for feedings and encounters with animal keepers.

Over 70 keepers take care of the animals; many of them meet visitors daily. From them, you'll learn the animals' names, what and how much they eat and the answers to any other questions the children might have.

Kesho Park (a 15-minute walk from the admission gate) is beautiful. Large bay windows allow you to watch the animals through rock walls. Along the trail, kids can go right inside a large baobab tree, peek inside a termite mound, look at footprints, spy zebras and touch elephant tusks.

Indoor zoo

The Malayan Woods, Indo-Malaya, African Rainforest, Americas and Australasia Pavilions make it possible to spend most of your visit indoors. With their jungles and tropical surroundings, they offer a great outing during very cold days and they're perfect on rainy days.

Personally, I really like these pavilions because they're enclosed spaces. Animals are within arm's reach... and so are the kids! Plus, they are perfect for winter outings.

In the Indo-Malaya Pavilion, have a close look into the amazingly intelligent eyes of the orangutan. We always spend a long time admiring them interacting with their babies in their beautiful environment. In Americas, children are fascinated by the incessant moves of the lively otters.

Inside the Africa Rainforest awaits the huge gorilla. Don't miss the intriguing (and very ugly) naked mole rats in their cross-sectioned maze of tunnels.

At the time of print, the Australasia Pavilion was finishing major renovations. Expect to see a stunning new great barrier reef with jelly fish, sea horses and more. Also note that polar bears have been removed while renovations are done around their den to make room for a new Tundra section in the zoo. Watch their website for updates.

You can still watch the Fur Seal pool, an attraction which always fascinates visitors.

TIPS (fun for 2 years +)

• **Toddle for Tots** has been cancelled.
• Fall colours are great at the zoo when the trails are covered with leaves.
• **Halloween** time brings **Boo at the Zoo**, a two-weekend event with special activities, when costumed children 12 years and under get in for free and receive treats at the exit.
• During the **Christmas Treat Walk** organized every Boxing Day (December 26), starting at 10 am, visitors walk with the keepers from one den to the next to watch them offering certain animals their favourite treat. Admission is half-price with a food bank donation. When we attended this event, three hundred people were gathering around the dens, leaving not much space for children to see anything. We had a good look at the tiger when everybody followed the keeper to the next animal. It had waited for the crowd to leave. The beast slowly walked to its treat, had a sniff at its red steak, and went back to sleep. Not exactly what we expected. The kids were frozen so we headed towards a pavilion to enjoy the tropical climate and all was fine.

• The keepers swear elephants, lions and tigers love to play in the snow.
• On **Easter** Sunday, children get a passport to stamp and get treats at the exit.
• During **March Break**, there are more daily feedings and meetings with the keepers.
• The zoo's gift shop is huge and filled with animal-related items.
• The Zoomobile (a trackless train) runs through the zoo in 40 minutes. You hop on and off of it all day long when you buy the $7 pass. BEWARE! Only collapsible strollers can get on. It runs daily from Victoria Day until Thanksgiving and on weekends in April and October.

NEARBY ATTRACTIONS

• Your family could sleep overnight during the family nights in the **Bush Camp** (6 years old minimum).
• **Glen Rouge Campground** is the closest campground to the zoo. It is located at 7450 Kingston Road in Scarborough. Call (416) 392-2541.
• On their website, the zoo advertizes a package with the hotel **Delta Toronto East**. Call 416-299-1500 or see **www.delta-hotels.com** for more information.
• There are several snack bars throughout the site.

Toronto Zoo • Scarborough (416) 392-5900 www.torontozoo.com	**D-3 N-E of downtown 25-min.**

Schedule: Open year-round (last admission always one hour before closing time) minimum from 9:30 am to 4:30 pm, extended hours in the summer. Splash Island (weather permitting) open weekends end of May to June and daily from end of June to end of August; then, weekends only until mid-September. **Kids Zoo** and **Splash Island** open at 10 am.

Admission: $29/13-64 years, $14/65 years +, $12/4-12 years, FREE for 3 years and under. Parking is $8 (cash only). If you plan to go more than once in the year, ask about membership!

Directions: Take Hwy 401 East. ATTENTION! Follow the signs to Morningside exit and stay in the collector lanes (you can't exit at Meadowvale directly from the express lanes).Then follow Meadowvale Rd. (#389) northbound to the main zoo parking.

ALL ABOUT PETS SHOW

A pet project

I would not trade my very allergic husband for a great dog or beautiful cat. I would not even add the weekly cleaning of a lizard's stinky cage or the troubled water of a fish tank to my already hectic schedule. So we are not about to get a pet. All this said, we love animals, so a pet show turned out to be a nice outing.

All About Pets Show is actually more ambitious than the pet show I visited with my kids a few years ago (which doesn't exist anymore). I have not seen it personally but this one is bigger, with over 180 exhibitors and experts, and has been going on for 15 years.

This kind of show obviously offers the latest pet products and services, and as we anticipated, there were plenty of dogs, cats, and fish. On the other hand, we did not expect to see hedgehogs, the cutest pets ever. There's no guarantee you'll see some when you go, exhibitors change from one year to the next, but you'll see plenty of rabbits (including the Easter Bunny).

Next to the exhibition hall is a dog demonstration ring which can seat 2,000 visitors. It showcases canine talent. There are parades of breeds in a separate area and dog fashion shows at the Centre Stage. The kind of action we won't see at our local pet shop.

TIPS (fun for 3 years +)
• Snacks, fast food and hot meals are sold on the premises.
• Read about **Toronto Humane Society** on p. 56.

NEARBY ATTRACTIONS
Pearson Airport (5-min.) .... p. 206

This show also includes a Pet Adoption Area coordinated by the **Humane Society** and **SPCA**. (Don't expect to leave with an animal on the spot.)

In another section (as far as possible from the dog shows) visitors can attend the **Championship Cat Show**.

One thing for sure, this is the right place to find out what you're really getting into if you are considering adding a pet member to the family (or why you shouldn't... yet).

All About Pets Show	D-3
• Mississauga	N-W
1-800-340-7387	of Toronto
www.pets-show.com	30-min.

 Schedule: Usually Friday to Sunday on Easter weekend, from 10 am to 6 pm, closes at 5 pm on Sunday.

 Admission: Around $12/ adults, $8/seniors and children 5-15 years old, FREE 4 years and under, $35/family of 4.

 Directions: International Centre, 6900 Airport Rd., Mississauga. Take Hwy 427 North. Exit Dixon Rd., turn west on Dixon, it becomes Airport Rd.

REPTILIA

Hungry anyone?

On the week we visited, *Newsweek* magazine had featured the best shots of the year and they included that of a zoo handler's arm coming out of the mouth of a crocodile. It was hard not to think about it as we watched Reptilia's staff poke at their biggest crocodile so it would come out of its inertia to eat its weekly feed.

Reptilia used to be a retail store and breeding facility with an education centre on the side. In 2006, it moved into a much bigger facility and became Canada's biggest reptile zoo, with animal handlers initiating encounters, special feeding sessions, larger displays, hatcheries... and a huge store on the side.

They got me from the start, with the washrooms' water streams from which to wash our hands and the large waterfall by the entrance.

Then you access the wide and sinuous corridor lined with reptile habitats, some of them simply beautiful. We mothers were enthralled by the Green Iguana. Not that the kids would notice, they were way too excited to see the small "crocodiles" (actually, they're caimans).

Most of the large snakes were quite lively, the Burmese Pythons raising vertically four feet off the ground, as if under the influence of a flute charmer. Even the turtles moved a lot! (We saw turtle eggs under lamps in one of the hatcheries.)

In the next hours, we attended an interactive reptile show (to be followed later by a snake show) hosted by a handler with an appropriate Australian accent in an amphitheatre.

The crocodile feeding (with raw chicken) took place near the theatre. We later saw the Viper swallowing a whole (dead) mouse. It is really impressive to see up close how they use their fangs to take in the body. Kids were fascinated. As a bonus, we even saw the handler walking with a gigantic snake wrapped around his body. What a sight!

TIPS (fun for 5 years +)
• Their store is huge. They sell reptiles along with everything to take care of them, as well as toys, posters, gadgets and t-shirts for the reptile fan.
• There's a snack bar selling pizza, burgers, fries, slushes and more. There's also a **Chuck E. Cheese** west of Reptilia, on the south side (3255 Rutherford, **www.chuckecheese.com**).

NEARBY ATTRACTIONS
Bass Pro/Vaughan Mills (10-min.) p. 344
Canada's Wonderland (10-min.) ... p. 20

Reptilia	**C-3**
• Vaughan	**North**
(905) 761-6223	**of Toronto**
www.reptilia.org	**35-min.**

 Schedule: Monday to Friday, 10 am to 8 pm, Saturday and Sunday, 10 am to 6 pm.

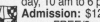 **Admission:** $12/adults, $8/4-15 years, FREE/3 years and under.

 Directions: 2501 Rutherford Rd., Vaughan. Take Hwy 400 northbound, exit at Rutherford eastbound. Reptilia is on the south side.

OSHAWA ZOO

Farm animals?

A cute lemur with fluffy white ears holds out his little paw to delicately pick the popcorn off my daughter's hand. He quietly starts to eat it while staring at her with interest. We are in the peaceful little Oshawa Zoo and enjoy every minute of it.

Despite its small size, the Oshawa Zoo holds a few surprises, the most awkward being the sight of a camel in the shade of a mature tree with lazy black and white cows grazing in the background! Thankfully, most enclosures are set in the middle of green pastures, adding to the quaint atmosphere of the place.

Further, we notice colourful pheasants on a grassy outcrop. The zoo counts an interesting variety of animals, including donkeys, llamas, goats, antelope and even a breed of rabbits from Argentina that look like kangaroos. The zoo is now home of Canada's only albino Wallaby (born in Oshawa Zoo).

While it doesn't take long to com-

plete your visit, children can take as much time as they want to feed the animals (popcorn is sold at the entrance for this purpose).

Oshawa Zoo • Oshawa (905) 655-5236 www.oshawazoo.ca	**C-4** **East** **of Toronto** **40-min.**

Schedule: Open daily in July and August, 10 am to 6 pm. Open on weekends from the time grass is green to the time there's snow, 10:30 am to 3:30 pm. Call to confirm.

Admission: (cash or Interac) $10/adults, $9/seniors and students, $6/3 years and up, FREE for children 2 years and under, $2/family. Popcorn bags cost around $2.

Directions: 3441 Grandview St. North. From Hwy 401 East, take exit #419/Harmony Rd. northbound. Turn right on Winchester Rd., then left on Grandview St. North, right on Columbus Rd. The zoo is on the left hand side.

TIPS (fun for 2 years +)

• You'll find picnic tables on site. We chose, however, to go back on pretty Columbus Road, westbound and down to Simcoe Street where we found a chip truck selling decadent fries and hamburgers by a gas station. We took our scrumptious lunch to the playground beside the adjacent church.

BOWMANVILLE ZOO

Please feed the animals

"Not in your mouth!" For the umpteenth time, my friend catches her little one as he is about to eat an animal treat. True, the biscuits in the greasy brown paper bag do look very appetizing. Undoubtedly, the Bowmanville Zoo gives its residents the royal treatment.

Unlike the **Toronto Zoo**, Bowmanville Zoo (the oldest private zoo in North America) gives visitors the opportunity to feed most of the animals, much to the delight of children. In fact, without supervision, kids would likely give their entire feed bag to the hungry and plump little goats that await them in the first compound located across the bridge.

The Bowmanville Zoo also contrasts with its big brother by its smaller size (42 acres compared to 710 acres at Toronto Zoo), and a more modest sampling of animals (205 animals). The upswing however, is the convenience of touring the zoo in a single visit and interacting with the animals.

The broad paths that criss-cross the zoo are generally well shaded by the bordering mature trees; a real plus on hot summer days. There is a lovely country feel to the site. We began our tour with the parrots, camels, reptiles, monkeys and llamas. We then crossed a small bridge over a river, that brought us to the elephants, lions and zebras.

There are various kinds of horned animals, large birds with impressive calls, intriguing large rodents and roaming peacocks, geese and ducks.

Daily performances involving lions, elephants or the many other kinds of animals, are presented in the impressive 400-seat indoor Animatheatre. Animal encounters also take place in and around an outdoor cage.

TIPS (fun for 2 years +)
• Since our last visit, they've added a splash pad! Bring the bathing suits!
• I recommend you buy a minimum of one animal feed bag per child (sold at the entrance for $2.50).
• Elephant or camel rides are offered for $6. A few small mechanical rides are located near the entrance. They are included with the admission fee in July and August.
• We had a picnic under the trees, but there is an air-conditioned snack bar near the entrance, with washrooms, tables and an aquarium to entertain visitors. Their gift shop is well stocked.

NEARBY ATTRACTIONS
Petticoat Creek (15-min.) .... p. 423
Cedar Park Resort (15-min.) .... p. 426

Bowmanville Zoo	C-4
• Bowmanville	**East**
(905) 623-5655	**of Toronto**
www.bowmanvillezoo.com	45-min.

 Schedule: Open daily from May to end of September, and weekends only in October until Thanksgiving, weather permitting. Open minimum from 10 am to 4 pm (closes at 6 pm on May and June weekends and daily in July and August). Shows daily in July and August, weekends only May through October.
 Admission: $17.50/adults, $15/ seniors and students, $10/2-12 years, FREE under 2 years.
 **Directions:** 340 King St. E. (Hwy 2), Bowmanville. From Hwy 401 East, exit #432/Liberty St. northbound. Turn east on King St.

JUNGLE CAT WORLD

"baby" of the moment. When I visited for the first time in 1996, I was surprised to discover a German Shepherd pup and a baby lion cohabiting like the best of friends. During my most recent visit, there was a young leopard gnawing a stuffed teddy.

We particularly enjoyed the otters and the small rabbit enclosure. Generally, the cages are relatively small, except those of the Siberian tigers (with its large pond) and of the white wolves. However, I saw wolves and tigers squabble happily.

Mommy is there!!!

"What's she doing?" a girl is cooing to a couple of tame tigers in a back cage, as her friend the keeper cleans their main cage. The big "kitties" brush their backs against the wired fence, allowing the girl to touch their beautiful fur. Then they engage in a friendly fight. Intimacy is the operative word in this privately owned accredited zoo.

Visitors are welcomed to Jungle Cat World by the strident "Hello" of a real parrot. A cage, located close to the zoo entrance, might temporarily house the

Amongst the zoo's many tenants, you'll also find lions, bobcats, leopards, cougars, lynx, a black jaguar, gibbons and marmoset monkeys, many of them born on site.

Jungle Cat World also features a small playground with free-roaming deer, pygmy goats, donkeys, sheep and peacocks. You can purchase a bag of grain to feed the animals.

Since our last visit, they've added a lookout tower to look into the wolf and tiger enclosures.

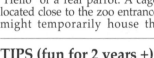

Photo: Courtesy of Jungle Cat World

TIPS (fun for 2 years +)

• Count on daily feeding sessions at 1:30 pm to see the felines in action.
• Ask about their **Night Safari** experience allowing groups to sleep over! And their new Bed & Breakfast on the premises allowing us to see the animals once the general public is gone!
• If your child is a big fan of tigers and you're near **Lake Scugog**, check **Northwood Buffalo & Exotic Animal Ranch**, 15 minutes north of Port Perry, off Simcoe Street (**www.northwoodranch.com**). You'll also find bears, wolves, monkeys and more in this licensed sanctuary.
• I recommend you eat at the **New Dutch Oven** instead of the zoo's snack bar. It is a family restaurant located across from the zoo, (905) 983-5001.

NEARBY ATTRACTIONS
Cedar Park Resort (20-min.) .... p. 326

Jungle Cat World
• Orono
(905) 983-5016
www.junglecatworld.com

C-5
East
of Toronto
55-min.

Schedule: Open year-round, 7 days, 10 am to 5 pm.

Admission: $15/adults, $12/ seniors and students, $7.50/2-13 years, FREE under 2 years old.

Directions: 3667 Concession Rd. 6, Orono. Take Hwy 401 East to Hwy 35/115 (exit #436) northbound. The zoo is on the southeast corner of Hwy 35/115 and Taunton Rd.

WHITE ROCK OSTRICH FARM

there. But not all are open to the public.

The owners of this farm housing some 75-130 big birds obviously have fun with their unusual herd. In the gift shop, you can admire carved ostrich eggs (watch the kids, as these are an expensive item to break!).

Visitors are not allowed to roam freely on the site. They are invited on a bumpy hay-wagon ride to the fields.

As the ostriches are called, the children can feed the huge birds with corn (at $2/cup). When the bravest bird sneaks its head through the wire fence, we can appreciate the flexibility of that long, muscled neck.

Now, that's interesting!

What has three pairs of eyelids, two toes and one toenail? An ostrich! Want to see for yourself? Go to this ostrich farm!

It seems that health-conscious North Americans are turning to low-cholesterol protein sources. In that light, ostrich meat is gaining in reputation. This could explain the ostrich farms that are popping up here and

TIPS (fun for 2 years +)

• The visit is not very long (approximately half an hour). It's a good stop to combine with an outing to another regional attraction.

• Usually over three weekends during **Halloween** time, the farm hosts a **Screamfest**. It seems to have gotten quite ambitious over the years with actors, intense sound and light effects, computers and pneumatic props. Suitable for 8 years and over, $11/12 years and older, $9/8-11 years. Check **www.screamfest.info** for more details.

• Ostrich burgers and hot dogs are sold on weekends. Frozen ostrich meat can be bought on the premises. If you wish to take some home, it would be a good idea to bring a cooler.

NEARBY ATTRACTIONS

White Rock Ostrich Farm

D-2
West
of Toronto
55-min.

· Rockwood
(519) 856-2629
www.whiterockostrichfarm.com

 Schedule: From June to October, open Saturdays from 10 am to 5 pm and Sundays from 12 noon to 5 pm (also open Fridays in June, then they add Thursdays in July and August, 10 am to 5 pm). Open for meat sales only on weekends in November and December.

Admission: Hay-wagon tours:$5/adults, $3/2 years and up, FREE under 2.

Directions: 13085 4th Line, Rockwood. From Hwy 401 West, take exit #320/Hwy 25 northbound. Turn west on Regional Rd. 12, then north on 4th Line.

AFRICAN LION SAFARI

Close encounters of the animal kind

Go figure why children are so attracted to animals! They're happy visiting a traditional zoo, but become literally ecstatic when encountering the fantastic opportunities offered by African Lion Safari. The park is huge and offers the unique opportunity to drive through the animals' living quarters, with your car windows as the only screen between your children and the animals.

African Lion Safari houses over 1,000 exotic animals and birds of 132 species. When we drove through the seven large game reserves, we first encountered big birds such as emus.

We then watched sleeping lions that didn't lift an eyebrow. The tigers were just as lethargic. The whole scenery lacked action... then a crowd of baboons started to jump on our car!

If you're able to live with the idea of a monkey's "little present" decorating the hood of your car, I strongly recommend using your own vehicle instead of the zoo's bus. Children become delirious with joy with baboons perched on the windshield.

Having tried both, I see some disadvantages to the bus option. First, you don't control the amount of time spent watching each animal (the Safari Tour Bus ride

takes approximately 1 hour. In your own vehicle, it lasts as long as you please).

Second, the bus offers little grip for the monkeys, while cars make comfortable perches.

Bears were strolling amongst the monkeys. Quite a mixed company!

You'll meet amongst others: a few tall giraffes (rather impressive from up close), some white rhinoceros, zebras and antelopes. My kids went wild when the tall giraffe licked our windshield with her black tongue.

Further on, you can witness the elephants swimming, pet the animals at the Pets Corner, watch shows by parrots and birds of prey and see other trained animal performances.

You can cross the pond on board the small boat named African Queen and ride the small train.

In the summer, children will enjoy playing in interactive water games at the Misumu Bay, located close to the restaurant's terrace.

You can also visit the Discovery Centre, including skulls, claws, teeth, eggs and more to touch.

Photo: Courtesy of African Lion Safari

TIPS (fun for 2 years +)

• Don't forget the bathing suits!
• Check their website for a list of hotels offering a package.

• The park's restaurant and gift shop are well stocked and affordable. In the gift shop, look carefully at the t-shirts. Some of them were painted by the elephants! Now, that's a unique souvenir.

NEARBY ATTRACTIONS

African Lion Safari	E-2
• Cambridge	S-W
1-800-461-9453	of Toronto
www.lionsafari.com	75-min.

Schedule: Open May to Thanksgiving, 10 am to 4 pm. Closes at 5 pm during weekends until end of June, then at 5:30 pm daily until Labour Day. Ground remains open for 2 hours after game reserves close.

Admission: (taxes not included) $28/13-54 years, $25/seniors, $23/3-12 years, FREE for children 2 years and under ($4 less during Spring and Fall). Tour bus costs approx. $5 extra per person.

Directions: From Hwy 401 West, take exit #299/Hwy 6 southbound for 14 kms and turn west (right) on Safari Rd.

THE FALCONRY CENTRE

In a flash

The small falcon leaves its stand in a flash. It takes us a few moments to locate it above the woodland at the back of the outdoor theatre. As the master falconer raises his arm, meat in his gauntlet, the bird dives back at amazing speed to catch its prey. Remarkably, the bird dismisses freedom, and this is telling of the complex relationship between falcon and master.

Don't go to the Falconry Centre expecting medieval costumes and references to chivalry. Instead, the centre serves primarily as a breeding centre for endangered or threatened birds of prey, with approximately a hundred birds hatching there each year.

Now open to the public, the centre offers self-guided visits via an audio commentary, programmed to be heard throughout the site. I learned it takes twelve weeks for a baby Bald Eagle the size of a chicken egg to reach its full size and an eight-foot wing span!

With cages made of particle board, the centre is no fancy zoo either. Strong odours are to be expected, as anyone owning a bird as a pet will know. Our visit to the mews, where rare wild birds are kept (along with hundreds of chicks used for feeding the birds of prey), proved to be quite trying for that reason. The falcon chambers brought a welcome contrast. Previously trained breeding birds live there, undisturbed by visitors. You can look at them comfortably through a series of narrow windows (kids need to be lifted to see).

Other spectacular sights of birds can be found along a pathway that runs a mere two metres away from an open site, where some twenty proud birds remain, simply tied to their stands.

TIPS (fun for 5 years +)

• The best time to see newly hatched birds is from May to July.
• They've reduced their hours in the past years, better confirm their hours before you go.
• You may buy raptor chow to feed the birds near the path.

NEARBY ATTRACTIONS

The Falconry Centre
• Tottenham
(905) 936-1033
www.falconrycentre.com

C-2
N-W
of Toronto
60-min.

Schedule: Open daily from mid-June to Labour Day, 12 noon to 3 pm. One show daily at 1 pm.
Admission: (excluding tax) Around $10/adults, $8/seniors, $7/3-12 years, $30/family of 4. Check their website for coupon.
Directions: 2nd Line, Tottenham. From Hwy 400 North, take exit #55/Hwy 9 westbound. Turn north on Tottenham Rd. and take first road westbound.

WINGS OF PARADISE

The butterfly effect

We had just spent fifteen minutes focusing on the impressive hatchery inhabited by dozens of still cocoons so it was quite a contrast to return to the path with free-flying butterflies where we were literally cut off by reckless flyers zooming by. It felt like this was the highway and we had to be careful.

There's action in the butterfly conservatory: babbling brooks, small cascading waterfalls and, at times, close to 3,000 butterflies, many of them frolicking about.

It is fascinating to observe the chrysalis set in different hatching stages in the hatchery. The cocoons come from Costa Rica and Malaysia. Nearby are resting specimens of the amazing Atlas Moth, a nocturnal insect wider than the face of a ten-year-old.

We have to watch where we walk to avoid crushing butterflies on the floor. A

staff member explains it's a sign they are getting weaker and closer to the end of their life cycle.

The weak beauties accept our hand as a perch when laid in front of them. The children understand intuitively how to behave with the fragile butterflies.

The vegetation surrounding us is tropical. The humid air smells of flowers and fruit (butterfly meals on plates). The controlled weather under the glassed roof ranges from 24 to 28 degrees Celsius. After a while, a visit to the cooler galleries is most welcome.

A large number of butterflies are framed in the "Flying Jewels" exhibit room. Some are endangered species. The "Insects of the World" includes intriguing displays of dead insects as well as a few live specimens such as a humongous millipede. Yuck!

A great time to visit the conservatory is during the **Monarch Days**, always the second weekend in September, when there's Monarch tagging (!!!) and releasing and migration exhibits.

TIPS (fun for 4 years +)

• They've added over 80 species of tropical flowering plants over the years. They've created an outdoor butterfly garden and a labyrinth is in the plans.

• They offer the drop-in **Bugfeast** event during the **March Break**: A lifetime opportunity to taste chocolate-dipped crickets!

• Ask about their **Brunch with Santa** and **Mystery in Paradise** events.

• The gift shop is well stocked with butterfly-themed toys, books, clothes and trinkets. My kids went crazy for chocolate butterfly lollypops.

• The **Paradise Café** is open daily March to September, 10 am to 3 pm. Reduced hours at other times.

NEARBY ATTRACTIONS
Shades' Mills C.A. (20-min.) .... p. 417

Wings of Paradise Butterfly Conservatory • Cambridge (519) 653-1234 www.wingsofparadise.com	**D-1 West of Toronto 85-min.**

 Schedule: Open daily from March to mid-October, 10 am to 5 pm. Closed on Mondays the rest of the year.

 Admission: $9.50/adults, $8.50/ seniors & students, $5/3-12 years, FREE under 3 years.

 Directions: 2500 Kossuth Rd., Cambridge. From Hwy 401 West, take exit #282/Hespeler Rd. North-Hwy 24. Turn west on Kossuth Rd. and follow signs. Niska St. is on the right.

BUTTERFLY CONSERVATORY

Butterfly-friendly attraction

The visit begins with the viewing of a short film. It is followed by a leisurely walk around the greenhouse for as long as we want. The conservatory layout includes trees, bushes and flower clumps, as well as a waterfall. The hot and humid air contributes to the overall exotic feel of the place.

We are told that over 40 butterfly species live freely at the Niagara Butterfly Conservatory. I couldn't tell most of them apart, yet I saw at close range all sorts of exotic kinds including blue, black, red, yellow and orange ones. Here and there,

fruit plates are left for the hungry butterflies, so that we may admire them while they feed. We can also observe their cocoons in each phase of development, suspended from the shelving in front of a large window with openings.

The beautiful winged insects are quite tame. In truth, they were born in this environment and have grown accustomed to the crowds that regularly and respectfully visit the hothouse.

My little naturalist miraculously stops moving for a minute, hoping that one of the two thousand butterflies in the greenhouse will mistake him for a flower and land on him.

A woman, looking through her camera, waits for the perfect moment to snap a picture, unaware that a wonderful specimen is resting on her head. I take my time to capture (on film) a superb green and black butterfly standing 10 centimetres away from me.

Don't miss the interactive stations in the entrance hall.

TIPS (fun for 4 years +)
• More on **Niagara Falls** on p. 269.
• Purchase your tickets as soon as you arrive at the conservatory, as only then will the time of your visit be assigned (often one hour later in the high season).
• If you arrive at opening time, chances are there will be many butterflies on the floor.
• Washrooms at the conservatory are less busy than those at the snack bar.
• You can end your outing with a visit to the adjacent outdoor gardens (the Conservatory sits at the centre of a botanical garden), have a bite at the snack bar or browse in the large gift shop.

Niagara Parks Butterfly Conservatory	E-4 Niagara Region 90-min.

• Niagara Falls
(905) 371-0254
1-877-642-7275
www.niagaraparks.com

Schedule: Open year-round from 9 am. Closes at 9 pm from mid-June to early September, sooner during other seasons (last admission 30 mins. prior to closing time).
Admission: (tax excluded) $11/adults, $6.50/6-12 years, FREE 5 years and under.
Directions: 2405 Niagara Pkwy., **Niagara Parks Botanical Gardens**. From QEW towards Niagara, take Hwy 405 towards Queenston, then exit at Stanley Ave. and follow the Butterfly Conservatory signs.

BIRD KINGDOM

Indonesian experience

If you find there's an Indonesian feeling to the site, it is because the main aviary is indeed a showcase for a pièce de résistance: a gorgeous original javanese house circa 1875, richly carved out of solid teak. Lets not forget the "Indiana Jones" feel of the Nocturnal Zone with bats, scorpions and crashed plane.

The noise takes you in as you enter the Main Aviary, with the birds' songs laced with the sound of the 40-foot waterfall. Then, your eyes are filled with the sight of the tall palm trees and the carved ruins amidst the walls of plants.

With all this distraction, we did not notice the birds right away. Then, we started an I Spy game, discovering the inhabitants one after the other.

There's a great story behind the beau-

tifully carved Java House! It was discovered by the owner of the aviary 30 km from Niagara, laying in pieces, forgotten in some farm's barn. It took over two years to figure out how to assemble the numbered pieces back into the house we now see in the Main Aviary. Instructions had been lost. Talk about a puzzle!

We arrived too late for the lorikeet and the bat feeding sessions, two big favourites here. But the kids had a blast with the parrot by the gift shop.

The Small Aviary was under construction during our visit so we did not experience it directly but you can do a virtual tour of it on their website. It features smaller birds than those living in the main section and offers a unique view of the Niagara Gorge.

TIPS (fun for 4 years +)

• Since our last visit, they've added a reptile exhibit, interactive reptile encounters and free-flight bird shows! Call for the exact schedule.

• The attraction's store is filled with great merchandise. The Java House now offers pizza, soups, drinks and more.

• Your ticket is a day pass so you can show up early and return later in the day after visiting other Niagara attractions. More on **Niagara Falls** on p. 269.

Bird Kingdom
• Niagara Falls
1-866-994-0090
www.birdkingdom.ca

E-4
Niagara Region
90-min.

Schedule: Open year-round at least from 10 am to 5 pm (extended hours in the summer). Check website for schedule of bat feedings, lorikeet feedings, bird shows and reptile encounters.

Admission: Around $17/13 years and older, $13/4-12 years old, FREE for 3 years and under. Extra for lorikeet food.

Directions: 5651 River Road. From QEW West, Niagara bound, take Hwy 420 exit to Niagara Falls, continue on Falls Ave., turn left at Clifton Hill, then left at River Rd.

MARINELAND

Not just another fish story...

As soon as kids try to feed one of the hundreds of deer Marineland is swarming with, they're swept away amidst a sea of white spots with dozens of wet noses and velvety antlers tickling their faces.

When you think of Marineland, the first thought that comes to mind is the sight of killer whales splashing the crowd or a dolphin show. Yet this attraction offers plenty of other activities too: a huge fish-feeding pond, a bear pit, a deer park, rides, a roller coaster and of course, a pool allowing a closer view of the killer whales and belugas.

Performances

As soon as you arrive, head for the theatre where the next performance will be held. Schedules for the shows are posted at the site's entrance. It's better to get there 15 minutes before performances begin. The animal shows last approximately half an hour.

Dolphin, walrus and sea lion shows are presented in the King Waldorf Theatre, left of the entrance. We walked along the amphitheatre's edge and reached a ramp that lead to the top of the auditorium and found seats in one of the last rows (where we had a good view of the show).

The best way to watch the killer whales is through the fabulous underwater viewing windows of Friendship Cove (located a 15-minute walk away from the admission gate). The first sight I had of them left me standing open-mouthed. It is incredible to watch these impressive forces of nature perform their number in unison.

For above-water viewing, it is surrounded by walkways. You might even get a chance to touch the whales. Camera holders, beware! You really can get wet when the beasts suddenly jump out of the water. There are more feeding and touching sessions with the beluga whales in a separate habitat called the Arctic Cove, more off the beaten track.

The Aquarium Dome with underwater viewing windows located in the basement of the theatre (where dolphins used to be) might eventually host walruses. Until then, there's freshwater aquariums located on this level.

One, two, three, GO!

There are three other points of interest not to be missed by animal lovers: the fish pond, the bear pit and the deer park. For the best effect, visit them in that order. A detailed map is given to visitors at the entrance.

You'll be surprised by the number of deer greeting you at the back of the deer park. Most of the 500 animals stay close to the stand where deer food is for sale. Don't expect your corn cup to last long and make sure to hold younger kids in your arms when they feed the deer.

When heading towards these attractions, you'll pass by the kiddie rides area. It includes a small roller coaster, especially designed for the younger crowd, that we really enjoyed. There's a Viking Boat carousel for the whole family and popular

TIPS (fun for 3 years +)

• During the summer, try to arrive no later than 10 am to avoid long line-ups, especially if you want to try the rides.

• Marineland's parking lot is set up lengthwise. If you're parked at one of the extremities, you'll have to walk more than 5 minutes before reaching the park entrance. Furthermore, the attraction is vast. You'll require a stroller for young children. Dolphin-shaped strollers can be rented on site for around $8.

• There's barely any shade on the Marineland site. Don't forget water bottles, hats and sunscreen!

• Don't do what my friend and I tried: to prop our children's caps up on their heads in order to make them reach the required height for a certain ride! The employee took a good 30 seconds to measure them carefully, then refused them access without batting an eye.

• The gift shop is huge and filled with small souvenirs. And by the entrance, there's a noisy (but air-conditioned) video arcade, with games galore.

• The closest campground, **King Waldorf's Tent & Trailer Park** is located behind Marineland at 9015 Stanley Avenue, (905) 295-8191.

• For lunch, expect to pay about $7 for a hamburger with fries at the Marineland cafeteria. You'll find large indoor and outdoor areas with tables by a playground, perfect for picnics.

NEARBY ATTRACTIONS

Wave Swinger (42" min.).

Beyond Friendship Cove, you can find the more elaborate rides, some way too testing for me but all included with the admission.

Dragon Mountain, going through a fake mountain amidst the trees is the world's longest steel roller coaster. It includes lots of tunnel travelling (48"). Even the entrance through a tunnel to access it is cool.

My daredevil went three times in a row into the Sky Screamers, a 450-foot triple tower (48"). It takes stamina to walk up the hill to the tower but you're rewarded by a great view from the lookout. The perfect place to stop for an ice cream cone.

Marineland
• Niagara Falls
1-877-700-0477
www.
marinelandcanada.com

**E-4
Niagara
Region
90-min.**

Schedule: Open from Victoria Day until Thanksgiving. From Victoria Day to late June, open from 10 am to 5 pm. In July and August, open daily from 9 am to 6 pm. Then, open from 10 am to 5 pm until Thanksgiving. All park activities remain in operation until dusk, after the admission gate closes.

Admission: (taxes not included) From the end of June until beginning of September:$40/10-59 years, $33/5 to 9 years and seniors, FREE 4 years and under.

Directions: 7657 Portage Rd., Niagara Falls.Take QEW west towards Niagara Falls, then take McLeod Rd. exit and follow signs.

MUSKOKA WILDLIFE CENTRE

Wild for animals

My young wolf lover and her friend are so thrilled by the promise of seeing three great specimens that they can't resist running wildly up and down the large trails until they reach their favourite animal's den.

This animal heaven is like no other I have visited. In true Muskoka fashion, it is set on uneven beds of rock. This makes for a lovely stroll through the forest with a new habitat to discover at every turn.

Signage by each den offers personal information on each tenant and once you've read one, you're hooked and have to read them all.

Here, we learn that Kootenay, the orphaned black bear, was raised by a B.C. family and now lives with his friend the cougar (they are separated only during feeding time!).

There, we read that Rufus was declawed with human nail clippers by a woman who wanted to keep him as a pet. Further, we meet the beaver. Its teeth were broken when it got to the centre. They healed him and have run all his food through the blender ever since.

During one of the "Meet the creatures" sessions offered indoors near the reception, we could pet a skunk, an opossum and a snapping turtle. Check the animal gallery on their website to see pictures of all their animals.

We took a break for lunch at family restaurant **Washago Village** and returned to the centre for more action. There was lots of choice on their menu and large windows (9620 Hwy 11 South, 705-689-0782, drive north from the centre to the next overpass, to acces Hwy 11 South, the restaurant is 10 minutes southound).

A few minutes further south on Hwy 11, you'll find the parking lot and overpass leading to a great burger place **Webers**. They have a train theme going on. You can eat your take-out meal inside a real train car.

Make sure you allow for some time to watch the cars from the viewpoint over the highway.

By the Hwy 11 South side parking lot, you'll find large beds of rocks to explore. It doesn't matter which way you're driving because there's parking on both sides of the road.

To top off this outing, stop at the **Candy Shoppe** (the "best candy store ever" say my daughter and her friend). Can't miss it, it has two locations on each side of Hwy 11, just north and 2-minutes south of **Webers** (**www.candyshoppe.ca**).

We drove back home, really pleased by all we'd seen. By the way, have you ever been face to face with a moose?

TIPS (fun for 2 years +)
• They don't show the same animals at every "Meet the creatures" session. It's worth seeing more than one!
• The centre's gift shop has a great collection of nature books with local content such as *Animal Tracks of Ontario*.
• Your admission is good for the day. You can go and have lunch outside the premises and come back for more fun.
• The picnic area near the beaver den is gorgeous and adjacent to the wolf space. They open a snack bar during the summer.

NEARBY ATTRACTIONS

Muskoka Wildlife
A-3 North of Toronto 1 hr 50

• **Severn Bridge**
(705) 689-0222
www.muskokawildlifecentre.com

Schedule: Open daily from Victoria Day to Thanksgiving, 10 am to 6 pm. Open on weekends the rest of the year, 12 noon to 5 pm, weather permitting.

Admission: Around 11$/adult, $9/senior & student, $8/3-12 years, $37/family of 5.

Directions: Take Hwy 400 northbound, then follow Hwy 11 northbound, 20 minutes past Orillia, by the highway.

ELMVALE JUNGLE ZOO

I spy...

If your child swears she is seeing a zebra in the woods as you drive along Hwy 27, she speaks the truth!

Elmvale Jungle Zoo houses more than 300 zoo-reared animals that have known no life in the wild: lemurs, tigers, snakes, flamingos, kangaroos, giraffes and more.

I really enjoyed the design of this small zoo. Trees everywhere make it the perfect place to hang out on a very hot day. Some cages are very nicely set along shaded trails in the woods. We bought bags of peanuts to feed the animals.

The trout pond has a small island inhabited by ducks and has a fountain that throws water way up in the air. We could feed the fish to generate some action. Parrots were fun to watch as they tried to grab the shells with their beaks.

There's a snack bar and playground.

Elmvale Jungle Zoo • Elmvale (705) 322-1112 www.elmvalejunglezoo.com	A-2 **Midland Region** 60-min.

 Schedule: Open daily late May to Labour Day from 9:30 (closing at 5 pm on weekdays and 6 pm on weekends until late June, then at 7 pm until Labour Day). Open daily until Thanksgiving, 10 am to 5 pm, weather permitting. Last admission one hour before closing time.

Admission: $12.50/adults, $10/seniors and students, $7/3-12 years, FREE for 2 years and under.

Directions: From Hwy 400 North, take exit #98/Hwy 26 northbound. Follow Hwy 26 into Hwy 27 to Elmvale.

BERGERON'S EXOTIC SANCTUARY

Discovery zone

Around the lane are big cages housing bigger animals: felines, bear, white wolves, fox and... goats, just to remind us that we are on a farm, after all. And the goats are getting along with llamas, just to remind us that we are not on a traditional farm.

In one lane, small cages are prettily invaded by wild plants and decorated with the domestic touch of flower pots. On the ground of a cage, my daughter spots a mother cat carrying her litter by the neck, one after the other. The kittens seem just like regular pets, but the adult looks like a tiny puma. They are jungle cats and are fed raw meat as we watch.

By the entrance, ducks roam free and chickens peck over a pile of fruit and vegetable crop rejects. On a cage next to this, we see Akira, a female timber wolf rejected by her pack and hand-raised by the owners.

As they say, this is a place to go for animals with nowhere to go.

Bergeron's Exotic Animal Sanctuary • Picton (613) 476-4212 www.bergerons.ca	C-6 **East of Toronto** 2 1/2 hrs

 Schedule: Open daily, early April to Thanksgiving, 10 am to 6 pm.

Admission: (cash only) $10/adults, $8/students and seniors, $5/3-12 years, FREE 2 years and under.

Directions: From Picton: Go east on Main St., it becomes County Rd 49. Turn left on County Rd 6, then right onto County Rd 5. They're at #967.

RIVERVIEW PARK & ZOO

On the right track

What a unique combination: a great outdoor playground and a beautiful little zoo. It comes with a small train ride along Otanabee River as a bonus. A definite must if you are in the Peterborough area.

The exhibits (over 27) offer a habitat well-adapted to the animals. Some are quite lovely! I am not the only one to think so, since the Peterborough Zoo was declared one of the two most ethical zoos in Canada by Zoocheck, a Toronto-based organization.

Yaks, various monkeys, snakes, camels, parrots, reindeer, ducks in a huge pond, pot-bellied pigs and other farm animals are nice. But if you ask my children, the playground is even nicer! Kids are attracted like magnets to the zip line, which allows them to fly above the ground over a distance of 15 metres. There's a long flume slide that stretches amongst wild flowers, many climbing structures and a spray pad.

We walked past the duck pond towards the train track, passing by a real plane jacked up on a post. We unfortunately missed the last train. The ride seemed like fun; it crosses over Otanabee River, goes through a tunnel, takes a loop and returns.

We reached the Monkey House and strolled on the trail along the river, back to the playground for more zip line rides.

At the time of print, they were building an Otter Exhibit with waterfall and underwater viewing!

TIPS (fun for 2 years +)

• Since my last visit, they've built a new splash pad promising buckets of water and sprays everywhere! Don't forget the bathing suits.
• Bring insect repellent if you want to go on the trails. It took us approximately 20 minutes to walk from the parking lot to the train stop at the other end of the park.
• During the summer, there are open-air concerts on Sundays at 1:30 pm.
• There's a snack bar and a gorgeous picnic spot down from the playground by the river, where we can walk to a tiny island across a small bridge.

NEARBY ATTRACTIONS
Wild Water & Wheels (15-min.) ..... p. 40

Riverview Park & Zoo
• Peterborough
(705) 748-9300
www.puc.org/zoo

B-5
N-E
of Toronto
2 1/4 hrs

Schedule: Open daily year-round, 8 am to 8:30 pm from May to Labour Day (closes at 4 pm the rest of the year). Train operates from Victoria Day to Labour Day, 10 am to 6 pm.
Admission: FREE, $1/train ride.
Directions: 1230 Water St. North, Peterborough. From Hwy 401 East, take exit #436/Hwy 35/115. Near Peterborough, exit at The Parkway, turn right on Lansdowne St. West, turn left on George St. South, turn right on Water St.

General tips about
Arts & Culture:

- BEWARE! If you buy tickets through services such as **Ticket Master** (**www.ticketmaster.ca**), there could be an extra charge of $5 per ticket or more! And they won't deliver if you buy at the last minute. You can usually buy tickets directly from the venue's box office to save the extra cost.
- Check **www.totix.ca** for discounted tickets sold at 12 noon for same-day shows.

ARTS
& CULTURE

See **Canadian Opera Company** on p. 105.

FUN SUPPLIERS

It's in the bag

I've given many children birthday parties at home and have found that a good supply of original craft material goes a long way.

I never really liked the idea of the additional cost of loot bags on top of those incurred by the birthday party, so I've developed the habit of investing the loot bag money into craft material to be used during an activity related to the theme of the party, which the guest would take home in the loot bag. Make sure you throw in a few candies and you're all set!

Here are a few of my favourite resources for material and craft ideas, for home or school events.

Sandylion Stickers

(905) 475-6771
www.sandylion.com
Directions: 400 Cochrane Dr., Markham (take Hwy 404 North, exit at Hwy 7 westbound, turn south on Cochrane).

Kids adore their stickers and parents adore the Sandylion warehouse bargains! You have to buy a minimum (around $15 worth) but instead of $1.50 for three little squares that you normally pay in a retail store, they'll cost approx. 5¢/square when you buy them in a roll. I strongly suggest you team with another parent to get and split a bigger assortment. They also carry sticker books, activity books and large stickers for decoration. An assorment of stickers makes great teachers' gifts (did you know teachers buy this kind of incentive with their own money?).

Creative Bag

(416) 631-6444
www.creativebag.com
Directions: 880 Steeprock Dr., Toronto (west of Allen Rd., south of Finch). Call (905) 670-2651 for Mississauga outlet.

This warehouse carries all sizes of bags and boxes, in all kinds of materials, as well as ribbon, tulle, tissue paper, gift wrap, etc. The best place I know to buy cute tiny clear loot or candy bags.

Retail Bag Company

(416) 504-0280
www.retailbag.com
Directions: 430 Adelaide West, Toronto (west of Spadina).

This downtown location is smaller than **Creative Bag** but still a great place for boxes and bags of all kinds and sizes. It is one of the few stores I know which sells cute Chinese takeout boxes (great as loot bags or to decorate as a craft activity).

The Palmer Group

(905) 670-7999
www.palmerkids.com

Louise Kool & Galt

(416) 293-0312
www.louisekool.com
Directions: 180 Middlefield Rd., Scarborough (east of McCowan Rd. and south of Finch).

Order these two suppliers' catalogues! They're full of affordable craft material we don't always see in retail stores. Palmer Group requires a minimum order of $100, no delivery charges. Louise Cool & Galt charges delivery but requires no minimum order and you save 10% if you pick it up at their warehouse (open to the public). They also carry toys, playroom furniture and more.

Sassy Bead

(416) 488-7400
www.thesassybeadco.com
Directions: 2076 Yonge St., Toronto.

This great store sells beads of all types. Every time I have been there, a great number of bead creations were displayed to inspire us. For bigger kids you could buy material to make spring or elastic bracelets.
The tiny bead boxes allow you to line up a 2-metre-long string of beads. There's a vast selection of fancy metal charms for under $2. For younger kids, I bought a $25 bag of large beads shaped like teddy bears (perfect for making necklaces with preschoolers). I noticed many $10-$15 bead kits to create animals. Ask about their birthday package.

Art Attacks
www.artattack.co.uk

I've been a great fan of Englishman Neil Buchanan, the creator of the outstanding craft show *Art Attack*, from the beginning and have followed him through all his haircuts since 1989. As soon as my son was old enough to understand the concept, he emulated Neil's big art attacks by arranging his toys on the floor into a giant "art installation" we could admire from the stairs. Neil's website is as funky as his television show and includes over 100 elaborate "art attacks": unique craft activities creating art you can use in your daily life. It provides a step-by-step description with pictures.

DeSerres
www.deserres.ca

It started as Omer DeSerres in Montreal, Quebec, then acquired Loomis & Toles art supply chain in Ontario in 1988. That's why stores all around the GTA called DeSerres or Loomis Art Store look alike. DeSerres is the largest retailer of art and craft supplies in Canada. They've developed a vast network of international suppliers which explains why this is the best place to find out about the latest new ideas and products. The stores are gorgeous and usually show many finished craft projects to inspire us.

R. Hiscott Theatrical Supplies

(416) 977-5247
www.hiscott.ca
Directions: 435 Yonge St., Toronto.

You might have noticed in the past the great artists of Kromatic turning children's faces into masterpieces during **Harbourfront Centre** events or at **Toronto Buskerfest**. I asked them where I could find the make-up they use to paint on skin and they sent me to this place. I found great colours in small compacts, perfect sponges and fabulous glittering powder so fine it is 100% safe to use on kids' faces. They also carry a wide selection of fancy Halloween make-up supplies like scars!

Family Fun
www.familyfun.com

For years, I've ripped and filed pages from the fantastic US magazine *Family Fun*. I would collect their craft suggestions, travel ideas, game descriptions and more. Now it's all available on their website. If you go to their **Arts + Crafts** section, you'll find a plethora of cute craft ideas with pictures of the end result. You can search by **Holidays & Seasonal** (including many ideas for **April Fool's Day**) or by **Age** (over 1,300 suggestions for 6 to 8 years old!).

DUSK DANCE

Dance to another tune

Going to the park takes on new meaning when the Dusk Dance event is on. Kids are in for a surprise! They might see white-clad people hiding in the forest under the spell of strange music, graceful women running around the field with flowing scarves, acrobat dancers jumping from trees...

Dusk Dance provides quite a refreshing approach to modern dance and clearly is an original way to expose our kids to contemporary dance.

The concept is clever: The public is led from one station to the next through a public park, to enjoy a series of five 10-minute choreographies inspired by the natural surroundings. Some pieces are more traditional; others are quite experimental or even hilarious. The dancers are often within arms reach of the wide-eyed kids. You can see many children impulsively mimicking the movements of the artists.

Even the presentation between choreographies is funny. As we walked to the next performance, following our host, he suggested, tongue in cheek, that we do a collective sound: "Lets all say bahhhhh!" Hundreds of us did; picture that!

TIPS (fun for 4 years +)

• Don't install yourself too comfortably before the event because you will keep changing places to watch the next choreography somewhere else in the park. A thick blanket could be useful.
• More about **Dufferin Grove Park** on p. 288. More on **Withrow Park** in the **Pape Subway Station** section on p. 443.

Dusk Dance (416) 504-6429, ext. 41 www.duskdances.ca	**D-3** **Downtown** **Toronto** **20-min.**

 Schedule: Usually several evenings in a row, starting end of June or beginning of July (depending on the dance companies' schedules). Normally at 7:30 pm.

Admission: Pay-what-you-can.

Directions: In Toronto, has been held in three different parks: **Withrow Park**, south of Danforth, between Carlaw Ave. and Logan Ave., **Dufferin Grove Park** on Dufferin, south of Bloor St. West, and **Firgrove Park**, south of Finch, west of Jane on Firgrove Crescent. More locations outside of Toronto. Check their website for locations selected for the current year.

FAMOUS PEOPLE PLAYERS

In the dark

Taking your child to Famous People Players' dinner theatre is as close as you'll get to a grown-up outing without incurring the cost of a sitter.

Your only concern here may be to maintain children's appropriate behaviour during the elaborate hour-long dinner. After the show, all guests come back to the dining room for a tasty dessert.

It is likely the white-gloved waiter serving your meal in the dining room will also perform on stage that evening. This you won't find out though until all performers remove their black hoods for the closing salute.

All productions are presented in black light, that is with performers who remain unseen to the public because they are dressed in black against a black backdrop, and who manipulate various fluorescent props that seemingly "float" around with a life of their own. Light-

hearted, the shows often include tall puppet characters (controlled by three performers), lip-syncing to original musical scores, and humourously designed objects miming scenes in a lively choreography.

Various musical productions are presented throughout the year, with some involving a story, while others simply present a series of great songs. All use the same concept.

I attended a **Christmas** show with two boys aged 7 and 9, and both just loved it. Musicals are appropriate for any child who likes lively songs.

Parents will be moved when they learn this company's mandate is to present world class stage productions and integrate, through training, people who are developmentally challenged. Between the reception, the restaurant, and the performance, these people run the whole show!

As the founder of the company, Diane Dupuy, puts it: "What you see is sensational... What you don't see is inspirational."

TIPS (fun for 7 years +)

• Stars' photos you'll see on the walls aren't there just for decorating purposes. These famous actors and singers have actually made financial contributions to Famous People Players.

NEARBY ATTRACTIONS
Ontario Place (10-min.) .... p. 18
High Park (15-min.) .... p. 286

Famous People Players Dine & Dream Theatre (416) 532-1137 www.fpp.org	**D-3** **Downtown** **Toronto** **10-min.**

  Schedule: Open year-round from Tuesday to Saturday. Dinner shows: arrival at 6 pm, dinner at 7 pm, show at 8 pm, dessert at 9:30 pm. Lunch shows: arrival at 11:30 am, lunch at 12 noon, show at 1 pm, dessert at 2:30 pm.
Admission: (tax not included) $52.50/adults, $45.50/seniors, $40/12 years and under.
Directions: 110 Sudbury St., Toronto. From Lake Shore, go north on Strachan. Turn west on King St. and turn right on Sudbury St. (west of Shaw St.).

MYSTERIOUSLY YOURS

Guess what?

Around dessert time, the extroverted members of a noisy family pour into the restaurant from every angle, entering into individual conversations with diners, in a joyous cacophony. A piano player swiftly replaces the taped music in the background and all of a sudden, we are in the midst of the Godfather's retirement party.

A nervous black-eyed man with unbuttoned tuxedo shirt asks my wide-eyed son if he has seen a little plastic bag somewhere while the Godfather, his dad, graciously welcomes "dear friends" at the next table. In the vicinity, his sister is fishing for compliments on her Versace party dress while a pink satin-clad woman is kissing an "old boyfriend" she had just "recognized" amongst the guests.

TIPS (fun for 10 years +)

• The restaurant opens at 6:30 pm but action only starts at around 8 pm. The mystery is solved before 10:30 pm.
• Drinks and soft drinks are not included in the fixed price of the meal.
• Most items offered on the menu won't appeal to the average child. You may arrive a bit before 8 pm and pay only for the play. Note there's a **Mandarin** at 2200 Yonge Street, in Canada Square, four blocks north of the theatre (with well-priced parking at the top of Canada Square). Reservations are a must, as you don't want to be late for the show; call (416) 486-2222.
• Matinee presentations are offered at least two Wednesdays each month at the **Toronto Historic Old Mill** Restaurant (lunch at 11:30 am, mystery at 1 pm); around $46/lunch and show, around $32/show only, plus tax.

People of all ages attend the show. The nice (and young) grandparents at our table are quick to offer repartees to the actors who come to visit us. The more we improvise, the funnier it gets. My companion is thrilled to watch adults play make-believe!

It doesn't take long for a murder to occur (the Godfather's son) and for Lieutenant Carumbo to appear, bearing an unmistakable resemblance to Peter Falk's Colombo. The subsequent interrogation launches into quick and witty dialogue between the comedians evenly spread throughout the restaurant.

Many of us end up acting a small staged part, adding to the interactive nature of the attraction (my 10-year-old was turned into a mobster offering his condolences to the Godfather, cigar in mouth). Throughout the play, clues are given away; little details that will help those who listen carefully solve the mystery. We are too busy laughing to pay attention.

The murders staged by Mysteriously Yours keep changing. Over thirty plays were created over the last seventeen years. You can expect a different mystery roughly every six months, investigated by the likes of Hercule Poirot, Miss Marple or Sherlock Holmes.

Mysteriously Yours (416) 486-7469 www. mysteriouslyyours.com	**D-3** **Downtown** **Toronto** **25-min.**

Schedule: Year-round, every Friday and Saturday and selected Thursdays (dinner from 6:30 pm, mystery at 8 pm).
Admission: (excluding tax) $65/dinner and show, $40/show only ($5 more on Saturdays). $5 off for seniors and full-time students.
Directions: 2026 Yonge St., Toronto (two blocks north of Davisville Subway).

STAGE WEST

Go West!

A buffet instead of a fixed menu makes a big difference, especially with young children. It allows them to stretch their legs, returning again and again to explore the exciting display of food. Then, they're ready to settle down to watch the show.

We remain at our table in the elegant theatre restaurant to enjoy the performance. Many seats in the large multi-level room are horseshoe-shaped booths. I love the cozy feeling of these and they were a great hit with my daughter. Covered with a long tablecloth, it made for a nice little fort to hide under with her little friend after dessert, before the play.

If you can't book a booth, don't worry. Conveniently, you'll have a good view of the stage from any of the well-padded seats.

The children's productions are lunch shows presented during the March Break and Christmas time. I've seen three different ones; they all lasted a bit less than one hour. While I found some better than

Photo: Courtesy of Stage West

others, my kids were equally thrilled by the whole experience on all three occasions.

All year round, they also produce dinner musicals and concerts, many suitable for families such as tributes to the Beatles, Abba and other legendary singers. They look like the real thing! I suspect these would be fun for pre-teens.

To give you an idea of the kind of plays they produce: In 2008, they present among other things *Beauty and the Beast* Broadway musical and *Little Horror Shop* the off-Broadway show.

Stage West is also a hotel! Their family packages are popular among local families who just want a change of scene. Must be the hotel's pool with a 3-storey-high water slide!

TIPS (fun for 4 years +)

• Their **Christmas** Getaway Package for a family of 4 includes: 2 nights in a suite, 4 tickets to kids' lunch show, buffet breakfast for 4 (2 mornings), use of pool and waterslide (around $400 plus tax).
• Their **March** Getaway Package for a family of 4 includes the same and more: craft room, games room, bingo, fun classes, Children's Museum on the Go exhibit and free shuttle to **Square One** (around $350 plus tax).

Stage West Theatre Restaurant	D-3 N-W of Toronto 35-min.

Stage West Theatre Restaurant
• **Mississauga**
(905) 238-0042
1-800-263-0684
www.stagewest.com

Schedule: Lunch normally from 12:30 pm, show at 1:45 pm. Call to confirm. **Christmas** shows on Saturdays, usually mid-November to first week of January. **March Break** shows on some Saturdays in March/April and during the March Break weekdays (except Wednesday). Check their website or call for the year-round program of concerts or plays.
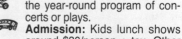
Admission: Kids lunch shows around $30/person + tax. Other dinner shows around $60 + tax.
Directions: 5400 Dixie Rd., Mississauga (south of Hwy 401, turn west on Matheson Blvd. to access entrance).

ART GALLERY OF ONTARIO

Off the Wall!

"My little artist's jaw drops once his tiny drawing on a minuscule plastic square is placed into a slide and changed into a huge and flamboyant mural that appears like magic on the dark wall. That's how AGO turns the newest generation into artists."

This is how I described our favourite feature at the AGO, prior to the renovations.

At the time of print, the AGO was closed for major renovations but I found out a few facts that will reassure the families who are fond of the Gallery: It will be even more family-friendly and interactive for all ages than before. They plan to offer hands on art activities in spaces throughout the Gallery.

TIPS (fun for 3 years +)

• It is pretty safe to assume that **AGO** will remain the sure bet it has always been for a successful **March Break** outing! Check their website for details.
• The new gift and book store will continue to include many great children's toys. It will be two levels and located at the corner of McCaul and Dundas, where we'll also find a casual café, a fine dining restaurant and a FREE contemporary art space for new projects.
• For a description of what's around **St. Patrick Subway Station**, a 5-minute walk from the AGO (including adjacent foodcourt), see p. 452.

Off the Wall!, the most popular discovery section for children, will remain at the same place but will undergo a dramatic redesign.

The Gallery School will also remain at the same location. This large studio sometimes offers drop-in activities during special events. At the time of print, they were already announcing **Smorgasbord Sundays** when we could choose from different workshops for the whole family, introducing new activities and art material every Sunday ($15/one adult + one child, $40/family of five, 416-979-6608).

On paper, the new AGO did not look as impressive as it felt when standing next to the 600-foot-long glass and wood façade along Dundas Street. It looked like Noah's ark in the making!

The new entrance will be aligned with Walker Court (flooded with natural light from a new glass roof) and **The Grange** historic house within the building. The new south façade will complement the **OCAD**'s funky architecture and offer a gorgeous background for **Grange Park** and its playground (with wading pool). Let's hope that part remains untouched!

A very important fact to know: The number of galleries will go from 50 to 110! That's what you get for $254 million.

Art Gallery of Ontario (AGO) (416) 979-6615 (family) or (416) 979-6649 www.ago.net	D-3 Downtown Toronto 10-min.

 Schedule: Should re-open in Fall 2008. Check their website for details.

 Admission: Not determined at the time of print.

 Directions: 317 Dundas St. West, Toronto (between McCaul and Beverley).

NEARBY ATTRACTIONS

Eaton Centre (5-min.) .... p. 168
Textile Museum (10-min walk.) ... p. 242

MOCCA

Queen buzz

Knitted muffins, Chiyogami paper, blue trees, antique brass elevator, funky characters... and you've not even entered the Mocca yet!

Start your Queen West journey with the Museum of Contemporary Canadian Art (MOCCA) as an anchor. Then, take it from there and see what comes along.

There are enough funky things to discover between **Trinity-Bellwoods Park** and Gladstone Avenue to spend a nice afternoon with older kids with artistic sensibility.

You'll recognize MOCCA's building by the blue trees erected by its entrance. When we visited it, we were greeted at the door by cheers and flashes. This art installation recreated for us the feeling of being rich and famous on the red carpet. That put us in a playful mood!

A pile of posters ornate with intricate drawings seemed to invite us to help ourselves... each of them warned us that it was printed with poison ivy. The adult in me played mental games, trying to figure out if an artist would dare punish me in such a way for touching her art. The youth accompanying me didn't even

think and grabbed one (with no harm).

In the rest of the large room, different exhibitions were calling for our attention: a movie on a wall, a sports circuit, collages, etc. Exhibits change but you'll always find art to fuel interesting conversations with young art buffs.

Walking eastbound from the Museum, you'll reach **Trinity-Bellwoods Park** where the **Queen West Art Crawl** is held every September (one of the best times to visit the area). Across the street is **The Paper Place** (887 Queen), offering an amazing selection of papers and related products, and the hip **Chippy's Fish & Chips** (893 Queen).

Go westbound and you'll see **The Knit Cafe** (1050 Queen), where you can buy unique yarn and simple patterns, knit and have a cappuccino. Check www.theknitcafetoronto.com (click on the door) to see how funky they are! First time I saw their shop, their window was filled with knitted muffins on plates.

You might want to check the bargains at **Woolfitt's Art Supplies** (1153 Queen). You'll definitely want to see the **Gladstone Hotel** (1214 Queen, 15-min. walk from the MOCCA) to feel the real buzz of Queen West. Show your young companions the room photos in the hotel's scrapbook at the reception. Each one was decorated by a different artist. Then, ride up the antique elevator to the upper floors where you'll find art exhibitions in the corridors.

TIPS (fun for 10 years +)

• The **Queen West Art Crawl** is organized by **Toronto Artscape**, an organization dedicated to unlocking "the creative potential of people and places". For details on their lively event (including an interactive kids zone), visit **www.toronto-artscape.on.ca** and click **Programs**.

Museum of Contemporary Canadian Art
(416) 395-0067
www.mocca.toronto.ca

D-3
Downtown
Toronto
10-min.

Schedule: Tuesday to Sunday, 11 am to 6 pm. Closed on Mondays and during change of exhibitions. Better call ahead.
Admission: FREE, donation accepted.
Directions: 952 Queen Street West, Toronto (between Ossington Ave. and **Trinity-Bellwoods Park**).

GARDINER MUSEUM

Great on all levels!

Hard to imagine a ceramic museum could be of much interest for the kids but put yourself in the I-Spy game state of mind and you'll find something to catch their imagination on all four levels of the Gardiner Museum.

The museum reopened in 2006, bigger, with an additional 14,000 square feet, and more beautiful, with an architectural make over.

Start your visit with a look at the original pieces in the Modern and Contemporary Ceramics section at the ground level. Not only will you be able to admire a Picasso vase and Chagall art but kids will be amazed to see that ceramic can be made to look like leather, metal, cement, glass, fabric or wood in the skilled hands of modern artists.

In the Ancient Americas gallery, you'll see fascinating artefacts dating from A.D. 200-850 (A.D. meaning Anno Domini, Latin for "in the year of our Lord", and not "After Djesus" as joked the mother accompanying me).

The colourful art in adjacent Italian Renaissance Maiolica gallery was detailed and beautiful. Don't miss the *Fiery Furnace* scene on a 1550's dish by Urbino!

On the second level, there are interesting battle scenes on the plates of the Chinese Porcelain section to your right, bathed with sunlight from the large windows.

In case you were wondering what exactly is Chinese porcelain, it is a mixture of kaolin (a pure white clay that forms when certain minerals break down) and petuntse or China stone (ground to a fine powder), fired at a very high temperature.

The most whimsical pieces are found in the European Porcelain gallery and date from mid-18th century. Among our favourites: the Monkey Orchestra figurines and the Pug dogs from Germany, the canine on a porcelain dog house and the scene of a wolf eating a deer on a plate from Austria, the life-size rabbit from England and the wall displaying one hundred tiny scent bottles.

The third level hosts a vast Special Exhibition Gallery where changing exhibitions are displayed, with plenty of space to circulate between the masterpieces. This is the level where you'll find the stylish Jamie Kennedy at the Gardiner restaurant and the two terraces from which you get a gorgeous view of Queen's Park and the **ROM**.

When the **Open Clay Studio** is open for drop-in sessions in the lower level, there's a professional ceramist on hand to help.

TIPS (fun for 8 years +)

• Tickets for the drop-in **Open Clay Studio** sessions go on sale 30 minutes prior to each session (does not include the admission cost).

• More about the **Twelve Trees of Christmas** on p. 171.

Gardiner Museum (416) 586-8080 www. gardinermuseum.com	**D-3** **Downtown** **Toronto** **10-min.**

 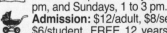 **Schedule:** Open daily at 10 am. Closes at 6 pm, Monday to Thursday, at 9 pm on Fridays, and at 5 pm on weekends. **Open Clay Studio** drop-in: Fridays, 6 to 8 pm, and Sundays, 1 to 3 pm. **Admission:** $12/adult, $8/senior, $6/student, FREE 12 years and under. FREE on Fridays, 4 to 9 pm and all day on first Friday of every month. **Open Clay Studio** drop-in: $10/adults, $8/seniors, $5/12 years and under, $3/firing fee per piece.

Directions: 111 Queen's Park, Toronto (just south of Bloor Street).

McMichael Art Collection

Inspired hands-on

There is no better way to introduce kids to art appreciation than by taking them to a drop-in studio activity in the heart of the McMichael gallery on a Family Sunday. Who knows what awaits them? They might create their own sketch book or cut and layer coloured tissue paper into a landscape.

When we were visiting, one hands-on workshop was held in the little studio located in front of the gallery. Our youngster got to choose from a mountain of socks adorned with glass eyes and rubber noses and made her own animal puppet.

No other painters have better depicted nature than Tom Thompson and the Group of Seven. The museum holds more than 2,000 of their masterpieces.

Seeing Group of Seven reproductions on placemats and stamps has never given me the feeling of being overexposed to their art. Each time, I rediscover them with the eyes of a child. But seeing these paintings with a child is another story, I must admit.

An easy way to do it is to select a theme and have them look for it in the paintings. This treasure hunt may lead to cries of excitement when they spot their theme but... galleries are not churches after all!

We criss-crossed all the rooms, looking for autumn leaves on the canvases. The gallery's walls seemed to my son like storybook pages on which he was looking for coloured trees.

Meanwhile, he was noticing that certain landscapes were covered in snow and that people were drawn on others. It became a great observation exercise on the sly.

Wide windows, framing the same nature painters seek to capture, are another reason to appreciate the gallery.

Just looking through them makes us want to go outside and play. That's exactly what we did after our tour. A wide path, lined with little trails, undulates through the site. On our way to the parking lot, we stopped to pet a few bronze wolves resting by the path!

TIPS (fun for 4 years +)

• For a great **March Break** off the beaten track, the gallery offers special drop-in craft activities, hands-on activities and entertainment in the lobby and in different galleries.

• The Discovery Space on the upper level is more interactive than the other galleries.

• The **McMichael Café** sells light lunches.

NEARBY ATTRACTIONS

McMichael Canadian Art Collection
· Kleinburg
(905) 893-1121
www.mcmichael.com

C-3
N-W
of Toronto
45-min.

Schedule: Open daily 10 am to 4 pm (closes at 5 pm from May to October). Family Sundays are held on the second Sunday each month, 11 am to 4 pm.
Admission: $15/adults, $12/6-18 years and seniors, $30/family of 5, FREE for 5 years and under. Parking is around $5.
Directions: 10365 Islington Ave., Kleinburg. From Hwy 400 North, take exit #35/Major Mackenzie Dr. westbound, then follow the signs to Kleinburg.

TORONTO PUBLIC LIBRARY

Kids flip... the pages

Through the Toronto Public Library, over 12 million items are put at our disposal: books, videos, CDs, CD-ROMs, cassettes, magazines and newspapers, in more than 100 languages. It is an invaluable free service.

To obtain a library card, go to any branch and bring identification on which your name and address appear.

We can borrow up to 50 items for a 21-day period, a manageable time limit

TIPS (fun for 2 years +)

• Obtain a library card under your child's name. The late fine is much lower for children than for adults! Take a sturdy bag to the library to bring back all the books the children want.

• Your child can hear a story on the phone 24 hours a day with the Dial-A-Story service! Stories for different age groups are told in over ten languages: (416) 395-5400.

• Toronto Public Library pays special attention to the March Break. In the What's On issue of January to March, you may consult the March Break Highlight pages or check the programs scheduled for each branch to find out about entertaining and free activities involving Reptilia, Stylamanders, Mad Science or clowns, to name a few cool options.

• Many branches also offer activities during Halloween.

for busy parents. Videos can be borrowed at no charge for a 7-day period.

Thanks to a computerized system, most books (except the current Best Bets) can be borrowed from and returned to any branch (which can be useful when visiting another part of the city). You can also request books to be shipped to your local branch from any of the 99 branches.

Library activities

Books are just the tip of the iceberg. You need to flip through a copy of the Toronto Public Library publication What's On to grasp the extent and variety of the free activities that take place at the different branches, many of which are drop-in activities. Most programs are less than one hour long.

Many branches offer programs for children: Babytime (for babies 0-18 months) or Toddler Time (19-35 months). Preschool Storytime is for those who are ready to be on their own in a group. Family Preschool Storytime is for children 1 to 5 with their parents or caregivers.

I have attended many activities with my children. Each time, we stayed afterwards to read books and came back with piles of them.

Lillian H. Smith Library

The Lillian H. Smith branch (located at 239 College Street, east of Spadina, (416) 393-7746) offers thousands of illustrated book titles, including hundreds of books for toddlers.

Younger children love to go there to see the spiral staircase and to sit in the pleasant reading corner for kids.

Toronto Public Library
(416) 393-7131
www.tpl.toronto.on.ca

 Schedule: Varies. Check online.
Admission: The late fine is 30¢ per day per item up to a maximum of $12 per item for adults;
 15¢ per day up to a maximum of $6 per item for teenagers and
 10¢ per day up to a maximum of $4 per item for children 12 years and under. To replace a lost card, it is $2/adults and $1/children (cash or cheque only).
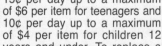 **Directions:** 99 locations around the GTA.

WORD ON THE S

Street smart

In the large Kidstreet section, you may see favourite children's hosts on the stage, hug Caillou, Franklin the Turtle or other popular characters. But more importantly, savvy young readers can see in the flesh Canadian Children's authors and browse through all the important children's book publishers and bookstores' booths.

visitors take advantage of this great cultural event every fall. They have done so for the last eighteen years. They know they can always rely on over 260 exhibitors under tents: Book and magazine publishers (including myself, come and meet me!), bookstores and more offering bargains or freebies.

The event's setting in and around Queen's Park is perfect. It is common to see visitors sitting on the grass, already involved in the reading of a new book.

There is a large food vendors' section offering a wide variety of takeout options to eat at the picnic tables.

For a site map and exhibitors listing check the *Toronto Star* the day before the event (Saturday).

Got kids in immersion?

Indoor book fairs have been a tradition for years in Quebec so it was natural for Toronto Francophones to import the concept.

Le Salon du livre de Toronto (Toronto French Book Fair) provides a space where you can buy French books and meet with authors from Quebec, Ontario, France and other Francophone countries, with a great emphasis on children's books.

Thousands of students flock from the French and immersion schools all around the GTA to attend workshops put together for them.

The event is usually scheduled Thursday to Saturday, on a week between the end of September and mid-October. Admission is around $10/adults, $5/children. In 2007, the event was held at the Moss Park Armoury on Queen Street East but the location for 2008 was still unknown at the time of print. Call or check their website closer to September (416-670-9847, www.salondulivredetoronto.org).

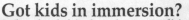

NEARBY ATTRACTIONS

Word On The Street	**D-3**
(416) 504-7241	**Downtown**
www.	**Toronto**
thewordonthestreet.ca	**10-min.**

 Schedule: Rain or shine. Usually on the last Sunday of September, from 11 am to 6 pm.
Admission: FREE.
Directions: The Toronto event runs on both sides of Queen's Park Circle, from Wellesley to Charles St., just south of the **Royal Ontario Museum** as well as in the park. The Kidstreet section is usually located on the west side of Queen's Park Cr. Closest subway access is **Museum Station.** (The event also runs in Kitchener, Victoria Park, on the same day!)

DRIVE-IN THEATRES

Don't remain seated

Some families are real pros at making themselves at home at the drive-in. One of them has parked its mini-van with open hatchback facing the screen, allowing two teenagers to lay down on their bellies to watch the movie. Their parents are comfortably seated wrapped in blankets on foldable chairs, beside the vehicle, feet up on a footstool and small dog on their lap.

Where else can your kids leave their seats to stretch their legs while watching a movie? At home, watching a video?… That's true. But here, you get to see the latest movies and you have a chance to socialize. Plus, smokers find

an obvious advantage to the outdoor drive-ins.

To get to the 5 Drive-In in Oakville, we drive through farmland (maybe not for long considering the way developments are catching up).

A big 5 Drive-In neon sign glows in the twilight. "Why do you call it 5 Drive-In if you have only three screens?" enquires my son. The man at the booth laughs and explains: "Cause we're located near Dundas, still called Hwy 5 by some!"

The three screens are placed back to back in a triangle. The biggest, Starlite(#1), can park 520 cars while the Sunset (#2) and Cosmic (#3) theatres respectively accommodate 330 and 150 cars with smaller screens.

It's 7:40 pm. We have to wait until the sun sets, at around 8:30 pm (we attended on a warm night in September). Kids play ball under the Sunset screen. My son is engaged in a game with new friends.

We admire a magnificent sunset, another advantage to a drive-in, and the double feature begins. Oops! I realize I should have brought Windex to clean my windshield!

TIPS (fun for 5 years +)

• You will catch the movie sound track on your car radio, through a local radio frequency, motor off. Don't worry, it won't drain your battery.
• You can play volleyball while you wait for the movie to start.
• There is a snack bar with the long and narrow look of diners from the 50's in the Starlite section. During the summer, it includes a BBQ pit from which you can get corn on the cob, sausages, chicken...
• See p. 352 for information on the only drive-in in Toronto at **Polson Pier**.
• The 3-screen **North York Drive-in Theatre**, in Newmarket, is located at 893 Mount Albert Rd. West, (905) 836-4444. Check **www.northyorkdrivein.com**.

NEARBY ATTRACTIONS
Shell Skate Park (15-min.) .... p. 357
Coronation Park (15-min.) .... p. 426

---

5 Drive-In
• Oakville
(905) 257-8272
www.5drivein.com

D-2
West
of Toronto
35-min.

 Schedule: Opens 3 days/week from late winter, daily during the summer, then 5 days until early winter, first feature starting at sundown. Go online for details.
Admission: $11/adult, $2/6-12 years, FREE for 5 years and under, $5/adults on Tuesdays, $15/car on Thursdays.
Directions: 2332, 9th Line in Oakville. Take QEW, exit at Ford Dr. North. It becomes the 9th Line, check east side.

IMAX AND OMNIMAX

Super-sized movie experience

You're flying over mountains, almost touching the rocky tops. Then the breathtaking sea reveals itself in all its splendour and you feel your plane taking a plunge until it levels a few metres above the waves. For a while, you can admire coral reefs through the turquoise water just before you dive under to follow a school of sharks...

I think Imax technology is used at its best when revealing an environment very few of us will ever get to see. My son disagrees, more inclined to appreciate Imax the most when it depicts extreme speed and sports.

Whatever the artistic themes behind the Imax movies, what makes them different from regular theatres is the technology. The film used to shoot the images is three times larger than standard film used in Hollywood productions. The resulting frame is 10 times bigger than the 35mm used in regular theatres.

In Imax theatres, a person's head in the row in front of you reaches your knee level. There's no question you'll have a perfect view of the 8-storey-high screen.

Imax screens are painted silver to better reflect the images and they are perforated with hundreds of thousands of tiny holes to let the sound go through perfectly.

The best place to understand the Imax technology is the **Omnimax Theatre (Imax Dome Theatre)** located under the noticeable dome of the **Ontario Science Centre** (p. 247). In the back of the Science Centre's lobby, you'll find large bay windows overlooking the impressive Imax projection room.

All Imax screens are designed to encompass our peripheral vision but it is at the **Omnimax Theatre** that the impression is the strongest. Its curved screen spreads over more than half of the vast surface of the dome. This allows the image to reach as high above and far to the right and the left as your eyes can normally see without moving your head!

Omnimax Theatre is also the only place screening a 15-minute presentation before the movies, an attraction in itself! It allows us to see the apparently solid dome disappear over our heads to reveal the 44 speakers. Sound effects will make you think an airplane is taking off right in front of you. Visual effects will make your kids throw their arms in a Superman fashion to fly through the universe in a tunnel of light.

Cinesphere at **Ontario Place** (p. 18) was the first Imax theatre to open in the world, in 1971. It is the biggest theatre, with 752 seats. **Scotiabank Theatre Imax** is the tallest with a 90-foot screen.

TIPS (fun for 5 years +)

• Documentaries with landscapes are more interesting than the ones with lots of close-ups. Watching the 3,600 sq. ft. image of a gorilla can be nauseating, especially on a curved screen.

• **Niagara Falls Imax Theatre** is another large theatre with 620 seats (see **Niagara Falls** on p. 269).

Imax Theatres
www.imax.com

Omnimax Theatre
(416) 696-1000
www.ontariosciencecentre.com

Ontario Place Cinesphere
(416) 314-9900
www.ontarioplace.com

Cineplex Imax
www.cineplex.com
  • **Scotiabank Theatre Toronto**
    (416) 368-5600
  • **Coliseum Mississauga**
    (905) 275-3456
  • **Colossus Woodbridge**
    (905) 851-1001

SPROCKETS FILM FESTIVAL

Reel fun

"Didn't we get the ticket already?" inquires a four-year-old girl standing in line in front of us at the Festival. "Yes sweetheart", replies her dad, "but that was the parking ticket".

TIPS (fun for 3 years +)
• When we visited, the doors opened at 9:45 am and some 10 am presentations were already sold out. It is better to reserve tickets online or by calling. Program information is available both ways. They start selling tickets by the end of March. You can order on the same day. They'll give you a confirmation number to present at the theatre.
• The English subtitles for many foreign language films are read aloud by a narrator.
• Sprockets' **Globetrotter Series** allows us to see international children's movies when the festival is over. Suitable for children 8 years and over, each monthly presentation comes with a detailed introduction to explain the film topics. The series now runs one Sunday every month from October to March at 12:30 pm ($11/adults, $10/children, $19/for one adult and one child). Check their website for details.
• While the festival is at **Canada Square**, you might want to combine a movie with a meal at the all-you-can-eat Chinese **Mandarin** in the same building, (416-486-2222, **www.mandarinbuffet.com**).
• **Hot Docs** is a 10-day international festival of documentaries usually held in April. It includes some documentaries interesting for children. Presented in various locations; around $10/adults, FREE for students and children. Check **www.hotdocs.ca** or call (416) 203-2155.

First held in 1998, the Sprockets Festival is the little brother of the famous **Toronto International Film Festival**. It aims to present the best films from around the world, made for children 4 to 17 years of age.

I am not one to think that big commercial successes are automatically lacking depth and meaningful messages, but it is a great opportunity to take a break from Disney! In many of the films for children 8 years and older, young viewers can relate to the way the young characters learn to overcome their difficulties. Some films include animation in various forms: claymation, digital, puppet or multi-media animation.

They usually try to thrill younger children with series of shorts normally held at the beginning of the day. In previous years, it was presented as the Reel Rascals presentations.

Looking for the next Atom Egoyan? Jump Cuts is another original event under the Toronto Film Festival Group umbrella, screening films and videos made by Ontarians from grade 3 to 12.

Sprockets Toronto International Film Festival for Children
(416) 968-3456
www.sprockets.ca

D-3
Downtown
Toronto
15-min.

Schedule: Usually runs 10 consecutive days from mid-April, 10 am to 9 pm, including an opening night for the whole family on Friday and the two weekends (on the weekdays, it 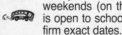is open to schools). Call to confirm exact dates.

Admission: Around $11/adults, $7/under 18 (usually cheaper for adults for Reel Rascals and Jump Cuts). Costs a bit more on opening night.

Directions: Was held at the Cineplex (formally Famous Players) Canada Square for the last few years (2190 Yonge, south of Eglinton Ave.). Will be there in 2008. Call to confirm following year location!

NFB MEDIATHEQUE

Photo: Courtesy of NFB

Culture doesn't get cooler than this!

My young movie buff casually slides behind a console in the cozy parlour, as if he had lived in this kind of futuristic environment all his life. Down goes the headrest with enclosed speakers, up goes the volume, tap-tap knock the fingers on the touch screen and off he boldly goes, in the universe of Canadian cinematic culture.

Just $2 and you get to use the viewing stations all day. The staff member gives you an access code to enter into the console and it's all yours.

The fact is, our tax dollars have allowed Canadian creators to explore their art for decades and the free Mediatheque is National Film Board's way of giving something in return while celebrating Canadian productions.

TIPS (fun for 5 years +)

• When viewing shorts with children at the consoles, it is better to select the **Children's Material** category under the **Film Genre** section. It will direct you to all productions appropriate for children.
• The animation workshop is a drop-in activity but it is very popular. It is better to reserve in advance and to arrive at the beginning of the workshop to ensure that your child will have enough time to complete his animation. An adult must accompany children.
• Bring a USB device to make a copy of your animated short or leave your e-mail and they will send it to you! Kids get to take home their clay creation.
• No food is allowed on the premises. Finish with a snack at neighbour **Indigo**.

I did not expect such a selection! Over 800 animated, documentary, short and feature films (roughly 10% of the entire NFB inventory), including over 200 in French. And they keep adding choices on a weekly basis.

The NFB went even further to stimulate the young visitors by offering $5 animation workshops where grateful parents watch their kids absorbed in the production of a real segment in claymation (remember Wallace and Gromit?) or other types of animation. Offered Saturdays and Sundays from 1 to 3 pm, the workshops can be combined with the free screening of a host of shorts in the 79-seat theatre on the second floor (also on Saturdays and Sundays, from 2 to 4 pm). Kids 3 to 5 years can rely on similar $5 workshops on Saturdays, from 10:30 am to 12 noon (including a special movie screening in a small viewing room on the first floor).

We attended the workshop. Every time a child finished his animation, the friendly and patient professional staff would play it on the two monitors and large screen for the benefit of everybody. And each time it never failed: every one in the room would cheerfully applaud the new production and its proud creator.

You can also rent or buy NFB productions at the Mediatheque.

NFB Mediatheque	**D-3**
(416) 973-3012 (general)	**Downtown**
(416) 973-2178 (families)	**Toronto**
www.nfb.ca/mediatheque/	**1-min.**

 Schedule: Monday and Tuesday, 1 to 7 pm; Wednesdays, 10 am to 7 pm; Thursday to Saturday, 10 am to 10 pm; Sundays, 12 noon to 5 pm.

 Admission: $2/day pass, $12/annual pass, $15/annual family pass. Workshops/$5 per child.

 Directions: 150 John St., Toronto (corner of Richmond St., just south of Queen St.).

NEARBY ATTRACTIONS

BABY-FRIENDLY THEATRES

No more cabin fever

When I was on maternity leave, I sneaked into matinee screenings with my baby. Sometimes, I was lucky and he would sleep through the whole presentation. Other times, I had to leave the theatre with a screaming baby. But that was before a trend that would fulfill the needs of a forever-grateful niche: movie buffs with babies.

The first to understand this craving new mothers have to just get out and see the latest movie was **Movies for Mommies**, which showed its first Toronto screening in 2001. From the beginning, this film event producer has favoured small independent cinemas, more suitable for moms networking, with their intimate environment.

On the day I attended one of their presentations in The Beaches Fox Cinema,

there was a line-up of moms with strollers waiting to get in. The back of the theatre was packed with strollers. A table offered free diapers, baby wipes, bottle warmer and free welcome packs were given by sponsors to first-time attendees.

During the screening, we could hear the babies cooing because there was no Dolby sound to bury their noise. When a baby cried, his mom would walk up and down the aisle and he would usually settle down. Of course, when they don't, the civil thing to do is to step out into the lobby, guilt-free, until the little one has quieted down.

I could see little heads sticking out behind the arms of nursing mothers. Some infants were jumping on their parent's knees (some dads were in the audience). Five moms stood in the aisles, rocking their babies to sleep as they watched the movie. One mom was even sitting in the aisle with her young toddler. All sorts of things mothers would not dare to try during regular presentations.

Of course, the major movie theatre chains joined in. **Cineplex** (which now includes the formerly Famous Players theatres) offers **Stars & Stroller**. **Empire Theatres** has jumped on the bandwagon with Reel Babies in Ontario.

Whatever the location, always count on reduced sound. New locations are added periodically. Bring on the popcorn!

TIPS (non-walking babies)

• Check **moviesformommies.com** for tips on how to make the most of the experience. They know, they started it all!

• You can bring toddler siblings if you feel they can sit through an adult movie (but bear in mind that most films screened are meant for adults).

• Food concessions are not necessarily open for these special screenings in the independent cinemas (in which case they will allow you in with your own coffee and popcorn).

• Check **www.cinemaclock.com** for current movie descriptions, theatre listings and more. You can also call (416) 444-FILM (3456) for similar information and to buy tickets in advance.

Movies for Mommies
(905) 707-8866
www.moviesformommies.com
(click **Locations** for independent theatres and listings)

Cineplex
www.cineplex.com
(search **Stars & Strollers** for chain theatres and listings)

Empire Reel Babies
www.empiretheatres.com
(click **Reel Babies** for chain theatres and listings)

CANADIAN ABORIGINAL FESTIVAL

Dance competitions, commonly known as the "SkyDome Powwow" (now called the Toronto Star Powwow), are the heart of the Festival, attracting over 800 dancers competing in different categories.

They are accompanied by the rhythm of several live drummers and singers who perform around what is known as a "dance circle".

The "Women's Jingle Dress Dance" is a high point with the clattering sounds of dresses covered with over 300 tin cones.

Regalia of sound and colours

Strolling the open space at the Rogers Centre during the Festival reminds me of the activity and excitement backstage of a show. Whether standing in a food line-up, checking out the market's many stalls or tidying fringes and feathers, dancers clad in beautiful traditional regalia are everywhere and mingle informally with visitors before the competitions.

Similarly, men move around with tiny bells attached around their ankles.

Most visitors prefer to stand near the "circle of dance" in the stadium. This allowed my 3-year-old great freedom to roam around without annoying spectators. In fact, children can stroll easily all over the grounds. But most of all, it was playing with newfound friends inside the large teepee that captivated my little papoose most.

TIPS (fun for 5 years +)
• More on **Rogers Centre** on p. 336.
• Toronto is an aboriginal word meaning "the gathering place."
• You'll find interesting things at the marketplace. We bought a nice wooden set of bow and arrows as well as a leather quiver (each around $10), on which an artist burned my daughter's name along with drawings of rabbits and beavers.
• Most activities are adult-oriented: traditional teachings, art exhibition and fashion show. Check the schedule at the entrance to find out more about the children's activities such as storytelling and games.
• See the **Six Nations Fall Festival** on p. 98.

NEARBY ATTRACTIONS	
CN Tower (2-min. walk)	p. 116
CBC Museum (5-min. walk)	p. 118

Canadian Aboriginal Festival (519) 751-0040 www.canab.com	D-3 Downtown Toronto 2-min.

Schedule: Usually starts last Friday in November, to Sunday.
Admission: $10/adults, $5/4-12 years, FREE for 3 years and under, $25/family of 4. Parking is approximately $15 across Bremmer Blvd.
Directions: Rogers Centre, Toronto (at the north-east corner of Front and John St., north of Bremmer Blvd.). Buy tickets at Gate 7.

SIX NATIONS FALL FAIR

Teenagers and grandparents, preschoolers and adults, male and female alike, all participate in the dance competitions.

I am really pleased that my daughter sees how great the kids are doing. She actually becomes so enthused that I have to restrain her

from joining the Powwow (which should never be confused with a dancing party). I tell her she could dance outside of the stadium instead.

Light feet in action

We hear the live singers and musicians as soon as we arrive at the fairground. In order to reach the dance circle, we have to cross a gravel road that has been blocked. With other visitors, we patiently wait (wondering why exactly). All of a sudden, a four-horse wagon flashes by, leaving a huge cloud of dust behind. Now I get it: Crossing the road in the middle of the chuck wagon race of the Six Nations Fall Fair would be a perilous affair!

Once the race is over, the gate is opened and we walk to the baseball diamond turned into the perfect spot for a great Powwow.

The dance circle is surrounded by sets of bleachers where all visitors can get a good look at participants, dressed in colourful regalia. We are close enough to appreciate the intricate steps performed with such light feet that the dancers seem to never rest their full weight on the ground.

After enjoying the dance competition, we spent a full hour alternating between the midway (offering some fifteen rides on a pay-as-you-play basis) and the food lane. The event may include birds of prey demonstration, rodeo or even a demolition derby. It changes every year.

TIPS (fun for 5 years +)

• The event actually starts on the Thursday following Labour Day. Expect fireworks on the Friday night. The powwow takes place during the weekend.
• Check the **Canadian Aboriginal Festival** on p. 97.

NEARBY ATTRACTIONS
Warplane Museum (20-min.) ...... p. 212

Six Nations Fall Fair	E-2
• Ohsweken	S-W
(519) 445-0783	of Toronto
www.sntourism.com	90-min.

Schedule: Always the weekend following Labour Day weekend.
Admission: (cash only) Around $10/ adults, $8/seniors, $5/6-12 years, FREE for 5 years and under, less on Sunday. Pay-per-ride midway.
Directions: Take QEW then follow Hwy 403 towards Hamilton. Exit Hwy 18 southbound, follow Hwy 54 past Onondaga. Turn right on Chiefswood Rd. to 4th Line.

CHINATOWN

Sticks to you!

My son digs into his plate of noodles after my crash course on how to handle the sticks. Then he slurps the tapioca balls from the bottom of his bubble tea. The outing is already a success.

Later, we hit **Furama Cake & Dessert**

TIPS (fun for 5 years +)

• It adds to the fun if you allow a small budget for your child to spend. Many shops offer cheap trinkets you would not find in a regular dollar store.

• For a great panorama of Chinatown, take the elevator to reach the **Sky Dragon Restaurant** (on the 4th floor of **Dragon City** at 280 Spadina). It is flanked with a long balcony overlooking Spadina and Dundas, with a view of the **CN Tower** to the south and the table-top like structure of the **OCAD** building on the east side.

• Want to see a real karaoke place with private rooms and all? See **Echo** on the 2nd floor of **Dragon City**.

• For a description of the adjacent **Kensington Market**, read **Funky Block Stroll** on p. 468.

Garden (248-50 Spadina) where we stack a decadent pile of inexpensive pastries on our tray (you know, to get "energy" for the stroll up and down Spadina).

Densely aligned signage is mainly in Chinese or Vietnamese. Most passers-by are of Asian descent. From the sidewalk, you can see the chefs at work through the restaurants' windows and the offerings on the outdoor stalls.

In a glance, I spot $1 glass eggs in a bowl of water, $1 tokens that look straight out of a treasure chest and $2 ornate metal nails to put on your fingertips.

My favourite places for great finds (bargains or merchandise I don't see anywhere else) are: **Pashmina Group** for its $10 pashminas in all colours (Unit 23B in the basement of **Chinatown Centre** at 222 Spadina), **Tap Phong Trading Co.** (366), **B & J Trading** (376) and **Harvest Int'l Trading** (406).

Flags International (422 Spadina) is the best place to find flags from every country in all sizes. There's a smaller flag store at 428 next to it.

When I checked the small **Gwartzman's Art Supplies** (448 Spadina), they had the biggest (affordable) collection of wood manikins I have ever seen: horses, robot, dinosaurs, hand, etc.

Bright Pearl Seafood Restaurant (a large room with wide windows on the 2nd floor of 346 Spadina) is famous for its wide selection of dim sum. (Check their menu on www.brightpearlseafood.com.)

Chinatown (416) 260-9800 www.chinatownbia.com	D-3 **Downtown** Toronto 5-min.

Schedule: Open year-round. Most shops open at least from 11 am to 7 pm.

Admission: FREE. Many stores or restaurants accept only cash.

Directions: Located along Spadina Avenue, between Queen and College.

LITTLE INDIA

What a feast!

Glittering wedding saris in the bright windows, tiny stores stocked with sparkling gods and goddesses, wood carvings and jewels, steaming roasted corn on the cob, colourful posters of the latest Bollywood movies. Quite a feast for the eyes.

There's nothing like walking along the strip of Gerard Street east of Coxwell on a warm summer evening. Indian music bursts from welcoming open-door shops, women are lovely in their saris, men look sharp in their crisp shirts and the whole street is lit in a festive way.

Street vendors offer exotic food: sugar cane juice mixed with lime, coconut milk directly from a freshly cut shell and fried pastries.

We don't try these yet because we're on our way to **Lahore Tikka**, my absolute favourite restaurant on the strip. If you've not visited the place lately, you're in for a surprise! The little covered patio, draped with silky fabrics in the summer, is gone but don't be sad! It's gone bigger, with the same owner. At the time of print, the unfinished restaurant was busy with customers amidst the renovations and already looked quite impressive.

Kids will enjoy climbing up the huge wooden wagon straight from India, adorned with the typical pompoms and flowers. Who knows, we might be able to ride on one of these some day.

After a great meal, we admire the exquisite **Rang Home Decor** (1413 Gerrard Street East). My little princess chooses pretty 10¢ metal bracelets from a bin in one of the small shops and I find myself a gorgeous gold and teal sari ($25 for a 5-yard sari) that I can admire in my office as I'm writing these lines!

TIPS (fun for 5 years +)

• For even more ambience, visit this neighbourhood during the **Vaiskhi Celebration** (Festival of Spring) normally taking place in April, or the **Diwali** (Hindu festival of lights) happening during the fall. The best time to get a henna temporary tattoo! Check their website for dates.

• Indian food is spicy. Let the kids gorge on white rice, warm naans and ice cream while you enjoy the attack on your taste buds.

NEARBY ATTRACTIONS

Little India
· Toronto
(416) 395-0067
www.
gerrardindiabazaar.com

D-3
East of
downtown
15-min.

Schedule: Open year-round. Most shops open at least between 12 noon and 9 pm.
Admission: FREE. Many stores accept only cash.
Directions: Located on Gerrard Street East, between Greenwood and Coxwell.

SWAMINARAYAN MANDIR

A vision

That's what you'll think you're having the first time you notice the creamy limestone towers of the Hindu temple by Hwy 427.

A building made out of 24,000 stones beautifully carved in India by over 1,800 craftsmen and assembled here with the help of hundreds of volunteers: kids get it.

More numbers for them? There are 132 archways and 101 ceilings, just on the first floor and 340 pillars, some of them so intricately carved it takes one artisan almost a year to create.

You could spend some time playing an I-Spy game with the breathtaking outer wall of the temple, sculpted in teak.

Inside, each sex leaves their shoes in their respective section and meet again by the prayer hall.

The most breathtaking part of the temple is the 16-sided Mandir, hosting five sacred deities on the second floor. We counted no less than 100 different musicians carved in white marble in one of the twelve circles inside its dome.

We really stood out amongst the worshippers. It was like wearing a "Tourist" sign on our foreheads but I felt the members of this community were more than open to sharing their culture.

TIPS (fun for 8 years +)

• The temple is open to the public but remains a place of worship where knees and shoulders must be covered. They graciously supply visitors with saris if need be. No photographs are allowed inside.

• The centre includes a **Canadian Museum of Cultural Heritage of Indo-Canadians**. It is small but nicely put together. Note that it focuses more on the Indian heritage than on the Indo-Canadian reality and that there is lots of reading involved.

• In the centre's gift shop, I noticed inexpensive comic books telling Sanskrit classic tales in English, and workbooks for kids to learn Gujarāti (spoken by about 46 million worldwide), an interesting way to expose kids to different writing systems created by mankind.

• We continued our immersion with Indian snacks from a nearby food store (**Shayona**, 46 Claireville Dr.). They sold colourful pastries, samosas and drinks we don't find in the major supermarkets.

NEARBY ATTRACTIONS	
Wild Water Kingdom (5-min.)	p. 431
Humber Arboretum (5-min.)	p. 294

Swaminarayan Mandir (416) 798-2277 www.baps.org	**D-3 North of Toronto 25-min.**

 Schedule: Open year-round, from 9 am to 8 pm.

Admission: Entrance to the temple is free, donations appreciated. The suggested donation is $5/adult and $3/child to access the Museum.

Directions: 61 Claireville Drive. From Hwy 427, take the eastbound exit to Finch, then turn north on Humberline Dr. and west on Claireville Dr.

CARABRAM

Remember Caravan?

It all started with Caravan, the first real multicultural festival launched in Toronto in the 70's. Then came Carabram in 1982, followed by Carassauga in 1985.

Carabram, Brampton; Carassauga, Mississauga. Get it? If they did one in Markham, they could call it Caraham! Or the City of Vaughan, Caravaughan. That would work. (OK, I'll stop here.)

The last **Caravan** unfortunately took place a few years ago but if you feel like a trip around the World in one day with your kids, you can turn to Brampton and Mississauga, where the two annual three-day festivals are going strong.

We visited Carabram, but judging from the info on **Carassauga**'s website, you can pretty much expect the same experience in Mississauga.

Both events last three days and include between 15 to 20 pavilions. Both cities offer free transportation and special shuttle buses for the occasion. Most importantly, at both events, you get a passport to stamp at each "country" you visit. Kids just love that!

The countries represented are not necessarily the same in both multicultural festivals.

At Carabram, most pavilions were less than a 10-minute drive apart. In "Hawaii", we were reminded that there is nothing cuter than a tiny hawaiian dancer. The market was very lively in "Philippines", where we saw a funny tease game (a bit like a mexican pinata). Displays were colourful in the pavilions of Pakistan and Caribbean.

TIPS (fun for 6 years +)

• At the time of print, there were hopes that **Caravan** could resume its activities (with a different concept). Check **www.caravan-org.com** to get the latest news.

• **Carassauga** normally takes place on the last weekend of May. Check **www.carassauga.com** or call (905) 615-3010 to confirm.

• There's a wading pool with water sprays in **Gage Park** on the south-west corner of Queen and Main Streets, downtown Brampton.

NEARBY ATTRACTIONS

Carabram
• Brampton
(416) 452-4917
www.carabram.org

D-2
N-W
of Toronto
35-min.

Schedule: Normally on the weekend after Canada Day, call to confirm.

Admission: Passports are $8 in advance and $10 at the door. FREE for children 12 years and under!

Directions: From Hwy 401, take Hwy 427 northbound to the end, then turn west to reach Brampton. Check their website for a map of the pavilions.

PACIFIC MALL

Ticket to Hong Kong

I have heard from several friends of Chinese friends, who've actually lived in Hong Kong, that going to Pacific Mall would be the closest to experiencing the real thing without catching a plane. Good enough for me! So I grabbed my 10-year-old and took him on a trip... to Markham.

I'm surprised by how small most stores are in the mall (self-proclaimed as the largest Pacific mall in North America). It includes some 300 indoor outlets plus 100 more outdoor stores and restaurants surrounding the building.

We can't understand one word anybody says and most signs are not in English. It is all really exotic to us! But the truth is, we feel quite at ease being the visible minority in this environment.

My son thinks he's in heaven when he spots a store selling the collector cards in fashion at the moment, with a dozen guys challenging each other at tables (**Pacific Gifts**, first floor, number E61). Then, on the second floor, is the **Orbit Entertainment Centre** (F83), a cool arcade where the teenage crowd plays on electronic guitar, keyboard and drums.

I can't resist buying the cutest Chinese outfit for my niece, pink and gold with the Chinese buttons and collar ($35, tax included in the price, cash only; many stores carry these). Adorable toddlers are actually wearing these colourful clothes in the mall.

We try bubble tea. Our pastel drinks are topped with huge straws and stocked with tapioca spheres at the bottom. We buy tons of nicely packaged snacks never seen before at **Ding Dong** (a large conve-

nience store located at C70/C72). I make a mental note to come back to stock up for my daughter's next party!

The second floor is where we find the most exotic section of the mall. Shops are even smaller. The entrance is adorned with dark wood and dragons greet us on large murals. In the small foodcourt, we eat a Japanese meal served in gorgeous bento boxes where everything has its own little compartment. Not your usual cafeteria tray. Let's hope they keep serving food in those!

My personal biggest find in this mall is the **MHQ Karaoke Box** (F33)! Behind a spectacular wall of brushed metal with portholes, are corridors with a series of doors leading to small rooms. Movie buffs will remember such rooms from the film *Lost in Translation* with Bill Murray! It does not get more exotic than that on this side of the planet!

TIPS (fun for 5 years +)
• Some stores only take cash.

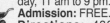

Pacific Mall
• Markham
(905) 947-9560
www.pacificmalltoronto.com

D-3
N-E
of Toronto
40-min.

 Schedule: Sunday to Thursday, 11 am to 8 pm; Friday and Saturday, 11 am to 9 pm.
Admission: FREE.
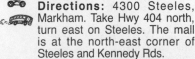 **Directions:** 4300 Steeles, Markham. Take Hwy 404 north, turn east on Steeles. The mall is at the north-east corner of Steeles and Kennedy Rds.

TORONTO SYMPHONY ORCHESTRA

A classic outing

A dark-clad man is testing his tuba, casually sitting on the edge of the stage and beating the tempo with his legs. Musicians and spectators alike are slowly reaching their respective seats and the joyous cacophony of a full orchestra tuning before the show fills the air.

I tease the two mature women in front of us who did not feel they needed to be accompanied by a child as an excuse to attend the **Young People's Concert** which is about to delight us. We came to see the animated movie based on Raymond Briggs' touching book *The Snowman*, with live music from the TSO!

On the program are printed *Jingle Bells* and *Frosty the Snowman* songs, for the sing-along part of the show. Among other things, we will also be treated to excerpts from a full orchestra version of the theme song of *Hockey Night in Canada* and Vivaldi's *Winter* enriched by the conductor's reading of Vivaldi's comments on the original score.

Storytelling, theatrical situations, dramatic conductors or even puppets, nothing is ruled out by the **Young People's Concerts** series in order to initiate children to the world of classical music. The roster varies from one year to the next but it always includes a **Christmas** show. Another TSO **Christmas** tradition is their Handel's *Messiah*, performed with the **Toronto Mendelssohn Choir** (this choir usually performs a great Festival of Carols in December at the **Roy Thomson Hall** but sometimes, it takes place in another venue, check **www.tmchoir.org**).

The younger body of TSO, the **Toronto Symphony Youth Orchestra,** involves musicians 22 years and under; a great model for young spectators! They perform throughout the season.

TIPS (fun for 5 years +)

• Children 5 years and older with purchased tickets are welcome to any TSO performance.

• TSO offers the **tsoundcheck** price of $12 on certain performances for spectators 15-29 years old. Check **www.tsoundcheck.com** on Mondays to find out what tickets are currently available.

• Also performing at Roy Thomson Hall is the **Toronto Children's Chorus.** We saw their **Christmas** show. Most memorable was the 300 children's passionate expressions as they sang carols. And what parent wouldn't wish for the level of attention these children so easily give their conductor!

• Fancy frozen deserts and refreshments are usually sold during intermission.

• Read the **Think Big! Stroll** on p. 466 for a description of things to see around **Roy Thomson Hall**.

NEARBY ATTRACTIONS
NFB Mediatheque (5-min. walk) ... p. 95
CN Tower (10-min. walk) .... p. 116

Toronto Symphony Orchestra (416) 598-3375 (TSO) (416) 593-4828 (Roy Thomson Hall) www.tso.ca	**D-3 Downtown** Toronto 5-min.

Schedule: Young People's Concerts run 5 times between October and May, at 1:30 and 3:30 pm on Saturdays.
Admission: $17-27/person (with the Desjardins Family Pack deal, buy one full-price ticket and bring up to 4 kids for $5/kid). This offer is also valid for the Sunday Light Classics performances.
Directions: 60 Simcoe St., Roy Thomson Hall, Toronto (south-west corner at King St.).

CANADIAN OPERA COMPANY

The **Four Seasons Centre** is the permanent home of the Canadian Opera Company (COC) as well as the performance venue of the **National Ballet of Canada**. It is internationally lauded for its acoustic design.

The seating was computer-tested to ensure one sees well from every row, and all the operas offer Surtitles TM (a concept of translations projected on a screen developed by the COC).

Make a note!

The entrance hall features the "world's longest free-span glass staircase". The horseshoe-shaped auditorium goes up so high I was told some people get vertigo in the highest rows. Breathtaking, and the opera hasn't started yet!

I was lucky enough to attend a dress rehearsal conducted by Richard Bradshaw himself, a few months before he died unexpectedly. A dress rehearsal is different from a normal performance. Orchestra and singers started with the second act. Bradshaw would comment out loud as he conducted. Following the last note, he casually asked the musicians to redo a specific measure, which the whole (over 100-piece) orchestra would instantly perform at unison after a quick "one-two-three" from the conductor. Amazing!

TIPS (fun for 10 years +)

• Their website offers a fantastic introduction to their operas! Go to **Performances**, click on the opera of your choice, then go to the right-hand menu **View Gallery** where I recommend you check **Synopsis**, **Historical Background** and **Musical Excerpts**.

• Public tours of the centre are offered on Saturdays at 11:45 am and noon when no matinee performance is planned. Call to confirm.

• Check their website for information on their **Take me out to the opera!** event, March Break public workshop, summer opera camp, operaworks for youth and saturday morning opera club, all taking place at the **Joey and Toby Tanenbaum Opera Centre** on 227 Front St. East.

• The **Canadian Children's Opera Chorus** is called to duty when an opera requires a children's chorus. Check **www. canadianchildrensopera.com** to find out about their performances at **St. James Cathedral** or with the TSO.

• More on the **National Ballet of Canada**'s **Nutcracker** on p. 175.

A cheap way to enjoy the amazing building is by attending one of the **Free Concerts Series** presented on weekdays from 12 to 1 pm or 5:30 to 6:30 pm in the **Richard Bradshaw Amphitheatre** (by the glass walls overlooking University Avenue). We attended a 12-string performance of Vivaldi and I thought it was fascinating to listen to this beautiful music from another time while cars were rushing by on the streets below.

Canadian Opera Company	**D-3** **Downtown** Toronto 5-min.
(416) 395-0067 www.coc.ca	

 Schedule: Box office open daily 11 am to 6 pm (closed on Sundays). Check their website for the schedule of performances.

Admission: Single tickets for operas are around $60-$275/adults, $30-$275/15 years and under. (Ask about their $20/30 years and under Rush Tickets.)

Directions: 145 Queen Street West, Toronto (just east of University Avenue).

NEARBY ATTRACTIONS
Around Queen Subway Station ... p. 450
Around Osgoode Subway Station p. 452

TORONTO CIRCUS FESTIVAL

Location, location...

"Have number, will perform. Just give me a place!" We don't realize it takes years for a young festival to find its venue and time slot amidst all the events happening in Toronto.

In 2007, we attended two small festivals that were not in their first year but were operating for the first time in their respective venues.

The **Toronto Circus Festival** took place in the new **Woodbine Park**. It had previously taken place at **The Distillery**. At the time of print, it had been decided it would now operate at **Harbourfront Centre**.

Woodbine Park was great for such a festival, with the giant gazebo hosting acrobats. Between numbers, kids would roll down the great hill or explore the large pond with fountain, trails and playground on the other side.

I expect **Harbourfront** to be equally great for this event. It offers more infrastructure to protect the artist from the elements and once again, between numbers, there will be things to explore (the pond,

the lake, the boats, the glass-blowers, etc.)

It definitely will fill the hole left by our beloved **Milk Festival**, which used to go on around that time at that location.

I would not be surprised if we were greeted by clowns on stilts, waving at us from Queen's Quay.

The day I visited another small festival (the **Clown Festival**), I stopped for coffee at a local café and noticed a nice fuzzy-haired guy with a bow tie who I naturally assumed was involved with the festival. As I waved at him, I started to doubt my assumption. Some people do look like that in real life! Then a girl in a crinoline skirt with a red nose came out of the washroom. Phew!

The **Clown festival** took place indoors at the **Pia Bouman School for Ballet and Creative Movement**. The previous year, it was at **The Distillery**. They offered a small roster of kid shows and adult shows. I liked what I saw but unfortunately, they've decided to continue catering only to adults. So, if you see advertising about this festival, don't mistake it for a family event. Those clowns lead a double life!

Bottom line, small festivals are not as tightly knit as the big ones. They can evolve a lot from one year to the next. Always check their websites. Wherever they'll be taking place in the coming years, they're a nice excuse to explore a different part of the city.

TIPS (fun for 4 years +)
• More on **Harbourfront Centre** on p. 25 and things to see around **Harbourfront** on pages 26-27.
• If the concept of a clown show for adults intrigues you, check **www.torontoclown.com** for details about the **Clown Festival** (2008: again at **Pia Bouman School** at the heart of hip western Queen Street West, probably on the second weeekend in June).

Toronto Circus Festival	D-3 Downtown Toronto 5-min.
www. TOcircusfestival.com	

 Schedule: For 2008, planned for May 17-18 at Harbourfront. Check their website.

 Admission: Pay-what-you-can for the outdoor shows, fees apply for the indoor performances.

Directions: For 2008, at Harbourfront Centre, 235 Queen's Quay West, Toronto. Call for exact location the following years.

TORONTO BUSKERFEST

Real urban fun

A menacing gladiator slowly walks towards my son and stops one foot short of his face. My son bravely sustains the look, at the same time shy and amused by the attention while people start to gather around us. Little did he know that he was about to be held hostage, serving as a shield between the heartless warrior and his enemy.

Now, we know first hand the Bus-kerFest qualities as an interactive event! In the next two hours as we walked from one attraction to the next, my 9-year-old keener took part in a sword fight, he shook hands with an extra-terrestrial, he was involved in a balloon sculpture contest and he passed the hat for a wacky cowgirl. I think his blond hair had something to do with being selected at every corner.

Among other skits, we saw a wacky black-belt performer from New York, the most interactive Men in Tights from Toronto and a Californian cowgirl who claimed she would "milk us for all our worth".

The following year, we saw a naughty Australian contortionist covered with tattoos, amazing break-dancers from New York, out-of-control acrobat dancers from the UK and a local favourite, Mark Cmor, who will grab your cell phone if it rings during his performance and engage in a conversation with your unsuspecting friend. Shy people beware! Expect great interaction and lots of jokes and teasing from these free-spirited street performers.

It is quite interesting to see how humour differs from one country to the next. Over the years, I have noticed that Australians are the most provocative, UK performers play with the absurd, Americans are more politically correct and Canadians have a tendency to downplay their act to better surprise you with something bold when you're off guard.

TIPS (fun for 4 years +)

• Make sure you bring a handful of loonies to the event. The shows are free but hats circulate at the end of every performance. Kids like to contribute their share. Buskers are not paid to perform during the event. Our donation is their bread and butter.

• The donations you make at the entrance to the car-free zone goes to **Epilepsy Toronto**. Toronto BuskerFest is actually an awareness event organized by this not-for-profit charity.

• The event includes free little workshops under the Scotiabank tent, allowing kids to learn more about the art of mime, drama, magic, etc. More children's activities are offered in other sections.

• Read **European Flair Stroll** on p. 476 about things to see in this part of town.

NEARBY ATTRACTIONS
St. James Cathedral (1-min. walk) p. 119
Hockey Hall (10-min. walk) .... p. 346

Toronto BuskerFest (416) 964-9095 www. torontobuskerfest.com	D-3 Downtown Toronto 5-min.

 Schedule: The organizers want to stick to the weekend before Labour Day, in August (including the Thursday and the Friday preceding this weekend), from 12 noon to 10 pm minimum (closes at 8 pm on Sunday). Call to confirm.

Admission: Donations for Epilepsy Toronto at the entrance. Pay-what-you-can for individual busker performances.

Directions: Front St., between Church and Jarvis. There's a public parking lot at the foot of Church, south of Front.

NUIT BLANCHE

Sleepless in Toronto

Here's an urban phenomenon you can show to your kids... except when stated otherwise in the 80-page brochure!

Your Nuit Blanche probably won't be sleepless if you're with kids (you've had your share of those nights in your younger years). The truth is, you can start at 7 pm, before the crowds kick in, and enjoy as many eclectic activities as they can bear. Warning, my friend's four kids were still going strong at midnight!

After attending different venues for the last two Nuit Blanche, I can tell you it is very hard to predict what awaits you. Activities created for the event can last anywhere from two minutes to half an hour. There can be a massive crowd attending, or hardly anyone. They can be extremely creative or very disappointing. The unknown is actually part of the fun. Control freaks will want to avoid this experience.

There were 195 options to choose from when we attended Nuit Blanche in 2007. After admiring giant helium balls lifting a fabric roof on Charles Street, we fled from the Bloor Street area, too crowded for our taste.

We drove to **The Distillery**. The setting was perfect with tiny lights adorning the trees and spot lights brushing changing colours over the historic chimney.

New artists stood in front of a large blank canvas every hour, to create art before our eyes. Actors created fixed scenes to accompany musicians. An installation by the **Balzac Café** featured white antique strollers covered with... mousetraps (working ones!).

Nearby, friends with kids attended an interesting play on an outdoor stage built for the occasion, where you'd think you've just come across a well-heeled woman in the middle of a life crisis, who has decided to talk to strangers.

My daring friends with the four kids opted for the **Kensington Market**. Among other things, they had a blast in the dumpster converted into some kind of living room.

TIPS (fun for 8 years +)
• Expect bigger crowds (and waiting lines) near Bloor and Avenue Road.
• Call them to learn where to find the event's brochure. It offers tons of information (including age recommendations) and is very useful to generate the treasure hunt feeling when strolling the city with kids.
• Take advantage of the TTC's extended services during the event, including special shuttle buses.

NEARBY ATTRACTIONS

The Distillery	p. 378
Kensington Market	p. 468

Nuit Blanche
(416) 338-0338 (Access Toronto)
www.scotiabanknuitblanche.ca

Schedule: Could be on last Saturday of September or first Saturday in October, from 7 pm to sunrise (2008: October 4).
Admission: FREE.
Directions: Check their website for the directions to the different venues.

THEATRE VENUES

Solar Stage
(416) 368-8031
www.solarstage.on.ca
Concourse Level of **Madison Centre**, 4950 Yonge St., North York. **Village Playhouse**, 2190 Bloor St. W., Toronto.
Admission: $13 + tax.

Live it up!

What a treat it is to watch children engaging with something other than a screen for a change. The palpable energy that comes from good live performances is simply irreplaceable.

For years, events such as the **Milk Festival** at Harbourfront or the **Mississauga Festival** were like a smorgasbord of high quality children's productions. They unfortunately don't exist anymore but you can count on other options to get your fix.

Note it is sometimes difficult from simple descriptions to know if performances involve actors or puppetry, if it's a musical or a simple storytelling. Better call the theatre beforehand to avoid any disappointment.

Solar Stage

Most plays at Solar Stage are mostly intended for children aged 3 to 8; some are meant for children up to 10 years old.

The younger crowd gathers in front of Solar Stage's intimate stage, comfortably seated on floor cushions. Parents of young children attending for the first time shouldn't worry about letting their child sit by themselves. Sooner or later most little ones join their parents during the performance; it's part of the deal and performers know it.

They've added a new venue and now offer children plays at the **Village Playhouse** as well (2190 Bloor Street West).

TIPS (fun for 3 years +)
• The Madison Centre's shops are closed on Mondays. You'll find a **Second Cup** on Yonge St., south of the building.

Lorraine Kimsa Theatre for Young People

Photo: Courtesy of LKTYP

Lorraine Kimsa Theatre for Young People (LKTYP) can be seen as the next level up in theatre initiation as it can also serve an older audience. The bigger stage allows for more ambitious productions. While their season is intended primarily for children 8 years and older, some productions, usually presented on a smaller stage, will interest younger audiences.

Here, my young designer has discovered wondrous theatre sets and props; my little animal lover has seen giant butterflies magically flying in the air. Both have been captivated by harmless villains, introduced to the magic of elegant puppetry and to the mystery of ancient tales (with a little help from pyrotechnic and sound effects).

TIPS (fun for 3 years +)
• When attending with younger children, I suggest you avoid the front rows of the balcony section as the railing sits at their eye level.
• To ensure LKTYP is accessible to all audiences, at least one performance of each production is Pay-What-You-Can. These tickets can be purchased in person (cash only) and they go on sale at 9 am on the day of the show. Call the box office for more information.
• There's a snack bar with tables at the lower level.

LKTYP
(416) 862-2222
www.lktyp.ca
165 Front St. East, Toronto.
Admission: $15-$20.

Family series

Many performing arts centres are committed to affordable and quality family shows at a cost of approximately $20 per show.

Popular productions, musicals or children's shows are often booked in more than one venue during the same season. If you've missed a favourite show at your local theatre, call other performing arts centres on the listing to see if it is being presented at any of them. They will mail their season's program upon request.

Performing Arts Centres:

· **The Sony Centre**
(416) 872-2262
www.sonycentre.ca
1 Front Street East, Toronto
· **St. Lawrence Centre for the Arts**
(Bluma Appel Theatre)
(416) 366-7723
www.stlc.com
27 Front Street East, Toronto
· **Rose Theatre Brampton**
(905) 793-4600
www.rosetheatre.ca
1 Theatre Lane, Brampton
· **Living Arts Centre**
(905) 306-6000
www.livingarts.on.ca
4141 Living Arts Dr., Mississauga
(west of Square One)
· **Meadowvale Theatre**
(905) 615-4720
www.mississauga.ca
6315 Montevideo Rd., Mississauga
· **Markham Theatre**
(905) 305-7469
www.markhamtheatre.ca
171 Town Centre Blvd., Markham
(north of Hwy 7, west of Warden Ave.)
· **Oakville Centre**
(905) 815-2021
www.oc4pa.com
130 Navy St., Oakville

TIPS (fun for 3 years +)

• **www.ticketmaster.ca** is very useful to get information regarding the venues and current shows, even if you don't intend to book through them (and pay the extra cost per ticket). You can view the seating chart of a venue by typing its name in the search box.
• Go to **www.torontoplus.ca** (created by the **Yellow Pages**), go to the excellent section **Guides & Features**. Under **Arts & Culture**, you'll find a **Seating Plans** link.
• The **Sony Centre** formerly was the **Hummingbird Centre**. Note that it sometimes features ice skating shows!
• **The Fringe** is Toronto's theatre festival including **Kidsvenue**, a selection of family theatre. Usually held for 12 days including the first week in July. For details, call (416) 966-1062 or check **www. fringetoronto.com**.

Arts in the school

Did you know that as a parent, you can help to bring a production to your school via its school council (the parents association)?

As a member of the board of **Prologue to the Performing Arts**, I know first hand that this non-profit organization is often the only way to ensure kids have access to performing arts.

For over 40 years, it has been assisting professional artists in creating and touring shows suitable for the schools.

Prologue provides a detailed catalogue (with booking information) upon request. Performances are presented under different categories such as dance, music, puppet shows, theatre, storytelling, etc. Schools can book shows for an average cost of $3 or less per student. Some school councils book as many as ten shows every year! Many share the costs with their school's administration.

The benefits are obvious. The school presentations enhance the curriculum, injecting arts back into the programs. It gives a break from routine programs and exposes many kids to performing arts they might not experience otherwise, for lack of money or time!

Prologue to the Performing Arts
(416) 591-9092
www.prologue.org

55 Mill St., The Case Goods Building, Suite 201, Toronto, ON, M5A 3C4.

OUTDOOR SUMMER THEATRE

Smooth theatre

I watch a little boy strolling along the park's path, unaware that a Shakespearean play is taking place right next to it. I laugh as I observe his astonished look when two big men engage in a fight. It caught the attention of other passers-by who decide to join in the crowd already following the play.

Withrow Park offers a perfect setting for an outdoor theatre. Two mature tress frame the stage, small pickets with lines mark imaginary aisles and spectators sit on the small slope, ensuring a good view.

When we attend, *Othello* is playing. The fact that we could see him coming from the grass field added a realistic touch impossible to recreate in an indoor theatre. Later on, as the scenes unfold, we can still watch a naughty Casio run-

ning after a playful Bianca in the far-away background.

Open-air plays also mean we can observe the actors "behind the scene". What I mistook for a flea market clothing sale was actually the actors' costume rack!

Some spectators come fully equipped to enjoy the show. The man in front of me brought his folding chair and coffee in a thermos. A mother of three offers an endless supply of snacks to her kids. Babies are quietly sleeping in their parent's arms. There's even a master petting a happy dog by his side.

The actor's voices are strong, which is a good thing with all those cicadas singing in the background!

When I attended, the play was performed by the company **Shakespeare in the Rough** (SiTR) but is closed after 2006 (and **Driftwood Theatre** took over in 2007). The artistic director of SiTR recently started **Humber River Shakespeare Company** which will perform along the **Humber River** (see p. 328). You'll have to google them for details later in 2008.

TIPS (fun for 8 years +)

• **Withrow Park** includes a gorgeous playground with wading pool much appreciated by local families. Danforth Avenue offers a wide choice of restaurants east and west of Logan. Read about what's around nearby **Pape** and **Chester Subway Stations** on p. 442.

• See **MOCCA** on p. 87 to find out what's around **Trinity-Bellwoods Park** and **Bradley Museum** on p. 148 (two other locations in the GTA where **Driftwood Theatre** is performing.

• **Dream in High Park** offers a Shakespeare play from the end of June to Labour Day at 8 pm, at the **Amphitheatre** in **High Park** (416-367-8243, www.canstage.com). Costumes and sets are more ambitious and the stage allows for dramatic lighting effects but it runs later and it is harder to leave the premises if your younger child loses interest. (Pay-what-you-can, they strongly suggest $20/person, FREE for 14 years and under).

STRATFORD FESTIVAL

Much ado!

Use Stratford as an excuse for a family getaway. Enjoy the town and theatre with your kids. (Then, come back with the girlfriends.)

I went twice to Stratford. Once with four girlfriends, once with a 12-year-old. No need to mention they were two totally different getaways, one of them involving much more shopping and dining but both revolving around great plays.

Every season, you can expect at least four productions of Shakespeare plays but you can also count on at least one musical, always very popular with families.

If you check the **Family Experience** menu of the **Festival**'s website, you'll find an **Age Recommendation** section. It states that most of the programming is accessible to children 10 years and older but don't forget: "accessible" doesn't mean "interesting"!

You'll find more specific information on each play in that section. They might say "not likely to be of interest to young children" or "on stage nudity, not recommended for children".

Once in a while, a play is recommended for kids younger than 10 years old, such as the musical *The Music Man* by Meredith Wilson (8 years and up), at the time of print.

The two great venues where the more ambitious plays and musicals are presented are the **Festival Theatre**, by the river (seating 1,824) and the **Avon Theatre** (seating 1,093). The other two venues seat less than 500 people.

We found **Festival Theatre** quite impressive when attending the musical *Oliver!* and everyone in that theatre could obviously get a good view of the stage.

Have a look at the Shakesperience newsletter (under the **Family Experience** menu) for fun insights from child actors (in 2006, *Oliver!* included 19 children), or... dogs (The 2007 production of *Comedy of Errors* requires a dog to chase a cat across the stage).

The best thing about staying overnight in Stratford is that it gives you time to visit the amazing costume warehouse where one can dress up at the end of the tour. They show you props, clothes, hats, wigs, shoes and more while giving you interesting details. "This head is anatomically correct" mentions the guide while holding a bloody prop used in a theatrical combat.

They also offer backstage tours of the **Festival Theatre**. You may book the tours while buying the play tickets. The tours really add to the experience.

Other things to do

If you go during the summertime, you could rent a paddle boat ($15/hour), a canoe or a kayak, or take a tour on a boat to explore the **Avon River** ($7/adult, $3/12 years and under) by the **Information Centre** on York Street. That's where you could also buy a $1 bag of corn to feed the swans.

TIPS (fun for 10 years +)

• An older child might better appreciate a Shakespeare play if he has seen a movie adaptation prior to the show. The **Festival**'s website points out such movies in their **Age Recommendation** section under **Family Experience**.

• We enjoyed a generous breakfast at an all-day breakfast place **Features Restaurant** (159 Ontario St.), and finished with better coffee at nearby **Balzac**'s (same one you find at Toronto's **The Distillery**). We had a delicious lunch at the colourful **York Street Kitchen** (41 York St.) and the whole family was more than satisfied with the dinner in one of the dark booths at **Bentley's**, where we played darts while waiting (99 Ontario St.).

• I recommend staying at the **Festival Inn** (1144 Ontario St., 1-800-463-3581, **www.festivalinnstratford.com**). It is at the edge of the action, modern, with a great indoor pool and a fabulous Sunday Brunch in their sunny dining room. We stayed at the **Victoria Inn** (10 Romeo St., 1-800-741-2135, **www.victoria-inn. on.ca**) because it had an indoor pool... but I didn't know about the **Festival Inn**.

• On our way to Stratford, we stopped at **The Best Little Pork Shoppe**, a funny little farm market selling lots of animal-related trinkets (2146 Hwy 7&8, Shakespeare, **www.porkshoppe.on.ca**).

Or you could walk to the new outdoor **Lions Pool** right across the bridge. It offers a waterplay area including a water umbrella, spraying palm trees, shooting streams, arch spray and small dumping buckets ($15/family of four, search **Lions Pool** on **www.city.stratford.on.ca**).

Make sure you take in the view of the bridge and surrounding stone buildings for a glimpse of England. Then stroll around the prettiest block in town (York and Ontario Streets), and stop at the very cool toy store **Family and Company** (6 Ontario St., **www.familyandcompany. com**) for a big finish.

Stratford Shakespeare Festival • Stratford 1-800-576-1600 www.stratfordfestival.ca	D-1 West of Toronto 1 hr 50

 Schedule: Most plays open end of May; most activities and plays go on from early June to early November. Most performances are presented at 2 pm or 8 pm. Check their calendar for dates and availability.

Admission: Musicals cost more than plays. Expect around $70 to $110/adult (depending on the seating). Children 18 years and under save about 40%, and Spring or Fall tickets cost roughly $30 less. Tours cost $7/person ($5/students or seniors).

Directions: From Hwy 401 westbound, take exit #278 at Kitchener, follow Hwy 8 West onto Hwy 7&8 to Stratford. It becomes Ontario Street, which runs through Stratford.

General tips about
Buildings:

- **Doors Open**, usually held in May, offers free tours in many buildings listed in this guide. Consult **www.doorsopenontario.on.ca** for details. Click **Events** on this website for a list of over 50 Doors Open events held in Ontario, including the main one **Doors Open Toronto** encompassing over 150 buildings throughout the city.

BUILDINGS

See **Flatiron Building** in the **European Flair Stroll** on p. 476.

CN TOWER

Broaden their horizons

With kids, you have to think big and tall... as tall as the CN Tower! It's great to see them looking up over and over again, attempting to make out the top of the 550-metre-high tower! It's well worth stopping at the base, just to see the great view from down there.

Arriving from Front Street, we walk over several railroad tracks via an enclosed bridge. This location is an excellent vantage point to see the sculptures of giant characters in their **Rogers Centre** balconies. Inside, before getting to the elevators, we walk across a spacious mezzanine housing displays and interactive computers.

There used to be funny visual simulators closer to the elevators, but I guess they got a bit outdated, as funny as they were. You'll find visual displays throughout the building with many fascinating stories about the engineering involved in the building of the tower.

Up! Up! And away!

Then comes the famous ride up the elevator: It's a one-minute climb on a fair day (over an hour if you climb the 1760 stairs), but it can take up to four minutes in high wind. Let your children go close to the glass door. The view will blow them away.

The elevator leads to the interior observation deck, 346 metres (1136 feet) from ground level, from where we can admire Lake Ontario and the four corners of the city. Children are allowed inside the **Horizons Café** located at this level.

One floor down is the fascinating glass floor surrounded by a beautiful mural depicting a construction site in the sky. When he was five, my little one didn't show any fear while walking on the glass floor. At six, he joined the rank of grown-ups cautiously remaining on the edge of the glass.

If you're wondering how such a surface can support visitors, a sign states that this glass floor can hold the weight of 14 large hippos!

We can read lots of interesting and fun information on large panels around the room, such as the fact that the **CN Tower** holds the world record for longest egg fall (it lost the tallest standing structure record to Burj Dubai Tower in 2007).

At this level, you can also access the exterior observation deck, to better feed your vertigo. We didn't feel the need to pay extra to go up to the Sky Pod. I suggest you do it only if there's no line-up. I must admit 100 metres more make a difference. The **Rogers Centre** really looks smaller from up there!

![image]

Special effect

That day, we completed the visit with a stop at the FX Shop where my teenager companions had their picture added to the background of their choice. The shop was replaced with a Souvenir Photo Booth but I was told you can get the same special effects. It costs $23 for the first copy and $16 for a second.

Other activities are offered at the base of the CN Tower. Films are presented in a mini-theatre equipped with seats that move to the rhythm of the movie projected on screen. There's also an arcade. Very few games are suitable for smaller children, but when we were there, my little one had a great time driving the motorcycles, and he and I teamed up, frantically rowing on a rubber dinghy, while attempting to avoid danger. I sweated up a storm and we laughed the whole time. The games keep changing but you get the idea.

TIPS (fun for 5 years +)

• Avoid foggy days, otherwise you'll be paying a lot just to have your head in the clouds...
• Try to visit the tower before or after the summer rush. We had a perfect visit during the **March Break** when it was not crowded by tourists (they offered special activities for the occasion).
• You can see a 15-min. movie on the building of the tower for $9/person at the Maple Leaf Theatre. You can also do the Himalamazon motion theatre ride (with wind and water effects) for $9/person. Both FREE for 3 years and under and located at the concourse level.
• The **Horizons Café** is not the expensive revolving restaurant but a fixed one underneath, with affordable menu, really worth the stop for the view!
• More on things to see around the area in the **Think Big! Stroll** on p. 466.

... and out!

For a better viewpoint of the tower in all its loftiness, stand on the outside terrace located between the tower and the **Rogers Centre**. You'll have to lay down on the ground to take a picture!

In June 2007, the CN Tower launched its 1,330-fixture programmable lighting system and has treated us ever since with myriads of colours and effects.

NEARBY ATTRACTIONS

CN Tower
(416) 868-6937
www.cntower.ca

D-3
Downtown
Toronto
at CN Tower

 Schedule: Open year-round, 9 am to 10 pm, closes at 10:30 pm on Fridays and Saturdays (extended hours during the summer).

 Admission: (taxes not included) $21.50/adults, $19.50/seniors, $14.50/4-12 years, FREE for children 3 years and under (extra fees for Sky Pod).

 Directions: 301 Front St. W. (corner of John St.).

CBC MUSEUM

Through the glass ceiling

When looking at the building from the outside, you'd never guess how breathtaking the ceiling of the CBC building is. Use the little museum as an excuse to admire some amazing architecture.

The CBC used to organize guided tours of its studios, which led us through corridors of fake bricks or unfinished sets of a new soap opera and the studio where they taped the Royal Canadian Air Farce in front of live audiences. We were initiated to the workings of a teleprompter used in reading the news in front of robotic cameras. They're not offered anymore but I'm leaving this description in case they change their minds.

From the main hall at the centre of the building, by the indoor café where many CBC staff have their meals, you can admire the Atrium's grandiose architecture and the spectacular skylight.

You can then carry on to visit the free CBC Museum on the west side of the building.

In the display by the entrance, there used to be the castle and costume of the *Friendly Giant* of my childhood but it was retrieved by the famous host's family in 2007.

Other kids shows' props can be seen (*Sesame Street, Mr. Dressup*). A large selection of clips from CBC programs for adults or kids can be watched.

In the back of the little museum are a series of displays explaining how they did the sound effects for the radio, with computer clip demonstrations. Kids can even listen to the sound they create by manipulating different objects.

TIPS (fun for 5 years +)
•   For a description of many attractions surrounding the CBC building, read the **Think Big! Stroll** on p. 466 (including details on all-day breakfast restaurant **Chez Cora** and **Wayne Gretzky's** restaurant, both less than a 5-min. walk away).

CBC Museum
(416) 205-5574
www.cbc.ca/museum

D-3
Downtown
Toronto
2-min. walk

Schedule: The CBC building is open daily. The museum is open Monday to Friday from 9 am to 5 pm.
Admission: FREE.
Directions: 250 Front St. West (across from the CN Tower), Toronto.

ST. JAMES CATHEDRAL

With its huge and gorgeous stained glass artwork framing the pulpit, and twelve colourful triptychs adorning the side walls, St. James is a beautiful cathedral of gothic architecture and proportions.

It is topped by a set of twelve ringing bells (the only such ring of 12 in North America). These are heavy bells, ranging from 631 lbs to 2418 lbs! Bell ringing practices take place every Monday at 6:30 pm. Visitors might have a chance to tour the bell tower afterwards (call in advance to let them know).

Free recitals are held Tuesdays at 1 pm, September to June, and year-round at 4 pm on Sundays (donations welcome).

During Christmas time, we are sometimes treated to a concert from the **Toronto Mendelssohn Youth Choir** (admission fees apply).

Got a cherished pet? St. James offers the **Blessing of the Animals** near St. Francis Day, end of September or early October! The special service usually gathers over 300 people with their pets (outside of the church of course), plus the Toronto Police on horseback, working dogs and exotic animals from Bowmanville Zoo.

The sound of music

I glance sideways at my little lad, amused by his reaction as music from the 87 ranks and 5,000 pipes of the St. James Cathedral's grand organ surrounds us.

Short concerts to broaden children's musical horizons, a lovely church to show them things of beauty grown-ups sometimes create and a cute little garden to stretch their legs; St. James Anglican Cathedral is one of those best kept secrets I'm glad to share with you.

TIPS (fun for 5 years +)

• See the **Crèche Exhibition** (p. 176) organized by **St. James Archives and Museum**.

• Check the **Sculpture Garden** right across King Street. It usually displays eye-catching outdoor installations!

• For a description of the nearby attractions, read the **European Flair Stroll** on p. 476, including **Le Petit Déjeuner** near the church, the **Flatiron Building** (seen on p. 115) and adjacent fountain and gelato place.

NEARBY ATTRACTIONS

St. James Cathedral
(416) 364-7865
www.
stjamescathedral.on.ca

**D-3
Downtown
Toronto
10-min.**

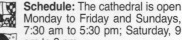
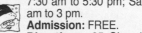

Schedule: The cathedral is open Monday to Friday and Sundays, 7:30 am to 5:30 pm; Saturday, 9 am to 3 pm.
Admission: FREE.
Directions: 65 Church St. (at the corner of King and Church), Toronto.

CASA LOMA

"I'm the king of the castle..."

Glancing at Casa Loma from the outside is enough to excite young minds. No mistake, we're about to enter a "real" castle. Inside, it seems like the fairy godmother waved her magic wand to transform the whole castle. It has regained the splendour of its younger days and a magical look worthy of Cinderella's Christmas. Those who visit Casa Loma at other times don't get to appreciate how great it is during the Christmas period and March Break.

During the **Christmas** holidays, the grandeur of Casa Loma awaits us. A 15-metre-high fir tree doesn't quite reach the main hall ceiling. Illuminated chandeliers and tinsel garlands contribute to the ambience of opulence, absent at other times of the year.

Between two performances, characters in the brief musical, produced for the occasion, mingle within the impressive decor.

One year, **Christmas** at Casa Loma was celebrated with Cinderella as a theme. We could see the handsome prince dressed in royal velvet answer a child's question in a gentlemanly fashion. The fairy godmoth-

er, in a cloud of pink tulle, held an ecstatic little girl in her arms. Further in the room, Cinderella's cruel sisters, seemingly not as mean as their reputation and splendid in their period dress, were flirtatious with visitors. On the three occasions I saw a show at Casa Loma, actors were always very nice with the little ones who were looking at them lost in wonder. And they never stepped out of character.

So far, we've seen Snow White, Robin Hood and Cinderella spread their magic. I didn't expect such high-quality musicals, presented several times daily in the castle library. Even if we're off-off-Broadway, voices are quite strong and well modulated, the five actors expressive and smart, the songs original and the musical arrangements harmonious. There are amusing, interactive dialogues aimed at the parents. The sets, mounted on curtains, compensated for the stage's limited size.

In the beautiful marble-floor conservatory, a second good clown or magic show is usually performed several times daily.

Walking up the imposing grand staircase, we arrive in a wide, richly decorated corridor lined with costumes or cut-out props. Kids can step behind them to have their pictures taken. Little adventurers will be thrilled when they find out they can also use the secret staircase hidden behind the wood panelling in Sir Henry's office!

From there, we can visit the former rooms of Sir Henry Mill Pellatt (the romantic Toronto financier who had the castle built in 1911) and his wife. These are also decorated along the year's theme.

During **Christmas** time, Santa awaits us in the billiard room on the ground floor, filled with multicoloured gifts and stuffed animals. You have time to take a picture of your little elves... if they cooperate.

Staircases located on the top floor lead to the castle's two towers, where you can enjoy a great view of the city. The Norman Tower (the one with access to an outdoor terrace) was under renovations at the time of print.

A 250-metre tunnel links the castle with the stables. The tunnel's entrance faces the Gift Shop located on the lower level of the castle. (Frankly, this level isn't more exotic than any basement, but nevertheless, it intrigues children.)

Furthermore, it leads to impressive stables. Their mahogany stalls and Spanish tile floors attest to Sir Henry's taste for luxury.

TIPS (fun for 3 years +)
• Parking is available on site. After 11:30 am, it is sometimes full, but spots free up rapidly at any hour.
• In the room where the musical performances are presented, the audience sits on the floor (there are a few chairs for adults). It is better to arrive fifteen minutes before a performance. Shows only last half an hour.
• The admission counter is inside a portico too small to contain the whole waiting line. Dress warmly!
• In the winter, the long tunnel is definitely cold. It's better to put on your coat before walking through there.
• Santa Claus arrives on the first day the castle presents its **Christmas** performances, and stays until December 24th. Ask about their **Breakfast with Santa** on Sundays in December!
• It is less interesting to visit Casa Loma when children's shows are not scheduled (the admission fee remains the same and the castle isn't decorated). On the plus side, the place is not as crowded.
• **March Break** is as much fun as **Christmas**. The same concept applies. And they now have added a similar **Halloween**-themed concept!
• A cafeteria located in the castle's basement offers an affordable menu with little variety. At the same level, the unfinished pool lies inside an enclosure. Decorations pertaining to the current theme are often displayed in it.

Casa Loma
(416) 923-1171
www.casaloma.org

D-3
North
of downtown
20-min.

 Schedule: The **Christmas** show is presented daily from end of November to early January, from 9:30 am to 5 pm, excluding December 25th and January 1. On December 24, the Castle closes at 1 pm. During **March Break**, the show is performed every day, from 9:30 am as well. (Last admission always at 4 pm.)
 Admission: At all times, even when shows for children are performed, $17/adults, $11/seniors and students, $9.25/4-13 years. FREE for children 3 and under. Parking max. is $8.25.
   Directions: 1 Austin Terrace, Toronto. (southbound from St.Clair Ave., Spadina Rd. becomes Austin Terrace).

NEARBY ATTRACTIONS

SHARON TEMPLE

A temple of light

While driving on Leslie Street, I look around for the temple. Despite having read comments regarding its amazing architecture, I don't quite know what to expect. Then it appears, with its dazzling whiteness contrasting with the blue autumn sky. Wow! The place holds its promise. Even my little adventurer, usually not inclined towards contemplation, recognizes that this building is different.

The Children of Peace, a sect fascinated by the spiritual value of art and music, built Sharon Temple between 1825 and 1832.

Everything here is symbolic. The three stories stand for the Holy Trinity. In the centre, the four columns surrounding the Ark of the Covenant are engraved with the words Hope, Faith, Love and Charity. The twelve pillars bear the apostles' names. On Jacob's ladder, the

bars supporting the ramp gradually reduce in height and width as we go up, giving the impression of rising towards Paradise.

I was impressed by the natural light shining through all the windows. There is no pulpit; priests didn't preach here. People came to meditate and listen to music while sitting in the mezzanines. The temple's acoustics are in fact remarkable.

We tour the 1819 house belonging to the builder-architect. At the back of the house, there's a small, peculiar round house. My little rascal was intrigued when he found out it was the architect's toilet, made in such a way "because the Devil hides in corners".

My son, being crazy about the movie *Back to the Future*, was impressed by photographs in the Exhibit Hall. First, we see the temple as it was in 1832 (without any vegetation around it), then as it is now, surrounded by mature trees (actually, many were cut without their permission in 2007, but that's a whole other story), and finally as it could become if no one takes care of it (abandoned, with broken windows and peeling paint).

TIPS (fun for 5 years +)

• Some sect traditions, highlighting the temple's inspired architecture and beauty, have been preserved. For example, in summer and autumn, shows featuring chamber music or choirs are held here. The **Musical Illumination** ceremony is still held on the evening of the first Friday of September. These events, though, are not suitable for children.

• There are picnic tables on the site.

NEARBY ATTRACTIONS
North York Drive-in (10-min.) .... p. 92
Live Steamers (15-min.) .... p. 221

Sharon Temple
• East Gwillimbury
(905) 478-2389
www.sharontemple.ca

C-3
North
of Toronto
45-min.

Schedule: Open mid-May to mid-October, Thursday to Sunday, 10 am to 4:30 pm.
Admission: $5/adults, FREE for 15 years and under.
Directions: 18974 Leslie, Sharon. From Hwy. 404 North, exit on Davis Dr. westbound, then turn north on Leslie St. The temple is on the south-west corner of Leslie and Mount Albert Sideroad.

CASTLE VILLAGE

Take a peek!

Slightly off the beaten track in the Georgian Bay area, the Castle is an intriguing sight in itself. But the little village hidden in its backyard was an even bigger surprise to us when we stopped there on our way back from a great weekend by the beach.

Delightful little houses awaited us in the Enchanted Kingdom Park, with inviting windows to peek through. Inside, we could see the Teddy Bears' Tea Party, Goldilocks and the Three Bears, Little Red Riding Hood and her grandmother and Mother Goose at reading time.

Since our last visit, Snow White with the Seven Dwarfs' house and Merlin the Magical Wizard's Tower were added. All the beautiful small interiors are skillfully decorated with painstaking attention to original detail.

There is also the old mill and dwarf village to climb and slide, the Hansel & Gretel Candy real snack bar with tiny tables and chairs, a 222-foot-deep well to taste crystal clear water (we were invited to fill our jugs) and a small educational trail.

TIPS (fun for 2 years +)

• The Castle houses a large gift shop and two indoor attractions: a series of small prisons inhabited by a few horror characters ($1) and a section showcasing medieval arms ($2). I was personally more impressed by the craft involved in the creation of the Enchanted Kingdom.

NEARBY ATTRACTIONS

Castle Village
· Midland
(705) 526-9683
www.castlevillage.ca

A-2 Midland Region 90-min.

Schedule: The park is open May to Thanksgiving (weather permitting) Tuesday to Saturday, 10 am to 5:30 pm (12 noon to 5 pm on Sundays). Open on Mondays as well in July, August and long weekends.
Admission: Enchanted Kingdom access is $2/person, FREE under 2.
Directions: 701 Balm Beach Rd., Midland. From Hwy 400 North, take exit #147/Hwy 12 westbound. Turn north on Hwy 93 and west on Balm Beach Rd.

General tips about
Farms:

- A good website to find a pick-your-own farm in your area is: **www.harvestontario.com** (click Farms).
- Here's a crop calendar for different Ontario fruit and vegetables. Always call to check the current crop report of the farms you want to visit. Mother Nature sometimes plays tricks on us! I remember picking a pumpkin from under a snow fall.
- Dogs are normally not allowed on the farms!

CROP CALENDAR	May	June	July	Aug.	Sept	Oct.
Asparagus	▬	▬				
Rhubard	▬	▬				
Strawberries		▬	▬			
Raspberries			▬	▬		
Flowers					▬	▬
Sweet Corn	▬	▬	▬	▬	▬	
Squash & Gourds					▬	▬
Apples					▬	▬
Indian Corn					▬	▬
Pumpkins						▬

FARMS

See **Yeehaw Adventure Farm** on p. 140.

ROYAL WINTER FAIR

Fair enough!

If you think this nearly 86-year-old fair is all about livestock and show-jumping competitions, you're in for a surprise when you first visit this huge event!

Strolling around, watching animals lined up in preparation for competitions is not particularly stimulating for younger children, yet, they are impressed when they meet large furry cows (nose to nose). Here, you'll find the obvious dairy cattle section (where we saw young beasts being lead by 10-year-old farmers), the large beef cattle stalls, along with the swine (there are cute piglets to see), rabbits and poultry sections.

There's also the Royal Horse Palace to the extreme west side of the site, with its imposing stalls, some heavily decorated with champions' medals; a world in itself.

Other animals can be touched at the petting farm. There are also paddocks where goats and sheep are competing for titles.

When visiting, we saw interesting demonstrations in one of the rings, such as the large animal Vet check-ups, which allowed young aspiring veterinarians to listen to a huge horse's heartbeat with a stethoscope. We also saw live auction simulations and sheep-shearing sessions. Activities and floor plan change every year but you get the picture.

The horse shows are usually ticketed (not included with general admission) but there might be some that are free. During our visit, we could see a large carriage demonstration in the **Ricoh Coliseum**. There was lots of action when the staff prepared the ring after the jumping competition. It took them less than 10 minutes to put away all the obstacles and make way for the shiny large carriages. Now, THAT was entertainment(!), according to my young builder.

Throughout the fair there are several educational displays, such as maple syrup making, egg grading, honey production and animal and sheep wool care.

Not to be missed are the butter sculptures. When we visited, over 12 creations were kept in a refrigerated room.

Of course, the Royal Fair is about seeing animals in action. Dog shows are included with admission. You can often see a keen dog barking enthusiastically at its master, begging her to start the routine through a series of obstacles. They seem to live for that kind of action. Check the schedule for the day as soon as you get to the fair.

TIPS (fun for 3 years +)
• Not all activities are presented daily. Call or check their website to select the best day to visit.
• A giant vegetable competition takes place. We found them a bit "deflated" by the end of the fair, but still impressive.
• In the **Ricoh Coliseum**, you will have to leave your stroller at the foot of the bleachers.
• Snack bars are found on site.

NEARBY ATTRACTIONS
Harbourfront Centre (10-min.) ...... p. 25
High Park (15-min.) .... p. 286

Royal Agricultural Winter Fair (416) 263-3400 www.royalfair.org	**D-3** **Downtown** **Toronto** **10-min.**

Schedule: 10 days long, usually starts around first week of November, 9 am to 9 pm (usually closes at 5 pm on last day).
Admission: Around $18/adults, $14/seniors and 5 to 17 years, FREE under 5, $40/family of 4. Parking around $15.
Directions: Direct Energy Centre in **Exhibition Place**. Take Lake Shore Blvd., go north on Strachan Ave. The entrance is to your left.

See **Royal Winter Fair** on p. 126.

RIVERDALE FARM FALL FESTIVAL

wait in summer

Best of the crop

Twelve kids have already given their attempt at the chicken-calling contest. My son stands next in line. I've never heard him imitate a hen. I see him whispering something to the host, who nods, smiling, announcing this contestant has requested permission to call a rooster. After a resounding try, he leaves with the second-best caller ribbon!

TIPS (fun for 3 years +)

• Over 30,000 people show up during this dual event so parking is hard to find around Cabbagetown. Come early or be prepared to walk. Get the small wagon out.

• The local residents have been organizing the **Forsythia Festival** on the first Sunday of May for over 30 years, a popular parade starting in front of Riverdale Farm at around 10 am (people arrive at around 9:30 am). Participants are asked to wear yellow and decorate their bike, stroller or dog! The parade heads to **Wellesley Park**, located a 5-minute walk north of the farm, and continues until 1:30 pm in the lovely park, with entertainment and food stands. To access this park, walk north on Sumach and turn east

on Amelia. Call **Cabbagetown Preservation Association** at (416) 964-8004, **www. cabbagetownpa.ca** for details.

• The farm usually organizes one day of **Halloween** activities, suitable for kids 10 years and under. For **Christmas**, they usually offer an evening of tree lighting, carolling and marshmallow roasting and a morning with Santa and treats. Call for exact date.

• More on **Riverdale Farm** on p. 55.

The farm gets very lively during the Fall Harvest Festival. Not only do they offer a wide range of activities within the farm's gates but **Cabbagetown Arts & Crafts Sale** takes place in adjacent **Riverdale Park** at the same time.

When I visited, the festival included line dancing, antique farm tools display, several demonstrations, kids crafts, potato-sack race, egg and spoon relay, horseshoe pitch, straw jump, hog and chicken calling contest, storytelling and more. Smaller kids could "fish" for little prizes, they could touch reptiles and admire scarecrows. On Sunday morning, they served breakfast for a fee.

In the park, we could admire the work of artisans and listen to musicians. When visiting, we even got to watch a children's play in the small chapel north of the farm! For more details, check **www. cabbagetownartandcrafts.org**.

Riverdale Farm
(416) 392-6794
www.toronto.ca/parks/
riverdalefarm.htm

D-3
Downtown
Toronto
15-min.

 Schedule: The **festival and the art and crafts show** take place on the weekend after Labour Day, from 9:30 am to 8 pm on Saturday and from 9:30 am to 3:30 pm on Sunday. Call to confirm dates of other seasonal events.

 Admission: FREE.
Directions: See p. 55.

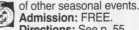

NEARBY ATTRACTIONS

✓ WHITTAMORE'S FARM

Snack time at the farm

When driving by, they had a frozen yogurt sign which caught my ever-hungry son's attention. I was happy we made that stop!

Not only was the snack bar's food delicious, the farm's market was well stocked with preserves, giftware and baked goods and it had an entertaining playground, complete with chickens and goats.

During their **Pumpkinland** event, you can catch a wagon ride through their haunted forest, see the pumpkin catapult in action (on weekends), go on a tree fort with slide, use the spider web tire climb, the barn bouncer, the mazes and more.

We went back to pick strawberries in their huge fields. Here, you can pick your own strawberries, raspberries, peas, peppers, tomatoes and pumpkins.

Whittamore's Farm • Markham (905) 294-3275 www.whittamoresfarm.com	C-3 N-E of Toronto 35-min.

 Schedule: The market is open early May to October 31. **Pumpkinland** open weekends from end of September to Halloween, 10 am to 5 pm.
Admission: Event is $8/weekends ($28/family); $4/weekdays.
Directions: 8100 Steeles Ave. East, Markham. From Hwy 401 West, take exit #389/Meadowvale Rd. northbound. Turn east on Steeles.

WATSON FARMS

Throughout the strawberry season and on weekends during apple season, wagon rides are provided to and from the fields.

You can pick your own strawberries, peas, raspberries, beans and apples. They organize a **Strawberry Festival** on **Canada Day** and an **Apple Festival** the weekend before Thanksgiving.

Surprise!

Out of sight, a great surprise awaits us in the middle of the fields at Ted Watson Farms. You find it by driving along a small road past the large farm's small produce market, on the side of the road.

When in Bowmanville, don't miss the unique free playground set up amidst Watson Farms. It is small but well laid out.

When we visited, there was a tractor to climb on, a hay jump shaded by a canopy to jump into, a large wooden structure to climb, a teepee and a slide.

Watson Farms • Bowmanville (905) 623-7252 www.whittamoresfarm.com	C-4 East of Toronto 50-min.

 Schedule: The market is open end of June until October 31. Pick your own weekdays from 9 am to 8 pm (6 pm on weekends).
Admission: FREE.
Directions: 2287 Hwy # 2, Bowmanville. From Hwy 401 West, take exit #431 northbound, turn west on Hwy 2/King St.

BROOKS FARMS

You'll have a blast!

Most of the farms around Toronto are strongly feeling the pressure of residential development. Not this one. It still stands in the middle of farmland, without one townhouse ruining the horizon, which is a good thing. You wouldn't want those pumpkin cannons disturbing a baby's nap!

Once you walk past the entrance, you can assess in a glimpse the wide range of activities going on here: pig races, pumpkin cannon demonstrations (they were one of the first farms to have one of these!), "train" ride to the pumpkin field, straw jumps, corn maze and my kid's favourite, the zip lines.

Wondering what a zip line is? It's a suspended metal line going downhill, with sliding handles kids hang from as they launch from a small platform. There's sand underneath so nobody gets hurt if they fall. The announcement of the cannon blast about to take place could not lure many young acrobats away from this activity!

Wondering how pumpkin cannons work? With propane gas and some crazy

guys loading wet newspapers and pumpkins into the cannons, which are aimed at some scarecrows, far away. The anticipation before each blast is just too much for the very excited kids. The strange muffled explosion doesn't disappoint them.

For the pig races, the same crazy guys encourage the crowd to cheer the pigs with resounding "Soo-ee" combined with a ridiculous dance step they demonstrate.

We went on Thanksgiving. Three hours went by in a flash at this most dynamic farm! It's a shame I had to take everybody back. I still had a turkey to cook, my first!

TIPS (fun for 3 years +)

• Pick-your-own strawberries, raspberries and pumpkins.
• They offer different activities during the summer weekends, for a lower admission fee.
• Their store sells pumpkins, jams, decorative corn and straw bales.
• They have a small snack bar which makes hot dogs and tasty small doughnuts (12 for $4.50), and a chip wagon. Bring a blanket to sit on the ground to eat lunch (not many tables around).

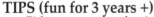

NEARBY ATTRACTIONS

North York Drive-in (15-min.) .... p. 92

Brooks Farms
• Mount Albert
(905) 473-3920
www.brooks-farms.com

C-3
N-E
of Toronto
45-min.

 Schedule: The **Fall Festival** runs on weekends from mid-September to October 31, 11 am to 5 pm. Check their website to confirm. Pick-your-own from end of June to mid-August.

 Admission: Around $9/person for the fall activities. FREE under 2 years. Get a discount coupon on their website.

Directions: 122 Ashworth Rd., Mount Albert. Take Hwy 404 North, exit at Vivian/Mulock eastbound. Turn north on Hwy 48, then Mount Albert Rd. East. Drive to Durham 30 and Ashworth Rd.

PINGLE'S FARM MARKET

Big field trip

At Pingle's Farm Market, the pumpkins are mighty impressive! There must be 10,000 of them, sitting in an amazing patch. We enter armed with a wheelbarrow, and pass through a winding corridor of lovely pumpkins standing at attention. It's well worth the trip, if only to take a look.

The farm's setting was nicely decorated for the season when we visited in the fall. An old wooden witch eyed my little one, and friendly scarecrows stared at us mischievously.

We visited the farm on a weekend during the **Fall Festival** when the outdoor playground was transformed into a Fun Farm Area accessible for a fee.

Kids bounced in the inflated structure, they rode on an amusing tricycle race track and they enjoyed the musical puppet shows presented on those weekends.

The farm has a Bunnyville (with rabbit inhabiting houses in a small fenced space). Then there's the elevated goats walk and mini-maze. They offer pumpkin cannon shows.

For an additional fee, you could carve or paint a small pumpkin or get your child's face painted.

TIPS (fun for 3 years +)
• Pick your own strawberries, fall raspberries, apples and pumpkins.
• During the **Easter** weekend, (excluding Monday) Pingles offers Easter egg hunts for around $7: Kids decorate their basket then fetch plastic eggs hidden by the Easter Bunny, which they trade for chocolate eggs and pot and seed to plant, earth provided on site.
• Pingles creates a different wide corn maze every year, which opens mid-August (additional fees apply). The maze gets haunted in October, when you can also stroll through the spooky orchard trail. Call for details and fees.
• You can buy snacks and baked goods in the relatively large market or fast food under a large tent.

NEARBY ATTRACTIONS
Jungle Cat World (10-min.) .... p. 64
Automotive Museum (25-min.) .... p. 217

Pingle's Farm Market
· Hampton
(905) 725-6089
www.pinglesfarmmarket.com

C-4
East
of Toronto
50-min.

Schedule: Opens for Easter, then daily, May 1 to October 31, 10 am to 5 pm. (Call to check if reopens during Christmas time.)

Fall Festival is offered during October weekends and Thanksgiving Monday, from 11 am to 4 pm. Call to confirm.

Admission: Extra fees apply during seasonal activities.

Directions: 1805 Taunton Rd. East, Hampton. From Hwy 401 East, take exit #425/Courtice Rd. northbound. Turn east on Taunton Rd.

FORSYTHE FAMILY FARMS

Come to your senses

Multicoloured flower baskets, delicious warm pies, smooth stacks of hay, apple turnovers fresh out of the oven, candied apples and children's laughter in the playground. You're at Forsythe Family Farms.

This farm-market isn't only a cornucopia of farm products, it also goes to great lengths to make us return to nature.

When we arrived at Forsythe Farms, we were struck by the beauty of the large, rustic market.

Further along, a decorated slide, a pony-shaped swing and rocking horses made from recycled tires, entertained the little ones.

A 10-minute cart ride brought us to the entrance of a tiny forest, where we were greeted by a funny face painted on a tree. A few wagons are put at the disposal of visitors at the edge of the forest.

Lovely paths carpeted with twigs

criss-cross the woods. From time to time they reveal scenes from several popular fairy tales.

For little ones, the simple act of taking a stroll in the woods is impressive in itself. I suggest you ask the older kids you are accompanying to identify the depicted fairy tales.

After the ride, there's the tricycle track, then the Barnyard Adventure with a Bunnyville. They've added a rope maze following the Little Red Hen theme (harder than it looks many parents have commented). There are also beehives in this section.

And straw to play with and animals in the barn, of course!

TIPS (fun for 2 years +)
• Pick-your-own peas, beans and pumpkins.
• Each weekend in October is **Harvest Festival** with **Halloween** activities (inflated pumpkin for jumping, scarecrow making) for an extra fee.
• During **Christmas** time, free hot cider is offered at the farm's market and the farm sells Christmas trees. Their store includes gift items and seasonal decorations.
• You may buy snacks at the market. Their outdoor snack bar is open only on certain weekends. Call to confirm.

Forsythe Family Farms
• Unionville
(905) 887-1087
www.forsythefamilyfarms.com

C-3
N-E
of Toronto
30-min.

Schedule: Open from the first weekend in May (weekends only in May), then daily from early June to October 31. Open Thursday to Sunday in November then daily again until December 24. Enchanted Forest is open until October 31. The corn maze opens on Labour Day weekend. The October Harvest Festival runs each weekend in October. Variable hours depending on crops. Call to confirm.
Admission: Admission to the Fun Area varies with the activities offered. FREE in December. Call to confirm.
Directions: 10539 Kennedy Rd., Unionville. From Hwy 404 North, take exit #31/Major Mackenzie eastbound, turn north on Kennedy Rd.

DOWNEY'S FARM MARKET

Mountain goats, sea of pumpkins

Navigating in an orange ocean, my tiny adventurer thinks he's dreaming. Then, we get into the action: jumping on hay-covered mattresses, visiting the haunted barn and the destabilizing black hole, racing on huge balloons, exploring the big corn field maze and sending feed to the mountain goats perched high above our heads.

During our visit in October, the Black-Hole Barn was a great attraction. Completely black inside, it included a trip through a turning cylinder, all black as well and studded with stars, with sound effects to boot. We literally lost our balance. My little one also lost her boot and we had problems finding it in the dark.

There were giant tires, bales of hay and a strolling pumpkin character. For an additional fee, you could make a big scarecrow, a great project for the whole family to create together!

During the **Pumpkinfest**, you can also expect a dump-truck slide, a trike track, a boo barn and more.

Their corn maze opens in mid-August and offers 7 km of trails!

The petting farm section is safe for children of all ages and filled with beautiful animals. We particularly enjoyed petting a small white goat with a soft coat. My little menace loved to chase the poor ducks.

Other farms have climbing goats but no other place has such an ambitious setting for them. At the crossing of four wooden corridors mounted on stilts, hungry goats bleat at us. The intelligent animals started to move only when I had filled a dish fastened to a rope and my little engineer had enthusiastically hauled it up using the pulley system.

Pony rides are offered for a fee on weekends during the Strawberry Festival and in the fall.

TIPS (fun for 2 years +)
• Pick-your-own strawberries, raspberries (wagon ride to the berry patch) and corn in August and September.
• The goats and the Kritter Corral are there from May to December. However, the best time to visit is during the events.
• During **Easter**, their Easterfest includes egg hunts with the Easter Bunny, egg decorating, wagon rides, puppet shows and children's entertainers.
• They celebrate **Canada Day** with a **Strawberry Festival** (free admission).
• The farm's market is brimming with goodies. We indulged ourselves with cheese bread and pumpkin doughnuts. They also sell fast food.
• **Christmas** trees are sold in December. Ask about their **Lunch with Santa!**

NEARBY ATTRACTIONS

Downey's Farm Market & Estate Winery	C-2 N-W of Toronto 45-min.

Downey's Farm Market & Estate Winery
• Inglewood
(905) 838-2990
www.downeysfarm.on.ca

 Schedule: Opens Easter weekend (Friday to Sunday, 10 am to 5 pm), then May to December, 9 am to 6 pm. **Pumpkinfest** is during October weekends (plus the last weekend in September or first weekend in November). Call to confirm.

 Admission: Around $9/person during the events, FREE under 3 years (admission to fun section varies by season).

 Directions: 13682 Heart Lake Rd., north of Brampton. Take Hwy 401 West, then Hwy 410 northbound until the end, where it becomes Heart Lake Rd.

ALBION ORCHARDS

Picking and walking

A few things distinguish this orchard from others: many tall apple trees, ladders to reach the upper branches, and a long winding road running down the beautiful scenery of Caledon.

There's something about climbing up a ladder that adds to the pleasure of apple picking. The orchard closest to the entrance included taller trees than the ones I'm used to seeing in the region. My little picker was thrilled to climb hers and grab the red apples that seemed inaccessible from the ground.

The biggest part of the orchard is located much farther, hidden from our sight by a hill. Up the hill, we observe an intriguing little graveyard under the shadow of a very large tree, where the likes of A. Lawyer, I.M. Gone and Lou Zer were buried...

Going downhill, we can take in the panorama of the white gravel sinuous road contrasting with the greenery of the apple trees and pumpkin field, with a tiny touch of orange in the background. As we get closer, the orange spot turns into a giant pumpkin decoration sitting next to the remains of an old orchard, creating a picture perfect Halloween scene.

We stop to eat sheep-shaped cookies we bought at the farm store and then off we go. We reach the entrance to the orchard where small red wagons to carry the apples (or the kids) are waiting for us. The tricky part here is to leave before the kids run out of energy. You still have to walk back up and down the hill to the starting point. A wagon ride can take you to the orchards during the weekends.

By the main building, there's a small play area where tires and hay are put to good use.

TIPS (fun for 4 years +)

• Pick-your-own apples and pumpkins. They have sold gift baskets, Christmas trees, pies, ice cream, hot dogs, and corn on the cob in their market. You'll need to call to confirm if they still do.

• I recommend you drive along Old Church Road, just north of Albion Orchards. It is as gorgeous a little country road as can be.

Albion Orchards

• Caledon East
(905) 584-0354
www.albionorchards.com

C-2
N-W
of Toronto
55-min.

Schedule: Normally open daily from mid-August to December 23, 10 am to 6 pm (to 5 pm on weekends in November and December. Please call ahead.

Admission: FREE. You pay for what you pick.

Directions: 14800 Innis Lake Rd., Caledon East. Take Hwy 400, exit at Hwy 7 going west. Turn north on Goreway Dr., it becomes Innis Lake Rd. The farm is 15 km away, on the west side of the road.

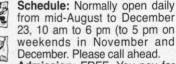

SPRINGRIDGE FARM

Happy ending

Less than a 15-minute drive from other attractions in the Milton and Guelph regions (mentioned in this guide), you will find Springridge Farm on the way back to Toronto. It is ideal to loosen little legs, grab a snack and finish off your outing nicely.

Springridge's farm market far exceeds what you would expect from a farm market. Inside the pleasantly decorated market you'll find a broad selection of seasonal decorative garden accessories, small toys, pre

serves and, best of all: excellent pies, tarts, cookies, muffins, cakes, breads, hot soups and delicious sandwiches. All of which you can eat sitting atop large barrels.

Everyday, visitors can climb haystacks of different heights or enter the open mouth of a witch that leads to a corn maze they can explore. They can feed the greedy sheep, goats, hens and roosters. They can play with the trucks in the large sandbox, climb up the old tractor and fly down the slide. They can "milk" a cut-out cow. All this for free.

Most weekends you can catch a pony ride or a tour of the property on a tractor-drawn cart for a fee. A section of the farmland is elevated, giving you a postcard perfect panoramic view.

In October, the wagon ride will take you to a huge corn **maze** you can't see from the farm.

TIPS (fun for 2 years +)

• Pick-your-own strawberries and pumpkins.

• Springridge closes at 5 pm. You will want to leave nearby attractions no later than 3 pm if you wish to include it in your itinerary.

• During the **Easter** 4-day weekend, kids may participate in a $7 egg hunt where plastic eggs are hidden by the Easter Bunny, which kids trade for treats and a little basket with hard-boiled chicken egg to decorate on the premises. Each child is sure to get one egg!

• Every weekend in October, **Fall Harvest Festival** and **Halloween** activities are offered for a fee: pumpkin painting, visit to the Boo Barn (cute rather than scary), wagon ride, etc.

• Every weekend from mid-November to mid-December, gingerbread making and glass ball painting are offered for around $4 and you get to visit Santa!

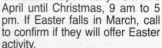

Springridge Farm
• Milton
(905) 878-4908
www.springridgefarm.com

D-2
West
of Toronto
45-min.

Schedule: Open daily from mid April until Christmas, 9 am to 5 pm. If Easter falls in March, call to confirm if they will offer Easter activity.

Admission: FREE (fees may apply to some activities).

Directions: 7256 Bell School Line, Milton. From Hwy 401, take exit #324/James Snow Pkwy southbound. Turn west on Derry Rd. and north on Bell School Line.

NEARBY ATTRACTIONS

CHUDLEIGH'S FARM

Hay! You!

"Something's bothering me!" my farm boy insists. For the third time, I stop the car at the side of the road to look for small pieces of straw slyly lodged in his clothes. This time, I extract the last intruders... from inside his underpants! That's what happens when you spend an afternoon running, jumping, sprawling and rolling in the play area at Chudleigh's Farm.

The site is huge, but the layout of the attractions gives it the charming and intimate character of a village fair. I doubt that your kids will let you begin by apple picking, as there are so many other tempting activities on site. I prefer to allow them to let off steam first in the playground. (It is actually worth going to the farm for the sole reason of having your children enjoy it.)

Their two giant slides offer an exciting sliding experience. When we visited, it was surrounded by a thick carpet of straw, topped by bales of hay that children climbed as if they were mountain goats (hence the straw!). The petting zoo is fun and includes climbing goats.

Afterwards, my kids were thrilled to ride to the orchard in a wagon drawn by a mighty tractor. My 3-year-old apple picker was quite satisfied by a half-hour harvest coming from a few trees, an operation made easier by the small size of the apple trees. From mid-July to end of October, there's a wide maze built with bales of hay. During the fall weekends, for an extra fee, you can take a 3-minute pony ride around a small orchard.

Chudleigh's Farm also grows pumpkins in a large patch by the orchard. After Thanksgiving, you can enjoy a wagon ride through the pumpkin patch to select your pumpkin.

Since our last visit, they've added a trail behind the bush with signs (to let your child guide you through the hardwood forest).

TIPS (fun for 2 years +)
• Pick-your-own apples and pumpkins.
• You get a $3 refund on admission when you purchase $20 worth of apples (about two of their bags, moderately filled), or pies or blossoms.
• Giant hot dogs, European sausages and corn barbecued in its husk are sold during the fall weekends. At the tempting outdoor market you can buy delicious homemade soup and eat it while observing the golden fish in the new pond.

NEARBY ATTRACTIONS

Chudleigh's Farm
• Milton
(905) 878-2725
www.chudleighs.com

**D-2
West
of Toronto
45-min.**

Schedule: Open daily early July to October 31, 10 am to 5 pm. Retail store stays open Friday, Saturday and Sunday to December 24.

Admission: Fee to use orchard and fun area is about $6.50/person, $4/senior, $25/family of 4, FREE for 3 years and under (read TIPS on refund).

Directions: 9528 Hwy 25, Milton. From Hwy 401 West, take exit #320/Hwy 25 northbound.

ANDREWS' SCENIC ACRES

Your pick

The first time we visited this farm, we picked strawberries. The ten-minute wagon ride led to the row assigned to us.

I must say my then 2-year-old son wasn't that fascinated by the picking itself. However, children 4 years and over seemed to be captivated by this activity. Furthermore, the rows of fruit were well spaced out, allowing little ones to run and explore easily.

After half an hour, our basket was full and my son's patience was coming to an end. Time to go back to the farm's big playground equipped with swings,

a giant tire, an old tractor to explore and an animal corral inhabited by rabbits, goats and chickens.

We returned in October to visit the small haunted forest located a short walk away from the playground. Don't expect a spooky trail but the winding trail created in the narrow forest made the experience interesting.

The mountain of straw was a hit with my family. There's real free play going on here. Try it! You'll be impressed by the straw's softness.

TIPS (fun for 3 years +)

• Pick-your-own rhubarb, asparagus, strawberries, raspberries, black currants, cherries, blueberries, flowers, gooseberries, apple, Indian corn and pumpkins.
• Wear comfortable, stainproof clothes. Don't forget hats and sunscreen.
• You can bring your own containers or buy them on site. As for the price of the fruit itself, it's about equivalent to what you would pay at your local store.
• The Haunted Forest trail is open most of September until end of October.
• Several picnic tables are located close to the playground. You can purchase delicious hot dogs and great cones of frozen yogurt. The farm market fills a large Mennonite barn with baked goods and produce as well as snacks.
• The farm is now producing a selection of 30 fruit wines through its **Scotch Block Winery**.

Andrews' Scenic Acres
· Milton
(905) 878-5807
www.andrewsscenicacres.com

D-2 West of Toronto 45-min.

  Schedule: Open 7 days from May 1 to October 31, 9 am to 6 pm (usually longer during summer) and weekends the rest of the year (closed on Holidays).
Admission: FREE ($2.50/person mid-September to October).
Directions: From Hwy 401, exit at #328/Trafalgar Rd. northbound, turn west on Ashgrove 10th Sideroad, to #9365.

NEARBY ATTRACTIONS

PUCK'S FARM

My little pony

Puck's Farm is a site where you can wander freely while giving children the opportunity to experience a real day at the farm.

The farm no longer offers piggy races but their pony ride is still unquestionably the best I've seen on a farm. It delighted my young cowboy.

Here, no sorry lads turning endlessly around a minuscule carousel. Ponies travel along a path bordering a pond inhabited by ducks.

You will find a large barn with familiar animals (a few lucky ones will even experience cow milking). Outside, you can pet lambs, cows and goats. You can take a ride on a horse-drawn wagon that takes you through a picture-perfect countryside.

The admission fee includes unlimited access to activities such as singing performances and pony rides.

It was corn-picking season when we visited and ears of corn, picked by the visitors, were cooking in huge bubbling cauldrons and were to be eaten on the premises. We thought it was quite exotic to roam inside a 2-metre-high cornfield!

They now offer a number of trail activities near the **Oak Ridges Moraine**.

TIPS (fun for 3 years +)

• Pick-your-own crops such as peas, pumpkins and corn, weather permitting.

• After rainy days, it is difficult to manoeuvre strollers on the muddy terrain. The sticky mud can suck boots in and may curb your appreciation of Puck's Farm's activities, otherwise so enjoyable on a drier day. Call to check ground conditions the day of your visit.

• Show up early on **Easter** weekend! We went on Easter Sunday. It seemed the whole city came along with us, we had to park far away from the farm. Easter Egg Hunts take place, rain or shine, on the two weekends prior to Easter as well as during the 4-day Easter Holiday. Chocolate eggs are hidden all over the place by the Easter Bunny. And he now does it all day long instead of 3-4 times a day, which makes it more fun.

• Ask about their **Pumpkinfest** in October.

• You can purchase hot dogs, pizza, hamburgers, fries and beverages from a snack bar in a Western wagon.

• Watch out for the hens as they'll keep an eye on your food. It's part of the fun!

NEARBY ATTRACTIONS	
South Simcoe Railway (15-min.)	p. 225
Albion Hills (20-min.)	p. 411

Puck's Farm
• Schomberg
(905) 939-7036
www.pucksfarm.com

C-2
N-W
of Toronto
45-min.

Schedule: Open two weekends prior to Easter and on Easter weekend (Friday to Monday), then weekends until end of June. Open daily from July 1 to Labour Day, then weekends only until Halloween, 10 am to 5 pm.
Admission: $8/person, $5/seniors, FREE for kids under 2 years old. Gives unlimited access to all activities. Check their website for a coupon.

Directions: From Hwy 400 North, take exit #55/Hwy 9 westbound. Turn south on Concession Rd. 11, to #16540.

HANES CORN MAZE

Fun at every corner

We had to think in three dimensions in order to figure out our position in the maze. "We're in the letter O!" understands my son, looking at the map. It turns out the framed letters on top of the map, which I mistook for a mere title, have actually been carved in the corn field. Amazing!

The corn stood ten feet high. The two 9-year-old boys I brought along couldn't get inside the 10-acre maze fast enough. They were armed with a map showing the contours of the five continents. Seven bullets on the map marked the places where they would find a box with codes: a series of letters and numbers plus interesting information about the continent on which it "sat".

This elaborate activity took them over an hour, after which they found the keys to the codes on a board, obtaining seven syllables to sort into a message. How clever! They had to spin a wheel to claim their prize.

The design varies every year. In 2007, it was over 12 acres!

My 6-year-old daughter never wanted to get near the maze! She was afraid of getting lost and scared of potential spiders. Fortunately, Farmland, the other section of the farm was just perfect for her and we could explore it while the older kids finished touring the maze. She was excited to pet animals. There was an assortment of animals to watch in the big barn in the back. She could play house in a tiny bungalow.

She could even "milk" a wooden cow by pulling its rubber udders, filling a bucket with the water spitting out of them. She was a very happy farmer.

TIPS (fun for 3 years +)
• Pick your own pumpkins.
• The maze experience can be fun for a 7-year-old if he's accompanied by older children. Otherwise, 9 years and over seems more appropriate. Don't enter a large maze with a young child if you are not convinced she could survive spending over an hour in it. I know dads who have found out it's a long time to hold a toddler on their shoulders. Bring flashlights for evening visits.
• Fridays and Saturdays in September, they offer Moonlight Mazes. Every night in October, it's **Haunted Mazes Nights**.
• There's a small farm market (closed on Sunday). Snacks and refreshments are sold at the admission stand.
• I noticed the **Dutch Mill Country Market** on our way back (east on Hwy 5, then north on Millgrove. This rustic place includes a Bakery & Deli and a Tea Room. It featured a funny outdoor playground with long wooden trains when we visited (533 Millgrove Sideroad, Waterdown, **www.dutchmill.on.ca**).

NEARBY ATTRACTIONS
Christie Lake C. A. (5-min.) .... p. 417

Hanes Corn Maze & Farmland • Dundas (905) 628-5280	E-2 S-W of Toronto 60-min.

 Schedule: Open daily 10 am to 5 pm late August to the end of October (please call for hours).

 Admission: $8.50/adults, $7.50/seniors, $6/5-15 years old, $2/2-4 years old, FREE under 2 years old ($2/person to access Farmland only). Ask for the family rate.

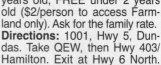 **Directions:** 1001, Hwy 5, Dundas. Take QEW, then Hwy 403/Hamilton. Exit at Hwy 6 North. Turn west on Hwy 5. Located across from Christie C. A.

YEEHAW ADVENTURE FARM

Fun family means family fun

How can it not be pure family fun when the members of the family involved in the creation of this great attraction are obviously enjoying themselves so much!

OK, not to sound like a groupie but last time I admired the attention to detail of an attraction this much, it was at Disney World.

The Walker family, three generations of them all costumed and staying in character, push the Hillbilly theme of their Annual Fall Halloween Harvest Hillbilly Hoedown as much as could be.

From the toothless girl welcoming us in her little shack with rugged roof to the hilarious gang awaiting to entertain us during the pig races down the hill, the whole adventure is a hoot.

Flo Gently, the host of an "educational" show going on in one of the barns,

strangely resembles Robin Williams in his famous role as the nanny Mrs. Doubtfire. Parents laugh out loud at the double meaning of Flo's jokes while kids are thrilled by the animals "she" brings in with the help of a funny ranger with his own agenda.

The Boo Barn featured the scariest sight of my childhood: the red fires of menacing burning furnaces. Kids could go up a silo ingeniously transformed into a climbing wall.

Adventurers used ropes to climb up the steep hill to get to the Sugar Shack stocked with old-fashioned candy, then went down the 30-foot slide to get to the other attractions.

Corn maze, haunted hay ride, pumpkin picking, animal pens, play barn, playground, even goat walk and pig racing that I've seen at other farms, they offer.

Many other features, I have never seen in a farm: authentic working outhouses, stilt walking, gold digging, hillbilly music fusing through speakers all over the place. The list goes on.

And to top it all, a picture perfect setting for a farm with entrance by a lovely country road leading to a spacious valley surrounded by a forest.

TIPS (fun for 2 years +)

• Certain activities you'll be allowed to do just once, by submitting a passport handed to you at the entrance.
• They have a great snack bar on the premises.
• On your way to or back from the farm, stop at **Dee's Bakery** on R.R. 97 for their self-proclaimed "to die for" butter tarts (1817 R.R. 97, Valens, **www.buttertartstodiefor.ca**).

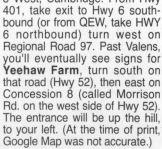

Yeehaw Adventure Farm
• Cambridge
(519) 624-0085
www.
yeehawadventurefarm.com

E-1
West
of Toronto
75-min.

Schedule: Open every weekend in October and Thanksgiving Monday, 11 am to 5:30 pm.

Admission: $13/3 years and older, $45/family of 4 (check for coupon on their website).

Directions: 1817 Concession 8 West, Cambridge. From Hwy 401, take exit to Hwy 6 southbound (or from QEW, take HWY 6 northbound) turn west on Regional Road 97. Past Valens, you'll eventually see signs for **Yeehaw Farm**, turn south on that road (Hwy 52), then east on Concession 8 (called Morrison Rd. on the west side of Hwy 52). The entrance will be up the hill, to your left. (At the time of print, Google Map was not accurate.)

NEARBY ATTRACTIONS

DYMENT'S FARM

low balls into which kids can plunge, a circuit offering bouncing ball races. There are also animals to pet and the Straw Fort filled with clean straw in which to frolic.

Since our visit, they've added a mini putt, a tall climber made out of rope and a zip line!

Simply awesome!

Dyment's keeps you so busy you tend to forget you came to pick a pumpkin in the first place!

Every year, Dyment's celebrates the ritual of pumpkin picking by opening its doors to the public every weekend in October.

I strongly recommend this unique and delightful farm located in the Hamilton area, despite the 1-hr drive from Toronto. This outing is also a wonderful opportunity to view the colourful landscapes of fall as you head towards the Niagara escarpment where Dyment's is nestled.

A traditional playground including a "Retired Tractor" and "Tired Horse Swings" greets us at the entrance. I was taken by the Trike Track activity. The fun tricycle track, located close to the barn, is outfitted with a small bridge, a tunnel and a traffic light which my young driver enjoyed obeying. Unfortunately, children older than 5 years old are often too big to fit the small tricycles.

Our kids were reluctant to leave the table filled with replicas (to scale) of farm machines to visit the other attractions: a small Spook Hut with cute light and sound effects, a Corn Bin with 10,000 yel-

En route to the hilly pumpkin fields, the tractor trail borders the Niagara escarpment, offering a lovely view through the trees and providing one of the most enjoyable farm rides I can remember.

An interactive exhibit called Agri-Maze, where you can learn about the daily life of a farmer named Jim, is one of the farm's most interesting features. It's full of amusing touches, including Jim with a television set as a head that speaks to the viewing public in the main barn.

Dyment's Farm
• Dundas
(905) 627-5477
www.dyments.com

E-2
S-W
of Toronto
60-min.

Schedule: Pumpkin farm open to the public from end of September to end of October, 10 am to 5 pm. The market is open year-round from 10 am to 7 pm.
Admission: Not decided at the time of print. Call to confirm.
Directions: 416 Fallsview Rd. East, Dundas. Take QEW then follow Hwy 403 towards Hamilton. Exit Hwy 6 northbound, turn west on Hwy 5, then south on Sydenham Rd. After the curve, turn right onto Fallsview Rd.

TIPS (fun for 2 years +)
• Remember not to pick a pumpkin up by the stem or you risk seeing it come crashing down on your feet.
• You can purchase fast food and yummy snacks on the premises.

NEARBY ATTRACTIONS

VAN-GO ADVENTURE FARM

It's a go!

Oblivious to the whole line-up of activities, my animal-lover and her new friends couldn't stay away from the animals and kept feeding them with grass from the surrounding lawn until dusk.

We visited Van-Go farm after a day of activities at the Waterford Pumpkinfest. There was so much to do in this attraction in itself that we couldn't see it all.

The farm was at the end of the circuit of the **Pumpkin Express** tractors offering free rides during the **Pumpkinfest**. It included a huge parking lot easily accessible once the **Pumpkinfest Parade** was over.

We were welcomed by a vast field, where the pumpkin cannon awaited its master. The farmer really loves his toy! I have seen such cannons fed by a regular BBQ gas tank but this baby was attached to the kind of tank you normally see on a train wagon! He was aiming at the old car way up in the field and reached his target, to cheers from the crowd.

Further, the climbing goats, alpacas, pigs (involved in pig races during the day), peacocks and pheasants. To the right, a bunny village, funny rubber duck races, sand pit, straw pile and jump castle, and more. The works!

We tried the pumpkin slingshot ourselves. Loaded it, pulled the bucket and... saw it come back full speed right at us... with the pumpkin still inside. That was close.

TIPS (fun for 2 years +)

• More on the **Pumpkinfest Parade** and a themed restaurant on the way back on p. 42.
• Check their website for a pretty map of their activities layout.
• They open their corn maze mid-August and turn it into a haunted maze in September and October.
• During the warm season, bring the bathing suits! They offer a water pad.
• In 2008, they intend to add **Christmas** fun, selling Christmas trees and offering activities: dogsled rides, light festival, ice sculptures, carolling, bonfire, Santa and the elves (call to confirm!).
• There's a snack bar on site.

Van-Go Adventure Farm
• Waterford
(519) 443-0001
www.vangoadventurefarm.com

E-2
S-W
of Toronto
90 min.

Schedule: Open late May to December 24 (call to confirm).
Admission: $10/adult, $8/4-14 years, FREE 3 years and under.
Directions: 710 Old Hwy 24, Waterford. From Hwy 403 southbound, take exit Rest Acres Road (Hwy 24 South), go southbound then turn east on Thompson Street, and south at the stoplight.

CHAPPELL FARMS

Did you see that?

I'm sure we looked like a bunch of hens in a red cage while riding a wagon through Chappell Farms' fields. Soon, our kids were competing to see who could spot the many surprises hidden in the cornstalks: pumpkin heads, old witches, a headless horseman and scarecrows who seemed to wave at us from their lawn chairs. This was no traditional wagon ride!

We arrived in the middle of the **Pumpkin Festival**. This means that in addition to the usual animal petting, cow milking sessions, entertainment, playground, maze, cut-out characters and seasonal displays the farm offers, we were also treated to a Boo Barn and a Haunted Barn.

I inadvertently entered the haunted barn with my 3-year-old, intending on the more suitable Boo Barn. Big mistake! Dimmed in light barely sufficient to appreciate the special effects, the place was so dark I could barely see my own hand, let alone the scary actors breathing

down my neck or the progressively narrowing fur-covered walls, with their unpredictable sharp turns.

The whole experience, successfully disorienting, left my younger one completely panicked, while my 7-year-old loved every minute of it. The Boo Barn, on the other hand, is lined with small friendly ghosts and funny characters.

The farm includes nanny mountain goats climbing around a silo, a big inflatable structure to jump in, trike track and more. My little performer joined the show in another barn and was asked to assist the skillful magician during a good card trick.

This farm has been in the Chappell family for over 175 years!

TIPS (fun for 3 years +)
- Pick your own pumpkins.
- They usually offer **Haunted Adventures** every night of the last week of October. Call to confirm.
- For **Easter**, they organize egg hunts (no more than 250 children at a time, scattered in a large area; kids are almost guaranteed to find candy), magic shows and wagon rides. Of course, there's always Bunny Village, with its own school, church, windmill and all.
- The big Old Barn Shoppe is packed with seasonal goodies and crafts.

NEARBY ATTRACTIONS

Chappell Farms
- Barrie
(705) 721-1547
www.chappellfarms.ca

B-2
North
of Toronto
60-min.

 Schedule: Open the weekend prior to Easter and on Easter weekend (Friday to Sunday, 10 am to 4 pm). The **Pumpkin Festival** runs daily from last week in September to October 31, 9 am to 5 pm. (Magic shows and inflated castle on weekends only.) Haunted Adventure daily on last week of October, 5 pm to 8 pm.

 Admission: During special events: $9/visitor on weekends and holidays, $5 on weekdays, FREE under 2 years old.

Directions: 617 Penetanguishene Rd., County Rd. 93, Barrie. Take Hwy 400 northbound, stay on centre lane onto Hwy 11, exit County Rd. 93/Penetanguishene Rd. westbound.

ROUNDS RANCH

Photos: Courtesy of G. Servinis

A round of applause

At this farm, you might find a special catapult that throws apples at a scarecrow and see free-roaming rabbits and hens. Kids will ride on large pedal carts and families will be challenged with a well-planned maze adventure.

My dentist is a big fan of labyrinths. So when I mentioned this one, he had to check it out with his three children in tow. His family enjoyed it so much that I decided to include it even though I did not personally see it.

When they visited, a pirate theme was going on. The next year, the theme was to be Australian Outback and the year after, Medieval Times. They have decided to stick to a Western theme for a while and built on it, only changing the design of the maze every year.

When my friends visited, the maze was shaped like a sailboat. At its entrance, a pirate greeted the family. Kids could dress up like pirates long enough for parents to take pictures. Everyone was given

a map with different information to find the nine pirate stations throughout the maze. It took my dentist and his two boys over two hours to get out of the labyrinth.

Back then, their maze covered 10 acres, including 5 km of pathways. Since then, they've reduced it to a more manageable 3.8 acres which should take no longer than one hour to complete.

My friend's daughter thought she was in heaven, petting the cute rabbits and other animals. The whole family eventually got onto the wagon to get a pumpkin from the field (after the boys had a turn on the pedal cart racetrack).

Another small maze hosts very popular pony rides. Parents can even lead the pony for 1/2 hour. There's also the colourful barnyard boxcar pulled by a tractor, the straw jump, the catapult...

TIPS (fun for 3 years +)
- Pick-your-own pumpkins.
- Read tips about mazes on p. 139.
- If **Easter** doesn't come too early, they organize fancy egg hunts, with their catapult shooting chocolate eggs into the air. Call to see if they offer it this year.
- Their **Pumpkin Mania** includes all kinds of games (seed spitting, pie eating, pumpkin hockey, baseball, toss and more) in addition to the Ranchland activities, the cornfield maze and a pumpkin.
- Ask about their 2-hour **Natural Horsemanship Trail Ride** for 10 years and older (one hour training and one hour trail ride on a horse for $75/person).
- There's a snack bar selling hot dogs, burgers, fries, corn on the cob and more.

NEARBY ATTRACTIONS	
Scenic Caves (30-min.)	p. 256
Wasaga Beach (15-min.)	p. 419

Rounds Ranch • Elmvale (705) 322-6293 www.roundsranch.com	B-2 N-W of Toronto 90-min.

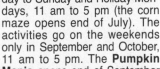

Schedule: The Ranchland activities start end of June, Wednesday to Sunday and Holiday Mondays, 11 am to 5 pm (the corn maze opens end of July). The activities go on the weekends only in September and October, 11 am to 5 pm. The **Pumpkin Mania** opens end of September to end of October.

Admission: (tax excluded) Ranchland: $10/10 years and older, $8/9 years and under; pony rides $4/10 min. Pony rental $17/30 min. **Pumpkin Mania** is $37/family or $9/person.

Directions: 1922 County Rd. 92, 4 kms west of Elmvale. Take Hwy 400 North. Exit at Hwy 26/27 North to Elmvale. In Elmvale, turn west at the second set of lights, to County Rd. 92.

BRUCE'S MILL MAPLE FESTIVAL

Hop on the wagon!

My little lumberjack is dying to put a log on the huge bonfire all by himself. Not far away, white smoke escapes from the sugar shack's chimney. The fire gives off an odour that blends beautifully with the pancakes' sweet smell. It's the busiest time of the year at Bruce's Mill.

At other times, Bruce's Mill Conservation Area is a rather modest attraction, its main asset being its proximity to Toronto. So I was really surprised to discover how well it was set up during maple syrup season.

Bruce's Mill Sugar Bush Trail is the most manicured of all those that I visited. The trees are scattered, the areas where the self-guided trail signs are located are bare. It takes about 15 minutes to do the trail, nonstop.

The course is lined with some characters cut out of wood, illustrating the different methods of maple syrup production. When we visited, "Buddy" (a maple leaf bud character) was teaching us, among other things, that the maple syrup season ends once he and other buds appear.

TIPS (fun for years +)
• More about **Bruce's Mill Conservation Area** on page 302.
• This sugar bush is my favourite when visiting with younger children. They can handle the short trail, and the wagon ride through the forest adds a feeling of adventure to the outing.
• The trails can be really muddy. Nice boots beware!
• They serve all-day pancake breakfasts during the festival.

The children particularly enjoyed going in the tall teepee (not there every year), which reminded us that the natives discovered the maple sap's properties. The kids also liked to pet the real horse in its pen, a reminder of the time when sap was collected in large barrels pulled by such horses. A jolly fellow, clad in overalls and checkered shirt, offered us a taste of syrup, prepared in a huge pot the old-fashioned way.

On weekends and during the March Break, a horse-drawn wagon runs around the site. Some years, they add a straw playground and animal pens.

Bruce's Mill Maple Syrup Festival
· Stouffville
(416) 667-6295
www.trca.on.ca

C-3
N-E
of Toronto
30-min.

Schedule: The season may start early March and last to mid-April (depends when Easter falls). Activities are offerred on weekends and daily during the March Break, 10 am to 4 pm. (Call to check the exact dates and hours.)
Admission: $6.50/adults, $5.50/seniors, $4.50/5-14 years, FREE under 5 years.
Directions: Between Warden and Kennedy, Stouffville. From Hwy 404 North, take exit #37/Stouffville Rd. eastbound.

KORTRIGHT MAPLE FESTIVAL

No wonder maple syrup is so precious to us. Kortright Centre moves heaven and earth to educate us on the subject.

You can cover the path crossing the sugar bush in half an hour. It begins with a steep downward slope that seems difficult to tackle, but the secret is to go slowly. Kids won't resist the call of gravity and will go down at full speed. However, they'll surely stop before the big turn if tools were left to drill tap holes the old-fashioned way, using a brace and bit!

On the path, buckets have been installed lower than usual, allowing children a peek at the dripping sap. Pioneers cook maple sap inside huge pots.

Mouth-watering

The sugar content of maple sap is between 2 and 3%, while maple syrup has at least 66%. It takes up to 40 buckets of the former to produce one bucket of the latter. It's not surprising that the cost of syrup is so high. It's only made in North America and 80% of the world production comes from Canada.

It's time to try the shoulder yokes.

Modern maple syrup production techniques are presented inside the sugar cabin. It's easy to see the modern maple sap collecting system and to explain its functioning to kids. My little engineer was fascinated by this gravity-fed system that moves the sap from the trees directly to storage tanks inside the cabin.

TIPS (fun for 4 years +)
• **March Break** is an excellent time to attend the festival, when they add a few activities to the line-up of maple-related things to see and do.
• During the **Maple Syrup Festival**, pancakes with syrup are sold at the **Kortright Centre Café**. Tasty snacks made with maple syrup are sold in the store.
• The first weekends of the festival are the quietest. Saturdays are quieter than Sundays. On weekdays during **March Break**, arrive after 2 pm when the school buses leave.
• The wagon rides are offered during the weekends only. I was disappointed by the ride as the course was uninteresting. On the bright side, the succulent maple popcorn we had bought kept my little companions' boredom at bay as we waited in the long line-up and the pleasant cart driver was very talkative. She taught us a lot about her horses and invited children to pet them.
• More about **Kortright Centre** on p. 296.

Kortright Maple Syrup Festival
• Maple
(905) 832-2289
or (416) 661-6600, ext. 5602
www.trca.on.ca

C-2
N-W
of Toronto
40-min.

Schedule: The season may start early March and last to mid-April. (Call to check the exact dates.) Open 9:30 am to 4 pm. (Demos stop half an hour prior to closing time).
Admission: $8/adults, $5/seniors and children, FREE 4 years and under. Parking is $3.
Directions: 9550 Pine Valley Dr., Maple. From Hwy 400 North, take exit #35/Major Mackenzie westbound, then turn south on Pine Valley Dr.

NEARBY ATTRACTIONS
McMichael Collection (10-min.) ..... p. 89
The Wave Pool (15-min.) .... p. 424

BRADLEY MUSEUM

Condensed sweetness

The sugar bush may be the smallest I have seen but nothing's missing: maple trees with spouts, sweet maple water smell around the fire pit, maple sugar molding demonstration in the pioneer house, horse-drawn wagon and a craft activity.

Maple syrup time is probably the best time to visit this heritage attraction. It is located in a residential area but nestled among trees and charming.

Bradley House itself is not big. We used the maple sugar molding demonstration as an excuse to visit it but we spent most of our time outside.

TIPS (fun for 4 years +)
- They serve pancake breakfasts in the Anchorage Tea Room during **March Break**.
- Ask about their **Shakespeare Under the Stars** event presented by the **Driftwood Outdoor Theatre Group**, usually on the mid-July Friday and Saturday, at 8 pm (call to confirm). Suggested donation. Come early, it is very popular.
- In mid-September, there's the **Fall Fair** (call for exact dates and fees). It includes musical entertainment, bake sale, children's area, wagon rides and contests.
- Call closer to December to find out about their official opening of the log cabin with Santa.

Our kids were just happy hiding in the little shack the museum had built the year we visited (not guaranteed every year) in the "Sweet Water Camp" section and checking out the maple sap level in the buckets on the trees.

We waited in line to catch a wagon ride (offered every day during the **March Break**). This reminded us that we are indeed in a residential area! Exploring **Bradley House** was a bit like time travel but the ride took us amidst modern houses and cars.

Then we did some small crafts in the big barn in the middle of the place. All in all, this was a short and sweet outing.

Bradley Museum • Mississauga (905) 615-4860 www.museumsof mississauga.com	**D-3** **West** **of Toronto** **30-min.**

     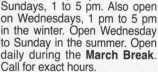 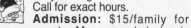

Schedule: Open year-round on Sundays, 1 to 5 pm. Also open on Wednesdays, 1 pm to 5 pm in the winter. Open Wednesday to Sunday in the summer. Open daily during the **March Break**. Call for exact hours.

Admission: $15/family for events. Museum admission is $5/adults, $3/seniors, students, $1.50/3-12 years, FREE under 3.

Directions: 1620 Orr Rd., Mississauga. From QEW, take exit # 126/ Southdown Rd. (Erin Mills Pkwy becomes Southdown Rd. south of the QEW). Turn east on Orr Rd. (south of Lakeshore).

NEARBY ATTRACTIONS

MOUNTSBERG MAPLE DAYS

Maple syrup time, with animals to boot

When you visit, if you are lucky, the hatchery in the Discovery Room might be bursting with little chirping chicks who undulate as one big yellow wave when children get close to them. What a great bonus!

The Mountsberg Conservation Area has a lot to offer during Maple Syrup Time.

Past the Visitors' Centre, there's a railroad crossing (it may be the first time your child walks over some tracks!) It gets us to a field from which you can walk to Mapletowne or wait for the $2 horse-drawn wagon. It will take you on a good ride through the sugar bush.

Mapletowne, a series of small, rustic houses, is in the heart of the action. In one of them, syrup is produced. In the next one, maple sugar is made (yes, everybody can have a taste). Another one is a country shop.

The Pancake pavilion is an enclosed shelter with picnic tables. We enjoyed eating at our table while admiring the surrounding landscape with lively music playing in the background.

Scenes recreating different maple syrup production techniques through the ages are displayed around the pavilion.

Bring your skates, you might be able to skate on their pond by the trails (from January to mid-March, weather permitting).

Maple Syrup Days usually starts with a **Flapjack Olympics** (they've had one for the last seven years) involving pancake-related events and a torch run. Check their calendar for the exact date.

TIPS (fun for 3 years +)
- During **March Break**, live raptor demonstrations, normally offered only on weekends and holidays at that time of the year, are shown at 12 noon and 2 pm.
- On **Easter** Saturday, expect an Easter Egg Hunt, baby chicks, wagon rides, crafts and more.
- More on the **Mountsberg Wildlife Centre** on page 298.

Mountsberg Maple Syrup Days	**D-2 West of Toronto 60-min.**

• Milton
(905) 854-2276
www.conservationhalton.on.ca

 Schedule: The season may start early March and last to mid-April (depends when Easter falls). Activities are offerred on weekends and daily during the March Break, 10 am to 4 pm. (Call to check the exact dates and hours.) **Admission:** $6.50/adults, $5.50/seniors, $4.50/5-14 years, FREE under 5 (extra for pancakes). **Directions:** From Hwy 401 West, exit #312/Guelph Line southbound. Turn west on Campbellville Rd., then north on Milborough Line to the park entrance.

NEARBY ATTRACTIONS
Hilton Falls (20-min.) .... p. 266

HORTON'S HOME FARM

It's personal

No fancy educational program here, just a few very informative signs to read when self-exploring or the down-to-earth tour by a friendly guide. No big scale, the trail around the sugar bush is short. No bells and whistles, just a little sap and maple tasting in tiny paper cups. So why bother coming here? For the timeless charm of the place, I would say. For the "monkey tree" would claim my children!

Is it because it is so off the beaten track you have to go through 500 metres of mud by foot or be pulled behind a tractor to reach it? When you discover this rustic little sugar shack, you feel like you've found the best kept secret in the region. Their "grandfather" maple tree is 450 years old and dying, but still standing.

After explaining to us the life cycle

of such a tree, it is noted on a sign: "We hope to be able to tap this bush through many generations of our family." It turns out our guide is one of the children of the couple from the 70's you'll see in the laminated press clippings on the wall inside the shack. The maple sugar bush has been family-run since 1963.

On another sign, we're reminded that each tap hole may yield 20-40 litres of sap in a season! A tree 25 cm in diameter will take one tap, three taps when over 45 cm. Among other things, the sign also states very clearly that "Tapping trees is a boring job!"

Everything about this place is laid-back. Your kids really want to climb up the tall "monkey tree"? "Be our guest; you know your own child's limits." This is actually the best climbing tree I have seen in ages, with lower branches perfectly set to help one climb way up! A lady clad in old-fashioned dress and cap serves us nice warm pancakes. The sun shining through the windowpanes inside the shack accentuates the warmth of the wooden walls and tables. Outside, it gives a dazzling glow to the snow.

Later, as I sit by a tree, I hear water dripping from the melting icicles and the laughter of the children involved in a snowball fight. It was so relaxing.

TIPS (fun for 5 years +)

• Don't confuse Horton's Home Farm with **Horton's Primrose Farm** or **Horton's Magic Hill Farm**. It is the only one with a sugar bush.

• There's a counter in the shack selling maple syrup, butter and sugar. They sell pancakes, coffee and hot chocolate in the adjacent kitchen.

• You can count on wet snow or good old mud so you might want to bring an extra set of clothes for the way back.

• In December, you can cut your own Christmas tree.

Horton's Home Farm	C-3 N-E of Toronto 40-min.

Horton's Home Farm
· Stouffville
(905) 888-1738
www.hortontreefarms.com

 Schedule: Saturdays and Sundays from 9 am to 4 pm, usually from mid-March to mid-April. Also open in December. Call to confirm hours.
Admission: $5/adults, $4/seniors and students, $3/5-12 years old.
Directions: 5924 Slater Rd., Stouffville. Take Hwy 404 North. Turn east on Aurora Rd., then south on Warden Ave., and west on Slater Rd.

SILOAM ORCHARDS

Off the beaten track

I was concerned there wasn't much of the white stuff left on the ground. But I had called to check if they still could offer taffy on the snow and they had confirmed it. I found out later that they've learned to store snow in the freezer after a fresh fall. Clever.

It was the end of the season so we ate our taffy off a batch of snow in a plastic container! So what? It was as good as ever!

Before reaching their 2,500-tree maple forest, we walked by the farm's orchards. At this time of the year, the naked apple trees revealed the funny shape of their trunks and we could easily discern abandoned nests through their branches.

The self-guided walk was as sim-

ple as can be but it explained well how the sap was collected from the green pipelines we saw emerging from the holes drilled into the maple trees. In a wooden box, we found portion-size paper cups to sample the sap in the buckets along the trail.

When we showed up, on the last weekend of the season, the sap wasn't running, neither was the tractor, but we still enjoyed the trail and the pancakes. And the maple taffy on the snow in itself was reason enough for this outing!

TIPS (fun for 5 years +)

• The sap flow is unpredictable so it is strongly recommended to phone ahead to check the conditions. Make sure they can offer their taffy on the snow!

• The trails can be quite muddy, bring boots.

• During the **Maple Season**, the **Cider Café** serves pancakes with maple syrup, breakfast sausage, coffee, apple cider, hot dogs and homemade apple pie.

• In the fall, you can pick your own apples at the orchards.

• There are not many attractions nearby that are open during the **Maple Season** but you could top the visit with a movie at the local downtown **Roxy Theatres**, 10 minutes away (46 Brock St. West, Uxbridge, **www.roxytheatre.com**, $8/adult, $5/13 and under.

Siloam Orchards • Uxbridge (905) 852-9418 www.siloamorchards.com	**C-3** **North** **of Toronto** **45-min.**

 Schedule: Maple Season is in March and early April, on the weekends from 9 am to 3 pm.

 Admission: $3/person (includes hot apple cider, taffy on the snow, access to self-guided walking tour and tractor ride to the bush if weather allows).

Directions: 7300-3rd Concession, Uxbridge. From Hwy 404 North, take exit #41 (Bloomington RR 40), follow to Goodwood, then turn left on Front St. It becomes 3rd Concession.

WARKWORTH MAPLE FESTIVAL

Have a taste of this!

"Her eyes are like maple syrup" declared my son as he closely observed his sister. A Canadian poet is born! Indeed, who else in the world would allude to this delectable brown gold that distinguishes us internationally? I must say that, thanks to the Warkworth Maple Syrup Festival, he had a taste of his first warm, amber-coloured ribbon, rolled around a wooden spoon. So he knows what he's talking about!

We parked in a field close to the **Sandy Flat Sugar Bush**. The snow was melting in the bright sunshine and getting mixed with the path's dirt. The resulting muddy cocktail would certainly prevent visitors from wearing their Sunday shoes to appreciate the event.

We'd just driven an hour and a half, leaving behind grey Toronto to go taste taffy poured on to white snow. (This activity isn't generally offered in sugar shacks neighbouring the city, as they suffer from a lack of the white stuff.) The country road we had been driving on for the last half an hour was charming and put us all in good spirits.

The place is very popular; there was a short line-up at the entrance booth.

The warm and friendly ambience reigning over the site is contagious. By observing closely, one understands why. Retired people from the area serve breakfast, boy scouts clean tables and local musicians play the violin. It seems that the whole Warkworth community is present!

All of the festival's activities revolve around a square, worthy of a postcard, where a happy crowd is gathered.

Here, onlookers watch how maple syrup is made, in the old-fashioned way and with the new method. There, two kids can't believe how lucky they are to be allowed to cut a slice off a log with a double-handled saw.

Further on, a group of people is waiting to take a place in one of the horse-drawn sleighs on which they'll take a tour of the maple grove. We join them and hear the mischievous driver's comments: "One of the engines is backfiring!" he says, when the horse starts to... (I'll leave it at that!).

They organize original competitions. We saw contestants being timed while they ran in the snow between the maple trees, wearing snowshoes and holding a pail of maple sap. It was pretty funny to watch!

The excitement rises each time a new pail of delicious taffy is ready. Grown-ups and kids alike line up eagerly in front of troughs full of snow where they can have a taste of the delicious treat.

But this wasn't the only thing we had to eat! Abundant breakfasts were served outside, including pancakes, sausages and maple syrup.

While we ate, we watched spontaneous dancers move to the sound of the fiddler's jig. (Wasn't that my son I saw dancing on the stage?) During the festival, you might even see step-dancing on the small stage.

TIPS (fun for 4 years +)

• There are two educational walking trails allowing visitors to burn off some of those maple syrup pancakes! The short one takes 20 minutes to complete, the other is one mile long. They include little bridges and plaques with the names and uses of the different trees.

• Wear old boots and bring a change of clothes for the kids. At the end of the day, they'll be so dirty with mud you may refuse to let them get in the car without a good cleanup!

• During the Maple Syrup Festival weekend, activities are held in Warkworth Village: Craft show, antique show, art show, pony rides and petting farm (check **www.maplesyrupfestival.com**).

• Every weekend after the festival, you can also visit **Sandy Flat Sugar Bush** to taste taffy, go on a sleigh ride (weather permitting) or to have breakfast in the little shack. When it's not festival time, the menu is different, even more diversified because there are fewer visitors to accommodate.

• Every weekend, chances are you'll see the owners and close relatives engaged in entertaining musical gigs in the rustic restaurant.

• Maple-flavoured cotton candy and many maple sugar treats are sold on site.

• I was told by a reader there's another sugar bush in the same spirit north of Peterborough. Check **Buckhorn Maplefest** at **McLean Berry Farm** at **www. mcleanberryfarm.com** or call (705) 657-2134. They offer taffy on the snow if fresh snow is available, musical shows, petting section, hay games, walking trail and much more during 3 weekends.

Warkworth Maple Syrup Festival • Warkworth (705) 924-2057 www.sandyflatsugarbush.com	B-6 **East** **of Toronto** **90-min.**

 Schedule: The annual festival is held the second weekend in March, 9 am to 4 pm. The sugar bush is open year-round but call ahead during the weekdays.

Admission: FREE taffy sampling. Small fees apply for the sleigh ride. Breakfast of pancakes and sausages with syrup costs $6/adults, $3/children.

Directions: Sandy Flat Sugar Bush, Warkworth. From Hwy 401 East, take exit #474/Hwy 45 northbound, then take County Rd. 29 eastbound towards Warkworth. Go to Burnley then turn left onto Noonan Rd. and follow the Sandy Flat Sugar Bush signs.

General tips about
Holiday outings:

- Days without school are what's driving our lives, aren't they? This chapter offers a quick reference to seasonal outings or seasonal activities offered in year-round attractions. It also describes unique seasonal attractions.
- You'll find a description of all the parades in the **Parades** section under the **Amusement Corner** chapter.

HOLIDAY
OUTINGS

See **Halloween** on p. 163.

MARCH BREAK

It's baaack!

March Break is such a misleading name! The only good news about this break for many parents is that there will be no homework to supervise and no lunch to prepare.

This listing is for those who choose (or have no choice but to) take a week off to be with the kids. Good time for a day trip!

Outdoor outings are much underrated during March Break, the busiest period of the year in many of the major indoor attractions. Put on rubber boots, pack some great snacks and a change of clothes and flip through the **Nature's Call** chapter (pp. 252-333) to choose a destination. Then watch your kids turn into young explorers.

This is also maple syrup time; check the maple syrup places described on pages 146 to 153. **Horton's Home Farm** and **Siloam Orchards** (pp. 150-51) are the least crowded; my favourite is **Warkworth's** (p. 152). Also consider **Lake Crawford Conservation Area** (p. 388), offering the advantage of great trails and the proximity of **Mount Nemo** (p. 263).

Many local families choose to "get away" in their own city with **Stage West's**

TIPS
• See our calendar of events on p. 9. Read about more good calendars of events on p. 15.
• Note that **March Break** is usually the last week most ski and snow tubing parks are open, weather permitting.
• If you are planning a vacation out of Ontario, be aware that the **March Break** doesn't fall on the same dates in the other provinces in Canada.

family package of hotel, pool and dinner theatre (p. 85). The **Delta Hotels** also offers very popular packages with pools and activities, and you can bring your pet under 50 lbs for an extra fee of $35. Check those with giant slides! **Delta Meadowvale Resort**/ Mississauga, **Delta Chelsea**/downtown Toronto and **Delta Toronto East**/Scarborough (**www.deltahotels.com**).

This time of the year is the best time to visit the **Bata Shoe Museum** (p. 243), the **Textile Museum** (p. 242) and **McMichael Canadian Art Collection** (p. 89) with their drop-in activities noticeably more interactive than usual.

The **Historic Fort York** becomes quite attractive with its musket drills for children (p. 379).

Casa Loma is also a winner during this period (p. 120), despite the fact it is quite busy; arrive early and enjoy special activities throughout the castle and a great show.

If you're looking for midways and big crowds, check the **Spring Fling** at the **Rogers Centre** (p. 336) and **Wizard World** at **Exhibition Place** (p. 32).

Finally, you'll find the best free activities in some of the **Toronto Public Library** branches (p. 90). Check their website to find one to suite your desire, they vary a lot from one branch to the next.

LOOK FOR THIS:
When you see the March Break pictogram on a page, it means the attraction offers special activities or schedule for these dates in March.

EASTER

Say what?

Wondering when Easter falls this year? Simple! It falls on the first Sunday following the first ecclesiastical moon (not astrological) that occurs on or after the day of the vernal equinox, that is March 21. Following me?

One thing for sure, it never occurs before March 22 and never after April 25. Even more simple, I can confirm it will fall on March 23/2008, April 12/2009, April 4/2010 and April 24/2011.

The **Beaches Easter Parade** (managed by the Beaches Lions Club) is an obvious choice on Easter Sunday. Read the tips on p. 39 to get the most out of this cute family event. On a more religious note, the **Good Friday Procession**, taking place in Little Italy, has been a Toronto tradition for over 40 years (p. 40).

A free visit to **Allan Gardens** greenhouses will give you a jump-start into

spring with their colourful and odorous display of spring flowers totally in the Easter spirit (p. 276).

Many farms create nice events during Easter weekend. Some of the farms start to offer Easter activities some weekends prior to Easter while others only offer them one day during the Easter weekend. Rule of thumb: Always call before you head to a farm.

We have been to **Chappell Farms** near Barrie during Easter and their range of activities was impressive (p. 144). **Drysdale Farms** near Alliston seems to be in the same line (p. 179). Both **Pingle's Farm Market** (p. 131) and **Springridge Farm** (p. 135) offer a nice craft activity.

Puck's Farm is sticking to real chocolate egg hunts (p. 138) while the others choose to do a plastic egg hunt which kids exchange for treats.

Easter time often overlaps with maple syrup time and **Mountsberg Wildlife Centre** is the best place to enjoy both (p. 149). It is also a good place to see cute little chicks.

Finally, the **Toronto Zoo** (p. 57) invites kids to collect stamps throughout the site to collect a treat.

TIPS

• See our calendar of events on p. 9. Read about more good calendars of events on p. 15.

• Beware! When the holiday occurs in March or early April, chances are the weather won't allow the farms to offer their event. But when it takes place in April, with a little help from Mother Nature, **Easter** activities at the farm can be lovely. Check with the farm!

• Always bring boots! This is the muddiest time of the year at the farm.

LOOK FOR THIS:
When you see the Easter pictogram on a page, it means the attraction offers special activities or schedule for the occasion.

VICTORIA DAY

n the air

ebration of Victoria Day occurs every year on the Monday prior to May 25th. It is the official celebration of the birthdays of Queen Victoria and Queen Elizabeth II, established as a national holiday in 1901.

Victoria Day and Canada Day are the only two days when we're allowed to have our own little fireworks in the local parks. Time to ask the neighbours to pitch in for a great local event kids will remember for the rest of their lives.

If you need a bigger fix, check one of the following public fireworks shows traditionally held during Victoria Day long weekend. **Canada's Wonderland** throws a big one on the Sunday of that weekend (p. 20), so does **Couchiching Beach Park** (p. 418).

On Victoria Day itself, check out the **Niagara Falls** fireworks (p. 269) or, closer to home, the one presented at **Ashbridges Bay Park** (p. 402), where a great ambience reigns on the beach while people wait and where the fireworks above the water give a great show!

Victoria Day is also one of the days when **Historic Fort York** is at its best (p. 379) and when **Black Creek Pioneer Village** gets even more interactive (p. 383) with its Fiddlers' contest and traditional games.

There used to be the **Milk Festival** at this time of the year at **Harbourfront Centre** but not anymore! For 2008, there could be the **Toronto Circus Festival** taking place instead (p. 106).

TIPS
• Read about the fireworks and good suppliers on p. 159.
• See our calendar of events on p. 9. Read about more good calendars of events on p. 15.

SIMCOE DAY

Last summer month!

The first Monday in August is a holiday in most of the provinces but it is in fact a municipal holiday called the August Civic Holiday in most municipalities. In 1968, the Toronto City Council officially called it "Simcoe Day" after John Graves Simcoe, first Lieutenant Governor of Upper Canada in 1791.

For some fireworks on Simcoe Day, check **Chinguacousy Park** (p. 297). It is

part of Brampton's Summer Festival, a whole day of family activities throughout the park (which already includes a pond, a petting zoo, a wading pool and minigolf).

Historic Fort York marks the event with interactive activities including the popular musket drill for children (p. 379). It is also a special day at **Gibson House Museum** (p. 382).

ABOUT FIREWORKS

Having a blast!

When about ten households in my neighbourhood got together to buy a fireworks kit, the kids had so much fun enjoying the modest show with all their friends, we decided to make it a tradition.

TIPS

• Read about **Victoria Day** and **Canada Day** fireworks on pages 158 and 160.

• You can catch fireworks at other times during the **Oakville Waterfront Festival** (p. 29), **Canada Dry Festival of Fire** at **Ontario Place** (p. 18), **Cavalcade of Lights** and **New Year's Eve** in **Nathan Phillips Square** (p. 170).

• Last summer, we watched **Ontario Place**'s fireworks from **Marilyn Bell Park** (we parked on Jameson Ave. near King and walked 15 minutes to the passageway leading to the waterfront). The ambience was relaxed. (Check the firework picture on this page to see what we saw.)

• To organize a safe fireworks display in a local park, you need a 30 m by 30 m space. You can download a pdf version of a City flyer on safety (**www.toronto.ca**, search **Firework safety**, or check **www.fireworksafety.com**.

• Note that many kids under 4 years are afraid of big noises, which are also stressful for many dogs. Make sure you've tested your kids before taking them to a major fireworks display!

• Expect traffic jams right after any major fireworks. Be prepared to entertain the kids in the car. Have snacks and water ready and make sure they've been to the local washroom before leaving!

• There are two fun websites where you can lauch your own little fireworks display: **www.cyberfireworks.com** and **www.fireworks.com** (click on **Fun Zone**, then select **Shoot Phantom Fireworks**).

For now, private fireworks are permitted in Toronto on designated holidays, such as Victoria Day. You have to check with your own municipality to find out about their regulations.

Amazing Party & Costume Store is the best store I know to buy pre-packaged kits of all sizes. They come with a suggested order of launch and a safety sheet. There's the family kit with noise, the family kit without noise, the driveway kit, the park kit, the cottage kit... You get the idea.

Lately, **Kaboom Fireworks** has started to advertize more heavily, now that they've opened a main store in Toronto near **Yorkdale Centre**.

Whether private or public, fireworks are more fun with sparklers (lots of them!), and glow-in-the-dark gadgets. The **Party Packagers** outlets always have a nice selection of these.

CANADA DAY

Blast call

Canada Day equals fireworks in my mind. Many attractions celebrate it with a blast. Whatever their size, you can always count on the fun of the collective anticipation and the exclamations of delight from kids and the young at heart.

There's something magical about fireworks by the water. **Ontario Place** is back with ambitious fireworks a few evenings during the summer, including on Canada Day (p. 18). Another large one is **Ashbridges Bay Park**'s fireworks (p. 402), which I really love because you get to watch it from the sandy beach.

Fireworks are sometimes worked into the schedule of a **Canada Day** weekend event. Last summer, we attended **Toronto Ribfest** at **Centennial Park** in Etobicoke (p. 216). They offered nice fireworks on **Canada Day** but we could also enjoy a midway and juicy ribs throughout the weekend.

Cobourg Beach's 4-day **Waterfront Festival** includes fireworks on **Canada Day** (p. 415) and so does **Couchiching Beach Park** (p. 418). Both locations are lovely and offer many family activities prior to the fireworks, along with a great beach and playground.

Downsview Park (p. 293) throws a free grand fireworks display.

Many local parks put together simple events that get kids really excited for the mere reason that they can enjoy them with their friends in the neighbourhood.

Jimmie Simpson Park, located at the corner of Booth Avenue and Queen Street East is a good example. Last **Canada Day**, its baseball diamond was turned into a pony trail. A temporary stage was put up for local dance groups. Belly dancing demonstrations were given in the adjacent community centre. Games and an inflatable structure were offered for a small fee. Arts and Crafts tables were displayed; BBQs threw a great smell in the air and kids could create flags.

Add to this the wading pool and big playground at the other end of the park and you get good old-fashioned fun. Call (416) 465-7554 for details.

Lots of activities are going on at **Thomson Park** (p. 291), including 19th century activities and **Strawberry Social** at the **Scarborough Historical Museum**. **Milliken Park** (p. 210) throws fireworks. **Chinguacousy Park** (p. 297) offers all-day family events complete with fireworks.

The 4-day **CHIN Picnic** free event with a big focus on musical entertainment always encompasses Canada Day. It is held at Exhibition Place (p. 32). **Mel Lastman Square** also hosts musical shows and tops it with a pyrotechnics display (read about **North York Subway Station** on p. 447).

Other attractions worth mentioning: **Downey's Farm and Market** throws a party (p. 133) and historic attractions **Fort York** (p. 379) and **Gibson House Museum** (p. 382) go the extra mile to entertain us.

TIPS
- Read about fireworks and good suppliers on p. 159.
- See our calendar of events on p. 9; read about more good calendars of events on p. 14.
- You may want to look at **www.toronto.ca** and search **Canada Day** to find out about local parks offering events. Last time I checked, they mentioned **East York's 50th Celebration** at **Stan Wadlow Park** (on Cosburn Avenue off Woodbine, just south of O'Connor Drive) starting with a parade at 9 am at Broadview and Danforth, midway, skatepark, pool and music in the afternoon at the park, topped with fireworks. Call (416) 396-2842 for details. There was also the 24th **Amesbury Park Canada Day** event (west of Keele on Lawrence W., **www.amesburycanadaday.ca**).

THANKSGIVING

Long weekend

Thanksgiving either means access to Halloween activities and fall colours on a Monday or the possibility of a long-weekend getaway with the family.

Of course, there's the Monday **Oktoberfest Thanksgiving Parade** in Kitchener-Waterloo (p. 41), which offers the perfect opportunity to visit the great **Children's Museum** in Kitchener (p. 238).

Thanksgiving is probably the best time to take a stroll in nature, to collect leaves and enjoy fall's special light through the trees. You just need to flip through the **Nature's Call** chapter to find an outing suggestion.

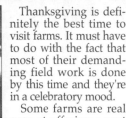

Thanksgiving is definitely the best time to visit farms. It must have to do with the fact that most of their demanding field work is done by this time and they're in a celebratory mood.

Some farms are real pros at offering a vast line-up of activitie during this time of the year, such as **Brooks Farms** (p. 130), **Downey's Farm Market** (p. 133), **Dyment's Farm** (p. 142), **Chappell Farms** (p.144), **Rounds Ranch** (p.145) and my new favourite farm **Yeehaw Adventure Farm** (p. 140).

This is traditionally a time to reflect on things in our lives we're grateful for and I heard about an inspiring family activity to help us do that. You create a special awards night where every family member gets to write down something they really appreciate about every other member, and then it is read aloud during the Thanksgiving dinner.

TIPS

• If you're planning a **Thanksgiving** getaway around **Niagara Falls** to take advantage of the fall colours, book way ahead of time. It is a very busy period of the year for this region (pp. 269 and 434).

• Note that **American Thanksgiving** happens in November, a few weeks later than **Canadian Thanksgiving**. Don't let American postings on the internet mislead you! You might want to double-check if the appealing offer which caught your attention indeed applies to our Canadian dates.

• Don't forget to thaw the turkey hours in advance (I had to boil my first turkey so 10 people could eat 4 hours later). Don't forget to remove the bag of giblets before you cook the bird (that was my second turkey story, witnessed by all the guests around the table).

LOOK FOR THIS:
When you see the Halloween pictogram on a page, it means the attraction offers special activities or schedule for the occasion, normally including Thanksgiving weekend.

LOOK FOR THIS:
When you see the Fall colours pictogram on a page, it means you will be able to admire fall colours at this location.

HALLOWEEN

Scary or cute?

It's always good to know where you're going during Halloween time. You don't want to traumatize your little pumpkin in the Barn from Hell but neither do you want to bore older siblings to tears in a cute Boo Barn.

I'll get straight to the point: The scariest farm we've visited is the **Magic Hill Haunted Adventure** in Stouffville (p. 164). They've honed their attraction for years. I would not go there with children under eight.

Since my last edition, **Canada's Wonderland** has created the **Halloween Haunt** set throughout the whole park. Expect ten scary attractions not normally offered, plus access to over 20 regular attractions (p. 20). They say it is not for children. Other places offering elaborate scary events are: **White**

Rock Ostrich Farm's Screamfest, which seems to have grown quite ambitious, judging by their website. Screamers at the **Exhibition Place** (p. 32), the scary indoor attraction in downtown Toronto, is also better suited for older kids.

Most farms in the **Farms** chapter are at their best during Halloween time. Our favourite place to jump into straw mountains is **Andrews Scenic Acres** (p. 137), followed by **Springridge Farm** (p. 135). **Chudleigh's Farm**'s slide into the straw is also a big hit (p. 136).

Last October, we saw the **Pumpkinfest Parade** in Waterford, which was really a great day trip, combined with a visit to **Van-Go Farm** (p. 143).

Our favourite store to drop by during Halloween is **Amazing Party & Costume Store**, south of QEW, west of Islington, **www.amazingpartystore.com**). All the fancy props you find on the front yards of the neighbours who put on a real show on Halloween night can be found in this store. When we visited, line-ups were huge at the cashiers but we didn't mind, it gave us time to observe the gory scenes created in the middle of the place, including a very convincing life-size hanged man wiggling above our head!

TIPS
• See our calendar of events on p. 9. Read about more good calendars of events on p. 15.
• Boo Barns can really scare young children. I can't count the times I saw kids under 5 years old exit from these, uncontrollably crying in the arms of their parent. We tend to over-estimate their level of tolerance for this kind of stress. Check the look on kids of similar age as yours as they exit the attraction.

LOOK FOR THIS:
When you see the Halloween pictogram on a page, it means the attraction offers special activities or schedule for the occasion, normally including Thanksgiving weekend.

HAUNTED ADVENTURE

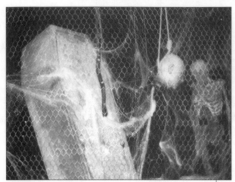

Good scare!

This is the best attraction of its kind in and around the GTA. It is located in the perfect setting of dark countryside, in woods and fields, and created by people who've shown a real passion for entertainment in the last 14 years, with the help of over 140 costumed actors.

When we got there on a Saturday at around 8:45 pm, it was so crowded that a policeman had to direct traffic on the small country road. By 9:30 pm, we were still far away from the living-dead cashier in the long line-up. My then 9-year-old son was falling asleep as he stood waiting, so we headed back home.

The following Friday, we went back shortly before 7 pm. We found parking in the field right next to the entrance. Only 70 people were waiting ahead of us. When the doors opened at 7 pm, it was almost dark.

We were told to go straight to the

Haunted Barn (the other attractions were not ready yet). As we waited our turn, we read one of the signs on the barn wall: "Rub the rock or you'll never see daylight again." My son kept bragging that he was not scared but I saw him rubbing the stone more than once!

The tour of the barn lasts less than 15 minutes. Among other things, we saw the kitchen from hell, a smoking electrical chair and sophisticated special effects. It ended with us being chased by a crazy man armed with a noisy chainsaw!

Before heading in a wagon for the Howling Hayride through the Field of Screams, we were invited to shout at the top of our lungs, to practise for what awaited us: a morbid car accident, chains raking the metal roof of our wagon, and UFOs, to name a few.

My favourite was the Terror Trail Trek. The trail was beautiful, on top of a hill, with red spots in the bushes and the city lights in the background. "Monsters" jumped out of the woods at every turn, quicksand effects, a hung dead man, a tricky labyrinth and more made for a stimulating walk.

The Black Cavern had narrower walls, scarier situations. My son was not enjoying it anymore even though the staff toned it down when they saw his reaction. I was so busy "protecting" him from the scare that I hardly remember what I saw. We had a good scare!

TIPS (fun for 8 years +)

• Try to get there around 7 pm, shortly after that, the line-ups are too scary! It is less crowded earlier in October and on Sundays. Ask about their VIP Express Pass to bypass the line for an extra fee.

• This attraction is not recommended for children under 8 years old. You might want to avoid the Black Cavern and the Murder Motel with children under 10. I suggest you see the haunted barn when they are not too tired so they can stomach it. My son said he preferred the Howling Hayride, but I saw him react and laugh much more in the Terror Trail Trek.

• There is a snack bar.

• More on **Magic Hill Farm** during the winter on p. 178.

CHRISTMAS TRADITIONS

Magic in the air

There's something magical about thousands of colourful light bulbs suddenly illuminating a huge tree. Christmas decorations on evergreens or at the mall, when skillfully done, are so pretty. Kids' excitement before a Santa Claus and the promise of gifts he represents is contagious. And, whatever your religion, a nativity re-enactment is a nice story to be heard.

A good way to start the season on a positive note (remembering it is not all about receiving!) is to get involved with **Operation Christmas Child**. When I first heard about this concept, I was seduced by the opportunity for my kids to discover they could create a magical moment in the life of another child by filling a shoe box with goodies before mid-November.

It seems I'm not the only one, last time I checked, in a year, Canadians alone had donated nearly 740,000 shoe boxes. Word-wide, six million children in over 95 countries had received a gift box. The boxes are distributed through a volunteer project created in 1993 by the Christian organization **Samaritan's Purse (www. samaritanspurse.ca)**. Orphanages, hospitals, refugee camps, schools and churches serve as distribution centres, regardless of their religious affiliation. The boxes get there by plane, then by boat, donkey, trucks or even helicopters.

The biggest tradition to launch Christmas time in Toronto has been the **Santa Claus Parade** (p. 43) for a century! Many smaller parades are offered on the main street of small towns and they always have a cozy intimate feeling to them (check the websites of Niagara-on-the-Lake, Unionville and Markham, to name a few).

The **Christmas Story**, a nativity re-enactment presented at the **Holy Trinity Church** for the last 60 years is another Toronto tradition (p. 172).

See what your options are if you want to take the kids to see **Santa at the mall** on p. 168. There's also the **Breakfast with Santa** on p. 167.

Colourful lights are the trademark for this jolly time of the year. The tree illumination launching the **Cavalcade of Lights** is quite exciting (p. 170). Then, there's the line-up of seasonal pleasures: the **Twelve Trees of Christmas** at **Gardiner Museum** (p. 171), the crèches exhibition of **St. James Cathedral** (p. 173) and, on a more nostalgic note, there's the opening of the **Victorian Christmas** at **Allan Gardens** (p. 176) and the **Pioneer Christmas** at **Black Creek Pioneer Village** (p. 177) and **Markham Village** (p. 385).

If you want to cut your own tree so your kids can see for themselves that they grow in fields, check **Magic Hill Tree Farm** (p. 178) or **Drysdale Tree Farms** (p. 179).

Looking for entertainment during this season? Consider the hilarious fairy tales of **Ross Petty Productions** (p. 180) or an exquisite **Nutcracker** presentation (p. 181). From time to time, **Soulpepper Theatre** also treats us with Dickens' great **Christmas Carol**.

Famous People Players always presents a fun show with huge puppets under black lights performing Christmas songs (p. 83). **Casa Loma**, at its best during Christmas time, usually offers a lively show and a roster of other activities, in addition to a visit with Santa (p. 120). **Stage West** is another sure bet, combining a Christmas play with a generous buffet meal (p. 85).

If you are into singing, the **Toronto Symphony Orchestra** often makes room for some carolling during its Christmas performance (p. 104). For serious singing, however, try the impressive **Sing-Along Messiah** (p. 182).

For a different kind of parade, you've got to attend the **Kensington Festival of Lights** (p. 183).

Throughout December, we can admire other festivals of lights where parks are adorned with structures covered by little lights. Niagara's **Festival of Lights** is the biggest of them all (p. 184). Burlington also offers a good one in **Spencer Smith Park** by the lake (**www. burlingtonfestivaloflights.com**).

You're not alone!

Wish you could join your extended family on the day of Christmas but can't make

it happen this year? Chase the blues and join the action at **Nathan Phillips Square**. We happened to be there last December 25 and the place was busy with families skating around the rink (bring your own skates because the rental shop is closed). They would head off to **Timothy's**, across the street, for a hot chocolate, then go to admire the gorgeous scenes in The Bay windows at the corner of Queen and Yonge as well as the lovely decorations inside the **Eaton Centre** (kept open for those using the subway).

We chose to walk down Yonge to lively **Richtree Market** for hot chocolate and yummy desserts (42 Yonge, **www. richtree.ca**).

TIPS

• I like to stock up on toys under $10 for last-minute birthday or Christmas gifts and loot bags. Popular **Samko** and **Miko** are two warehouses open seasonally. Both locations offer the same merchandise: end of the line brand-name toys (Little Tykes, Fisher-Price, Mattel, Crayola, Tonka, etc.), craft material, books and gadgets that might catch your fancy, all at really affordable prices. Children used to not be allowed in Samko but they've changed their policy. The Toronto location has changed (now south of QEW, west of Kipling) and there's a Richmond Hill location (north of Hwy 7, west of Hwy 404), (**www.samkosales.com**).

LOOK FOR THIS:
When you see the Santa pictogram on a page, it means the attraction offers special activities or schedule for the occasion.

BREAKFAST WITH SANTA

high ceiling, suspended chandelier and marble floors offers the perfect setting for a breakfast with Santa.

Most girls did not want to miss a chance to dress up so we see a parade of pretty dresses and the colour red reigns. People are still arriving at 9:30 am when the breakfast buffet opens. Don't go expecting fancy eggs Benedict or French toast soaked in maple syrup. Nevertheless, the buffet concept is enough to excite most kids and mine are thrilled at the sight of the scrambled eggs, sausage, bacon, small potatoes, pancakes, small muffins, fruit, yogurt and juice. Parents are content with the bottomless cups of coffee and tea.

As we eat at our table covered in fine linen, an interactive singer warms the place with his **Christmas** songs. Meanwhile, clowns are creating shapes with balloons and offering face paint to the kids between bites.

See you in Court

It feels so weird to enter into the deserted The Bay store at 9 am that it makes me doubt we are in the right building. Yet, when the elevator's doors open on the eighth floor, the **Arcadian Court is already buzzing with the excitement of families gathering around their tables.**

Even though there has been a restaurant on The Bay's eighth floor since 1889, I had never been to the **Arcadian Court** restaurant open daily to the public. The large white and cream room with

When Santa arrives, a stampede is contained by the promise that each table would be called in its turn to visit the jolly man waiting in his large chair (all tables were previously assigned a colour). By 10:30 am, all food is removed.

The Breakfast with Santa has become a tradition for many extended families to launch the festive season.

TIPS (fun for 2 years +)

• At this kind of event, kids will have more fun if they come with cousins or friends to dance and sing with.
• You can access the **Eaton Centre** from the overpass on The Bay's second floor to admire the beautiful **Christmas** decorations (no need to put the coats back on). BEWARE! "Santa" is also there! Be prepared with a good explanation.
• **Arcadian Court** is open for fancy lunches Monday to Saturday, 11:30 am to 2:30 pm (might be closed for private functions, call to confirm).
• **Casa Loma** also organizes popular breakfasts with Santa, normally from 8:30 to 9:30 am on the three Sundays prior to Christmas (p. 120). It includes the visit of the castle after breakfast and Christmas carols at some point and costs around $21/adult, $19/children, plus tax.

NEARBY ATTRACTIONS
Nathan Phillips Rink (1-min.walk) p. 358

Breakfast with Santa (416) 861-6611 www.arcadiancourt.ca	**D-3** **Dowtown** **Toronto** **10-min.**

  Schedule: They try to offer it on Saturdays and Sundays of the three weekends prior to Christmas, from 9 am to 10:30 am. Call to confirm. (Reservations are a must.)
Admission: Around $22/adults, $15/12 years and under. Call to confirm.
Directions: In the Arcadian Court, on the 8th floor of The Bay, at the corner of Bay and Queen.

SANTA AT THE MALL

Spotted in shopping malls: He really exists!

Does your neighbourhood mall host the real Santa in a magical setting? Does it house your favourite shops? Does it offer a drop-in child-care service? Some malls do, but... which ones?

Starting mid-November until December 24th (inclusive), you can visit Santa Claus in several shopping malls. It is an adventure that requires some determination. Line-ups can be long and impatient children, who have waited for an hour, may decide to opt out at the last minute.

Sherway Gardens

The Santa Claus display is always enchanting and colourful, and it is the only one I know which incorporates distractions into the line-up, year after year.

For a few years now, they've offered a great concept. They gave timed-tickets allowing groups of kids to meet Santa for 30 minutes at once, for some interactive storytelling and song. No official photo sessions. Parents could take all the pictures they wanted of their kids in action. They are continuing to offer the experience in 2008.

Sherway Gardens houses over 200 stores, including **Holt Renfrew**, **The Bay**, **Sporting Life**, **Sears**, and many children's clothing stores.

Square One

Less interactive in nature, yet the most spectacular, the tall Christmas Castle at this shopping centre enthuses every year. Last time we visited, a sleigh crossed a shower of lights and descended on the many turrets, and an electric train travelled through the castle with its many colourful passengers. They're rebuilding the castle for 2008 but assured me it would be as big and even better.

Square One houses over 350 stores including **The Bay**, **Sears**, **Wal-Mart**, **Zellers**, **Toys, Toys, Toys**, **P.J's Pet Centre**, many children's clothing stores and **Empire Studio 10**, (905) 275-2640. **Coliseum Mississauga** sits across Rathburn, (905) 275-3456.

Eaton Centre

I recommend a ride in the glass elevator near the large water fountain in the Eaton Centre. It gives you a good view of the overall Christmas display: a large reindeer-pulled sleigh, travelling through a multitude of lights, suspended amidst giant **Christmas** trees and the 4-storey-high water spray that spurts out at regular intervals. There should also be a giant **Christmas** tree covered with crystal.

This downtown mall is home to some 300 stores including **Disney Store**, **Toys, Toys, Toys**, **Gymboree** and many children's clothing stores. Read about what's around **Queen** and **Dundas Subway Stations** on p. 450.

An overpass links it to The Bay. A good place to eat is the **Cityview Café** along the window side on the 8th floor of **The Bay**, with breakfasts and very affordable meals (Monday-Wednesday, 10 am to 5 pm; Thursday-Friday closes at 7 pm; Saturday, 9:30 am to 5 pm; Sunday, 12 noon to 5 pm).

Yorkdale Centre

Its Santa Claus Rotunda shows the same refined aesthetic as the rest of the centre. It usually is dressed in wood and velvet, in shades of forest green and burgundy or red, it mirrors a picture perfect display in a Bombay Company catalogue.

Here, you will find over 240 stores including the **Rainforest Café**, **Holt Renfrew**, **The Bay**, **Sears**, **Disney Store**, many children's clothing boutiques, as well as **Silvercity Yorkdale**, (416) 787-2052. Read about what's around **Yorkdale Subway Station** on p. 454.

Woodbine Centre

Located close to **Pearson Airport**, with some 150 stores, it includes **The Bay**, **Sears**, **Zellers** and some children's clothing stores, as well as the movie theatres **Rainbow Cinemas Woodbine**, (416) 213-9048. It also houses the large indoor amusement park **Fantasy Fair** (p. 35), which adds to the fun (or torture) of seeing Santa.

Scarborough Town Centre

When we visited, Santa was awaiting in a Victorian living room. This mall is the only one with a daycare offering a drop-off service. This can be a life saver during the trying Christmas shopping spree (**Kornelia's Korner**, (416) 296-0901).

The mall is home to more than 200 stores, including **The Bay**, **Sears**, **Wal-Mart**, **P.J's Pet Centre**, Toys, Toys, Toys, **Disney Store** and many children's cloth-ing stores. It also hosts the **Coliseum Scarborough**, (416) 290-5217.

Dufferin Mall

Years ago, their Santa was more of a St. Nicholas, with a magnificent long coat. Considering the artistic community involved with **Dufferin Grove Park** across the street (p. 288), I was not surprised.

The mall was fully renovated this year. It includes over 110 stores and is the only one I know offering **Toys "R" Us**, **Wal-Mart** and **Winners** under the same roof.

Vaughan Mills

I have not visited this mall during **Christmas** time but in addition to over 250 stores including **Toys "R" Us** and **Winners**, it offers an entertainment complex with bowling and a restaurant, a go-kart track and an arcade.

Shopping centres

- **Eaton Centre/Toronto**
(416) 598-8700
www.torontoeatoncentre.com
(Yonge St. and Queen St.)
- **Dufferin Mall/Toronto**
(416)532-1152
www.dufferinmall.ca
(900 Dufferin St., south of Bloor St. W.)
- **Sherway Gardens/Etobicoke**
(416) 621-1070
www.sherwaygardens.ca
(QEW, exit Browns Line, take Evans Ave.)
- **Yorkdale Centre/North York**
(416) 789-3261
www.yorkdale.com (Hwy 401, Allen Rd. exit, take Yorkdale Ave. southbound)
- **Woodbine Centre/Etobicoke**
(416) 674-5200
www.woodbinecentre.ca
(Hwy 427 North, exit Rexdale East)
- **Scarborough Town Centre**
(416) 296-0296
www.scarboroughtowncentre.com
(Hwy 401, McCowan exit southbound)
- **Square One/Mississauga**
(905) 279-7467
www.shopsquareone.com
(Hwy 403, exit Hurontario southbound)
- **Vaughan Mills/Vaughan**
(905) 879-1777
www.vaughanmills.com
(1 Bass Pro Mills Dr., east of Hwy 400)

CAVALCADE OF LIGHTS

Photo: Courtesy of City of Toronto

High-spirited countdown

Our eyes are riveted on the lighted skating rink, shining in the frigid darkness. In less than one minute, the event we've all been expecting will take place. The 300,000 lights adorning the square and the tall Christmas tree will light up at once. Anticipation is building among the excited crowd.

Children delight in excited expectation and they, like us, marvel at the magical effect of this illumination. It's not surprising the City has been organizing this event for over 34 years!

You can arrive as late as a half-hour prior to the illumination, and easily find a spot in **Nathan Phillips Square**'s large underground parking lot, and a viewing spot (providing you perch your little one on your shoulders).

The Cavalcade of Lights includes skating parties with DJ, free concerts and fireworks on all four Saturdays prior to Christmas. The opening night offers a holiday concert so most of the performers sing holiday songs for the delight of the crowd.

Don't forget to visit inside **City Hall** while you're there to view a model of the city sure to amaze the kids.

On Cavalcade's home page, you'll find a link to the different lighting displays which have spread throughout the city in the last years.

TIPS (fun for 5 years +)

- More on the Square's rink on p. 358.
- **Nathan Phillips Square** is also host to a **New Year's Eve** celebration that begins at 10 pm on December 31 and ends with fireworks.
- The **CN Tower** has joined the **Cavalcade of Lights** by offering access to its glass floor at a lower price to admire the lights of the city and a **New Year's Countdown** with special effects with its programmable lighting system (p. 116).

NEARBY ATTRACTIONS
Eaton Centre (3-min. walk) .... p. 168
Christmas Story (3-min. walk) ..... p. 172

Cavalcade of Lights | **D-3**
(416) 338-0338 | **Dowtown**
www. | **Toronto**
toronto.ca/special_events | **10-min.**

  Schedule: Cavalcade of Lights line-up of activities normally takes place on the four Saturdays prior to Christmas. Lighting celebration is on the opening night of Cavalcade at around 8 pm. Check exact hour closer to the event. The lights are usually brought down by mid-January.
Admission: FREE.
Directions: Nathan Phillips Square, Toronto (corner of Queen St. West and Bay St.).

TWELVE TREES OF CHRISTMAS

Gardiner's trees

Every year, designers are given "carte blanche" to their wildest fantasies with the decorating of twelve christmas trees, which are then displayed throughout the museum. The result is lavish, if somewhat loaded, with a myriad of lovely details that small eyes enjoy discovering.

While this is one of those places where the "do not touch" prevails, I mention it nevertheless for those who get swept away by glittering Christmas trees.

When we visited, it was *Christmas through the decades*, an exhibit where each designer created a tree evocative of a decade between 1888 and 2008. It included a tree reminiscent of 1938, decorated as a Monopoly game. I enjoyed the tree of 1908 with its dolls and "Anne of Green Gables" memorabilia. Children preferred the 1968 "Space Race" tree with its rockets, or the moving disco balls and plastic jewellery of the 1978 "Groovy Christmas", or again, the dozens of Beanie Babies on the 1998 tree.

The trees are auctioned to raise funds, which explains why they're taken away so early in December.

Read p. 88 about the **Gardiner Museum**, for a description of the many ceramic pieces of interest for children.

TIPS (fun for 4 years +)

• While you are in this neighbourhood, you might want to see the Christmas lights in the **Yorkville Village Park** on Cumberland and finish the outing with a movie at the **Cumberland** (159 Cumberland St.) or the **Varsity** (55 Bloor St. West).

• After seeing all this porcelain, why not push it to **Ashley's** (5-min. walk east on Bloor) for a look at their trademark "Wall of China".

NEARBY ATTRACTIONS

Gardiner Museum (416) 586-8080 www. gardinermuseum.com	D-3 **Downtown** Toronto 10-min.

 Schedule: Usually from mid-November to early December. The museum is open daily at 10 am; closes at 6 pm, Monday to Thursday; 9 pm on Fridays; 5 pm on weekends.

 Admission: $12/adult, $8/senior, $6/student, FREE 12 years and under. FREE admission on Fridays, 4 to 9 pm and all day on the first Friday of every month.

 Directions: 111 Queen's Park, Toronto (just south of Bloor Street).

THE CHRISTMAS STORY

A time for rituals

A tiny house of worship dating from 1847 is caught in a stranglehold by the buildings that have sprung up since then. For over 60 years, it has been telling the story of Christmas to Torontonians, with the assistance of its great organ, accompanied by a singing quartet and amateur actors of all ages miming the narrators' words.

The Christmas Story performances held at the **Holy Trinity Church** are certainly the most concrete way to explain to children the story of the nativity scene displayed at Christmas time. The Anglican church is modest but gorgeous. The great organ plays softly while we wait for the show to begin. The first two rows of pews, as well as two large carpets at the front, are reserved for young spectators.

Children hold their breath when all the lights go out, emphasizing the large stained-glass windows at the back of the altar, before a spotlight shines on the two narrators. For the remainder of the perfor-mance, the actors perform within islands of light standing out against the darkness. The amateur production offers studied and harmonious scenes, and the costumes are very nice. The Annunciation angel has majestic wings, the shepherds' clothing is meticulously draped, and the Three Wise Men are dressed in rich fabrics.

The actors are all volunteers, generous with their time and enthusiasm, but they're confined in a relatively static formula (you don't attend "Christmas Story" for acting performances).

I was charmed by many of the child actors: a pageboy with the giggles, a little angel forgetting to leave the stage, baby Jesus happily babbling as the myrrh is shown to him and quivering with joy during the offering of the third Wise Man, with the audience laughing. When I visited, Jesus was played by... eight-month-old twins, sharing the role according to their mood of the moment!

TIPS (fun for 5 years +)

• The performance lasts about an hour and combines perfectly with a short visit to admire **Eaton Centre**'s **Christmas** decorations (p. 168) and **Nathan Phillips Square**'s Cavalcade of lights and skating rink (p. 170).
• The rest of the year, you can enjoy this lovely church by attending their free concerts: the **Taddle Creek Fiddlers** (October to end of May, 1st and 3rd Tuesday from 7 to 9 pm) and the **Music Mondays** (in the summertime, at 12 noon).

NEARBY ATTRACTIONS	
Hidden Treasure Stroll	p. 473

The Christmas Story

(416) 598-4521
www.
holytrinitytoronto.org
(click Arts)

D-3
**Downtown
Toronto
10-min.**

  Schedule: Usually on the three weekends before Christmas: Friday and Saturday evenings, 7:30 pm; Saturdays and Sundays, 4:30 pm. (Call to confirm and to reserve.)

 Admission: Suggested donation: $10/adults, $5/children.

 Directions: Church of the Holy Trinity, 10 Trinity Square, Toronto (west side of Eaton Centre).

ST. JAMES & CRÈCHE EXHIBIT

I spy...

Find the crèche made out of walnut. Which crèche figures are actually flutes? Where's the one with a pine cone roof? Can you see the shepherd feeding his sheep from a basket? These are a few of the items children are asked to find throughout the exhibition.

St. James Cathedral's annual crèche exhibit has grown to include over two hundred Nativity scenes. Most of them are quite modest in size. This actually adds to the pleasure of the hunt!

They come from over forty countries and are made with every possible material: gingerbread, straw, clay, fabric, wool, stone, wood, shells, tin cans... They were knit, carved, modelled, painted, sewn or baked. No need to be Christian to appreciate the lovely figures. Kids won't want to leave.

TIPS (fun for 4 years +)

• Every year, the **St. James Archives and Museum** puts together well researched exhibits. At the time of print, it featured a major exhibit on the life of St. James and the pilgrimage to Santiago de Compostela, including paintings of scenes along the road and photos taken by pilgrims during their trek.

• Don't forget to admire the daylight shining through the beautiful stained-glass window inside the cathedral! More on **St. James Cathedral** on p. 119.

• Read the **European Flair Stroll** on p. 476 for a description of atttractions and restaurant suggestions around **St. James Cathedral**.

NEARBY ATTRACTIONS
Around Dundas Subway Station ... p. 450

St. James Cathedral & Crèche Exhibit
(416) 364-7865, ext. 233
www.stjamescathedral.on.ca

D-3
Downtown
Toronto
10-min.

Schedule: Open daily from early December to December 22, maybe beyond. Call to confirm.

Admission: FREE.

Directions: The exhibit takes place in the St. James Archives and Museum located on the second floor of the parish house, which you access from Church St., south of St. James Cathedral. BEWARE! The building could undergo renovations in 2008, in which case the exhibition would be temporarily relocated in the downtown area. Check their website in November for details.

The Bay's enchanting Christmas windows at Yonge and Queen.

NATIVITY SCENES

Things of the past?

I have seen Stouffville's "Bethlehem Live" organized by the Christian Blind Mission, Lake Simcoe's "Walk to Bethlehem" of the Cedarvale Church of the Nazarene, Burlington's Kids Christmas Stable from the Park Bible Church. But unfortunately, these events are now things of the past.

Now, I have to add Stayner's great Journey of Love, organized by the Evangelical Missionary Church to my list of such events to be missed. Their church burned in January 2008, with all the costumes and most of the props used to recreate nativity scenes. It will take them a few years to reinvent the concept.

All is not lost. Here are promising options I have not visited.

The Timothy Eaton Memorial Church in Toronto offers The Night Before Christmas on December 24: a nativity pageant with live animals performed at 3 and 5 pm. Doors open one hour before the performances (food bank donations or free-will offering accepted).

Then, there's the Footprints of Christmas which came highly recommended by one of my readers. It is organized by St. Andrew's Memorial Presbyterian Church in Port Credit, Mississauga. It offers the experience I really enjoyed in an event I visited in the past. You get to travel as a family of shepherds from one scene to the next and meet the tax collectors, Roman guards, merchants, the angel appearing to Mary and Joseph and live animals! It normally runs on the first weekend in December, starting at 6:30 pm.

The Park Bible Church in Burling-

ton has merged with another church to form the Compass Point Bible Church. At the time of print, they were in the process of finding a new Christmas tradition for a willing public. The reality of a shrinking pool of aging volunteers renders the more ambitious events impossible but their great space allows for the planning of something that should be interesting. I can only suggest you check their website closer to November.

One I'd really like to see is the Walk to Bethlehem at the Country Heritage Village in Milton. It is a re-enactment of the nativity throughout the site, ending with Jesus in a manger in the log barn. It is usually held on four consecutive evenings from 6:30 to 9 pm, end of November or early December.

VICTORIAN CHRISTMAS

Allan Gardens' most interactive day

The opening day of Allan Gardens Victorian Christmas is the only time of the year when activities are planned for children.

The greenhouses have donned reds, pinks, greens and whites for a few months. Under the big glass dome, we admire a few Christmas shapes covered with plants (in the past, we've seen a toy soldier, a rocking horse and a fireplace).

During opening day, singers in Victorian costumes perform Christmas carols under that same beautiful dome.

A "make-and-take" activity takes place in the cactus room. More activities are held outside the conservatories.

When visiting, we could grab free Christmas cookies and hot cider and enjoy them in front of the bonfire.

We even caught a glimpse of a Victorian Santa (St. Nicholas) and took a horse-drawn wagon ride around the site.

There were a couple of farm animals to pet and a very pretty snowman and snowwoman with cut out holes to throw sandbags through. (Some Allan Gardens staff entertained the kids with this game.)

TIPS (fun for 4 years +)
• A craft activity is usually offered every year.
• More about **Allan Gardens Conservatory** on page 276.

Adults and children even had a chance to toss balls into the air with a huge colourful parachute.

Victorian Christmas Opening Day

**D-3
Downtown**
Toronto
20-min.

(416) 392-7288
www.toronto.ca (click **Parks & Gardens**, and **Gardens & Conservatories**)

Schedule: Usually first Sunday of December, 12 noon to 4:30 pm. Call to confirm.

Admission: FREE with non-perishable food donation.

Directions: Allan Gardens, 160 Gerrard St. East, Toronto (between Jarvis and Sherbourne, south of Carlton).

NEARBY ATTRACTIONS	
Riverdale Farm (5-min.)	p. 55
Riverdale Park (5-min.)	p. 366

PIONEER CHRISTMAS

Victorian Christmas

During the Victorian Christmas, the village is adorned with decorations. Don't go expecting glittering frills and colours however, as decorations were humble and home-made. The village's old houses are quite bare and pioneers certainly did not waste money on candles. As a result, it is likely your children won't even notice they are decorated!

When we last visited, we got to craft home-made presents and taste some treats. We toured the village muffled by white snow.

One of the most popular events at Black Creek Pioneer Village is **Christmas By Lamplight** for which you need advance reservations. For the occasion, candles and lanterns lend a magical feel to the village. Singers dressed in costumes of the times present **Christmas** carols in the streets.

When we attended this event, chestnuts were cooked on a bonfire and hot cider was served. Kids could do make-and-take **Christmas** crafts, and have old-fashioned wagon rides in the dark.

TIPS (fun for 5 years +)

• The **Christmas By Lamplight** event is so popular, try to reserve as early as October. They give priority to people booking the **Christmas** dinner as well (which I prefer not to attend with kids) but you can ask to be put on the waiting list!

• More on **Black Creek Pioneer Village** on p. 383.

NEARBY ATTRACTIONS
Reptilia (15-min.) .... p. 61

Black Creek Pioneer Village
• North York
(416) 736-1733
www.blackcreek.ca

D-3
North
of downtown
35-min.

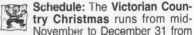
Schedule: The **Victorian Country Christmas** runs from mid-November to December 31 from 9:30 am to 4 pm on weekdays and from 11 am to 4:30 pm during the weekends (more activities offered on the weekends in December before Christmas).

Christmas by Lamplight is offered at least three Saturday evenings in December.

Admission: Regular activities: $13/ adults, $12/ seniors, $9/5-14 years, FREE 4 years and under, tax not included. Parking is around $6. **Christmas by Lamplight** is $30/person without the dinner.

Directions: 1000 Murry Ross Pkwy, North York (at the corner of Steeles Ave. and Jane St.; east of Hwy 400 and south of Hwy 407). The entrance is east of Jane St.

MAGIC HILL TREE FARM

"O, Christmas Tree"...

After our wagon ride had taken us, ax in hand, to the heart of the fir tree farm, we pulled our little green elf at full speed in his toboggan. Then, we stopped to assess the potential of the tree in front of us. "What do you think, pumpkin?" With all the conviction in the world, the miniature expert replies: "It's PERFECT!"

Cutting your own tree is a great family activity. It brings kids in close contact with the great outdoors. After helping to select and cut the tree, my son looked at our **Christmas** tree with new eyes.

There's more to the adventure. A tractor-pulled cart shuttles the young lumberjacks to the field every 15 minutes. An impressive bonfire burns to warm the families in the fields.

On your way back, you may buy a hot chocolate and cookies at the Munch House. You can play in the big barn hayloft. You can see Santa circulating among the visitors.

The tree-wrapping machine stringing the evergreens to reduce their volume was a good show in itself!

Finally, visitors have access to some of the attractions in the giant playground Magic Hill Farm normally only offers to private functions.

TIPS (fun for 4 years +)

• It's colder here than in Toronto. Dress warmly, but not too elegantly, because sticky mud is often present on the paths. I had to undress my son before he entered the car. A warm change of clothes could be useful.

• They don't provide toboggans anymore (it was harmful to the baby trees). They can lend you tools but you might have to wait for some to become available. It is better to bring your own saw.

• While you're at it, bring your own toboggan as there are hills on the site.

• Cutting your own tree doesn't save money! You have a better chance of finding a deal at your local corner store. I like to consider the cost of the tree we cut ourselves as the admission fee to a great family outing.

• More about **Magic Hill Haunted Adventure** during **Halloween** on p. 164.

More about **Magic Hill Haunted Adventure** during **Halloween** on p. 164.

NEARBY ATTRACTIONS
Forsythe Farm (15-min.) .... p. 132

Magic Hill Tree Farm	C-3
• Stouffville	N-E
(905) 888-1738	of Toronto
www.magichillfarm.com	30-min.

Schedule: Open weekends in December up to weekend prior to Christmas, 9 am to 4:30 pm. Call to enquire if planning to come after mid-December.

Admission: FREE for tree buyers (Cut-your-own trees cost approx. $35).

Directions: 13953, 9th Line, Stouffville. From Hwy 404 North, take exit #41/ Bloomington Rd. eastbound. Turn north at 9th Line.

DRYSDALE'S

That's the spirit!

It's the beginning of December and a snowfall has yet to happen. It is actually raining as my husband tucks under low branches on all fours, deep in mud, to cut our Christmas tree. He is on the verge of losing his spirits when the kids reward him with ecstatic exclamations as the tree finally falls.

Drysdale's tree farm is beautiful and very popular. The owner's house is picture perfect, all dressed up in decorative lighting. The parking lot is almost full when we arrive shortly after 3 pm. We catch a $1 ride on a horse-drawn wagon, expecting it will lead us to the cutting zone, only to find ourselves

back at the departure point 20 minutes later. The kids enjoy the ride nonetheless, and we hop out to warm up by a bonfire. We will eventually get to the cutting area (in the back of the farmyard) on a large wagon fit to hold everybody's trees.

Back at the farm, we drag our designer tree to a counter, where we pay while a machine wraps our tree so it will fit on top of our vehicle. Mr. and Mrs. Claus

have their own little hut where families enter one at a time. They look like the "real" thing so bring your camera!

Afterwards, we reach the farm's **Christmas** store where we are greeted by an impressive herd of wooden deer and moose (for sale). It was redesigned since my last visit and offers an even wider selection of housewares, gifts and seasonal novelties as well as treats such as handmade chocolate and fudge.

TIPS (fun for 4 years +)
• If you intend to bring toddlers, remember it is difficult to cut a tree and care for highly mobile little ones.
• The farm could lend us a saw when we attended but it is always better to bring your own tools.
• For more cut-your-own Christmas-tree places, check **www.harvestontario. com**.
• During **Easter** time they do Easter Egg Hunts and wagon rides. Kids look for plastic eggs to trade for generous loot bags (hence the admission price of $15). Call to pre-register.
• During October weekends, **Halloween** activities include: pick-your-own-pumpkins, wagon rides and the one-acre-large hay maze (approx. $7/family).
• There's a food concession on site and they sell snacks in the store.

NEARBY ATTRACTIONS
Albion Hills (25-min.) .... p. 392

Drysdale's · Alliston (705) 424-9719 www.drysdales.ca	**B-2** **N-W** **of Toronto** **70-min.**

 Schedule: Open week prior to Easter and Easter weekend (Friday-Sunday), then daily from first week of May until December 24, 9 am to 6 pm (closes at 5 pm from October to December).

 Admission: FREE admission. Trees cost approximately $40.

 Directions: 6635 Simcoe Rd. #56, Alliston. From Hwy 400 North, take exit #75/Hwy 89 westbound. Turn north on 7th Concession Road (Simcoe Rd. #56).

ROSS PETTY PRODUCTIONS

Photos: Courtesy of Ross Petty Productions

Silly, very silly

For years, Ross Petty Productions has presented pantomime versions of fairy tales such as Robin Hood, Aladdin, Snow White and Peter Pan at the beautiful Elgin Theatre. These presentations are pure entertainment for the whole family.

Traditionally, the Ross Petty Productions involve a villain impersonated by Ross Petty himself, who everyone loves to hate. I always find it hilarious when first time adult spectators want to prevent their kids from booing at the villain when it is exactly what he wants them to do. He would be very disapppointed if they didn't!

For the fun of it, performers take liberties from the original tale and talk directly to children as if they were part of the action, adding as many modern references as can be.

From songs complete with dances that are choreographed in a hilarious cartoon-like fashion, to elaborate costumes and decor, all contribute to the success of this goofy entertainment!

They always choose a funny way to acknowledge their sponsors and they're totally unapologetic about this (and all the other politically incorrect faux-pas they make on purpose). Throughout the show, parents will find double-meaning to the jokes.

In every production, expect a star from another discipline. In the past years, we've seen a ballet dancer, television host, ice skater and even a wrestler. Most of the time, you can also count on a male actor playing a female role, the trademark of a good pantomime.

TIPS (fun for 5 years +)

• To avoid the extra charge of around $5 per ticket from **Ticket Master**, buy your tickets directly at the **Elgin Theatre**'s box office (on a day when you're visiting the Eaton Centre). The box office is open Monday to Saturday from 11 am to 5 pm and prior to the shows.

• For a description of things to see around the Eaton Centre, read the description of the **Hidden Treasure Stroll** on p. 473.

NEARBY ATTRACTIONS
Cavalcade of lights (10-min walk) p. 170
Crèche Exhibition (5-min. walk) ... p. 173

Ross Petty Productions
(416) 872-5555
www.rosspetty.com

D-3
Downtown
Toronto
5-min.

Schedule: From late November to early January at around 7 pm, with matinees at around 1 or 2 pm. Call for exact schedule.
Admission: Around $54-$74/ adults, $49/12 years and under, $196/4 people.
Directions: Elgin Theatre, 189 Yonge St., across from the **Eaton Centre**.

THE NUTCRACKER

Great on all points

A ballet that involves a rat, horse, ram, rooster, fox, bee, sheep, unicorns, mice, bears, cats and dogs will get their attention, believe me!

Whether or not you intend to get tickets to the **National Ballet of Canada**'s lavish **Nutcracker** accompanied by the **National Ballet Orchestra**, you must visit their website.

After clicking **Performances** and selecting **Nutcracker**, choose **About the Show**, then **Story** to access the video excerpts worth a thousand words to describe the dazzling magic of their performance in a Russian setting.

Still under **About the Show**, you'll find **About the Nutcracker** offering a **Nutcracker** history (where I learned that the **National Ballet** first performed the

Nutcracker in 1964). The current choreography was created by James Kudelka in 1995.

The **Costumes** section under **Explore the Making of the Nutcracker** impressed me. It features clips of a wardrobe tour, a dance rehearsal for the two dancers in the very realistic horse costume and a fascinating explanation on the making of a tutu (they cost thousands of dollars!). Note that all these website references were valid at the time of print.

The **Nutcracker Story Time** is a 45-minute bonus event offered prior to the show to introduce kids to the storyline. To download their activity book, go to the **About the Show** section in their **Nutcracker** home page, click on **Special offers and Events**, then **Nutcracker Story Time**.

The seating plan of the **Four Seasons Centre** includes Orchestra, Grand Ring, Ring 3, Ring 4 and Ring 5 (the latter being the least expensive). We sat in Ring 5 to test it and found we had a very nice view of the whole ensemble of dancers from there. We did not realize that we were missing the upper part of the spectacular set until we toured the lower levels after the show! Note that Ring 3 tickets would cost around $40 more per person. Your call.

TIPS (fun for 5 years +)

• More about the **Four Seasons Centre for the Performing Arts** and the **Canadian Opera Company** on p. 105.
• I wanted to test the $30 **Rush Tickets** option (which you can buy on the same day as the show) so I went to the box office on a Wednesday at noon. They had tickets available in Ring 3 (normally worth $70-$78!). At 6 pm, they still had many Ring 5 tickets (worth $31-$41).
• For the first time in December 2007, a matinee performance of the **Nutcracker** was presented, live from the **Four Seasons Centre**, in sixty-nine **Cineplex** theatres across Canada, at the cost of $20/adults, $10/children and $50 for a family of 4. Let's hope it becomes a tradition!
• If this is your child's first **Nutcracker**, why not take her first to a more modest version? The following companies have created their own **Nutcracker**, look them up to see if they're offering it this year: www.balletjorgen.ca, www.ontarioballet-theatre.com, www.piaboumanschool.org, and **Canadian Ballet Theatre** at www.starsofthe21stcentury.com. Rule of thumb, expect their best tickets to cost near the price of **National Ballet**'s cheapest ones.

NEARBY ATTRACTIONS	
Cavalcade of Lights (3-min. walk) p. 170	
Eaton Centre (5-min. walk) .... p. 168	

The National Ballet of Canada	D-3 **Downtown** Toronto 5-min.
(416) 345-9595 www.thenutcracker.ca www.national.ballet.ca	

Schedule: The Nutcracker is normally offered throughout December (but not daily).

Admission: Around $40-$110/ adult, $30-$100/13 years and under, $140-$370/4 people. Ask about their $30 Rush Tickets.

Directions: Four Seasons Centre, 145 Queen St. W., Toronto (at University Ave.).

SING-ALONG MESSIAH

Photo: Courtesy of Tafelmusik

Hallelujah!

As he's talking to us, Maestro Handel is interrupted by... a bawling baby. Tongue-in-cheek, he comments on the great potential of the future singer (while the mother sheepishly reaches the exit) and goes on introducing the great masterpiece we've all come to sing.

When we handed in our ticket at the entrance, we were asked in what register we sang. I used to contribute a thin soprano voice to a choir in my life b.c. (before children) but I was accompanying a friend of mine with his two young daughters so we opted for the mixed section selected by many families.

TIPS (fun for 8 years +)

• Arrive early if you want to buy the Messiah's score. Consult the Sing-Along program to find out which portion of the score will be performed. (You can also get it at Remenyi stores, www.remenyi.com).

• Handel interacts with us again after the intermission. Remember it is only in the second part that you will be able to belch the famous "Hallelujah! Hallelujah! Halleeluujaaah!"

• The **Tafelmusik Baroque Orchestra and Chamber Choir** also present their *Messiah* (although not in the sing-along version) at the **Trinity St. Paul's Centre**. They usually offer a few performances mid-December. Call to confirm.

• See what's around Dundas Subway Station on p. 450.

To reach it we had to climb way up through the narrow backstairs of the old 1804 **Massey Hall**.

From our seats, we could get quite a view of the happy crowd, most spectators eagerly holding on to their score. Later on, I realized that most of them had been there before and just could not wait for the magic to start.

The maestro, quite handsome in his overcoat and wig, encouraged us to "zing along" with his strong German accent and helped us warm up. The **Tafelmusik Baroque Orchestra and Chamber Choir** and special soloists were accompanying us.

Listening to thousands of voices joining in to present Handel's *Messiah* is an amazing experience. You literally become the music. One has to know that Handel composed his masterpiece in 21 days, partially paralyzed from a stroke!

At one point, I was totally lost and frantically flipping through the complicated score when I felt a gentle tap on my shoulder. Alia and Alex, aged 10 and 11, earnestly wanting to help, quietly pointed out to me the right spot on the right page. Hallelujah! (It makes one wonder what do they teach these kids in whatever school they attend?)

Sing-Along Messiah	D-3 Downtown Toronto 10-min.
(416) 872-4255 (box office) www.masseyhall.com **(416) 964-6337 (company)** www.tafelmusik.org	

Schedule: Usually at 2 pm on the Sunday right before Christmas, call in September to reserve!

Admission: Around $30/adults, $22/ others.

Directions: Massey Hall, on Shuter St., just east of Yonge St. by Eaton Centre's parking lot entrance.

NEARBY ATTRACTIONS
St. James Crèches (5-min. walk) p. 173
Eaton Centre (1-min. walk) .... p. 168

KENSINGTON FESTIVAL OF LIGHTS

The longest night

On the night of December 21, a wave of madness sweeps through Kensington Market, as the cars give way to pedestrians and to the joyous parade engulfing stunned passers-by.

Along the lively streets filled with musicians and people in disguise, everyone is won over by the spirit of the celebration.

Kensington Market is renowned for its coloured effervescence, but many don't know about the Festival of Lights, an annual ritual now in its 20th year.

We're not talking about standard, tiny Christmas lights. Rather, we mean the lights of sun and fire, symbolic or genuine: Hanukkah candles, the fire of Christian faith, the pagan celebration of the solstice, and the joyful party to salute Earth's last revolution of the year around the sun.

This is not a parade that people watch passively. We are the parade and move along. All the people attending are warmly dressed, and walk the course where several attractions await. Playful families hold elaborate paper lanterns dancing over the crowd.

When we attended the event, the story of the people of Israel was told with theatrical humour. Giant marionettes mimed a solstice story. Actors (a real baby among them) acted out the Nativity scene… on the roof of a store.

Then, we went on to **Bellevue Square**, where a giant sculpture was burned with cries of joy. The ambience is unique, and so is the event!

TIPS (fun for 4 years +)

• **Red Pepper Spectacle Arts**, behind the festival, is a non-profit community arts organization and storefront production facility in Kensington Market. It organizes drop-in lantern-making workshops where participants can create lanterns out of bamboo and paper. They normally take place on the weekend prior to December 21, from 12 noon to 5 pm in different locations within Kensington Market. The cost of the workshop is pay-what-you-can ($10 suggested donation). Kids must be accompanied by an adult. I recommand it for children over 5.

• December 21, 2008 will be the 20th Festival of Lights. Expect more workshops, in more locations, and more action during the Festival!

• More about **Kensington Market** on p. 468.

NEARBY ATTRACTIONS

Kensington Festival of Lights (416) 598-3729 www. redpepper.spectaclearts.org	D-3 **Downtown** Toronto 15-min.

 Schedule: December 21, starting with ongoing performances at around 5:30 pm. The parade starts at 6 pm and lasts approximately an hour with fun continuing until 8 pm.

 Admission: FREE, you can buy $8 handmade lanterns.

Directions: The parade begins at Augusta and Oxford (Augusta, south of College is closed to traffic from 5 pm).

NIAGARA'S FESTIVAL OF LIGHTS

Photo: Courtesy of E. Ritson

An enlightening discovery

It's ironic that Niagara Falls should be a viable family destination given all the jokes that refer to it as the honeymooners' haven. Yet, this is what you get with the Winter Festival of Lights.

Created over fifteen years ago, the Niagara Winter Festival of Lights comes to life at dusk. Nightfall brings twenty lighted animated scenes (many representing Walt Disney characters), in a park facing the Falls.

The waterfalls themselves are lit by a powerful system, with sweeping colour spots that change throughout the evening. The light reflects nicely on the surrounding ice-laden trees.

It is preferable to take your car to view the scenes on **Dufferin Islands**, located south of the Niagara Parkway, bordering the Falls. Most visitors observe the displays from their cars, and traffic is understandably slow on the small road that travels the islands. You can stop in certain areas along the road, if you manage to find a spot. In addition to the lovely displays (such as Noah's Ark), we spotted an owl in lights perched on a tree and a small sparkling doe behind a bush, when we visited.

TIPS (fun for 4 years +)

• The Festival of Lights includes an outdoor show on a stage next to the light displays most Saturdays at 7:30 pm.

• I strongly recommend you arrive in **Niagara Falls** at the beginning of the afternoon to enjoy the wealth of family attractions available in the area.

• I have visited many other festivals of lights. All of them offer smaller and fewer displays than Niagara's Festival. Regardless of the size, displays are done following the same concept of lights fixed on a metal frame outlining a flat scene. These smaller festivals are worth a visit when located near another attraction. They are pretty after a snow fall.

• More on attractions around **Niagara Falls** on p. 269.

NEARBY ATTRACTIONS
Bird Kingdom (5-min.) .... p. 71
Fallsview Waterpark (5-min.) .... p. 434

Niagara Falls Winter Festival of Lights	E-4 Niagara Region 90-min.

Niagara Falls Winter Festival of Lights
• Niagara Falls
(905) 374-1616
www.tourismniagara.com

Schedule: From mid-November until mid-January, 5 to 11 pm.
Admission: FREE (voluntary contribution suggested during outdoor shows).
Directions: See Niagara Falls on p. 302.

NEW YEAR'S EVE

In the (time) zone

New Year's Eve is all about the build-up to the countdown. It's so much fun, why stick to celebrating only once when there's a countdown going on at every hour somewhere around the world.

If you don't think the kids will be able to stay up late (or for the mere fun of doing more countdowns), you can always celebrate the New Year's countdown happening earlier in other time zones.

For your information, on New Years's Eve, when it is 7 pm sharp in Ontario, it is midnight in Dakar (Senegal) and London (England). When it is 8 pm here, it is midnight in the Azores (Portugal) in the Atlantic Ocean; 9 pm here, midnight in Rio de Janeiro (Brazil); 10 pm here, midnight in Santiago (Chile); 11 pm here, midnight in Nova Scotia and New Brunswick (Canada). And one last: when it is 10:30 pm in Ontario and Quebec, it is midnight in St. John's, Newfoundland (and Labrador). Perfect time for a geography lesson!

Celebrations

There used to be **First Night Toronto** at **Harbourfront Centre**, then **The Distillery** but it's been gone for a while.

Toronto Zoo has been offering for a few years now its own version of a **New Year's Eve** party for families. The countdown takes place at 9 pm after three hours of musical entertainment and activities (p. 57).

Of course, there's the **Nathan Phillips Square** party with music on the outdoor stage, culminating with an exciting countdown. It is not really suited for children (too loud, too long, too late) but it is broadcast live on City TV and CP 24. This year, we watched the last 15 seconds to do our own countdown during a private party.

Family fun

If you want to make it memorable, here's an idea we tried last year, which was a true success! In a room, we filmed ten family members each shouting a number in the countdown. We plugged it into the television and played it for the real countdown. It was hilarious!

Our family's favourite for New Year's Eve is a roll filled with metallic confetti that pop up when you twist its base. Ask for them at stores, they will know. These are very user-friendly. Your only concern is to make sure kids don't twist it before the right time in their excitement. (We always leave the confetti for the kids to play with in the morning and then make them clean it up!).

In order to make noise to welcome the New Year, we bought bubble wrap from an office supplier (the kind with one-inch bubbles) and lined it on the floor for everyone to step on. We had a blast.

TIPS

• A fun website to find out about how New Year's is celebrated throughout the world is: **www.newyearfestival.com**. That's where we learned that Julius Caesar officially declared January 1 to be the beginning of a new year in 46 B.C. Not that everybody listened, we had to wait until the Gregorian calendar in 1582 for it to become a sure thing.

• If you want to know the current local time in cities and countries in all the time zones around the world, go to the **World Clock** on **www.timeanddate.com**. (Note that the time on the screen will be frozen to the time at which you logged in.).

• Check the list of suppliers on p. 159 for good addresses to find party supplies.

General tips about
Indoor playgrounds:

- Even in the middle of the summer when they're wearing sandals, always have socks handy for your kids when visiting an indoor playground. Some sell them on the premises but many don't!
- Most playgrounds' bread & butter comes from birthday parties so it happens that they often close earlier to accommodate such parties. In some cases, the playgrounds create special events for the benefit of their regular customers, with an extra fee involved. They often request people book in advance for these events. Bottom line: always call before going to an indoor playground.

INDOOR
PLAYGROUNDS

See **Kidsports** on p. 194.

DROP-IN CENTRES

Just drop in!

My preschooler rushes to the sand box, what a treat given that we are in the middle of winter! She then embarks on a creative game with her 3-year-old friend, involving a doll house, an army of plastic animals and a tow truck. Meanwhile, I sit in the baby section surrounded by age-appropriate toys and play with my friend's infant who lies on a floor cushion.

Drop-in centres vary in size, activities and members' involvement. Yet, all offer an opportunity for preschoolers and their parents or caregivers to meet other children and grown-ups and enjoy informal playtime. Kids also love the opportunity to play with toys different from those at home.

In most of the drop-ins I have visited, there was a kindergarten feeling to the place; from the layout of the room with their craft and snack tables, to an array of well categorized toys.

Most mornings, there is a circle time where adults and children are encouraged to sing or listen to a story. A healthy snack is usually provided in each of the morning and afternoon sessions.

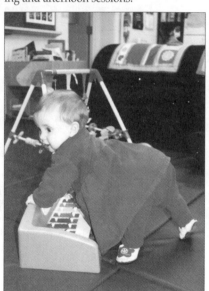

TIPS (fun for 5 years & under)

• Call the **Metro Association of Family Resources Programs** to find the closest drop-in in your area. If it is not to your liking, try the next closest to you. Once you find one you like, adopt it! You and your child will eventually create a valuable network of friends.

• The biggest drop-in I have visited lately (the one shown in the pictures) is the **Applegrove Centre**, located at 60 Woodfield Rd., near Queen Street E., (416) 461-8143.

• A mother told me about a very special drop-in centre catering to children (6 years and under) with hearing problems at the **Rumball Family Resource Centre for the Deaf and Hard-of-Hearing** (2395 Bayview Ave., 416-449-9651, ext. 105, **www. rumballfamilyresource.org**). The staff is fluent in sign language. Call for exact schedule.

Metro Association of Family Resources Programs
(416) 463-7974

 Schedule: Many are open during school time and only on certain days.
 Admission: FREE.
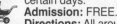 **Directions:** All around Toronto.

PLAYGROUND PARADISE

A divine mural

Playground Paradise's walls and ceiling are covered by a magnificent painted birch forest. The mural successfully gives an intimate feel to this vast area. This meadow-like atmosphere brightens up gloomy days.

Two-thirds of the space is occupied by a two-storey play structure designed to get muscles working. Children can circulate underneath it. Inside, there is an 8,000-ball pool with targets, as well as spiral and straight slides.

I was charmed by several of the place's original features: a zip line, a distorting mirror, big punching bags and long talk tubes used as a telephone system to chat from one crawl tube to the other. (These might have changed since.)

The rest of the space included a myriad of vinyl shapes used by children to build shelters. For preschoolers, there was a Duplo table, a wide activity board and a few abacus tables.

There are only a few benches for parents to sit on. Instead of sitting on the ground, you might as well... join the kids on the play structures!

TIPS (fun for 3 years +)

- Socks are required for everyone.
- They offer the cheapest birthday party package in town but you need to reserve way in advance.
- They have a small spray pad with a giant flower on the side of the building. Bring bathing suits... and sun screen (there's no shade).
- Kids can also play in the good outdoor playground in nearby **Flemingdon Park**, a few minutes walk away.
- The playground offers an affordable snack bar and machines.

NEARBY ATTRACTIONS

Playground Paradise
(416) 395-6014

D-3
North
of downtown
20-min.

Schedule: Normally open year-round on weekends, 12:30 to 5 pm (closed December 24, 25, 26 and 31). Varies a lot on weekdays throughout the year, call before you go! (At the time of print, they opened in blocks of 9:30 to 11:30 am, 1 to 3 or 4 pm, 4:30 to 8:30 pm or 6:30 to 8:30 pm, but not every day, with summer Monday mornings reserved for 6 years and under.

Admission: (cash only) $2/child on weekdays, $2/hour/child on weekends and holidays. FREE for accompanying adults.

Directions: 150 Grenoble Dr., Toronto. From Don Mills Rd. (south of Eglinton), turn east on Gateway Blvd.

KIDSWORKS

They'll dig that one!

Fifty tons of indoor sand untouched by cats, dogs or raccoons! Huge castle-like climbing structure with long slides to land in the sand complete with a twelve-foot climbing wall. All makes for a unique indoor playground.

I chose to include the place in my guide even though they're not open to the public most of the week because I loved their choice of covering half their playground with sand. There is plenty of sandy playground outdoors but the novelty of seeing it indoors makes it fun.

There's also a toddler centre with bouncing inflated castle, swings, wavy tracks (plastic slides toddlers ride down on sturdy vehicles) and train table. Stools are lined up along the sandy play area for parents' convenience. A dragon stares at the kids playing and lovely decorations adorn the reception area.

Since my last visit, they've added a zip line. Even better!

TIPS (fun for 8 years & under)
• Younger kids will be encouraged to climb sideways, for safety reasons.
• They don't sell coffee or juice but can point you to many coffee shops in the surrounding area.
• One of the owners of this playground is also a partner in **Fantasy Castle**, a whimsical party place located next door! Their birthday packages are expensive but judging by the pictures on their website, the space is gorgeous and parties allow for action and dress-up fun. Check **www.fantasycastletoronto.com**, (416) 422-2253, 105 Vanderhoof Avenue, Unit 8, Toronto.

NEARBY ATTRACTIONS
Leonard Linton Park (2-min.) .... p. 354

Kidsworks
(416) 483-1367
www.
kidsworkstoronto.com

**D-3
North
of downtown
25-min.**

Schedule: Open for drop-in Tuesday to Friday, 10 am to 3 pm (reserved for birthday parties at other times).

Admission: $7/first child, $5/for each additional child.

Directions: 105 Vanderhoof Ave., Unit 5, Toronto (one street south of Eglinton, east of Laird).

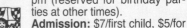

IT'S PLAYTIME

Play date

The narrow facade is misleading. The place is big, with an additional room attached to the back, used for the day-care. The range of activities is good, from imagination games with small toys, karaoke machine, costumes, to physical play, with climbing wall and wooden structure.

Here, the layout is different; more like a house school than an indoor playground. It is because in addition to the drop-in service, the place offers Play Group allowing children to socialize without their parents! It involves singing, storytelling, playtime, and arts & crafts.

It is one of the only places I know which offers this kind of service, which could be very handy if you need a last minute solution.

There's a sofa and large square table fit with small chairs. Murals line the walls and a wooden climbing structure with slide stands in the middle of the main room.

When I visited, the owner was on the floor. She was playing with a toddler and engaged in conversation with a pre-schooler while she keeps an eye on the baby sleeping in a bassinet. She was so good with them, I assumed they were her kids. Then, I saw their moms returning for them!

When I drive by the place, I often see mothers peeking though the window to reassure themselves that their kid is happily playing, before taking off.

Note that because of the structure required to manage a drop-off service, you might feel there's less free play involved here than in the other indoor playgrounds.

TIPS (fun for 7 years & under)

- You don't need to subscribe to the drop-off Play Group sessions for a series of days. Your child may attend only one half-day or the whole day (ending at 3:30 pm). They will take you on the spot if they have availability but I suggest you call ahead to reserve a spot.
- They offer different programs such as beginner Mandarin classes.
- They don't sell snacks. Bring your own.
- Read about **Monarch Park** (a 10-min. walk from It's Playtime) in the **Greenwood Subway Station** section on p. 444.

NEARBY ATTRACTIONS
Around Pape Subway Station ..... p. 443

It's Playtime
(416) 465-6688
www.itsplaytime.ca

**D-3
East
of downtown
20-min.**

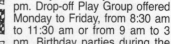 **Schedule:** Open for drop-in Monday to Friday, 9 am to 4 pm. Drop-off Play Group offered Monday to Friday, from 8:30 am to 11:30 am or from 9 am to 3 pm. Birthday parties during the weekends.

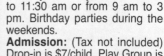 **Admission:** (Tax not included) Drop-in is $7/child, Play Group is $26/morning or $45 for full day.

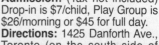 **Directions:** 1425 Danforth Ave., Toronto (on the south side of Danforth, west of Coxwell Ave.).

AMAZON INDOOR PLAYGROUND

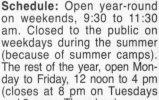

They're at that stage...

I watch my little butterfly flash by me and disappear into the climbing structure. A moment later, she reappears in the... eye of a huge monkey's head.

This place is special. It is one of the few I have visited that offers costumes to play dress-up and the only one with a small stage, complete with background curtains to fire up children's imaginations.

A puppet theatre comes as a bonus. This indoor playground also comes with the big climbing structure supporting the monkey head, ball pits, soft blocks and rider toys with some space to circulate.

I liked the large bay windows. Parents are allowed in the structure. Or they can rest on the large sofas.

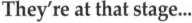

TIPS (fun for 7 years & under)
• Socks are mandatory.
• They now offer drop-off child care for $6/hour! Call before you go.
• They offer complimentary coffee and tea and sell candy.
• Check the ice cream shop **Dutch Dream** (10-minute walk away) on p. 454.

NEARBY ATTRACTIONS
Winston Churchill Park (5-min.) ... p. 368

Amazon Indoor Playground
(416) 656-5832
www.
amazondowntown.com

D-3
West
of downtown
25-min.

Schedule: Open year-round on weekends, 9:30 to 11:30 am. Closed to the public on weekdays during the summer (because of summer camps). The rest of the year, open Monday to Friday, 12 noon to 4 pm (closes at 8 pm on Tuesdays and 6 pm on Thursdays).

Admission: $8/child 2 years and older, $5/child under 2 years old.

Directions: 21 Vaughan Rd., Unit 108, Toronto (located on a v-shaped block south of St. Clair West, at the corner of Bathurst St., in front of Wychwood Library).

MARY'S PLAYLAND

Life on a mini scale

When he was three years old, my little brother, seeing his mother suffering from a painful attack, hurried to get his medical kit to relieve her while the ambulance was coming. That's when I understood how seriously children take role-playing games. The owners of Mary's Playland also clued in to this by offering us an indoor street, scaled perfectly to its miniature visitors.

TIPS (fun 7 years & under)
• Socks are mandatory.
• Snacks are available. They also sell many trinkets and small toys for parties.
• They offer spa services conveniently located upstairs from the playground. Their **Tranquility Family Day Spa** includes: massage, body exfoliation, manicure & pedicure, facial, hair cut (adult and kids) and perms. When you use one of those services, they will charge a sitter fee including admission to the playground: $10/one child, $15/for two, $20/for three, for the duration of the service! Now, we're talking!
• If you have errands in the neighbourhood, they offer a drop-off service: $15/one child per hour, $7/hour for extra child. You need to call ahead to reserve a spot.

It actually was created by the previous owners under the name of **Kidsway** but the new administration has kept everything.

Children fidget impatiently as they enter the place; they sense this is a different kind of store. Those who can't stand the noise level of vast indoor playing fields can be reassured; the place is quiet, well-lit and intimate.

The concept is simple, yet not an obvious one. Lovely displays that incorporate the best products of the Little Tikes line, have been created to encourage creative play. You will find, side-by-side, a little house fully equipped with kitchen, dining room and living room on the second floor, a beauty salon that can accommodate a few clients, a garage (tools and hard-hat included), a grocery store (a real hit with my aspiring home economist) outfitted with food carts and produce displays.

You will also find a grey carpeted road, with its miniature cars and gas pump, sitting against a green carpet. Distorting mirrors, a couple of computers equipped with great software packages, games for the very young, a basketball hoop, a multicoloured ballroom and other similar outlets for energy surplus are also found at Mary's Playland.

Mary's Playland
• Etobicoke
(416) 236-5437
www.marysplayland.net

| D-3 |
| West |
| of downtown |
| 20-min. |

 Schedule: Monday to Friday, 9:30 am to 5 pm; weekends, 9 am to 12 noon.

 Admission: $10/one child, $7/ extra child. Read TIPS about drop-off and babysitting services.

 Directions: 2885 Bloor St. West, Etobicoke (west of Prince Edward Dr.).

KIDSPORTS

Fun network

Once again, a net partition separates us from our destination: a net corridor with deep holes filled with balls, located on the top level of the 3-storey-high structure. Finding the right entrance to get there is a real mind game and it's part of the fun.

Colourful houses dressed in turquoise, fuchsia, corals and blues mark the food area by Kidsports' entrance.

The apparent low height of the building from the outside is misleading because the interior is designed in split levels, with the play area actually nestled below ground level.

The impressive indoor climbing structure is topped with a bright papier mâché dragon. It is the best climber we have tried!

Adults and kids alike crouch to climb from one level of a net labyrinth to the next. It is the only way to reach the many slides, fire poles, tunnels, corridors outfitted with punching bags and ball rooms located in the vertical maze. (Grown-ups beware: The nets are hard on the feet.) Some twenty token games are scattered around the structure, including an air hockey table which could make a few tokens go a long way!

There is a smaller structure for younger kids at the other end of the building, as well as a room filled with big toys and gym cushions ideal for toddlers.

TIPS (fun for 3 years +)
• The combination of hundreds of happy kids and token machines in action creates high decibels.
• Most machines reward the players with tickets they can trade for trinkets at a counter. This is an irresistible concept for kids over 5 years old. I strongly suggest you budget an additional $3 to $5 per child to give them the pleasure of winning something ($10 gets 36 tokens). Kidsports conveniently offers gadgets you can get for only a few tickets.

NEARBY ATTRACTIONS
Pearson Int'l Airport (10-min.) ...... p. 206
Centennial Mini-Indy (5-min.) ...... p. 216

Kidsports
• Mississauga
(905) 624-9400
www.
kidsports.sites.toronto.com

D-3
West
of Toronto
35-min.

 Schedule: Monday to Sunday, 10 am to 8 pm (closes at 9 pm on Fridays).

 Admission: $8/children 3 years and up, $5/under 3 years, $2/under one year, $1/adults. Check their website for monthly specials.

Directions: 4500 Dixie Rd., Mississauga (south of Eglinton).

CHUCK E. CHEESE

the machines, my daughter climbs next to Chuck E. Cheese and dances along as the big plush mechanical mouse sings a lively tune with its musicians. A video clip is shown on a couple of monitors by the stage and every song is followed by a five minute shut down of the mechanical band. Let's party!

Games on the menu

At first, the place looks like a well-staffed family restaurant (which it is). Then, the noise level reminds you this is an amusement centre above all!

As we get settled in a booth located by a huge maze structure of tubes and tunnels, we notice an army of kids free-roaming the site. Between the short, free of charge shows, the climbing structure (where adults are also welcome) and some 40 token games (most of them requiring only one token), the kids had enough fun to spare (allowing me the luxury of a few chapters in the book I had the good foresight to bring!).

Food is ordered at the counter but waiters serve at your table.

While her brother is enthralled by

TIPS (fun for 3 years +)

• Tickets are dispensed from the machines according to the player's skill. Tickets can also be exchanged for trinkets.

• I suggest you avoid these types of outings unless you are prepared to spend a few dollars on tokens. Even with dollars in hand, it seems you need loads of tickets to win anything remotely interesting (to you). As for my kids, all they really wanted was to win something... anything!

• We visited during **Christmas** time and the Chuck E. Cheese band's songs and clips were in the Christmas spirit.

• Pizza is Chuck E. Cheese's specialty. There is also a salad bar and hot sandwiches. Some value packages are real savers if you intend to buy tokens.

Chuck E. Cheese
www.chuckecheese.com

  Schedule: Most locations are open daily, 9 am to 10 pm (closing at 11 pm on Fridays and Saturdays).

 Admission: FREE (free refills on all soft drinks). See food coupons on website.

 Willowdale: 2452 Sheppard Ave. East (just west of Victoria Park), 416-497-8855.

 Newmarket: 17380 Yonge St. (south of Davis Dr.), 905-953-8664.

 Whitby: 75 Consumer Dr., Bldg J (from Hwy 401, take exit #412/Thickson Rd. northbound, turn west on Consumer Dr.), 905-665-2142.

Mississauga: 4141 Dixie Rd., (south of Rathburn Rd.), 905-602-4090.

Vaughan: 3255 Rutherford Rd. (east of Hwy 400), 905-532-0241.

Mississauga West: 2945 Argentina Rd. (east of Winston Churchill Blvd., south of Hwy 401), 905-785-3593.

Cambridge: 42 Pine Bush Rd. (from Hwy 401, take exit #282/Hespeler Rd. southbound, turn east on Pine Bush), 519-621-7752.

WOODIE WOOD CHUCK'S

A kid-friendly interior

There's a major heat wave going on, and your house is not air-conditioned. The children are bursting with energy, but it's raining cats and dogs and the neighbourhood playground looks like a duck pond. So many good reasons to resort to the services of large playgrounds such as that of Woodie Wood Chuck's!

Neon lights, machine noises and children's screams bouncing off cement walls, all combine in a cacophony for the senses that makes me want to turn around as soon as we step in. A quick glance at my child's excited look convinces me we're here to stay… at least a couple of hours! Once I've come to terms with the idea, there are in fact several good surprises that await.

This indoor park is huge. It includes a section of sixty "pay-as-you-play" token games, where you can test your throwing,

pushing and hitting skills. Woodie Wood Chuck's main attraction, however, is its huge play area spread over two floors.

The imposing structure in itself is well worth the visit. Large modules are connected by transparent tunnels or suspended bridges. All abound with hidden corners to explore. Ropes, slides, an enclosure filled with colourful balls, boxing cushions, tunnels and ladders; everything has been planned for the enjoyment of young climbers.

A note of caution however: It is very easy to lose sight of a child in this maze of corridors, and while adults are allowed on the structure, they can only go on when the playground is not too busy. Younger ones should therefore be encouraged to stay in the smaller playing area.

The place includes a small stage with characters playing in a band.

TIPS (fun for 3 years +)
• Socks are mandatory.
• Look carefully. You can't see the Scarborough location's façade from Sheppard Avenue. It faces Brimley Road.
• Both places sell pizza and include table sections. In the Scarborough location, there is also a large central area with tables, surrounded by bay windows. It is a great refuge for adults with sensitive hearing. They don't have one in the Mississauga location.

Woodie Wood Chuck's Indoor Playland
(416) 298-3555
www.woodiewoodchucks.ca

Schedule: Monday to Thursday, 11 am to 9 pm, Friday, 11 am to 10 pm, Saturday, 10 am to 10 pm, Sunday 10 am to 9 pm.
Admission: Only $1/child, FREE for accompanying adult.
Scarborough: 4466 Sheppard Ave. East (from Hwy 401 West, take exit #379/ Kennedy Rd. northbound, turn east on Sheppard. It is east of Brimley Rd.
Mississauga: 1248 Dundas St. East, west of Dixie Rd.

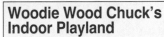

AMAZON WEST END

Action!

The pretty mural featuring trees and animals and the wooden structures give an overall warm feeling to the place.

This used to be a Peanut Club. The space is still as big and absolutely spotless. Great attention has been paid to the layout, with low walls and climbing structures placed on an angle that breaks the monotony of the big rectangular space.

Check their website for more pictures.

The owner of the playground is also at the head of **Loot Lady**. That's why you'll see a small display of loot bags for sale in the playground. You can ask to see any of their loot bags, they will bring them upstairs for you from the warehouse basement. See **www.lootlady.com** for details.

Photo: Courtesy of Amazon

Amazon Indoor Playground	D-3
• Etobicoke	N-W
(416) 245-1459	of downtown
www.amazonindoorplayground.com	30-min.

 Schedule: Monday to Friday, 10 am to 3 pm. Summer hours vary and open on weekends only when no private parties are on. Call to confirm.

 Admission: Around $10/first child, $7/second child, $5/infant, FREE for parents and infant with paid admission for another child.

 Directions: 1500 Royal York Rd., Etobicoke (north of Eglinton).

PEANUT CLUB (NORTH YORK)

Monkey fun

The place is bright and colourful with house façades adorning the walls. The climbing structure is fit for little monkeys. An enclosure with a wall to wall castle interior holds all the toys to play house. It creates a feeling of intimacy quite appreciated by little homemakers.

Note there's a **Bowlerama** in the same building (**www.bathurstbowlerama.com**).

Peanut Club	D-3
• North York	N-W
(416) 782-8735	of downtown
www.peanutclub.com	25-min.

 Schedule: Monday to Friday, 9:30 am to 3 pm. Closes at 2 pm during the summer.

 Admission: $6/child (ask about their packages).

Directions: 2788 Bathurst St., North York (south of Lawrence).

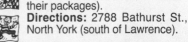

PLAY-&-PARTY-A-SAURUS

So pretty!

In general, the largest, noisiest playgrounds do little to cater to the needs of preschoolers. Others choose to target the 7-year and under clientele.

I fell for the zany murals that cover whole walls. The studied decor helps create an intimate ambience. An intelligent layout allows parents to watch their brood at all times, without difficulty.

The playground is lovely, from the turquoise ceiling to the colourful murals covering the walls. Huge dinosaurs relax on the couch painted above the parents' section. Other dinosaurs on the mural seem as busy as the kids on the floor and in the large climbing structure.

Kids slide into the huge ball pit filled with turquoise, pink and purple balls that match the decor.

For even more fun, they now have an inflated jumping castle.

TIPS (fun for 7 years & under)

- Socks are required at all times.
- Ask about their special evenings with characters during **Halloween**, **Christmas**, **Easter** and other special occasions. Admission cost is $15 per child and it includes pizza and juice (FREE for accompanying adult). They are even considering adding puppet shows.
- They sell snacks.
- **Erin Mills Town Centre** (**www.erinmills.ca**) is 10 minutes away (at Eglinton and Erin Mills Pkwy).

Play-A-Saurus
- Mississauga
(905) 828-7088
www.
playandpartyasaurus.com

**D-3
West
of Toronto
35-min.**

 Schedule: Open Monday to Friday, 9:30 am to 6 pm. Private parties on the weekends. Call to confirm dates of special events.
 Admission: $5/child. FREE for adult and infant with older sibling.
 Directions: 3355 The Collegeway (Units 30 & 31), Mississauga. From QEW West, take exit #124/ Winston Churchill northbound. Turn west on The Collegeway.

PLAYGROUNDS WITH INFLATABLES

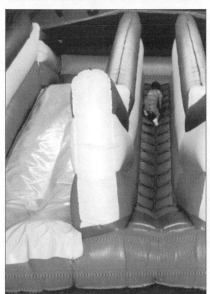

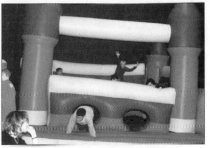

Slam-bam fun

These have to be the noisiest places, with all those air pumps at work. Chances are your kids will accidentally knock each other's heads (my kids did) in the midst of such excitement! And yet, bouncing and jumping on the inflated structures remains a favourite of energetic children.

Such play centres can be a life-saver during cold winter days, and a welcome air-conditioned break during hot summer days.

Now under separate ownerships, the two centres offer similar attractions that include inflatable structures, token machines and a large food area filled with tables.

The Pickering one (the only one I have visited) also offers a glow-in-the-dark 9-hole minigolf room with dark fluorescent minigolf lit under black light. Beware, the minigolf could be in use for birthday parties when you visit.

TIPS (fun for 4 years +)
- Socks are mandatory.
- Parents are not allowed on the inflatable structures. These could be suitable for kids under 4 years old only if they are very strong on their feet.
- Children have way more fun when attending places like these with friends.

Air Zone Party & Play Centre
- Pickering
(905) 839-1047

C-4
East
of Toronto
35-min.

Schedule: Open Monday to Saturday, 10 am to 8 pm; Sunday, 10 am to 6 pm.
Admission: $6/child on weekends, $1 less on weekdays, FREE for adults. Extra fees/minigolf.
Directions: 1095 Kingston Rd., Pickering (from Hwy 401, take exit #394/Whites Rd. northbound, turn east on Kingston Rd.).

Airzone Oshawa
- Oshawa
(905) 377-9663
www.airzoneoshawa.com

C-4
East
of Toronto
45-min.

Schedule: Tuesday to Friday, 10 am to 8 pm; weekends, 10 am to 6 pm (closes at 7 pm on Saturdays in winter). Open Monday in the summer, 10 am to 5 pm.
Admission: $6 per child on weekends, $5 on weekdays, 2-for-1 on Tuesdays.
Directions: 385 Bloor Street, Oshawa (from Hwy 401, take exit #416 towards RR-54/Park Rd., then follow Bloor St. East ramp toward RR-54 and turn east on Bloor St.

RAINBOW PLAYLAND

Photos: Courtesy of Rainbow Playland

No hard sales!

The Rainbow Company sells fabulous wooden play structures that can be found in the best playgrounds. To help us test their products, the company opened Rainbow Playland, not a mere showcase but a genuine indoor playground.

They have moved their playground next door, in a bigger space than the one I visited. The new place is not as cozy but it offers much more space. Some murals adorn the walls and, of course, it features a huge Rainbow structure. Several big toys are also available.

Smaller children will appreciate the padded area, equipped with a few toys and with cushions to climb on. It's conveniently located close to the area with sofas

| **Rainbow Playland & Party Centre** • Richmond Hill (905) 886-0306 www.playrainbow.ca | C-3 North of Toronto 30-min. |

 Schedule: Tuesday to Friday, 10 am to 3 pm. Closed to the public on Mondays and weekends.

 Admission: (cash only) $7 per child.

 Directions: 28 Fulton Way, unit 7, Richmond Hill. Take Hwy 404 North, exit Hwy 7 westbound. Turn north on East Beaver Creek, then west on Fulton Way.

KIDS ZONE

The zone

The climbing structure in this playground is fun and original with two levels.

Among other things, it includes an area with a giant ball, a suspended bridge and a pipe system allowing kids to talk from one tunnel to the next. Plus, adults are allowed to climb! The place also offers a section for smaller children with kiddie rides and arcade, a cafeteria with numerous tables and six birthday party rooms.

Since my last visit, they've added **Laser Tag**, a laser game for kids 8 to 16 years old (minimum 48 inches high at the shoulder) and a **Teddy Bear Workshop** (stuff-your-own-bear activity).

| **Kids Zone Family Fun Centre** • Whitby (905) 666-5437 www.kidszonedurham.com | C-4 East of Toronto 40-min. |

 Schedule: Normally open year-round on weekends, 10 am to 6:30 pm minimum, and Monday to Friday, 10 am to 4 pm minimum (extended seasonal hours). Check website for Laser and Teddy Bear hours.

 Admission: $8.50/2-12 years, $6/12-23 months, FREE for accompanying adults. Extra cost for Laser Tag and workshop.

 Directions: 12 Stanley Court, Whitby. From Hwy 401, take exit #410/Brock St. northbound, turn east on Consumer Dr., north on Garden St., east again on Burns St.; Stanley Court is on the right.

Looking for the best outdoor playground? It is found in **High Park (see** p. 286).

The best outdoor sand pit is in **Dufferin Grove Park** on p. 288.

MORE PLAYGROUNDS

For a change

I've never visited a small playground that wouldn't do the job if your main goal is to meet other parents/caretakers or give your child a chance to play with big toys you don't have at home. But if you want a change of scenery from your local playground, here are a few suggestions of places with a little twist.

I have not had the chance to visit personally the indoor playgrounds listed below but based on my experience, these will be worth the drive.

Mess for Fun
• North York
(416) 736-7101
www.messforfun.com
This playground with inflated structures, play structure and large toys is also a ceramic studio. Now, that's an interesting combination!

Schedule: Closed on Mondays, call for current hours.
Admission: (For up to 2 hours) Playground: $7/child under 8; Studio time: $7/adult and $5/14 years and under, plus the cost of the ceramic piece. Glaze is $1 per piece. Paint & Play combo: $11 plus the cost of the piece.
Directions: 73 Alness Street, Unit #3, North York (north of Finch, off Dufferin, turn west on Martin Ross Ave., then south on Alness.
Nearby: Yorkdale Shopping Centre (www.yorkdale.com), **Party Packagers** main store (1225 Finch, www.partypackagers.com).

Kidz Castle Playground
• Maple
(905) 417-2626
www.kidzcastleplayground.com
They offer drop-off services! The place includes a play structure that looks like a castle, a bouncing castle and a climbing wall, among other things. Plus, there's a mini-lounge and they sell cappucinos.

Schedule: Monday to Friday, 8:30 am to 5 pm.
Admission: $6/child, FREE under 1 year. Ask about their drop-off service.
Directions: 2338 Major Mackenzie Drive, Unit #7, Maple. From Hwy 400, take exit #35 to Major Mackenzie Dr. eastbound.
Nearby: Vaughan Mills (www.vaughanmills.com)

Mega FUN 4 Kids
• Scarborough
(416) 282-6531
www.megafun4kids.com
I've been to this one with my Mother's Group when our kids were younger and the name was different but it has not changed. We really liked it because of the play structure put together like a giant pirate ship that gave a very lively feeling to the place. It includes riding toys, a ball pit, an infant play area, a costume corner and a reading area as well as a train table and a play kitchen area.

Schedule: Monday to Friday 9 am to 5 pm (closes at 7 pm on Thursdays).
Admission: $5/child ($4 on Tuesdays).
Directions: The Villages of Abbey Lane Plaza, 91 Rylander Blvd., Scarborough. From Hwy 401 eastbound, stay on collector lanes and take exit #390 (Port Union Rd.). Turn east on Kingston Rd., then north on Rylander.
Nearby: Toronto Zoo (see p. 57).

Busy Bodies Playground
• Oakville
(905) 337-8535
www.busybodiesplayground.com
Here, the high ceiling allows for a tall play structure, with climbing ropes and many slides, and includes a section with giant balls. There's also basketball hoops, air hockey, infant/toddler room and more.

Schedule: Monday to Friday, 9:15 am to 3 pm; Saturday and Sunday, 9 am to 12 noon.
Admission: $8/2 years and older, $5/under 2, $4/extra sibling ($3 if under 2).
Directions: 245 Wyecroft Road, Oakville. From QEW, take exit #117 (Kerr Street) southbound, then turn west on Wyecroft.
Nearby: Coronation Park (see p. 426).

Amazing Adventures Playland

• Burlington
(905) 639-6544

The place includes an inflated obstacle course! There's also a bouncing structure, a 17-foot-high play structure with swirl slide, triple slide, trolley ride and more. They offer an enclosed area with motorized "motorcycles" for younger kids and a toddler section. That should help them blow off some steam!

Schedule: Open daily from 9:30 am, closes at 3:30 pm Monday to Wednesday, 7:30 pm on Thursdays, 9 pm on Fridays and 12 noon on weekends.
www.amazingadventuresplayland.ca
Admission: $6-$8/child (depending on day), FREE for under 12 months with full-price sibling.
Directions: 4325 Harvester Road, Burlington. From QEW, take exit #107 (Appleby Line) southbound, then turn west on Harvester.
Nearby: Bronte Creek P.P. (see p. 308).

Lil' Explorers Clubhouse

• Markham
(905) 910-7529
www.lilexplorers.ca

This one caught my attention because it is one of the few that offers an ambitious climbing wall behind a raised play area and a "helicopter". It doesn't seem really big but it includes an area for smaller kids. They offer drop-off service.

Schedule: Tuesday-Friday 10 am to 3 pm.
Admission: $8/18 months and over, $6/siblings and 12-18 months, FREE under 12 months with paying sibling. Call to confirm drop-off fees.
Directions: 190 Bullock Dr., Markham.
Nearby: Forsythe Farms (see p. 132).

Photo: Courtesy of Zooz Indoor Playground

Zooz Indoor Playground

• Aurora
(905) 713-1800
www.zoozindoorplayground.com

Great murals in this one! The large play structure is adorned with a giant toucan's head. They have climbing walls, air hockey table, video games, bouncing structure, costume section, small animals and more.

Schedule: Monday 9:30 to 12 noon, Tuesday to Friday 9:30 am to 2:30 pm, Tuesday evening 5.30 to 7:30 pm.
Admission: $8/first child, $6/siblings, $4/under 1 year.
Directions: 73 Industrial Parkway North, Unit 2B, Aurora. From Hwy 404 (north of 401), take exit #45 (Wellington St.) westbound, turn north on Industrial Pkwy).
Nearby: Cineplex Odeon Aurora Cinemas (www.cinemaclock.com).

Little Feet Fitness

• Oshawa
(905) 433-4668
www.littlefeetfitness.com

Now this is original! This is a unique centre focussing on children four years and under: Any first time parent with a toddler knows the feeling when their little treasure is knocked over by an energetic older child. Slides, climbs and balances are size-appropriate and meant for them to move.

Schedule: Open to the public Tuesdays to Sundays, call for current hours.
Admission: $8/child, $5/child in a group of 5 children or more, $3/babies (FREE if they accompany a full-price sibling).
Directions: 1077 Boundary Road, Unit 108, Oshawa. From Hwy 401 East, take exit #412 (Thickson Rd./RR-26), turn south on Thickson, then east on Wentworth St., and north on Boundary Rd.
Nearby: Canadian Automotive Museum (see p. 217).

General tips about
Machines:

- In this chapter, you'll find attractions, events or places to observe things that roll, float, fly or work.

MACHINES

See **HMCS Haida** on p. 230.

PEARSON INTERNATIONAL AIRPORT

There!

"You're serious?
You mean there
is not one single
viewing window in
the entire airport?"
I asked baffled. I
squeezed my little
guy's hand, glanc-
ing at him side-
ways checking for
his reaction. Since
morning I had
been promising him beautiful planes
and for the last half hour had been drag-
ging him around from one end of Pearson airport to the other, in search of an
elusive viewing spot.

When you're accompanying travel-
lers, you don't get to see the planes. You
don't even really see them when you're on
the other side of the gate!

The disappointingly sad reality
prompted me to investigate the issue. The
only place on the airport's premises where
you can observe the planes (unless you
are a passenger waiting to board) is from
the top parking lots (the longer you stay
the more you pay and you don't even see
very well).

One of the runways borders the
north side of Hwy 401 and planes that
circulate on it fly just above Hwy 427. A
good way to view them for free is from
Carlingview Street, a parallel street east
of Hwy 427. Two east-west runways share
the bulk of flights.

You can see planes at closer range
from outside the **Coffee Time** restaurant
on Carlingview Street, which is quite
practical. Between two planes, you can
treat the kids to a snack.

The other east-west runway borders the south side of Derry Road and
planes that circulate on it fly just above
Airport Road. You can view them land
on the ground from Airport Road, just
a bit east of the **Toronto International
Centre** located at 6900 Airport Road.

Judging by the number of cars
during our visit, this is a well-known
spot for serious observers with cameras.

There's a Petro Canada with convenience store across the street not too far
east of this viewing spot.

TIPS (fun for 4 years +)

• In the mid-afternoon to early evening, you might see a new plane every 4 to 5 minutes around Pearson Airport.

• Got a child passionate about aviation? Check the **Prop Shop** in **Buttonville Municipal Airport** in Markham. It is baffling to think there is no equivalent at Pearson Airport: posters, clothes, models, pins, birthday cards, cake decorations, trinkets, puzzles, videos. It's all there! (2833, 16th Ave., 905-477-8100; from Hwy 404 North, take exit #29/16th Avenue eastbound).

NEARBY ATTRACTIONS
Fantasy Fair (15-min.) .... p. 35
Humber Arboretum (15-min.) .... p. 294

Pearson International Airport
· Mississauga
(416) 247-7678

D-3
N-W
of Toronto
30-min.

 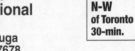 **Schedule:** Heavy air traffic peaks daily between 3 and 7 pm, with most impressive sightings on weekends.

Admission: FREE admission to unofficial observation points.

Directions: The Coffee Time is located at 215 Carlingview St., just east of Hwy 427. You reach it via Dixon Rd. eastbound. You can reach the viewing spot on Airport Rd. via Dixon Rd. westbound (it is the west-end extension of Dixon Rd.).

Plane watching from Airport Road.

TORONTO AEROSPACE MUSEUM

Photo: Courtesy of Toronto Aerospace Museum

This one takes off!

The museum is located in the original factory of the manufacturer The de Havilland Aircraft of Canada Ltd (currently Bombardier). Bombardier continues to use the adjacent runway for testing and delivery of aircraft, and planes continue to be restored on the premises.

Other things displayed among the eclectic collection: a huge grey aircraft with folded wings (the last Canadian tracker built at Downsview, initially used to detect submarines) and the Ornithopter (an experimental craft designed by researchers from the University of Toronto to fly by flapping its wings), an aerobatic kit aircraft, a glider and a simulator from the 40's.

Volunteer staff involved with the museum are obviously skilled in collecting and restoring artifacts from the aviation heritage of the GTA but I was surprised by their visible effort to exhibit it in an interesting manner to the best of their abilities.

If a staff member proudly shows you the full-scale replica of the Avro Arrow under construction, learn why he's so enthusiastic about it. It turns out the Arrow has quite an intriguing story. Built around 1958, it was capable of going at twice the speed of sound, still accelerating at over 1,000 mph while climbing 50,000 feet. Experts agreed that it was 20 years ahead of its time. Yet, the government of the day ordered the production stopped and destroyed all aircrafts and plans! An order that wasn't followed through apparently! When completed (which should be soon!) visitors will be able to activate some basic controls on the replica.

You can watch the work-in-progress restoration of the Lancaster, a famous Second World War bomber Torontonians used to see on a pedestal in front of the CNE. Kids will love to see the ejector seat (which they can't touch) and the cockpit simulator, which they can touch, but this is basically the only thing you can touch when self-exploring the museum.

In the "Blue Room" you'll find old machinery and panels about early women pilots, competitive flying and more, along with rows of real passenger aircraft seats.

TIPS (fun for 8 years +)

• Their small shop offers a wide selection of original trinkets, videos, books and models related to airplanes.

• Check their **Wings & Wheels Heritage Festival** on the last Saturday of May including the flying of dozens of aircraft, continuous demonstrations of model flight and a vintage automobile parade.

NEARBY ATTRACTIONS
Downsview Park (2-min.) .... p. 293

Toronto Aerospace Museum	D-3 N-W of downtown 35-min.

• North York
(416) 638-6078
www.torontoaerospacemuseum.com

  Schedule: Wednesday to Saturday and Holiday Mondays, 10 am to 4 pm (closes at 8 pm on Wednesdays). Sunday, 12 noon to 4 pm.

Admission: $8/adults, $6/seniors, $5/students 6-17 years old, FREE under 6, $20/family (little extra for interesting guided tour).

Directions: 65 Carl Hall Rd., North York. From Hwy 401, take Allen Rd. North and turn west on Sheppard Ave. The Downsview Park's entrance is south of Sheppard and east of Keele. Take John Drury Dr. once in the park and turn left on Carl Hall Rd, past the railway tracks.

INDUSTRIAL ALLIANCE KITEFEST

Go fly a kite!

Everybody's nose is pointing up. Everywhere we look into the open sky, there's a kite punctuating the blue background. I have never seen so many of them at once. One looks like an electric ray swimming above our heads. Others are huge and crazy. Every child wants to emulate the adults by making their own little kites lift up into the air in the open flying field.

The last time I visited **Milliken Park**, it was dwarfed by the huge sky. I thought it was a shame that all the tall trees were found in a tiny patch of forest by the pond, leaving the rest of the park without shaded spots. Now that I see it as the site of a great kite festival, it seems perfect.

Kite flying is an art which originated in China many thousands of years ago. It is not surprising that the whole Chinese community seems to be meeting at this event. The KiteFest is organized by the Mandarin Club of Toronto (assisted by the Toronto Kite Fliers).

Industrial Alliance KiteFest offers professional kite flying demonstrations by teams from around the world, and usually includes free kite flying classes for the

public, international kite exhibits and kite design competitions.

We saw, floating in the air, a three-dimensional kite shaped like two gigantic legs with running shoes and shorts as well as a huge character dressed like Superman from a favourite children's television program.

The park's playground comes in very handy for parents who wish to try kite flying themselves (it keeps the kids busy!).

TIPS (fun for 4 years +)
• More on **Milliken Park** on p. 292.
• The City staff have nothing to do with the organization of the festival. The park is rented by the Mandarin Club, a private group, for the occasion. Alliance has been the sponsor for many years. It could change in the future and therefore change the official name of the event. You can check **Toronto Kite Fliers'** website for the exact date of the KiteFest and for a list of kite flying events (**www.tkf.toronto.on.ca**).
• It would be real torture for children to show up at such an event without having access to a kite. Traditionally, the festival offers a paper kite make-and-take craft activity for a minimal fee. Also, kite vendors are on the premises, offering affordable or unusual kites for sale.
• Snacks and Chinese food are sold on the premises.

NEARBY ATTRACTIONS
Woodie Wood Chucks (15-min.) ..... p. 196
Agincourt Pool (15-min.) .... p. 421

Industrial Alliance KiteFest · Scarborough www.tkf.toronto.on.ca	D-3 N-E of downtown 35-min.

  Schedule: Usually on a mid-September weekend, 11 am to 4 pm (check event calendar on Toronto Kite Flier's website).
Admission: FREE (approximately $2 charge for material to build a small kite).
Directions: Milliken Park, Scarborough (at the intersection of Steeles Ave. East and McCowan Rd.).

FOUR WINDS KITE FESTIVAL

wind was rather timid! As a result, only the experienced participants managed to raise their flying apparatus into the air. The smaller amateurs' kites only went up slightly, thanks to air drafts generated by laughing children pulling on their toys' tight cords. We had a lot of fun, regardless.

Most young children remain within the small valleys surrounding the Visitor Centre. Farther, past a vast field, is the site where real pros compete for two days.

High four!

Need to get out for some air (with the kids in tow)? During the first weekend in May, if Mother Nature bestows good winds upon us, you'll want to take advantage of this event. When decent wind is part of the picture, loads of large, graceful kites colour the sky.

The few times we attended the festival held at the Kortright Centre, the

TIPS (fun for 4 years +)

• More about **Kortright Centre** on pages 147 and 296.
• If it has rained for a few days prior to the festival, rubber boots are a must.
• Upon arrival, check if they've planned a "Teddy Bear Drop" (they've done this in the past) which involves the dropping from flying kites of a couple of furry creatures equipped with parachutes, which gently fall before young spectators' eyes.
• Around **Kortright Centre**'s main building, kids pull small kites that they build themselves. The centre supplies little builders with the instructions, paper, balsam sticks, glue and string. This craft is suitable for children aged 4 years and up and costs around $5. The gift shop normally sells some kites.
• Check the **Industrial Alliance Kite-Fest** held in September, on p. 210.

These artists, solo or as part of a team, create impressive ballets with their splendid kites, to the sound of music. The public can get a close look at their kites before they fly. There are individual precision and ballet disciplines, as well as "quad-line" kites (pulled by four strings), and team competitions.

Four Winds Festival	C-2
• Maple (905) 832-2289 or (416) 661-6600 ext. 5602 www.kortright.org	**North** of Toronto **40-min.**

Schedule: Last weekend in April or the first weekend in May, from 10 am to 4 pm. Call to check the exact date. (2008: May 3 & 4)
Admission: $6/adults, $5/children, FREE for children 4 years and under. Parking $3.
Directions: From Hwy 400 North, take exit #35/Major Mackenzie Dr. westbound. Turn south on Pine Valley Dr., follow signs.

CANADIAN WARPLANE MUSEUM

Down-to-Earth airplanes

When we arrive, children's imaginations are fired up by a real jet, its nose pointing towards the sky like a church steeple. More than forty, genuine, functioning specimens now await in the museum's immense hangar. Add cabins, cockpits, switches and buttons to explore and you get a great family outing!

Before entering the hangar, we saw a display on the use of planes in Canadian military history. Budding pilots enjoyed operating the model airplanes. (Note that the displays change every four months.) Then, we circulated among the impressive hangar's fleet bathed in natural light.

The wheels of certain planes were as tall as my future pilot. Part of the site is dedicated to the restoration of a few vintage models. It's an excellent opportunity to appreciate aeronautical engineering while examining airplanes from every angle.

We're not allowed to touch most of the gleaming aircraft, but don't worry, we can access a few specimens and their engaging cockpits: a real WWII trainer or a real CF-100 jet aircraft. We can also manipulate (from the outside) the array of controls in a Silver T-33 training aircraft. Not often do we get the chance to see a plane's landing gear in action! Children love the two-seat Flying Boxcar simulator, with its wall-to-wall switches and dials.

Stairs at the back of the hangar lead to an observation deck, from which we have an overview of the museum's squadron.

Higher up the stairs, we can access the exterior terrace, from which other planes can be seen. At the bottom of the stairs is a cafeteria-style restaurant in a vast room and, best of all, a panoramic view of the outside. Paved roads connect with the **Hamilton International Airport**'s runways, located 1 km away.

TIPS (fun for 4 years +)

• Most aircraft are maintained in flying condition. On most days (weather permitting), you will have the chance to observe a vintage aircraft in flight.
• During the 2008 Father's Day weekend, the museum will offer a **Fly Fest** when all of the planes are out and there's a midway for kids.
• A company has started to offer **Ultimate Children's Party** on the museum's grounds, with $15 admission including unlimited midway rides, shows, access to the museum and more (2008: March 8 & 9, November 8 & 9). Check **www.hamiltonshows.com** for details.
• The museum's gift shop is well stocked.

Canadian Warplane Heritage Museum • Mount Hope (905) 679-4183 www.warplane.com	E-2 S-W of Toronto 70-min.

Schedule: Open year-round, 9 am to 5 pm.
Admission: Around $10/adults, $9/seniors and students, $6/6-12 years, FREE for children 5 years and under.
Directions: Hamilton International Airport, 9280 Airport Rd., Mount Hope. Take QEW West, follow Hwy 403 towards Hamilton, exit at Hwy 6 South and follow the museum's signs.

ABOUT FIRE STATIONS

Dare to ask

Firefighters and their red fire trucks are fascinating (and I'm not even considering their calendars in the equation). They're the heroes in our cities and we can always count on them.

I knocked at the door of a fire station in my neighbourhood to enquire about their policy regarding children dropping in to meet with them. A young fireman in his socks opened the door, flashing a Tom Cruise smile. It felt like I had entered someone's living room, which is basically what I had done since firefighters often work shifts of 24 hours during which their station is their home.

I learned that between two runs, they normally will take a few minutes to talk to wide-eyed children and let them touch the fire truck. Chances are they will even let the child sit in the driver's seat.

I read somewhere that a small station can be called 5 to 8 times a day, approximately 1,500 times a year (half of these being related to fire).

Do you know why the old fire stations have high towers? No, it is not so

they could build in a giant clock for the neighbourhood to see. Firefighters use it to hang the fire hoses in to dry!

Today's Parent Kidsummer (p. 28) usually includes a special evening presenting a unique chance to watch live firefighting demonstrations at the firefighter's training station on 895 Eastern Avenue in Toronto. Check **Kidsummer**'s calendar to learn when it is offered this year.

During the **Fire Prevention Week** (on the second week of October), they also offer activities, displays and firefighting demonstrations on their Eastern location.

TIPS (fun for 3 years +)

• It is possible for your school or other organizations to book a fire station tour or to have a fire truck visit a specific event! Send your request to fire@toronto.ca at least three weeks in advance. It is free and the worst that can happen is that the tour is cancelled because they have to respond to an emergency.

• There's the **Canadian Fire Fighter's Museum** in Port Hope. I haven't had a chance to visit it but it seems to have a lot to offer and it is located near a beach. See **www.firemuseumcanada.com** for details (95 Mill Street South, Port Hope, (905) 885-8985, open daily from Victoria Day to Thanksgiving, 9 am to 5 pm, admission by donation).

Toronto Fire Services
(416) 338-9050
www.toronto.ca/fire

 Schedule: Drop by to the fire station of your choice to see if you can do a short tour. Check their website in the summer and closer to October for the dates of their open houses with firefighting demonstrations (or call Access Toronto: 416-338-0338).

Admission: FREE.
Directions: Check the **Fire Station Locations** section on their website.

DOUBLE-DECKER RIDES

On top of things

"I have not had a good hair day since I started this job" claims the tour operator. I believe her. As we drive under the Gardiner, we feel quite a draft!

Hop-On Hop-Off City Tour used to be the only ones offering this tour. Now, Shop-Dine-Tour Toronto offers a similar double-decker guided tour called **Jump On & Jump Off**. Both last two hours and include at least 20 stops.

There are a few things you can experience only if you've taken a ride on the top of a double-decker. You get to see the top of the TTC buses, your head is at times only a metre away from the traffic

lights, and branches get close enough to brush your hair.

My daughter also enjoyed having a closer look at the **CN Tower**. She saw the huge characters fooling around on the **Rogers Centre** balcony, bronze workers on top of a bridge, a restaurant's roof turned into a hockey table with rotating players and the Flatiron building's mural looking like a painting peeling off its facade.

Your ticket gives you the right to step on and off as you wish, throughout the day, at any of the stops. I recommend combining this ride with a visit to one of the attractions along the circuit: **Harbourfront Centre**, **Hockey Hall of Fame**, **Royal Ontario Museum**, **Casa Loma** and the likes (it would save you the parking fees!). Make sure you know the time of the last departure from that attraction!

TIPS (fun for 5 years +)

• You can buy your ticket online and print it.
• Tickets from both operators are valid for two consecutive days.
• This kind of ride is meant for tourists. As a Torontonian, I think too many stops take place in front of hotels in uninteresting areas to justify the ride for the sheer pleasure of admiring the city I live in. But it is really worth it if, like my son, your child has shown a fascination for double-deckers.

NEARBY ATTRACTIONS	
Around Dundas Subway Station	p. 450
Think Big! Stroll	p. 466
Hidden Treasure Stroll	p. 473

Jump On & Jump Off
(416) 463-7467
www. sightseeingtoronto.com

D-3
Downtown Toronto by CN Tower

Schedule: From May to October, runs every hour from 9 am to 5 pm. Call for winter schedule.
Admission: $33/adults, $30/seniors and students, $20/3-12 years old, $95/family of 4.
Directions: Advisable to depart from the Hard Rock Café at 279 Yonge St. near the Eaton Centre.

Hop-On Hop-Off City Tour
1-800-595-3310
www.grayline.ca (click **Toronto**)
Schedule: North-South loop offered year-round; East-West loop from May to September. Call for exact hours.
Admission: $34/adults, $30/seniors and students, $23/4-11 years old, $100/family of 4 ($15 for additional child).
Directions: Advisable to depart from Nicholby's Souvenir Shop, 123 Front St. West, near the CN Tower.

SOAP BOX DERBY

Watching over you

The soap box cars are lined up along the top of Centre Road in High Park. Feverishly, Big and Little Brothers add the finishing touches to their creations: calibrating wheels, polishing hoods and fixing gadgets as they wait for the derby to start. Each in their own way, the kids are so proud; it is pure pleasure to read the emotion on their faces. What a fabulous project for them to undertake and for us to watch!

Two by two, in categories previously established in time trials, the young racers get ready for the signal. The small crowd at the bottom of the hill is already cheering.

The 10-year-old I am observing dries his hands on his pants before grabbing the steering wheel. His smile could not be broader. As his Big Brother pushes him down the hill, he gently reminds him to lean forward to increase his speed by becoming more aerodynamic. I laugh out loud as I read "Eat my Dust" on the Little Brother's bumper!

Many cars are pretty basic, built out of wood, screws and metal wire from a pre-made kit. This is usually a telltale sign of new teams participating in their first race. Veterans have had all year to improve their vehicles.

Some cars are covered with silvery metal or aerodynamically-shaped fibreglass, others have flames painted on their sides. One ambitious Little Brother claims that next year, he'll have a radio in his car.

My son was so impressed by the cars that he started to recycle garbage in order to build a car of his own. Watching other boys driving cars at a soap box derby will do that to you!

Since my last edition, the derby has been expanded to include Big and Little Sisters as well! That should spice up the race!

TIPS (fun for 5 years +)
• More about **High Park** on p. 286.
• See **All Fired Up** in the Royal York Subway Station section on p. 438.

NEARBY ATTRACTIONS
Sunnyside Café (10-min.) .... p. 404

Soap Box Derby (416) 925-8981, ext. 4138 www.bbbst.com	**D-3** **West** **of downtown** **20-min.**

Schedule: Usually a mid-September Saturday. If raining, it takes place the following day. The whole Derby runs from 12 noon to 4:30 pm but the part where the Little Brothers compete one against the other starts at around 2 pm until 5 pm.

Admission: FREE.

Directions: Centre Rd. in High Park, Toronto (on southwest corner of Bloor St. West and Parkside Dr.). From the Bloor entrance, drive to Grenadier Restaurant and walk east to Centre Rd.

CENTENNIAL PARK MINI-INDY

Step on it!

According to my young co-pilot, I drive my go-kart like a grandma on a Sunday outing. Since everybody is passing us, I must admit he has a point, so I step on it!

To drive on the 2km (1 1/2 mile) clover leaf track, one has to be at least 54 inches tall or 10 years of age and older. Anyone however, can be a co-pilot and ride for free.

Younger drivers (5 to 9 years old), can try their hand riding smaller cars on the kiddie track. Considering the expression on my pint-size Villeneuve, I would say he felt empowered by the whole experience!

After a couple of rides, we bought tokens to play with some 30 machines in the 3,000-sq.-ft. arcade by the ticket booth.

TIPS (fun for 5 years +)

• It is advisable to call ahead as the attractions are sometimes closed for private or corporate functions.
• At the south end of the park, you will find a big wading pool with spray pads, and a greenhouse you can visit for free. These are fun alternatives for little ones who can't accompany their older siblings on the go-kart rides.
• Ask about **401 Mini-Indy**, their indoor go-kart track with more powerful vehicles and Junior go-karts only children 10 to 15 years old and 54" can drive during Family Hours, located at 37 Stoffel Rd., North York, (416) 614-6789, **www.mini-indy.com**.
• More on **Centennial Park** during the winter on p. 369.

NEARBY ATTRACTIONS
Playdium Mississauga (20-min.) ... p. 22
Pearson Int'l Airport (5-min.) .... p. 206

Centennial Park Mini-Indy	D-3 N-W of downtown 30-min.

Centennial Park Mini-Indy
• Etobicoke
(416) 620-6669 (go-kart)
(416) 394-8750 (park)
www.centennialmini-indy.com

Schedule: Usually open daily mid-June to mid-September, 11 am to 10 pm. Open Friday to Sunday, 11 am to 9 pm, mid-September to end of October. Call for exact hours.

Admission: $4.25/lap on the big track (passenger does not pay), $21.50/6 rides, $4.25/5 laps on the kiddie track.

Directions: 575 Centennial Park Blvd, Toronto. From Hwy 427 North, take exit Rathburn Rd. westbound, turn north on Centennial Park. FREE on-site parking.

CANADIAN AUTOMOTIVE MUSEUM

Hot wheels

This Museum is the only place I know where I could feed my son's passion for cars. It is probably the least interactive museum I've visited with children. But I couldn't resist including it in this guide. It is filled with over 60 vehicles from 1898 to 1980 displayed in an authentic car dealership.

The Canadian Automotive Museum (CAM) itself is not fancy. The first floor is made of cement, pipes run on the low ceilings and there's not much room for all the beautiful cars. However, memorabilia related to the different periods of vehicles make it fun to explore. Don't forget to raise your head at the entrance. You wouldn't want to miss the vintage red racing car pinned to the ceiling!

The children who know the movie *Chitty Chitty Bang Bang* will think they recognize it in many of the cars displayed. There are also a couple of antique fire trucks.

On the second floor it's easy to observe the progression from horse carriages to cars. We can see wooden vehicles that were made by a carriage builder from Oshawa named McLaughlin. When increasing speed made the windshield a necessity, roofs were added and the look of cars changed dramatically from carriages (although it's funny we're still talking about horse power!).

TIPS (fun for 5 years +)

• The CAM was created for big kids with a driver's license! Don't go expecting interactive activities. In addition, the classy 1926 Bentley, sassy 1931 Alfa Romeo, gorgeous 1939 Rolls Royce, and all the other shiny cars are not to be touched, a rule which can be extremely frustrating for a young child.

• If you've come this far, pay a visit to the **Oshawa Aeronautical, Military and Industrial Museum**. In the last few years, they have reorganized the space around the time line of the origin and evolution

of the militia (King Louis X1V ordered Frontenac to create the first "milice" in Canada in 1669), with a focus on all the generals up to today. Paul Dolly, who gives tours, is passionate on the subject. The museum owns 71 restored and working war vehicles, of which we can see some 30 around the site. Kids 7 years and older will appreciate these and displays of uniforms and weapons.

NEARBY ATTRACTIONS

Kids Zone (15-min.) .... p. 200

Canadian Automotive Museum	C-4 East of Toronto 40-min.
• Oshawa (905) 576-1222	

Schedule: Open year-round Monday to Friday, 9 am to 5 pm; Saturday and Sunday, 10 am to 6 pm.
Admission: $5/adults, $4.50/seniors and students, $3.50/6-11 years, $13.50/family of 4, FREE for 5 years and under.
Directions: 99 Simcoe St. South, Oshawa. From Hwy 401 East, take exit #417/Simcoe Stree northbound; the museum is on the east side.

Oshawa Military & Industrial Museum
(905) 728-6199
(905) 723-9930 (to book a tour)
Schedule: Friday, Saturday and Sunday, 1 pm to 5 pm, Easter to November 1 (call for tours rest of year).
Admission: Around $4/adults, $3/seniors, FREE 12 years and under.
Directions: 1000 Stevenson Rd. North, Oshawa. From the Automotive Museum, take Simcoe St. northbound, turn west on Rossland Rd., then turn north on Stevenson Rd.

For both museums:
 www.oshawa.ca (click **Things to do**, then **Attractions**, then **Museums**)

GO TRAIN RIDE

One, two, three... GO!

For children fascinated by anything on wheels, the GO Train offers the ultimate experience of a real train journey. Most importantly, it costs a fraction of the price of a regular train ride and you don't end up far from home. Lets not forget it's just as important to enjoy the scenery as it is to know where you're going!

Union Station, on Front Street, is a great starting point for a child's first ride on the GO Train. Suburban and intercity trains are next to one another and children get the chance to see imposing locomotives from up close.

Green and white signs lead us to the GO Train's ticket office and customer service department. When we stopped there to ask for information, we got lucky, they gave my son a few gadgets to celebrate his initiation. (Ask if they have some handy!)

After admiring a large mural decorating the outside of a railcar, we sat on the train's second level in order to see far-

ther. We were facing south to take in the view of Lake Ontario. Seats are very comfortable and each car is equipped with restrooms... A real train!

After analyzing GO destinations, we decided the most interesting was Pickering with the varied panorama of its itinerary: downtown skyscrapers, residential neighbourhoods, countryside and most of all, long stretches alongside Lake Ontario (and in our case, this line passes right in front of our house!). The ride to Pickering lasts 40 minutes and doesn't require a transfer. Pickering is the 6th stop.

To prolong the excursion, you can take the local bus from **Pickering Station** up to the **Pickering Town Centre** (www.pickeringtowncentre.com). We went there to have a bite to eat and check the **Mastermind Toys**. You'll also find the movie theatre **Cineplex Pickering 8**.

TIPS (fun for 3 years +)

• A day pass is sold at the cost of two single fares and allows one person unlimited rides between two specified zones throughout the day of purchase. This is perfect if you want to get off at different stations and catch the following train.

• There's a fare calculator on their website.

• I recommend that you avoid the stress of rush hour, favouring departures between 9:30 am and 2:30 pm. You'll be sure to get a window seat, as there are fewer passengers on board outside peak times! Little ones can be rambunctious without disturbing too much.

NEARBY ATTRACTIONS

GO Transit
(416) 869-3200
www.gotransit.com

D-3
Downtown
Toronto
5-min.

Schedule: Daily, from early in the morning to late at night.
Admission: An adult day pass for Union-Pickering-Union costs about $11. It is half the price for children under 12 years and FREE for 4 years and under per each accompanying adult.
Directions to Union Station: On Front St., Toronto (between Bay and York St.).

CHRISTMAS TRAIN SHOW

Adults play too!

My action-driven son is fascinated by the small trains riding full speed on parallel tracks. His friend, the observant type, is absorbed in the examination of detailed small-scale landscapes. My young daughter is delighted by every display featuring a cow in a field. Whatever their personality, a child's attention is sure to be caught at a train show.

The model train shows I have visited never had a unified look to them. But each model railway association represented there was a small world in itself.

One association tested children's observation skills by providing a list of funny details to spot on the landscape and allowed them to pick chocolate balls from the display. Another was quite interactive, allowing visitors to play with remote controls moving lifts up and down, handle baggage, control the saw mills and more.

One long train track was set on the floor. We saw a couple of miniature circuses by the railway in small towns.

Some buildings along the track in some exhibits were real pieces of art. We could even observe some exhibitors in the process of building copper trains from scratch. Such shows could easily become more interactive but let's not forget that their main purpose is not to amuse small kids. It is to delight the child within big people...

TIPS (fun for 3 years +)

• I saw a dad carrying a little stool for his 4-year-old. It is a great idea since many displays are 48" high, preventing the younger ones from seeing without help.
• Not all exhibitors have the same attitude towards children. Some get really nervous with them. Make sure you are in control of your little ones' hands unless you want to see a grown man cry!
• There was nothing really "festive" about the Toronto Christmas Train Show (except for a few small Santas here and there) but it offered enough train displays to make it worth the visit.
• There are tables and a snack bar on the premises.
• For a good list of train shows around the GTA, I suggest you check **www.railtronics.com** and click on **Schedules**.

MODEL RAILROAD CLUB

Children are up to this attraction

Fascinated children of all ages are perched on steps running alongside the huge raised table. They watch small locomotives pulling long strings of railcars through villages, mountains and a harbour. Behind them, impressed adults admire the genius of miniaturization. This is the result of 180,000 hours of work by passionate people!

You can forget the metric system as everything displayed here is built to a one-forty-eighth scale! Railcars that measure 40 feet in reality barely make 10 inches. The entire set, inspired by the styles of the 1955-62 period, comprises the equivalent of 10 miles of track.

The installation sits approximately a metre and a half off the floor. One has to actually walk around it to truly measure the magnitude of this ambitious set.

All the children in our small group easily found an observation point, changing places frequently so as to capture every angle of the fourteen moving trains. It took them more than an hour to get their visual fill!

Cargo and passenger trains, even circus trains, move along cliffs taken on by mountain climbers. They border a little harbour with its busy docks, construction sites, villages, factories and warehouses. Here, a fisherman indulges in his sport. There, a tow truck is pulling a car out of the ditch. Together, these contribute to making the installation incredibly realistic along with tunnels, huge suspended bridge, aqueducts, turntable, overpasses with real light signals and even a soundtrack of moving trains!

Installed at the centre of the set with remote controls in hand, switchmen are directing railway traffic. They are members of the Model Railroad Club of Toronto, the 70-year-old association responsible for this wondrous display.

TIPS (fun for 3 years +)

• The association is located within a large complex of numbered warehouses. Follow the parking signs from King Street West and Atlantic Ave.
• As visitors circulate within a two-metre-wide corridor around the set, manoeuvering strollers is impossible. Comfortably nestled in my arms, my little one did not mind and was perfectly positioned to view the railway activity.
• If your kids are truly hooked and ask for more, make sure to read the association's posted notices advertising other similar events and activities held regularly by other regional associations.
• There is a food vendor on site where beverages and snacks are available at a reasonable price.

NEARBY ATTRACTIONS
High Park (10-min.) .... p. 286

Model Railroad Club of Toronto (416) 536-8927 www. modelrailroadclub.com	D-3 Downtown Toronto 10-min.

Schedule: Usually on the last three Sundays of February, 12 noon to 4:30 pm, call for exact dates.
Admission: $8/adults, $5/seniors, $4/children.
Directions: 171 East Liberty St., Suite B1, Toronto (note it is the same building as before, which now has a different civic address, formerly 37 Hanna Ave.). From King St. West, take Atlantic Ave. southbound, then Liberty St. eastbound.

RICHMOND HILL LIVE STEAMERS

I found the (rail) way!

The track site lies in a beautiful woodland setting, in harmony with the trees. From the road, we can barely see it, but can hear the whistles' wet hissing, as the small steam engines rustle along the 7 1/4-inch wide tracks.

On location, you see marvels of miniature trains, their steam puffing high; those little guys use real coal to produce their steam! At close range, you can even feel droplets coming down on your shoulders as they quickly condense; a refreshing mist on a hot summer day.

In addition to the miniature track, there are two larger tracks that cover the entire site. Many trains circulate on them, and they are conducted for the most part by enthusiasts, outfitted with overalls and caps. Some of these hand-built steam engines range in cost up to $40,000. This is the achievement of some passionate members of the Richmond Hill Live Steam-

ers, dedicated to the craft for more than twenty years.

On the central track, the shortest, the steam engines carry one passenger at a time. Conductor and passenger are literally straddling the small but solid locomotives. They go past a water tower and over a bridge. As for the track that surrounds the site, it boasts larger and stronger trains that can carry up to 16 passengers on their small cars, and travel through the forest site.

Richmond Hill Live Steamers • Stouffville (416) 261-9789 www.geocities.com/ richmondhill_livesteam	C-3 N-E of Toronto 45-min.

Schedule: Open Houses usually held the weekend after Canada Day and the weekend after Labour Day, 10:30 am to 4 pm. Check website for exact dates. For 2008, gates are open June to September most Sundays, 1 pm to 3 pm, weather permitting.
Admission: Donations appreciated.
Directions: 15922 McCowan Road, Stouffville. From Hwy 404 North, take exit #45/Aurora Sideroad eastbound, turn north on McCowan Rd. The site is on the south-west corner of St. John's Sideroad and McCowan.

TIPS (fun for 3 years +)

• I recommend you arrive before noon to avoid long line-ups leading to the individual rides. Otherwise, we waited no more than 10 minutes for a ride on the larger train with wagons.
• You can buy snacks, burgers and hot dogs on site during the Open House events. Washrooms are also available.

NEARBY ATTRACTIONS
Whitchurch (5-min.) .... p. 305
Burd's Family Fishing (15-min.) ..... p. 342

ABERFOYLE JUNCTION

A labour of love

So many details, such a beautiful layout recreating the Southern Ontario of the 50's, so many little stories going on... There's no doubt this attraction is a labour of love undertaken by very keen-eyed and patient artisans.

One of the most original features of this miniature world is the night fall (a 10-minute dusk to dawn sequence every 40 minutes or so).

At one point during your visit, the light will gradually fade until all that's left to see is the little bright rectangles of the windows lit from within the small buildings and trains.

Then, you start to distinguish details you hadn't noticed before: passengers in the wagons, customers inside the tiny restaurants and shops, and street lights.

"I saw the Polar Express!" swears a little boy by my side. Maybe not, but

if you look closely, you could see: campers on the verge of being bothered by a bear, a mother petting a cat and waving at her kids in the water, a fisherman and his dog, a musician playing the banjo and kids selling lemonade. You'll even see someone escaping from a hotel's window with the help of good old sheets tied together, and a life model posing in the nude for a painter.

The miniatures are done in "O" scale (or 1/4 inch for every foot), which means a 40-foot wagon would measure 10 inches on the model railway. Most of what you see was hand built with only basic purchased parts rearranged according to the artists imagination. Amazing!

High rises are being raised, houses are being built and streets are being repaired. It's a busy town.

When you notice a restaurant called Sam & Ella's, you realize the creators had fun with the signage too.

A few families are visiting. "Duck!" shouts a mother to her husband holding their son on his shoulders. They were so taken by all the action that they had not seen the floor of the control tower running the trains, two metres above the ground.

There's also real amateurs talking shop and gathering ideas for their own projects. "We could do a hole in the wall", says a woman. "I don't think the basement could take it structurally", answers the husband. These people mean business!

TIPS (fun for 3 years +)
• A dad brought in a rubber stool for his son, the best thing to make sure kids can see (without touching).
• There's a cozy little snack bar selling hot dogs and snacks.
• In the tiny gift shop they sell, among other things, a die-cast set of trains for $9, posters for $15 and a DVD of the attraction for $30 (which you can watch while sitting at the tables in the snack bar.

NEARBY ATTRACTIONS
Yeehaw Farm (20 min.) .... p. 140
Mountsberg Wildlife (15-min.) ..... p. 298

Aberfoyle Junction
• Aberfoyle
(519) 836-2720
(905) 527-5474
www.
aberfoylejunction.com

D-2
N-W
of Toronto
50-min.

 Schedule: Spring show, usually first two weekends in May; Fall Show, usually the three weekends following Thanksgiving; from 10 am to 4:30 pm.
Admission: $7/adults, $5/seniors, $4/children.
Directions: From Hwy 401, take exit #299, go northbound on Brock Rd. for 1.5 km (it is on the east side).

YORK-DURHAM RAILWAY

Its windows don't open very wide, but the car is comfortable and, above all, there's a space between the seats big enough for children to hide in.

There, my young Captain Kirk imagined a spaceship, while others saw it as a tent or a little house. At that age, it's impossible to look at the scenery for two hours!

Chug-a-chug-a-chug-a... Choo-choo!

The train ride from Stouffville to Uxbridge can be summarized with the above words. It's a two-hour ride for the return trip on a 1900's diesel train. That's enough "choo-choos" to fill young railroad men's (and women's) ears for quite a while, believe me!

Don't forget this excursion's goal isn't to go somewhere, but rather to offer children the experience of a train ride.

If you can, visit the railcars before choosing one, as there are different types. I opted for one with wine-red upholstery.

Conductors are attentive to children and answer all their questions. I also recommend you take your children for a walk through the moving train. They'll love to watch the tracks from the last wagon.

The railroad passes through fields and woods. We only got off to stretch our legs at the last train station, in Uxbridge, and chose to catch our train back right away.

If you go on an early departure you can choose to stay in Stouffville while you wait for the next train (make sure there is a next train!).

TIPS (fun for 4 years +)

• Watch the children while they walk through the train. They could pinch their fingers in the joints between cars, as it moves with each bump.
• The Stouffville-Uxbridge railroad crosses many rural roads and has to blow its whistle each time. My two-month old daughter was stressed by the "CHOO... CHOO's" that delighted her brother!
• They sell snacks on the train. There's no food available at the Uxbridge station. However, you'll find portable toilets on the station's grounds and you have just enough time to walk to Brock Street to buy drinks and snacks for your return trip.
• Call to find out about the railway's special events: **Teddy Bear Run**, **Halloween** trains, **Ride with Santa** and more (must reserve seats).

NEARBY ATTRACTIONS

York-Durham Heritage Railway • Stouffville (905) 852-3696 www.ydhr.on.ca	C-3 N-E of Toronto 40-min.

 Schedule: Open weekends, June to mid-October. Trains will depart from Uxbridge and Stouffville at least two times daily (check website for exact time).

 Admission: Return fare is $22/adults, $20/seniors and students, $18/2-12 years,$65/family of 5, FREE for children under 2 years.

 Directions: Stouffville Go Station, Stouffville. From Hwy 404 North, take exit #37/Stouffville Rd. eastbound; the road becomes Main St. The Stouffville station is located east of 9th Line, on the north side of Main Rd.

SOUTH SIMCOE RAILWAY

Full steam ahead !

Here we are, my son and I, in the middle of nowhere, an hour away from Toronto. Fortunately, the return trip is included. We'll come back to our starting point after a charming 45-minute ride in a vintage 1920's railcar pulled by a steam engine dating back to 1883.

You have to see the children's eyes when they watch the small train in the distance get closer and finally appear as the colossus it really is, with its whistle and its plume of steam.

Because there's only one track, the

locomotive has no other choice but to move forward and then to back up. Mind you, it makes no difference from a passenger's point of view. For part of the ride, we see backyards full of flowers and a few commercial plots of land. Then comes the countryside with farms, cows, cornfields and trees. Most trees along the track are deciduous and must take on beautiful colours during the fall.

When you're riding, try to make your children listen to what the conductor says, especially when he is telling the story of the train that disappeared into the river on a foggy night, a long time ago. To put us in the mood, the conductor stops the train and blows the whistle three times, hoping that the ghost of the missing train will answer back...

At the end of the line, we wait a few minutes before heading back. "We're waiting, because all the wheels must be reinstalled for us before we head in the other direction" the conductor seriously explains. It takes kids a few seconds to wrap their minds around that one!

TIPS (fun for 4 years +)
• It's best to get there 30 minutes before departure time. After you've parked and paid for your ticket, you'll be able to wait for the train to arrive (and hear it coming as well).
• Inside the railcars, don't expect luxury. Giving some of the seats a good knock could release a 50-year-old cloud of dust! Just in case, don't wear white pants...
• There's a small gift shop.
• Call to find out about their **Santa Train.** (You must buy tickets in advance.)
• On hot summer days, you'll be happy to take advantage of the **Tottenham Conservation Area**'s beach and playground, located less than 5 minutes from the train station on Mill Street.

NEARBY ATTRACTIONS	
Falconry Centre (5-min.)	p. 68
Puck's Farm (15-min.)	p. 138

South Simcoe Railway • Tottenham (905) 936-5815 www.steamtrain.com	C-2 N-W of Toronto 60-min.

Schedule: Open every Sunday and Holiday Monday, from Victoria Day weekend to one week after Thanksgiving (plus Monday and Tuesday in July and August as well as last Saturday of September and first two Saturdays in October). There are usually 4 departures between 10:30 am and 3 pm.
Admission: Return fares is $12/adults, $10/seniors, $7/children 3-15 years, FREE for children 2 years and under.
Directions: From Hwy 400 North, take exit #55/Hwy 9 westbound. Turn north on Simcoe Rd. #10/Tottenham Rd. then west on Mill St. (first set of lights in the town).

Halton Radial Railway

On the right track

We climb into the first vehicle ready to leave. It is a superbly renovated passenger train car from the 1915 – 1960 period. It has elegant woodwork, velvet upholstery and copper tin ceiling decorations. Before long, the car heads towards a lavish green forest.

The streetcar museum differs from other railway attractions in the region. First, because its primary activity is the collection and renovation of trains, electric tramways and buses. Second, its track system is short (2km). Instead of offering long rides, the museum offers as many short ones as you wish, on any of the different vehicles available that day.

The museum's collection is large and vehicles are primed for service according to drivers' availability. When we visited, we took a ride aboard the elegant "#8-Steel Car passenger", as well as an open-roof wagon replica of the 1890s, reminiscent of ancient carriages, in which we enjoyed a ride in nature.

Ten minutes later, our train reached the end of the line, not far from a lovely pond. The kids looked at some old abandoned railcars (most likely future renovation projects), including a run down, but amusing caboose that entertained children. Young visitors also enjoyed the opportunity to walk along the tracks.

Upon your return, you may jump into another train ready to leave, or hang around to admire those displayed in the warehouses or in the yards.

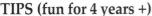

TIPS (fun for 4 years +)

• Make sure to pack some insect repellent; the little bugs are overtly present in the many bushes surrounding Meadowvale Station.

• Call to find out about their **Halloween** events (with haunted car barn and subway car) and **Christmas** special evening events.

• Since my last visit, they've added a gift shop and the **East End Café** in a vintage streetcar!

NEARBY ATTRACTIONS

Halton County Radial Railway
• Milton
(519) 856-9802
www.hcry.org

D-2 West of Toronto 60-min.

 Schedule: Open weekends May to October, 11 am to 4 pm, plus weekdays in July and August, 11 am to 4 pm.

 Admission: Return fares is Around $9.50/adults, $8.50/ seniors, $6.50/4 to 17 years, FREE for children 3 years and under.

 Directions: 13629 Guelph Line, Milton. From Hwy 401 West, take exit #312/Guelph Line northbound.

KAJAMA, THE TALL SHIP

As they came in, guests rearranged the chairs to their liking all over the large and unobstructed deck. Half an hour later, the Kajama left its mooring spot, motors on. The wind was blowing very gently. We headed towards Ontario Place.

Everything looked different from that angle: the amusement park, **Toronto Islands**, the **CN Tower**. My daughter undertook a thorough exploration of the 165-foot deck.

Merrily, merrily...

My 5-year-old was not excited by the promise of the 7,000-square-feet of sail we could potentially put up if the wind allowed, but she was thrilled when the captain summoned us with mock authority to help his crew pull the ropes to set sails. She would have loved the fact that they now fire their own canon on every cruise!

We climbed aboard the Kajama, in the midst of a colourful and lively event at **Harbourfront**, accompanied by a whimsical chaos of music and vendors teasing the crowd, under a blazing sun. The illusion of playing tourists on some exotic cruise in the Islands was perfect.

After a while, I noticed people were more cheerful and relaxed. Each small group seemed involved in its own little private party. Only then, did I realize the captain had shut down the engine and we were actually sailing!

Don't expect the soothing sound of the wind against the sails and the waves brushing the hull. We are in Toronto and it's noisy: with hoards of motor boats in the harbour and planes landing and taking off at Porter Airport, when it is not helicopters flying over our heads.

Still, as my small crew member played hide-and-seek with her dad in the lower deck, I admired the sparkling blue water dotted with dozens of tiny boats right under the nose of the Kajama for the next hour. Now, that's my kind of outing!

TIPS (fun for 5 years +)
• Don't spend too much time trying to figure out the best spot to stay away from the sun. The boat keeps moving and so do the shadows. Bring hats!
• The return sail trip takes around two hours, boarding included.
• You can order from a menu on board.
• There are many other boat tours offered in the harbour: less ambitious, with no need to pre-book. And there's always the ferry! (See **Toronto Islands** on p. 398.)

NEARBY ATTRACTIONS
Harbourfront Centre .... p. 25
Music Gardens (5-min. walk) ...... p. 275

Kajama
(416) 203-2322
www.tallship
cruisestoronto.com

D-3
Downtown
Toronto
5-min.

  Schedule: Daily from July to Labour Day (check website for June's schedule). Boardings at 11:30 am, 1:30 pm and 3:30 pm (departure half an hour later, sailing time is 90 minutes).
Admission: $20/adults, $18/seniors, $11/5 to 15 years old, FREE under 5.
Directions: Harbourfront Centre, Toronto (at the corner of Queen's Quay and Lower Simcoe St. behind Power Plant).

TORONTO HIPPO TOURS

It's a bus! It's a boat! No, it's a Hippo!

We notice something peculiar underneath the vehicle... Long wet weeds! You know, like the ones that can be observed at the bottom of Lake Ontario. The fact is, Hippo's drivers have to be licensed marine captains to be allowed to pilot the intriguing Canadian-made amphibious buses.

The kids are already excited by the overall look of the vehicle, adorned with colourful depictions of hippos in the water. Accessing the bus from a rear entrance just adds to the novelty. The windows are large and part of the ceiling is glass so we know we'll get a good view of Toronto's tall buildings throughout the tour. (Some of their buses have such glass ceilings, others have canvas).

My young companions feel like royalty when they see the reactions our hippo gets from the people along the sidewalks. Kids are laughing and pointing at us as we pass by the Hockey Hall of Fame.We ride along Yonge Street, Parliament, University of Toronto then along McCaul Street by the **AGO** and the intriguing table-like architecture of the **Ontario College of Art**

and **Design**. Next, it's hip Queen Street to Bathurst and down to **Ontario Place**, our launching point.

It makes one feel uneasy to watch one's vehicle get nearer to the water than reason would dictate, then definitely too close... Then it's too late, we're in it with a splash, floating! We undertake our smooth ride on the lake amidst the elegant structures of **Ontario Place**. Our captain leads us up to the end of the channel opening into Lake Ontario.

Our guide, who's been commenting all along on Toronto's landmarks as we drove by, now cedes her front seat and microphone to a few young riders who pretend for a while they've got the job.

We leave the water with regret and drive towards **Harbourfront Centre**, by **Air Canada Centre** and around the **Rogers Centre** before reaching the finish line on Front Street.

TIPS (fun for 5 years +)
• You can reserve by calling. There's a service charge when you book online.
• They can store strollers in the Tours office.

NEARBY ATTRACTIONS
Think Big! Stroll (5-min. walk) ...... p. 466

Toronto Hippo Tours	D-3 **Downtown** Toronto 1-min.
(416) 703-4476 1-877-635-5510 www.torontohippotours.com	

 Schedule: Open May to October, from 11 am to 5 pm (last departure at 6 pm in July and August).

 Admission: $38/adults, $33/seniors and students, $25/3-12 years old, $110/family of 4, $3/under 3 years if sitting on lap.

Directions: Departs from 151 Front St. West (near Simcoe St.), Toronto.

YOUR FANNY DOWN THE GANNY

Among others, we admire a crew of eight rowers in their rail-car-boat, the Flintstones in their prehistoric craft and an airplane-shaped raft. But the golfers on a floating green, who'll reach the shore without getting wet, definitely take the cake!

About 20 years ago, the Ganaraska River burst its banks; Port Hope was officially declared a disaster area. Since then, during

That sinking feeling

A brave pooch barks frantically, running along the banks of the Ganaraska River. A small boat has just capsized in the current... to the audience's great delight! The good dog doesn't realize he's in the middle of Port Hope's annual event. He tries to rescue the laughing crew, who clumsily attempt to reach their home made craft to finish the race.

To my little landlubber, a grown-up reluctantly immersed in cold water is the funniest sight he's ever seen! Most crews take the plunge. Their craft is usually precarious: pieces of Styrofoam, wood, metal or plastic barrels piled or tied together, sometimes quite artistically.

TIPS (fun for 4 years +)

• Along Cavan Street, close to where it crosses Barrett Street, the banks are lined with flat stones and slope down gently. It forms a natural amphitheatre, stroller accessible with a great view.
• Many people bring blankets to sit on the ground, which can sometimes be muddy at this time of year.
• It's best to get to your observation point before 10:30 am. At 11 am, the first boats can be seen from downtown.
• Temporary toilets are available. Stands sell hot dogs and coffee.
• Port Hope hosts the only "atmospheric theatre" in Canada. Built in 1930, the **Capitol Theatre**'s interior was painted like a medieval castle, with clouds projected on the ceiling. Check their website for up-coming plays, films, and concerts at **www.capitoltheatre.com** or call 1-800-434-5092.

the sudden spring rise in the water level, the city has been organizing this race for canoes, kayaks and floating creations.

Each year, participants create their boat. Usually, about fifty crazy crafts are expected, but they don't all finish the race. A technical error happens so fast!

The ten-kilometre course followed by the boats ends downtown, where the crowd gathers to applaud the participants. The ambience is great; it shows that people know each other.

Float Your Fanny Down the Ganny River Race	C-5 East of Toronto 60-min.

• **Port Hope**
1-888-767-8467
www.floatyourfanny.ca

Schedule: Usually the first Saturday in April or the Saturday following Easter. Starts at 10 am. (2008: April 5) Call for exact date for the following years.

Admission: FREE.

Directions: From Hwy 401 East, take exit #464/Port Hope/Hwy 28 southbound (it becomes Mill St.). Turn right on Walton St., then left on Queen St. to find parking. On foot, go back to Walton St. (Cavan St. is located west of the River, north of Walton St.).

NEARBY ATTRACTIONS
Jungle Cat World (20-min.) .... p. 64

HMCS HAIDA

Afloat and well

Ontario Place visitors remember the huge destroyer that used to greet them by the entrance of the amusement park. We visited it in its new setting in Hamilton, better looking than ever.

HMCS Haida is the last survivor of 27 Tribal destroyers having served in three Commonwealth navies. More rooms were restored since its Ontario Place days so we could get a better feeling of what the life on the warship must have been like.

At arrival, grab a self-guided tour brochure and start what will feel to kids like a treasure hunt.

They'll be oblivious to shiny brass and varnished woods but torpedo tubes, all kinds of big guns, mortar barrels and catwalks will do the trick.

Reading the signs really adds to the visit, putting things into perspective. On the mess deck, we learn that 40 men lived there, with an 18-inch space to hook their hammock, lockers doubling as seats.

We all agreed that the highlight of our visit was the engine room. So many nooks and crannies between boilers and turbines! Pipes, instruments, and throttles were everywhere. It was easy to imagine the noise, smell and heat in that section when the destroyer was in action.

From the main deck, we could see the QEW Skyway Bridge far away and cormorants fishing nearby.

TIPS (fun for 4 years +)

• More on **Parks Canada Discovery Centre** on p. 246.

• You could get to Haida from Hwy 403 but I recommend driving over the QEW Skyway Bridge, then along the Dofasco and Stelco industrial complex. Kids don't get to see that kind of panorama (and smell) very often!

• You'll have to do lots of contortions to cross through the numerous hatchways. Not recommended with a baby in arms or in a backpack!

• Interesting items noticed in their small gift shop: a $2 old-fashioned comic book *HMCS Haida Rescue at Sea* which brings Haida back to life, all kinds of badges for 50¢, $1 ribbons printed with HMCS and name of a city, to decorate a hat.

NEARBY ATTRACTIONS
Parks Canada (7-min.walk) .... p. 246
Dundarn Castle (5-min.) .... p. 391

HMCS Haida • Hamilton (905) 526-0911 www.hmcshaida.ca	E-2 S-W of Toronto 60-min.

Schedule: Open 10 am to 5 pm, daily from Victoria Day weekend until Labour Day weekend, then Thursday to Sunday until Thanksgiving. Closed for the winter.

Admission: Dual entry with Parks Canada is around $9.50/adults, $5/6-16 years, $24/family of 5, FREE for 5 years and under, FREE for all on Canada Day.

Directions: Pier 9, 658 Catherine St. North. Take Q.E.W. toward Niagara, go over the bridge, then take exit #89 (Burlington Street). Drive past the industrial complex, keeping left, turn right at John St. (past Wellington St.), right at Guise, then left at Catherine. Haida's entrance is to the right.

Steer a boat at the **Parks Canada Discovery Centre** on p. 246.

WELLAND CANALS CENTRE

The ups and downs of a canal

A drawbridge lets the freighter go by with its iron ore cargo. The gigantic lock gates shut heavily behind the 225-metre-long ship finishing its course through the canal. Tons of water lift the boat. It gets even better when sailors working on the main deck wave at the children. The kids, confined to the observation platform, look at them with envy. Here in St. Catharines, at Welland Canals' lock number 3, we're swimming amidst a world of *Mighty Machines*.

The Welland Canals' eight locks allow ships from thirty countries to cross the Niagara escarpment, which brings about a 100-metre level difference between Lakes Ontario and Erie. Because of its ideal set-up for visitors, lock number 3 is the best place to initiate children to the science of locks. It boasts an Interactive Centre, a souvenir shop and the great little **St. Catharines Museum**. And best of all, the lock's observation platform offers a breathtaking view.

A bulletin board can be which lists the boats that will pass through the lock during the day. It mentions each boat's name, port of registry, length, destination, type of cargo it carries and its approximate time of arrival at the lock. This helps to put young minds to work...

A question of time

During our visit, a good half hour went by between the moment we saw the arriving freighter passing under the drawbridge and the time it entered the lock. The

kids weren't expecting it to be so gigantic!

To help them pass the time while waiting for a ship, we went to the snack bar and explored the playground. We also visited the St. Catharines Museum. Don't hesitate to go there at any time, as speakers inside the museum will announce the arrival of each ship. You can then return to the lock and when the ship has finished passing through, resume your visit to the museum.

It took 15 minutes for the Canadian cargo, called the *Jean Parisien*, to station itself inside the lock. This allowed us time to admire it from every angle. The little sailors accompanying me had many questions: "Why is the bridge watered by those hoses? Why are there only a few life boats?"

It takes about 10 minutes for the lock to fill with water. The freighter was rising before our very eyes and the kids enjoyed identifying the objects that were getting closer. "Wow, look at the lifebuoy! Can you see the white stairs? And the blue basket?" Finally, the lock opened on the other side.

The freighter's engines restarted and caused the water to swirl around. The ship continued its slow course upstream. It was about time, as my little sailors' level of interest was beginning to sink dangerously low! We improved the situation by visiting the enjoyable museum.

TIPS (fun for 5 years +)

• The lock can remain empty for more than 5 consecutive hours. For a successful visit, it is best to call Lock 3's information service before you leave. It states the daily schedule, with the approximate arrival time of each ship. It is best to go to the site when three or four ships are scheduled to pass through the lock within a 3-hour period.

• The perspective is best when you watch a ship rising from "upbound", that is when it goes upstream from Lake Ontario towards Lake Erie.

• At the museum entrance, ask for a very interesting booklet titled *ABC's of the Seaway*, free with admission. Using simple terms, it describes the functioning of the locks that the kids have just seen live.

• There's a snack bar on site open at least from April to October.

NEARBY ATTRACTIONS

The St. Catharines Museum

The museum includes various activities around the naval theme and several time-travel exhibits. The Lacrosse Hall of Fame comes with a shooting gallery, where kids can throw balls into a net. There are more hands-on pioneer artefacts to play with.

My little inspectors fell for the captain's wheel with a moving landscape seen through portholes in the background. We can watch a 15-minute video presentation to learn more about the four remakes of the canal system.

Welland Canals Centre	**E-3**
• St. Catharines	**Niagara Region**
1-800-305-5134	**75-min.**
or (905) 984-8880	
www.stcatharineslock3museum.ca	

Schedule: Ship viewing possible between April up to shortly before Christmas. The museum is open Monday to Friday, 9 am to 5 pm and weekends, 11 am to 4 pm.

Admission: FREE admission to the centre. Museum admission is around $4.25/ adults, $4/seniors, $3.25/students, $2.50/6-13 years, FREE for children 5 years and under.

Directions: Lock 3, 1932 Welland Canals Pkwy., St. Catharines. Take QEW Niagara to St. Catharines, exit at Glendale Ave. West, cross the lift-bridge and turn right on Welland Canals Pkwy. (formerly Government Rd.).

General tips about
Museums:

- Museums change their exhibits on a regular basis. Points of interest described in this guide were accurate at the time of print. Based on my experience, they rarely change for the worse!

- In most cases, if you intend to visit a specific museum more than once during the year, it is worth considering a membership (normally no more than the price of two admissions). It will give you priviledges and most importantly, it will give you the liberty to come for a quick visit whenever you have a chance, without being concerned about not getting your money's worth!

MUSEUMS

See **the Royal Ontario Museum** on p. 244.

JEWISH DISCOVERY MUSEUM

Filled with good faith!

"He'll read all this?" asks my son bewildered as he looks at the series of small papers inserted between the bricks of the Western Wall. I just finished explaining these are children's prayers to God. With that, he sits down before a blank page and....draws a plane (he'd like to go for a ride). He quickly slips his drawing in a crack in the wall.

Jewish or not, young visitors equally enjoy the small interactive museum. It is dedicated to children 5 years and under (older kids welcome).

Years ago, the Discovery Museum really seemed to be inspired by a precise theme: the history of the Jewish religion and its current life experience.

When I visited it recently, it was less like a museum and more like a cozy drop-in, with a costume section, a play kitchen, a climbing structure, a two-seat plane, a craft area and a Window around the world section where kids get to lift flaps to discover video clips.

The place has developed more six-week programs especially designed to cater to the needs of Jewish families with young kids (Singing in Hebrew, Hands on Jewish, Purim, Passover & Shavuaot around the world, and more).

They also offer drop-in programs (not requiring pre-registration) on Thursdays and Fridays at 10:30 am. They involve storytelling, games and crafts and are included with the admission.

This is also the place to turn to celebrate Jewish Holidays with kids during their **Chanukah** and **Purim Carnivals**, or on December 25, when everything else is closed.

Near the parking lot runs the Don River where kids will be able to see ducks.

TIPS (fun for 5 years & under)
• The community centre holds a well-stocked kosher cafeteria.
• There's an indoor pool accessible to non-members for a fee.
• ATTENTION! Major construction was going on at the time of print. The Museum will probably be moved in September 2009 into the new building currently being built at the back of the actual centre. At the beginning of 2008, they were still developing the concept for the Family Place in its new location. The drop-in programs will be maintained but the physical layout could change drastically. Check their website later in 2009 to find out about the latest developments.

NEARBY ATTRACTIONS
Bathurst Bowlerama (5-min.) .... p. 45
Black Creek Village (15-min.) ...... p. 383

The Family Place @ The Jewish Discovery Museum
• North York
D-3
North of downtown 30-min.
(416) 636-1880 ext. 242
www.bjcc.ca

 Schedule: Open Sunday to Friday, 9:30 am to 5 pm (sometimes more depending on the activities or events). Call in 2009 for new schedule.

 Admission: $2/adults, $2.50/children.

Directions: Bathurst Jewish Community Centre, 4588 Bathurst St., North York (north of Sheppard). ATTENTION! The community centre is under construction. Around September 2009, expect many services to move into the new buildings and some (such as the pool) to be stopped for a time.

HAMILTON CHILDREN'S MUSEUM

Photos: Courtesy of Hamilton Children's Museum

Hamilton for kids

Don't be disappointed by the building's small size. The philosophy of the Hamilton Children's Museum is to maximize the use of space.

The museum is constantly reinventing itself. For every new edition, I have had to rewrite this page to follow the changes.

Last edition, I had to rely on the nice curator's descriptions and pictures to describe the latest activities.

There was a room where kids constructed a ball course on a wall out of see-through pipes. They could climb into a 12-foot-high tree made out of recycled tires, pieces of carpet and other items. They could use a periscope and a pulley system. In another room, they'd play with horns, rocks, fossils and minerals which they explored with microscope, magnifying glass, metal detectors and more.

At the time of print, the new exhibits were under construction so no pictures were available (I'm leaving the old pictures to give you an idea of the ambience).

For 2008, expect a "Kitchen Works" exhibit involving games, stories, play and kitchen "chemistry"!

TIPS (fun for 2 years +)

• The museum's visit lasts approximately one hour, a good choice to combine with another local outing.

• There's a colourful room adjacent to the exhibition called the Sensorium. It is used for birthday parties and pre-registered craft activities (check their calendar of events for a description of these interesting crafts offered on Saturdays or Sundays (around $7 to $12 per person).

• They normally offer special activities included with regular admission everyday during the **March Break** and the **Christmas Break** between Christmas and the return to school. They also offer special **New Year's Eve** activities with a countdown at 3 pm.

• A small outdoor playground is located beside the museum. A very large playground including a wading pool and a spray pad is a 5-minute walk away, at the back of **Gage Park** on which the museum sits.

• There is no snack bar in this park but there is a **McDonald's** located on a parallel street in front of the museum.

NEARBY ATTRACTIONS

Hamilton Children's Museum · Hamilton (905) 546-4848 www.myhamilton.ca (click on **Arts, Sports & Recreation**)	E-2 S-W of Toronto 60-min.

  Schedule: Open Tuesday to Saturday, 9:30 am to 3:30 pm (from April to September). Closed on Tuesdays but open on Sundays, 11 am to 4 pm, from October to March, plus the whole week of **March Break** and the **Christmas Break** from Boxing Day to before school starts again. Closes between new exhibits, better call ahead to confirm it is open.

    Admission: $3/1-13 years old, $1/adults, $7/family of 4.

 Directions: 1072 Main St. East, Hamilton. Take QEW West, then Hwy 403 towards Hamilton, exit Main St. East.

THE CHILDREN'S MUSEUM

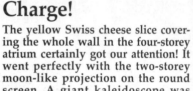

Charge!

The yellow Swiss cheese slice covering the whole wall in the four-storey atrium certainly got our attention! It went perfectly with the two-storey moon-like projection on the round screen. A giant kaleidoscope was throwing its ever-moving light on it, while enlarged shadows of kids danced on the screen. My companions could not get through the gate fast enough.

Don't be fooled by the stiff facade of the building. It used to be a department store, which sat vacant for 15 years.

To see its inner beauty, enter through the child-size doors (next to the full-size ones), even 10-year-olds find it amusing). Go past the huge round reception counter and admire natural light pouring from skylights and the glass front, three mezzanines and a gorgeous tempered glass staircase bordered with glass guardrails, wooden floors and a line-up of creative activities.

The Children's Museum (formerly called the **Waterloo Children's Museum** even though it was in Kitchener) opened in September 2003. It is a bit like a bigger version of the whimsical KidSpark section in the Ontario Science Centre (see p. 247), with many scientific activities geared towards older kids.

On the street level (emphasizing mathematics and patterns), the Atrium area by the giant kaleidoscope is quite popular with kids. Several building systems are at their disposal.

Another hit is the enclosed and carpeted area TotSpot in a corner of the vast floor. Meant for preschoolers and babies, the cocoon-like room is mesmerizing for anyone, with five bubbling water tubes lit in the dark and a ceiling covered with wavy mesh.

The second level focuses on mechanics and hydraulics. We loved the Construction Alley with its sails of stretch-fabric panels we could hook with the help of fasteners on poles to create labyrinths. The two-sided pin walls next to it were a blast. Kids could leave a life-size impression on it. (Beware, make sure no other explorer is simultaneously pushing pins on the other side while you're pushing on yours.)

ing to the projection of a space launch.

It offers interesting scientific activities as long as you have the patience to figure them out (tip: you have to wait for buttons to light-up before pushing them and wait a few seconds to leave time for the experiment to start).

The highlight of this floor was the opportunity to lay down on a bed of nails which would come out of a plexiglass sheet under your body with the help of a control button.

The fourth level hosts travelling exhibitions. Expect something interactive. When visiting, we saw displays on the chimpanzees in Jane Goodall's world. The kids could wear a primate's long arms to walk like them, hop on a Chimp's nest, fish for termites and more!

The water section used to include a 15-metre-long stream when the museum opened but it has been downsized to a 4-metre water table, still fun enough for my two 10-year-old companions to spend 30 minutes steering boats between sections.

This floor also offers a craft section and a large magnetic board.

On the third level was an infrared pod with a screen registering our body temperatures (the more layers of clothing, the colder it registers!). There was a section with a few vibrating seats react-

TIPS (fun for 2 years +)
• Make sure there's an exhibition on the 4th floor when you visit. There can be a few weeks between exhibitions.
• The **Exhibit Café** sells organic meals.
• If you walk a few blocks to your right when exiting the museum, you'll find Kitchener's City Hall with a nice fountain in the summer, which turns into a rink in the winter. Bring the skates! (There's a **Williams Coffee Pub** right next to it).
• Check the theatre company **K-W Children's Drama Workshop**. It presents plays by children for children and families at the **Registry Theatre** (122 Frederick, a few minutes from the museum) at **Christmas**, **Easter** and in the Spring. Their Saturday presentation at 7 pm would be a nice complement to the museum visit. In 2008, they were offering the *Nuncrackers* (a Nunsense Christmas musical), *Charlie & the Chocolate Factory* and the broadway musical *Annie Jr.* ($17/adults, $12/seniors and children 12 years and older, $8/children under 12, **www.kwdramakids.ca**).
• More on the **Oktoberfest Parade** taking place on King Street on p. 41.

NEARBY ATTRACTIONS
Wings of Paradise (20-min.) .... p. 69
Shade's Mills C.A. (20-min.) .... p. 417

The Children's Museum
• Kitchener
(519) 749-9387
www.thechildrensmuseum.ca

D-1 West of Toronto 85-min.

Schedule: Wednesday to Friday, 10 am to 4 pm; Saturday, 10 am to 5 pm; Sunday, 12 noon to 5 pm. Open Mondays and Tuesdays early July to Labour Day, 10 am to 4 pm. Closed for two weeks after Labour Day.

Admission: $7/person, FREE for children 2 and under ($10/person when there's a visiting exhibition).

Directions: 10 King St. West, Kitchener. From Hwy 401 West, take exit#278/Hwy #8 West towards Kitchener-Waterloo. Keep right, it becomes King St. The museum is past Queen. There's a parking lot on Duke St., just north of King St. and west of the museum.

LONDON CHILDREN'S MUSEUM

Fun space

The museum's large dimensions and its lovely setting inside a former three-storey school, enchanted me. My son loved its child-sized village, then it was the Space gallery that thrilled him.

It took us more than two hours to explore the London Regional Children's Museum.

On one side, the prehistoric room boasts two complete dinosaur skeletons and a deep cave, with its dark and realistic nooks and crannies, prehistoric drawings and cleverly designed sandbox, in which children can dig for stones with genuine fossils. On the other side, you will find an Inuit room, complete with a snowmobile!

TIPS (fun for 2 years +)

• Hot food service is available (but not weekdays in the off season). There is an interesting outdoor playground.

• The museum offers many special activities during their Summer Carnival. They also offer special fun during **Easter**, **Canada Day**, **Halloween**, **Christmas** and **March Break**.

• The **London International Children's Festival** is the only such festival left (Milk and Missisauga Children's Festivals have been cancelled). It usually runs for 5 consecutive days including the first or second weekend in June. It takes place in and around **Victoria Park** in London. Check **www.londonchildfest.com** or call (519) 645-6739. Good time for a getaway!

NEARBY ATTRACTIONS
London StoryBook (10-min.) .... p. 50
Fanshawe Village (15-min.) .... p. 395

In the mezzanine on the second floor is the Jellyfish Junction with underwater theme and sand floor. The miniature rendition of a village is also located on the second floor. Its small buildings depict the decor, accessories and costumes of various businesses you'd find in any town.

On the third floor, there's a room where kids can enjoy a huge tree that houses a slide and hiding places. The rest of the room was much in need of renovation when we visited. There were a few other displays on the science of the senses but we did not explore them, the Space Gallery nearby was way too attractive!

Wow! What a beautiful gallery to look at and to explore too! You're inside a space station with a central control module with large bay windows and monitors allowing you to see the visitors in all the other sections of the station. Cargo, docking, experiment module and habitation module complete the gallery, along with projected constellations in the dark on the dome ceiling of the Observation Lab.

My kids looked like astronauts when they wore the silver costumes at their disposal. My daughter felt like a real one when she heard the noise after she had pushed the launch button in her space shuttle. Clever!

London Children's Museum • London (519) 434-5726 www.londonchildrensmuseum.ca	E-1 S-W of Toronto 2 hrs

Schedule: Open Tuesday to Sunday, 10 am to 5 pm (closes at 8 pm on Fridays). Open Mondays also, from Victoria Day to Labour Day and during holidays.
Admission: $6/visitor, FREE under 2 years.
Directions: 21 Wharncliffe Rd. South, London. From Hwy 401 West, take exit at Wellington Rd. northbound, turn west on Commisionner's Rd., then north on Wharncliffe Rd. (past Horton St. and railway bridge). The museum is located on the left side.

TORONTO POLICE MUSEUM

Good guys, bad guys

Police work is so attractive and conducive to play-acting with its good guys, bad guys and elaborate gear, it will take children twenty years to realize the world of crime isn't cool at all. Until then, the Police Museum makes every effort to impress its visitors.

The architecture of the Police Headquarters building is magnificent. The museum, up with the best, offers plenty of activities which took us an hour to explore.

At the entrance, officers in uniform impressed my little citizen, but not as much as the gleaming police edition Harley-Davidson posted nearby. He happily (and legally!) hopped on the motorcycle. Mannequins display uniforms dating from the 1850's to the present. There's even a Mountie riding a life-size horse.

While your children inspect the genuine police car, read the captions inside the display cases containing exhibits from true criminal cases. Afterwards, initiate your miniature CSI ingestigator to the Forensic Evidence Area. You can show them several pieces of evidence: a drinking glass covered with fingerprints, a victim's jewels recovered from the murderer's house and nails stuck in garden hoses used by robbers to slow down the police during a chase.

Adults appreciate watching the short videos covering various topics. An interactive fingerprint screen offered an interesting display.

In the replica station, there's a prison cell, (which was unfortunately closed when we visited). Further on, my son saw his first real car wreck. It faces an officer on a 1950's road sign encouraging us to drive safely. The sign compares the number of automobile accident deaths from the current and previous year. The billboard is old, but the statistics are current and updated weekly!

TIPS (fun for 5 years +)
• Kids can ask for a free police button at the duty desk.
• They have a Cop Shop in the lobby, selling gift items, clothing (adult and children sizes) and more.
• In the winter time, bring the skates! There's a great outdoor artificial ice rink in **College Park**, across the street, behind the large building including the Winners outlet. You can walk into the building and go underground to access it. See **College Subway Station** on p. 450.

See **College Subway Station** on p. 450.

NEARBY ATTRACTIONS
Textile Museum (5-min.) .... p. 242

Toronto Police Museum
(416) 808-7020
www.torontopolice.on.ca

D-3 Downtown Toronto 15-min.

Schedule: Open Monday to Friday, 8:30 am to 4 pm (call before visiting). Book ahead if you want a guided tour.

Admission: Charitable donation of $1 per person.

Directions: 40 College St., Toronto (one block west of Yonge St.).

TEXTILE MUSEUM

finally get to see what a silkworm looks like and touch real cocoons, so white and soft between my fingers. The fibre-space education gallery within the Textile Museum is filled with such things to discover. There's also the Discover Textiles corner with a "knitted zoo", hooked rugs and lace making trials, and the Discover

Strong artistic fibre

In the Discover Fibre section, there's a discovery drawer to learn about the living things producing fibres. I really enjoyed the exercise but my five-year-old couldn't care less. She's too distracted by the alignment of colourful threads inside a large cage in the Discover Colour section.

It doesn't take long for her to rearrange the threads into an artful display. Then, she makes patterns using a wide choice of pre-cut patterns.

While she's busy, I can't believe I

Meaning section where activities constantly change to coincide with specific exhibitions.

You can expect up to six exhibitions going on in the three exhibition spaces throughout the year. They're always intriguing and interesting for adults, like the one on geotextiles, which taught me how fabrics were used in construction and agriculture, or the one on the molecular structure of fabrics.

You can usually count on artistic installations involving fabric in some way. Once, a dramatic organza curtain pinned with thousands of rose petals by the artist stunned me. And the installation "I've got balls" was quite a sight, with its twenty-one white nylon legs suspended from clothes lines, heavy with baseballs in their feet, and one full pair of red nylons also with baseballs, nicely contrasting. Even my daughter reacted to that one.

TIPS (fun for 5 years +)

• The **March Break** is a great time to drop in with artsy kids who would like to create textile art! Special craft activities are then adapted to the current exhibitions.
• The store is filled with original works of some 50 artisans. It also carries a great selection of textile-related books, for adults and children (even some storybooks involving fabrics). Kids' stuff also includes textile-related kits, learning activity books and craft projects.
• Check their virtual exhibitions on their website! It is exquisitely designed, very informative, both in English and in French.
• There's no restaurant on the site but the museum is only a 10-minute walk from the **Eaton Centre**.

Textile Museum of Canada (416) 599-5321 www.textilemuseum.ca	**D-3 Downtown** Toronto 10-min.

 Schedule: Open daily, 11 am to 5 pm, (closes at 8 pm on Wednesday.

 Admission: $12/adults, $8/seniors, $6/5-14, $25/family of 5, FREE under 5 years old, FREE for all on Wednesdays, 5 to 8 pm.

Directions: 55 Centre Ave., Toronto. Just south of Dundas, one block east of University Ave.

NEARBY ATTRACTIONS

THE BATA SHOE MUSEUM

The shoe fits!

Since the company has always focused on low-end shoes, I was quite curious to see what the Bata Shoe Museum had to offer. Well, I was impressed! The museum is gorgeous and Bata has shown great skill in putting itself into its young visitors' shoes to get their attention.

The All About Shoes semi-permanent exhibition reviews the history of shoes, from prehistoric times until the present, using many props: art reproductions, informative text, mannequins, lighting effects and fascinating artefacts. They change the displays from time to time to feature different shows from their vast collection.

TIPS (fun for 5 years +)

• **March Break** activities are original. Last time I was there during this period, visitors could play with Brio-like tracks and "shoe" trains. They could create socks and shoes for a multi-legged dragon. The activities vary but you can always count on crafts, dress-up and clog making demonstration (pre-registration is recommended).

• Check out their website to find out about special family activities on Saturdays, **Easter**, **Halloween**, **Christmas** and more.

Once, when visiting, we saw the oldest closed shoe dating from the 1400's! Among other things, I learned that in 14th Century England, length of the shoe tip was related to social status and regulated by law. That explains the disproportionately long shoes seen in some medieval paintings!

Children can't appreciate the historic value of ancient shoes. But they'll be impressed by the variety of footwear displayed here, especially if you explain the use of certain shoes to them. At the time of print, we could see astronaut training boots, chestnut crushing clogs, Dutch smugglers' clogs designed to create a footprint! And what can we say about the ancient Chinese shoes used to reduce the foot size of women victims of their time?

We then move on to the Star Turns display, showcasing some famous footwear: one of the Beatles' ankle boots, Marilyn Monroe's red pumps, Picasso's pony-skin boots. Kids will favour the size 20 EEE Reebok shoes of basketball player Shaquille O'Neil.

Three other galleries feature special exhibitions under diverse themes. These have exhibited collections of dancing shoes, athletic footwear and evolution of fashionable footwear, among others.

The Bata Shoe Museum (416) 979-7799 www.batashoemuseum.ca	D-3 **Downtown** Toronto **15-min.**

 Schedule: Open on weekdays and Saturdays, 10 am to 5 pm (closes at 8 pm on Thursdays). Open Sunday, 12 noon to 5 pm.

 Admission: $12/adults, $10/seniors, $6/students, $4/5-17 years, $18/one adult + 4 kids, $30/two adults + 3 kids, FREE for children 4 years and under. FREE on Thursdays, 5 pm to 8 pm.

 Directions: 327 Bloor St. West, Toronto (at corner of St. George St., in front of St. George Subway Station).

NEARBY ATTRACTIONS
ROM (15-min. walk) .... p. 244

ROYAL ONTARIO MUSEUM

Extreme makeover

The ROM so dramatically changed in the last years, in and out, that you won't recognize the place if you've not been since 2004.

The Bat Cave (with its swarm of flying bats), Gallery of Birds (with the series of discovery drawers under the glass displays), Gallery of Reptiles and Gallery of Hands-On Biodiversity (a whole little museum in itself with stuffed forest mammals, displays giving us the impression of being on a field trip in Canada's lake and cottage regions, guessing games, hands-on tables, costumes, a tunnel and real beehive): All these have remained relatively untouched on the second level of the historical building. They've added a new interactive CIBC Discovery Gallery which is becoming a family favourite.

Everything else has pretty much been scrapped or re-invented, starting with a new entrance on Bloor through the "crystal" structure now attached to the old building.

Remember the Dinosaurs Gallery, where the skeletons stood on prehistoric flora, with great trompe-l'oeil in the

background? It's gone, but don't cry yet! If you stand on Bloor and look up at the windows on the second floor, you'll see the full length of the largest dinosaur now featured in the new gallery.

Don't take the elevators to the second floor or you'll miss the amazing new staircases built in **Michael Lee-Chin Crystal**. They are breathtaking and include a few collections encased like gems in a cave.

The first room in the Temerty Dinosaurs Gallery is interesting, with the largest fossils I have ever seen and the longest skeleton of the collection: the Barosaurus. In the second room, across the corridor, huge marine specimens hung over our heads, Tyranosaurus Rex in all its splendour and the Tryceratops skull were all great, but what blew us away was the adjacent Gallery of the Age of Mammals with the display of contemporary skeletons next to those of their prehistoric ancestors... and the mammoth from Welland, Ontario!

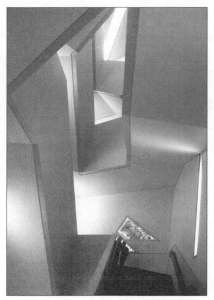

You might want to see the mummies in the Egypt section of the Galleries of Africa on Level 3. Many more galleries will open in 2008 on this level (including the Gallery of Middle East with display of Islamic arms and armour and a promising Gallery of Textiles and Costume).

There's no more Gallery of Earth Science on Level 1, with its volcano, passage through an impressive crack of quartz and no more Big Bang story. Instead, new Earth Sciences Galleries will open in December 2008 on Level 2 in the Weston Family Wing. It will include the Gallery of Minerals and the Gallery of Gold and Gems, among other things.

On Level 1, don't miss the Gallery of Chinese Architecture with its full-scale replica of the corner of an imperial palace hall. And check the Gallery of Canada! Its original displays have nothing to do with the gallery which used to be on Level B1.

TIPS (fun for 3 years +)

• There's a Toronto Parking Authority affordable parking lot on Bedford Street, north of Bloor Street, west of Avenue Rd.

• Every weekend is **ROM Family Weekend** with more activities and solo artists strolling through the Museum.

• The ROM offers even more interactive activities during the **March Break** and around **Christmas** time.

• During peak periods, timed tickets will be issued for the Discovery Gallery at the entrance of the gallery.

• The large ROM Museum Store by the entrance is amazing. There's also a small ROMkids Store on Level B1.

• The new cafeteria-style **Food Studio** on Level B1 offers great food for all tastes.

• The new fancy restaurant **c5** on Level 5 of the Crystal is breathtaking (I know what I want for my next birthday!).

NEARBY ATTRACTIONS
Bata Shoe Museum (15-min. walk) p. 243
Around Bay Subway Station .... p. 441

Royal Ontario Museum (416) 586-8000 www.rom.on.ca	**D-3** **Downtown** **Toronto** **15-min.**

 Schedule: Open daily, 10 am to 5:30 pm, closes at 9:30 pm on Fridays.

 Admission: $20/adults, $17/ seniors and students, $14/5 to 14 years, FREE for 4 years and under. Half-price admission on Fridays, 4:30 to 9:30 pm. Temporary exhibitons included with general admission.

 Directions: 100 Queen's Park (at the corner of Bloor St. West). Note the entrance is on Bloor St.

PARKS CANADA DISCOVERY

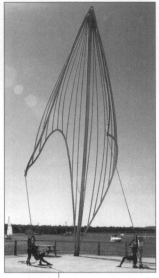

Pier pressure

Our friends couldn't thank us enough for convincing them to drive to Hamilton for what turned out to be a highly-rated outing by parents and kids alike.
We went to Hamilton Harbour to visit the warship Haida and thought we might as well check its neighbour the Parks Canada Discovery Centre since it was suggested as a combo.

What a great idea! The Centre turned out to be a gorgeous building with the best view of the beautiful harbour from its café's tables.

Sailboats were roaming the harbour, sea gulls in the air were fighting the wind and we could fly the small kites we had just built in the craft section of the Centre.

Everything in the Discovery Centre is well designed. Parents won't mind that there's lots of interesting reading involved with the interactive screens. Kids will prefer the electronic games by the entrance, the stuffed black bear to pet, interactive screens reacting to your steering of a boat's wheel and the model lock with water to play with.

We walked around the harbour to check out the intriguing sculpture of a 60-foot stylized sail. Then we drove a few minutes away to **Hutch's**, a burger joint straight out of the 50's, by **Bayfront Park**. We stopped on our way back to play in the **Pier 4 Park**'s boat playground by the floating docks (all of these attractions clearly pointed out in the Hamilton waterfront brochure handed out at the Centre).

TIPS (fun for 6 years +)
- More on **HMCS Haida** on p. 230.
- You can buy a ticket for the 12-km trolley ride but I recommend it only if you intend to stay in the trolley for the whole tour. Even if there's an on/off privilege, line-ups are long and you might have to wait a very long time for a ride back to your car!
- The electronic games displayed by the entrance of the Centre are accessible on Parks Canada's website. Go to their **Educational Resources** section, then click on **Youth Zone**.
- You'll find an ice cream parlour by the trolley station, near the **Williams Coffee Pub** and its lovely patio.

Parks Canada Discovery Centre • Hamilton (905) 526-0911 www.pc.gc.ca	E-2 S-W of Toronto 60-min.

 Schedule: Fall and winter, Thursday to Sunday, 10 am to 5 pm.

Admission: Dual entry with HMCS Haida: approx. $9.50/adults, $5/6-16 years, $24/family of 5. FREE for 5 years and under and FREE for all on Canada Day.

Directions: 57 Guise St. East, Pier 8, Hamilton Harbour. Take QEW toward Niagara, go over the bridge, then take exit #89 (Burlington St.). Drive past the industrial complex, keeping left, turn right at James St. (past John St.), right at Guise and left at Discovery Dr.

ONTARIO SCIENCE CENTRE

The science of fun

What a unique playground! Cave, 5-metre-high tornado, rocket chair, interactive floors, magnetic liquid, wall of bubbles; the list goes on. Mind you, nobody has to see it all in just one visit!

Those who haven't been to the Science Centre in the last few years are in for a surprise! Major funds (private and public) were invested to improve the attraction, beginning with the Teluscape space created outdoors in front of the Centre.

On your way to the escalators, you'll cross the Great Hall adorned with the Cloud, the permanent art work that now hangs from its ceiling. It consists of 100 rotating shafts, each one rotating at a slightly different speed, catching the light at a changing angle over a 20-minute cycle. What we have here is the best example of science meeting the arts!

Another gorgeous addition is the Lotic Meander on the outdoor KRG Terrace overlooking the valley (use the door from the Great Hall). The overall effect of this artistic representation of a river's meandering path is simply whimsical. It includes a 300-foot-long sinuous path

adorned with 860 discs, glass eggs and polished stone boulders.

I recommend starting the indoor visit with The Living Earth, three escalators down to Level D and to your far right. (For younger kids, this ride is an adventure in itself!)

Start slowly with the tropical rain forest, to feel the climate and see the waterfall. (There used to be leaf-cutting ants circulating through transparent pipes; they've been gone for a while but they're supposed to get a new ant colony for summer 2008!)

Then, get them excited with the 5-metre-high tornado (which vanishes when you blow on it) and the large cave with a TV monitor showing the visitors inside. Up the stairs in that room, you can lay on your belly and watch a short movie of a flight from the perspective of the flying bird!

Further in this section, you'll see the Science Arcade (which was relocated there). Don't be too sad if you're not greeted by the "cling clang" of metal balls rolling through the orange circuits which the children loved so much to reload. They've just moved it near KidSpark!

Not all the exhibits from the old Arcade are in the new section, but it is still where you'll find the famous hair-raising ball used during daily electrical demonstrations. Then, it's shadow tunnel, pedal power, jiggling sculpture, steel drums, optical effects, exhibits testing friction, resonance, vibration and more exhibits for bigger kids to pump and pull.

Next to the rain forest, The Living Earth includes live bugs and reptiles and a popular exhibit where a column fills with water to illustrate the volume of water contained in your body.

Older kids will appreciate the confinement chamber in the adjacent A Question of Truth or the exhibit on the 256 symbols learned by chimpanzees to communicate with humans in Communication.

Returning to the centre of Level D, try the interactive floor! Can you figure out how it works? Every time I introduce visitors to this floor, they go wild (whatever the age).

If you want to keep moving, get to the Sport room where you'll be able to race on a wheelchair, or on a bobsleigh, measure how high you can jump or how heavily you can fall and more.

Temporary exhibitions are featured further in the back of the Sport room.

After this, we normally split our group: younger kids and a few adults going to KidSpark (Level C, two escalators up) while teenagers head to the fantastic Weston Family Innovation Centre.

This centre was a stroke of genius, kind of like finding the missing link. It was created with teenagers and young adults in mind.

They can make short animated films, record and replay weird sounds they make on special DJ's tables, make a magnetic liquid react to sound, have their picture reproduced on a wall of bubbles, play music with lights, create shoes, and so much more.

With all of these options, it is easy to miss the Human Body on Level E (check their map). The modules you will find there are quite daring, covering the reproductive system and contraception.

Ask your little explorers to stand in front of a smiling little girl's picture. Then, open the "window" around her face. Behind this opening, her face contracts and a hidden water spray system reproduces a generous sneeze. It's quite funny when you don't expect it. Don't give it away!

On Level C, the Space section is a good place for older kids to hang around while the younger ones are still playing in nearby Kid-Spark (we've never been able to play less than an hour in this section, parents just need to go with the flow!)

Space has been fully renovated. The air-lifted rocket chair is still there and worth trying! We were fascinated by the room focusing on cosmic rays, with the amazing table allowing us to "see" the passage of particles using a condensation process. You've got to see this.

Thanks to Hubble's telescope, the universe gets all the attention it deserves. The pictures will give the kids a sense of the vastness of it all, from our solar system to the confines of the universe.

As for KidSpark, it is located in two adjacent rooms and simply lovely. It was designed for kids 8 years and under, but my son really enjoyed it beyond that age (they would allow older siblings to play if the place is not too busy).

Hard to say what my kids preferred: the stage where you lip-sync while playing fake instruments and creating light effects, the construction site with lifts and blocks and the floating balls in the first room, or the water table, the tree house, the screen with special motion effects or the igloo with multiple mirrors, in the other room with large windows overlooking the pond (yes, there's a pond at the Science Centre!).

TIPS (fun for 2 years +)

• More about the **Omnimax Theatre** on p. 93. On Fridays and Saturdays at 7 pm, you can see two consecutive Imax® Dome films ($18/adults, $16/seniors & students, $14/4-12 years, FREE for 3 years and under). The exhibits close at 5 pm but the snack bar by the entrance remains open.

• During busy times, check KidSpark section as soon as you arrive on the premises to see if they are giving timed tickets.

• Don't be afraid to take young kids to this museum. They won't understand much but they will be elated by the concept of being allowed to touch everything.

• They offer even more activities during the **March Break**. Beware! It's their busiest time of the year.

• The gift shop on Level A is a **Mastermind Educational Toys** store. Their selection is actually different from the other **Mastermind** stores. It is a fabulous place to buy educational toys, books, posters and $10 science gadgets. It offers a huge selection of activity books.

• By the entrance of Level D, there are vending machines and a cafeteria. In the summer, you can eat outside and take advantage of the natural surroundings of the ravine... along with the raccoons.

NEARBY ATTRACTIONS
Toronto Botanical Garden (5-min.) p. 278

Ontario Science Centre
(416) 696-3127
www.ontariosciencecentre.ca

D-3
North
of downtown
25-min.

Schedule: Open year-round, 10 am to 5 pm (extended hours during the March Break, July and August).

Admission: $18/adults, $13.50/seniors and students, $11/4-12 years, FREE for 3 years and under. Parking costs $8. (With one Imax® Dome film, it is $25/adults, $19/seniors and students, $15/children). Ask about their membership rates if you intend to visit more than twice in a year!

Directions: 770 Don Mills Rd., Toronto. Take Don Valley Pkwy., exit Don Mills Rd. North.

Interactive floor at the **Ontario Science Centre**.

HAMILTON MUSEUM OF STEAM

19th century techies

Our guide puts an oily paper hat on my nephew's head, turning him into one of the kids hired in the 19th century to keep the pumps well oiled. We all laugh at his funny "oiler" look until we are told this was the only protection those working children had when working in that environment. What about their little fingers?

The steam engines before us are quite impressive, at 70 tons each and 45 feet high. We're actually too close to see them in one shot as we look at them from the mezzanine. Canadian made, they're the oldest surviving examples in the nation and we can see them in operation under our noses.

Before we were allowed to see this phenomenon, our guide took great pains to explain to us the "beauty" of the technology involved by means of an interactive demonstration perfectly adapted for children. During the tour (which lasted 40 minutes), kids were allowed to use a lever to make the huge wheel turn.

We could also admire a model of the pump house, in a large barn-like display room filled with charts explaining the system. Each of the 12,000 parts of this model were handmade by a Hamilton resident in the 80's and it is functioning.

TIPS (fun for 6 years +)

• Every now and then during a Golden Horseshoe Live Steamer Day, you can catch a ride on a miniature steam-powered locomotive. On **Canada Day**, they always show up. Call for specific dates.

• During **March Break**, including the weekends before and after (and opening at 10 am) they offer more drop-in special demonstrations and craft activities.

• During **Christmas** break, they offer a special activity including two crafts and a craft bag to take home (for an extra fee).

• They offer some nice trinkets in their small gift shop. We bought a train whistle and a cute little tin boat moving with the heat of a candle!

• Read about nearby restaurants in the tips section of **Wild Waterworks**, p. 432.

Hamilton Museum of Steam & Technology

E-2
S-W
of Toronto
65-min.

· Hamilton
(905) 546-4797
www.myhamilton.ca
(search for **Arts, Sports & Recreation**)

 Schedule: From June 1 to Labour Day, Tuesday to Sunday, 11 am to 4 pm (opens at 12 noon the rest of the year). Closed on Mondays.

 Admission: $6/adults, $5/seniors and students, $4/children, $15/family, FREE for 5 years and under.

 Directions: 900 Woodward Ave., Hamilton. Take QEW towards Niagara, exit at Woodward Ave. and follow signs.

General tips about
Nature's call:

• Did you know poison ivy often climbs up larger trees? Me neither! In case you were wondering, here's what poison ivy looks like.

Look for shrubs with distinctive three-part pointed leaves, the central of which has a longer stem than the two side leaflets. The edges of the leaves can be smooth or very jagged. It loves sunny areas along trails, roads and beaches.

The rash appears 24-48 hours after contact. Beware! You can get it from touching your pet if it has brushed itself against it in the woods.

We can complain about it but let's not forget it is a good source of food for fall and winter animals!

• In the summer, have bathing suits handy! You never know when you'll find a swimming hole.

• In the spring and the fall, it is a good idea to have a change of clothes in case young kids fall in the mud!

NATURE'S
CALL

See **Albion Falls** on p. 268.

ABOUT CONSERVATION AREAS

Most affordable recreation!

Twenty-three conservation areas are described in this guide. Every single one we visited offered a good day-trip under $20... and Ontario has over 300 of them!

Conservation areas were initially based on the Ontario watershed. Back in the early 1940's, wide areas of the province were strained by deforestation and erosion. Worsening spring floods were followed by low summer flows of polluted water. Eventually, the province encouraged the creation of locally based conservation authorities who were petitioned by municipalities to solve ecological problems. Dams and reservoirs were built.

Today, flooding has virtually been eliminated. The conservation authorities have broadened their activities to include restoration, recreation and education.

TIPS (fun for all)
• For details on the conservation areas, go to www.conservation-ontario. on.ca and click on Find Your C.A.
• **Conservation Halton** offers a $105 vehicle pass giving one year access to its conservation areas, all mentioned in this guide; see **Rattlesnake Point** (p. 262), **Mount Nemo** (p. 263), **Hilton Falls** (p. 266), **Mountsberg Wildlife Centre** (p. 298), **Crawford Lake** (p. 388) and **Kelso** (p. 416). On a given day, admission to one conservation area gives you free access to any other conservation area under Conservation Halton's authority.
• **Credit Valley Conservation** vehicle pass is $95; see **Rattray Marsh** (p. 304) and **Belfountain** (p. 331).
• **Lake Simcoe Conservation**: **Whitchurch** and **Scanlon Creek** (p. 305) don't offer a pass.
• **Hamilton Conservation Authority** vehicle pass costs $85; see **Webster's Falls** (p. 267), **Westfield Heritage Village** (p. 390), **Christie Lake** (p. 417) and **Confederation Park/Wild Waterworks** (p. 432).
• **Grand River Conservation Authority** vehicle pass is $110; see **Rockwood** (p. 300), **Elora Quarry** (p. 413), **Shade's Mills** (p. 417) and **Elora Gorge** (p. 428).

About Toronto Conservation

Conservation Journeys Membership costs $65 for individuals and $125 for families of 4 (two adults and children under 18 years old), plus taxes. It gives unlimited access for an entire year to most Toronto conservation areas, FREE parking, plus discounts on certain events. See **Boyd** (p. 295), **Kortright Centre** (p. 296), **Bruce's Mill** (p. 302), **Glen Haffy** (p. 344) and **Black Creek Pioneer Village** (p. 383), **Heart Lake** (p. 410) and **Albion Hills** (p. 411).

You can upgrade your membership to include unlimited cross country skiing at **Albion Hills** (p. 372) or swimming in **Petticoat Creek**'s pool (p. 423), it would then cost you $95/individual or $155/family of 4.

You can also get membership for **Black Creek Pioneer Village** only ($50/individual, $85/family of 4) or **Kortright Centre** ($40/individual, $75/family of 4).

These options are available in all the Toronto and region conservation areas or call their customer service at (416) 667-6295. You may also download membership forms from their website.

Conservation Authorities
• **Toronto and Region Conservation**
(416) 667-6299 (TRCA info line)
(416) 667-6295 (customer service)
www.trca.on.ca
• **Conservation Halton**
(905) 336-1158
www.conservationhalton.on.ca
• **Credit Valley Conservation**
(905) 670-1615
www.creditvalleycons.com
• **Lake Simcoe Conservation**
(905) 895-1281
www.lsrca.on.ca
• **Hamilton Conservation Authority**
1-888-319-4722
www.conservationhamilton.ca
• **Grand River Conservation Authority**
(519) 621-2761
www.grandriver.ca

ABOUT BEACHES

My kids have been swimming in Lake Ontario since they were toddlers... and they survived. Many people don't realize that many beaches hardly have to be closed throughout the season, especially the beaches on the south side of Toronto Islands. All you need to do is learn the water condition on the beach you want to go to, on that day.

During the warm season, Toronto daily tests eleven beaches, ten of which are included in the **Water Fun** chapter in this guide: **Hanlan's Point Beach, Gibraltar Point Beach, Centre Island Beach** and **Ward's Island Beach** (p. 398), **Cherry/Clarke Beach** (p. 401), **Woodbine Beach** and **Kew Balmy Beach** (p. 402), **Sunnyside Beach** (p. 404), **Bluffer's Beach Park** (p. 405) and **Rouge Beach** (p. 406). The results of the last test are posted daily on a website, along with a picture of the beach and a map.

Testing, testing

We live near one of the biggest lakes in the world. Sometimes, when the sun hits it just right, it takes on shades of turquoise. When there's humidity in the air, the horizon line is blurred and makes us feel like we're standing by the sea.

The question is: Will there be a sign awaiting you, warning that the water is unsafe to swim, thanks to a high ratio of E. Coli? Will you have to spend the rest of the outing refraining your toddler from throwing himself into the water?

You can avoid any disappointment by checking the water condition before you go to the beach.

For information about beaches in Mississauga, Caledon and Brampton, go to the Peel Region's website. It provides information about **Jack Darling Park** (p. 304), **Professor's Lake** (p. 407), **Heart Lake C.A.** (p. 410), **Albion Hills C.A.** (p. 411) and others not mentioned in this guide.

Halton Region manages beaches in Burlington, Oakville and Milton, among them **Bronte Park Beach** (p. 357), **Beachway Park** (p. 408), **Kelso C.A.** (p. 416) and **Coronation Park** (p. 426).

TIPS (fun for all ages)

• A rule of thumb: Chances are the water conditions won't be good within two days following a rain storm.

• Whatever the beach you're going to, call ahead to check the water conditions. In the height of summer, I've seen closed beaches in conservation areas.

• The Toronto Beach website includes old pictures and historic information about the beaches. That's where I saw for the first time a picture of the amusement park and the diving horse that used to jump off a high structure at **Hanlan's Point** in the early 1900's (go to the **Toronto's Beaches** section in **www.torontobeach.ca**, select **Toronto Beach History**, then **Central Beaches**).

• It is a good idea to freeze plastic bottles of water or juice the night before you go to the beach. It will slowly melt during the day and remain cold.

Toronto Beaches
(416) 392-7161 (hotline)
www.torontobeach.ca (click on the name of the beach on the map)

Peel Region Beaches
www.peelregion.ca (go to **Health Services**, then **Beach Testing** under the letter B in the **A-Z Topic List**)

Halton Region Beaches
(905) 825-6000
www.halton.ca (go to **Services**, then **Beach Water Testing Results** under the letter B)

SCENIC CAVES ADVENTURES

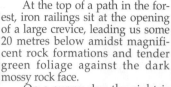

Get to the bottom of it!

At the beginning of the path, you cross the Ice Cave, a natural fridge which maintains a cool 4 degrees Celsius in summertime. Even its exterior walls are cold. Hugging my small baby, I remain in the cave's narrow and cool vestibule, while **father and son explore further down a corridor that descends into the even cooler part.**

TIPS (fun for 5 years +)

•   The trail system is accessible for the entire family but not stroller accessible!

•   Running or hiking shoes are a must, and take extra care when ground is wet.

•   Equip your children with flashlights, it will enhance their explorations.

•   The self-guided visit and the suspension bridge experience take approximately two hours.

•   There is a large pond filled with enormous trout you can feed. For an extra fee, you can enjoy minigolf or Gemstone Mining, a great "panning" structure allowing kids to find semi-precious gems from bags of mine rough.

•   The **Treetop Walking** experience of their **Eco Adventure Tour** includes zip lines (one of them 1,100 feet long) you slide down, hanging 40 feet above the ground. Check their website for details or to make reservations. The 2 1/2 hr tour is $95/adults, $85/seniors, $75/10-17 years old, plus the GST.

At the top of a path in the forest, iron railings sit at the opening of a large crevice, leading us some 20 metres below amidst magnificent rock formations and tender green foliage against the dark mossy rock face.

On a sunny day the sight is breathtaking. An information plaque tells us that some 300 years ago, Hurons used the natural fortress of the Scenic Caves to protect themselves from the enemy. That sparks the imaginations of young visitors!

The trail is filled with spots to explore and includes a few benches. You can easily recognize George Washington's profile, naturally sculpted by the shapes in the wall above our heads. While we didn't see any bears in the Bear's Cave, a small bat escaped. My young speleologist just loved the Fat Man's Misery passage. Its 36-centimetre width, at its narrowest, is not for everyone. Fortunately, there is an alternative path that circumnavigates the rock.

Since my last visit, they have added a 126-metre-long suspension bridge, the longest in Ontario, included with the admission to the caves. A wagon ride takes you there (or a 10-minute walk). It is 4 feet wide and I was told we feel lots of exciting sway in the middle, 25 metres above the valley and the stream. Wow!

Scenic Caves Nature Adventures	B-1 N-W of Toronto 2 hrs

· Collingwood
(705) 446-0256
www.sceniccaves.com

Schedule: Open daily from early May to end of October, 10 am to 5 pm (9 am to 7 pm in July and August).Last admission two hours prior to closing.

Admission: Caves (including bridge) around $18/adults, $16/ seniors, $14/5-17 years, FREE 4 years and under. Minigolf is $4.50/adults, $4/children. Gemstone Mining is $7.50/person.

Directions: From Hwy 400 North, take exit #98/Hwy 26/27, then follow Hwy 26. At Collingwood, take Blue Mountain Rd., which will cross the Scenic Caves Rd.

NEARBY ATTRACTIONS
Wasaga Beach (30-min.) .... p. 419

WARSAW CAVES C. A.

Underground experience

A while ago, I visited Warsaw Caves at the end of a cold afternoon, on a wet fall day, with a two-year old and no flash light. You might as well say I did not see them. Still, we were there long enough to assess what a unique underground adventure it offers to young explorers.

Some of the seven biggest caves marked along the trails are up to 100 metres (300 feet) long. Some go as deep as 15 metres into the ground. Ice may be found in one of them all year round. The average temperature in the other caves is approximately 15°C.

The trail to the caves is indicated on a map by the parking lot. It starts out smoothly but is soon covered by large plates of rock (at times slippery), which offer a unique scene. We easily lose track of the trail but the caves are not too far apart.

Bright green touches of moss cover the stones, and straight tall trees have popped up wherever they can. Some have actually managed to grow from the bottom of 2-metre-deep crevices. Everywhere, there are natural nooks and crannies to explore.

Approximately 20 minutes further, another trail leads to a lookout. Off the path, you will observe kettles, which are holes created by the movement of melting glaciers. They can be quite small but the biggest in the conservation area measures over 5 feet wide.

TIPS (fun for 7 years +)

• It is a must to bring flashlights and good shoes for everyone!
• As of May 2008, you'll be able to print a great *Spelunkers Guide to the Caves* from their website (go to their **Maps** section and find the downloads at the bottom of the page).
• Our pint-size paleontologist never wanted to go deeper than one metre into the caves. The guide I talked to told me she recommends exploring the caves with children 7 years or older. They need to be a certain height to stroll more at ease in the underground corridors.
• During the summer, visitors can swim in a calm river only three feet deep, accessible from a beach where canoes and kayaks can be rented. There's also a campground in the conservation area.
• The staff sells ice cream bars and drinks during the summer. I was told there is a great chip truck in the town of Warsaw, five minutes away from the Warsaw Caves.

Warsaw Caves Conservation Area · Warsaw (705) 652-3161 **Campground** 1-877-816-7604 www.warsawcaves.com	B-5 N-E of Toronto 2 hrs

 Schedule: Open to vehicles from Victoria Day to Thanksgiving, from 8 am to sunset.

Admission: (cash only) around $9/vehicle. Canoe rental is $15/2 hours or $30/day. (Headlamp sold for $4-$6.)

Directions: From Hwy 401 East, take exit #436/Hwy 35/115 northbound. It becomes Hwy 7 near Peterborough. Follow it east of Peterborough. Turn north on Regional Rd. 38 (2nd Line Rd.), then take County Rd. 4 to Caves Rd.

SCARBOROUGH BLUFFS PARK

No bluffing!

The stunning Scarborough Bluffs can reach 60 metres in height. In some places, the sandstone cliffs are beautifully carved in such a way to have inspired the name The Cathedrals. You'll add to your enjoyment of this natural phenomenon if you explore it from top to bottom in one visit.

To get the best panoramic view of the lake, visit the **Rosetta McClain Gardens** perched atop the Bluffs (see p. 313). But you'll get the finest lookout from the cathedral-shaped cliffs in Cathedral Bluffs Park a few minutes drive from the gardens.

Don't be put off by the simple look of the Scarborough Bluffs Park, as you can't readily see some fifteen benches sitting at the back. Nothing announces the breathtakingly beautiful panoramic view you'll get from each one. Try them all!

Facing us, the lake spreads endlessly. On the west side, we discover cliffs covered with trees, while the east side reveals the park's 400 acres, with its marina and the cliffs with their rocky peaks.

On the park's eastern side, there is a lovely path that borders the cliffs. There, I noticed (just before it heads north), another steeper path going down towards **Bluffers Park**; a natural slide my son really enjoyed (don't try this with toddlers).

Last year, we discovered another way to explore the Bluffs from top to bottom: **Scarborough Heights Park**, just west of **Rosetta Gardens**!

Once again, the park doesn't look too appealing but as you get closer to the edge the gorgeous view of the lake emerges. This time, we took one of the makeshift trails leading down the cliff. Boy! It was steep!

We loved it but I suspected there was a safer way down. There is! Between the park and **Rosetta Gardens** is a closed road accessible from a small opening to the left of the gate.

The paved road faded into a hard pressed dirt road following the shore and bordered by huge boulders. We walked for 10 minutes and got a breathtaking view of the white cliffs, the best I have seen so far, completely surreal so close to Toronto.

The bushes along the trail were host to several butterflies.

Keep some energy to go up the slope on your way back!

TIPS (fun for 3 years +)

• I did not notice washrooms in these two parks.

• During a visit I made at the beginning of October, I spotted dozens of Monarch butterflies in a patch of wild flowers east of Scarborough Bluffs Park. The park is located on their migratory route. I was also intrigued by the multitude of red ladybugs I found every second step along the shore.

• As you stroll along Kingston Road, between Warden and Midland Roads, it is amusing to ask children accompanying you to spot the ten murals to be found there, commissioned by the Scarborough Arts Council. See if they can find the race car, ladies in gowns, a row boat and some tubas and drums. I particularly enjoyed the one with a row boat approaching the cliffs, while my young arts critic was awestruck by the military band.

• Read about **Bluffer's Park** (including information on **Dog Fish Pub** at **Bluffer's Park Marina** and nearby **Lick's Homeburgers** a few minutes west of Midland on Kingston Road) on p. 405.

NEARBY ATTRACTIONS
Rosetta McClain Gardens .... p. 280

Scarborough Bluffs Park

D-3
East
of downtown
35-min.

• Scarborough
(416) 392-1111
www.toronto.ca/parks

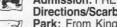

Schedule: Open year-round.
Admission: FREE.
Directions/Scarborough Bluffs Park: From Kingston Rd., take the short street west of Midland Ave. to access Midland southbound. Turn west on Romana St. and south on Scarboro Cr.
Directions/Scarborough Heights Park: From Kingston Rd., take Glen Everest Rd. southbound, then turn right on Fishleigh Dr., look for the Pumping Station.

DORIS MCCARTHY TRAIL

A passage worth exploring

Nature was quite an artist. The turquoise shade of Lake Ontario I saw, walking down the trail, was mesmerizing with the sun lighting thousands of gems on the water. Powerful waves were brushing the shore. I was alone and everything seemed so exotic. Then, it revealed itself, at the foot of the trail, blending so lovingly with the surroundings: *Passage*, a work of art from one artist to celebrate another.

I had noticed a little sign announcing the Doris McCarthy Trail. Curious is my middle name, plus I'm always on the lookout for new ways to access the waterfront, so I propelled myself down the ravine, not expecting much from the trail.

It started predictably, enclosed by tall thin trees blocking the view. But very soon it widened and cleared to reveal the sky. Then, I heard the whimsical sound of a small stream. As I went down, I would peak through the bushes to watch it flow between large rock plates. The bed of the stream eventually got two metres lower than the level of the trail, forming an irresistible corridor I just had to explore.

I jumped into it and started to hop from one plate to another over pockets of water.

When I looked upstream, I saw that the layered plates created moss-covered stairs from which tiny falls fell. The blocks of rock framing the whole scene added to the impression of being amidst ancient ruins.

I'm not sure my 10-year-old would have appreciated the beauty of the site but I know for a fact that he would have loved this adventure on the bed of the small brook.

Down stream, the water pockets were getting larger and the plates fewer so I climbed back onto the trail. Moments later, I discovered the strange sculpture. The *Passage* stood like the remnants of an ancient canoe or the rib cage of a strange aquatic mammal, overlooking the cliffs along the shore.

When I got home, I looked up Doris McCarthy on the Internet and was put to shame for not yet recognizing this amazing painter, now over 90 years old, who has spent her life capturing the beauty of the light on Canadian landscapes and passing on that passion to students.

It also turns out that she was the owner of the scenic property nestled on the **Scarborough Bluffs** east of the Doris McCarthy Trail: The Fool's Paradise. She has donated it to the Ontario Heritage Foundation along with funds to maintain the property as an artist's retreat.

This inspiring woman also wrote a biography titled *A Fool's Paradise*, relating her journey from childhood, in the Beaches neighbourhood, to a mature painter on top of the bluffs.

The trail was officially named after Doris in May 2001 and *Passage*, the work of Marlene Hilton-Moore, was unveiled in October 2002 in her honour.

TIPS (fun for 5 years +)

• It takes less than 15 minutes to go down the trail; more if you go the harder way, along the bed of the stream. BEWARE! There are thorns on the bushes bordering it. It takes longer to climb your way back up the trail, especially with tired children (not for under 8 years).

• There's a beach, east of the trail. I was told you could reach the **Guild Inn** property if you keep going in that direction.

NEARBY ATTRACTIONS

Rosetta Gardens (5-min.) .... p. 280
The Guild Inn Gardens (5-min.) .... p. 281

Doris McCarthy Trail
· Scarborough
(416) 392-1111
www.toronto.ca
www.dorismccarthy.com

**D-3
East
of downtown
35-min.**

 Schedule: The trail is open year-round.
Admission: FREE access.
 Directions: Take Kingston Rd. eastward, turn south on Ravine Dr. (which is named Bellamy Rd. on the north side of Kingston). You can park on the street past the sign marking the entrance to the trail off Ravine Dr.

RATTLESNAKE POINT C. A.

Shortcut

I first visited Rattlesnake Point with an energetic mom carrying her chubby baby on her back. I didn't dare bring my five-year-old explorer close to 25-metre cliffs before having inspected the surroundings first. What's the verdict? Well... With a firm hand and a strong heart, you can take children along to see the panorama from Rattlesnake, extending as far as the eye can see. The area's many natural assets are worth it.

The cliffs are a five-minute walk away from the first parking lot, giving children instant gratification!

The first parking lot is accessible via a small, one-way loop road to the left. The

Vista trail beginning in that area leads you directly to the Nelson observation point and to the stairway. The stairs lead down to the foot of the cliff. This gives visitors a totally different perspective of the rock. Furthermore, the rock formations in this area allow sturdy little explorers to climb enthusiastically, emulating the rock climbers who are most likely on the premises.

Rattlesnake Point is indeed a great spot for rock climbing (a waiver form must be signed). While walking along the path, you might spot seemingly abandoned backpacks, but look closely. You'll eventually notice brightly coloured ropes wrapped around trees, with climbers silently perched at their ends.

Before reaching the stairs, you'll notice a small path leading to the nearby Trafalgar observation point. You'll find another viewing point overlooking Nassagaweya canyon, a fifteen-minute walk away to the right, also accessible from another parking lot.

You'd have to walk another half-hour beyond that to reach the last observation point, Buffalo Crag, lengthening the return trek by about an hour. When you're accompanying kids, that's a serious consideration to ponder.

TIPS (fun for 5 years +)

• You need good walking shoes. As soon as a child is less than ten metres away from the escarpment, you should hold his hand. A ratio of one adult per young child is advisable.

• Depending on which way the wind blows, your nose may be bothered by a smell emanating from a nearby mushroom-growing farm. Had to mention it.

• A most moving detail seen on the course: a 40-cm-wide flat stone with a plaque mentioning "Baby Nina Anna Glinny Copas, June 23, 1996". I was assured this child didn't fall off the cliff. Still, this is a real commemorative plaque placed by parents... Should still be there.

• Some readers told me they found small caves along the rock walls, barely noticeable through shady cracks.

• Remember to keep your Rattlesnake Point entrance ticket. During the same day, it gives you free access to other conservation areas such as **Hilton Falls** (see p. 266) or **Crawford Lake** (see p. 388), ten minutes away.

Rattlesnake Point Conservation Area · Milton (905) 878-1147 www.conservationhalton.on.ca	D-2 West of Toronto 50-min.

 Schedule: Open year-round, from 8:30 am to dusk.
Admission: $5/adults, $4/ seniors, $3.50/5-14 years, FREE 4 years and under, ($5/vehicle in self-serve fee box when no attendant on duty).
Directions: From Hwy 401 West, take exit #320/Hwy 25 northbound. Turn west on Campbellville Rd., south on Tremaine Rd., west again on Steeles Ave., then turn south on Appleby Line.

MOUNT NEMO C. A.

Don't worry

From here, catch the most breathtaking views of the Niagara escarpment. Between the fragrant cedars, you can even admire the turkey vultures' wingspans while they silently glide at eye level, against a backdrop of checkered fields. Don't worry, there's very little chance that your little ones will fall from this 85-metre cliff without rails. The crevices will prevent this from happening!

Seriously, I was enthralled by the Mount Nemo Conservation Area when I realized that here, children could discover the natural phenomena of cliffs and crevices. During our last visit, we accompanied two mountain climbers, aged four and five, who thoroughly enjoyed these famous crevices.

For little ones on foot or in strollers, there's a wide gravel path (Bruce Side Trail), a shortcut leading to the Brock Harris observation point in 10 minutes. From behind a solid, safe low wall, this belvedere offers a superb panorama. On a clear day, we can make out the **CN Tower**, 60 kilometres to the right.

The crevices most accessible to young adventurers are located just left of the belvedere. The two we explored were about 30 metres from the cliff. Their narrow openings slope gently. Five metres down, their bottoms are lined with large stones. Natural footbridges cross over the crevices and give access to the edge of the cliff.

Beyond the first two crevices, the path sometimes gets as close as two metres from the escarpment, and crevices abound. Incredibly tortuous, criss-crossed by roots, lined with moss-covered rocks, with spots of light piercing through the trees, this trail is one of the most beautiful I've seen. Its course is clearly marked by white paint on tree trunks. It leads you back to the parking lot in an hour.

TIPS (fun for 4 years +)
• With children 7 years and older, I recommend you take the 2.3 km North Loop (the first one to the left when you walk on the gravel path by the parking lot, with orange markers). Kids will love to spot the **Bruce Trail**'s white marks (two marks on a tree means that there's a turn). The South Loop is less interesting.
• Accompanying adults who fear for their children's safety may want to stick to the first two crevices along the trail.
• Good walking shoes are a must; increased attention is required on certain slippery patches.
• You may use a stroller only on the gravel road leading to the belvedere.

NEARBY ATTRACTIONS
Kelso Beach (10-min.) .... p. 416
Crawford Lake C. A. (10-min.) .... p. 388

Mount Nemo Conservation Area	**D-2 West of Toronto 45-min.**
• Mount Nemo	
(905) 336-1158	
www.conservationhalton.on.ca	

Schedule: Open year-round, 8:30 am to dusk.
Admission: $5/vehicle. Deposit the exact amount in an envelope provided at the entrance, or place your same-day entrance receipt to another Halton conservation area on your dashboard.
Directions: From QEW West, take exit #102/Guelph Line northbound. From Hwy 401 West, take exit #312/Guelph Line southbound. Turn east on Colling Rd. (north of Mount Nemo).

SANDBANKS PROVINCIAL PARK

Three beaches, three worlds

As soon as my son and his friends reached the top of the golden dunes overlooking the lake 30 metres below, they playfully fell on their knees, thanking Heaven like grateful desert survivors who just realized they're saved.

The first time I visited Sandbanks Park, I literally missed Dunes Beach. We went straight to Outlet Beach and stayed there for the whole day. Upon returning later, I was better able to appreciate the uniqueness of Sandbanks Beach and Dunes Beach which remained to be explored.

Dunes Beach

Dunes Beach is definitely unique. As you observe the tall dunes bordering the east side of the beach adjacent to the parking lot, you realize that your eyes are not accustomed to this kind of panorama. You must get closer to the lake shore to better gauge the size of this natural playground.

You must then hike the highest peak of the dunes. The scenery is grandiose and conducive to daydreaming. Then, gravity calls and kids can't resist sliding down the silky slope all the way to the water. Others, of all ages, run wildly or simply tumble down with glee. The sandy water lake bottom is calling them.

Because of its location, the water of the beach at the foot of the dunes is the quietest of the Sandbanks Park. Located close to West Lake, it doesn't face Lake Ontario like the others (one has to consult a map to figure that one out). Well isolated, its water is warmer! This is great since I, unlike my little tomboy, found the water temperature at the other two beaches a little too cool for my liking. The school of small fish moving at our feet and the tiny frogs in the reeds added to the kids' enjoyment.

You can walk a lot farther through the dunes along the lake. The further you go, the less crowded it gets, naturally. Don't forget bottles of water!

Outlet Beach

Outlet Beach's wonderfully fine and pebble-free sand is outstanding for building castles or digging a maze of interconnected waterways. Also, the very large area of shallow water along its shores is ideal for swimming toddlers, and great for parents' peace of mind.

The Beach stretches along three kilometres, reaching depths of 30 metres in some places, which the surrounding tall trees can't completely shade.

The Beach's name changes to Camper's Beach, where it meets the River Outlet (which you can cross by foot). There's a specially designated pet area nearby!

Photo: Courtesy of D. De Oliveira

TIPS (fun for all ages)

• More on provincial parks on p. 307.

• If you want to go to **Dunes Beach** directly, don't follow the signs leading to the main gate; stay on Road 12 to reach Dunes Beach's day-use parking lot and pay the admission at the automatic machine (accepts coins and credit cards).

• The beautiful semi-wild **Outlet River Campground** has 270 campsites. **Cedars Campground**, set further back from Outlet Beach has 190 more sites. **Richardson's Campground** sits in a young and sparse forest near Sandbanks Beach, and offers less privacy than the two other sites.

• A Visitor Centre and a Nature Shop are located at the entrance of **Outlet Beach**, close to Parking lots #1 and #2. This beach is well outfitted with picnic tables; you can easily get a hold of one before 11 am. A well-stocked snack bar is also located near Parking lot #7. There's another one at **Dunes Beach**.

• We overnighted at the **Bloomfield Inn**, a motel located in Bloomfield. A room with two double beds costs $115/ double occupancy in summertime with a cost of $10 per person for additional guests (children up to 10 years old stay for free). The motel belongs to the owners of **Angeline**, a French gastronomic restaurant located on the same property. We also booked babysitting services to fully enjoy a great meal. See **www.angelinesinn-spa.com** or call 1-877-391-3301.

• Check **www.pecchamber.com** and click on **Business Directory** to find out about other accommodations in the area.

• Last time we visited the area, we took the time to visit Picton's **Birdhouse City**. It is actually a vast park with a few trees here and there and over 100 birdhouses mounted on poles. Most are miniature reproductions of historic buildings done as a community involvement project. The Friends of Birdhouse City have built, and maintain the houses, (613) 476-1659. From Main Street in Picton, take  Union Street, it becomes County Rd. 8, the park is on the right hand side.

NEARBY ATTRACTIONS	
Bergeron's Sanctuary (20-min.)	.... p. 77
The Big Apple (60-min.)	.... p. 415

Sandbanks Beach

Sandbanks Beach offers 8 kilometres of sand; an obvious favourite for hikers. Lovely trails surround the slopes on these shores.

Here, the beach is not as wide as that of **Outlet Beach**. With a few pebbles here and there, its water is a bit deeper and nice waves usually form, greatly pleasing the young swimmers.

Last time we went, end of June, early July, hundreds of small silver fish were washed up on the shore, a natural phenomena I was told occurs often at this time of the year. If you think it would gross you out, call the park to see if it is currently going on.

Sandbanks Provincial Park
• Picton
(613) 393-3319
www.ontarioparks.com

**C-6
East
of Toronto
2 1/2 hrs**

Schedule: Open April 1 to end of October from 8 am to dusk.
Admission: $8-$13 per vehicle for day use.
Directions: R.R. 1, Picton. From Hwy 401 West, take exit #522/ Wooler Rd. southbound, then follow Regional Rd. 33 through Bloomfield. Turn south on County Rd. 12 and follow the signs. (Read TIPS!)

HILTON FALLS C. A.

Falls 101

We're on the way back. I'm puffing like an old locomotive while I pull my little "bundle", comfortably seated in the red wagon. I then hear his voice, somewhat concealed by the noise of wheels crunching on the gravel, chanting: "I think I can, I think I can." I burst out laughing when I recognize the chant from *The Little Engine that Could*. Those who know the classic tale will smile as I did when faced with my son's empathy. This goes to show how our children never miss a beat when we take them on outings!

The Hilton Falls are a 30-minute walk away from the parking lot. With good shoes, you can easily get close to the falls (there may be a cold shower included!). Here and there, makeshift bridges are made of tree trunks. If little explorers are able to cross the river on these, they're big enough to romp about in this natural playground: a cave, rock climbing and the discovery of a "secret" passage inside the ruins (even so, tell them to be careful on the sawmill wall).

Go for a short walk on the trail downstream from the falls. A huge round pothole was formed 12,000 years ago by the movement of rocks on the riverbed. It's quite safe for children to go down into it. However, they (and you) should be vigilant in areas closer to the cliff's edge.

From the belvedere in front of the falls, an unexpected view reveals the ruins of a 19th century sawmill. Further ahead, along the **Bruce Trail**, stairs lead to the riverbank.

To return, I recommend taking the Beaver Dam Trail marked in orange until it crosses another trail. The red circles of the Red Oak Trail will then lead you to the parking lot. This trail crosses a small river that flows down into a wide reservoir.

TIPS (fun for 4 years +)
• More on **conservation areas** on page 262.
• During spring and summer, black-flies might swoop down on visitors as soon as they stop on bare trails: Bring insect repellent. They're nearly absent close to the falls and in the woods.
• The gravel paths are wide and stroller-accessible except for the first hundred metres of the yellow trail going up hill.
• There are single tracks for mountain bikes (helmet mandatory).
• In wintertime, the falls surrounded by ice make for an original family outing. There's also cross-country skiing.

NEARBY ATTRACTIONS
Ostrich Farm (15-min.) .... p. 65
Halton Museum (15-min.) .... p. 226

Hilton Falls Conservation Area	**D-2 West of Toronto 50-min.**

• Campbellville
(905) 854-0262
www.conservationhalton.on.ca

 Schedule: Open year-round from 8:30 am until dusk.

 Admission: $5/adults, $4/seniors, $3.50/5-14 years ($7/mountain bike fee).

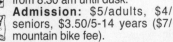 **Directions:** From Hwy 401 West, take exit #312/Guelph Line northbound. Turn east on Campbellville Rd. Park is on the north side.

STER'S FALLS C. A.

We walked for 30 minutes before heading back (to maintain the children's momentum to the end).

A small sign from the parking lot indicated a trail leading to Tew's Falls. We were told it would take approximately 20 minutes to reach it but the kid had had it by that time so we drove to get there.

Many written sources described it as towering 41 metres, "only a few metres short of **Niagara Falls**"... It was tall indeed but nobody had mentioned that it was only a metre wide!

Double feature

A majestic gorge and powerful falls, plus the rainbow effect, the mist on our face and the gorgeous trail: I did not expect such a wholesome program! I'll just have to go by the usual cliché: This is the best-kept secret in the region.

Let your ears guide you to the falls from the parking lot but don't miss the tiny cemetery nearby to find out who they are named after.

You'll need to cross the cobblestone bridge to get a good view from the top and then to get to the trail leading down the falls. The adventure starts with the stairs. They were stiff and slippery when we visited but will be refurbished soon.

I just love the thundering noise of falls, and this is a good 79-foot one, with the bonus of a full rainbow when you look at the right place at the right time. The beauty of the trail bordering the river is that it is at the water level and the river cascades and dances all along.

Webster's Falls Conservation Area
· Dundas
(905) 628-3060
www.conservationhamilton.ca

E-2
S-W
of Toronto
60-min.

 Schedule: Open year-round.
Admission: $5 per vehicle.
 Directions: From QEW/Hwy 403, exit at Hwy 6 North then turn west on Hwy 5. Turn south on Brock Rd., then east on Harvest Rd. Turn south on Short Rd. (it becomes Fallsview Rd.) to get to Webster's Falls or drive a bit further on Harvest Rd. to reach Tew's Falls.

TIPS (fun for 4 years +)
• There's a trail along the edge of the escarpment accessible from the parking lot at Webster's Falls. It offers nice panoramas but the kids preferred the forested depths of the gorge.
• We were told the site is beautiful in the winter when part of the waterfalls are frozen and sparkling.

NEARBY ATTRACTIONS

ALBION FALLS

Rock and roll!

You could go the easy way and use the stairs for instant gratification... or build your kids' anticipation (and their muscles) by taking a 30-minute upstream trail to reach the impressive falls.

The 10-minute trail by the parking lot took us down to the **Red Hill Creek**. We could have walked on large boulders to cross the creek but started instead to walk upstream into a luscious ravine. Previous visitors had cut different trails along the stream, some of them quite steep.

As I was wondering what age recommendations I would make for this attraction, we came across

a brave father and his three young "entomologists" hopping across the creek, taking advantage of the rocks revealed by the lower level of the water during the fall season.

After a 20-minute walk in the gorgeous forest, accompanied by the whimsical sound of the water, we finally saw the falls through the trees. Only once we reached past those trees could we appreciate the 18-metre-wide body of water cascading down the 19 metres of natural stairs. What a sight!

You realize how impressive the scale is when you actually see someone walking on the humongous boulders at the foot of the falls.

We noticed a young man rummaging through some rusting metal junk unfortunately gathered by the boulders. I assumed he was one of those artists using recycled material for weird installations. Turns out he was just a nature lover understanding the value of small gestures, picking up one piece of junk every time he goes on a trail. Inspiring, isn't it?

Stairs took us to the top of the falls where we followed a small trail along the road leading back to the parking lot in 5 minutes.

TIPS (fun for 8 years +)
• There's a parking lot in **Upper King's Forest Park** by Mountain Brow Blvd., on the west side of the falls, a few minutes walk from the stairs located on the east side of Albion Falls.
• Good shoes are a must.
• To get the Conservation's great *Cascades & Waterfalls* brochure listing 32 waterfalls, go to **Contact Us** of their website, then click **Request Brochures**.

NEARBY ATTRACTIONS
Canadian Warplane (15-min.) .... p. 21
Children's Museum (15-min.) ...... p. 237

Albion Falls
• Hamilton
(905) 525-2181
www.
conservationhamilton.ca

E-2
S-W
of Toronto
60-min.

 Schedule: Open year-round.
Admission: FREE.
 Directions: From Hwy 403 towards Hamilton, take Lincoln Alexander Pkwy east (for about 9 kms), exit at Gage St., go northbound, then east on Mohawk Rd. until you reach Mountain Brow Blvd. The parking lot is past Pritchard Rd.

NIAGARA FALLS

Fall for them

A couple of kilometres upstream along the Niagara Parkway, we observe the large cascades as they roar into the falls. Through the car's open window, we can hear their thundering sound and feel a mist blowing towards us.

Even though it is midweek on the summer afternoon we visit, we are caught in the long line-ups, and the closest available parking space is located on Upper Rapids Drive, two kilometres away from the Niagara Falls.

Don't worry if it happens to you, it does not mean you will have to walk that distance or watch it all from your car! A free shuttle will take you from the Rapidsview Parking to the falls. Or you could buy the People Movers pass directly at the parking lot, allowing you to travel all day long in the air-conditioned buses going up and down the Niagara Parkway. They are simply the best way to enjoy the area if you don't find parking right away and kids love to ride them.

Upstream

Upstream from the falls is the **Floral Showhouse** (formerly the **Greenhouse**). Its admission is free… and so are the exotic birds flying over our heads. It is a good observation game for the children to spot them among the colourful plants.

A five-minute walk away upstream leads you to the **Dufferin Islands**. These are eleven little islands linked by small bridges. We got close enough to touch the doz-

ens of wild ducks swimming around the bridges in the fall.

At the Falls

The **Table Rock Center** (the renovation of which will be finished by June 2008) is right at the falls, so is the attraction **Journey Behind the Falls**. My children's favourite part of this attraction is the ride in the elevator down to the tunnels. You may observe the white wall of water falling from a terrace or through the viewing portals.

A new, multi-million dollar attraction was on its way at the time of print: **The Fury**. They didn't want to give away details but I expect an interactive multi-media experience exploring the formation of the falls from the ice age to the present! Check **www.niagarasfury.com** for upcoming details.

The **Table Rock Restaurant** is being replaced by **Elements on the Falls**. It should still offer the best view of the falls from the panoramic windows and I was told the price range and menu would remain affordable and interesting for families. We really enjoyed our lunch time experience in the old restaurant.

A ride on the **Maid of the Mist**, a bit further down the river, is your surest bet to get in the middle of the action. I think "Maid of the Shower" would be a more accurate name for this boat. Don't go expecting not to get wet! After my ride, I started to notice all the visitors with wet pant legs.

The truth is, you don't get to see much of the falls as the boat approaches them, because your eyes are shut to protect them from the water spray. But you get to hear them pretty well!

Our greatest surprise was the beautiful rainbow above our heads. Later on, as we took the 15-minute walk back to the **Table Rock Center**, we could again admire a rainbow from the railing of the boardwalk. It was also the best spot to admire the ever-changing lights on the falls in the evening.

The **Incline Railway** ride linking the **Table Rock Center** to upper Fallsview area costs $2. It is a big hit with children! The People Movers pass also gives access to the **Incline Railway** for the entire day. Note that this ride and the **People Movers** buses are not wheelchair accessible.

Downstream

I think the visit to the **White Water Walk** (formerly called the **Great Gorge Adventure**), a few kms down the river is underrated. It is usually less busy than the other attractions and shows you the river from a different but equally powerful point of view.

The elevator ride down to the dark and cool tunnel is as much fun for the kids as the one at **Journey Behind the Falls**.

It leads us to a boardwalk by the spectacular rapids. The river, being 38 metres (125 feet) deep at this level, makes the water gush down in large impressive swirls at the speed of over 60 km/h. Our 15-minute walk on the boardwalk was beautiful, safe and refreshing (in mid-summer), without soaking us, and the kids enjoyed climbing up the giant boulders.

It takes approximately 10 minutes to walk from the gorge to the **Whirlpool Aero Car**. This car hangs 76 metres (250 feet) above the river. The track cable system that moves the car was invented by a Spanish engineer also responsible for the world's first computer (Leonardo Torres Quevedo). I have not tried it, but from what I saw, young kids won't be tall enough to see above the railing of the car.

Further along, another attraction I want to visit next time we go is the **Niagara Glen Trail** which leads us down 60 metres (200 feet) to the water level in approximately 20 minutes, and **Niagara Totem Pole & Wood-Carving Park** featuring over 500 totem poles!

Bikers and hikers can admire the gorge from the trail running along the road. My husband has often cycled from Niagara-on-the-Lake to this point and back (in 4 hours) and finds it beautiful.

Dry fun

The area is chock-a-block with attractions of all kinds in and around Clifton Hill Centre Street. **Guiness World of Records** (**www.guinessniagarafalls.com**) and the **Ripley's Believe It or Not Museum** (**www.ripleysniagara.com**), despite some displays of questionable taste, are likely to strike children's imaginations, whether with "the biggest man in the world" or a sculpture made with one grain of rice. One! (Some displays of nature's anomaly can disturb kids under seven.)

Visits to the non-interactive wax and horror museums are too short for their cost.

Last time we went, the kids enjoyed **BrickCity** (4943 Clifton) featuring impressive constructions all made by one single guy out of the kids' favourite blocks, including a model of the falls!

Don't miss the huge marble ball and the giant chair by the entrance of the **Guiness World of Records**.

TIPS (fun for 4 years +)

- See **Butterfly Conservatory** on p. 70.
- See **Niagara's Winter Festival of Lights** on p. 184.
- First time we went to the Falls, we visited the **Niagara Falls Imax Theatre**, at the end of the day, to watch the movie *Miracles, Myths & Magic*. I wish we had started our outing with it. The legends, accidents and stories of daredevils, which were re-enacted on the huge screen, shed a new light on the falls. The daredevil artefacts shown in the lobby and the museum are fascinating when seen after the movie (6170 Fallsview Blvd., 1-866-405-4629, **www.imaxniagara.com**).
- Wondering how the Falls generate electricity? Tons of water are channelled through underground tunnels on each side of the river, into huge reservoirs behind the power plants downstream from the whirlpool. **Sir Adam Beck 2 Generating Station** is open for tours to explain it all!
- No need to wait in line-ups! You can buy timed tickets in advance at the attractions' ticket booths and show up 15 minutes before the booked time slot.
- Check their website and click **Plan a visit** for information about their **Adventure Pass** including admission to **Journey Behind the Falls**, **White Water Walk**, **Maid of the Mist** and **Butterfly Conservatory** (which you don't have to see all in one day) with **People Movers** transportation (valid for one day only).
- My 3-year-old was a bit distressed by the showers of water falling over her on the **Maid of the Mist**. Kids normally scared by thunderstorms will probably not enjoy this noisy attraction. I don't recommend you go on with a stroller either.
- Free **fireworks** can be seen every Friday and Sunday at 10 pm, from mid-May to early September as well as Wednesdays in July and August and Fridays from September to early October. They're also offered on **Victoria Day**, **Memorial Day**, **Canada Day**, **Independance Day and Simcoe Day**. The falls are illuminated at night year-round. Check their website under **What to do** for the fireworks and illumination schedules.
- The **Rainforest Café** and the **Hard Rock Café** are both in the middle of the action and great restaurants the kids will enjoy. Check **Restaurants** on **cliftonhill.com**.
- For the best value in the summer, to the all-you-can-eat breakfast/lunch/ dinner buffet at **Almacs Buffet** (5435 Ferry Street, 905-357-6227 (seasonal), go up Clifton Hill, then left on Victoria., it becomes Ferry Street). With a 200-seat patio, kids rates, a really wide selection, we were in heaven. It is just on the way out of Niagara, west of Stanley Ave. leading to Hwy 420.
- Read about our stay at the **Skyline Inn** on p. 434, to take advantage of the amazing indoor **Fallsview Waterpark**.

Niagara Parks Commission	E-4 Niagara Region 90-min.
• Niagara Falls 1-877-642-7275 (info line) or (905) 356-2241 www.niagaraparks.com	

 Niagara Parks attractions Schedule: Journey Behind the Falls is open year-round. Other outdoor attractions are open as early as March to as late as November. All are at least open from 10 am to 5 pm. Call for exact dates and times.

People Movers Schedule: From April 1 to October 31, the shuttles run daily from 9 am to 11 pm in the summer (shorter hours for the rest of the season).

Admission: All attractions are FREE for children 5 years and under. **Journey Behind the Falls** is around $12/ adults, $7/6-12 years; **Maid of the Mist** is $14.50/adults, $9/6 to 12 years; **White Water Walk** is $8.50/adults, $5/6-12 years; **Whirlpool Aero Car** is $11/adults, $6.50/6-12 years; **Sir Adam Beck 2 Generating Station** is $8.50/ adults, $5/6-12 years; **People Movers** day pass is $7.50/adults, $4.50/6 to 12 years.

Directions/Rainbow Bridge: From QEW towards Hamilton and St. Catharines, exit at Hwy 420. Follow Hwy 420/ Roberts St. and signs to the Bridge to the US. Remain on Falls Ave. Turn left on Clifton Hill, then right on Niagara Pkwy to reach the falls.

Rapidsview Parking: (open May to early October) From QEW towards Hamilton and St. Catharines, exit at McLeod Rd., turn left on McLeod, it becomes Marineland Pkwy. Turn left at Rapidsview, it leads to Niagara Pkwy. Turn left.

NEARBY ATTRACTIONS	

HIGH FALLS

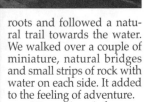

Small adventure

My son just loves exploring natural wonders full of nooks and crannies. High Falls is filled with these.

First, we tried to get as close as we could to the thundering High Falls. The powerful white body of water was fascinating to my then 5-year-old. In some spots, we had to jump more than one metre down onto lower rocks, to get closer.

All around the park, the ground is covered with big slabs of rock. Vegetation has tried to grow over and hold on to as much as it could with the help of really long running roots.

We slid down a steep hill filled with roots and followed a natural trail towards the water. We walked over a couple of miniature, natural bridges and small strips of rock with water on each side. It added to the feeling of adventure.

We explored the surroundings of a stream running into the woods. Part of the stream had enough water for it to expand into a nice wading pool among the trees. I wanted to stop for a while to listen to the musical sound of the water flowing over the stones, but my son felt like a pioneer, stick in hand and wanted to keep going.

TIPS (fun for 5 years +)

• The rocks and ground can be quite slippery. Bring rubber boots or shoes to better explore the stream.

• Bring insect repellent if you want to explore the stream.

• Since our last visit, the **Trans-Canada Trail** has reached High Falls. There is now a bridge running over High Falls offering a great panorama.

NEARBY ATTRACTIONS

High Falls
· **Bracebridge**
(705) 645-5264

A-3
North
of Toronto
2 1/4 hrs.

Schedule: Open year-round.
Admission: FREE.
Directions: North of Bracebridge. Take Hwy 400 North then follow Hwy 11 northbound. Take exit #193 (R.R. #117 on the east side, Cedar Lane on the west side), drive over Hwy 11, enter High Falls Resort and drive up the hill.

WONDERS OF THE EARTH

A real gem

This gem show has been organized by the **Gem & Mineral Club of Scarborough** for the last 35 years. It is a great starting point for young geologists.

My kids were thrilled by the Kids Quarry where we could get a sandbag of minerals for 50¢. They would dump its content into a sifter and discover at least 6 specimens. A little plastic pouch included contained labels to identify the rocks. There were also hands on soapstone carving and fossil preparation.

The show is held in a large gym. Many members exhibit their collections. You can watch lapidary work and jewelry making, gem cutting, soapstone carving and fossil preparation.

There's also a Mineral Identification Table where your child can take the "precious" stone he found for the experts to identify (but maybe he doesn't really want to know...).

There were many 50¢ to $1 minerals to choose from. My daughter went for a $2 fabric surprise bag holding three stones. We could buy strands of fresh water pearls for $5.

TIPS (fun for 6 years +)

• To find a local gem club, go to the website of the **Central Canadian Federation of Minerological Societies** (**www.ccfms.ca**) and click on **Member Clubs**.

Wonders of the Earth
• **Scarborough**
(905) 396-4043
(community centre)
www.scarbgemclub.ca

D-3
N-E
of downtown
35-min.

 Schedule: On the second weekend after Labour Day, Saturday, 10 am to 6 pm, Sunday, 11 am to 5 pm.

 Admission: $3/adult, $1/child.

Directions: Mid-Scarborough Community Centre, 2467 Eglinton Ave. East, Scarborough (between Kennedy Rd. and Midland Ave.).

ROCK POINT PROVINCIAL PARK

On this rock, I will build... a park

Romantic picnic lovers and those longing for Cuban sand, stay away from Rock Point Park. Make way for miniature paleontologists, ornithologists, pebble collectors... and arachnid enthusiasts.

Photo: Courtesy of E. Ritson

When you arrive, ask at the gate for the trail leading to the fossils. On our visit, we parked not too far from a beaten dirt path which led us to the lake (where we intended to picnic...). What I saw was quite unexpected!

A rock floor covered the whole ribbon of "beach". The breaking waves were loaded with slimy moss and gave off a fishy smell. There was also the odour of the stagnant water evaporating from various natural basins carved in stone.

We had to choose between mosquito bites under shady trees and sunburn in open areas. At any rate, rock spiders heavily patrol the place.

If they don't decide to leave, park visitors are rewarded. From up close, we noticed that the fissures trapping the stagnant water were covered with fossils, dating back 350 million years!

Three-year-old tots aren't impressed by this discovery, but it will surely have an effect on older kids, especially if you do research before the outing. Personally, I was fascinated.

While I was examining the rocks, my two companions settled into a small, pebble-lined cove, fairly moss-free, where they "fished" with sticks for quite a while. Later, we walked to a viewing tower. We then drove to the beach on the other side of the park where beautifully rounded pebbles formed the lake bed. A great occasion to start a rock collection!

TIPS (fun for 4 years +)
• Beach shoes are helpful to deal with the pebbles rolling under your feet in the water at the day-use beach.
• The green space adjoining the beach by the parking lot is too bare for my liking; not what I would expect in a provincial park.
• There's a nicer sandy beach by the campgrounds.
• Camping areas are surrounded by quite a bit of greenery. The level of privacy isn't great (campers have a direct view of neighbours camping across the road), but it's far from the sardine can concept found in several campgrounds.

Rock Point Provincial Park
• Dunnville
(905) 774-6642
www.ontarioparks.com

E-2
S-W
of Toronto
2 1/2 hrs

Schedule: Open mid-May until mid-October.
Admission: $8-$11/vehicle pass.
Directions: Take QEW towards Niagara, exit Hwy 20/Centennial Park southbound (it becomes Hwy 56). Take Hwy 3 eastbound through Dunville, then follow the park signs.

TORONTO MUSIC GARDEN

On a fun note

It seems nobody thinks to walk west of the popular Harbourfront Centre so this part of the water's edge feels like an oasis in the midst of the city.

The garden is developed following a dance theme. Accessible from Spadina, we first encounter the Minuet, impressive with beautiful hand-made ornamental steel adorning its rotunda.

Walking down from the rotunda (kids will actually run), we reach a gentle slope of grass broken with grass stairs forming a sort of curved amphitheatre facing the water. At the foot stands a small stone stage. This whole section is called the Gigue. Both the Gigue and the Minuet are the chosen stages for dance and music shows during the summer.

The Sarabande offers a small trail spiralling down to a huge stone carved with a tiny pool of running water. Ever-

green trees, turning this corner into a nice little retreat, surround the rock.

The Courante stands out with its tall Maypole spinning in the wind, competing with the **CN Tower** against the sky. It is surrounded by luscious borders of flowers. Numerous granite boulders greet us in the Prelude section. It is also the best spot to observe the planes taking off and landing at Porter Airport across the water.

Just east of the Toronto Music Garden lies the **Spadina Quay Wetland**, an old parking lot transformed into a small marsh decorated with funny birdhouses.

If you use the headphones for a self-guided tour, you'll hear candid comments from the kids of a neighbourhood school who were involved in the landscaping of the garden. You'll also be able to hear music segments associated with the different dances.

TIPS (fun for 3 years +)

• It takes less than 5 minutes to walk along the garden on Queen's Quay West. **Harbourfront Centre** is 10 minutes east of the garden's entrance. The western part of the Music Garden is 2 minutes away from Bathurst Street.

• The **Marina Quay West** located at 539 Queen's Quay, near the garden's western entrance, offers underground parking at $7-$10. It is the place to rent $5 headphones for a self-guided tour of the garden, (416) 203-1212.

• For a description of attractions along the waterfront, read **Stroll around Harbourfront Centre** on p. 26.

Toronto Music Garden
(416) 973-4000
www.toronto.ca

D-3
Downtown
Toronto
5-min.

Schedule: Open year-round. Guided or self-guided audio tours and shows offered from June to September.
Admission: FREE admission, $5 to rent headphones.
Directions: Runs along Queen's Quay between Lower Spadina Ave. and Bathurst St.

ALLAN GARDENS CONSERVATORY

An oasis in the city

I tell my son we'll be visiting a greenhouse. "Is the house all painted in green?" he asks incredulously. "No, it's a house made out of glass and full of green plants that believe it's summer all year long!" I reply.

Talk about a greenhouse effect! Five buildings with large windows, covering over 16,000 sq. feet are filled with plants for all occasions. Some are filled with exhibits which gradually change into new ones according to the plants' life cycles. And it's free!

Enter through the building with the high palm tree filled dome. Stepping through a curtain of fine roots, you enter a tropical hothouse with hibiscus set amidst a tapestry-like leafy backdrop. Beyond it, a large selection of hairy, prickly, and fluffy cactuses await the little ones' impatient hands.

Retracing your steps to the other side of the dome, you'll find a cooler space with a small waterfall and a lovely red fish pond, with its penny-carpeted bottom, at the foot of a nymph statuette.

Further, the tropical mood is definitely on with its hot and humid climate. Here, orchids bloom against the roar of water going through a paddle wheel attached to a small house. In winter, you can admire shapes covered with flowers installed amidst hundreds of poinsettias and palm trees.

For two weeks during **Easter** time, a new selection of flowers adds its sweet perfume to the conservatory. The first **Easter** we visited the hot houses, we were struck by the sweet bouquet and the visual richness of the settings. What a contrast with those of wintertime!

Chrysanthemums bring an autumn look to the Allan Gardens, while December marks the return of the **Victorian Christmas** display.

TIPS (fun for 3 years +)

- More on their **Victorian Christmas** opening ceremony on p. 176.
- We played at guessing from which plant the fallen leaves belonged. A fun initiation to botany!
- GOOD NEWS! There's a revitalisation plan going on. It will eventually add a Children's Garden and play area, a South Garden Terrace and Artists' Gardens.

NEARBY ATTRACTIONS
Riverdale Farm (5-min.) .... p. 55
Mt. Pleasant Cemetery (15-min.) p. 277

Allan Gardens Conservatory (416) 392-7288 www.toronto.ca (click **Parks & Gardens**, then **Gardens & Conservatories**)	D-3 **Downtown** Toronto 15-min.

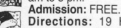

Schedule: Open year-round, 10 am to 5 pm.
Admission: FREE.
Directions: 19 Horticultural Ave., Toronto (south of Carlton, between Jarvis and Sherbourne St.).

MOUNT PLEASANT CEMETERY

The circle of life

"Is it true?" asks my anguished son. A smart little girl had just concluded the dispute she had been having with him by striking with an ultimate, irrefutable argument, that had nothing to do with their quarrel: "Oh yeah? Well, girls live longer than boys!" My little live one was shattered when I confirmed this dire statistic. He was ready for a visit to the cemetery to help us approach this delicate but very natural topic in a more realistic fashion.

Few people realize that the Mount Pleasant Cemetery is far from being sinister. The setting is so pretty, it attracts walkers, joggers and cyclists.

Sculptures adorning numerous graves give the visit an interesting cultural quality. If you go to Mount Pleasant Cemetery with children, I suggest you try finding, by car or by foot, the works of art I've photographed for you.

Bayview Avenue and Yonge Street

border the Cemetery. It's easier to enter by Yonge Street, north of St. Clair Avenue. Paved roads criss-cross the site and cars can stop wherever they please. A tunnel allows vehicles to circulate under Mt. Pleasant Road, which separates the cemetery into two sections.

After reading for my son a few dates written on gravestones, I was able to discuss with him the random nature of death. Here, parents bid farewell to their child; there, a woman said good-bye to her husband waiting for the time she'll join him; farther away, an entire family was buried a long time ago.

Many tombstones from plots 37 to 47 even show a picture of the deceased. This confers a more concrete image to the experience. The cemetery really is a fertile ground for discussion.

TIPS (fun for 6 years +)

• A great variety of trees can be found in this cemetery. During the fall, it becomes a great harvesting ground for young leaf collectors.

NEARBY ATTRACTIONS
David A. Balfour Park (5-min.) .... p. 319
Around Davisville Subway Station p. 448

Mount Pleasant Cemetery
(416) 485-9129

D-3
North
of downtown
20-min.

Schedule: Open daily, year-round from 8 am to 8 pm.
Admission: FREE.
Directions: 375 Mt. Pleasant Rd, Toronto (entrance on Yonge St., north of St. Clair Ave.).

TORONTO BOTANICAL GARDEN

It has blossomed!

A 5,000 square-foot glass pavilion and a 4-acre garden have been added to Edwards Gardens since my last visit, turning the place into a real botanical garden. What an elegant setting!

The new facility gracefully mingles with the landscaped surroundings, the architectural form of the plants blending with the natural texture of the walls.

A wall of water welcomes us by the main entrance of the building. We explore it on both sides which leads us to the Floral Hall Courtyard. We can see the shadow of the trees through the acid-etched glass. It is like being in our own little japanese world. A stone bridge runs over a small canal by a waterfall in the Garden Halls Terrace. From there, we can see the plants on the sloping green roof and the Spiral Mound, a viewing platform three metres above the ground.

TIPS (fun for 6 years +)

• Grab a visitor's map inside the main building to better enjoy the stroll.
• You'll need to register in advance for their programs or family events but they offer drop-in storytime in their library on Wednesdays at 11 am.
• Wilket Creek's wide paved trail starts at the southern edge of Edwards Gardens. Along its course, you'll find a few benches, a singing river flowing underneath several small bridges, beautiful undergrowth facing the river as well as 30-metre-tall maple trees and several other species of deciduous trees that take on magnificent hues in autumn. Beware, cyclists sometimes rush through the trail. Within 30 minutes, you'll reach the road going through Sunnybrook Park (where you can find washrooms). You can continue your stroll on Serena Gundy Park trail located across Sunnybrook Road.
• The TBG store offers a gorgeous selection of home and garden accessories as well as interesting toys and books.
• The TGB Café is open daily from May to October from 10 am to 4:30 pm (closes at 6 pm on weekends).

This section of the garden is so popular with kids (it allows a 360-degree perspective of the site and a view of the adjacent Knot Garden) that it was under renovations during my visit, to make it sturdier.

Five minutes down the west side of Edwards Gardens, past the weeping willow and the small valley, you'll find a Teaching Garden open to the public when not in use for the programs. It includes a giant butterfly sundial.

Behind the Carpet Bed Garden by the parking lot, you can access the Wilket Creek ravine.

NEARBY ATTRACTIONS
Ontario Science Centre (5-min.) p. 247

Toronto Botanical Gardens
• North York
(416) 397-1340
www.torontobotanicalgarden.ca

D-3 North of downtown 25-min.

Schedule: Open year-round.
Admission: FREE.
Directions: 777 Lawrence Ave. E., North York (at the corner of Lawrence Ave. and Leslie St.). There are a few pedestrian entrances to Wilket Creek Park on Leslie, south of Lawrence Ave.

JAMES GARDENS

viewpoint. A small pebble trail has been designed parallel to an asphalt one along the Humber River. It is reserved for pedestrians, so as to avoid collisions with cyclists and roller blade enthusiasts.

Heading towards the small forest of **Lambton**

Cool picnic!

The flowerbeds full of tulips and other spring blooms don't impress my little thrill-seeker. However, he really falls for James Gardens after he discovers the stairs. They climb 30 metres up towards the panoramic viewpoint overlooking the Humber River. To add to the picturesque character of this surprising city outing, we walk the trails through Lambton Woods and we head for a picnic on a bridge over the river.

The James Gardens are not particularly imposing, yet they have lovely symmetrical flower displays as well as several small ponds straddled by footbridges where ducks and chipmunks cavort here and there.

Small paths require the odd portage for those visiting with strollers, while a gentle slope offers a convenient alternative to the stairs leading to a terrace with a great

Woods, my aspiring botanist noticed curiously shaped and knotted trees and many tame birds with red wings. We observed with great interest a female duck in her nest... perched atop the chopped trunk of what would have been a mature tree.

After a 15-minute walk, the path turns onto a long footbridge leading to a bridge with benches. We stopped there and enjoyed our picnic. Below, the river cascaded down, glistening in the sun. Some 40 metres above, trains rolled down tracks set on high pillars. The overall effect was stunning!

TIPS (fun for 4 years +)
• **Lambton Woods** is well-known for spring wildflowers and the area is a favourite for birders.
• If you picnic on the bridge, make sure to sit on the sidewalk stretching along its railing to avoid cyclists travelling in the middle on the bike trail.

NEARBY ATTRACTIONS

James Gardens
• Etobicoke
(416) 392-1111
www.toronto.ca/parks

D-3
N-W
of downtown
35-min.

 Schedule: Open year-round.
Admission: FREE.
Directions: From Royal York Rd. (south of Eglinton Ave.), take Edenbridge St. eastbound.

ROSETTA MCCLAIN GARDENS

Perched garden

If you're in Scarborough to admire the Bluffs, don't forget to stop by the Rosetta McClain Gardens, perched atop the cliffs. You'll catch a breathtaking view of Lake Ontario, 60 metres below.

You can go round the gardens' paved trails in about twenty minutes. In the centre, there are symmetrical raised planter beds adorned with a few large stones. A scent garden filled with fragrant plants will titillate little noses. Numerous benches allow visitors a chance to admire the landscaping.

Young visitors like to take refuge underneath a beautiful bandshell located at one end of the gardens.

I went with my family on a beautiful autumn day. The sun was shining on Lake Ontario and the ground was littered with large leaves in bright yellow and red hues.

TIPS (fun for 4 years +)

• During my first visit, on a rainy day, fog created a white screen that completely hid the lake from my view! The atmosphere was magical; I felt cut off from the rest of the world... but I did not get to see Lake Ontario.

NEARBY ATTRACTIONS
Scarborough Bluffs (5-min.) .... p. 258
Birchmount Pool (5-min.) .... p. 421

Rosetta McClain Gardens
• Scarborough
(416) 392-1111
www.toronto.ca/parks

**D-3
East of downtown
30-min.**

Schedule: Open year-round.
Admission: FREE.

Directions: From Kingston Rd., access the gardens' parking lot, just before Glen Everest Rd.

THE GUILD INN GARDENS

Art comes naturally

We usually walk by the architectural details of downtown Toronto's buildings without giving it a thought, but here, in the natural setting, they regain all their beauty.

It is almost poetic, these wall fragments amidst the forest. One could imagine the ruins of an ancient civilization.

In the 50's, when Toronto began to tear down the downtown area to make room for the new, there was not much concern about preserving historical buildings. The owners of the Guild, already offering an outdoor sculpture garden, decided to collect the pieces of historical sites they came across.

Nowadays, among other things, you

can admire fragments of the Imperial Bank of Canada, built in 1928, and the Toronto Star Building, erected in 1929. You can see animal bas-relief panels, angel panels, lion's head keystone, column fragments, archways, bear sculpture and more, spread all around the site.

But the pièce de résistance is the central entrance to the Bank of Toronto, built in 1912 and turned into the impressive Greek Theatre. There used to be a theatre company that would produce a play every summer in this setting but not anymore.

We loved the plays but exploring the architectural fragments all around was as much fun. And we would top it off with a stroll along the westbound trail bordering the cliff.

TIPS (fun for 5 years +)

• There has been an **Art Naturally Festival** for years, normally on the weekend following Simcoe Day. Check **www.scarborougharts.com** or call (416) 698-7322 to find out about events organized by the Scarborough Arts Council.

• The place has belonged to the City of Toronto for a while now and the City, which used to manage the Guild Inn hotel for weddings and conferences, has closed down the venue. Talks to build a hotel, spa and cooking school, while maintaining the original artistic mandate fell through. At the time of print, you could still download a 2-page *Guild Sculpture Walking Tour* from the City of Toronto website.

The Guild Inn Gardens	D-3
• Scarborough (416) 392-1111 http://www.toronto.ca/culture/ the_guild.htm	East of downtown 30-min.

Schedule: Open year-round.
Admission: FREE.
Directions: 201 Guildwood Parkway, Scarborough. Take Kingston Rd. East to Guildwood Pkwy, then turn south.

NEARBY ATTRACTIONS

ROYAL BOTANICAL GARDENS

Royal treat!

As we walk down towards the lilacs, the vivid greens among the tall trees of the luscious valley catch my breath. To top it off, a live jazz tune is filling the air along with the sweet fragrance of the lilacs. This is what I call a well-cultivated event!

The **Lilac Celebration** is my favourite time of the year to visit the Royal Botanical Gardens (RBG). The weather is mild and the event takes us to the Arboretum, a large section 3 km from the RBG Centre, home to lilacs and magnolias and surrounded by fun nature trails to explore with the kids. One needs to explore the Arboretum to begin to grasp how vast and wild the RBG really is.

The RBG is comprised of 30 kms of nature trails, five separate gardens and four nature sanctuaries, one of which is the **Cootes Paradise Marsh**, right at the edge of the Arboretum.

You want to stop at the Arboretum's Nature Interpretive Centre, by the parking lot, to get trail maps and check out their interactive displays (with stuffed animals, microscope, live turtles and more) and their little shop, well stocked with trinkets.

During the **Lilac Celebration**, we were handed a map of the lilac dell with sections indicated by letters (the letters are actually shown on signs in the valley). Don't fail to cross section "S" to get to section "T" where you'll find all the gorgeous yellow, pink and white magnolia trees. Bring your camera, the contrast between the dark

branches and the delicate petals when the sun is shining through is simply beautiful!

You can access the North Shore trail from that section or from section "G". It runs along the **Cootes Paradise Marsh**. It was amazing to stop on the boardwalk just to listen to the birds and quite captivating to watch dozens of Cormorants hanging over their nests on the trees of a small island.

As a bonus for children, at different times and in different gardens throughout the year, the RBG displays interactive Discovery Carts filled with things to touch. During the **Lilac Celebration**, kids could compare the odours of different lilacs. Some really stink! They were invited to draw a lilac flower, choosing from the numerous characteristics: single, double, small, medium or large with lobes cupped, flat or curled down. Then, they could check on a chart if it already existed and where they could find it in the lilac dell.

The Rock Gardens, much appreciated by the children, offered a different kind of fun. Built in 1929, it was the first major display at the RBG. The huge mature trees are a testimony to that. Tulips and rocks take over the show in that garden. Rock stairs leading to secret corners, rocks becoming small bridges over the pond, huge rocks to climb on. This is a great spot for little explorers!

The fish in the pond of the indoor Mediterranean Gardens were a hit along with some huge flowers. The outdoor Discovery Garden was fun with its giant leaves and hollow tree trunk (both accessible from the centre).

TIPS (fun for 5 years +)

• The **Lilac Celebration** is usually held on the last two weekends of May but call before going to make sure the lilacs have blossomed.

• Here's a calendar of some blooms to expect (but call ahead to confirm): spring flowering bulbs in April; lilacs, flowering trees and spring wildflowers in May; irises, roses and annual flowers in June; lilies in July and August. In September and October, you still can see annual flowers, roses, dahlias and chrysanthemums, (although not at their best!). From November to March, there's always the indoor Mediterranean Gardens in the RBG Centre.

• Rock Gardens, RBG Centre and Rose Gardens are stroller accessible. I would dare to push a stroller across the Arboretum and part of the South Shore when it is not too muddy. Expect to lift it over stairs here and there.

• There's a double-decker service hopping from one garden to the next (included with admission). It runs Wednesday to Sunday and Holiday Mondays, every 30 minutes, from 10 am to 6 pm. Bear in mind that you might not be able to get on during very busy periods and the frequent stops mean it'll take the shuttle 25 minutes to go from the **Rock Gardens** to the **Arboretum** while you could do it in five minutes by car. (It took us 30 minutes to walk from the **Rock Gardens** to the **Arboretum Nature Centre**, following an unofficial narrow trail along the road.)

• There's no food service at the Arboretum. Bring your own water and snacks (including small nuts you could share with the chipmunks). If you are planning a picnic during the Lilac Festival, bring a thick blanket and some plastic garbage bags to line it! The ground might still be a bit wet.

• The **Rock Garden Tea House** is very nice with its elevated terrace (in the Rock garden). We also enjoyed locally famous **Easterbrook's Foot Long Hot Dog** snack bar (at 694 Spring Garden Rd. near the parking lot of RBG, 905-527-9679).

We have not had a chance to visit the other sanctuaries. There is the **Hendrie Valley** with 5 km of trails starting at the Rose Gardens parking lot. The Berry Tract is connected to **Cootes Paradise Marsh** and **Rock Chapel** by the **Bruce Trail**. **Rock Chapel** I have to see next time. It boasts a 25-m waterfall and 3.5 km of trails along the **Niagara Escarpment**, coinciding with the **Bruce Trail**).

The South Shore trails (not accessible from the North Shore trails) also seem quite interesting, with more hilly paths facing the **Niagara Escarpment**.

For Summer 2008, they will feature **Earthart**, an international environmentally appropriate art exhibition, throughout all the gardens.

Royal Botanical Gardens • Burlington (905) 527-1158 www.rbg.ca	E-2 S-W of Toronto 50 min.

   Schedule: The outdoor garden areas are open from 9:30 am until dusk. The **Nature Interpretive Centre** near the **Arboretum** opens from 10 am to 4 pm. The **RBG Centre** opens from 9 am to dusk and the **Mediterranean Gardens** (the greenhouse inside the **RBG Centre**) is open from 9 am to 5 pm.

Admission: $10/adults, $8/seniors & students, $6/5-11 years old, FREE under 5 ($4 less during off-season).

Directions: 680 Plains Rd. West, Burlington. Take the QEW to Hwy 403 West, then catch Hwy 6 North and take the first exit to Plains Rd. West.

LITTLE NORWAY PARK

Who knew?

I never expected to find such a tall and beautiful totem in such a secluded little park. And there was much more to discover as we walked further in: a giant lion leaning on a slide, the small labyrinth, a little forest and the pier behind, overlooking the glittering water of Lake Ontario.

When you read the plaques by the entrance, you learn that this used to be a training camp for Norway's Air Force during World War II and that it was officially opened by the King of Nor-

way in 1987. I don't know when it fell into oblivion but this little park is a keeper.

There were many details to observe on the 12-metre totem, from the large whales at the bottom to the small people climbing stairs way up high. Then my little mountain goats explored the rock stairs under the metal bridge.

The playground, located by the water, was hidden from our view so the huge concrete lion adorning it came as a great surprise.

A long pier is accessible through the little patch of evergreens (providing nice shade for picnics). We walked on it towards the lake until we reached the open water of Lake Ontario sprinkled with tiny sailboats. Small planes landed on the runway on the island as a bonus. It made us forget where we were!

TIPS (fun for 2 years +)

• There's no rail along the pier so you'll need to be extra careful with children. I don't recommend it with toddlers. The edges are too tempting…
• There's a wading pool in the playground. Bring bathing suits in case it should be open when you visit.
• The ferry ride to **Toronto City Centre Airport** is free and takes less than one minute.
• **Harbourfront Community Centre** (627 Queen's Quay West, just east of the park) offers $1 drop-in sessions to children 6 years and under. No need to pre-register. Call (416) 392-1509 or check **www.harbourfrontcc.ca**, go to **What we offer**, then **Family** to print their flyer.
• You'll find a great convenience store at the corner of Bathurst and Queens Quay perfect for an impromptu picnic.

Little Norway Park (416) 392-1111 www.toronto.ca/parks	D-3 **Downtown** Toronto 5-min.

Schedule: Open year-round.
Admission: FREE.
Directions: Runs along Queen's Quay between Bathurst St. and Little Norway Cr. There's public parking on the southwest side of Bathurst.

WOODBINE PARK

Downhill from there

Forget the 30-foot-high fountain, the bulrushes, the big frog, the giant gazebo or the little climbing wall. If you ask my kids, they'll tell you the park's best feature is the hill.

Woodbine Park popped out along with the new developments by Lake Shore in the Beach neighbourhood. It will show a very different face depending where you access it.

TIPS (fun for 2 years +)

• The parking lot on the south side of Eastern Avenue costs only $2. I would not be surprised if they eventually raise the price for those who don't attend the cinema.

• I think **Alliance Atlantis Beach Cinemas**, across the parking lot, is the best movie theatre in town: perfect seats, adjacent parking lot, great coffee, live jazz on weekends. For a movie listing, look for **Beach Cinemas** on **www.cinemaclock. com**.

• At the time of print, the construction of a large skatepark at the north-west corner of Lake Shore and Coxwell had been put on hold. To be continued?

We usually park in the parking lot by Eastern (across from the movie theatre) and walk southbound around the lot along Coxwell.

I think it is the best way to access the park because it is the least pretty. It allows for a dramatic effect when we get up the steep hill past the giant gazebo.

From this vantage point, you can admire Toronto's skyline with its trademark **CN Tower** on one side and the vast pond and 30-foot-high fountain on the other.

Cyclists like to ride the winding paths before reaching Ashbridges trails across Lake Shore.

Kids can climb up a small wall in the playground or get wet while hanging near the giant frog on the spray pad.

Woodbine Park (416) 392-1111 www.toronto.ca/parks	**D-3** **East** of downtown 15-min.

Schedule: Open year-round.
Admission: FREE.
Directions: Located east of Coxwell Ave., between Eastern Ave. and Lake Shoe Blvd. East, Toronto. You can park in the $2 parking lot on Eastern, east of Coxwell.

NEARBY ATTRACTIONS
Cherry Beach (5-min.) .... p. 401
Beach Neighbourhood (2-min.) ... p. 402

HIGH PARK

Toronto's true nature

It's all a question of perspective. Previously, I associated High Park with romantic walks along Grenadier Pond and Shakespeare at the fascinating outdoor theatre. Now, when I think of High Park, I see a baby bison living in one of Deer Pen Street's many animal paddocks, I hear the little train's bell joyfully ringing through the park's 161 hectares and I see a castle...

There's a trackless little train operating on a nine-station circuit around the park from spring to autumn. You can get on the train at the station of your choice, get off where you want to, and stay as long as you wish before hopping back on. You have the privilege of getting back on at the same station or at the next one, to complete the circuit to your starting point.

The High Park train's flexibility allows visitors to build an itinerary suited to their schedule, to take advantage of the various pleasures offered at the Park. For us, it usually starts with the playground.

High Park's is simply the most original playground in town. Guess how long it took High Park volunteers to build it from scratch? Ten days! OK, fine, there were about three thousand volunteers and planning had been a long-term affair. Even so, I admire the results of what people can achieve when they put their heart into it.

The masterpiece is shaped like a fortified castle, decorated with engravings and mosaics of children's drawings. It occupies 10,000 sq. ft. A third of this area is dedicated to small children and is enclosed with a fence, for parents' peace of mind.

The section for smaller children is full of nooks and crannies to explore and includes an amusing vibraphone. The staircase in the area for older children gives a labyrinth-like impression (if you let small children go there, step up the supervision).

The playground is next to the big duck pond, the animal pens which house bison, goats, llamas and sheep, a snack bar as well as one of the train's stops.

When the children have played all they want, I suggest that you let the little train take you to Grenadier Pond, a few stations further (about a fifteen-minute ride for young conductors).

In this corner of the park, the weeping willows that brush against the pond tempt visitors to picnic. Birds are so used to human presence that a Canada goose nearly left a few feathers between the fingers of my little rascal when he was only two years old.

After exploring this area of the park, you can hop back on the train to come back, ten minutes later, to your starting point. From there, you can visit Deer Pen Road's animals.

TIPS (fun for 2 years +)

• More about Shakespeare's **Dream in High Park** on p. 111 (in Tips section).
• See the **Soap Box Derby** in High Park on p. 215.
• More about **Colborne Lodge** and **Easter** activities at High Park on p. 380.
• BEWARE. From May 1 to October 1, on Sundays and holidays, the park can only be accessed from the Bloor Street entrance and you can only drive down to the restaurant.
• We prefer to enter the site through High Park Boulevard (accessible from Parkside Road) and turn left to park by the animal paddocks or at the end of Spring Drive. These parking lots are the closest to the castle playground. Otherwise, we park beside **Grenadier Restaurant** and walk 5 minutes.
• The **Keele Subway Station** is closer to the castle playground but still a 15-min. walk away (down Parkside Road).
• High Park includes a large outdoor pool as well as a wading pool, closer to the Bloor Street entrance, near **High Park Subway Station**.
• High Park Children's Garden, near **Colborne Lodge**, offers FREE drop-in programs for families every Thursday from 10 am to noon, in July and August. It includes garden games, crafts and gardening activities for children 3 to 12 years old (call 416-392-1329).
• There are snack bars in the park, near the big playground and by the Bloor entrance. There's also the **Grenadier Restaurant** with a dining room and a takeout counter (great fries!). Open year-round, from 7 am to 10 pm during the summer, (closes earlier the rest of the year). Call (416) 769-9870.

NEARBY ATTRACTIONS
Sunnyside Pavilion Café .... p. 404

High Park
D-3
West of downtown
15-min.
(416) 392-1111
(905) 652-6890 (train)
www.toronto.ca/parks

 Schedule: Open year-round. (The train operates daily from early May to Labour Day, from 10:30 am to dusk (weekends only in April and the rest of October, weather permitting).

 Admission: FREE. Train ticket (sold by train operator, cash only): $4/adults, $3/seniors and children 2 years and older, FREE under 2 years.

Directions: At the intersection of Bloor St. West and Parkside Dr., Toronto (Parkside Dr. is accessible northbound from Lake Shore Blvd.). Read tips!

DUFFERIN GROVE PARK

lic park: a gigantic sandpit. It lay in front of us, complete with running water, garden shovels and long logs.

Imagine what small engineers can do here! They build labyrinths of water streams and bridges. They dig holes. They create mini ponds...

Community centre without a roof

I was surfing through a very interesting site the other day: Project for Public Spaces, a non-profit organization dedicated to promoting great community places giving a new wholesome meaning to urban life. Guess what I found on their list of the 105 best public parks seen during their walk around the world in 1,000 neighbourhoods, 46 states and 12 countries? Our own Dufferin Grove Park!

This park might have been considered a seedy one back in the 90's but those days are over! The Friends of the Grove, a neighbourhood association, turned it around.

As soon as we entered the park we saw acrobats casually practicing their walk on stilts along the sinuous path that runs up and down hill.

Families were busy fixing individual pizzas to cook in one of the two outdoor wood ovens. Isn't it the most clever idea to bring a community together? Some people had brought toppings they offered to share with us. Another wonderful touch of colour in the vicinity: a huge border of tall sunflowers.

Further, a large playground surrounded by a split-rail fence (much prettier than the usual wire fence) was filled with a laughing crowd. As we walked towards it, we discovered the best and most daring feature I have seen in a pub-

It was so cute to see a bunch of preschoolers surrounding my 10-year-old boy scout, eager to help him as he undertook an ambitious bridge project. Many had the astonished look kids have when they can't believe their luck: "At last! A place where I'm allowed to get dirty and play with the garden faucet. Too good to be true; must hurry before someone stops me!"

You've got to see the details on the funny little house they recently built to offer sinks for the public (to comply with the City's sanitary requirements)!

TIPS (fun for 2 years +)

• The park is less than a 10-minute walk from **Dufferin Subway Station**.

• You'll find free parking at **Dufferin Mall** across the street. By the way, this mall includes **Wal-Mart**, **Toys 'R Us** and **Winners**!

• There's a large wading pool right next to the playground.

• Weather permitting, from May to September, the **Pizza Days** take place on Tuesdays and Wednesdays, 12 noon to 2 pm, and Sundays, 1 to 3 pm. A piece of dough, tomato sauce and cheese are included in the $2 fee.

• **Friday Night Suppers** take place, weather permitting. The park suppers cost $6. They are cooked in the community kitchen and served outside when the weather is good, lit with torches and candles. Sometimes films are projected outdoors after the supper, at 8 pm, against the field house wall (on a bed sheet)... Can you get more retro?

• The **Clay and Paper Theatre** has been involved with the park for years. Once a year, around October 31, they organize the interactive **October Night of Dread Parade**, starting and ending at the park and followed by a big bonfire, food and music. Call (416) 537-9105 or check **www.clayandpapertheatre.org** for the exact date and to find out about their drop-in mask-making workshops prior to the event.

• In the winter, if you go skating on the park's rink, you can enjoy a campfire and hot chocolate on most Sundays. The **Zamboni Café** sells light meals.

• Go to the **Project for Public Spaces** website to read the good feedback that is written about our park (**www.pps.org**, search for **Dufferin Grove Park**)! This website gives valuable tips for those who want to improve their local park.

I saw some resigned parents who watched their kids getting covered with mud in their Sunday clothes. Had they known, they would have brought a change of clothes.

Another original initiative in this park: There are two fire pits, which you can use with a permit! Think about it! You can actually roast marshmallows in the middle of the city! Call to ask about their $10 campfire permit and short training session.

As a bonus, when we visited the park, there was the **Children's Powwow** going full blast on the soccer field, with huge teepee, traditional drummers and dancers, adults and children so cute in their elaborate regalia. For a small fee, we could make a button, a dance shawl or a necklace. Wow! Native Child and Family Services has organized this annual **Children's Powwow** for the last ten years at the park. It usually takes place on the third or fourth Saturday of September. Call (416) 969-8510 to confirm.

There's an organic farmers' market every Thursday from 3:30 to 7 pm, year-round.

Dufferin Grove Park | D-3 West of downtown 15-min.
(416) 392-0913
www.dufferinpark.ca

 Schedule: Open year-round.
Admission: FREE access to the park.

 Directions: On the east side of Dufferin St., across from Dufferin Mall (two blocks south of Bloor St. West and the Dufferin subway station).

NEARBY ATTRACTIONS
Around Christie Subway Station   p. 439

YORK MILLS VALLEY PARK

Where am I?

The tall buildings at York Mills and Yonge are flanked with trees but there's still no country in sight. Walk south of Mills Street, and you're in another world altogether.

You can easily reach the paved trail off Mills Street from the south of the park's parking lot. There, you'll see water running down the ramp of a canal by a white house that looks like a fancy cottage. The illusion of being in the country is perfect even though the stream, actually the **West Don River**, is quite manicured at this point.

Further, the path reaches a very nice playground with a great hill as a background. If you keep going, you'll get to the viaduct. That's the best spot to access the water and view the cars driving over the viaduct.

From Donino Avenue, you can walk back to the parking lot off Mills Street or take another paved path at the corner of Mills and Campbell Crescent, by the statue of C. W. Jefferys (an artist and historian who lived nearby).

This will lead you to the subway station where you'll want to take the outdoor stairs down, to explore the graffiti in the long tunnel under Yonge Street and see the glistening water of the winding river.

If you have a chance, drive through the quiet streets accessible from Donido Avenue. They all lead to gorgeous dead-ends where no house looks like the next and all are beautifully set amidst luxurious vegetation.

TIPS (fun for 5 years +)

• There's a parking lot with machines by the park, which you can access from Yonge Street.
• There's a gas station with washrooms and a convenience store selling coffee in front of **York Mills Subway Station**.
• The hill by the playground seems perfect for some serious tobogganing on its south part. A more gentle slope on the north will cater to the younger crowd.

NEARBY ATTRACTIONS
Around Sheppard/Yonge Station p. 447
Around Lawrence Subway Station p. 448

York Mills Valley Park
• North York
(416) 392-2273
www.toronto.ca/parks

D-3
North
of downtown
20-min.

Schedule: Open year-round.
Admission: FREE.
Directions: Just east of Yonge Street, on both sides of Mill Street, North York. It is adjacent to York Mills Subway Station.

THOMSON & BIRKDALE PARKS

Paved with good intentions

While on a quest for stroller- and wagon-friendly paved trails, my wheels brought me to Scarborough. There I found great little asphalt paths in two adjoining parks: Birkdale and Thomson Memorial. Bathed in sunlight, the lush, leafy woods were abundantly laden with the autumn hues and shadows I enjoy so much. In addition, both parks offered a playground.

Usually, I'm not crazy about manicured parks. Nevertheless, I really enjoyed the intimate aspect of **Birkdale Park**. It is narrow, with plenty of curves and small valleys. The views are so diverse that you never know what awaits you around the next bend. It may be a small river, a pastoral valley, maple trees, either gigantically tall or short and stubby, or majestic weeping willows.

After a twenty-minute fun stroll, we got to a playground alongside Brimley Street. Last stop! Everybody off the wagon to move a bit!

If you wish to walk some more, you can cross Brimley Street (unfortunately, there are no traffic lights at this location, so be careful) and join **Thomson Memorial Park** by taking the path across the street. You'll need to walk another 15 minutes before reaching the middle of this park. It has large picnic areas and woods carpeted with leaves. The trails along the border of the park are less interesting (at the east exit, you pass under electrical towers).

The picnic sites are pretty, and several are located under the trees. On the south side of the park, there's a small pond. It's a marvelously landscaped oasis located between two playgrounds and close to pens housing several farm animals (in July and August, depending on the City of Toronto's agreement with a private petting zoo).

When we were there, children were wading about in a brook emerging from the pond. Grandparents sitting on a bench under the weeping willows were observing children hidden inside flowering bushes along the river side. Simply lovely!

TIPS (fun for 2 years +)
* Both parks offer free parking.
* Thomson Memorial Park hosts the **Scarborough Historical Museum** (416-338-8807), right next to its playground. During the summer weekends, costumed staff greet us in the four small buildings. On **Canada Day**, it usually offers a Strawberry Social and there's a big party at Thomson park with different activities from 10 am to 5 pm.

NEARBY ATTRACTIONS

Thomson & Birkdale Parks · Scarborough (416) 392-1111 www.toronto.ca/parks	**D-3** **N-E** **of downtown** **30-min.**

Schedule: Open year-round.
Admission: FREE.
Directions: Birkdale Park's entrance is on Ellesmere Rd., between Midland Ave. and Brimley Rd. Thomson Memorial Park's entrance is on Brimley Rd., between Lawrence Ave. and Ellesmere Rd.

L'AMOREAUX & MILLIKEN PARKS

Ponds in the "hood"

For those short on time to explore the countryside, you can find a small oasis of nature in the suburbs.

Milliken Park offers paved trails, a large pond and a small island of trees. Those trees are mature and the variety of trails quite entertaining for young explorers. The forest sits next to the pond and a few picnic tables have been installed along the water under the trees.

The rest of the park is rather bare and offers little shade. We enjoyed, however, the nearby playground and its wading pool.

In the same region, you will find **L'Amoreaux Park**, adjacent to the community centre of the same name. It holds a treasure of small paved trails that border a large pond. Interestingly, the cranes I saw resting along the edge seemed unaware they were in the middle of a residential neighbourhood!

Some of the paths lead to a small island of tall leafy trees that looks like some kind of a dense forest housing the neighbourhood's entire vegetation. It is circled by a woodchip covered trail (yet practical with a stroller), framed by trees. You can travel the entire trail in approximately 15 minutes, excluding the time to explore the selection of wild flowers.

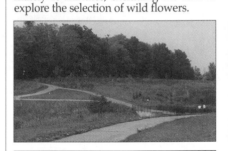

TIPS (fun for 2 years +)

• L'Amoreaux Park South hosts the **Kidstown Water Park**. More about this great water playground on page 380.

• Read about the **Industrial Alliance Kitefest** at Milliken Park on p. 210.

• I don't recommend you go out of your way to visit these two parks. Should you find yourself in the area during the fall however, take the time to enjoy the colourful foliage.

• There usually are fireworks at Milliken Park on **Canada Day**, at around 10 pm. Call to confirm.

NEARBY ATTRACTIONS
Woodie Wood Chucks (5-min.) ... p. 196

L'Amoreaux & Milliken Parks
• Scarborough
(416) 392-1111 or
(416) 396-7757
www.toronto.ca/parks

D-3
N-E
of downtown
35-min.

 Schedule: Open year-round.
Admission: FREE.
 Directions: Both parks are located north of Hwy 401. L'Amoreaux Park is north of McNicoll Ave. and west of Kennedy Rd., Milliken is south of Steeles Ave. and east of McCowan Rd.

DOWNSVIEW PARK

The missing link

The former military base was a bit of a no man's land for a while. It is slowly turning into an urban park. Tree City, the phased plan for Downsview Park's transformation, intends to integrate it into the system of wooded river valleys, ravines, parks and public paths already in existence in adjacent areas. Make way for the raccoons!

Until then, since the land is owned by the Government of Canada, **Canada Day** is the obvious best time to visit the park. The free event presents a roster of stage performers and a large midway topped with an ambitious fireworks show.

When we visited, a circus had erect-

TIPS (fun for 5 years +)

• In addition to the **Canada Day** celebration, the park has offered varying events and activities throughout the years. Check their website for exact dates of current events.
• They've been busy since my last visit, creating partnerships with different businesses: **The Rail**, a huge indoor skatepark with no age minimum (**www.therailskatepark.com**), equally huge **Grand Prix Kartways**, an electric go-kart place where 10-year-olds and older (at least 50 inches) can drive the junior karts (**www.gpkartways.com**), **Area 51 Paintball Park**, where they accept kids 10 years old but recommend it for 12 years and over (**www.a51pb.com**).
• There is a very big farmers' market selling much more than produce at the entrance of the park (**www.dpmarket.com**). It is open Saturdays and Sundays from 10 am to 6 pm.

ed a tent on the site, for additional fun for a fee. A shuttle took us from the parking lot to the centre of the action. We only saw the fireworks but during the day, several children's activities had been offered: petting zoo, buskers, dog shows and the likes.

Officials envision Downsview Park becoming to Toronto what Central park is to New York. It seems far-fetched but apparently, back in 1857, Central Park did not look better than Downsview does now.

Meanwhile, and for the years to come, the main interest of the park is the special events it can host and year-round community programs and activities it can offer. Remember the Pope's visit to Toronto, drawing 800,000 pilgrims together? The Rolling Stones concert during the SARS scare? They took place in Downsview Park.

The Tree City project will be a very long time in the making. As of January 2007, 30,000 trees had been planted in the Canada Forest. It will need to self-finance its implementation. Right now, the park still doesn't look too appealing with huge fields of grass with very few mature trees. The project aims to add 25% forest coverage, meadows, playing fields and gardens. The first phase involves soil preparation, path making and planting.

For a bit of history, it is interesting to know that by the end of WWII, over 7,000 people worked at de Havilland Aircraft (currently Bombardier), completing 1.5 to 3 aircrafts every day. Now, people play soccer or volleyball in the hangar formerly used for aircraft assembly. Times change.

Downsview Park • **North York** **(416) 952-2227 (hotline)** **www.pdp.ca**	**D-3** **North** **of downtown** **35-min.**

 Schedule: Open year-round.
Admission: FREE access to the park.

 Directions: Take Allen Rd. northbound (go north of Hwy 401). Turn west on Sheppard Ave., then turn north on John Drury Dr. in North York.

NEARBY ATTRACTIONS
Aerospace Museum (2-min.) .... p. 209

HUMBER ARBORETUM

Urban ecology

A tiny house lies on a stump in the middle of the trail. As we approach, birds fly away and I explain to my 3-year-old that this is the local restaurant for birds. She collects seeds on the ground and intends to stand still until they come back to feed from her hand.

The nature trail leading to the woods by the Arboretum's gardens begins nicely with rustic stairs.

We spend some time in a small ravine near a curiously shaped old tree, then follow a path down to the meadow. We discover many nests in the high bushes and play with velvety cocoons from which seeds lazily escape, carried by their shiny umbrellas in the fall breeze.

The path leads us towards a large garden section. Its educational value seems most appropriate for a school trip.

We prefer to wander informally in the gardens by the Arboretum entrance, with its pond, small pergola and little bridges.

They have recently finished the new **Eco-Centre**: A world class centre for urban ecology.

The **West Humber River** runs at the edge of the woodland. There's a paved path beside it that leads to the main **Humber River Trail** towards Lake Ontario.

TIPS (fun for 4 years +)

• From their website, you can download a *Discovery Walk* brochure to explore the surroundings.

• Most of the Arboretum activites are programs you need to register for and camps. One of their only drop-in events, the **Winter Festival**, usually takes place the first Saturday in December from 10 am to 3 pm. It includes hay rides, a visit from **Santa Claus**, Christmas tree sale and children's crafts ($5/passport, $8/for two or pay-as-you-play).

• They offer a **Halloween** party with a walk through the forest to a Jack-O-Lantern tree. You need to register.

NEARBY ATTRACTIONS

Humber Arboretum
· Etobicoke
(416) 675-6622, ext. 4467
www.humberarboretum.on.ca

D-3
N-W
of downtown
30-min.

 Schedule: Open year-round.
Admission: FREE.
 Directions: 205 Humber College Blvd., Etobicoke. Take Hwy 427 North, exit at Finch Ave. eastbound. Turn south on Humber College Blvd. Obtain an Arboretum pass at the College's parking kiosk, go to Lot #1.

BOYD CONSERVATION AREA

Look Mom! Toads!

Some of the mature trees look impressive in these woods where the sun can't reach through the thick canopy of leaves. Many toads can be spotted on the dirt ground, as well as intriguing little man-made constructions from dead wood. The adventure begins!

A small playground greets us close to the parking lot at the end of the park's only road.

We walk back onto the road to the first entrance in the woods, and soon reach a fork. We opt for the left trail where our kids run wildly, until they are slowed down by a steep section with stairs made of running roots.

Soon, our little scouts are inspired by strange lean-tos made out of branches. Building our own becomes our family project for a good half hour.

Back on this trail, we soon reach a picnic shelter. From there, we headed right onto the first little road along the river (no swimming!) and discovered a great picnic spot. (You can also walk back to the gravel road, towards the parking lot.)

While the trail is a bit confusing, there's no fear of getting lost! Simply stand still, and the sounds of traffic on Islington Avenue will remind you this oasis still sits in the middle of civilization.

TIPS (fun for 4 years +)

• We went with a couple of 3-year-olds, one of whom was scared by the darkness of the woods (made darker by cloudy skies). They both had a tough time exploring the steeper sections of the trail, but really enjoyed the toads!

• Bug repellent is a must, especially after a rain fall.

• When in this area, we like to drop by **Humber Nurseries Butterfly Conservatory** (15-minute drive). Admission is $3 and it is set in the back of the largest garden centre I have ever seen, selling life-size bronze statues and marble furniture and featuring an aquatic section with some 40 little pools. Take Hwy 427 northbound, turn west on Hwy 7, then south on Hwy 50 (8386 Hwy 50, Brampton, (905) 794-0555, **www.humbernurseries.com**).

NEARBY ATTRACTIONS
Reptilia (15-min.) .... p. 61

Boyd Conservation Area
• Vaughan
(416) 661-6600, ext. 5203
www.trca.on.ca

C-3
North
of Toronto
35-min.

Schedule: Open end of April to early October, 9 am until dusk.
Admission: $6/adults, $5/ seniors, FREE for infant to 15 years with accompanying adult.
Directions: Islington Ave., Vaughan. Take Hwy 427 North, exit Hwy 7 eastbound. Turn north on Islington Ave.

KORTRIGHT CENTRE

Green power

Kortright Centre went "green" way before it became trendy and now it can boast that it features one of Canada's largest educational demonstrations of renewable energy and energy efficient technologies.

There have always been enough trails throughout Kortright Centre to overwhelm newcomers. You can now add the Power Trip Trail to the roster. Fortunately, the centre has designed self-guided tours you can download from their website to find your way.

The Power Trip Trail reaches the Bee Space (home to over 2 million bees), a 15-minute walk from the Visitor Centre.

Along the way, you'll have the opportunity to see the following systems in action: grid-connected photovoltaic, solar shingle roof, water pumping, wind turbines, solar hot water heating, wetland waste water treatment, composting toilets and an energy efficient cottage entirely powered by solar and wind energy.

On occasion, we've wandered on the wooden trails surrounding the centre (where nature gets a little more imposing) and enjoyed the path running through the fields to a marsh.

Inside the Visitor Centre, small naturalists will appreciate the displays of animals camouflaged in recreated environments. Some of them were borrowed from the Royal Ontario Museum.

TIPS (fun for 4 years +)

• The **March Break** takes place during the **Kortright Maple Syrup Festival**. More about it on page 147.

• Special **Easter Egg Hunts** with Easter Bunny often coincide with the **Maple Syrup Festival** (Easter Sunday and Monday, call for exact hours).

• See **Four Winds Kite Festival** on page 211.

• Check Kortright's Weekend Programming calendar on their website (click on **What's on**, then **Weekend Programming**). It includes special hikes (including Mother's Day brunch & hike and a **Natural Christmas** hike), slide shows and films.

• The Kortright Centre Café serves hot meals.

NEARBY ATTRACTIONS
Putting Edge (15-min.) .... p. 47
McMichael Collection (10-min.) ..... p. 89

Kortright Centre for Conservation • Maple (905) 832-2289 or (416) 661-6600 ext. 5602 www.kortright.org	C-2 North of Toronto 40-min.

 Schedule: Open year-round, 9 am to 4 pm on weekdays. Opens at 10 am on weekends and during the Maple Syrup Festival.

 Admission: $6/adults, $5/seniors and children, FREE 4 years and under (small extra fee during special events). Parking is $3.

 Directions: 9550 Pine Valley Dr., Maple.Take Hwy 400 North, exit Major Mackenzie Dr. (exit # 35) westbound and follow the signs.

CHINGUACOUSY PARK

Anything else?

This park has everything! Animals? Check. Pond? Yep. Splash pool? Got it. Minigolf? Skateboarding pipe? Ski hill? Yes, yes and yes. Add a greenhouse, a teahouse, tennis courts, a playground, paddle boats, a band shell and a couple of ambitious events and you get a really dynamic municipal park indeed!

Chinguacousy Park is big but you can still walk from one attraction to the next. When visiting, we parked in the south lot off Central Park Drive and were seduced right away by the weeping willows throwing their shade over ducks on the sandy beach. A crane just happened to be standing there. It's always amazing to find spots like this in the middle of a city.

Right next to it, we saw several pens with different farm animals: pigs, lambs, goats, horses, hens and more. On the weekends, you can ride a pony for $3.

Further, we visited a large greenhouse amidst manicured gardens with a paved path leading to fields of grass. The teahouse with patio was adjacent to it.

Following the road back to the centre of the park, we found the snack bar, where you can rent the gear to play minigolf. Closer to the bigger section of the pond, there was a busy splash pool within a fenced area and a playground. On that side of the pond, you can rent paddle boats to use on both sections of the pond.

Then, there were the skateboarding features (two quarter-pipes and a slope) with the tiny ski hill in the background.

At the time of print, many of the installations in the park were a bit outdated and tired, but it still added up to a nice place to have a picnic and spend time with the kids. Most of all, it convinced me that any family event could be perfect in such a setting.

TIPS (fun for 2 years +)
• More on **Chinguacousy Skatepark** on p. 356.
• Check their website to find out about potential events in the park such as: **Canada Day** (with fireworks) and Brampton's **Summer Festival** (a whole day of activities with fireworks during **Simcoe Day** in August).
• Along Queen Street (Hwy 7) just southeast of Chinguacousy Park, between Bramalea and Airport Road, you'll find a strip of fast food outlets and family restaurants as well as a large movie theatre: a good combo after an afternoon at the park.

NEARBY ATTRACTIONS	
Carabram	p. 102
Professor's Lake (15-min.)	p. 407

Chinguacousy Park	D-2
· **Brampton**	**N-W**
(905) 458-6555	**of Toronto**
(905) 791-1884 (teahouse)	**45-min.**
www.city.brampton.on.ca	

Schedule: The park is open year-round. Most activities are available daily from late June to Labour Day weekend.
Admission: Small fees apply to wading pool and minigolf. Paddle boat rental around $8/1/2 hr.
Directions: Take Hwy 427 North to the end of the road, turn west on Hwy 7. Turn north on Central Park Dr. Go into the first parking lot. It is the closest to the pond and animal farm.

MOUNTSBERG WILDLIFE CENTRE

Wild!

I see a free-roaming rabbit by the trees. Geese are flocking by the reservoir. After we've strolled through the Raptors Walkway including several cages with hawks and owls, we head towards a large field where the weird cry of the elks greets us! This conservation area is almost a zoo!

Many birds of prey are injured every year. Some fly through power lines or step in traps. Others are struck by vehicles or their nest is accidentally cut down by landowners. On signs, we could read about some birds' misfortunes: wing tip lost in wolf snare, permanent wing muscle deformity, etc.

The Raptor Centre at the Mountsberg Wildlife Centre site offers them a hospital with treatment and recovery areas. The birds we saw in the Raptor Walkway were non-releasable residents due to permanent injuries. Weather permitting, the centre holds live raptor presentations in a 6,000-square-foot netted outdoor enclosure. Check out the round windows on the curved wall surrounding the enclosure. They allow you to peek into more bird cages.

Otherwise, presentations are held indoors, in the Aerie Theatre. We can also catch an audiovisual presentation in this theatre and peek into the Raptors' hospital through a one-way viewing window. The exhibit gallery artistically displays many mounted specimens.

Another time we went we were lucky enough to see the bisons staring at us impassively at the end of the short Raptor Centre Trail. Not this time. It seems the herd often hides in the back woods behind the vast field. But we saw an elk.

On our way back, we watched the ducks from the Lookout Blind by the reservoir (a good spot to see frogs).

The Lookout Trail is 6 km long but the observation tower overlooking the reservoir is less than 15 minutes away from the Visitor Centre. On our way, we notice Swallowville: a "village" of 25 bird-houses standing on poles. We walked 15 minutes more and could observe a flock of geese from a quiet spot by the shore.

Ten minutes further, we caught a trail to our right, going up a hill back to our starting point. It offered a very pretty view of the area.

Back to the Visitor Centre, we checked out their wonderful **play barn**.

TIPS (fun for 3 years +)

• See **Mountsberg Maple Syrup Time** for **March Break** and **Easter** activities on page 149.

• During weekends in the **Fall Harvest Season** (end of September to end of October), there are $2 horse-drawn wagon rides, craft activities for kids, a 5-acre maze, pumpkin carving, straw piles and more.

• You can pre-book as early as beginning of September for the very popular event **ChristmasTown.** On the weekends from the end of November to right before Christmas, the **Mapletowne** section is transformed into Santa's, with decorations and all including Santa's visit, crafts, cookies and more, $14/adults, $12/seniors and 5-15 years, $8/4 and under.

• Ask about their **New Year's Eve Hoopla** on December 31, 6 pm to 9 pm (you'll need to buy tickets).

• From January to part of March, weather permitting, you can skate on the old farm's pond.

NEARBY ATTRACTIONS

Mount Nemo (15-min.) .... p. 263
Kelso Beach (15-min.) .... p. 416

With fire fighter's pole, zip line, ladders, slides, climbing ropes and tons of straw, this was heaven for the kids! I was seduced by the picture perfect barn scenery of blinding rays of sunlight shooting through the cracks of the wooden walls on the golden straw, like some laser beams.

The Visitor Centre includes a gift shop and displays.

Mountsberg Wildlife Centre
• Milton
(905) 854-2276
www.conservationhalton.on.ca

D-2 West of Toronto 45-min.

 Schedule: Birds of Prey shows are at 12 noon and 2 pm on weekends year-round. The area is accessible year-round, 10 am to 4 pm.

 Admission: $6.50/adults, $5.50/seniors, $4.50/5-14 years, FREE under 5.

 Directions: From Hwy 401 West, take exit #312/Guelph Line southbound. Turn west on Campbellville Rd., then north on Milborough Line, to the park's entrance.

ROCKWOOD C. A.

Stunning!

Rockwood Park Conservation Area is a stunningly beautiful place that offers a complete change of scenery, with ruins, caves and natural reservoirs.

I still can't get over it: so much beauty, so close to Toronto and open to everyone. We're lucky…

As you arrive, take the first path on your left after Rockwood's entrance and you will reach large ruins; the site's first attraction.

This old windmill stopped functioning in 1925. It burned down in 1967 and only a few pieces of the stone walls remain today as my aspiring historian discovered. He was captivated by these explanations while he pursued his explorations of the site.

Another road, accessible by stroller, borders the ruins. It leads to two large caves a half-kilometre further, which I found fascinating. Daylight enters the grottos and children find them amusing to explore. Outside the caves, along

the rock walls, make them shout and listen to the echo. It is amazing.

There's actually more to it than meets the eye! The conservation area has a network of twelve caves. It is one of the most extensive in Ontario and includes stalactites and stalacmites (but I don't think we can access these).

On the other side of the parking lot, you will discover a path that travels around over 200 potholes: Some kind of natural tanks of all sizes created by the abrasive whirlpools from glaciers that melted over 15,000 years ago.

While you can't access the path with a stroller, it is nevertheless safe and inviting as it turns into small wooden bridges here and there. It borders the Eramosa, a narrow river that runs lazily amidst a fabulous landscape of rock and trees. Visitors explore it with canoes and paddle boats,

which you can rent daily at the beach a little further inside the park.

With young children, it is preferable to take your car to reach this beach. There, you will also find a small snack bar and washrooms. The beach is really nice with pleasantly smooth sand.

TIPS (fun for 4 years +)
• Bring a flashlight for the children to explore the small cave.
• There's a minigolf course on the site. It is available at the cost of around $4, weather permitting.

NEARBY ATTRACTIONS	
Ostrich Farm (10-min.)	p. 65
Halton Museum (5-min.)	p. 226

Rockwood Conservation Area • Rockwood (519) 856-9543 1-866-668-2267 (camp reservation) www.grandriver.ca	D-2 West of Toronto 60-min.

 Schedule: Open from end of April to mid-October, 8 am to 9 pm.

 Admission: $4.25/adults, $2.50/6-14, FREE 5 years and under. Kayak, canoe and paddle boat rental is around $10 an hour.

 Directions: From Hwy 401 West, take exit #312/Guelph Line northbound. Turn east on Hwy 7 to Falls St.

BRUCE'S MILL C. A.

TIPS (fun for 4 years +)
- More about **Bruce's Mill Maple Syrup Festival** on page 146.
- A local parent mentioned to me she always combines an outing to Bruce's Mills with a visit to **Applewood Farm**  **Winery** (12442 McCowan Rd., a short distance north of Stouffville Side Rd). You can pick your own strawberries, apples and pumpkins. They have a small playground (with an old functioning water pump) and wagon rides to take you to the fields as well as a small store; www.applewoodfarmwinery.com, (905) 640-5357.
- Nearby, we visited **Lionel's Pony Farm and Petting Zoo** at 11714 McCowan Rd., north of 19th Ave. It costs $4 for a pony ride (only on Sundays, 12 noon to 5 pm in the summer). It is free to visit  their petting zoo from May to November, 9 am to dusk, Monday to Saturday (905) 640-7669, **www.lionelsfarm.com**.

NEARBY ATTRACTIONS
Burd's Family Fishing (15-min.) ..... p. 342

Conservation 101

The recreational pond created by the dam was affecting the natural watershed system, an important component of the Rouge River. So goodbye beach. Native grasses are overtaking the place.

When I did my third edition in 2004, we had lost the beach. As we go to print for this fourth edition in 2008, I learn that we've lost the pond as well (I had to relocate this attraction under the Leisure Parks category at the last minute, which explains why it is featured at the end even if it is not the farthest from Toronto).

Good news is we've gained a private pool available for rental in this conservation area. It is near the Beech Tree area and is not open to the public but we can reserve it for $100/one hour. Up to 50 people can swim at a time and the rental price includes the services of a lifeguard. (To rent, call 416-667-6295.)

The pond has been dried up to undertake a renaturalization project. Meanwhile, the conservation area continues to include trails which fork into several paths covered with boardwalks in their most spongy areas. They are regularly maintained but still, should you take the stroller along, be prepared for a few portages.

There's also a playground on the premises, between the Spruce Tree and the Beech Tree areas.

The park now hosts a driving range, past the gate on the left hand side. It is managed by a different administration (905-887-1072). If you're only going to the driving range, mention it at the gate so they don't charge you the admission cost.

Bruce's Mill Conservation Area
· Stouffville
(905) 887-5531
or (416) 661-6600, ext. 5203
www.trca.on.ca

C-3
N-E
of Toronto
35-min.

 Schedule: Open early March to mid-October, 9 am to dusk (closes earlier in April and October).

 Admission: $5/adults, $4/seniors, FREE 15 years and under with accompanying adult.

 Directions: Stouffville Rd, Stouffville. From Hwy 404 North, take exit #37/Stouffville Rd. eastbound (drive past Warden Ave.).

DON VALLEY BRICKWORKS

Surprise, surprise

The bricks mingle with the sand and pebbles on the path. They remind us there was a brick factory for a whole century on this site! It seems impossible. The place has become such a precious little enclave hidden in the big megacity. We could mistake the walls of the old quarry for a small natural escarpment shielding us from the urban noise.

Following the pleasure of observing the fish in the large pond amidst the water lilies, my little naturalist was ecstatic to discover a whole encampment of snails along the path of the Weston Quarry Garden farther in the back. We actually had to be careful not to crush them.

Bulrushes, wildflower meadows, small creek with rocks to jump, small trails climbing up slopes; the place is perfect for young explorers.

Moore Ravine (p. 320) is even accessible above the "West Wall" on the western part of the site.

TIPS (fun for 4 years +)
• My son's friend found a fossil among the rocks!
• Since my last visit, a lookout has been established at the top of the east slope.

NEARBY ATTRACTIONS
Riverdale Farm (10-min.) .... p. 55

Don Valley Brickworks (416) 392-1111 www.toronto.ca/parks	D-3 North of downtown 20-min.

Schedule: Open year-round.
Admission: FREE.
Directions: 550 Bayview Ave., Toronto. It is on the west side of Bayview Ave. It is safer to access it from the southbound off Bayview. The entrance is south of Pottery Rd. (a good way to access Bayview Ave. if you're coming from the east side of Don Valley Pkwy).

RATTRAY MARSH C. A.

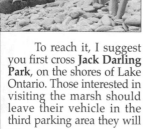

A real enclave

A marsh is an unusual site in a residential neighbourhood, yet, Rattray Marsh sits, sheltered deep within the conservation area sandwiched between Mississauga and Oakville.

Rattray Marsh, with its many viewpoints along tree-bordered walkways, attracts young explorers and bird watchers.

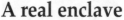

TIPS (fun for 4 years +)

• There are no washrooms at Rattray Marsh. The closest is located in **Jack Darling Park** and is closed in the winter.

• The long path that borders **Jack Darling Park** is stroller friendly. The boardwalk, however, has too many stairs for comfort. We left ours at the entrance to Rattray Marsh.

• Stay close to young children on the viewing platform bordering the marsh. While the boardwalks are solid, watch the children don't escape to the small slopes.

• Rubber boots are recommended after a rainfall.

• Make sure to stop from time to time and invite children to listen to, and locate, the many birds. Ornithologists have identified some 277 species here! There is a wide range of wildflowers as well.

• It used to be possible to hire a private interpreter from the Rattray Marsh Protection Association but not anymore due to liability issues. You can call them if you need information regarding the marsh (905-823-1572).

To reach it, I suggest you first cross **Jack Darling Park**, on the shores of Lake Ontario. Those interested in visiting the marsh should leave their vehicle in the third parking area they will see.

Anticipate a 20-minute walk through several beaches and another interesting playground before you reach the conservation area. I have friends whose kids had so much fun in that part of the park that they never got to the marsh! (Read the directions for a quicker access.)

The path to your left that you cross just before you reach the marsh is worth the detour. It opens onto a wide pebble beach. It will take you a good half-hour to stroll along the boardwalk. More trails lead you through the marsh.

NEARBY ATTRACTIONS
Bradley Museum (5-min.) .... p. 148
Scooter's Roller Palace (5-min.) p. 350

Rattray Marsh Conservation Area	**D-3 West of Toronto 30-min.**

· Mississauga
(905) 670-1615
www.creditvalleycons.com

Schedule: Open year-round.
Admission: FREE (donation).
Directions: Take QEW West, exit Mississauga Rd. southbound. Turn west on Lakeshore Rd. Enter through Jack Darling Park on the south side. Or exit at Erin Mills Pkwy southbound, it becomes Southdown. Turn left on Orr, then left on Meadow Wood, and right on Green Glade and park in the school's parking lot. Access to the marsh is in the school's backyard.

SCANLON CREEK C. A.

Nice boardwalk!

Swimming is not allowed anymore in the reservoir. Now, we go there for the lovely trail around the marsh, the boardwalk, the wildlife and the fall colours.

We prefer to park in the farthest parking lot, closer to **Scanlon Reservoir** and the boardwalk at the western end of what used to be the beach. The trail runs over the reservoir on a boardwalk across marshland.

When we visited, the trail climbed up a forested hill and went east towards a bridge crossing the creek, leading us back to the beach at its other end in less than 45 minutes. But the trail map shown on **www.simcoecountytrails.net** seems to indicate it has changed since...

Scanlon Creek Conservation Area • Caledon 1-800-465-0437 www.lsrca.on.ca	C-2 N-W of Toronto 45-min.

 Schedule: Open year-round from 9 am to dusk.
Admission: $4/adults, $3/seniors, $2/children 5-14, FREE 4 years and under.
Directions: From Hwy 400 North, take exit #64/Simcoe Rd. 88 eastbound, turn north on County Rd. 4 (formerly Hwy 11), then east on 9th Concession.

WHITCHURCH C. A.

sound of a loud frog.

As we get even closer, the kids jump on a thin strip of sandy shore behind a wild flower bush. They are not a big threat to the small quicksilver fish they try to catch with their bare hands. BEWARE! The water is not tested.

Memories

When was the last time you saw a real frog? And a school of tiny fish? The intimate Whitchurch Conservation Area is a beautiful spot to enjoy the small joys of nature.

We stroll for five minutes on a trail before we reach a clearing. The pond is located down a small hill and we have to get closer to take it all in; it is beautiful! Tall trees and bushes on the other side of the water are reflected on the still pond's mirror-like surface. Everything is so quiet that we can hear the living creatures that surround us: the song of birds, the humming of insects and the funny "Daow!"

Whitchurch Conservation Area • Stouffville (905) 895-1281 www.lsrca.on.ca	C-3 N-E of Toronto 35-min.

 Schedule: Open year-round.
Admission: FREE.
 Directions: Aurora Rd., Stouffville. From Hwy 404 North, take exit #45/Aurora Rd. eastbound. The park is on the south side, between Warden Ave. and Kennedy Rd.

WYE MARSH WILDLIFE CENTRE

Water lily land

How about a canoe excursion amidst water lilies and turtles, paddling through corridors of tall grass and bulrushes? Interested? Then, Wye Marsh may be just what you need!

In July and August, you can reserve a seat on one of the seven-metre-long canoes that traverse the water of Wye Marsh. As father and son embarked on this one-hour adventure, I took off for a stroll with my younger one towards the beautiful boardwalk that spans the marsh.

As we approached the wooden trail, we could hear trumpet sounds blowing high and strong. As we moved closer to the large water hole, we discovered that, yes indeed, the noise came from spectacular white Trumpeter Swans, dozens of them, swimming through the channels. A three-storey-high tower afforded us a better view of the colony of birds.

On the boardwalk, we found a sheltered section with long landing nets to explore the marsh's bed. Quite a hands-on experience! In two places, the trail turns into a bridge and from there, my happy girl greeted her canoeist dad and big brother as they paddled along underneath us. My preschooler could not contain his excitement when he caught a glimpse of some turtles between the water lilies and rocked the boat in a manner none of the other passengers appreciated!

On our way back, we spent some time at the Visitor Centre. There, we listened to samples of waterfowl calls and watched an interesting documentary on the Great Lakes (if not shown when you visit, you may ask for it specifically). My son fell for the poor canoeist who gets caught in time travel and many transformations of his environment (melting of ice, receding of water, etc). Ask for it!

Since my last visit, they've added 25 kms of bike trails and two wind mills.

Included with the visit are Meet the Creatures sessions on the weekends at 11:30 am and 2:30 pm.

TIPS (fun for 4 years +)

• Six years is the required minimum age for canoe trips with an adult. Five canoe trips depart daily, call for exact hours. You need reservations.
• They offer free guided walks.
• In the winter, there are cross country and snowshoe trails.
• Ask about their Moonlight Survival workshops, Winter Snowshoe Ecotours, falconry workshops or geocoaching sessions (treasure hunt games in the wilderness with GPS)!

NEARBY ATTRACTIONS

Wye Marsh Wildlife Centre
· Midland
(705) 526-7809
www.wyemarsh.com

A-2
Midland
Region
90-min.

Schedule: Open year-round, 9 am to 5 pm (open 10 am to 6 pm from May to Labour Day).
Admission: $10/adults, $6.50/seniors and children, $25/family of 4, FREE under 3 years. Canoe trip is $6/person ($10 on Sundays).
Directions: Same entrance as Sainte-Marie among the Hurons, Midland. Take Hwy 400 North, exit Hwy 12 westbound. Wye Marsh is just east of Midland.

ABOUT PROVINCIAL PARKS

Naturally yours!

Twenty-one of the 280 provincial parks in Ontario are located within a 2-hour drive of Toronto. Twelve of these are mentioned in this guide for their special assets: the golden dunes of Sandbanks, Rock Point's fossils, Earl Rowe's giant pool and beach... And that's just the tip of the iceberg!

One-day visitors might only want to focus on the beaches and nature trails but many provincial parks have much more to offer: kids' programs, guided hikes,

campfires and star-gazing and myriads of special events.

Others might want to watch the Monarch butterflies gather at **Presqu'ile** (p. 310) for their autumn journey to Central Mexico. Others will want to visit **Bronte Creek** (p. 308) for its tobogganing, skating and original play barn.

After a few years of day trips, my family is finally getting it. The best way to change a great outing into an outstanding family experience will be to turn ourselves into... happy campers.

About camping reservations

You can book a campsite in advance at 76 provincial parks (12 more are on a first-come first-served basis). You will actually have to book many months in advance for the most popular parks. For reservations, call 1-888-668-7275.

Even better, do it online! Click **Reservation** on the **Ontario Parks** website. Then log in and use the **New Reservation** section where you enter your preferred dates, then selected park. Available campsites in that park will be marked with a green dot.

Click on a specific dot and you'll get information on site quality, privacy, shade, ground cover and more. Amazing!

Use **Browse Maps** if you don't know the parks. You then select a region. All parks in that area will show up. Click on specific parks for campground layout and specific site information.

TIPS (fun for all ages)

• **Ontario Parks** has put together an attractive free booklet packed with information titled: *Nearby and Natural*. Call **Ontario Travel** to get one mailed to you or get the PDF version on their website.
• If camping is not your thing, you can rent furnished all-season yurts (tent-like and mounted on platforms), rustic cabins or even cottages. Reserve way in advance!
• Two availability tools are provided under the online **Reservation**. The **Site Availability** allows you to see the availibility of a specific camp site in the park of your choice. The **Park Availability** displays probable availability by park based on average weekday and weekend use.
• A summer season pass provides unlimited daily vehicle entry to all Ontario provincial parks, $80 from early April to early November. The winter pass is $55. An annual pass is also available for $120.

Ontario Parks Campsites
1-888-668-7275
www.ontarioparks.com

Ontario Travel
1-800-668-2746
www.ontariotravel.net

Schedule: Parks open, in general, from the second weekend in May until the end of October. Some parks, particularly those in the North, open mid-June until the end of the Labour Day weekend. Only a dozen parks operate year-round.
Admission: Day-use vehicle permits vary from $8 to $16 per day. It does not include camping fees.
Other costs: Camping fees range from around $23 to $36 per day depending on the facilities and services provided. They include the cost of the day-use vehicle permit.

BRONTE CREEK PROVINCIAL PARK

Old MacDonald had a pool...

What a gorgeous summer day! Where can you go with children? To the farm? To the pool? There's no need to take a vote. Half an hour away from Toronto, Bronte Creek Park offers a great farm-pool combination, as well as many other sport and leisure activities.

Not only does Bronte Creek Provincial Park have the usual walks and nature centre, it also boasts farmyard animals, a Victorian-style farm where they work the soil in the traditional way, and a barn transformed into an original playground. To complete this unique mixture of activities, it offers one of the largest pools in North America.

In this vast park, wanting to try every activity in a single day would be too ambitious. Hardy walkers can move from one attraction to the next by taking the trails and roads laid out on the site. However, young families would be better advised to travel by car between activity centres, in order to spare everyone's energy.

Around Spruce Lane Farm

The Bronte Creek visit begins with a walk in the morning (while children are still full of energy!). Park at lot F to access the trails by **Spruce Farm**.

On your way, you have a good chance of seeing one-metre-long remote-controlled airplanes doing loops in a field reserved for that purpose.

The Half Moon Valley trail is an excellent starting point for the whole family. It offers a two-kilometre walk, and is bordered by wildflowers and old trees of unusual shapes.

In certain locations, the wide path runs alongside the cliff bordering the wide Bronte Creek.

The two storeys of **Spruce Lane Farm**, built in 1899, were laid out in accordance with the times. During July and August, costumed actors move about, showing visitors a glimpse of rural life in the early part of the last century.

In the kitchen, there's usually a little something for us to taste.

The play barn

Turtles, snakes and fish await us inside the small nature centre near parking lot C. Bees go in and out through a long pipe connected to the outside. Not far from there, various buildings house rabbits, hens, chicks, pigs and horses.

All that becomes less interesting when kids spot the great play barn with its hanging bridges, tunnels, large tires to climb on and its second storey platform from which children can jump into the big cushions, without breaking their necks. It even has a heated section for parents who are waiting while their kids go wild, during the colder months!

TIPS (fun for 2 years +)

• More on **Bronte Creek** during the winter on p. 373.
• Bring mosquito repellent if you intend to stroll on the trails. We had some on and really enjoyed ourselves, but I've seen families fleeing from the woods because they weren't protected.
• Bronte Creek's **Maple Syrup Festival** is usually offered on March weekends and daily during **March Break**. It includes a pancake house, candy making demonstrations, syrup trail and horse-drawn wagon rides.
• Lately, there have been no **Halloween** or **Christmas** activities but the park is offering an interesting New Year's Eve activity: **Howl'n Hikes** on December 31st. It includes a guided evening coyote howl hike where we learn a few secrets about this misunderstood mammal, then gather around the fire. There's a countdown at around 8:15 pm for the kids. The rink is open late, so is the food concession and they rent skates. Now, that's different!
• The park's campground is located 5 minutes away, on another piece of land. Its 144 lots are relatively secluded.

NEARBY ATTRACTIONS
Coronation Park (10-min.) .... p. 426

Take the plunge

The Bronte Creek pool, located near parking lot D, holds 1.3 million gallons of water spread over a 1.8-acre area. An adult must walk 500 steps to go around it! It is fabulous for children: no more than two metres deep in the middle, more than half its area is like a gigantic wading pool where little swimmers can frolic without swallowing mouthfuls of water.

Naturally heated by the sun, the pool's shallow water is very comfortable during the afternoon. Those who seek shade can plant their umbrellas on the grass around it. Several picnic tables and a snack bar are located outside the pool grounds.

Bronte Creek Provincial Park
• Burlington
(905) 827-6911
www.brontecreek.org

E-2
West
of Toronto
35-min.

 Schedule: Park is open year-round, 8 am to dusk (play barn, 9 am to 4 pm). Farm and Nature Centre open May 1 to Labour Day,10 am to 4 pm (weekends only the rest of the year, 11 am to 3 pm). Pool opens July 1 to Labour Day, 11 am to 5 pm.
 Admission: $13 fee per vehicle. Additional fees to access pool: $3/adults, $2/4-17 years, FREE for 3 years and under.
 Directions: 1219 Burloak Dr., Burlington. From the QEW westbound, take exit #109/Burloak Dr. northbound. To go to the campground, take exit #111/ Bronte Rd. northbound, turn west on Upper Middle Rd.

PRESQU'ILE PROVINCIAL PARK

Bulrushes and sand on the menu

The appetizer: a smooth ribbon of sand separated from the shore by a natural barrier of shrubs (ideal for playing and picnicking). Beyond, the 200-metre-long beach leading to the main course: a vast, shallow, glistening body of water. To add a bit of green: a stroll among the bulrushes on the boardwalk overlooking the marshes. What a feast for the little ones' eyes!

The beach at Presqu'ile Park spreads for 2 kilometres along Lake Ontario. You can access it from four different entrances within the park. By entering via entry 2 and 3 you will take full advantage of all of the sites' appeal. Their parking spaces are located closer to the beach, which you access by going through a sandy enclosure bordered by bushes. The spot proved ideal for a picnic, and on a windy day, this secluded oasis was warmer than the nearby larger, wind-swept beach on the lake shore.

When we visited, the sand looked more like a neat harvested field than an idyllic beach. However, in places where the fine blond sand got licked by the waves, it had the tight and regular furrowed quality we prefer (it resists under the foot). It extends like this for more than 100 metres under shallow and warm water; just heaven for kids.

You would need to take your car again to reach the path that leads to the marsh's boardwalk, further along the peninsula. Unfortunately, the boardwalk shown on the picture below was deemed unsafe and is supposed to be under construction in 2008. The Friends of Presqu'ile Park are currently raising the funds for this project. Check their website for more information.

Lets hope it doesn't take too long. When we visited, the tightly pressed bulrushes bordering the decking reached taller than the head of my little naturalist. He was fascinated by the myriad of water lilies adorned with yellow flowers we could see at our feet.

My little boy agreed to stop and listen to the birds' various and surprising calls. They fascinated him. This marsh is a mecca for birdwatchers every spring and fall.

TIPS (fun for all ages)

• At the beginning of September, Presqu'ile serves as a meeting point for thousands of Monarch butterflies preparing for their migratory flight to Mexico. The event is celebrated by the **Monarch Weekend** held on Labour Day weekend.
• Presqu'ile includes two Interpretive Visitor Centres, an old lighthouse and 394 campsites surrounded by beautiful trees (some facing a pebble beach).

NEARBY ATTRACTIONS
Big Apple (15-min.) (read tips on p. 415)

Presqu'ile Provincial Park
• Brighton
(613) 475-4324
www.ontarioparks.com

C-6
East
of Toronto
90-min.

Schedule: Open year-round.
Admission: $8-$11/vehicle pass
Directions: R.R. 4, Brighton.

From Hwy 401 East, take exit #509 to Brighton/Regional Rd. 30. Turn west on Regional Rd. 2, then north on Regional Rd. 66.

McRae Point & Mara Parks

TIPS (fun for all ages)

• You can fish in both parks. Both provincial parks include campgrounds.

• I recently revisited this area with girlfriens (to see a show at the **Casino Rama**). I noticed an ice cream stand **Sweet Dreams** by Hwy 12 on the way to the provincial parks. It sat by the small beach with playground of **JD Tudhope Memorial Park**. We followed the trail along Couchiching Lake (see lower right picture). It is a great place to bike. The 8 km trail reaches **Couchiching Beach** (p. 418).

• We stopped in Orillia to check out the main street and fell in love with the **Mariposa Market** (109 Mississauga St., 705-325-8885, **www.mariposamarket.ca**). This store with restaurant doesn't look huge from the outside but it is! It includes a clothing and accessories section, a gift shop, a counter restaurant with delicious and very affordable food, a kitchen store and shelves loaded with goodies.

Best family picnic

Lake Couchiching and Lake Simcoe are separated by a shallow strip of land called the Narrows. Mara Provincial Park sits right by the Narrows. McRae Point Provincial Park lays further along the shores of Lake Simcoe.

We stopped for a swim at **Mara**'s wide beach with shallow water and great sand. Picnic tables were set in the shade of tall trees; unfortunately, they were too far from the water for my liking.

We preferred to spend the rest of the afternoon at **McRae Point** (10-min. drive further). We really fell for **McRae**'s narrow beach bordered by grass, pretty trees and tables (as shown on the upper left picture).

As the day was fading away we had a great picnic, accompanied by the music of the lazy waves stroking the shore.

McRae Point P. Park (705) 325-7290 Mara P. Park (705) 326-4451 (seasonal) • Orillia www.ontarioparks.com	A-3 North of Toronto 75-min.

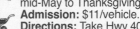

Schedule: Mara opens mid-May to Labour Day. McRae opens mid-May to Thanksgiving.
Admission: $11/vehicle.
Directions: Take Hwy 400 North, then follow Hwy 11. Take Hwy 12 eastbound and follow signs. Mara comes first.

SIBBALD POINT PROVINCIAL PARK

Swimming, sand & snacks

People who aren't inspired by Lake Ontario can turn to Lake Simcoe, the next closest large natural lake in the Greater Toronto vicinity.

The Sibbald Point Provincial Park, located on the shores of **Lake Simcoe**, is quite busy. One goes there to mingle with the crowd rather than to return to nature. The decibel level in the park doesn't exactly make it relaxing, as motor boats are allowed on the lake. On the other hand, adult swimmers can take advantage of great waves challenging those swimming beyond the buoys.

The beach is long. The sand is mixed with a few pebbles, but you can easily walk on it with bare feet. There's a very nice playground facing the beach. The children in our group spent their time vis-

iting it, in between a swim and an ice cream cone. Walking on the west side of Sibbald Point, across the farthest parking lot, you will find a tall pine and cedar forest where picnic tables are set up.

Various natural clearings reveal a narrow pebble beach, much more isolated and not marked by buoys. The waves are stronger and more fun for big kids who can swim well.

Here, people settle in the patches of sun shining through the mature trees. You can hear the sound of the waves and the birds singing. This area of the park is perfect for little trappers and for those who are looking for a quieter location.

TIPS (fun for all ages)
• More about provincial parks on p. 307.
• More about provincial parks on p. 307.
• Sibbald Point offers more than 800 campsites made private by tall, deciduous trees.
• Several picnic tables await under the shade of tall trees by the most crowded beach. I recommend getting there before 11 am if you wish to use one.
• There's a well-stocked store and a snack bar by the main beach. It seems their boat rental concession is back.

NEARBY ATTRACTIONS
Sharon Temple (25-min.) .... p. 122

Sibbald Point Provincial Park	**B-3**
• Sutton	**North of Toronto 60-min.**
(905) 722-8061	
www.ontarioparks.com	

Schedule: Open mid-May to early October.
Admission: $11-$16/per vehicle for day use.
Directions: 26465 Hedge Rd., R. R. 2, Sutton West. Take Hwy 404 North to the end, take exit #51 (Davis Dr./Hwy 31) eastbound. Turn north on Hwy 48, then follow Rd. 18/Park Rd. northbound.

EARL ROWE PROVINCIAL PARK

Some water holes!

Beaches offer everything pleasing to children: space to run, sand to build castles and water to float and swim. Add to this a pool the size of a football field, and you get a feel for Earl Rowe Provincial Park.

Beaches at Earl Rowe Provincial Park are not as busy as those located around Lake Simcoe. The two large beaches are connected by small wooden bridges straddling the reservoir (the bottom of the lake is slightly muddy).

TIPS (fun for all ages)

• More about provincial parks on page 307.
• There's a 5-km lookout trail at the northern part of the park. The main trail is 8 kms long. For a good description of this trail, go to **www.simcoecountytrails.net** and click on **Trails**.
• BEWARE! The beaches are closed on average twice through the summer due to high bacterial counts (lots of geese visit the park). Call before you go!
• Earl Rowe includes some 365 campsites.

NEARBY ATTRACTIONS
South Simcoe Railway (20-min.) .... p. 225

Children will enjoy crossing over the wooden bridge to reach the park store by the western beach. You may rent canoes and paddle boats, as well as bicycles, at the Information Centre.

Those who settle on the eastern beach will also enjoy the gigantic shallow pool (it took me 350 long strides to circumnavigate it), and a small playground.

When we visited, we missed the fish ladder in the dam across the Boyne River! It is only a few minutes from the two parking lots by the entrance.

Earl Rowe Provincial Park

· Alliston
(705) 435-2498
www.ontarioparks.com

B-2	N-W
of Toronto	90-min.

Schedule: Open mid-May to Thanksgiving (pool opens end of June to Labour Day).

Admission: Vehicle day pass is $11. The pool's entrance fee is $2.50/adults, $1.50/children, FREE 4 years and under. Canoe or paddle boat rental is around $10/hour.

Directions: From Hwy 400 North, take exit #75/Hwy 89 westbound. Turn north on Regional Rd. 15.

AWENDA PROVINCIAL PARK

A clear choice!

One of the best ways to enjoy Georgian Bay's clear water is to visit one of the four beaches in beautiful Awenda Provincial Park.

The first beach you encounter, a short walk from the first and second parking lots, is our favourite, with gulls resting on rocks sitting above the water, and small pebbles nestled in the fine sand.

From there, you can walk to the second beach (also a short walk from the second parking lot), crossing over a small rocky section in the water. Last time we visited, the water had receded so much that what used to be a narrow stretch of pebbles had turned into a sea of rocks, great for imaginative play!

A half-hour walk from the second parking lot, along the wide and well-groomed Beach Trail (time to get the bikes!), you'll find the third beach.

Located in a small tree-sheltered bay, this beach is everybody else's favourite because of its emerald water and perfect sand.

There are some serious bike trails throughout the park.

The two pictures below were taken five years apart. Notice how we did not see the sand strip by the trees in the top one! The water has really dropped.

A 10-minute walk brings you to the fourth beach, for a completely different panorama that embraces a wide view of Georgian Bay. Good news: Very few people choose to do the extra walking, and when we visited, we felt like we owned this sandy beach adorned with dunes and plants.

At last, on our most recent visit, we were able to pull the kids from the beach to explore Awenda's trails. We did the Dunes Trail, a 3-km trail which took us to a steep sandy slope. We actually walked to that slope and turned back, which was as much as my 6-year-old could bare; bring water!

We also enjoyed the 1-km trail strolling around Beaver Pond and walked a bit on Wendat Trail around Kettle's Lake (a 5-km trail). You can bring your own canoe.

TIPS (fun for all ages)

• More on provincial parks on p. 165.

• Awenda Park's more than 320 campsites are really popular. Nicely set under tall trees, they offer great privacy. If you can't get a campsite there, you may try **Camping Lafontaine** on Lafontaine Rd., (705) 533-2961 or **www.lafontaine-ent. on.ca**. It offers very decent campsites amidst trees. From there, you can return to Awenda Park for day use.

NEARBY ATTRACTIONS

**Awenda
Provincial Park**
• Penetanguishene
(705) 549-2231
www.ontarioparks.com

**A-2
Midland
Region
90-min.**

Schedule: Open year-round (facilities available from mid-May to Thanksgiving).

Admission: $11/vehicle.

Directions: Take Hwy 400 North, exit Hwy 26/27 (exit #98), then follow Hwy 27 northbound. After Elmvale, follow Simcoe Rd. 6 North. Turn east on Lafontaine Rd (it becomes Concession Rd 16) and follow signs.

KILLBEAR PROVINCIAL PARK

The families gathering along the beach were cooking their dinners and enjoying the final hours of day light. A few sailboats were slowly heading back home. Leaving this little piece of paradise was the hardest thing to do!

I totally missed the Visitor Centre offering 3,000 square feet of displays. Oops!

Life up there

As we're wondering if the park "bears" its name because it is actually inhabited by those animals, we see a sign that reads "Active bear in campground". Further, another sign begs us to "Please brake for snakes". This park is the real thing!

The truth is, I only spent a few hours at Killbear on my way from the rock camp where a friend and I had just dropped our sons. We thought a dip in Georgian Bay would be a nice treat for our trouble.

The site was so beautiful and our short visit so satisfying that I had to include it in this guide.

We did the Lighthouse Point Trail, a 1-km stroll. It emerged from the trees into a majestic rocky shoreline offering a breathtaking view of the bay (and the 30,000 Islands).

Most of the visitors seemed to gather on the beach located on the east side of Lighthouse Point. We chose to go to a more secluded one on the west side, accessible from a small trail on the north side of the parking lot. The water here was quite shallow. Any child could easily swim to reach a tiny rock island to "explore".

We also tried a section of the 2-km Twin Point Trail near the day use beach on Kilcoursie Bay. Brochures describing the trail were available in a guide box.

A very soothing lap of gentle waves brushed a sand bar pushing into the bay.

TIPS (fun for all ages)

• Killbear Park offers 881 campsites spread over 7 campgrounds. I've checked the "premium rate" campsites (indicated as such on the park's map) of Kilcoursie Bay, from 53 to 63, and Beaver Dams, 316 to 326 and 328 to 336, and they were truly fantastic, with an amazing view right on the beach. Harold Point and Lighthouse Point also offer such premium rate campsites.

• There's a 6-km bike trail parallel to the park's main road.

• Check **www.friendsofkillbear.com** to see their photo gallery of events taking place at Killbear: pancake breakfast on the 1st of July, Bike Rodeos in July and August, Maple Syrup festival in March.

• Parry Sound's waterfront is worth the detour! (20-min. drive). Have a bite at the **Bay Street Café** (22 Bay Street, 705-746-2882); they have a kids menu and a wrap-around porch. Then stroll around the town dock.

• One annual event to check out in August: **The Georgian Bay Parry Sound Tugfest**, featuring tugboat races, Festival of Lights parade and more (**www.tugfest. net**).

• One local attraction that should interest many is the **Hall of Fame** of hockey legend **Bobby Orr** from Parry Sound (**www.bobbyorrhalloffame.com**).

Killbear Park • Parry Sound (705) 342-5492 www.ontarioparks.com	A-2 **North** of Midland 3 hrs

Schedule: Visitor Centre open daily, 10 am to 5 pm during the summer, and 10 am to 3 pm in the spring and fall. Park open from 8 am to dusk.

Admission: Around $9-$17 per vehicle.

Directions: Hwy 559, Parry Sound. From Hwy 400 North, follow Hwy 69/Parry Sound/Sudbury. Continue on Hwy 69/Trans Canada then turn west on Hwy 559.

GLEN STEWART RAVINE

City trappers

As we happily complete our visit to the Glen Stewart Ravine, my son emerges from our expedition with muddy shoe soles, filthy elbows and knees, soiled pants and a sweater full of twigs, having climbed, slid, splashed about and crawled everywhere. We're perfect candidates for a detergent commercial!

TIPS (fun for 3 years +)
• See tobogganing at **Glen Manor Drive Park** on p. 366.
• To avoid exhausting your kids, I recommend you park on Glen Manor Drive East near the ravine entry. You'll find a place, even on weekends.
• Bring a small plastic or paper-made boat and follow its course down the stream. It won't be hard to retrieve when you are finished with the game.
• Warning! If you plan on returning thereafter to civilization on Queen Street, bring a change of clothes for the kids.
• Every year, locals enjoy **Carolling in the Park** event by the rink, when 800-2,000 show up (depending on the weather) to hear Christmas music in a magical setting (on the second Tuesday before Christmas, 7:30 to 8:30 pm, 416-694-0617).
• **Garden Gate** is a popular local family restaurant a few minutes east on Queen (2379 Queens St. East, 416-694-3605).

Past the boutiques of Queen Street East in the **Beaches** and next to Glen Manor Drive, sits a gorgeous rock garden with many water fountains. From there, follow a path to a quaint and leafy park bordering the surrounding mansions.

Walk further, up the stairs and across Glen Manor Drive East, and you find yourself at the mouth of the Glen Stewart Ravine, a paradise worthy of any small Robin Hood! Its "unmanicured" qualities reminded me of the countryside forests of my childhood and won the interest of my young naturalist.

The small and narrow valley in the ravine is crossed by a log-straddled stream a few feet in width. Surrounded by steep tree-filled slopes, some paths and naturally-formed stairs are accessible and comfortably shaded by abundant undergrowth and sit desirably isolated from neighbouring houses.

Walking to the end of the main path bordering the ravine takes about fifteen minutes. Children love to climb the wooden stairs reaching the street, just for the sake of it. The rugged terrain is not recommended for strollers, and I recommend vigilance with young kids as they can easily slide down (more fright than harm).

Glen Stewart Ravine (416) 392-1111 www.toronto.ca/parks	D-3 East of downtown 20-min.

 Schedule: Open year-round.
Admission: FREE.
 Directions: Located by Glen Manor Dr. East, Toronto (accessible from Queen St. East).

NEARBY ATTRACTIONS
Movies for Mommies (5-min.) .... p. 96
The Beach (15-min. walk) .... p. 402

DAVID A. BALFOUR PARK

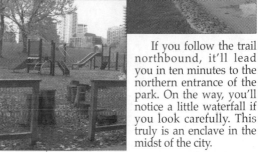

By the water...

Before you reach the Balfour Park, you've got to check out the cluster of reflecting pools on the western part of the adjacent Rosehill Reservoir. It is big enough to show on a city map!

I visited this spot in the fall, when the fountain had been shut down and the three blue reflecting pools emptied but it was nevertheless impressive, with its little bridges and molecule-shaped sculpture, framed by high-rises.

Small signs warned us that entering the pools is prohibited. Can't imagine how one would prevent kids from dipping one toe... All is not lost, there's a wading pool in the southern part of the park.

Behind the slope east of the wading pool, you'll find a pretty playground and the entrance to the nature trail.

It is a real treat to go down this trail as you quickly see the ravine closing on you.

From the upper ramp, you see a small bridge way down there. Were you to go down that road, you'd be able to reach the **Belt Line Trail** running along the **Don Valley Brickworks Park**, then the **Moore Park Ravine**, roughly 3 kilometres away.

If you follow the trail northbound, it'll lead you in ten minutes to the northern entrance of the park. On the way, you'll notice a little waterfall if you look carefully. This truly is an enclave in the midst of the city.

TIPS (fun for 5 years +)

• More on **Moore Park Ravine** on p. 320.
• There's a municipal parking lot on Pleasant Blvd. just south of St. Clair, east of Yonge.

NEARBY ATTRACTIONS
Mt. Pleasant Cemetery (5-min.) .... p. 277
Don Valley Brickworks (5-min.) ..... p. 303

David Balfour Park	D-3
(416) 392-1111 www.toronto.ca/parks	**North** of downtown **20-min.**

 Schedule: Open year-round.
Admission: FREE.
 Directions: East of Yonge and south of St. Clair Avenue, along Rosehill Avenue, Toronto.

MOORE PARK RAVINE

Darkest corners of the city

The sun beats down on our heads. Our sandals barely shield us from the hot asphalt. On the street, the heat bounces from one building facade to the next, their walls blocking a breeze that would otherwise clear away the heat. Not to complain about summer, but we can't wait to hit the shade of Moore Park Ravine.

Moore Park Ravine is undoubtedly the jewel of Toronto's natural crown. You enter the ravine through a steep little path, towards a magnificent forest of spectacularly high trees. The undergrowth is different from that of **Glen Stewart Ravine**, it's much bushier.

Here, you'll find a large and powerful stream with birds' songs playing against the ruffling of leaves. There, a pond potentially inhabited by frogs, and further, a large tree trunk inviting you to a moment of rest.

From this main path, many smaller trails depart, haphazardly fashioned by previous hikers. The main path travels under a couple of imposing bridges, and continues towards a large opening we reach after a half-hour walk. It runs along Bayview Avenue.

TIPS (fun for 4 years +)
• Be cautious when visiting with young children as some slopes are exceedingly steep and there are no railings. However, you can manoeuvre a stroller without much difficulty.

NEARBY ATTRACTIONS
Mt. Pleasant Cemetery (10-min.) p. 277
Don Brickworks (2-min. walk) ..... p. 303

Moore Park
(416) 392-1111
www.toronto.ca/parks

D-3
North
of downtown
20-min.

Schedule: Open year-round.
Admission: FREE.
Directions: Located south of Moore Ave. (between Mount Pleasant Rd. and Bayview Ave.

CHATSWORTH RAVINE

Little wild thing

It's all there, in a nut shell: steep access, tree trunks to jump over, dirt paths to explore, and the small creek under a tiny bridge.

It is as if Duplex Avenue suffered from a split personality! On the east side, Duplex Parkette is as groomed as the houses' landscaping in the neighbourhood.

On the west side, Chatsworth Ravine presents a totally different setting. I just like the contrast between the two and think they offer a great combo for a small outing.

It will take you only a few minutes to walk from Duplex Avenue to the west end of Chatsworth Ravine. There, you'll find Glenview School and nearby **Otter Creek Outdoor Rink**. This one is a real asset in the winter when you can combine skating with tobogganing down the gentle slopes of the schoolyard.

The steeper slope of **Duplex Parquette**, by Duplex Avenue, is a great place for daredevils to go tobogganing. All in all, a great combo!

TIPS (fun for 5 years +)
• For more information on **Otter Creek Rink**, call 416-392-0919 or check **www.cityrinks.ca**, the unofficial website of Toronto's outdoor rinks.

NEARBY ATTRACTIONS
Sherwood Park (5-min.) .... p. 322

Chatsworth Ravine — D-3 **North** of downtown 25-min.
(416) 392-1111
www.toronto.ca/parks

Schedule: Open year-round.
Admission: FREE.
Directions: West of Duplex Avenue, between Chatsworth Dr. and Glenview Ave., Toronto (south of Lawrence Avenue West and west of Yonge Street).

SHERWOOD PARK RAVINE

Diamond in the rough

As you walk down the path from Blythwood Road, you'll discover what has to be one of the nicest playgrounds in the whole city! With new and interesting equipment, it sits like a jewel in the midst of tall trees, next to a beautiful wading pool adorned with giant water-spraying bulrushes.

It gets quite busy when summer camp children invade the place, but there is still plenty of room to comfortably roam the trails of this vast oasis.

The playground includes a small climbing wall much appreciated by the children.

After a good play and nice picnic, we walked past the wading pool and reached long stairs leading up to a great trail. Kids enjoyed the wooden stairs in the middle of the forest, and hopped from rock to rock over a shallow stream.

In all, it took us 40 minutes to complete the trail's return trip by foot.

TIPS (fun for 4 years +)

• The summer camps usually leave around 4 pm, perfect timing to enjoy the park for a couple of hours and a picnic dinner.
• Parts of the trails can be challenging for a 3-year-old, hold on to their hand.
• With a stroller, it took us over twenty minutes to cross Blythwood Road from Sherwood Park, and walk through **Blythwood Ravine Park** (not particularly interesting) to the **Alexander Muir Memorial Gardens** (on Yonge Street, south of Lawrence Avenue). The gardens are very pretty but hard to stroll around because of stairs.

Sherwood Park
(416) 392-1111
www.toronto.ca/parks

D-3
North
of downtown
25-min.

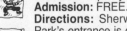

Schedule: Open year-round.
Admission: FREE.
Directions: Sherwood Ravine Park's entrance is off Blythwood Rd., Toronto (south of Lawrence Ave. between Mount Pleasant Rd. and Bayview Ave).

MORNINGSIDE PARK

Morning glory

Very few things satisfy me as much as sunshine's glittery reflection on a stream. The stream that runs through Morningside Park is broad and long. With its short tree-filled hills, it is a wonderful site to explore with children.

For a guaranteed change of scenery, go to Morningside Park's furthest parking lot. From there, as you take the large path of fine gravel, you will hear the lovely sound of water running through stones.

A few minutes later, you will discover **Highland Creek**, a broad body of water some 20 metres wide, lying at the bottom of a valley, like a fine jewel nestled in a bushy bower.

The stream is shallow and its partly rocky shores attract hikers who can walk along it without getting wet. On one side, little clear rapids emerge through large flat rocks, while the water follows a more sinuous path between the big rocks on the other side. A few tree trunks provide children with ample distractions and many cyclists rest while admiring the shores from their trail above.

TIPS (fun for 5 years +)

• Sandals might not allow a sure grip on the rocks. However, in summertime we went barefoot along the stream, up to the muddier section (much to my little friends' delight). I nevertheless recommend rubber shoes to protect small feet in the water. While wet rocks can be slippery, fear nothing more serious than a wet bottom; you may want to pack a change of clothes. Rubber boots are ideal on colder days.
• They say it is an excellent site for cross-country skiing during the winter.

NEARBY ATTRACTIONS
Woodie Wood Chucks (15-min.)   p. 196
Kidstown (15-min.) .... p. 425

Morningside Park • Scarborough (416) 392-1111 www.toronto.ca/parks	D-3 N-E of downtown 30-min.

Schedule: Open year-round.
Admission: FREE.
Directions: From Hwy 401 East, take exit #387/Morningside Ave.southbound. The park's entrance is south of Ellesmere Ave.

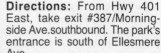

TOM RILEY PARK

turers who stroll along the dirt trail following the creek upstream will discover funky graffiti under another viaduct.

This path will lead you over a second bridge, to the northern entrance of the park. It will take you less than 15 minutes to walk back to the southern entrance.

White noise

Listen carefully, past the noise of the trains rolling on the tracks, past the cars whooshing by all around the urban setting... This sound you hear doesn't come from the subway's air vent. It's Mimico Creek!

You'll notice a lovely community garden by the southern entrance to the park off Bloor Street.

Kids will love to watch the TTC trains flash by over the viaduct. A sight we normally don't see up close!

Different dirt trails have been worn by previous visitors to reach the creek. The ease of access of these paths vary but young explorers are bound to find one that suits their capabilities.

Walking northbound on the winding paved trail running through the long and wide park, you'll reach a playground nicely set by tall trees.

A bit further on the east side, you'll see a small bridge, the perfect spot to see the wild ducks. Adven-

TIPS (fun for 4 years +)

• There's a municipal parking lot on Bloor, by the southern entrance of the park. Beware, the parking lot by the northern entrance seems to require a permit.

• The paved path is less than 1 km long and winding, great for young cyclists.

NEARBY ATTRACTIONS
Montgomery's Inn (10-min. walk)   p. 384
Around Royal York Subway Station p. 438

Thomas (Tom) Riley Park
· Etobicoke
(416) 392-1111
www.toronto.ca/parks

D-3
West
of downtown
20-min.

Schedule: Open year-round.
Admission: FREE.
Directions: Entrance from Bloor Street (east of Islington) or from Islington (north of Cordova Ave.).

WARDEN WOODS PARK

Woods in the hood

After a short walk along the TTC's grey parking lots by the 6-lane wide Warden Avenue, the last thing I expected was the sight of a willow tree brushing the water of a bouncing creek strutting over large rocks at the bottom of a curvy valley.

Just a few minutes from Warden subway station starts a 2-km trail running south of St. Clair East down to Pharmacy Road near a parking lot.

The paved trail is a little uneven but wide: the perfect place to bike with older kids when they're sturdier on their wheels. It is sinuous, goes up and down through a mature forest and runs along the Massey Creek. The works!

If you access the park from St. Clair, the creek will reveal itself to your right after the country-style fence. It is easy to get to the river side in this section of the stream. If you decide to do so, make sure your young explorers see the "secret vault" by the willow tree (a cement structure that will look like the real thing to them but which is actually a storm sewer outlet).

Halfway from either entrance, you'll find some stairs formed by beams encased among the roots on the hill. They lead to a great park with a small playground. Note that the climb up is quite steep and not stroller accessible!

Nearby, if you hear the wooshing sound of water, it doesn't come from the creek but from the waste water running underground. A little reminder that we are still in the city. On a more poetic note, I heard the song of birds I don't normally hear in Toronto.

Further, you'll see a pretty bridge crossing over the river. It leads to a series of other dirt trails. If you remain on the main trail (also called the Gus Harris Trail), you'll reach the parking lot adjacent to Pharmacy Avenue in a few minutes.

TIPS (fun for 8 years +)

• There's a convenience store in the apartment building at the corner of Teesdale Place and Pharmacy, just south of the park.

• In the winter, people do cross-country skiing in the park.

NEARBY ATTRACTIONS
Beach Fairway Minigolf (10-min.) ... p. 44
Scarborough Bluffs (15-min.) .... p. 258

Warden Woods Park	D-3
· Scarborough (416) 392-1111 www.toronto.ca/parks	**East** of downtown **30-min.**

 Schedule: Open year-round. Beware of the river if visit after a rainstorm or a big melt.

 Admission: FREE.

Directions: West of Warden Avenue and south of St. Clair Avenue East, Scarborough. The other entrance is on Pharmacy Ave., north of Danforth Ave.

ROUGE PARK

So long, civilization

The trail had led us to the river; we heard the clear sound of splashing water. Standing still, we heard it again, this time identifying the source of this noise: A 60-cm-long trout, jumping upstream! It is a shame my 3-year-old could not appreciate the wonder of such a scene. Mind you, everything she saw that day was a first for her.

You can't explore Rouge Park in a single day. It is huge, with the Toronto Zoo occupying only a tenth of its area. It offers a wide variety of natural settings accessible from different points.

Resort Road access

I visited during the fall with my 3-year-old and I thought it was the perfect place to enjoy fall colours with a little one. A cascade of leaves would fall from the tall trees every time the wind blew, and the ground was covered with crisp leaves.

The easy trail runs along the river and, in many places, we had access to it over a wide band of pebbles. The river is very shallow. I was flabbergasted to discover a huge dead fish on the pebbles! Observing the fish's sharp teeth, my little one declared it was nothing less than a shark. Later on, I learned that trout and pike, even though they don't travel upstream to spawn like salmon, still like to roam up and down the river.

We laid out our picnic on a fallen tree by the river. Further on, the trail was narrower and bushier so we turned back. We were only twenty minutes away from the parking lot.

I was told there is a trail along the Little Rouge River which would take us to Pearse House in approximately two hours.

Pearse House access

In the backyard of the pretty Victorian house that holds the Rouge Valley Conservation Centre, we found a circle of intriguing and nicely painted rocks between a tent made out of cedar branches and the entrance to the trail. The beginning of this trail was steep and winding, and lead to an easier stretch.

Our first glimpse of the Little Rouge River was simply gorgeous. The stream was shining like diamonds under the sun, framed by colourful leaves, with white cliffs and dark evergreens in the background.

Upstream, we explored the river banks. Large flat stones that popped through the shallow water allowed for a great hopping session. We reached the gravel road in twenty minutes.

Twyn Rivers Drive access

During the fall, Twyn Rivers is a real gem of a road in the midst of civilization! Breathtaking colourful leaves, white cliffs, a crossroad passing over two small bridges... and not a single house in sight!

The drive led to a large parking lot. From there, we took a trail along the river leading towards the bridge, which we crossed. Then we took the trail off the road. It eventually started to run up a steep hill to our right. For a little while, we explored the right-hand side of the fork up the hill. The path was really pretty, the dark trunks contrasting with a colourful patchwork of trees on a hill in the far background.

The left-hand side of the fork offered quite an interesting stroll. Roots were running across the path. We took the first downhill trail to our right, aiming at the river.

A strange vision of dark trees with peeling bark and tortuous branches among standing dead trunks awaited us. Soon after, following the sound of the river, we reached a postcard landscape of river and fall colours, complete with 50-cm trout jumping against the current! The manoeuvres required to succeed at this complicated task were fascinating. I just could not believe we could observe such a phenomenon so close to Toronto!

It took us approximately an hour to walk the whole loop back to the asphalt road and to the parking lot.

Kingston Road access

The path near the **Glen Rouge Campground** is the one that leads to the Riverside trail, which has the biggest trees. The high canopy scarcely allows sunbeams to penetrate the forest. At the height of the summer, it is a great place to hide from the heat of the day.

When we were visiting, the riverside trail was closed to be rejuvenated. The path we took, steep at times, ran through the forest and reached a clearing in half an hour. It would take approximately one hour to walk from Kingston Road to Twyn Rivers.

TIPS (fun for 5 years +)

• See **Rouge Beach** on p. 406.
• Exploring the shores would be even more fun with high rubber boots.
• The section of Rouge Park accessible from Twyn Rivers Drive is more fun to visit with energetic children 6 years and older with a taste for adventure.
• **Toronto Kayak & Canoe Adventures** offers trips on the Rouge River, starting below Old Kingston Rd. and ending at **Rouge River Beach** ($50/person, equipment and life jackets included). Check **www.torontoadventures.ca** for details. Children under 8 must be with an adult.
• **Glen Rouge Campground** is located by the Kingston Road access. To reserve a campsite, call (416) 338-2267 or e-mail at **camping@toronto.ca**.

NEARBY ATTRACTIONS	
Toronto Zoo (5-min.)	p. 57
Petticoat Creek (10-min.)	p. 423

Rouge Park	D-3
• Scarborough	N-E
(416) 392-1111	of downtown
www.rougepark.com	30-min.

 Schedule: Open year-round.
Admission: FREE.
 Directions: Kingston Road access: From Hwy 401 East, take exit #392/Port Union northbound, turn east on Kingston Rd., the entrance is on the north side.
Twyn Rivers Drive access: Driving from Meadowvale, turn east on Sheppard Ave and take the first fork to the left (The Twyn Rivers Dr.). Pay attention, as this branch is easy to miss if you are coming from Sheppard Ave. eastbound.
Pearse House access: Go east on the overpass over Meadowvale Rd. (in front of the Toronto Zoo entrance).
Resort Road access: Take Meadowvale northbound, turn west on Old Finch, then north on Resort Rd. There is a small parking lot just south of Steeles. The park entrance lies at the end of a small clearing, not too far from the Little Rouge River.

CREDIT RIVER

To Mississauga's credit

A friend of mine was anticipating the reaction of his sibling visiting from Quebec when he took him on a casual walk along the Credit River. It did not fail! His wide-eyed brother saw a man lure out of the water, right under his nose, the kind of salmon fishermen dream about. And this happened here, in the heart of the most urban part of Canada!

Credit River is a wild trout and salmon river where you can see huge fish swimming upstream into the shallow water.

We explored it from different access points all the way up to northern Mississauga, each offering a unique experience of the river, regardless of the season.

At the foot of Mississauga Road lies **J.C. Saddington Park**. Kids will enjoy exploring the large boulders along Lake Ontario's shore. I was impressed by the large area with picnic tables one can reserve for a large family gathering by the lake. The park includes a cute stream not too far from a playground. The pond is lively with ducks, geese and a fountain, great willow trees almost brushing the water.

The eastern part of the park runs along the Credit River. We saw people fishing from the large rocks, under the watchful eye of a couple of swans. On Front Street, bordering the river, the boats of the companies offering fishing and

cruising fares from spring to fall are located. You'll find the small and pretty **J.J. Plaus Park** on the east shore of the river.

Erindale Park is the best spot from which to observe fishermen during the month of September (the ride along Misissauga Road to get to **Erindale Park** is beautiful during the fall). The Credit River is less than a 5-minute walk from the vast parking lot. Downstream, right under Dundas Street Bridge, the shallow river joyfully cascades over the rock bed.

Upstream, the river is lined with high boulders overlooking deeper water. Many stone stairs offer lovely openings through the bushes leading to a large trail along the river, partly shaded by large trees. The trail is lovely and stretches past Hwy 403, approximately an hour walk away northbound.

During the winter, we took this path, the **Culham Trail**, from Wellsborough Place, north of Hwy 403. I strongly recommend trying this winter outing.

The sun shining on the stream bordered with ice and snow, with the added contrast of the dark rocks and trees, can be breathtaking! And it offers quite a playground for young explorers! It took us an hour to walk back and forth between the trail entrance and Burnhamthorpe Road Bridge, not counting the time allowed for exploration.

Streetsville Memorial Park is the access point to another lovely stretch of the **Culham Trail** going upstream along the Credit River. Mature trees are found on both sides of the river. We loved the colourful carpet of leaves during our fall visit. It includes a playground and an outdoor pool. I encourage you to get closer to the cluster of huge trees in the wide field, across the bridge. One of them forms an intriguing figure that really looks like a hooded person sitting by the trunk.

the river, for nice panoramas. One of them was running down the shore, to an appealing stone path crossing the shallow river (not suitable for younger kids). At the end of the trail awaited the gorgeous **River Grove Community Centre** and its amazing indoor swimming pool (see p. 383).

It will take you 15 minutes to reach the Main Street Bridge if you stay on the western shore. You'll get a great view of the Credit River from that bridge. On the north-east side of it you'll find the entrance to **Timothy Park**. The trail is gorgeous and leads you in less than 40 minutes to the elevated part of **River Grove Park**.

Don't hesitate to take any little path leading to the edge of the hill overlooking

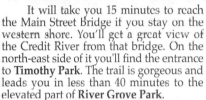

TIPS (fun for 5 years +)

• **Toronto Kayak & Canoe Adventures** offers trips on the Credit River, starting at Dundas Street West and ending at Port Credit, Lake Ontario ($50/person, minimum 3 persons, equipemnt and life jackets included). Check **www.torontoadventures.ca** for details. Children under 8 must be with an adult.

• A **Fish & Chips** and a **Starbucks** are conveniently located at the corner of Front and Lakeshore Road.

• The **Streetsville Bread and Honey Festival** usually takes place at Streetsville Memorial Park on the first weekend of June (including parade, midway rides, petting zoo, kids' entertainment, main stage, crafts. Call (905) 816-1640 or check **www.breadandhoney.com**; $5/adults, $3/children 6-12 years old.

• Stop at the **Town Talk Bakery** at 206C Queen Street South in Streetsville, (905) 821-1166. It is closed on Sundays and Mondays but the other days you can buy scrumptious pastries and lovely themed baked goodies according to the season.

Credit River • Mississauga (905) 896-5384 www.mississauga.ca	D-3 W & N-W of Toronto 30-min.

 Schedule: Accessible year-round.

Admission: FREE.

 Directions: J.C. Saddington Park: from QEW, take exit # 130/ Mississauga Rd. South to the end of the road.

 J.J. Plaus Park is on the other side of Credit River, at the foot of Stavebanks Rd. South.

Erindale Park: Take Mississauga Rd. North, turn east on Dundas St., the entrance is on the north side.

Southern access to Culham Trail: Take Mississauga Rd. North, turn east on Eglinton Ave., then south on Inverness Blvd. Follow Credit Point Dr. to your left, turn left on Wellsborough Place.

Streetville Memorial Park: Take Mississauga Rd. North, it becomes Queen St. South, turn east on Beech St.

Timothy Street Park: Keep going on Queen St. South, turn east on Main St., it becomes Bristol Rd. The park's entrance is north of Bristol. There's a cemetery with parking space on the south side.

Northern access to Culham Trail: Keep going on Bristol Rd., turn north on River Grove Ave. Park at the River Grove Community Centre. The trail's entrance is at the back of the centre.

HUMBER RIVER

Dam if you don't

I'm walking on a side trail bordering the cliff from which I can admire the river down below when a walker who just appeared on the edge of the cliff surprises me.

"How did you climb up here?" I marvel. "...I climbed" he says, matter-of-factly. I look closer to the edge and indeed spot very steep trails going down. I think I'll stick to my leafy trail.

A 15-minute walk west of the nice **Sunnyside Pavilion Café** by Lake Ontario is a footbridge you might have noticed when driving along the Gardiner. It is the crossing over the mouth of the Humber River. Streets often interrupt the trail leading to the next access point to the river so I decided to drive to the next public parking lot by the stream at the end of Humber Valley Road.

Many use this parking lot as a starting point for bike rides. The scenery is not particularly pretty but if you walk 5 minutes, you reach the entrance of the trail by the Toronto Humber Yacht Club and some gorgeous spots overlooking the river. From there, it takes some 15 minutes to get to the Old Mill overpass. Nothing striking about this trail through **Kings Mill Park** but kids will find it intriguing to walk under the bridges.

The best way to appreciate the Humber River is to park by **Étienne Brûlé Park** right by the stream. Two trails follow the river, one for bicycles and one for pedestrians. The trail is bordered by tall tress and even cliffs on both sides at some points, creating unique intimate scenery. Six low dams, spread along its course between Old Mill Road and Dundas Street, control the river's flow, hence the lovely sound of cascades we hear as we walk. With kids, it would take half an hour to walk to the Dundas overpass. The trail along the west shore of the river leads back to Old Mill Road Bridge. It offers one of the nicest bike rides for families.

TIPS (fun for 4 years +)
• **Toronto Kayak & Canoe Adventures** offers trips on the Humber River, starting at the Old Mill Subway Station and ending at **Sunnyside Pavilion Café**, weather permitting, ($35/person, equipment and life jackets included). Check **www.torontoadventures.ca** for details. Children under 8 must be with an adult.
• The **Old Mill Inn** (very popular for its fancy Sunday brunches) is located near Étienne Brûlé Park (21 Old Mill Rd., **www.oldmilltoronto.com**).

NEARBY ATTRACTIONS

Humber River	D-3
• Etobicoke	**West**
(416) 392-1111	**of downtown**
www.toronto.ca/parks	**25-min.**

Schedule: Open year-round.
Admission: FREE.
Directions: Humber Valley Road: From The Queensway (north of the Q.E.W.), take Stephen Dr. northbound, turn west (left) on Riverwood Pkwy and take Humber Valley Rd. to your right. **Kings Mill Park:** From Bloor St. West (east of Royal York Rd.) take Old Mill Rd. northbound. The parking lot's entrance is just before the bridge. **Étienne Brûlé Park**'s entrance is just after the bridge, to your left.

BELFOUNTAIN C. A.

Small is beautiful

It's tiny. A 1.5-km trail goes round the park. However, it's so beautiful! No wonder so many people have their wedding pictures taken here.

It boasts a fountain, a pond, a "cave", a rumbling waterfall and a suspension bridge. The winding path starts up the escarpment and leads us into the depths of the ravine, towards another bridge crossing the crystalline river. Indeed, the park offers all the elements of a great family outing.

I stumbled upon Belfountain while driving on the beautiful Forks of the Credit Road during the fall. My young wanderer enjoyed this small, tree-lined country road built over several sizeable hills. It leads to Belfountain and to the Belfountain Conservation Area located just before the village.

Bringing a stroller along wasn't a great idea. I had to go down a long series of low steps leading to the river, then continue on rocky trails, while pushing my napping heavyweight angel.

Nice picnic spots lie at the bottom of the steps, by the water. Barbecues are available on site. Swimming is not allowed anymore but fishing is. The cold, spring-fed water of the **West Credit River** is the perfect habitat for trout and other fish.

TIPS (fun for 5 years +)
• To make the most of the stream, bring along rubber shoes or boots.
• After leaving the park, if you head towards Belfountain, you should find a snack bar selling ice cream, the perfect grand finale to an outing. The village itself is small, but has a general store that seemed friendly and well stocked.

The original owner, who put up all the other existing structures at the beginning of the last century, built the park's dam. The fountain is a favourite spot for newlyweds. During our visit, we admired a bride with her elegant wedding party.

The man-made Yellow Stone "mini-cave" fires up fertile imaginations with its stalactites. The suspension bridge just downstream from the dam is long enough to impress children.

A stone path begins beside the fountain. It disappears under the trees and runs alongside the roaring river that lies 25 metres below. Now's the time to hold on to your little ones! At times, the path's inclination is quite steep. It eventually leads to a small boardwalk that stands one metre above a large stream. This area is magnificent during the fall. The kids stopped and played a good while with the stream's running water. The boardwalk continues on the other side and heads back to the suspension bridge.

Belfountain Conservation Area	D-2 N-W of Toronto 45-min.
• Belfountain (519) 927-5838 or 1 800 668 5557 www.creditvalleycons.com	

Schedule: From late April to late June, open on Fridays, weekends and holidays, 10 am to 5 pm. From late June to Labour Day, open daily 9 am to 9 pm. From early September to mid-October, Monday to Friday, 11 am to 6 pm and weekends and holidays, 9 am to 7:30 pm.
Admission: $4.25/adults, $2.25/seniors and 6-12 years, FREE 5 years and under. Maximum per vehicle is $18.
Directions: 10 Credit St., Belfountain. Take Hwy 401 West, exit Hwy 410 North, turn west on Hwy 7 then north on Hwy 10. Turn west at The Forks of the Credit Rd.

NEARBY ATTRACTIONS
South Simcoe Railway (20-min.)   p. 225
Albion Hills C. A. (15-min.) .... p. 411

HALIBURTON FOREST & RESERVE

Walk in the clouds

"Wow! Hooking on to the web takes on a new meaning!" comments a guy in the group as he literally hooks himself to the lifeline some twenty metres above the ground.

As I carefully walk on the 12-inch wide boardwalk suspended in the air by an elaborate series of ropes knotted into a handrail, I realize I would be very nervous doing the same with my son, had he met the required minimum age of 10.

Our guide assures me he's never had to turn back because of a scared child, adding he remembers some kids who got bored by the experience! Bored?! If my children got bored by such an experience, it would be time to lock up the video games and throw away the key!

The four-hour round-trip starts with a 15-minute van ride through the reserve, catching a glimpse of some of the campsites located in semi-wilderness along beautiful lakes. We then take a 10-minute walk along a scenic creek before canoeing for 15 more minutes to a large stand of old growth White Pine. It would not surprise us to see a moose in such a landscape.

Our guide demonstrates how to put on our harness (to be hooked to a lifeline, a short walk from there). And we're off to the canopy trail.

It consists of half a kilometre of suspended boardwalk, painstakingly installed to ensure no harm comes to the tall White Pines. "The owner wanted to spruce up the forest trail" jokes the guide. We are each assigned a buddy before we hook ourselves and climb the ladder to our first section of boardwalk.

We walk from one tree to the next. Every time we change direction, we have to hook ourselves to a new lifeline while our extra hook remains attached to the line under which we stand. Taller bud-

dies often have to lower the lines to allow shorter partners to hook themselves (that would be the tricky part for parents).

A large platform surrounds a very tall and straight pine, suspended from the tree top. We stop for a snack and to take in the amazing panorama while our guide tells us more about the crazy adventure in the building of this one-of-a- kind canopy boardwalk.

The Wolf Centre

The **Wolf Centre**, also located in Haliburton Forest, is only a few minutes drive

TIPS (fun for 10 years +)

• Bring bug repellent in the spring.

• If you do the morning excursion, you will be back in time to attend the 1:30 pm feeding session at the **Wolf Centre** (best way to see the wolves). In July and August, if you attend the afternoon excursion, try to book it on a Thursday, when they offer a Wolf Howl session at around 8 pm ($1/person). You might be lucky enough to hear the wolves howl back at the guide.

• 17 of the 50 lakes in this privately owned 50,000-acre forest, are accessible by car. It is possible to buy a day pass ($15/adult, free for kids) to hike in the park and swim in the lakes. This is a great family outing for children under 10 years old and their parents, while older siblings tackle the canopy trail. A detailed map is available on site.

• Haliburton Forest is renowned for its mountain bike trails (over 300 kms). Trail pass is $15/day. Bike rental is $35/day or $25 after 1 pm (15" frames and up).

• They have a small wooden observatory the roof can roll off, equipped with two (10 and 12-inch) telescopes. Presentations (pre-registration required) are offered every Tuesday, Wednesday, Friday and Saturday at 9 pm in May and August, 9:30 pm in June and July and 8 pm in September and October ($20/adults, $15/under 18 years old).

• These lakes host great campsites but most are leased annually, except for 20 designated sites available for short term use ($15 plus the cost of day use permit). They also rent 2- or 3-bedroom housekeeping units for $59 per night, per person ($89 in the winter) and log cabins for small groups. It includes the day use permit and taxes. These are popular among the snowmobile amateurs. BEWARE! The roaring motors will trouble the quietness of the natural setting. Better rent during the fall to enjoy the colours.

• Ask about their dog sledding excursions!

• They were the first to offer a canopy trail attraction in Ontario. There are now two other such trails within 2 hours of Toronto. Check the **Treetop Walk** of **Eco Adventure Tours** in Collingwood (**www.sceniccaves.com**) and the trails of **Arbraska Treetop Trekking** in Barrie (**www.horseshoeresort.com**).

from Base Camp. It was feeding time when we arrived (at around 1:30 pm).

A big line-up of visitors stood by the large bay windows overlooking a tiny part of the 15-acre enclosure, anxious to catch a glimpse of the wolves feeding on beaver carcasses. Through loud speakers we could hear the animals' growls as the leaders grabbed the best pieces and the tiny cubs patiently awaited their share.

Inside the **Wolf Centre**, there are many exhibits and some interactive displays, as well as a book section and an art gallery featuring works on wolves.

Haliburton Forest & Wildlife Reserve • Haliburton (705) 754-2198 www.haliburtonforest.com	A-4 N-E of Toronto 2 1/2 hrs.

Schedule: Open year-round 8 am to 5 pm (extended hours in July and August and during the winter). The **Wolf Centre** is open daily from Victoria Day to Thanksgiving and Friday to Sunday only the rest of the year, from 10 am to 5 pm. The **Canopy Trail** runs daily from early May to late October, starting at 9 am and 1:30 pm.

Admission: The daily use permit is $15/adult ($35 during the winter).Wolf Centre is $9/adults, $6/under 18 years old, $20/family.The **Canopy Tour** is $95/adults and $70/10-17 years old. (includes daily use permit and admission to Wolf Centre.)

Directions: R. R. #1, Haliburton. From Hwy 404 North, take exit #51/Davis Rd. eastbound. Follow Hwy 48 North to Coboconk. Take Hwy 35 North to Minden (do not take Hwy 121 South to Kinmount!). Take Hwy 118 East to West Guilford. Cross the bridge and take County Rd. 7 for approximately 20 kms to the Base Camp.

General tips about
Sports:

- Sunscreen, hats and enough bottles of water are a must during summer sports.
- A change of clothes is always a good idea when playing outside where there's a potential for mud!
- Extra layers of clothes that you can add or take off could save the day during a winter outing. Bottles of water and snacks are also important since concessions are often closed for the season.

SPORTS

See **the Raptors at Air Canada Centre** on p. 337.

ROGERS CENTRE

Duck!

The two boys were only 4 and 6 but already great baseball fans; the time was ripe to take them to their first game at the former SkyDome. They brought their little baseball gloves. When their dad shouted: "It's coming!" they never doubted the authenticity of the ball as he picked up a brand new ball (that he had bought for the occasion) off the floor! It was the best day of their lives!

TIPS (fun for 5 years +)

•   **Spring Fling** is the **March Break** week-long event at the Rogers Centre. With the admission fee, you get to see the stadium and enjoy unlimited access to a large midway ($20/8 years and up, $14/2-7 years, $10/ground admission only, $30/all-week pass).

•   Rogers Centre hosts the **Monster Jam** event on a weekend in mid-January. My 10-year-old has begged me to go for years! Demolition derby, biggest trucks in the world on the biggest wheels; the works! Just never had the time to go. It costs $15-$27. Check if they still offer their pit party ticket (extra cost) to have access to the floor to get closer to the trucks two hours before the show.

•   Planning to attend a circus show at the Rogers Centre (or any other venue)? BEWARE! The cost of elephant rides and more is not included with the ticket and the intermissions are big commercials to promote $10 gadgets all kids want.

•   See **Wayne Gretzky's** restaurant and **Chez Cora** described in the **Think Big! Stroll** on p. 466.

NEARBY ATTRACTIONS
CN Tower (1-min. walk) .... p. 116

I am not a baseball fan but when my dentist told me how he tricked his sons to create this magical moment, it made me want to rush to a baseball game, kids in tow. My son doesn't know anything about baseball but he is into buildings, models and how things work, so we had a Rogers Tour Experience. We learned that the Rogers Centre required twice as much concrete as the **CN Tower** to build, enough concrete to stretch a sidewalk between Toronto and Montreal.

As we waited for the tour to begin, we watched a short film fast-forward two years of building the former **SkyDome** into a two-minute clip made from a time-lapse camera. The tour began with a short movie in a small theatre, on the construction from the architects and the workers' points of view. (Note that these films are not automatically shown anymore but you can ask for them when you're purchasing the tour tickets. You've got nothing to lose.)

We looked at a model of the building. We then had a peek at a giant baseball bat. The first glimpse into the huge stadium (with a seating capacity of 50,600 during a baseball game) was impressive!

My then 8-year-old son was not thrilled by the tour itself, but he loved visiting the Hall of Fame box with its trophies and photos of the Blue Jays as they were, winning the World Series.

Rogers Centre	**D-3**
(416) 341-2770 (tours)	**Downtown**
(416) 341-1234 (Blue Jays)	**Toronto**
(416) 341-2746	**2-min.**
(Argonauts)	
www.rogerscentre.com	

 Schedule: Open year-round but schedule varies depending on special events. Call to confirm.
 The baseball season runs from early April to late September.
Admission: Tour: $13.50/adults, $9.50/seniors and students, $8/5-11 years, FREE under 5.
 Game: Baseball starts at around $9, football starts at $35.
Directions: At the corner of Front and Peter St., Toronto (entrance to the tour is between Gates # 1 and 2).

RAPTORS AT AIR CANADA CENTRE

"Thanks Dad!"

I had to see it to believe it: boys and girls, some barely five years old, eagerly following the game!

The truth is the enthusiasm of a roaring crowd is contagious and every minute when the teams are not competing is filled with action. When it's not the mascot Raptor fooling around with spectators by the aisles, it's the Raptors Dance Pack hitting the floor, or the half-time act. No wonder I heard a grateful boy exclaim, on the way back to their car: "Thanks Dad for taking me!"

A quick stop at the store to get some Raptors paraphernalia to show our support and another one to grab a mandatory hot dog and we were ready to find our seats. The Raptors and their visitors were already warming up and the mascot was stretching along with them. Then, a rain of metre-long balloons fell from the ceiling over the spectators in the Lower Bowl Endzone and Baseline Prime sections behind the visitors' basket. We later found out these were to be used by the Raptors fans to distract any opponent focusing on their free throws.

Foul play, rebounds, assists, running jump shots, one-handed jams... we saw it all. What we did not expect was the ever-present music and hilarious sound effects: sound of a bouncing spring when the ball would stray off the court, breaking glass noise when a player crashed into a panel.

We were lucky enough to be attending the game the Raptors won 84-76 against the Hornets during the 2004 season. Even for amateurs like us, it was a thing of beauty to watch Vince Carter do a half-court running jump-shot sinking into the basket as the buzzer announced the end of the third quarter.

That day, we saw the Raptors' 16-point lead melt down to six, two minutes before the end of the game. Talk about tension! And imagine the standing ovation when they won! But my guess is any Raptors game will always win the approval of young fans.

TIPS (fun for 5 years +)

• Parking beside Air Canada Centre during a game costs around $25! We found a $5 spot in the parking lot on Windsor St., just north of Front St. and west of John St. (10-minute walk from the centre).
• We were in the first rows of the Upper Bowl seating area, at $59 per ticket, and had a ball. But I checked it out and can assure you you'll see well wherever you sit in Air Canada Centre!
• Up to two hours before the game, ticket holders have free access to the BMO Fan Zone and its interactive basketball and hockey stations.
• On Sunday home games, kids used to be invited on the floor after the game to throw once into the basket. Lets hope they still are!
• More about what's around **Union Subway Station** on p. 451.

Air Canada Centre
(416) 815-5500 (info)
(416) 872-5000 (sports)
www.raptors.com
www.mapleleafs.com
www.theaircanadacentre.com

D-3
Downtown
Toronto
5-min.

Schedule: Basketball season runs from October to mid-April. Hockey goes from October to April. The tours are offered year-round, variable hours depending on the season.

Admission: Basketball tickets range from $12.50 to over $900! Individual hockey tickets are almost impossible to get. Try to call in September!

Directions: Between York and Bay St., north of Lake Shore Blvd. There's a covered passage to Union Subway Station, on Front St.

LESLIE SPIT

Urban wilderness

This is the place where people come to drop their brick, cement, asphalt, etc. from demolished buildings and other construction. This is also the best place to feel like you're biking by the ocean.

You can remain on the smooth trail for 3 kilometres, or take one of the sandier side trails to different lookout points all around the peninsula.

We took an off the beaten track trail through a field and saw the most intriguing scene: a fully-blown white sail towering over the tall grass, the only indication that we were by the water.

In other parts of the park, we would have a full view of the glittering water taking turquoise shades under the summer sun.

Somewhere else, we saw weird sculptures made out of metal rods and bricks found in the landfill.

We saw a lighthouse on top of a hill on one side of the path, and the **CN Tower** on top of the horizon on the opposite side.

We crossed a small bridge, we cycled by ponds, we even came across a bird sanctuary where cormorants nest in May.

It was past the time of the year when we're not allowed to enter the sanctuary and were in for a surprise (sensible souls beware): hundreds of dried bird skeletons were scattered all over the place. (We were later told by a park worker that many youngsters unfortunately fall off their crowded nests!)

It seems there are turtles, owls, snakes and frogs along with the butterflies and over 300 species of birds amidst the 400 plant species found on Leslie Spit.

Of course you won't see any of that if your main goal, when coming here, was to enjoy the feel of the wind through your hair and the sun on your face as you're swooshing by on your bike.

TIPS (fun for 5 years +)

• It will take you 45 minutes to bike on the looped trail of Leslie Spit at an average speed.

• Beware if you park in the parking lot adjacent to the entrance. It will be locked after the official hours! There's parking along Leslie Street and Unwin Avenue.

• There are normally chip trucks selling food and drinks by the entrance.

Leslie Street Spit
www.friendsofthespit.ca

D-3
East
of downtown
15-min.

Schedule: Open year-round on weekends, 9 am to 6 pm. The bird sanctuary is closed from April 1 to September 1.

Admission: FREE.
Directions: Leslie Street Spit (Tommy Thompson Park), Toronto. From Lakeshore Blvd., turn south on Leslie Street until you reach the park.

ASHBRIDGES BAY PARK & BEACH

In the loop

Past the boulders and the boardwalk by Woodbine Beach, the paved path turns into a sinuous loop that goes up and down, surrounded by the bay and the lake. A real adventure for beginner bikers.

It only takes 15 minutes to bike around the loop but you can stop at the tip of the peninsula to take in a view of the lake. You can even access a pebble beach through the shrubberies.

On your way back, you can take the right branch of the fork leading you to the Beach area along the water, past the **Boardwalk Pub**.

The path offers a wide-open view of the beach. You can ride for 10 minutes to reach another loop amidst mature trees offering nice shade in the summer. There's a snack bar in this section and a playground further east.

The whole ride from the **Boardwalk Pub** to the eastern end takes approximately 15 minutes. Be careful! It is busy and pedestrians walking in couples tend to use the whole width of the path.

TIPS (fun for 5 years +)

• When I use a car to get to the bike trails and only intend to stay a couple of hours, I often park in the parking lots of **Canadian Tire** or **Loblaws**, at the corner of Lake Shore Blvd. and Leslie Street. It is a 15-min. bike ride from there to Ashbridges Bay Park, going eastbound on the trail along Lake Shore. Leslie Spit bike trail is only a 5-min. bike ride southbound down Leslie.

NEARBY ATTRACTIONS
Woodbine Park (2-min. walk) ...... p. 285
Cherry Beach (5-min.) .... p. 401

Ashbridges Bay Park & Beach	D-3
(416) 392-1111 www.toronto.ca/parks	East of downtown 15-min.

Schedule: Open year-round.
Admission: FREE. Parking fees at Ashbridges Bay Park and Boardwalk Pub's parking lots.
Directions: From Gardiner Expressway eastbound, exit at Lake Shore Blvd. Turn south at Coxwell Ave. The Ashbridges Bay parking lot is straight ahead. It is a few minutes away from the bike path.

OTHER BIKING OPTIONS

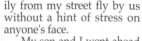

Going down this path

In a big city where cars rule, a simple bike ride can turn into a parent's worst nightmare. Bike paths come to the rescue.

A few years ago, I decided my family would explore all the GTA's bike trails interesting for the whole family. I pictured a whole chapter... but you won't find it in this guide. And here's the reason why.

On our first outing to be documented, my then 5-year-old had her big brother's old 4-wheeler. He was using his brand new bike. I had a good bike myself but no helmet. My husband had the 10-speed bike from his teenage years. On the other hand, my son's godmother was fully equipped with a top-of-the-line shiny bike, complete with odometer and first aid kit.

As we're about to set off on the bike path near Cherry Beach, my daughter hits herself with her own bike. The first aid kit is taken out to find a band-aid.

My son has three false starts. He just can't stay put on his bike. Then the chain falls off. Dad is getting annoyed, he wants to get going. Finally, we take off and as I'm wondering if it is as complicated for everyone with kids, I see a whole fam-

ily from my street fly by us without a hint of stress on anyone's face.

My son and I went ahead and eventually have to wait for my daughter, who is finally seen around the corner, followed by her dad walking his bike.

There's a narrow sidewalk on a bridge, which we will never be able to convince our little girl to cross. I go back to the beach with her while we wait for the rest of the gang.

You see? But I can still point out a few paths, fun for beginner bikers, which I noticed when visiting parks and rivers.

Upper left picture shows the recreational path of **Cherry Beach** (p. 401). From the beach's parking lot, it leads to the entrance of **Leslie Spit** in 15 minutes (p. 338).

In the upper right picture, you see a portion of **Cedarvale Park**, a few minutes south of Eglinton West. The northern part offers a wide open valley where beginners will enjoy going up and down. Southbound, it leads to a pretty trail down the ravine. The whole trail is around 2 kms long.

The middle picture shows the path which runs approximately 2 kms along **Humber River** (p. 330) in **Étienne Brûlé Park**, then across Dundas Street and back on the other side of the river. Half way, you'll find a playground.

Finally, the picture below was taken on the recreational path of Toronto Islands. There's a bike rental shop which rents these four-seat bikes at Gibraltar Beach. On weekends, you can't catch the Centre Island ferry with your bike but the two other ferries accept them. There are approximately 5 kms between Hanlan's Point and Ward's Island.

TIPS (fun for 5 years +)

• You can download **Toronto Cycling Map** from **www.toronto.ca/cycling** or call 416-392-7592 to order a colour copy of this detailed map including all kinds of biking-related information.

DOGSLED AT ROB ROY FARM

"Hike! Hike!"

Before seeing the Farm's Siberian Huskies, we hear their high-pitched barking. They're smaller than I expected, and are harnessed to the sleds in groups of three. They let out febrile howls, excited by the anticipation of an outing. However, they rapidly calm down when my little trail blazer pets them.

We walk towards a large clearing, where I receive my first sled-driving lesson. Meanwhile, my son takes his place in the front of the dog handler's sled, on the only passenger seat.

I learn basic concepts. I have to place my feet on the sled's skates. In order to turn to one side, I need to lean my body the right way.

Photo: Courtesy of Rob Roy Farm

When I want the dogs to move forward, I must yell "Hike!" And, most importantly, I must slam on the brakes immediately if my sled starts to pass its own dogs or if our team threatens to charge the sled ahead of us!

"Don't worry" says a member of the staff, "everyone falls…" How reassuring! In fact, I did fall once. I didn't hurt myself, and had plenty of time to hop back on.

An employee rides a snowmobile behind us. He's there to catch up with the sleds that have lost their drivers. My son is clinging to his sled and loudly encouraging the dogs to go faster.

When the sled slides without resistance, the speed is exhilarating and the huskies' joy is contagious. The ride lasts around 30 minutes. It's not very long, but in my case it was intense enough to leave me the following day with aches and pains in several arm muscles I didn't even know existed!

Meanwhile, my 21-month-old daughter stayed in Daddy's arms. They admired the farm animals: donkeys, pigs, guinea hens and barn cats. After the dogsled ride, we met at the barn and drank a hot chocolate.

TIPS (fun for 5 years +)

• Young passengers have to be old enough to be able to hang on to both sides of the dog handler's sled. Young children are not allowed to ride alone with inexperienced parents.
• The braking manoeuvre is a bit difficult for children to handle but the owner assured me many succeed and drive a sled. If they don't, they can always be passengers.
• Expect an igloo, their new thing in the last few years!
• They also rent snowshoes for $15/hour.
• They are located 30 minutes away from **Talisman Resort** (**www.talisman.ca**) and **Blue Mountain** (**www.bluemountain.ca**).

Rob Roy Farm • Singhampton (519) 922-2706 www.dogsledfarm.com	B-1 N-W of Toronto 2 1/2 hrs

 Schedule: Open mid-December to end of March, weather permitting. Call for snow conditions.
Admission: 30-min. ride is $65/adults, $45/12 years and under.
Directions: 469358 Grey Rd. 31. From the Talisman Centre, take County Rd. #13 southbound, then take County Rd. #31 eastbound.

BURD'S FAMILY FISHING

The line is busy

You need fishing gear? They rent it out. The very idea of putting a desperate worm on a hook grosses you out? They'll do the dirty work for you. And most of all, you're afraid your pint-size fisherman (or woman) might return without a catch? Well, you can't come home empty-handed with the thousands of trout that inhabit the ponds at Burd's Trout Fishing. From now on, nothing stands between your child and the intriguing experience of fishing.

The tree-lined farm is a pretty sight with its two, one-acre ponds, each adorned with a lazy paddle wheel that gently stirs the water. A small brick path runs alongside the bigger pond, allowing for strollers and wheelchairs to circulate.

TIPS (fun for 4 years +)
• No permit required.
• One rod might actually be enough for two young children since one can bring the trout ashore with the rod while the other catches it with the net.
• Trout sells for around $1.75 per 100 g. so you could run a high bill. Note that it is sold at the market price which may vary depending on the season.
• During our visit, the seven fish we caught measured between 18 and 25 cm and cost around $30. The farm accepted payment by cash or credit card.

NEARBY ATTRACTIONS
Live Steamers (15-min.) .... p. 221
Bruce's Mill (10-min.) .... p. 302

The bigger pond, for general public use) is stocked every week. The other pond is reserved for group use.

There's a laid-back country feeling to the place. But don't be fooled: no stone was left unturned in order to cater to our needs. The employees, dressed in sweatshirts printed with the farm's logo, offer courteous service. There is also a rain shelter, washrooms, the sale of beverages and snacks and, oh bliss, a small outdoor playground with sandbox (complete with toys!).

After weighing our catch, an employee killed, cut and cleaned our fish way too fast to trouble my little Nosey Parker, who was observing the whole scene with big... fish eyes.

Later on, we found out that the trout, being so fresh, were incredibly tasty. True, they weren't really a bargain compared to the market price, but watching my little guy frantically winding his reel to bring in the fighting fish was worth a million.

The proud look on his face while we were eating his catch wasn't bad either.

Burd's Family Fishing
• Stouffville
(905) 640-2928
www.burdsfamilyfishing.com

C-3
N-E
of Toronto
30-min.

 Schedule: Season runs daily from Victoria Day to Labour Day, weather permitting (weekends only from Easter to Victoria Day, and from Labour Day to Thanksgiving, 9 am to 6 pm (7 pm in the summer).

Admission: Around $5/visitor, FREE for 12 years and under, $5/rod rental and bait.

Directions: 13077 Hwy 48, Stouffville. From Hwy 404 North, take exit #37/ Stouffville Rd. eastbound. Turn north on Hwy 48, look on the east side.

PRIMEROSE TROUT FARM

Simple pleasures

This one is off the beaten track so you don't really hear the cars from the highway. You're surrounded by nature. Everyone who's there is relaxed... except my kids when they catch their first fish!

Here, you won't find staff wearing the farm's logo on a sweatshirt and no one will clean the fish for you. But the owner who was observing my son in action from afar quietly came to offer some welcomed fishing advice.

TIPS (fun for 4 years +)

• We really enjoyed our lunch at **Superburger**, a hamburger joint in an air-conditioned streetcar located a few minutes from the trout farm on the north-west corner of Hwy 89 and Hwy 10.

• I did not know at the time but a fun thing to do after our fishing session (bring a cooler to keep the fish fresh) would have been to drive south to downtown Orangeville, a 20-minute drive on our way back to Toronto, to check out their **Art Walk of Tree Sculptures**! (Go east on Hwy 89, then south on Hwy 24 to Orangeville and turn west on Broadway.) To download the map of this walk running around Broadway, go to **www.orangeville.org**, click **Tourism**, then **Attractions** and go to **Related Information**. The brochure features over 40 sculptures.

My daughter was more than happy to rely on her big brother to put the worm on the hook (the apple didn't fall too far from the tree for this one).

I thought it funny how she kept changing spots. At one point, she lost patience and thought she would have a better chance to catch the fish with her net. Big brother was more patient and got a good one which she helped bring in.

They provide the fish cleaning facilities.

Primrose Trout Farm · Shelburne (519) 925-3846 www.primrosetroutfarm.com	C-2 **North** of Toronto 75-min.

 Schedule: Open daily from April to October, 8 am to 6 pm. Call to see if they are open at other times. I've seen it open in the winter!

Admission: $3/admission per rod (kids can share their rod). Rod rental is $5. They sell ice and bait. The trout from the Family Pond is around $4.50 per lb.

Directions: R.R. #4, Shelburne. From Hwy 400 northbound, take exit to Hwy 89 westbound. Drive past Hwy 10, turn south on Blind Line.

ABOUT FISHING

Fun for shore!

I don't know about your children but as far as mine are concerned, fishing is the only fun way to remain calm for half an hour: There's the hope, the surrounding nature, and the thrill of the catch. So I decided to get to the bottom of this sport to indulge their passion.

In years of visiting the region inside out, I have noticed people fishing everywhere, at all times of the year. I've always wondered if they were allowed, how they knew which fish were edible, how they got their permit, etc.

Fishing regulations

The bottom line is that kids and youth under 18 years old don't need a fishing permit. And if you just want to watch your kids fish, you don't need a permit either.

Only residents between 18 and 64 require a fishing licence. Licences are available from camps and lodges, summer camps, sporting goods stores or bait dealers. In smaller communities, they're often sold in general stores.

When buying a licence from one of the 2,000 licence issuers across the province, you fill out an Outdoors Card Application. An Outdoors Card bearing your one-year fishing licence tag will be mailed to you. It is a plastic identification card good for 3 years, to which the fishing licence is affixed. Meanwhile, you'll get a temporary licence on the spot. A renewal package is automatically mailed to you before your card expires.

If you want to fish with your kids, you'll need to get at least the $10 One-Day Fishing Licence. If you intend to join them more than one day, you'll need to get the $20 Conservation Fishing Licence or the $30 Sport Fishing Licence, both good for one year and including the cost of the Outdoors Card Annual Licence. (In most cases, you'll be allowed to catch more fish with a sport licence.)

The daily catch limit varies a lot depending on the species, the location, time of year and kind of licence you've got.

MNR publications

Could not distinguish one from the other? No problem! Get the Ontario Ministry of Natural Resources (MNR) brochure *Fishing Regulations Summary* with a colour fish identification chart at the end.

This free publication is now divided into 20 zones. Each is broken into fishing divisions, with specific regulations applying to them. There's of course more information than you'll need in it. For example, we learn that salamanders may NOT be used as bait. Yuck! The very idea they need to specify that!

You may download this publication and the ones listed below from their website. At the time of print, they were revamping their website but it is a safe bet to assume you'll find a **Publications** section (look past the new publications).

My favourite is the great 40-page brochure *Take a Kid Fishing Guide*. It is filled with lovely pictures and very useful information for neophytes. It covers it all: tackle, hooks, sinkers, bobbers, bait, lures, etc. Illustrations will show you how to put together your tackle, how to make basic knots, how to cast.

The last two pages include colour charts to identify your catch. In it, I learned that the best beginner's fishing gear to buy for a child should be a light reel on a 4 1/2 to 5 ft. lightweight rod with 6 to 12-lb. line which should be easily found for around $30.

The pictures in their other publication, the 32-page *Fish Ontario*, are even more beautiful. Here, you'll have a better look at the different species, with some amazing pictures of prize catches that will make your young fisher dream. For each species, they give you the Ontario record catch, average size of fish, information on biology, temperature and habitat as well as concrete tips on bait and fishing techniques.

It mentions that Ontario includes over 400,000 lakes, roughly 15% of the world's fresh water. It also states that the record lake trout caught in an Ontario lake was 63.12 lbs. (28.65 kg)... Really!

Around the city

If you want to know where the fishing spots are in and around the GTA, you must get a free copy of the flyer *Urban Fishing Opportunities in Toronto & Surrounding Areas* put together by the Aurora District of the Ontario Ministry of Natural Resources.

It includes a list of the GTA fishing sites as well as the fish you're bound to find in them! Many of those sites are described in this guide: **Albion Hills C.A.**, **Heart Lake C.A.**, **Chinguacousy Park**, **Professor's Lake**, **Centennial Park**, Grenadier Pond in **High Park**, **Toronto Islands**, **Ashbridges Bay**, the mouth of the **Humber River**, **Bluffer's Park**, Rouge River Marsh by **Rouge Beach**, **Mill Pond**, **Willcox Lake**, **Bruce's Mill C.A.**, **Petticoat Creek C.A.** and **Kelso C.A.**

A conservation area I don't describe in my guide but which is probably the best for fishing is **Glen Haffy** at 19305 Airport Road, north of Caledon East, (416) 667-6299. It has two trout ponds regularly stocked and fishing equipment for rent. It even has two private ponds for groups to rent (**www.thehillsofheadwaters.com**)

TIPS (fun for 4 years +)

• The picture on page 344 was taken at **Christie C. A.** (see p. 417).
• You've got to check the **Picture Gallery** on the **Credit River Anglers Association**'s website to see the kind of monsters we can get out of the urban river (**www.craa.on.ca**).
• A visit to **Bass Pro Shops** in **Vaughan Mills Mall** is an outing in itself! The huge store's layout is amazing. It includes many mounted animals in a realistic setting, with a waterfall and a huge aquarium where they were offering fly fishing demonstrations when we visited! (**www.basspro.com**). They sell fishing licences.

Family Fishing Weekend

Ontario Family Fishing Weekend is an official three-day weekend of unlicenced fishing. Usually held on the second weekend of July, this event allows adults to fish without a permit. It is locally driven, meaning that what's done during this event varies from one municipality to the next.

Some locations offer games for the children and prizes, others offer free use of equipment and bait. Many will feature fly fishing demonstrations and give fish identification tips. Check their website or call for details about local events.

Ministry of Natural Resources
1-800-667-1940 (info line)
1-800-387-7011 (for Outdoors Cards)
www.mnr.gov.on.ca/mnr/fishing

Family Fishing Weekend
1-800-667-1940 (info line)
www.familyfishingweekend.com
Schedule: Usually on the first or second weekend of July, Friday to Sunday.

HOCKEY HALL OF FAME

Shoot and score!

The Hockey Hall of Fame reflects the colourful palette of the world's many hockey teams and is as bright as any rink during play-offs. There is no need to be a serious fan to enjoy the many attractions displayed throughout the labyrinth-shaped path of discoveries.

The museum fills a large space in the underground of the eye-catching **Brookfield Place**. Devoted aficionados could easily spend an entire day reading the texts adjoining each gorgeous window display but there are also sufficient interactive displays to entertain children six years and older, particularly if they are hooked on the national sport.

My companions thoroughly enjoyed the NHLPA Be A Player Zone!

In the glassed rooms of Lay's Shut Out, they positioned themselves in front of a goal and tried to intercept soft pucks shot full blast by a virtual Marc Messier and Wayne Gretzky. Then, they'd stop shots fired by four virtual players (and watch themselves on the 8-by-10-foot screen.

On the other side, they waited anxiously for their turn at the Source For Sports Shoot Out, where they shot real pucks towards a virtual Eddie Belfour guarding the goal. Data such as their speed, precision and reaction time would show up on a screen.

A mezzanine area overlooks the game zone. It is part of the TSN/RDS Broadcast Zone and includes several broadcast pods where visitors can transform into sports commentators.

ing Stanley Cup, located in the Bell Great Hall. The room is capped by a dome 15 metres above, adorned with magnificent stained glass. The heavy doors of this ex-bank's vaults are an intriguing sight for children's active imaginations.

Last time I visited, we could have our photo taken by the Cup (one glossy 8-by-10-inch picture for $10, ready in a few minutes).

They watch clips of real games from a menu of classic moments as their comments are taped. (They find it challenging, except for yelling "He scores!") They can compare with the actual comments from legendary broadcasters. They also get a private access code to hear their play-by-play via www.hhof.com! It will stay on the web for a few days.

The Production Mobile is for older kids (and adults). The simulator allows us to compose our own clip, selecting camera angles, audio mix, broadcast pace and more.

Make sure to photograph your aspiring players in front of the gleam-

TIPS (fun for 6 years +)
• Parking at the **Brookfield Place** is expensive on weekdays but O.K. on weekends.
• Jerseys from most professional teams are available in small sizes in the store (strategically located at the museum's exit).
• There is a food court out of the attraction. Also read about the **Richtree Market** on p. 450.

NEARBY ATTRACTIONS
Air Canada Centre (5-min. walk) p. 337
European Flair Stroll (5-min. walk) p. 476

Hockey Hall of Fame
(416) 360-7765
www.hhof.com

D-3 Downtown Toronto 5-min.

Schedule: From end of June to Labour Day, during Christmas and March Breaks, 9:30 am to 6 pm (opens at 10 am on Sundays). Fall/winter/spring: Monday to Friday, 10 am to 5 pm, Saturday, 9:30 am to 6 pm; Sunday, 10:30 am to 5 pm.
Admission: $13/adults, $9/ seniors and 4-13 years, FREE for children 3 years and under. (You can leave and re-enter.)
Directions: Brookfield Place (formerly BCE Place), Concourse Level, Toronto (north-west corner of Yonge and Front St.).

CLAIREVILLE RANCH

Conservation indeed

Some people have gone through all kinds of hoops to turn this huge piece of land into a golf course but, thanks to its Conservation Area status, it's been preserved, ensuring the survival of one of the last horseback riding ranches in the GTA at the same time.

I have tried to include horseback riding in my two previous editions but the ranches we visited would be gone before I would go to print. You could literally see the housing developments creeping close to those ranches.

Claireville Ranch has room to breath. Its one-hour trail rides guide you through woods and fields, and along a glittering river.

TIPS (fun for 10 years +)

• Kids must be 10 years old and most importantly, have a 27-inch minimum length of inseam (measure them from the crotch to the ground. My 10-year-old barely made it.) Closed shoes are a must.
• There are good old outhouses. The ranch normally sells some snacks and beverages but they might be out of stock. Better bring your own.
• Ask about their three-hour breakfast ride ($60 for this special experience).
• I recommend you come earlier to give your name and reserve a time slot. It would leave you time to have lunch in Brampton (just keep going west on Road 7, it becomes Queen Street, lined with the usual restaurant chains), then come back without waiting. We did not do that and had to wait 45 minutes for a spot.

When we were riding, a bird almost flew into my daughter and we admired two blue herons taking off from a turn in the stream. To think that we were just between Toronto and Brampton was mind-boggling!

I discovered my child was scared of trotting in the middle of our trail ride, when there's no way out! Fortunately, we were at the end of the line, so we could make our horses walk while the others trotted without being in the way. Of course, there's always the possibility that trail horses will just follow the horse in front at whatever speed they go.

Parents can lead their kids on a pony ride in an enclosed area in the field, if they are too small or scared.

Claireville Ranch	D-2
· Brampton	N-W
(905) 794-0700	of Toronto
www.clairevilleranch.com	35-min.

Schedule: May to October, open every day but Tuesday (weekends only during wintertime, weather permitting). Call for exact hours.
Admission: $25/one hour ride (check their website for a discount coupon), $5 for a pony ride. Credit cards accepted.
Directions: Drive northbound on Hwy 427 to the end, turn west on Road 7. Pass The Gore Road, the small road leading to the ranch is on the south side, just across the road from McVean Drive.

NEARBY ATTRACTIONS
Chinguacousy Park (10-min.) ..... p. 297
Wild Water Kingdom (5-min.) ...... p. 431

TORONTO CLIMBING ACADEMY

"There you go!"

"Is it the paparazzi corner?" teases a father. "Actually, we all work for the Globe!" I joke back. Truth is, if I am the only one writing about today's experience, I also have the least impressive equipment to catch the moment when my child conquers the 55-foot wall!

I did not expect all parents wanting to stay for the whole two-hour program. Most of all, I did not expect them to cheer each climber in unison!

The young supervisor coaches each child during the climb, with step-by-step instructions punctuated by plenty of "Awesome!" or "There you go!" encouragements. I read 5.4 at the bottom of the first wall. I am told 5 means "vertical", and 4, the degree of difficulty. Some impossible walls rate 5. 14!

The other wall they climbed (a 5.5) was 55 feet tall; more than twice the height of the first one. Those who reach the top hit a button which turns on a red light. Thankfully, all the kids succeed.

The third climb was a corner wall. On his last climb, my son is bypassed by a spider woman on the "wall" above his head. She eventually falls, dangling safely at the end of her rope. "What happened?" asks a girl in the group. What did you expect? She was climbing on a... ceiling!

"Was it fun?" I later ask my little monkey when he comes down. "Yes!" "Does it hurt anywhere?" I inquire. "Everywhere!" is his reply. Go figure!

TIPS (fun for 6 years +)

• Shy children beware! Children climb with all eyes on them.
• I felt my tall 7-year-old's legs and arms were just long enough to reach the holds. A six-year-old in the group almost did not make it to the top. Bring good shoes or rent climbing shoes for $5.
• For $35, parents can be certified and learn how to supervise their child.
• If you want some down time while your child is in the program, just go five minutes east of Broadview on Queen Street, for a perfect croissant at **Bonjour Brioche** (812 Queen Street E., (416) 406-1250) or great coffee at **Dark Horse** (682 Queen Street E., (416) 898-6235).
• **Joe Rockheads** at 29 Fraser Ave. offers the Kids Klimb program for $25/child, any time of the week (min. three, 8 to 13-year-old kids). A good flexible birthday party solution! (416) 538-7670 or www.joerockheads.com.

NEARBY ATTRACTIONS
Cherry Beach (10-min.) .... p. 401

Toronto Climbing Academy
(416) 406-5900
www. climbingacademy.com

D-3 East of downtown 10-min.

 Schedule: Monday to Friday, 12 noon to 11 pm; Saturday and Sunday, 10 am to 10 pm; Holidays, 10 am to 6 pm. **Kids Love To Climb** for 6-12 years: Saturday from 11 am to 1 pm.

 Admission: One Day pass $14/adults, $12/student, $9/6-12 years. Harness rental is $6. Kids Love to Climb is $22.

 Directions: 100A Broadview Ave., Toronto (south of Queen St. East, on the west side of Broadview Ave.).

SCOOTER'S ROLLER PALACE

Hold on!

It was a hot summer night outside when we visited the Palace so the light air-conditioning cooling the place was most welcome. A few minutes later, I was breaking a sweat just fitting my two kids into their skates. Still, it was nothing compared to what I felt the second I hit the rink!

Trying rollerblades for the first time while holding the hand of my unsteady 6-year-old daughter on roller skates was a very bad idea! I held on to the boards and crawled back onto the carpet, went back to the rental counter and got myself good sturdy four-wheel retro leather skates.

There were very few people on that Wednesday night. The good thing about it was that it meant fewer potential collisions with fellow skaters. The bad thing was that there was nowhere for me to hide to preserve my dignity.

There's a "disco" feeling to roller-skating. Add a ceiling punctuated with colour spotlights and a mirror ball reflecting on the shiny floor and you're back into the 80's... (or is it the 50's)! Add a couple of slow songs playing by the end of the evening and you might even get a flashback from your teenage years.

The skate floor is huge. Some loops are printed on it, for the keeners who want to practise routines. Scooter's Roller Palace actually offers affordable skating lessons for the young on Saturdays and for adults on some evenings. They also host All Night skating from time to time (going from 8 pm to 3 am!). I even heard about Christian Gospel skating nights!? The night we were there, the music sounded more like a very annoying radio station, not that I really noticed since I was in survival mode. They now have a disc jockey every night.

The place also includes some small bowling lanes and a few arcade machines. They sell glow pendants, bracelets and necklaces (from $2) which anybody aware of the roller skate culture knows is really cool when skating in a dark room under black lights.

TIPS (fun for 6 years +)
• You can use a bike helmet. Knee and elbow pads are recommended.
• The more friends you take with you, the more fun your kids will have. It is actually a great place to bring a birthday party. You can rent a private room or the whole place for skating, blading or roller hockey parties.
• I was not impressed by the food at the snack bar. I suggest you stick to buying refreshments there. If a meal is part of the outing, you might want to go to **Harvey's** next door.

NEARBY ATTRACTIONS
Rattray Marsh (5-min.) .... p. 304

Scooter's Roller Palace
• Mississauga
(905) 823-4001
www.scooters.on.ca

D-3
West
of Toronto
30-min.

Schedule: The schedule varies throughout the year. Look on their website for the Family All Ages sessions. Some sessions cater to adults only. They are open for children on most holidays and P.D. days.

Admission: $6 to $10 depending on the day. Rental: $2/roller skates, $3.50/rollerblades, $3.50/pads (limited inventory available).

Directions: 2105 Royal Windsor Dr., Mississauga. Take QEW, exit at Winston Churchill southbound, and turn east on Royal Windsor Dr. (an extension of Lakeshore).

ABOUT SKATEBOARDING

Join the club

It happens without warning. One day they're babies and the next they want wheels! So you take a deep breath and buy them their first skateboard... and skate shoes... and skate helmet (this sport doesn't come cheap!) Now, where's a skate park when you need one?

You owe this section to my buddy Cody, a very resourceful young expert I met a few years ago at a skate park in Cobourg (see picture above), after a nice day at the lovely beach there (p. 415). It took him fifteen minutes to point me to all the good spots he'd been to around the GTA (with the help of a dedicated dad, I am sure!) and to convince me that my research would not be lost on all the parents with kids with a strong inclination towards this sport.

On the following pages I describe the most popular parks we've visited around the GTA but they seem to be popping up more and more. And I've seen indoor skateparks come and go, so always call before you go!

Your best bet to find the latest or closest skatepark in your area is to call a local skate store. These guys usually know everything skateboarding-related that happens in the region! In these stores, you might even find some tapes offering an introduction to the sport.

One indoor skaterpark I really wish I had time to visit is **The Rail**, which opened in 2007 in **Downsview Park (www.therailskatepark.com)**.

Wherever you go, make sure your skaters always have a good supply of water with them. It is amazing how much this sport makes them perspire!

TIPS (fun for 6 years +)
In my first weeks of indulging my son in his new passion I learned a few things:
*   Don't look!
*   In most parks, rollerblades and BMX bikes are allowed as well.
*   No! A $20 skateboard won't do! The cheap bearings make it very hard and frustrating for the new skater to learn to get some control. Better to start with $50ish ones.
*   Try to borrow a board or find a second-hand one to verify how serious your child is about it before investing in the real stuff (new, it will cost over $200).
*   By the way, whatever the look of your child's new board, it won't take long for it to look old! That's why they sell those huge stickers in the skate stores: to cover up the scratches. Stickers are part of the skate culture (sK8 for the insiders). When visiting a skate store, you can always ask if they give some away.
*   Yes! Good shoes are a good idea! Skating is really rough on normal shoes and on tender heels.
*   Ski helmets are way too warm for summer use. We tried! Helmets and elbow pads are mandatory in most paying parks.

POLSON PIER

Formerly The Docks

Everyone has heard about The Docks' loud parties advertised by bikini-clad gals, in a Florida March Break fashion. Now under new management and a new name, Polson Pier is in the process of reinventing itself.

I put it in the skateboarding category of my guide before finding out that the indoor structures would not stay up year-round. The skatepark was built in a section normally covered with tables and chairs in the summer. Therefore, it will be taken away when the warm weather returns. They intend to put it back next year.

The **Ripley's Urban Rail Park** includes the skatepark and a snowboarding structure they also built by the water (see p. 362). These two winter additions allow for fun demonstrations from pros. The winter of 2007 had a false start in November and we had to wait until February 2008 to get real snow (too late to have it tested by my in-house snowboarder).

The driving range is open year-round. When spring is back, you can still expect minigolf and a rock climbing wall. At the time of print, they were not sure the go-kart track would be back (it might just change location on the premises, call to confirm).

What really does the trick for me is the 40,000 square foot waterfront patio. The best place from which to admire Lake

Ontario and the city's lights.

There's action to observe from this patio: police boats, tall ships, ferries, with **Ward's Point** on **Toronto's Islands** as a backdrop on one side and the **CN Tower** by the lake shore on the other.

Last time we visited during the summer, my kids wanted to swim in the octagonal pool in the middle of the patio. Denied! Me? Paying to be among the only ones to play, in a bathing suit, in a fenced pool surrounded by customers leisurely watching? I don't think so!

In the spring, weather permitting, the driving range turns into a drive-in theatre some nights every week, screening a double-feature of the latest movies. Think about it! A drive-in theatre. In downtown Toronto...

Polson Pier
(416) 469-5655
www.polsonpier.com

D-3
Downtown
Toronto
5-min.

  Schedule: Check their website in the fall to find out when the skatepark opens for the season until Victoria Day. The snowboard slope opens daily, weather permitting. The driving range is open year-round. The other outdoor activities open from Victoria Day to mid-September, weather permitting. **The Drive-in Theatre** opens Friday and Saturday (screening starting at 9:30-10 pm). The patio opens at 12 noon, kids not allowed after 9 pm.

Admission: The skatepark access is $10/day. Snowboard park is $20/day but includes access to the skatepark. Swimming Pool: $8/adults, $6/12 years and under ($10/person on weekends). Rock Climbing: $15/unlimited climbs. Mini Putt: $6/adults, $4/12 years and under ($2 more on the weekends). **Drive-in Theatre**'s double feature is $13/adults, $4/3-12 years old. Parking is $7-$15.

Directions: 11 Polson St., Toronto. Turn south on Cherry St. (from Lake Shore Blvd. eastbound), turn west on Polson.

TIPS (fun for 8 years +)

• A waiver must be signed by one parent on the premises the first time children under 18 years old use the skatepark.
• Kids are allowed on the patio until 9 pm. Bring a sweater!

NEARBY ATTRACTIONS
Cherry Beach (2-min.) .... p. 401

SHRED CENTRAL

Über cool

Some of you who reigned over an unfinished basement in your teenage years will know exactly what to expect at Shred Central. Those dusty hand-me-down sofas on the mezzanine (behind chain-link fence to protect the visitors) will bring back memories...

Seriously, the place is über cool. And yet, the staff is really nice with anybody over thirty and under ten.

TIPS (fun for 7 years +)
• ATTENTION! A release form must be signed for skaters under 18 years old by one of the parents on the first visit. They will then keep it on file for a year.
• One of the first skills a new skater will have to learn is to get out of the way as soon as he or she falls. The place is not as big as most outdoor parks.
• You may rent the space for birthday parties before regular weekend hours.
• Shred Central's small store is well stocked with shoes and other skate equipment. They have some vending machines for drinks and snacks.
• Your child does not need to be accompanied when skating on the premises. (There are a few cafés on Yonge Street, in the vicinity.)
• **Adrift** is the only other indoor skatepark downtown Toronto and it is tiny, in the back of a skateboarding store. It is open from 12 noon to 8 pm (opens at 3 pm on Mondays, closes at 7 pm on Sundays). It costs $4/person to use the park, bring your own equipment. An adult will have to sign a waiver the first time for kids under 18 (299 Augusta, 416-515-0550, **www.adriftskateshop.com**).

In the winter, it's pretty much the only option for serious downtown skaters (especially those who want to try out the new skateboard they got for Christmas!).

You access it through an alley. The façade is covered with large graffiti. Graffiti also covers the indoor walls, the columns, the pipes and the ramps.

NEARBY ATTRACTIONS
Police Museum (5-min. walk) ...... p. 241

Shred Central
(416) 923-9842
www.shredcentral.com

D-3
Downtown
Toronto
15-min.

 Schedule: Tuesday to Friday, 3 to 9 pm; Saturdays, 12 noon to 9 pm; Sundays, noon to 7 pm.
 Admission: $10 for a day pass, minimum age is 7 years old. FREE for girls!
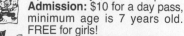 **Directions:** 19 Nicholas St., Toronto (a backstreet just west of Yonge and north of Wellesley St.).

WALLACE EMERSON CENTRE

Hidden treasure

The area is busy with stores, I almost missed it, hidden in the back of the community centre.

Daredevils are riding their BMX bike with skill; they've been at it for hours. Encouraged by the adult (me) observing them, they give their best shots.

Even though they're all with bikes (the park was created with them in mind), they confirm to me that kids also come with skateboards.

There's a great playground surrounded by trees and the centre includes an indoor pool, which younger siblings could enjoy while the oldest indulge in their extreme sport. Check the pool's schedule on their website.

Wallace Emerson Community Centre (416) 392-0039 www.toronto.ca/parks/torontofun	D-3 N-W of downtown 25-min.

Schedule: Open year-round.
Admission: FREE.

Direction: 1260 Dufferin Street, Toronto (south of Dupont).

LEONARD LINTON PARK

Super bowl time

This skatepark is reminiscent of those days when pioneer skaters started to hone their skills in the empty pools of the suburbs.

Leonard Linton park includes a great U-shaped bowl with an ambitious deep end and a separate section with ramps and stairs. A paved path links it all for a nice flow. And it is covered with graffiti.

Younger kids should try to go early. I know brave ones who show up at 7 am on the weekends, before the teenagers take over.

Last time we visited, there was an ice cream truck nearby, to add to the pleasure.

A few blocks west on Vanderhoof is the indoor playground **KidsWorks** (p. 190), perfect for younger siblings.

If you just want to drop your teenager and do some errands, the area is surrounded by big box stores: **Winners, Home Depot, Canadian Tire, Pier 1 Imports** and more.

Leonard Linton Park	D-3 North of downtown 25-min.

Schedule: Open year-round.
Admission: FREE.
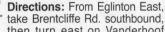
Directions: From Eglinton East, take Brentcliffe Rd. southbound, then turn east on Vanderhoof Ave., Toronto. The skatepark is

way back in the park.

CUMMER SKATEBOARD PARK

Action!

When we approach the side of the skatepark, a guy we had not noticed flies off from nowhere and flips back in a flash.

As we observed his routine, we realized that there was a slope, farther and higher in the back, which allowed him and other daredevils to gain an impressive speed before they threw themselves into what seemed like an empty pool and what I will learn to call a bowl.

This skatepark, adjacent to the **Cummer Community Centre**, is small but packed with features with which the skaters seem to be very creative: stairs, ramps, concrete corridors, different levels and the deep bowl. We can see it all in a glimpse.

It's around lunchtime and groups of teenagers arrive to watch their friends, armed with boxes of steamy pizza bought at the nearby strip-mall. The strip of concrete surrounding the park is quite narrow so we have to be careful to stay out of the way of the skaters in action. It's our first visit to a skatepark and we are learning as we go.

An older guy gives my 10-year-old son a tip or two after seeing him enduring a few painful-looking falls. I am immensely grateful to know that someone is watching over him because... personally, I can't watch!

When I dare to look at my newly extreme-sport-infatuated-one, he is as red as a tomato and soaked, I'm assuming from the adrenaline rush every time he tries a new move. Will he survive? An hour later, he's still at it!

Good news! There's a great indoor pool in the community centre, with giant slide and shallow area. I take a mental note to come back with my younger one for a swim next time I drive my son to this park.

In the back of the huge community park, there's also a small playground and four tennis courts.

TIPS (fun for 6 years +)
• **Cummer Pool** (indoor, with a big slide) is open for family leisure swim on weekends, 2 to 4 pm. More hours in July and August. Call to confirm.
• There's a snack bar in the community centre and some food outlets on the other side of Leslie St. We opted for the **Pickle Barrel** with its kids' menu and real "adult" food.

Cummer Skateboard Park	D-3 North of downtown 35-min.

Cummer Skateboard Park
• North York
(416) 392-1111 (City)
(416) 395-7803 (pool)
www.toronto.ca

Schedule: The outdoor park is open year-round. Call for the recreational swim schedule at the centre's indoor pool.
Admission: FREE access to the skatepark. FREE swim.
Directions: 6000 Leslie St., North York (north of Finch, just south of Cummer Ave.).

MISSISSAUGA SKATEPARK

Cool... but hot!

A sea of concrete waves is rippling before us. This skatepark seems bigger than the others!

Angles are not as accentuated as in other parks and slopes are not as high. As far as I can judge (from the humble point of view of a non-skater) the riders can't build as much speed here as in other parks but they can go for ever, not unlike a good back street lined with obstacles... without the cars (but we certainly hear

them! The park is located along Highway 403, so it is noisy.

The municipal park includes a large kidney shaped bowl going 6 feet down, slopes and quarter-pipes.

In the midst of summer, in 30-degree heat, the sun is burning hot. Steamy skaters are ready to throw themselves face first into the nearby snow bank formed by the Zamboni's discharge! (This park is located by **Iceland**, a complex with four indoor ice rinks.) Good news! There's a spray pad right next to **Iceland**.

Mississauga Skatepark • Mississauga (905) 615-4100 www.mississauga.ca	D-3 N-W of Toronto 35-min.

  Schedule: Open year-round.
Admission: FREE.
Directions: 705 Matheson Blvd. East, Mississauga. Take Hwy 403 West, exit at Eglinton westbound, turn right on Kennedy and right again on Matheson.

CHINGUACOUSY SKATEPARK

In the dirt

This skatepark is also BMX heaven, with parallel dirt paths, allowing healthy competitions between friends.

As we watch the skaters and riders in the small skatepark on cement, with a few half-pipes, we see MBX bikes in the background going up and down on the dirt paths. It sure looks tempting!

I don't know of another place in the GTA where young riders can have this kind of fun in a city.

A couple of minutes from the skatepark, you can access **Chinguacousy Park**

and its other attractions: wading pool, paddleboat rental, playground and more (p. 297).

Chinguacousy Skatepark • Brampton (905) 458-6555 www.city.brampton.on.ca	D-3 N-W of Toronto 35-min.

  Schedule: Open year-round.
Admission: FREE.
Directions: Take Hwy 427 North to the end of the road, turn west on Hwy 7, then north on Bramalea Rd. The skatepark is by the parking lot.

SHELL PARK

In a nutshell... loved it!

This is by far my favourite skatepark, strictly from an esthetic point of view. The place obviously belongs to the skaters.

I love the fact that the City of Oakville allowed colourful graffiti to blossom on the concrete instead of covering it with grey paint as soon as it appears. Let's hope nobody changes that! We've been to this park a couple of times and I could see that the graffiti is evolving!

The skatepark is contained in a large basin bordered by a large concrete sidewalk. When standing on it, you glimpse

the whole park down below, with plenty of trees in the background. It is nicely laid-out with slopes, quarter-pipes and ramps.

The skatepark is located on the edge of a small forest with a trail and next to a playground and a lovely garden. It is a perfect spot for a picnic while you wait for your skater to throw in the towel.

If you feel confident enough to leave your capable skater behind, you can explore the trail in **Sheldon Creek Park** leading to the lake, on the other side of Lakeshore.

TIPS (fun for 6 years +)

• After the skating session, I recommend you take a 2-minute drive back towards Bronte Harbour, at the foot of Twelve Mile Creek Lands, to check out the little **Bronte Beach**. Turn south on West River Street (on the west side of the creek); you'll find a public parking lot with

access to the beach. We especially loved the western section of it, a tiny secluded sandy spot hidden by the trees. The small park on the east side of Bronte Harbour is also quite pretty.

• Read about nearby **Fire Hall** restaurant under Riverview Park on p. 359.

Shell Park
• Oakville
(905) 845-6601
www.oakville.ca/
skateboardpark.htm

D-2
West
of Toronto
35-min.

Schedule: Open year-round.
Admission: FREE.
Directions: From QEW, take exit #111/ Bronte Rd. southbound, turn west on Lakeshore. Shell Park is on the north side.

MAJOR RINKS

By the lake

From one side, it looks as if the rink extends all the way to Lake Ontario. From another, the sun shines on the imposing CN Tower.

From the **Lakeside EATS** outdoor terrace, visitors observe skaters while eating or sipping a hot chocolate. The **Natrel Rink** at **Harbourfront Centre** is decidedly a cool skating spot!

It is here, at **Harbourfront Centre**, that we decided to introduce our little one to the trials and tribulations (and fun) of outdoor skating. He was quite surprised when his blades hit the slippery surface...

In the hour that followed, as we pulled him along between us, he would drop like a dead weight – a prisoner being brought to death row. At least he was laughing!

Some object to skating in the crowd-ed conditions on the weekend. However, you won't find that many skaters at all between 10 and 11 am. Moreover, given the rink's odd shape, there are some secluded spots to be enjoyed by those not too eager on speed skating.

A good time to visit is during **Harbourfront Centre**'s **Swedish Christmas Fair** and **Mennonite Christmas Festival** (p. 25).

In the square

Nathan Phillips Square and **Mel Lastman Square** also boast large outdoor artificial ice rinks with rental services. They too are open from the end of November to mid-March, weather permitting, and their admission is free.

TIPS (fun for 5 years +)

• Don't count on cheering your dear one's arabesques, standing on the rink with your boots on. Skates only are permitted on the ice.
• The **Natrel Rink** offers blade sharpening service.
• The ice of these rinks is artificially maintained at freezing level, providing the external temperature does not exceed 8° C, and the sun doesn't shine too aggressively.
• More on **Cavalcade of Lights** at **Nathan Phillips Square** on p. 170 and **WinterCity Festival** on p. 31.

NEARBY ATTRACTIONS
AGO (15-min.) .... p. 86
CN Tower (10-min.) .... p. 116

Major rinks
(416) 395-7584 (rink hotline)

Schedule: Open from mid-November to mid-March, 10 am to 10 pm (weather permitting). (Lakeside EATS at Harbourfront is closed on Mondays.)

Admission: FREE. Skate rental is usually around $7/adults, $6/seniors and children. Sharpening is $5.

Directions: Natrel Rink: 235 Queens Quay West, Toronto (west of York St., south of York Quay Centre).
Nathan Phillips Square: 100 Queen St. West, Toronto, west of Bay.
Mel Lastman Square: 5100 Yonge St., North York.

POND SKATING

Bring on the shovel!

There's something about skating on natural ice... I think it is this mix of beauty and imperfection that gives us the feeling we're OK as we are and we fit into our environment. Plus, being surrounded by a wide surface of snow and trees certainly beats looking at hockey boards!

Riverview Park

This park is buzzing with action! It is the unofficial town meeting place for those who love to play outside. In addition to pond skating, visitors can enjoy a good tobogganing slope. The skating pond is located on the western side of the **Twelve Mile Creek** in front of Riverview Park, where a marsh has formed (an official fish sanctuary).

On the day we went local families had cleared a dozen rinks in different sizes and shapes. Hockey games were going on the bigger ones and parents were initiating their toddlers on the smaller ones. The ice was not bumpy at all, the result of a fast freeze overnight.

There was tobogganing going on by the entrance of the park. But if you really want more serious tobogganing check **Appleby College Hill** on p. 370, 5 minutes away.

I found one fun restaurant in the area to finish a nice outdoor outing: the **Fire Hall**. This one really plays the fire hall theme, with fire hydrants, firemen's gear, hoses, small fire truck ride and pictures of real fires on the walls.

The menu boasts items such as extinguisher dip, fire crackers, three alarm chicken etc. Food is tasty. They offer a kids' menu. They even sell kid-size fire-fighter hats for $6 (2441 Lakeshore Rd. West, 905-827-4445, **www.thefirehall.ca**).

A funny tradition in **Oakville Coronation Park** (p. 426) is the annual **New Year's Day Polar Bear Dip** involving over 400 dippers and some 5,000 spectators to raise money for World Vision. For details, see **www.polarbeardip.ca**.

Mill Pond Park

The whole pond is cleared and managed by the Town of Richmond Hill. A sign indicates the ice conditions. You can call their Parks & Recreation Department to find out the conditions at (905) 884-8013.

There's an outdoor place to put on your skates and leave your boots as well as a small playground and some cages with geese and swans. There's even a parking lot and washrooms across the street from Mill Pond Park. A paved trail runs along the pond into a small forest. With gorgeous weeping willows brushing the pond, the place is a great picnic spot in the summer.

Check **www.wintercarnival.net** about **Richmond Hill's Winter Carnival** on the first weekend in February.

Saddington Park

The City of Mississauga used to manage this v-shaped pond. Now, locals still come and clear it off. It is set by Lake Ontario and surrounded by trees. Hockey players seem to stick to one branch of the "v" while leisure skaters hang around the other one. Check p. 328 for a description of this great park by **Credit River** in the summer.

TIPS (fun for 5 years +)

• We need a couple of weeks with serious sub-zero temperatures in order for the pond's ice to be  safe. Rule of thumb: If dozens of people are already skating, it is safe. If you're first, scratch the ice to judge its state. If it is slushy, don't go there. Ice by the shore is always thinner.

• When you go pond skating, bring a shovel! If you're the first to show up, you'll need it! Or you can help widen an already existing rink and those who have cleaned the ice before you will be convinced of your good faith. If you are plain lazy (or have to hold a kid's hand instead of a shovel) I suggest you go on a Sunday. Chances are the other skaters will have worked for you the day before.

• Other potential sites for natural-ice skating: **L'Amoraux** and **Milliken Park** (p. 292), **Mountsberg Wildlife Centre** (p. 149) and **Markham Museum** (p. 385).

Pond skating

 Schedule: The ice is normally safe after two weeks of freezing weather. Our best bet is from mid-January to mid-February but it's all in Mother Nature's hands.
Admission: FREE.
Directions:
Riverview Park/Oakville: Take the QEW, exit at Bronte Rd. southbound. Turn west on Lakeshore Rd. and north on Mississauga St. The first street on your right is Riverview St. It is a dead-end leading directly to the front of Riverview Park. People park along this street.
J.C. Saddington Park/Mississauga: See p. 350.
Mill Pond Park/Richmond Hill: Go west of Yonge, on Major Mackenzie St. Turn north on Trench St. to Mill St.

CEDARENA

Old-fashioned way

Interested in a small rustic ice rink, managed by volunteers for over eighty years and located in the backcountry, thirty minutes from Toronto? Then head for Cedarena.

At first sight, we were

charmed by the tortuous path that leads down to the Cedarena ice rink, which sits nestled amidst cedar trees.

At the end of the path, there is a small woodstove-heated cabin, where many families sit tightly against each other, as they put on their skates. Outside, an even smaller porch can hardly contain the overflow of eager skaters ready to embark on the ice.

It was a bit of a disappointment then to see boards surrounding the medium-sized rink, making it look somewhat choked. In addition, when we visited, the ice was dented and the music rinky-dink. Yet, it did not keep skaters from having a great time. The intimate character of the place must have something to do with it. It has been a local tradition for over 80 years!

Cedarena	**C-3**
• Markham	**N-E**
(905) 294-0038	**of Toronto**
(seasonal phone number)	**35-min.**
www.tourismmarkham.ca	

Schedule: The hours depend on volunteers' availability and may vary from one year to the next. Usually open Sundays, 1 to 4 pm and some evenings, 7:30 to 10 pm, weather permitting.

Admission: Around $2.50/adults, $2/seniors and $1/children.

Directions: 7373 Reesor St., Markham. From Hwy 401 East, take exit # 383/Markham Rd. northbound. Turn east on Steeles Ave., then north on Reesor Rd.

TIPS (fun for 5 years +)
• There are washrooms on site and a little snack bar that serves cider and hot chocolate.

SKIING IN TOWN?

The real thing!

From the "schlink" sound of the double chairlift, to the "swoosch" of skis scraping the slopes and the huge fireplace that sits in the ski chalet, Earl Bales looks like the real thing.

You won't see slopes running down to the **North York Ski Centre** as

TIPS (fun for 5 years +)

• More on tobogganing at **Centennial Park** on p. 369.
• Both ski centres have snowmaking equipment, night lighting and a snack bar. They also offer Alpine ski and snowboard lessons, and full sets of ski or snowboard equipment rentals as well.
• In the winter of 2007-08, **Polson Pier** (formerly **The Docks**) constructed a snowboard hill on their premises by the lake. Weather was unfortunately not on our side at the time of print so the experience was not really conclusive yet. They're supposed to put it up again in 2008 (**www.polsonpier.com**). See p. 352.

Photo: Courtesy of Polson Pier

you would expect at a ski resort. That's because they run down a ravine behind the centre.

Hidden from view, you'll discover them when you walk over and stand at the top of the chairlift. There you'll find a gentle slope for beginners equipped with a Tow Rope. It is the best place to be introduced to this winter sport.

Don't expect great hills, but the high-rises you spot on the horizon are there to remind you this is the middle of the city. This ski centre is a little miracle in itself!

Centennial Park Ski Hill

Centennial Park Ski Hill is the ski centre located in **Centennial Park**. It offers two shorter hills equipped with a T-bar and a Magic Carpet Lift, and a slope for tobogganing.

North York Ski Centre & Centennial Park Ski Hill	D-3 North of downtown 35-min.

(416) 338-6754
(info & snow conditions)
www.toronto.ca/ski

Schedule: Usually from mid-December to mid-March. Open minimum from 10 am to 8 pm (closes at 6 pm on Sundays).
Admission: Prices are the same for both parks. Varying prices depending on age. No more than $25 for snow pass, no more than $25 for full rental. $8 for beginner slope.
Directions/North York Ski Centre: Earl Bales Park, 4169 Bathurst St., North York (south of Sheppard Ave.).
Centennial Park Ski Hill: 256 Centennial Park Rd., Etobicoke (south of Eglinton Ave. West).

GLEN EDEN SNOW TUBING

Start here

Reluctant parents who've decided to give in and offer their enthusiastic kids the experience of snow tubing will love this one. It is the closest tube park to Toronto, and probably the one with the mildest slopes. Not that you could not gain some speed on these slopes. On a good night, the staff have seen people fly by at 80 km/h on radar.

The **Glen Eden Ski and Snowboard Centre** is located in the heart of **Kelso Conservation Area** in Milton. Its tube park includes four chutes and one low lift. When we visited, the February weather was so mild, one of the staff members was wearing shorts.

I thought the slopes a bit lame when I first saw them, but the ride down was quite fast. I was getting concerned by the acceleration that was building as I got really close to the end of the run when black rubber patches abruptly slowed me down. I recommend this tube park for parents of kids 5 to 8 years old.

Older kids know to visit the place in the evening, when the weather is colder and the chutes get icier. Younger kids will prefer day time, when warmer temperatures create more friction under the tube.

Beginner skiers use the Galaxy Learning Centre, a series of mild slopes located on the north side of the train track. You access the ski hills on the south side of the track through a funny low tunnel right next to the rental shop.

TIPS (fun for 4 years +)
- See the **Halton Museum** on p. 387.
- Kids need to be a minimum of 42 inches (106cm) tall to ride. Only one person per tube is allowed but you can hold another rider's tube handles to ride down in twoa (or threes).
- The farthest parking spot is located 1/2 km from the ski chalet on the eastern part of the ski hills and the Galaxy Learning Centre. It's a long way to walk back to the car with tired little skiers. Good news! A pedestrian walkway was built and now allows skiers to buy their ticket at the western chalet, by the parking lot.
- There's a snack bar inside the eastern chalet and exterior food counters in both lodges.

NEARBY ATTRACTIONS	
Crawford Lake (15 min.)	p. 388

Glen Eden Snow Tubing • Milton (905) 878-8455 www.gleneden.on.ca	**D-2** **West** **of Toronto** **50-min.**

 Schedule: Call to confirm when the season starts, it depends on the weather. Always call to confirm tubing runs are open. They're confident the season can go until end of March Break. Glen Eden is open for night use but closes at around 4 pm in the spring. Check exact schedule.

Admission: Around $3/one ride, $15/six rides. Note that unused rides can be used anytime within the same season. Ask about special nights.

Directions: In Kelso Conservation Area. From Hwy 401 West, take exit #320/Hwy 25 northbound. Turn west on Sideroad #5 (Campbellville Rd.), then south on Tremaine Rd. and enter Kelso C. A., west on Kelso Rd.

SNOW VALLEY SNOW TUBING

Are you game?

The expanse of snow before us seems abruptly severed horizontally. Beyond this divide, long corridors stretch out, lined with a carpet of snow. Farther still, dark forests alternate with white fields. We need to walk right up to the edge of this imaginary line to discover a slope equivalent to a ten-storey descent.

My six-year-old friends stamp their feet with impatience as they await the attendant's signal... but not me! In a split second, I feel like I am on a free-falling, four-storey elevator ride.

Then I am showered with snow that rushes from under my tube (all the more surprising because my eyes were shut and my mouth was wide open). I speed up even more, and my tube starts revolving around itself. I grasp my handles, barely catching a glimpse of my two lads stand-ing alongside the slope, laughing at my adventure. My pint-sized Olympic bobsledders are already asking for more!

The tubes are covered with a thick canvas, equipped with a strap that you tie to the lift, to be brought up the hill. But you must be careful, it's not the time to wipe your glasses: you get to the summit faster than you think! Both your hands are required to hang on to the tube when it is unhitched from the lift.

TIPS (fun for 4 years +)

• Minimum height to ride down the slopes is 42". Smaller kids have two options: the Chicken Chutes (without a lift, where parents and kids can form groups to slide down) and the Kidz Play Area (a miniature 3-chute tube park, without a lift, reserved for kids under 42"). They have kid-sized tubes.
• The first set of slopes is steeper. Tubers that choose a second group of gentler trails, located behind a row of trees, still come down at great speeds.
• On the day we visited, it took us ten minutes to go up, tube down and walk back to the lift. It was more advantageous to pay for a two-hour block of time. When there are long line-ups, it is recommended instead to buy a series of tickets, good for six descents.
• There are lockers and a cafeteria on site (and **Ski Snow Valley Barrie** next door offers 2 hour ski passes!).
• They now offer 7 kms of snow shoe trails. The cost of $15 includes snowshoe rental and the trail pass.

NEARBY ATTRACTIONS
Drysdale Tree Farm (35-min.) ..... p. 179

**Snow Valley
Snow Tubing Park**
• Barrie
1-877-404-4744
www.skisnowvalley.com

**B-2
North
of Toronto
70-min.**

Schedule: Open daily from mid-December to late March (weather permitting). Call for exact schedule.
Admission: Around $25/person for 4 hours or $20/6 rides. One ride is $4. Around $7 to use the Kidz Play Area. $16/weekdays except Christmas and March Breaks.
Directions: From Hwy 400 North, take exit Dunlop St. (#96B) westbound, turn north on George Johnson Rd., then east on Snow Valley Rd.

ABOUT SWIMMING

In the **Water Fun** chapter on pp. 397-436, you'll find all the beaches and pools.

TORONTO SLOPES

Off the beaten tracks

When snow finally graces our city, it's time to run to the slopes.

Glen Manor Drive

After a hearty brunch on Queen Street East in the Beaches, I recommend you drive to Glen Manor Drive, and continue the day at **Glen Stewart Ravine** (p. 318). On the north side of Queen Street, Glen Manor divides in two at the beginning of the ravine.

There, an ice rink has been installed (somewhat bumpy when we visited).

A little further, the ravine deepens and the two facing slopes are sufficiently steep, despite their lack of length, to entertain kids of all ages.

From the top of the stairs at the entrance to the ravine, you can catch a lovely view of the area and the gorgeous residences and mature trees that overlook the slopes. Read about **Carolling in the Park** in the tips section on p. 318.

Riverdale Park East & West

On a different scale, Toronto's most challenging slope sits at **Riverdale Park**, west of Broadview Avenue. It is quite broad, steep and long, and offers a stunning view of downtown Toronto's skyline.

Hang on to your hats though if the slopes are even just slightly icy! In fact, it is best to avoid the area altogether when the shiny crust covers the slopes, as it becomes nearly impossible to climb back up.

The western face of Riverdale Park, on the west side of the Don Valley Pkwy, is not as broad but is equally fun and challenging. Plus, it includes shorter sections, better for younger kids. The **Riverdale Farm** is a 5-minute walk from this slope (see p. 55).

Lawrence Park Ravine

Beautiful **Lawrence Park** (see above picture) is bowl-shaped, free of obstacles in the middle and surrounded by mature trees.

You can access the slope from all sides. The height varies so the site is suitable for different age groups. Bigger kids usually manage to create huge bumps to challenge themselves on the slope adjacent to Yonge Street.

Read about the steep hill in adjacent **Duplex Parquette** on p. 321.

Christie Pits Park

Snow was pretty much gone on the steep slope next to the rink but I could still see the toboggan tracks. This hill must be a thrill for big kids, but beware of the poles 15 metres apart at the bottom of the hill. This is not where most people go.

Rather, they will use the wide slope

TIPS (fun for 3 years +)

• You will easily find parking on Glen Manor Drive along the park of the same name, as well as on Broadview Avenue along **Riverdale Park**.

• **Riverdale** and **Glen Manor Parks** have no washroom facilities. **Christie Pits** does. **Lawrence Park** visitors could use the **George H. Locke Library** branch (at the corner of Lawrence Ave. and Yonge St.) where kids could warm up as they choose some books to take back home.

near the corner of Bloor and Crawford. The youngsters go down a gentle slope in front of the playground.

There are snack machines in the Christie Pits Centre and the rink might be open for free skating when you are visiting, so bring the skates.

Bickford Park

A few minutes walk south of Bloor on Christie, there's a more secluded and gorgeous park with slopes of varying heights on both sides. It is conveniently located near **Linux Caffe**, selling hot chocolates and more.

Toronto slopes
(416) 392-1111
www.toronto.ca/parks

Schedule: Weather permitting.
Admission: FREE.
Directions:

Riverdale Park: On Broadview Ave., between Danforth Ave. and Gerrard St.
Glen Manor Park: North of Queen St. East, between Glen Manor Dr. East and West, five blocks east of Kew Gardens.
Christie Pits Park: 779 Crawford St. The slope is just north of Bloor St., between Christie and Crawford Streets. Rink: (416) 392-0745.
Bickford Park: At the south east corner of Grace and Harbord Streets. Linux Caffe is on the north-east corner of this intersection.
Lawrence Park Ravine: South of Lawrence Ave., at the south-east corner of Yonge St. and Weybourne Cr.

SIR WINSTON CHURCHILL PARK

When I checked this slope, I did not have my young inspectors with me but I saw a whole class with their teacher joyfully walking from their local elementary school, armed with toboggans.

The upper part of the hill is blocked with fences. The lower section is shorter and less steep on the eastern side, more suitable for younger kids. From wherever you attack the slope, it is so long, the snow will slow you to a stop before you can hit anything. On the down side, kids will need to take a good walk back up the hill. Not for the lazy ones!

The small Roycroft Wet Forest lays at the bottom of the hill. In other seasons, it offers quite a change of scenery from the big city: a 5-minute walk amidst native shrubs and wildflowers and tall trees.

Prime location!

The snowy slope is endlessly winding down. When I looked at it from the bottom of the hill, I was impressed by the white panorama stretching high in front of me. That's a long and wide slope for the energetic ones.

Under the bridge taking Spadina over the ravine, I discovered stone stairs leading to Russell Hill Drive. When my daughter was exploring them, in the middle of the summer when it was invaded by plants, it looked like she was climbing the ruins of an ancient Mayan city.

TIPS (fun for 5 years +)

• A hot chocolate in the café of the **Forest Hill Market**, the **Loblaws** on St. Clair just west of Spadina, is the perfect way to start or finish this tobogganing outing. The grocery store offers plenty of parking (to its loyal customers) and you can catch a 5-minute trail leading to the park in front of it.

• Also check the ice-cream parlour **Dutch Dream**, open year-round, in the description of what's around **St. Clair West Subway Station** on p. 453.

NEARBY ATTRACTIONS
Casa Loma (5-min.) .... p. 120

Sir Winston Churchill Park
(416) 392-1111
www.toronto.ca/parks

D-3
North
of downtown
25-min.

Schedule: Open year-round.
Admission: FREE.
Directions: At the south-east corner of St. Clair Ave. West and Spadina Rd., in Toronto. There's street parking on Ardwold Gate just south of the park.

CENTENNIAL PARK

Off the record

At Centennial Park, there's the designated tobogganing area, and then there's the unofficial one where a sign, at the bottom of the hill, reads: "No hang-gliding or parasailing permitted." You get the picture.

When you, along with fifty other people, use the unofficial slope, you do so at your own risk. The hill is really steep, lasts a long stretch, and has a great panorama at the top.

The official hill is located next to the parking lot accessible from Eglinton Avenue. The slope is not steep but it goes down forever (which means parents will feel they are climbing up the hill forever with their younger child's toboggan in tow). It is lots of fun for the young crowd with a good toboggan.

TIPS (fun for 3 years +)

- See skiing at **Centennial** on p. 362.
- It is better to go on the steep hill only with children old enough to know better than to take their time at the bottom of the hill. You don't want your child to be hit by a full-speed teenager on a tube!
- There is a greenhouse in Centennial Park, located by the parking lot closer to Rathburn Road. It offers a nice contrast to winter, with colourful flowers, cactus, fish and turtles in a pond. An exotic way to end the outing.

NEARBY ATTRACTIONS
Fantasy Fair (15-min.) .... p. 35

Centennial Park
· Etobicoke
(416) 392-1111
www.toronto.ca/parks

D-3
N-W
of downtown
30-min.

Schedule: Open year-round.
Admission: FREE.

Directions: 56 Centennial Park Rd., Etobicoke. Take Hwy 427 North, exit Rathburn Rd. westbound, turn north on Centennial Park Rd. The official hill is at the southeast corner of Centennial Park Rd. and Eglinton Ave.

RICHMOND HILL LIBRARY

One for the books

The slope by the Richmond Hill Library is long, moderately steep and... facing Atkinson Street.

Daredevils can't resist the part of the hill where big bumps give enough speed to require them to "put on the brakes" before they reach the street.

You will want the younger ones to use the safer slope closer to the parking lot. Inside the Library, a café sells great hot chocolate and coffee to warm up. There are washrooms.

See **The Wave Pool** on p. 424.

Richmond Hill Central Library	C-3
• Richmond Hill (905) 884-9288 (library) www.richmondhill.ca	North of Toronto 30-min.

Schedule: Weather permitting.
Admission: FREE.
Directions: 1 Atkinson St., Richmond Hill. From Hwy 404 North, take exit #31/Major Mackenzie Dr. westbound. The hill is south of the Library (at the corner of Yonge).

APPLEBY COLLEGE HILL

This hill gets an A+

When we saw this slope as we were driving by on Lakeshore, we just had to join the fun. It was wide and long. Trees were surrounding it and we could admire the blue lake on the horizon.

This gorgeous spot certainly is a favourite in Oakville, judging by the dozens of local families with kids of all ages enjoying it. But it's wide enough that everybody spreads out nicely. There's a large visitor's parking lot on the college's grounds. During the weekend, we could even park closer to the hill, on the western part of the school.

A one-minute drive away to the east, on the prettiest strip of Lakeshore Road in Old Oakville, there are lots of nice cafés selling hot chocolate, to top off the outing.

Read about nearby **Fire Hall restaurant** under **Riverview Park** on p. 359.

Appleby College Hill	D-2
• Oakville	West of Toronto 35-min.

Schedule: Open year-round.
Admission: FREE.
Directions: 540 Lakeshore Rd. West, Oakville. Take QEW, exit at Dorval Dr. southbound, turn west on Lakeshore Rd. West. Appleby College is on the south side of the road.

ROUGE PARK

Unofficial fun

"Now I understand why there are so many broken toboggans along the slope!" comments my 7-year-old, rubbing his bottom after his first try from the top of the very steep hill.

In the midst of winter, everybody walks over the frozen (shallow) river to get to the hill located next to the parking lot off Twyn Rivers Drive in Rouge Park.

Trees buffer the noise of the city. Two hills are separated by a line of trees. One has to be in good shape to walk up the steep slope.

From above, it is a real pleasure to admire the forest panorama and to hear the laughter of the families sliding down the unofficial slope (at their own risk, I might add). Many teenagers go down on their snowboards.

For the next two hours, my son and his friend will feel more comfortable sticking to the lower half of the hill.

TIPS (fun for 7 years +)
• More about the **Rouge Park** trails near Twyn Rivers Drive on p. 326.
• There are no washrooms on site.

NEARBY ATTRACTIONS
Toronto Zoo (5-min.) .... p. 57

Rouge Park
• Scarborough
(416) 392-1111
www.toronto.ca/parks

D-3
N-E
of downtown
5-min.

Schedule: Open year-round.
Admission: FREE.
Directions: From Hwy 401 East, take exit #389/Meadowvale Rd. northbound (keep to the right lanes as soon as you reach Morningside to catch this exit), turn east on Sheppard Ave. and take the first fork to the left, Twyn Rivers Dr. (easy to miss when you are driving eastbound on Sheppard). You'll see a parking lot on your right.

ALBION HILLS C. A.

Panoramic tobogganing

It took us 40 minutes to reach Albion Hills, where I had been assured we'd find great tobogganing hills. Indeed, a long and wonderful slope awaited us, sitting against a breathtaking panorama! It promised an even acceleration without being too risky, and I know my little appraiser would have loved it... had I been able to wake him up! Kiddies' naps and snow conditions are undoubtedly the two unpredictables for family outings!

Our son did not bat an eye for the two hours of our visit but we tested the site ourselves. The slope's incline was long enough to provide lots of excitement, and not too steep to make the climb back unpleasant.

TIPS (fun for 3 years +)

• More about **Albion Hills Conservation Area** during the summer on p. 411.
• When Toronto's snow begins to melt, call Albion Hills to enquire about snow conditions, as the tobogganing season is often prolonged for another few weeks in that region.
• You can park your car not far from the centre's admission booth, close to a sign indicating "tobogganing". The slope is located on the left. Then drive to the ski chalet (follow the signs), where you will find washrooms, a snack bar, and ski rentals. They rent toboggans for $5!

NEARBY ATTRACTIONS
Kortright Centre (25-min.) .... p. 296

The day we visited, while Toronto's tobogganing hills were icy at best, those at Albion Hills boasted a lovely coat of fresh snow, completely enjoyable for sliding afficionados, perfect for cross-country skiers, many of whom passed us with beaming smiles!

Albion Hills Conservation Area
· Caledon
(416) 661-6600, ext. 5203
or (905) 880-0227
www.trca.on.ca

| C-2 |
| N-W |
| of Toronto |
| 45-min. |

 Schedule: Open year-round from 9 am to dusk.
Admission:$6/adults, $5/ seniors, FREE for 15 years and under with their family (more than double this price to use the cross-country trails).
Directions: From Hwy 400 North, take exit #55/Hwy 9 westbound. Turn south on Hwy 50 and follow the signs.

BRONTE CREEK PROVINCIAL PARK

Hill addiction

Each time we go tobogganing, it's the same story. At the top of the hill, our little adrenaline addict smiles with anticipation, then lets out a long happy shout as he toboggans down. At the end of the descent, he bursts out with the laugh of victory, only to be towed back up (thanks to the private chairlift he finds in his stamina-filled daddy), again and again, happy to relive the experience.

Bronte Creek Park is a great summer outing. In the wintertime however, our attention shifts from the big pool to the large, well-maintained ice rink.

The rink's natural surroundings are quite pleasing.

There is a wide path climbing to the top of a hill overlooking the park. Its two faces hold much to be enjoyed by young toboggan fans. The view is far-reaching from both sides of the hill, offering athletes an unusually rare panorama.

You can access these activities via parking lot D.

After the winter sports, I suggest you drive to parking lot C, and walk to the farm's playground in a barn and its area with various farm animals. I strongly recommend you dress warmly as the barn is not heated in winter time. On the other hand, they've added a heated room within the barn for the parents patiently waiting for their kids to be done.

Spruce Farm, the visitor centre and animal barns are open in winter.

TIPS (fun for 3 years +)
- More about **Bronte Creek** on p. 308.
- They rent skates. Note that they don't rent cross-country skis anymore.
- A washroom and small snack bar are available close to the rink. Washrooms are also available next to the visitor centre.
- Check the Lakeside Festival of Lights in **Spencer Smith Park**, Burlington (**www.burlingtonfestivaloflights.com**).

More about **Bronte Creek** on p. 308.

NEARBY ATTRACTIONS

Bronte Creek Provincial Park
· Burlington
(905) 827-6911
www.ontarioparks.com

E-2
West of Toronto 35-min.

Schedule: Open year-round from 8 am to dusk. Most activities are offered on weekends only during the fall, winter and spring.
Admission: $13 per vehicle.
Directions: From QEW West, take exit #109/Burloak Rd. northbound and follow signs.

General tips about Time travel:

- All these places normally involve staff members or volunteers dressed in period costumes to play the part.
- You too can dress up! It will add to the experience and you'll get a good reaction from the staff, volunteers and other visitors.
- Most of these attractions rely on volunteers, which explains why activities may vary a lot, one year to the next. It all depends on who's available, and when.

TIME TRAVEL

See **Westfield Heritage Village** on p. 390.

MEDIEVAL TIMES

Good times!

"Is that real metal?" asked my son, pointing towards the spear held by the knight greeting us. With just enough authority, the guard scraped the blade on the stone wall. Gritting our teeth, we concluded that the metal was definitely genuine. "Mi'lady, may I help you?" asked the ticket office attendant, before showing us the way to the table where we would all be crowned.

We found ourselves inside the "castle" ante-chamber, in front of a camera, alongside a count and countess (we were then pushed gently towards the next activities). During the meal, the photo they took was presented to us, which we are free to purchase. It did appeal to us, with its medieval-style frame and our hosts' superb costumes!

Inside, the 110,000 sq. ft. space has been turned into a dark, 11th Century castle, complete with coats of arms and murals depicting scenes of chivalry.

To the right of the grand hall, the stables are equipped with windows allowing us to admire the stallions with braided manes. On the other side, royal thrones are surrounded by suits of armour. With great pomp, those who pay an extra fee are knighted during a short ceremony.

The master of ceremonies, to the sound of genuine resounding trumpets, invited us to enter the 1350-seat banquet hall. Wearing yellow crowns, the colour of

the knight that we would be rooting for, we headed for the tables bearing the same colour.

Over the sand-covered arena, powerful spotlights projected an entertaining ballet of coloured lights on a smoke screen. This captivated us until the show began.

We see an act featuring well-trained horses. Then, the handsome, long-haired equestrian warriors were introduced. Guests in each

section were greeting their knight as noisily as possible. Everyone burst out laughing when the master of ceremonies described the people greeting the green knight as "scum" from the bad part of town, invited only thanks to the king's great generosity.

In the cheering department, we could not manage to outdo the blue section, completely filled by a group of friends, who encouraged each other to produce a happy clamour. The knights confronted each other at games of skill, and the queen rewarded the best with a flower, which they promptly threw at a beauty sitting in the audience.

Later, costumed waiters invaded the field, armed with chicken-covered trays. "You will love the taste of baby dragon!" our waiter confided to my incredulous son. We were also served spareribs, followed by coffee and dessert.

The story line has changed since my last visit but it remains the justification for games, joust and a tournament to choose a new champion. In the former version, the champion was needed to fight the revengeful son of an enemy killed by the king. Now, it's the king himself who's seeking revenge for his brother's death.

When the knights fought each other in mortal combats (what a waste!) to determine the champion, my son very nearly climbed on his chair to better cheer for our yellow knight.

"Is he really dead?" anxiously inquired my young humanist when our knight collapses on the floor after a fatal blow.

In the darkness, real sparks were flying from swords clashing together.

I must say that the

Photos: Courtesy of Medieval Times

fights resembled a choreography, which had to be well orchestrated! It is obvious that the well trained actors could easily suffer serious injuries while manipulating the really heavy weapons.

When the final confrontation took place between the champion and his enemy, *Carmina Burana* was thundering as a musical background. I was told the musical score of the new version is even more dramatic. Expect a grande finale!

When we returned to the hall, we got down on the dance floor to the beat of non-medieval music!

Despite the fact that Medieval Times is an expensive outing (even more so with all the extras that can be purchased), the experience is worth the trip, thanks to dynamic actors and a very entertaining show.

TIPS (fun for 6 years +)

• I recommend avoiding the small dungeon with an exhibit of reproductions of medieval torture instruments. Accompanied by graphic drawings, these apparatus bear witness to horrors very difficult to explain to children. After a fabulous show, visiting this dungeon left a bitter taste in my mouth.

• The gift shop area is chock-full of varied "medieval" goods, from small accessories for children priced at $7 to metal swords going for more than $500.

• They normally offer interesting specials during **March Break**, Mother or Father's Day and other such occasions. Call to find out about these.

• The meal is served with soft drinks or water and we eat with our fingers. You will eat to your heart's content, but do not expect a gastronomic feast. (Alcoholic beverages are also available for an additional cost.)

NEARBY ATTRACTIONS

Medieval Times | D-3
1-888-935-6878 | **Downtown**
www.medievaltimes.com | **Toronto**
 | **5-min.**

Schedule: July & August, Tuesday to Sunday; April, May & June, Wednesday to Sunday; October, November & December, Thursday to Sunday; September, January & February, Friday to Sunday. Open during March Break weekdays. Check their website for exact hours.
Admission: (tax not included) Show is $63/adults, $43.50/12 years and under. Parking fees vary throughout the year. You can upgrade your ticket for $10 to get preferred seating, cheering banner and commemorative program and DVD.
Directions: Exhibition Place,Toronto. Take Lake Shore Blvd., go north on Strachan Ave. Turn west into the grounds of Exhibition Place. Follow Princes Blvd. to Saskatchewan Rd. There is a parking lot right next to the Medieval building.

THE DISTILLERY

A pedestrian village

This national historic site set in downtown Toronto includes over forty red brick buildings proclaimed "the best preserved collection of Victorian industrial architecture in North America".

Kids won't care that this was once the largest distillery in the world but they certainly will notice the brick lined and carless streets.

TIPS (fun for 8 years +)

• Check www.soulpepper.ca for the **Soulpepper Theatre Company** program presented at the **Young Centre for the Performing Arts** (Tank House Lane). Every other year, they present a **Christmas Carol** that gets rave reviews.

• If you are involved in a parent school council, you might want to drop by the head office of **Prologue of the Performing Arts** (Bldg 74, suite 201 inside Bldg 74 on Case Goods Lane) to grab their catalogue of shows especially made for schools. It features some 40 artists and companies presenting over 3,000 quality performances in schools every year, at the same price throughout the province.

• There's a **Crêperie** for sit down or takeout (suite 102 inside Bldg #47 on Tank House Lane) and **Café Uno** for lighter meals (Distillery Lane).

They won't think much of the freshly roasted coffee smell at **Balzac's Coffee** (last building at the end of Trinity Street) but they will be impressed by the amazing chandelier or the bean bags in the backroom on the way to the washroom. And they will enjoy the treats and home-made lemonade.

The public spaces surrounded by the beautifully restored buildings are really welcoming, especially when their trees are adorned with hundreds of small white lights. They often host craft shows and farmers' markets. In the evening, they sometimes show movie segments on a giant screen at the plaza near the Brewery Lane.

The Distillery is especially appealing when there's an event going on, and there's plenty of those year-round. We've seen a Wolf Howl, a Dance Festival, Nuit Blanche, LuminaTO...

My personal favourite stops on the site are: **Pikto**, a photo shop and gallery stocked with funky merchandise (Case Goods Lane), the fabulous **Sandra Ainsly** glass gallery (Trinity Street) with some incredible pieces worth over $30,000, and **SOMA Chocolate & Gelato** (Tank House Lane) where you can taste the most amazing spicy hot chocolate in a (very) tiny cup.

Kids enjoy the **Auto Grotto**, filled with anything related to cars, with old-fashioned candy corner as a bonus.

The Distillery (416) 364-1177 www. thedistillerydistrict.com	D-3 **Downtown** Toronto 10-min.

Schedule: Open year-round.
Admission: FREE.
Directions: 55 Mill Street, Toronto (between Parliament and Cherry Streets, south of Front St.).

NEARBY ATTRACTIONS
Cherry Beach (5-min.) .... p. 401
European Flair Stroll (5-min.) ...... p. 476

FORT YORK

Kids hold the fort

Little soldiers learn how to hold the wooden rifle, to walk in step, to present arms and to fire at the order of a lenient officer. Giggles are guaranteed; bring out your cameras!

When they discover the historical and archaeological wealth of this Fort, Torontonians are surprised, as they've been passing by for years without noticing it. Nestled between buildings and highways, Fort York is in fact, one of Toronto's well kept secrets.

On this site, the City of Toronto, initially named Fort York, was founded in 1793, following the demise of the French Fort Rouillé around 1750.

Historic Fort York really comes to life in July and August with its daily historic military demonstrations of music, drill and artillery, all performed by costumed employees. You're also treated to an historic tasting in the kitchens.

You can explore the basement of the Officers' Brick Barracks, built in 1815. More than 12,000 artefacts were found during the archaeological digs performed there from 1987 to 1990.

The Centre Block House houses the military museum full of arms and uniforms from different times.

TIPS (fun for 4 years +)
• Fort York's favourite activity for children, the drill, is only offered during special events. Dates to remember: **Victoria Day**, **Canada Day** and **Simcoe Day**, when they usually offer special activities.
• During the **March Break**, you can pre-register for the **March Through Time** event for children 10 years and under (also including a kid's drill).
• Ask about their intriguing **Ghosts of the Garrison** events a few nights in October, involving storytelling under candlelight (pre-registration, $10/adults, $5/12 years and under.
• Fort York has had battle re-enactments in the past. Call to confirm if it is offered this year. For more battle re-enactments, see the other attractions in the **Time Travel** chapter.

NEARBY ATTRACTIONS

Fort York	D-3
(416) 392-6907	**Downtown**
or (416) 338-3888 (events)	Toronto
www.toronto.ca/museums	10-min.

 Schedule: Open year-round, 10 am to 5 pm (closes at 4 pm on weekdays after Labour Day until Victoria Day). Closed mid-December to January 1. Check the website for March Break hours.

 Admission: Around $6/adults, $3.25/seniors and students, $3/6-12 years, FREE 5 years and under. Parking is FREE.

 Directions: At the end of Garrison Rd., Toronto. Take Lake Shore Blvd., go north on Strachan Ave., east on Fleet St.

COLBORNE LODGE

Easter traditions

Last spring when we visited High Park, several geese were walking over the pond ice and kids warmed up in the gorgeous nearby playground. The year before, the sun had been warm enough to melt the little chocolate eggs fallen from the kids' baskets on their way back from the egg hunt. Easter time is a tricky time of the year but one sure thing during this period is the Easter fun at Colborne Lodge.

Colborne Lodge was built in 1837 and still contains many of the original artefacts, but the adults better appreciate this. The best time to visit the historic museum is around Easter, for their traditional Easter activities.

First, there's the **Spring Egg Fun Day** on Palm Sunday, one week prior to Easter. The event's activities vary from one year

to the next, depending on the volunteers involved. You can always count on egg dyeing in the lodge's kitchen, for a small fee, and chocolate egg hunts divided by age group in and around the Children's Garden by the lodge.

The **Easter Traditions** activities are usually offered on a few consecutive weekends around Easter time. The event includes a house tour, egg dyeing in the historic kitchen, using natural vegetable dye, and a game to spot hidden eggs around the house.

TIPS (fun for 4 years +)
• See **High Park** on p. 286.
• During **Easter** time, you can enter the park from High Park Blvd. off Parkside Rd. and park by the animal pens. An unofficial trail leads up the hill to Colborne Lodge. Anytime of the year, you can also park by **Grenadier** restaurant and take a 5-min. walk to the Lodge.
• During **Christmas** time, you can pre-register for half-day Christmas activities.
• Ask about **Haunted High Park** involving scary storytelling in the dark house a few nights at the end of October (pre-registration, $10/adults, $5/8 years and older).

NEARBY ATTRACTIONS
Around Royal York Subway Station p. 438

Colborne Lodge
(416) 392-6916
www.
toronto.ca/museums

D-3
West
of downtown
15-min.

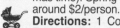

Schedule: Open Friday to Sunday only from January through April. Open Tuesday to Sunday during March Break and from May through December, noon to 4 pm (closes at 5 pm May to September and at 3 pm on Christmas and New Year's Eves). Closed on Mondays. Spring Egg Fun Day is always on the Sunday before Easter, usually noon to 3 pm).
Admission: $4/adults, $2.75/seniors and students, $2.50/children (a bit more during Christmas time). Spring Fun Day costs around $2/person.
Directions: 1 Colborne Lodge Drive, Toronto (in the south end of High Park, see this park's directions on p. 286.

SPADINA STRAWBERRY FESTIVAL

Garden party

It feels like the whole family has been invited to the garden party of very rich relatives. After behaving nicely when visiting the elegant Spadina House, children run wild under the shade of the huge trees to burn off energy. Others stroll with their kites in tow under the indulgent gaze of proper ladies. They have all donned their fancy hats for the occasion.

Spadina House is a gorgeous 19th-century home set on an enormous property, by Toronto standards, with adjoining gardens.

Only a few hundred very privileged guests could rate doing the same back in 1900 when the Austin family was holding its annual private strawberry social.

Now, many line up to get refreshments and a piece of strawberry shortcake drowned in whipped cream.

Old-fashioned activities were offered when we attended: tossing games, stilt walking, shaker making and ice cream making demonstrations. The activities vary from year to year, depending on the theme for the festival.

A more ambitious craft activity was offered when we visited: kite making. Once again, the craft varies depending on the theme. Live musicians entertained children on the lawn.

This was one great garden party!

TIPS (fun for 4 years +)

• I recommend you buy your food or refreshment tickets as soon as you get in. There's a line-up to buy tickets and another one to actually get the food. Strawberry shortcakes could sell out before the end of the event! Consider bringing a blanket to sit on the grass for the picnic.

• Ask about their **Christmas** event **Sharing our Traditions**, exploring the seasonal celebrations in a different country each year (three Sundays in December, from 12 noon to 5 pm, $8/adult, $6/children).

NEARBY ATTRACTIONS

Spadina Museum
(416) 392-6910
www.
toronto.ca/museums

D-3
North
of downtown
20 min.

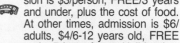

Schedule: The Strawberry Festival is usually held on the third or last Sunday of June, from noon to 4 pm. The museum is open for tours year-round on weekends, 12 noon to 5 pm, then Tuesday to Sunday from April to early January. Check their website for exact dates and hours.

Admission: The festival's admission is $3/person, FREE/3 years and under, plus the cost of food. At other times, admission is $6/ adults, $4/6-12 years old, FREE under 5 (extra fee on Holidays).

Directions: 285 Spadina Rd., Toronto (located just east of Casa Loma).

GIBSON HOUSE MUSEUM

Hands-on history

The Gibson House Museum is the historic house offering the most hands-on activities. In the minds of young visitors, the museum's great discovery room for children makes the actual visit to the 1851 house look like a mere bonus.

Our costumed guide has all the patience in the world for the children's questions. The **Gibson House**'s staff members and volunteers are used to dealing with young visitors.

During the Holiday season when we visit, we are allowed to touch a few old-fashioned toys, peek into a few bedrooms and stop at the kitchen for a taste of hot cider and a cookie.

Usually, in most other historic houses, once visitors have no more questions for the guide, the visit is over. Here, we head towards the modern-looking Discovery Gallery, where the real fun starts for children.

Some fifteen boxes, each bearing a label describing its contents, await us on the shelves. In the "Sheep" box, you'll find real wool kids can glue on a drawing of

a sheep and take back home! The boxes vary from one year to the next.

I loved the quilt puzzles with wooden triangles and quilt designs to reproduce. Then there's the weaving box with materials to create our weaving device from scratch, great drawings to colour and more.

Clothing and accessories for boys and girls are available next to full mirrors. Beside a beautiful mural are two heavy buckets with a yoke.

Once your children have tried to carry this apparatus, tell them that on a regular day, the Gibson children had to carry 15 buckets for cooking, many more for laundry or baths, and as drinking water for people or animals. The very idea should make their bed-making, toy-tidying and pet-feeding chores more bearable!

TIPS (fun for 4 years +)

• More free activities on **Canada Day** (including free ice cream) and on **Simcoe Day**.

• On selected days during **March Break** children can register for activity-filled programs, usually involving more hands-on fun in the old kitchen. Programs are also offered some days during **Christmas** time. Call for exact prices.

• During the fall and **Easter**, you could have the chance to see a cooking demonstration in the historic kitchen (included with regular admission).

Gibson House Museum • North York (416) 395-7432 www.toronto.ca/museums	D-3 **North** of downtown 35-min.

    Schedule: Closed in September, open the rest of the year Tuesday to Sunday, noon to 5 pm (also open on Holiday Mondays). **Admission:** Around $3.75/adults, $2.25/seniors and students, $1.75/2-12 years (a bit more from mid-November to end of Christmas activities). **Directions:** 5172 Yonge St., North York (at Park Home Ave., south of Finch Ave., on the west side of Yonge).

NEARBY ATTRACTIONS
Around North York Subway Station p. 447

BLACK CREEK PIONEER VILLAGE

Sneak in!

Here, the blacksmith hammers hot red iron; there, a weaver hums as she works. Elsewhere, a homemaker in her long dress bustles about in front of her ovens, while the harness maker handcrafts leather articles. This is Black Creek Pioneer Village: a fascinating replica of a small cluster of some 35 houses and businesses of the 1860's.

In fact, Black Creek Pioneer Village satisfies the "voyeur" within each one of us. Here, you can enter anywhere without bothering to knock! (I make sure to point this out to children when we visit.) I found it captivating to watch my young explorer open doors by himself and discover new territories.

Many of the rooms, inside the houses you'll visit, cannot be entered. You may however, view them from the doorway. Thankfully, there is generally an area inside these buildings where you may roam freely and feel as if you are truly in a private house.

If you come with younger children (as I did with my then 3-year-old son), anticipate their attention span will not exceed 15 seconds for a woodworker silently planing down a plank in the making of a barrel, or a weaver calmly working at her loom. But they might enjoy watching the shoemaker or the broom-maker at work.

Other details however, will satisfy their curiosity. For instance, there are farm animals in various parts of the site, and after all, the blacksmith makes lots of noise as he hits the red hot iron! We can't forget the treats sold at the old post office! Every day, you can smell fresh bread baking in the kitchens of the village's **Half Way House** restaurant.

TIPS (fun for 4 years +)
• See Christmas activities and **Christmas by the Lamplight** on p. 177.
• Wagon rides are offered during some special events.
• **Black Creek Village** offers much old-fashioned family fun during special events: **Fiddlers' Contest** on **Victoria Day**, the **Battle of Black Creek** (with re-enactment) on Father's Day weekend, **Canada Day Celebration**, the **Pioneer Festival** on the second or third weekend of September and the **Howling Hootenanny**, usually on the weekend prior to **Halloween**, to name a few.

NEARBY ATTRACTIONS

Black Creek Pioneer Village
• North York
(416) 736-1733
www.blackcreek.ca

D-3
North
of downtown
35-min.

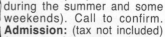

 Schedule: Open only May 1 to December 31, at least from 11 am to 4 pm (extended hours during the summer and some weekends). Call to confirm.
Admission: (tax not included) $13/adults, $12/ seniors, $9/5-14 years, FREE 4 years and under.
Parking is around $6.
Directions: See p. 177.

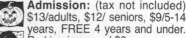
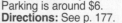

MONTGOMERY'S INN

Tea is served

Some events are more interactive than others at Montgomery's Inn, but you can always count on their tearoom experience to complement your visit to this old Inn, dating from the 1830's.

Most historical buildings that can be visited in the region used to be private houses. The Montgomery family lived and made a living at Montgomery's Inn. The rooms' settings are therefore different than historical houses.

There is a worn-out floor in front of the bar counter, with tables and checkerboards. There's a small ballroom, and guest rooms with many beds (in those days, you rented a place in a bed, not a room!).

We visited during a special program requiring pre-registration during Christmas, when crafts and games were organized for young visitors. These might change from year to year, but the spirit remains the same.

TIPS (fun for 4 years +)

• Call to find out about special events involving storytelling, usually during **Halloween** and **Christmas** time (advanced registration required, fees apply, call to confirm dates).

• In the tearoom, they serve tea and snacks for $4 per person. On special occasions, they serve "special teas" for a higher fee.

NEARBY ATTRACTIONS
James Gardens (15-min.) .... p. 279
Tom Riley Park (5 min.) .... p. 424

When we visited, the kids made New Year's crackers. They created a game from the old days, made out of a button and a string, to take home.

They tried their hand at old-fashioned games: cup-a-ball, marbles and "traumat-ropes".

They ground spices, grated lemon and cinnamon and rolled dough in the kitchen, supervised by a cook in costume.

The tearoom was our obvious next stop.

The small pastries were delicious. I rediscovered the pleasure of pouring myself some good tea from a teapot. My 3-year-old was thrilled when I transferred her lemonade into my teacup on a plate for her to taste.

Montgomery's Inn **D-3**
• Etobicoke **West**
(416) 394-8113 **of downtown**
www. **35-min.**
montgomerysinn.com

 Schedule: Open year-round, Tuesday to Sunday, 1 to 5 pm. Closed on Mondays. Tea served from 2 to 4:30 pm.

 Admission: Around $4/adults, $2/ seniors and students, $1/12 and under, $10/family of 6. Tea with pastry is $4/visitor.

 Directions: 4709 Dundas St. West, Etobicoke (east of Islington Ave., on the south side of Dundas).

MARKHAM MUSEUM

It takes a village...

Use the Museum as an excuse to introduce yourself to historic Markham Village during one of its dynamic events when the Main Street is closed to traffic.

The idea here is to combine a visit to the Museum (preferably during one of their own special events) with a stroll down Main Street Markham when it is in a carless party mode, for maximum fun.

The Markham Museum is located at the end of Main Street and set in the origi-

nal Mount Joy Public School built in 1907.

The surrounding Historic Village includes a blacksmith shop, Markham's oldest church, a sawmill, a general store and historic homes to visit. You can even climb into a railway car.

The buildings seem a bit lost on the site, for lack of a forest like at the Black Creek Pioneer Village, but the attraction offers an amazing list of events that greatly add to the ambience.

Check their website for dates and details on their **Springfest Easter Egg Hunt**, Springfest, Family Camp-in, Family Star-Gazing Night, International Museums Day (free event in May), Applefest, **Haunted Museum**, Winter Carnival (free event in February) and more.

TIPS (fun for 4 years +)

• During winter, you'll find outdoor rinks (weather permitting). Bring your skates!

• My favourite combo would be to go skating at the Museum, then enjoy their **Village Lantern Tours** (from 6:30 pm to 8 pm, many days around **Christmas** until beginning of February) and finish up with a stroll down the Main Street to admire the **Festival of Lights**.

• If it seems too late for your troopers, try the Main Street **Markham's Santa Claus Parade** (last Saturday of November at 10 am), have lunch there, then go to Markham Museum for a visit and some skating.

• Among other Markham street events, there's **Markham Village Music Festival** (always on the third weekend in June) and **Auto Classic Car Show and Rally** (on the Sunday after Labour Day weekend). Both include a large Kids Play Zone.

NEARBY ATTRACTIONS

Markham Museum	C-3
• Markham	N-E
(905) 294-4576	of Toronto
www.markham.ca	35-min.
(click **Attractions**)	

Schedule: Closed on Victoria Day. After that to Labour Day, open daily, 12 noon to 5 pm (closes at 8 pm Thursday to Saturday).The rest of the year, open Tuesday to Sunday, 12 noon to 5 pm (closed on Easter Friday, Sunday and Monday). Daily tours at 1 pm and 3 pm, except Mondays.

Admission: $6/adult, $5/student and seniors, $4/3-12 years, $15.50/family of 4. FREE/ two years and under. Fees may vary during special events.

Directions: 9350 Hwy 48. From Hwy 401, take exit #383/ Markham Rd. northbound.Go past Hwy 407, where it becomes Main Street Markham, then Hwy 48. The Museum is just north of 16th Ave. on the west side.

COUNTRY HERITAGE PARK

A close shave!

A big sheep, held firmly in the grip of a farmer, sits, literally, on the cushion of her own wool, ready for "a close shave". As soon as she starts to bleat, the sheep in the pen walk towards her as if offering moral support.

When the newly shaven beast joins them, they all push her away. Really concerned for her well-being, the kids ask why this is. "They don't recognize her odour", explains the farmer. Poor thing!

It was Sheep Day when we visited the Country Heritage Park. This special event has been dropped since, but you must have a look at their website to see the extent of the line-up of events they have going on year-round. We headed towards the nearby school. A teacher in a long skirt invites us to write with a grey stone on a black slate. We eventually sneak out to catch a tractor ride around the farmstead. There are some thirty buildings on site. Located in one area of the park, the Dairy Industry Display, the All About Apples barn and the Steam Power buildings offer the most interaction.

There, my little farmers "drove" a dairy delivery truck, and felt the suction of a milk pump (for cows, of course). They observed the workings of a steam machine, tested a hay bed, peeled and pressed apples the old-fashioned way and pet animals in the small pioneer farm.

Since our last visit, they've acquired two cute miniature horses and they've added a very popular kids' playfarm.

TIPS (fun for 4 years +)

• You can hop on and off of the tractor ride as much as you want, which turns out to be really handy for the site is huge.

• Activities vary from one year to the next. At the time of print, their calendar of events included a kids' weekend with heritage toys, games and crafts, an **Antique Tractor and Toy Show** and even an **American Civil War** re-enactment. Call for specific dates.

• They are also open during the year for some special events. I will have to go back to check out their **Walk to Bethlehem**, a re-enactment of the nativity throughout the site, ending with Jesus in a manger in the log barn. It is held on four consecutive evenings from 6:30 to 9 pm, end of November or early December). Ask about their **Parade of Lights** in November with tractors decorated with lights, music in the barn and Santa's visit.

• There's a snack bar and a small gift shop on the premises during the summer.

NEARBY ATTRACTIONS	
Hilton Falls (5-min.)	p. 266
Kelso (5-min.)	p. 416

Country Heritage Park	D-2
· Milton	West
1-888-307-3276	of Toronto
or (905) 878-8151	45-min.
www.countryheritagepark.com	

 Schedule: Open to the public weekends only, in July and August, noon to 5 pm, and year-round during special events.

 Admission: (cash only) $7/ adults, $6/seniors, $4/6-12 years, FREE 5 years and under, $20/family of 5.

 Directions: 8560 Tremaine Rd., Milton. From Hwy 401 West, take exit #320/Hwy 25 northbound. Turn west on Regional Rd. 9, then south on Tremaine Rd.

HALTON REGION MUSEUM

... and surroundings

On my way back from the snow-tubing park located in the Kelso Conservation Area, I decided to check out the museum on site. When I entered the large red barn bearing the museum's name in big letters, I almost turned back right away. Although it seemed like a beautiful banquet room to rent, it didn't look like much to visit. It's a good thing a nice staff member insisted on showing me the place.

TIPS (fun for 4 years +)
• More on **Kelso Beach** on p. 416.
• More on **Glen Eden's Snow Tubing Park** on p. 364.
• The third floor is maintained at a cool temperature to better preserve the artefacts. It offers a great break for the kids to cool down after some time under the sun at the beach. It is open upon request during the museum hours, don't be shy!
• During **Thanksgiving** weekend, **Kelso Conservation Area** offers **Fall Colours**, an event allowing us to catch a ski lift ride up the escarpment to admire fall colours! Fee included with park's admission. Check their website closer to Thanksgiving.
• This whole park encompasses 16 km of overlapping trails for hiking and/or mountain biking with three levels of difficulty. You can get a detailed map at the park's entrance or at the museum's Visitor's Centre.
• When I asked about the trail to the top of the cliff, I was told that in a 25-minute walk on the way up, we would find an old quarry with lots of fossils! That would make it worth the trip for young paleontologists. The top is only minutes away from then on. You access the trail from the cute tunnel by the ski chalet.

NEARBY ATTRACTIONS
Country Heritage Park (5-min.) ... p. 386

We had been here a number of times to enjoy the lake. Each time, the kids were so involved in water fun that I never got to visit the museum or stroll along the trail leading to the top of the Niagara escarpment.

Turns out that within the first room I entered, there was an interesting display of the turbine developed by the Alexander family in 1898 to generate water power and electricity, using water from a natural spring up on the escarpment. The museum is actually located on the former site of the Alexander family farm. This family settled in 1836 and farmed the land until 1961!

A few galleries featuring carriages, lamps and lanterns was found on the second level but the real fun was on the third floor. There awaited a casual showcase of some of the 35,000-artefact collection of the Halton Region Museum.
I noticed many antiques kids would like to see: wreaths made out of dried flowers and human hair, chairs made out of buffalo horns or branches, seats with a hole (adult-size potty chairs), ancient washing machines and antique toys, to name a few. All are stored by categories on shelves, in a warehouse fashion.
More objects are currently stored in other buildings on the site. They are planning to build a new Artefact Centre.

Halton Region Museum	D-2 West of Toronto 50-min.
• Milton (905) 875-2200 www.conservationhalton.on.ca	

 Schedule: Open year-round Monday to Friday, noon to 4 pm (also open on weekends from noon to 5 pm from Victoria Day to Thanksgiving. The park is open year-round from 8:30 am until dusk.
Admission: FREE, with park's admission ($7/adults, $5/children).
Directions: From Hwy 401 West, take exit #320/Hwy 25 northbound, turn west on Campbellville Rd., then south on Tremaine Rd., follow signs.

CRAWFORD LAKE C. A.

An Indian village

Walking into the fortified village through a corridor lined with 5-metre-high stakes is like entering another world. From the top of the palisade, my young warrior inspects his territory with a watchful eye. In such a setting, it's easy to imagine the life of native people who lived here in the 15th Century.

Inside the palisade is the Crawford Lake Indian Village, which was reconstructed using data collected during an extensive archaeological dig. The Turtle Clan House stands close to the central square. With an austere exterior, it doesn't reveal the exoticism of its interior layout: roof openings to let the smoke out and the sunshine in, fur-covered sleeping areas, animal skins hung here and there, tools, clothing and jewellery.

Inside the second longhouse, the Wolf House, a short educational film was shown in a mini-theatre. A third of the Wolf House has regained its original look. To help visitors visualize the daily life of the Iroquois of yesteryear, big family clan pictures are hidden behind large pelts. Children enjoy peeking through the holes to discover these worlds.

In the pretty Visitor Centre (which abounds in interactive information), we learned that the Village's presence was discovered after analyzing Crawford Lake's bed. When corn pollen was identified in a sedimentation sample, it became evident that there had been agriculture close by. Research confirmed the hypothesis, and the remains of the Village were then unearthed. A well marked trail leads to Crawford Lake. You can go around it by taking a wooden trail, relatively safe for young children. The walk lasts about half an hour. A couple of picnic tables are available by the lake.

Opposite to the lake trail, a stroller-accessible path leads to a belvedere offering a view of the **Niagara Escarpment** in about fifteen minutes. Another winding path offers a one-hour return hike into the forest, between roots and crevices, to the viewpoint.

TIPS (fun for 4 years +)
• Ask for a trail map at the **Visitor Centre** or download it from their website.
• During the weekends of the **Sweet Water Season** (March/April), you can watch maple syrup being made from sap, sitting on a log around the fire. A staff member prepares and cooks corn flatbread that can be dipped in syrup at the end of the presentation.
• The list of themed activities offered throughout the year is too long! Check their website.

Crawford Lake Conservation Area
• Milton
(905) 854-0234
www.conservationhalton.on.ca

D-2
West
of Toronto
45-min.

Schedule: The site is open year-round. Full access to all facilities is offered weekends and holidays year-round and during the March Break, from 10 am to 4 pm.
Admission: $6/adults, $4/seniors and 5-14 years, FREE 4 years and under.
Directions: From Hwy 401, take exit #312/Guelph Line southbound, then follow the signs.

BATTLE OF STONEY CREEK

The muskets were good for one shot for each charge. Still, there is lots of firing and many artillery shots during the re-enactment. The noise creates quite an atmosphere with, of course, many soldiers "dying" on the battlefield.

Don't expect any hand-to-hand combat however, as soldiers of the time moved slowly and in straight lines towards the enemy, stopping to shoot or recharge as they went.

Time travel at its best!

Upon your arrival, you'll notice the military encampment, with its small white tents facing the Battlefield Museum. Women under their umbrellas, gather around campfires with their long dresses, while soldiers practice formations. Costumed children play with antique toys, and Native Warriors, in full make-up regalia, add a touch of authenticity. We find ourselves deep in 1813.

For the sole pleasure of acting, volunteers from all over Canada (some flying from the States) join in and don their costumes, put up their tents, prepare their authentic food and most of all, get ready to re-enact the Battle of Stoney Creek, which involved about 3,000 Americans and 700 British troops in 1813.

As a general rule, tents with open doors mean you can sneak in and admire the historic furniture, made without nails, and different objects for daily use these passionate people have gathered.

The powder bullets, used with historic muskets, explode in a muffled sound as they are shot during the military drills.

Next to the battlefield is an amusing section with old-fashioned games: fishing pond, wooden muskets firing rubber bands and wooden frames to entrap prisoners' heads and hands (for a small fee). Other attractions include the high monument to climb, the museum with costumed staff handing out cookies from the kitchen, horse and wagon rides and shooting demonstrations.

TIPS (fun for 4 years +)

• There's no parking on site. Free parking and bus shuttle service are available at the St. David's Elementary School, on Centennial Parkway. Follow signs or ask the locals.

• Ask about their **Lantern Tours** in October and their **Christmas** day in December.

NEARBY ATTRACTIONS
Welland Canals (15-min.) .... p. 232
Albion Falls (10-min.) .... p. 268

Battle of Stoney Creek	E-2 S-W of Toronto 65-min.

Battle of Stoney Creek
· Stoney Creek
(905) 662-8458
www.battlefieldhouse.ca

   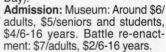

Schedule: Usually takes place the first weekend of June (call for exact time and date). When we were there, there were re-enactments on both afternoons plus Saturday evening (at 8:30 pm, followed by fireworks). The museum is open year-round, Tuesday to Sunday, 1 to 4 pm (opens at 11 am from mid-June to Labour Day).

Admission: Museum: Around $6/adults, $5/seniors and students, $4/6-16 years. Battle re-enactment: $7/adults, $2/6-16 years.

Directions: 77 King St. West, Stoney Creek. From QEW towards Niagara, take exit #88 (Centennial Pkwy/Hwy 20) southbound. From Centennial, turn left on King St. (museum is on your right).

WESTFIELD HERITAGE VILLAGE

Wonderful events

If our visit on Anne of Green Gables Day reflects the quality of all events organized at the Westfield Heritage Village, my family could easily become addicted to the place.

At the fence, a trio of Anne of Green Gables look-alikes are greeting arriving friends, similarly clad. We look around and see dozens of young Annes. Later on, we'll be able to admire 45 of them, with genuine red hair or wigs and period dresses all lined up by the train station where they will be presented to the judges.

My son spends thirty minutes in the game zone, learning to walk on tin cans. I thought it was hilarious to watch a bunch of girls, sporting straw hats with red wool braids, compete in a tug-of-war game. Alongside the village bandstand, people line up to dance to the fiddle. My daughter also shakes it up, until a parade of antique cars starts to race around the place.

The Village includes 33 buildings. At the General Store, we buy old-fashioned candy. At the Doctor's house, we take a look at the old-fashioned pill-making technique. My daughter is busy exploring the inside of… the coffin exhibited at the workshop door.

A fire burns near the log house, one of the buildings located off the beaten track. Next to it, the trading post is interesting, with pelts to touch and traps used by pioneers to catch animals. We walk across a covered bridge to return to the action.

TIPS (fun for 4 years +)

- Sundays in March as well as some weekdays during the **March Break**, it is maple syrup time with demonstrations of native, pioneer and modern methods. They serve pancakes at the restaurant and wagon rides to tour the village.
- Ask if they're having a battle re-enactment this year. Westfield offers the perfect setting for it.
- There's something going on **Canada Day** (with regular admission fee) and they offer haunted **Halloween** nights in October (additional fees apply). Check their website for a description of many more events (Ice Cream Festival, Steam and Machine Show...).
- They traditionally offer **Christmas** evenings in the country with carol singers, toy makers and St. Nick's visit (a few Saturdays before Christmas, additional fees apply).
- There is a restaurant on the premises ofering full food services.

NEARBY ATTRACTIONS
African Lion Safari (15-min.) .... p. 66
Wild Waterworks (20-min.) .... p. 432

Westfield Heritage Village · Rockton (519) 621-8851 www.westfieldheritage.ca	E-2 S-W of Toronto 70-min.

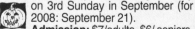

Schedule: The Village is open and alive with staff in period dress any Sunday and holidays from early April to late October, 12:30 to 4 pm (also open Wednesday and Thursday during the March Break and other days for special occasions). **Anne Day** usually on 3rd Sunday in September (for 2008: September 21).

Admission: $7/adults, $6/ seniors, $4/6-12 years, FREE under 6 (a few dollars more during special events).

Directions: 1049 Kirkwall Rd., Rockton. Take QEW West to Hwy 403, then turn north on Hwy 6 to Hwy 5. Turn west on Hwy 5, then keep right on Hwy 8 to Kirkwall Rd. (also called Regional Rd. 552) just past Rockton. The Village is on the west side.

DUNDURN CASTLE

Yes, Sir!

Outside the 1832 building, a woman in a long dress is plowing the garden. To go inside, we have to walk through an interior courtyard. At the entrance, children play with antique toys while waiting for the guided tour to begin.

Dundurn Castle is in fact a superb manor that once belonged to one of Ontario's first Premiers, Sir Allan MacNab. The building has been preserved with much of its initial splendour, with magnificent furniture, trompe-l'oeil walls and original artwork.

The guided tour, which lasts a bit more than an hour, allows us to admire the manor's three floors. Not interactive enough for my then 5-year-old son, he made us leave after 30 minutes. It's a shame! During the last third of the visit his patience would have been rewarded when visitors get to the Castle's basement (looking like an underground passage to a 3-year-old).

These stone-floor corridors are the part of the manor that younger children will readily relate to a true castle. At the end of the visit, they're expected in the kitchen for a treat served by employees in period dress.

Back outside, children inevitably stop to look at the large cannon sitting by the **Hamilton Military Museum**. Small but efficient, this museum traces military history from the War of 1812 until World War I, using many photos, military uniforms and artillery pieces. Inside the museum, in a small, dark corridor, a trench has been reconstructed. The sound effects are very effective; you will have the uneasy feeling of really being at war!

The **Military Museum** now includes a Discovery Gallery for children, with hands-on activities allowing them to wear costumes, load a cannon, build a fort and more.

TIPS (fun for 4 years +)
• The gift shop is usually well stocked with children's books on castles.
• During **March Break**, expect an Activity Centre with a dress-up area, puzzles and games.
• From the end of November until the beginning of January, Dundurn Castle puts on its **Christmas** finery: cedar garlands, red ribbons and flowers add to the Castle's rich Victorian ambience. They offer special tours and workshop for an extra fee (pre-registration needed).
• **The Coach House** (Dundurn's restaurant) is closing in 2008.
• The gift shop sells snacks.

NEARBY ATTRACTIONS
Warplane Museum (15-min.) .... p. 212
Children's Museum (5-min.) .... p. 238

Dundurn Castle & Hamilton Military Museum
E-2 S-W of Toronto 60-min.

· Hamilton
(905) 546-2872
www.myhamilton.ca

 Schedule: Open from Victoria Day to Labour Day, 10 am to 4 pm. The rest of the year, open Tuesday to Sunday, noon to 4 pm.

 Admission: (includes both attractions) $10/adults, $8/ seniors and students, $5/6-14 years, $25/family (around $2/person for museum admission only).

 Directions: 610 York Blvd., Hamilton. Take QEW West, then Hwy 403 towards Hamilton, exit York Blvd. and follow the signs.

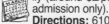

SIMCOE COUNTY MUSEUM

To explore inside out

Maybe I was just lucky but when I was there, the soft light of the fall sun bathing the historical small village made everything look picture perfect. It was the last week in the season to visit the buildings and there were hardly any other visitors. The carpet of red needles on the ground muffled my steps. The tall trees ruling the parkland hid the highway. For a moment, I thought I was back in the good old 1870's.

I was glad I made an impulse stop at this museum on my way back from another attraction in the area. I had noticed it several times over the years, being so close to Hwy 26, so it was now or never.

Imagine my surprise when I discovered a full-size Huron longhouse inside the main complex. Corn was drying in a corner and fur lay on furniture made out of branches. Nearby was a small activity centre with archaeological digging bins.

Around the corner awaited a strip of a Victorian street lined with shops. Through the window, I could see a Santa consulting a list of names. In another were antique toys. Further, a vast room was filled with antique furniture, arranged to

reconstruct whole Victorian rooms.

There was a display of musical instruments and old cameras. There was a model bridge and miniature trains. After all this, the sixteen outdoor historical buildings felt like a bonus.

Right by the tiny school was a large bell one could ring. The train station was funny, with just a few metres of track in front of it. One could explore the Spearin House, which was home to Barrie's Spearin family for over five generations.

During the summer, they offer demonstrations and activities with a different historical theme each week.

TIPS (fun for 4 years +)

• They offer special activities throughout the **March Break** and one Victorian **Christmas** day usually around mid-December. Their **Halloween** and **Easter** evenings are offered on week days.

• During the summer, you can count on special activities and demonstrations on Sundays.

Simcoe County Museum
• Minesing
(705) 728-3721
www.county.simcoe.on.ca

**B-2
North
of Toronto
70-min.**

 Schedule: Open year-round Monday to Saturday, 9 am to 4:30 pm and Sunday, 1 pm to 4:30 pm. The outside buildings are open to the public from May 1 to the end of November.

 Admission: $4/adults, $3.50/ students & seniors, $2.50/5-14 years old. FREE for 4 years and under.

Directions: 1151 Hwy 26, Minesing. Take Hwy 400 northbound to Barrie. From Barrie, follow Bayfield St. North and exit at Hwy 26.

 Look on south side.

DISCOVERY HARBOUR

Past and present in the same boat

My son had heard about feathers being used as pens, so he was intrigued by the real one on display in the office of the "Clerk-in-Charge". He could hardly believe his luck when the guide invited him to dip it into the inkwell and write his name in the official register. From then on, my child was hooked for the rest of the excellent summer tour.

In the Sailor's Barracks, the guide introduced us to sailors' sleeping habits as she hopped into one of the hammocks that hung one metre over my preschooler's head.

He tried a few times before settling into one. We then played a tossing game the sailors used to play. In the kitchen, attached to the Commanding Officer's House, my young cook pretended to mix one pound of this and one pound of that to make a pound cake.

In another barrack, he was absolutely thrilled to sit at a workbench and work with old-fashioned tools, while my youngest one was seriously "re-arranging" the logs in the shed.

Trotting through the Assistant Surgeon's House, the Home of the Clerk-in-Charge, the Naval Surveyor's House and Keating House with its long table set for a family, we visited one intimate interior after another and observed a wide range of artefacts from the daily life of the 19th Century.

At the outer limits of Discovery Harbour (a full 30-minute walk from our starting point), we found the site's sole remaining original building: the impressive Officer's Quarters, built in the 1840's. The children loved to stroll along its many corridors.

After the tour, we explored two replica schooners, *Bee* and *Tecumseth*, moored at the King's Wharf, on our own. We explored the vessels' nooks and crannies, tackled the bells and examined more hammocks in the ships' holds.

TIPS (fun for 4 years +)
• When muddy, it is hard to push a stroller on the slightly sloped trails; a wagon would be a better option.
• Most activities are offered only in the summer.
• There's the **King's Wharf Theatre** on site, presenting professionnal summer theatre (**www.kingswharftheatre.com**).
• Their restaurant serves light lunches and snacks but you might want to stop at the **Dock Lunch** in the port of Penetanguishene, for tasty fast food and ice cream at outdoor tables by the water, (705) 549-8111.

Discovery Harbour	A-2
• Penetanguishene	**Midland**
(705) 549-8064	**Region**
www.discoveryharbour.on.ca	**90-min.**

Schedule: Open Monday to Friday, 10 am to 5 pm, from end of May to mid-June and weekends as well after that, until Labour Day. Last admission at 4:30 pm. Open Wednesday evenings for the Lantern Tours offered end of June to end of August. (Re-opens a few days for special Halloween and Christmas events).

Admission: Around $6.50/adults, $5.50/seniors and students, $4.50/6-12 years old, FREE 5 years and under.

Directions: From Hwy 400, take exit #121/Hwy 93 to Penetanguishene, turn right at the water and follow ship logo.

SAINTE MARIE AMONG THE HURONS

Kids on a mission

Those who received a Catholic education might remember the stories in the history books of their youth. Father Brébeuf? The Jesuit mission? Well, it all happened in Midland (close by, actually) in 1649, at Sainte Marie among the Hurons.

This unique site is a vibrant testimony to the far-reaching impact of European cultural influence and the Christian religion. Judging by the multitude of languages heard during our visit, Europeans know about this and the word-of-mouth mill is going strong!

On the other side of the fence, we found costumed attendants busying themselves with chores reminiscent of the times. A native storyteller was talking

with a few visitors while stirring the contents of a large pot.

Children loved to explore the buildings freely. We adopted their rhythm and therefore, did not see everything. Yet, we took time to view the river from above the bastion. The little ones were intrigued by the canoes built in the old tradition. We climbed up and down the stairs inside the Jesuits' residence, and tried their small beds.

Everything here was sculpted in wood, even the plates. We tried on clothing in the shoemaker's shop. My young trapper was flabbergasted by the small fire an attendant started in the hearth with sparks that flew from two stones he was hitting against one another. Children loved the wigwam and three-metre-high sunflowers.

At the end of our visit we enjoyed the **Sainte Marie Museum** and its refreshing coolness. It is decorated with great refinement, even in the texture of its wall coverings. The result of careful and extensive research, the museum harmoniously blends and juxtaposes expressions of 17th Century French culture, the frugal materialism of Canada's early settlers and the native culture (and it has been upgraded and digitized since our last visit. Even better)!

TIPS (fun for 4 years +)

• Get a map of the site at the entrance. Before you begin your visit, you may wish to view a 20-minute audio-visual presentation to get yourself in the mood.
• Various craft activities are offered daily to kids in July and August.
• They do a **Thanksgiving Harvest Festival** with lots of hands-on activities and a First Light event with **Christmas** activities, end of November or early December.
• A **Powwow** is offered in the park across from the attraction in September (for 2008: September 6 & 7).
• Ask about their **Aboriginal Festival and Paddlefest**.
• The main building includes a cafeteria-style restaurant.

NEARBY ATTRACTIONS

Sainte Marie among the Hurons • Midland **(705) 526-7838** **www. saintemarieamongthehurons.on.ca**	**A-2** **Midland** **Region** **90-min.**

 Schedule: Open daily mid-May to mid-October, 10 am to 5 pm. Open for self-guided tours only a few weeks prior and after the prime season, Monday to Friday. See website for exact hours and dates.

Admission: Around $11/adults, $10/ seniors and students, $8/6-12 years old, FREE for 5 years and under.

Directions: From Hwy 400 North to Hwy 93 (Midland/Penetang), travel on Hwy 93 North to Midland, follow Hwy 12 eastbound to Sainte Marie (across from Martyrs' Shrine Church).

FANSHAWE PIONEER VILLAGE

Back to the past

Here, kids can actually scrub to their hearts content at the washboard. We all know how much fun doing the laundry can be...

Many of the thirty buildings at Fanshawe are open to the public, displaying various antiques within reach.

The Fanshawe School, built in 1871, is charming with its rows of small wooden desks. Make sure to read the rules observed by the pupils of the time!

TIPS (fun for 4 years +)

• Call the Village to find out about special events. They normally plan a **Canada Day** event, a **Harvest Fest** in late August, an **1812 Re-enactment** end of August, **Haunted Village Hayrides** the last three weekends of October, and **Christmas** activities on December weekends.

• **Fanshawe Conservation Area** is located right next to the Pioneer Village. It includes a nice and long unsupervised beach and over 650 campsites. We really enjoyed it after our visit to the Village. For reservations: (519) 451-2800.

• The **London Museum of Archaeology** is located at 1600 Attawandaron Road. See **www.uwo.ca/museum** or call (519) 473-1360. It includes indoor exhibits, a longhouse and on-going excavation and reconstruction of a 500-year-old native village, open to the public.

In a replica of the *Canadian Free Press* Building, a predecessor to the *London Free Press* founded in 1853, children can look at typesetting letters and engravings that were patiently set for the printing of the newspaper.

My little one enjoyed exploring the kitchen of London-born Canadian painter Paul Peel's childhood house, with its utensils and fridges of another era, and other curiosities. Last but not least, was a pedal-activated sewing machine.

The log house is a good example of the type of house built by the settlers who arrived in 1865. The Pioneer Farm shows the type of house they subsequently built, on wooden foundations this time, once they were better settled on their land. The Jury's House, which recently was fully restored, displays all the comforts available at the end of the 19th Century.

NEARBY ATTRACTIONS
London StoryBook (20-min.) .... p. 50
Children's Museum (20-min.) ...... p. 240

Fanshawe Pioneer Village	E-1
• London	**West of Toronto**
(519) 457-1296	**2 1/4 hrs**
www.fanshawepioneervillage.ca	

Schedule: Open from Victoria Day weekend to Thanksgiving Day, Tuesday to Sunday and Holiday Mondays, 10 am to 4:30 pm (also open at other times for special events).

Admission: $5/adults, $4/students and seniors, $3/3-12 years old, $15/family of 4 (a bit more for special events).

Directions: 2609 Fanshawe Park Rd. East, London. From Hwy 401 West, take exit #194/Veterans Memorial Hwy northbound. Turn west on Oxford St., then north on Clarke Rd. to Fanshawe Park Rd.

General tips about
Water Fun

- This is the chapter to turn to when you want to enjoy some wet fun. It includes:

  - beaches
  - lakes
  - wading pools
  - spray pads
  - pools
  - waterparks
  - water tubing

WATER FUN

See **Wild Water Kingdom** on p. 431.

TORONTO ISLANDS

Islanders for a day

Did you know that an amusement park existed in 1800 at the very same place today's Toronto City Centre Airport sits? In 1909, a baseball stadium was added to this park. Did you know that it's in this very stadium that Babe Ruth hit his first professional home run?

The Toronto Islands might have lost their identity as centres of recreation after the 1930's when the stadium was closed, the amusement park demolished and the airport constructed, but they have since reclaimed the title with a vengeance, with over 1.2 million visitors a year.

Ferry ride

The adventure starts before you even reach the Islands with a 15-minute ferry ride, the only way to reach them.

My little sailor was tickled pink, unsure whether to check the panoramic view of the **CN Tower** and the tall buildings close to it, look at planes taking off from the airport, gaze at the white sailboats manoeuvring on Lake Ontario, or to simply explore the many bridges on the ferry itself.

Three ferry boats service the Islands. The ferry that reaches **Centre Island** brings you closest to the **Centreville Amusement Park** and

the bicycle rentals. It is the most popular, crossing every 15 minutes on weekends (for most of the day). The **Hanlan's Point** ferry services the western end of Toronto Islands, while **Ward's Island** ferry reaches the eastern point. These two ferries cross every half-hour throughout the day.

Centre Island

In addition to the popular **Centreville Amusement Park** (p. 34), Centre Island offers two great wading pools on both sides of the path across the bridge.

Walk further south and you'll reach the **Toronto Islands Bike Rental**, on the south shore of the island where you can rent bicycles, tandems, double-seaters or 4-seaters to ride along 20 kms of bike trails.

Nearby is **Gibraltar Beach** with a wide deck over the lake, that will make you feel you are by the ocean!

If you walk further east, you'll reach a boardwalk heading towards Ward's Beach and passing by the cute teahouse.

Ward's Island

The eastern part of the Islands is where the year-round residents live. It is almost impossible to resist a nosy peek as you stroll by the little postcard cottages close to the board-walk or within a short walk east from the ferry dock.

It is fun to see regular munici-pal street signs indicating we're on Lakeshore Ave. or Third Street as we walk along the carless paths between the houses.

Within a short walk of the ferry dock, past the snack bar, you can reach the boardwalk and the intimate **Ward's Beach** (the least frequented beach on the Islands). The **Rectory Café** is accessible from the board-walk, not too far west of the beach. They serve great food on the quaint patio. When I sit here with a glass of wine after a great day at the beach, it feels like Toronto's best kept secret.

Hanlan's Point

The **Hanlan's Point** ferry reaches the western end of the Islands. This part of the Islands includes Porter Air-port, tennis courts, 2 wading pools, a trout pond and the great **Hanlan Beach**, a 15-minute walk from the ferry dock.

At a glance, we take in the endless stretch of pristine water, with its swimmers frolicking against a backdrop of lazy white sailboats. On the right hand side of the beach, we can watch small planes taking off from the airport, stretched out against the city landscape. The **CN Tower** emerges behind the tree line, reminding us we are still in the heart of Toronto.

The sand is burning our feet on our way to the shore. By the water, it is cooled by the breeze and so soft our kids beg us to bury them in it! The water along the south shore of the **Toronto Islands** is the cleanest water in the area. The Islands act as a filter. It remains shallow for a great distance, reaching no higher than an adult's waist for at least 50 metres. The beach is well patrolled by lifeguards on shore and water.

When we last visited, the beach seemed relatively deserted. Further to our left however, a fenced area with the sign "You are entering a clothing optional area" attracted a larger crowd. Without being at close range, you see nothing out of the ordinary. Yet, those uncomfortable with the situation can move away along a wide stretch of beach to the right.

A small playground and a wading pool mark the entrance to the beach. Beyond the wading pool, a number of smaller sandy trails, some looking like real tiny dunes, branch off from the main trail leading to the beach.

From the paved trails beside the wading pool, plan on a 20-minute walk to reach Gibraltar Beach and another ten minutes to reach the **Centreville Amusement Park**.

TIPS (fun for 2 years +)

• More on **Centreville Amusement Park** on page 34.

• The **Centre Island** ferry won't allow bikes aboard on summer weekends but the other two ferries always welcome them.

• Try to avoid going to **Centre Island** during **Wakestock** in July (a wakeboarding festival very popular with youths). The line-up to the ferry is longer than usual and very loud music is blasting from the festival's stage by the bridge.

• A snack bar and washrooms are located near the wading pool by the entrance to **Hanlan Beach**. There are other snack bars by Gibraltar Beach, near Ward's Island ferry dock and in the amusement park. The tearoom by the boardwalk on **Ward's Island** offers great homemade desserts during the summer.

NEARBY ATTRACTIONS
Stroll around Harbourfront .... p. 26

Toronto Islands	D-3
(416) 392-8193 (ferry)	Toronto
(416) 392-1111 (city)	Islands
(416) 203-0009 (bike rental)	15-min.
(416) 392-7161 (beach hotline)	

www.toronto.ca/parks

Schedule: During the summer, the three ferries operate from 8 am until 11:45 pm. Schedules vary on weekdays.

Admission: Return fare is $5/adults, $3/seniors and students, $2/2-14 years, FREE for children less than 2 years old.

Directions: The Toronto Islands Ferry Terminal is located on Queen's Quay West, east of Bay St. No cars allowed on the ferry.

CHERRY BEACH

Cherry on top of the Sunday

Sorry for the easy pun but it was irresistible. It also describes very well our impression when we visited this beach on a hot summer Sunday when the Beaches area was overloaded with visitors and the Ashbridges Bay parking lot was full!

Unlike in the Beaches area, where beaches are wide open to the lake, Cherry Beach sits right in front of Toronto Islands so it offers a different panorama. You will see several small sailboats zigzagging between the two shores.

The sand is not as fine as what you'll find more to the east but there are many pebbles worth prospecting, according to my kids. On the eastern part of the beach, many tall trees offer shady spots for large families to picnic.

Another great advantage is the direct access to the bicycle trail leading towards **Leslie Spit**, offering Toronto's least-crowded ride along the water. (This trail starts at the end of Leslie Street and reaches the lighthouse at the tip of the land, 5 km away.)

The place was already great when we visited but it will get better. It is the lead-in project to the more than 500 acres of revitalization planned for Toronto's central waterfront.

At the time of print, they were already in the process of doing an major cleanup, improving and adding to the **Martin Goodman Trail**, constructing a trail to **Cherry Point** (to the west), creating a grand entrance, restoring the 1933 historic buildings, building a boardwalk and adding new benches, BBQ grills and picnic tables. Something to look forward to!

TIPS (fun for all ages)
• Cherry Beach is also known as **Clarke Beach** but the Cherry name is sticking with the locals since the beach is located at the foot of Cherry Street.
• There's usually a chip truck by the parking lot or you can get something from the take-out counter of the huge **Asian Supermarket** which opened at 222 Cherry Street (**www.tnt-supermarket.com**).

NEARBY ATTRACTIONS
Polson Pier (2-min.) .... p. 352
The Distillery (5-min.) .... p. 378

Cherry Beach
(416) 392-7161
(beach hotline)
www.towaterfront.ca
www.toronto.ca/parks

D-3
Downtown
Toronto
10-min.

Schedule: Open year-round.
Admission: FREE.
Directions: Going eastbound on Lake Shore Blvd., turn south on Cherry St. Note that you can not turn south on Cherry St. going westbound. You'll have to turn north on Cherry and find a way to U-turn back southbound.

THE BEACH NEIGHBOURHOOD

Life on the (water)front

Queen Street East, enlivened by small shops, cafés and great parks along the water-front, indiscriminately attracts three catego-ries of people: those being pulled by their dog, those follow-ing their stroller and finally, those who can enjoy a long brunch.

We early risers always begin an out-ing to the **Beaches** by having breakfast at one of the district's restau-rants in front of **Kew Gardens**.

We then explore the **Kew Gardens** play-ground. It offers a love-ly castle-like climbing structure built around the central mature tree and a wading pool.

After playing hide and seek around the bandstand in the middle of the park, we head for **Kew Beach**, a 3-minute walk away.

It's a renewed pleasure each time I look at the water. It sometimes appears turquoise beyond the boardwalk running

alongside. With the sand, pebbles and seagulls, you'd think you were star-ing at the ocean, as far as your eye can see. A long bicycle trail runs along the boardwalk. Towards the east, it is lined with trees and there's a snack bar. Last time we visited, locals had created a labyrinth with rocks nearby.

The boardwalk ends 20 minutes farther, east-bound, at **Balmy Beach**. Along the way, you'll see another snack bar with some tables during the summer, near the private Balmy Beach Club. There's a nice playground in the adjacent little park.

Further east, you'll reach a secluded section of the beach, where you can sneak into the backyards of some great properties.

TIPS (fun for all ages)

• In the spring or the fall, bring an extra sweater. The breeze that sweeps across the beach makes it cooler than on Queen Street.

• Fireworks are usually offered at Ashbridges Bay Park on **Victoria Day** and **Canada Day**. Call **Access Toronto** closer to the dates for event updates, check **www.toronto.ca/special_events** or call (416) 338-0338.

• The Alliance **Beach Cinemas** are right behind **Woodbine Park**, at 1651 Queen Street East. It is our favourite theatre, with spacious seats, live jazz on Saturday nights, patio, cafe with lots of tables, chess games, puzzles and magazines at our disposal. And here, movies are hardly ever sold out. There's also **Fox**, the independant theatre in the eastern end of the Beach at 2236 Queen, where you pay $10/ adults and $7/3-12 years. (Check listing for both on www.cinemaclock.com).

• You'll find a snack bar at **Kew Beach** and **Balmy Beach**.

• Our favourite place to eat on Queen is **Green Eggplant** where the plates always look great and fresh and the prices are unbeatable for the quality (1968 Queen, **www.greeneggplant.com**). We enjoy all-day breakfasts at **Sunset Grill** (especially in the back under the skylights) (2006 Queen, 416-690-9985, opens at 7 am). A favourite with the locals is **Garden Gate** with choices for everyone at very affordable prices (2379 Queen, 416-694-3605). Check the lovely green backyard patio of **Michelle's Beach House** (1955 Queen, **www.michellesbeachhouse. ca**) and **Dufflet's** amazing decor in the restaurant section in the back of the store (1917 Queen, **www.dufflet.com**).

• More on **Ashbridges Bay Park** and its bike path on p. 339.

• More on the **Beaches Easter Parade** on p. 39.

If you walk ten minutes westbound from **Kew Beach**, there's a playground located by the beach as well as the huge **Donald D. Summerville** outdoor pool. Along the way, if you're lucky, you'll see odd towers of rocks defying gravity, left by anonymous artists.

Beyond, the beach widens a lot and the sand becomes finer, you've reached **Woodbine Beach** from which we can see Ashbridges' fireworks during special events. This is where you'll see volleyball nets during the summer.

Another 10-minute walk and you'll see the playground located in front of the **Boardwalk Pub** and snack bar.

We really enjoy the western part of the bay in that area. It offers huge stones on which older children love to leap about, tall trees and a scenic lookout of the bay and access to **Ashbridges Park**.

Note that when you park near Ashbridges Bay Park, it takes 10 minutes to walk to **Woodbine Beach**.

The Beaches (416) 392-7161 (beach hotline) www. beachestoronto.com	D-3 East of downtown 20-min.

Schedule: Open year-round.
Admission: FREE (during the summer weekends and statutory holidays, there is a parking fee to park in the Ashbridge's Bay parking lot (the major lot located at the foot of Coxwell).
Directions: The Beach neighbourhood is located between Coxwell and Victoria Park Ave., along the waterfront. Take Gardiner Expwy. eastbound to the end, exit at Lake Shore Blvd.

SUNNYSIDE PAVILION CAFÉ

Someone pinch me, please!

I'm seated in a café. Facing me, the blues of sky and water merge in an unending horizon. I gaze at two swans flying over the shoreline, hearing the rustle of their majestic white wings. Thirty metres away from me, my son is building a short-lived dam in the fine sand. Beside me, my little one is asleep in her stroller. Sighing with contentment, a flavourful cappuccino in hand, I'm getting ready to relax. Where am I? Here in Toronto, at the Sunnyside Pavilion Café!

Along Lake Shore Boulevard West, you will notice a large, white building beside a long municipal pool. If you venture to the other side of this building, you'll discover a facade with arches and columns and a patio full of tables topped by umbrellas. The structure efficiently muffles the roar of motor vehicles circulat-

ing on the adjacent boulevard! Only the boardwalk separates the terrace from the beach.

An inner courtyard boasts other tables set amid fountain, trees and flowers, completing the illusion of being at a European café. It makes you feel like writing postcards to friends you've left behind.

The restaurant offers an elaborate choice of hearty breakfasts. You can order coffee any way you like it. Salads are large and fresh. Gourmet pizzas are delicious.

The patio is the perfect spot for adults with children. Parents can finish their meal while watching their little ones play on the beach.

TIPS (fun for all ages)
• On rainy days, the restaurant might be closed. When the weather is grey, it is better to call before you go.
• East of the restaurant (beyond the huge outdoor public **Gus Ryder/Sunnyside Pool**) you'll find a great shaded playground, a large wading pool and a few dinosaurs to climb on! Let's not forget the ice cream stand and snack bar on the west side of the café.

NEARBY ATTRACTIONS	
Ontario Place (15-min.)	p. 18
High Park (5-min.)	p. 286

Sunnyside Pavilion Café
(416) 531-2233
(416) 392-7161
(beach hotline)
www.sunnysidecafe.ca
www.torontobeach.ca

D-3
West
of downtown
25-min.

Schedule: Usually open daily from May through September (weather permitting), with variable hours, usually from around 9:30 am to at least 11 pm during the summer. Call to confirm.
Admission: FREE admission to the beach (you will pay around $8 for a fancy burger, $11 for a pizza).
Directions: 1755 Lake Shore Blvd. West, Toronto. If on Lake Shore westbound, drive past Ellis Ave. and take the exit for Lake Shore East to your left. A few parking lots are located on the south side of Lake Shore Blvd.

BLUFFER'S PARK

Cliffs from below

This beach, at first quite broad, narrows gradually. When dry, its sand is one of the finest I've seen in the area. My little lad threw himself down and made an angel with his arms and legs.

The beach spreads at the end of the fourth parking lot to the east. You reach it via a small road that borders the base of the cliffs which sit blazing in the summer light.

As you walk further east along the beach, you'll discover another source of playful inspiration in the pieces of polished beachwood lying here and there.

When visiting in early October, there was a multitude of red ladybugs every second step on the beach.

TIPS (fun for all ages)
• More on the **Scarborough Bluffs** on p. 258.
• **DogFish Pub** is a restaurant located at 7 Brimley Road South (in the **Bluffer's Park Marina**) offering a nice view of the marina from its patio. Check their menu on **www.bluffersparkmarina.com**.

• There's a **Lick's** hamburger joint a few minutes west of Midland on Kingston Rd. (2383 Kingston Rd., 416-267-3249, **www.lickshomeburgers.com**).

Bluffer's Park	D-3
• Scarborough	**East**
(416) 392-1111	**of downtown**
www.toronto.ca/parks	**25-min.**

Schedule: Open year-round.
Admission: FREE.
Directions: Take Kingston Rd. eastbound. Turn south on Brimley St. (east of Midland). Go to the end of the fourth parking lot to the east.

ROUGE BEACH

Spread of Rouge

We climb up stairs, cross over a bridge and arrive at a boardwalk where we get a superb panorama of the lake, with a strip of sand pointing out from the shore of Rouge Beach, looking like the seashore during low tide.

The trail eventually takes off from the edge of the cliff, so we come down the path to get to the beach itself.

Rouge Beach is relatively long and wide, with great sand, and is equipped with changing rooms. When we were visiting, the kids had fun chasing nice tiny waves created by the wind.

Many people fish in the **Rouge Marsh** adjacent to the parking lot (accompanied by a large population of geese).

Some launch their canoes into **Little Rouge Creek**, visible from the shore. Others come from Lake Ontario, into the creek.

There's an undercurrent in that area but not at the beach.

TIPS (fun for all ages)
• Note that this beach is more often not suitable for swimming due to the many geese visiting this site. Check the Beach hotline before you go.
• More about **Rouge River** on p. 326.
• **Toronto Kayak & Canoe Adventures** offers trips on the Rouge River, starting below Old Kingston Rd. and ending at Rouge River Beach ($50/person, equipment and life jackets included). Check **www.torontoadventures.ca** for details. Children under 8 must be with an adult.

NEARBY ATTRACTIONS
Toronto Zoo (10-min.) .... p. 57
Pettycoat Creek C.A.(10-min.) .... p. 423

Rouge Beach
· Scarborough
(416) 392-1111
(416) 392-7161
(beach hotline)
www.toronto.ca

**D-3
East
of downtown
30-min.**

Schedule: Open year-round.
Admission: FREE.
Directions: Take Hwy 401 East, follow Port Union signs, exit Port Union southbound. Turn east on Lawrence Ave., to the parking.

PROFESSOR'S LAKE

Spring-fed and urban

When I was told about this lake smack in the middle of a large suburban housing development, I envisioned... well, I just could not envision it! No wonder. The man-made lake is a first attempt of this kind in eastern Canada. It offers the best water in the region, a twisting water slide, a raft to jump from for the better swimmers and a large sandy beach. It is also surrounded by 750 housing units.

To access Professor's Lake, one has to go through a hallway in the recreation centre, which hides the lake from our view. When the beach revealed itself, I took in the panorama of the wide beach covered with pale sand, some 300 visitors (much less than I had expected for a great summer day) and the 65-acre mass of blue water. My kids ran like wild horses to try the fun slide throwing happy children into the lake.

My 5-year-old spent the next four hours on the slide while her 9-year-old brother kept jumping off the raft, more than 30 metres from shore. Like many kids, mine could not care less about water attributes vital to me such as quality, temperature, colour or odour. Whatever water will do the job, as long as I allow them to swim in it.

I was really taken by the sensation of swimming in Professor's Lake, and so were the moms I introduced to this attraction. It felt... clean and refreshing!

There are many reasons for it. The former gravel pit is spring-fed. It offers a large shallow area but reaches 42 feet in its greatest depth. And unlike many lakes in the region, a storm drainage system was designed to bypass the lake so it is protected from water run-off from farms, houses and roads, following heavy rains.

Add lifeguards on the beach, at the raft and at both ends of the slide and you get a very relaxing outing for parents! Add plenty of canoes, kayaks and paddle boats for rental at affordable prices to take advantage of the lake, and you get an outing suitable for all ages and genders.

TIPS (fun for all ages)

• You need to be 42 inches or taller to use the slide. Adults are welcome.
• An **Annual Beach Party** run by the neighbourhood community group is usually offered on the last Saturday in June. You can expect water-ski shows, live entertainment, ice cream eating contests, maybe a sandcastle contest, and fireworks. Call to confirm.
• A trail runs around the lake outside of the gated area.
• A snack bar sells hot dogs, snacks, popsicles and slush.
• There is a **Gateway Six (Cineplex)** on 5 Gateway Drive, just off Queen Street (www.cinemaclock.com). A family movie would be a nice way to finish a great outing (especially since the beach closes at 6 pm). You'll find many fast food chains and family restaurants in the area, a 5-min. drive from the lake.

NEARBY ATTRACTIONS
Chinguacousy Park (5-min.) .... p. 297

Professor's Lake	**D-2**
• Brampton	**N-W**
(905) 791-7751	**of Toronto**
www.professorslake.com	**50-min.**

Schedule: Open daily late June to Labour Day, 10 am to 6 pm.
Admission: Around $4/adults, $3/others. **Rental costs:** Around $5/30 min. for paddle boat, $5/1 hr for canoe, $8/1 hr for kayak. Call to confirm.
Directions: From Hwy 401, take Hwy 427 northbound to the end, turn west on Hwy 7, then north on Torbram Rd. and west on North Park Dr.

BEACHWAY PARK

The beach pavilion, with changing rooms and outdoor showers and arty wall adorned with a modern mosaic is very nice and is surrounded by tall grass and trees. Many families were already enjoying the water. The sun was hot and some trees were offering spots in the shade.

After some fries at the snack bar, we went for a dip. The water was quite shallow. The kids could run out over 20 metres without having water over the waist. A minus for serious swimmers, a major plus for kids who want to play tag.

If a lift bridge is something that could be a hit with your kids, don't forget to check the 380-foot-long **Burlington Canal**

Lift Bridge at the western end of the beach. It will take you 20 minutes to walk from the beach pavilion to the canal or one minute to drive.

It lifts on demand for the large vessels and every hour and a half for leisure boats (approximately 4,000 times in a year). Chances are you'll see it in action.

Sandbar is open

Beachway Park is part of the sandbar linking Burlington to Hamilton. It ends at the Burlington Canal, first opened in 1826 to provide Hamilton Harbour with navigable access to the Atlantic Ocean.

With Stelco and Dofasco as neighbours, the "Burlington Beach" hasn't had good press in the last decades. It was covered with black coal dust or light coloured ash in the 70's, it suffered persistent bacteria warnings in the 80's, dead ducks in 1989, black paint-like water in 1995. To top it off, Hydro towers line up all along the beach. But, not knowing any of that, we arrived unbiased at the beach.. and loved it!

TIPS (fun for all ages)
•   There's free parking on the south side of Lakeshore.
•   You can get all you need for a last minute picnic at the grocery store in **Brant Plaza**, four blocks north of Lakeshore on Brant St.
•   You might want to finish the day with a movie at the independent movie theatre **Encore Upper Canada Place** (460 Brant St., three blocks north of Lakeshore, (905) 681-FILM).

NEARBY ATTRACTIONS	
Royal Botanical (15-min.)	p. 282
Wild Waterworks (5-min.)	p. 432

Beachway Park	E-2
• Burlington	S-W
(905) 825-6000	of Toronto
(ask for beach hotline)	50-min.
www.cms.burlington.ca	
(click Parks & Recreation,	
then Waterfront)	

Schedule: Open year-round.
Admission: FREE.
Directions: From QEW, take exit #101/Brant Street southbound. Follow Brant. Turn west on Lakeshore Rd. You'll find free parking on the south side along the park.

Hutch's restaurant from the 50's in Hamilton, read tips section on p. 432.

Photo: Courtesy of Baranga's

Baranga's on the Beach in Hamilton, read tips section on p. 432.

HEART LAKE C. A.

Dive into nature

Heart Lake's swimming hole is a well-kept secret. Its sandy beach is wide, and licensed fishermen can enjoy their sport looking for a few farmed trout, comfortably installed in the willows' shade. Beyond the area reserved for swimmers, paddle boats criss-cross the heart-shaped pond, escorted by dragonflies.

The valley's picnic sites bordering the parking lot closest to the lake offer an inviting panorama. There, you feel the urge to roll on the grass. Big families are gathering for large picnics and the air is filled with the appetizing smells of meat sizzling on the barbecues. Unfortunately, you don't get a view of the lake from those sites.

The lake is stocked with rainbow trout every spring. You may fish from the shore if you pay the daily angling fees ($5.50/adults, $2.65/5-14 years, FREE under 5 years old) or rent a paddle boat to fish out on the water.

Half a kilometre from the parking lot by the lake, you'll find another parking lot that borders a lovely nature trail, past the Hill & Dale picnic lot. The whole family can stroll on it for 30 minutes, while enjoying the shade of 40-metre-high trees.

Heart Lake Conservation Area
· Brampton
(905) 846-2494
or (416) 661-6600, ext. 5203
www.trca.on.ca

D-2
N-W
of Toronto
35-min.

Schedule: Open end of April to October 31, 9 am until dusk (variable closing time for each month).

Admission: $6/adults, $5/seniors, FREE for 15 years and under with their family, $2/child to use the new splash pad. Canoe/paddle boat rental is around $14 per hour.

Directions: Take Hwy 410 North until it becomes Heart Lake Rd., then go 2 km north on Road #7.

TIPS (fun for all ages)

• Since my last visit, they've added a splash pad by Birchview picnic lot!
• The snack bar is not always open on weekdays; better to bring a lunch.

NEARBY ATTRACTIONS
Chinguacousy Park (15-min.) ...... p. 297

ALBION HILLS C. A.

A quiet sandy hide-out

Albion Hills' beach is wide in certain areas, and sufficiently long to satisfy those seeking a quiet sandy hide-out at its far end.

At the end of the more quiet sandy point, you can take a trail running up the hill bordering the water.

From the highest point, you will get a great view and be able to go down a sandy slope bringing you to the shores of the small lake.

If you cross the road by the entrance of the trail, you'll reach the narrow Humber River, complete with picnic areas along the way. It eventually leads to the campground. You must take your car to access other hiking trails of 1.6 to 5.8 kilometre-long paths. You can rent a paddle boat or canoe (or bring your own) to enjoy on the lake.

TIPS (fun for all ages)

• More about **Albion Hills** tobogganing in the winter on p. 372.

• During a visit in May, we observed hundreds of tiny tadpoles in the water!

• Albion Hills' trails are open for mountain biking from the end of April to the end of October, weather permitting. All trails start at Cedar Grove parking lot.

• Albion Hills offers around 260 **campsites**, quite close to one another, yet equipped with a lovely playground.

• The snack bar is mainly open during the weekends. You should bring your lunch on weekdays. There is a small playground by the beach.

NEARBY ATTRACTIONS
South Simcoe Railway (15-min.) ... p. 225

Albion Hills Conservation Area
• Caledon
(905) 880-0227
or (416) 661-6600, ext. 5203
www.trca.on.ca

C-2
N-W
of Toronto
50-min.

Schedule: Open year-round from 9 am until dusk. Swimming is allowed June to Labour Day.

Admission: $4/adults, $3/seniors, $2/5-14 years, FREE 4 years and under. Canoe or paddle boat rental is around $14 per hour, camping, around $25/night.

Directions: 16500 Hwy 50, Caledon. From Hwy 400 North, take exit #55/Hwy 9 westbound. Turn south on Hwy 50.

EMERALD LAKE

A little gem!

This natural setting is utterly unique in the region. This is your chance to swim in the pristine green water of a spring-fed lake. This is your kids' opportunity to jump off a diving board into a real lake.

Even better! They've added water toys since our last visit such as a water trampoline.

The lakeshore consists of natural rock plates descending into the water like some man-made stairs. The water doesn't have the usual muddy texture of the small lakes with sandy bottoms. This one sits on pale bedrock, hence the nice emerald shade. Being spring-fed, it is cold!

Emerald Lake is a trailer resort and waterpark doing its job to entertain the customers with: a 200-foot water slide with small receiving pool (48"+), a large kids pool with deck and water sprays, many volleyball courts and paddle boat and kayak rentals. Nothing too fancy.

But when I swam in the farthest part of the pollution-free lake, enclosed by overhanging boughs of trees, it felt like Eden...

From the water, I had a great spot to observe the daredevils, my 8-year-old

included, jumping off the board atop the small cliff.

Later on, we rented a paddle boat (they also rent kayaks) and explored another section of the small lake with weeds and... big snails! My kids enjoyed jumping from the paddleboat and were glad to rest on it for a while.

Since my visit, they've added a 3,400 sq ft splash pad near the kids' pool. The rock plates on the lake's shore don't offer a gradual entrance into the water and they are slippery. I found that section stressful for parents of toddlers. The new spray pad is solving this problem. Toddlers will be more than happy to stick to the water games area. Good old-fashioned fun! This is definitely a great reason to escape the city.

TIPS (fun for 2 years +)
- The trailer resort also includes family campsites for tents. Call them one month in advance to reserve if you want a space during a long weekend.
- There's a snack bar and they have BBQ pits throughout the park. Bring your own charcoal.

NEARBY ATTRACTIONS	
African Lion Safari (15-min.)	p. 66
Westfield Village (15-min.)	p. 390

Emerald Lake	E-2
• Puslinch	West
1-800-679-1853	of Toronto
(905) 659-7923	60-min.
www.emeraldlake.ca	

Schedule: Waterpark is open daily mid-June to Labour Day, 10 am to 8 pm. Campground is open May 1 to mid-October.

Admission: Around $10/over 12 years, $5/seniors, $9/3-12 years ($1 less on weekdays), FREE 2 years and under.

Directions: 4248 Gore Rd., R.R. #2, Puslinch. From Hwy 401, take exit to Hwy 6 south. Turn west at West Flamborough Concession 11, for approx. 5 km. The lake is on your right hand side.

ELORA QUARRY C. A.

Old-fashioned hole

With the passing years, a basin has formed at the bottom of Elora Quarry, abandoned since the 1930's. On hot summer days, you can dip into this water fed by pure springs.

We accessed the quarry through a small beach offering an excellent view of the 12-metre-high walls surrounding the body of water. Seen from the beach, the panorama is unique.

On the other side of the quarry runs the **Grand River** where we saw some people fishing.

Last time we visited, our little pioneer just loved the manual water pump, still in working order, located on the beach. At the time of print, I could not confirm if it is still there. Let's hope so!

TIPS (fun for all ages)
• Jumping or diving is not permitted for insurance reasons.
• More about nearby **Elora Gorge Conservation Area** on p. 428.

Elora Quarry Conservation Area
· Elora
(519) 846-5234
www.grandriver.ca

D-1
West
of Toronto
50-min.

Schedule: Open mid-June until Labour Day, from 10 am to dusk.
Admission: Around $4/adults, $2.50/6-14 years, FREE 5 years and under.
Directions: From Hwy 401 West, take exit #295/Hwy 6 northbound, then follow County Rd. 7 to Elora. Turn east on County Rd. 18 (also called Fergus-Elora Rd.). Elora Quarry is located between Elora and Fergus.

CEDAR BEACH PARK

A private matter

The sign atop the stone gate with its gothic lettering, brings to mind the look of a summer camp from the 50's. The entrance's iron doors frame a blue square of water, and as we reach the top of steep stairs, the wide private beach reveals itself, promising an afternoon of fun.

The sand works well for elaborate "engineering" projects of bridges and tunnels. The shores of Musselman's Lake are comfortably shallow for a distance, and the deeper water is well marked with buoys. Since my last visit, they've added two water trampolines and water logs. They're lots of fun but be warned, they require parent's careful surveillance!

The two parks near the parking lot include nice playgrounds, making a picnic even more enjoyable for the kids.

TIPS (fun for all ages)

• There's a slight algae smell to the water, typically in the midst of summer, though it was quite clear and refreshing when we visited. The water quality is monitored. You might want to call and check if the beach is open before you go.
• Kayaks, canoes and paddle boats used to be available for rent for day users at the campground. (You might have to drive to the office to get a key to unlock the boat's padlock.) Call to confirm.
• They usually offer a fireworks display on Labour Day. Call for exact date.
• The trailer park includes 41 campsites for tents. The use of the pools and spray pad is for overnight campers only.
• There's a snack bar on site. Picnic tables are lined up along the iron railing and we enjoyed eating there watching swimmers down below.

Cedar Beach Trailer Park & Pavilion	C-3
• Stouffville	N-E
(905) 642-1700	of Toronto
www.cedarbeach.com	50-min.

 Schedule: The beach is open early April to late October, 8 am to dusk, weather permitting.
Admission: (cash only) $8/adults, $4/children, FREE for babies (On weekdays: $6/adults, $3/children).
Directions: 15014 9th Line, Musselmans Lake/Stouffville. From Hwy 404 North, take exit #45/Aurora Rd. eastbound, turn south on 9th Line (Regional Rd. 69).

NEARBY ATTRACTIONS

COBOURG BEACH

The shallow water is pleasantly refreshing, yet it warms up quickly in the middle of summer. Swimmers walk through the waves some 50 metres ahead of us, while my daughter embarks on a digging engineering project in the water. She soon joins new friends for a game of wave catching and burying in the sand!

The spray pad by the boardwalk is lovely and colourful. There's also minigolf in the park.

A two-minute drive away, there's a skatepark. We usually like to grab a take-out dinner and sit by this skatepark to watch the skaters in action. (Take Queen or King Street east until you reach D'Arcy Street, then go towards the lake.)

Adjacent **Breakers Motel** has its own private beach. They rent nice cottages. This would offer a really cool weekend getaway! (94 Green Street, 905-372-9231).

The **Cobourg Waterfront Festival** returns every year during 3-4 consecutive days including **Canada Day**. It involves **fireworks** on July 1. There's also the new **Sandcastle Festival** to look forward to on the first weekend in August (competition on Saturday only). Both take place by the beach.

Charge!

As soon as my little mermaid sees the wide and long beach at Victoria Park, she darts off, sure of her way, to a day of water fun.

TIPS (fun for all ages)

• You'll find a nice ice cream parlour at the corner of Division and Charles Streets by the park before the beach entrance.

• If you want to push 15 minutes further east on Hwy 401, you'll reach the **Big Apple** in Colborne (take exit #497 southbound, then turn east on Big Apple Drive). In addition to the trademark 10-metre-high red apple visible from the highway (in which you can climb), there are free-roaming rabbits, llamas, deer and sheep to feed, a small trail to explore,

minigolf and a small train offering rides on a track. You can see them make apple pies and more through large windows. Their cafeteria is huge, and so is their gift shop. They close at 9 pm in the summer (905-355-2574).

Cobourg Beach

· Cobourg
1-888-262-6874 (festival)
or (905) 372-5831
www.cobourgtourism.ca

C-5
East
of Toronto
70-min.

Schedule: Open year-round.
Admission: FREE.
Directions: Victoria Park, Cobourg. From Hwy 401 East, take exit #472/Regional Hwy 2 southbound. Turn east on King St., then south on Division St.

KELSO CONSERVATION AREA

Milton's water spot

For a successful outing in the Milton region, I recommend including a swim at Kelso Conservation Area.

Kelso Beach sits by a grassy park with lots of shade. The length of the beach is covered with long transparent wires hung some ten metres above, to prevent bird visits. Needless to say the sand is clean! It is the ideal spot for a picnic but expect hordes of visitors after 1 pm. With children 7 years and older, you may wish to hike all the way to the top of the escarpment. I have heard it takes more than

45 minutes to reach, but the panoramic view is amazing and you'll find an old quarry with fossils on the way! Kelso is known in the region for its series of trails for serious mountain bikers. More on this conservation area and the **Halton Region Museum** on p. 387! See **Glen Eden Snow Tubing** on p. 363.

Kelso Conservation Area • Milton (905) 878-5011 www.conservationhalton.on.ca	D-2 West of Toronto 50-min.

 Schedule: Open year-round (summertime, from 8 am to 8 pm).

 Admission: $5/adults, $4/seniors, $3.50/5 to 14 years, FREE 4 years and under. Bike pass is $7. Canoe, paddle boat or kayak rental is around $12 per hour.

Directions: From Hwy 401 West, take exit #320/Hwy 25 northbound, turn west on Campbellville Rd., then south on Tremaine Rd., follow signs.

CHRISTIE LAKE C. A.

Check this out!

This sandy beach is 360 metres long and the swimming area is... chlorinated!

A fabric shield separates the swimming area from the rest. It protects the water from the pollution of bird droppings but the down side is that the muddy sand at the bottom stays suspended longer, giving a murky colour to that section. The truth is that happy bathers do lots of stirring in that water, never deeper than five feet, perfect for parents to toss their ecstatic kids like potato sacks into the lake. There are no lifeguards on duty.

You can rent large inner tubes to play on inside the boundaries, or paddle boats, canoes and... hydro bikes to explore the rest of the lake.

We're not allowed to eat on the narrow beach to keep it clean but we have our picnic on the grass right next to it. One of the trails runs around the lake for 5.6 km (get a map at the entrance).

Attention fishermen! Christie includes nine ponds (note that Pond 8 is wheelchair accessible). They sell bait.

Christie Lake Conservation Area • Dundas (905) 628-3060 or 1-888-319-4722 www.conservationhamilton.ca	E-2 S-W of Toronto 55-min.

 Schedule: Open year-round.

Admission: $8 per vehicle and driver, $3/add. passenger, to a max. of $17. Canoe, paddle boat and hydro bike rental is around $7 for 30 minutes.

 Directions: From QEW/403, take exit Hwy 6 North. Turn west on Hwy 5. Christie is on the south side.

SHADE'S MILLS C. A.

Paddle time

We were grateful for this nice swim almost right in town on our way back from other attractions in this region.

Regardless of the name, the beach is not in the shade but there are plenty of trees around the boat rental. Renting a canoe or a paddle boat was very tempting because of the shape of the reservoir, with a long arm of water to explore, stretching out one side. It would have taken the whole day to try everything. The conservation area's map showed a footbridge

and 12 km of nature trails (turned into cross-country ski trails in the winter).

Ask about their ice fishing and heated ice huts renting.

Shade's Mill Conservation Area
· Cambridge
(519) 621-3697
www.grandriver.ca

E-1
S-W
of Toronto
75-min

Schedule: Open year-round.
Admission: $4/adults, $2.50/6-14 years old, FREE 5 years and under. Canoe or paddle boat rental, $10/hr.

Directions: 412 Avenue Rd., Cambridge. From Hwy 401 West, take exit #282 at Hespeler Rd. South. Turn east on Avenue Rd.

Sandbanks P. P., p. 264. Look for more beach options in the **Provincial Parks** category under the **Nature's Call** chapter on pp. 307-316.

COUCHICHING BEACH

You can expect fireworks at dusk in the park on Sunday during **Victoria Day** and an even bigger celebration on **Canada Day**, also complete with fireworks at dusk.

The **Trans-Canada Trail** now includes a 7-km trail running through the City of Orillia. I've seen part of it east of Orillia and it was the perfect trail for a family bike outing.

Summer treat

Ice cream, a playground by the beach, with a swing just a few metres from the water, soft sand. What more could a child want?

How about a miniature engine blowing its whistle in the park to invite the visitors on a one-km- long track?

TIPS (fun for all ages)

• More about the **Mariposa Market** in the tips section of **McRae Provincial Park** on p. 311.

• During a girlfriends outing to the **Casino Rama** (10 minutes from Couchiching Beach), I was surprised to discover a splendid building which incorporated the Native culture into the architecture in a way I would expect to see in British Columbia, not in Ontario! There's no need to go to the casino to enjoy it. It includes an indoor waterfall near the gorgeous casual dining restaurant **The Weirs**, a great ceiling projection and a wonderful store with native art for every budget (**www.casinorama.com**).

Couchiching Beach Park	**A-3**
• Orillia	**North**
(705) 326-4424	**of Toronto**
www.orillia.com	**75-min**

 Schedule: Open year-round. The train runs weekends from Victoria Day to Canada Day, then daily until Labour Day.
Admission: FREE park access. Train ride is around $2/person.
Directions: Take Hwy 11, exit eastbound on Coldwater Rd. Turn right on Front St., left on Mississauga St., to the Port of Orillia and the beach.

NEARBY ATTRACTIONS
Muskoka Wildlife (20-min.) .... p. 74

WASAGA BEACH

"The world's longest freshwater beach"

We only hear about the portion of Wasaga Beach which resembles an American ocean city on March Break. This is only part of the reality. As a matter of fact, Wasaga Beach is 14 kms long.

In some spots, the hot and soft sand is cooled by the shade from tall trees and it feels like paradise. Some other spots count bathers by the dozens instead of the hundreds. You'll even find a perfect playground if you go to the right section of the beach!

What makes Wasaga Beach so popular is that pretty much everywhere along the strip of beach, a 6-year-old can walk 100 metres into the water and still maintain her head above the water. In addition, being shallow, the water never gets as cold as the pristine water of Georgian Bay everywhere else.

The downside is if you want to have a good swim, you'll need to go quite far from the beach to have enough water to move in. But then, there's the threat of sea-doos and motorboats. On the bright side, those noisy vehicles make fun waves!

You'll be glad to know that the big fire of 2007 did not destroy the buildings along Beach Drive, which borders only the western side of **Beach Area 1**. This is the hot spot with cars parked everywhere, traffic on the road as well as on the sidewalk, restaurants, ice cream parlours, beach

shops, pierced navels and loud music.

As a rule of thumb, the further you go east and west of this area the less noisy and crowded it will be. You want to go there for a glimpse of the action but it's much better to move on in order to find a better beach spot to spend the afternoon.

The **Beach Area 1** access is at the foot of Spruce Street, to the right just after the bridge taking Main Street across Nottawasaga River. When I saw the beautiful white sand overflowing from the beach to the parking lot, it reminded me of ocean cities. Quite a change from Toronto!

There's no road along that part of **Beach Area 1** so it's much prettier than its western neighbour in front of Beach Drive. It is noisy from all the boats motoring around between the lake and the river but the shops are far away.

Away from the boardwalk, you will find tall birch throwing their most appreciated shade. Come early if you want one of those for your family. There are no more trees along Beach Drive.

Beach Area 2, accessible from 3rd Street, is quieter than the western part of **Beach Area 1** but it might change soon. Major development plans are in the air.

Beach Area 3 is narrower on its eastern part. Trees are back but they are shorter. You see bushes near the entrance and more grass on the eastern part of that area. It is accessible from 22nd Street. You may access **Beach Area 4** from 24th Street. From then on, the sand is not as fluid, more packed.

Beach Area 5, which you access from 36th Street, might be your best bet with a young family. The children will split their time between the beach and its original playground amidst the trees (a nice way to cool down from the sun). I really liked its wooden structures. My kids enjoyed its many corners for hiding.

TIPS (fun for all ages)

• Even though the water is shallow, you need to keep a good eye on your younger children. When they fall, water does get over their heads! There is also the problem of an undertow that can take away inflatable toys.

• If you feel like going to a waterpark, go to **Wasaga Waterworld**, a nearby attraction. It includes speed slides, serpent slide, bumper boats, wave pool, whirlpool and more(1-800-809-0896, **www.wasagawaterworld.com**). Note that this attraction is under new management and they are planning to revamp the place.

• Special events take place at the **Beach Area 1**. We were there on Labour Day weekend and saw a dog show during the day and great fireworks on the Sunday evening (they called it the Memories of Summer Fireworks Display). Activities vary from one year to the next.

• Note most shops are closed after Labour Day weekend.

• The Beaches Loop, is a **10-km trail** of beaches and parks for bikers and hikers, sometimes running along a town road.

• If you are looking for a campground, it is a good idea to consider **Craigleith Provincial Park**, located 25 minutes from Wasaga Beach. It includes 165 campsites by a strip of slippery rocky shore on Georgian Bay. The advantage is that your vehicle pass to that provincial park saves you the $15 fee to access Wasaga Beach Provincial Park. There's also the **Cedar Grove Park**, self-described as family camping with 1,000 ft of sandy beach, (705) 429-2134.

Many large rocks were popping out from the water at **Beach Area 6**, accessible from 45th Street. The eastern beaches of **New Wasaga** and **Allenwood**, which I did not get a chance to check out, are respectively accessible from Albert Street and Concession 11. Locals go there.

Wasaga Beach is such a good getaway destination, it is worth staying overnight. The plain motel room we rented last minute was expensive and off the beach, like most of the area's accommodations.

A good way to find an accommodation is through the website **www.wasagabeach.com**. Click on **Visitors**, then in the **Where to stay** section, click on the list of accomodations.

Unless you are choosing an accommodation located near the beach or offering rustic charm and some privacy, I strongly recommend at least selecting something with a pool. Note that hotels closer to the beach in the "hot" section in **Beach Area 1** risk being noisier at night.

Wasaga Beach Provincial Park

B-2
N-W
of Toronto
1 3/4 hr

• Wasaga Beach
(705) 429-2516 (park)
1-866-292-7242 (town)
www.wasagabeach.com

 Schedule: Open year-round (facilities available from mid-June to Thanksgiving).

Admission: Around $15/day per vehicle, good for all the parking lots (less after Labour Day).

Directions: Along Mosley St. in Wasaga Beach. From Hwy 400 North, take exit #98/Hwy 26/27 westbound, then follow Hwy 27 to Elmvale. Turn west on Hwy 92, it will lead you to Main St. and Mosley St.

AGINCOURT LEISURE POOL

other little pirates launched an attack on the fun, shipwreck-shaped waterslide. Since my last visit, the coconut trees seen in the pictures have been replaced by palm trees, but they're still spraying water over our heads.

Behind the wading pool is the small, intermediate pool, perfect for introducing children to swimming.

Under the palm trees

We often crave turquoise water and palm trees. The Agincourt Recreation Centre pool offers an innovative alternative. It includes aqua-coloured water, water slides, an adjoining Jacuzzi, a waterside restaurant and... spraying trees as a bonus!

As soon as we went in, the aquatic complex's originality, revealed by wide bay windows, caught my little one's admiring eye and made him walk towards the admission counter, wriggling with impatience.

It wasn't long before my son and

Further to the right, swimmers 48 inches and over are going down the gigantic, spiral-shaped waterslide into a small pool lined with tall palm trees. They are greeted with a loud SPLASH!

To the left, adults can soak in the warm water of the Jacuzzi, reserved for bathers aged 12 years and up. Nearby, there's a sauna.

Tables are especially set up for swimmers in their bathing suits, overlooking palm trees and the pool area. They can order off the counter from the adjacent Country Style concession! When we visited, the illusion of being down South would have been perfect if observers hadn't been standing on the other side of the bay window, wearing their winter coats!

TIPS (fun for all ages)
• Bring your own lock if you wish to use the changing room lockers.
• The slide is open during the programs: Recreational Swim, Family Swim. Call for the schedule of the day.
• The Parent and Tot program is reserved for adults accompanying children 6 years and under. It is usually less crowded.
• The **Country Style** is usually open on weekends, and some evenings.
• **Birchmount Pool** is similar with huge slide and tables by the pool. It is located at 93 Birchmount Road, call (416) 396-4018 for information.

NEARBY ATTRACTIONS
Chuck E. Cheese (20-min.) .... p. 195
Woodie Wood Chucks (15-min.) p. 196

Agincourt Leisure Pool
• Scarborough
(416) 396-8343 (pool)
(416) 396-4037 (centre)
www.toronto.ca

D-3 N-E of downtown 35-min.

 Schedule: School year and summer hours are different. Expect extended hours during Christmas and March Break. Call the pool number to confirm what program runs for the day.

 Admission: FREE, $2.50/adults for lane swim.

 Directions: 31 Glen Watford Dr., Scarborough. From Hwy 401 East, take exit #379/ Kennedy Rd. northbound (Glen Watford is north of Sheppard Ave. and east of Midland Ave.).

DOUGLAS SNOW CENTRE

Me Tarzan, me sad

It was the only pool in Toronto with a Tarzan rope and now it's gone! But there are still two great slides.

With or without the tarzan rope, this a beautiful pool! The huge pool offers a wide section with beach-like access, perfect for younger kids, and a profusion of water toys at your disposal in a separate room (you just need to ask the staff). They even have duck decoys!

Bigger kids will spend their time at the long, bumpy white slide and the huge flume slide with a few loops. Both land in the shallow section. Only those who pass a deep-end test will be allowed to use the flume slide.

The slide is available during Recreational Swim.

The Tarzan rope fans will want to know that there is one in the aquatic centre of Mississauga Valley Community Centre (1275 Mississauga Valley Blvd., 905-615-4670, **www.mississauga.ca**).

Douglas Snow Aquatic Centre • North York **(416) 395-7585** **www.toronto.ca/parks**	**D-3** **North** **of downtown** **40-min.**

 Schedule: School year and summer hours are different. (Check their website under **The FUN Guide** then **Swimming** section). Call to confirm if Recreational Swim runs for the day.

 Admission: FREE ($2.50 for adult lane swim).

 Directions: 5100 Yonge St., North York. Turn west on North York Blvd. (north of Sheppard). The pool is at the corner of Beecroft Rd. (public parking).

RIVER GROVE AQUATICS

Lighten up!

The Nature is so nicely framed by the glass wall and the whole architecture of the pool that one would think they are swimming inside the McMichael Canadian Art Collection building!

Very high wooden ceiling, smooth arches and huge bay windows catch the daylight, beautifully filtered by the tall trees. Quite a setting for a community pool! Kids just love the triple loop red slide ending in shallow water and the blue one in the deeper end. Most of the pool is actually shallow. Balls, floaters and life jackets are provided. A big whirlpool completes the experience. A large mezzanine on the second floor allows parents to watch their kids.

There are vending machines on site. The **Culham Trail** running along the **Credit River** is accessible from the back of the community centre (see p. 350).

River Grove Community Centre • Mississauga **(905) 615-4780 (pool)** **www.mississauga.ca**	**D-3** **N-W** **of Toronto** **35-min.**

 Schedule: School year and summer hours are different. Expect extended hours during Christmas and March Break. Call the pool number to confirm if Family and Fun Swim programs run for the day (when the slide is open).

 Admission: $3.60/person, $9.34/family of 5.

Directions: 5800 River Grove Ave., Mississauga. From the QEW, take exit #130/ Mississauga Rd. North. Turn east on Main St. (in Streetsville), it becomes Bristol Rd. Turn north on River Grove. Ave.

PETTICOAT CREEK C. A.

Not a petty pool!

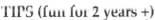

The Petticoat Creek wading pool is huge and nicely surrounded by green lawn and small trees! It took me over 350 full steps to circumnavigate the edge of this blue wading pool.

We found ourselves a spot in the shade of a coniferous tree and we watched our kids run wildly into the shallow water. Some lines drawn at the bottom of the pool mark the vast shallow area.

There's enough water to allow bigger kids to swim in the centre of the pool (where I had water below the shoulders).

Petticoat Creek is located on the shores of Lake Ontario. Outside the fenced pool area are picnic tables and a trail leading to the lakeshore below the bluffs. The view from above is great, however, don't go expecting a fabulous shoreline.

TIPS (fun for 2 years +)
• The pool's water isn't heated and remains quite cool in the deeper areas. The sun warms up the shallow section by the afternoon. If you think of bringing along some water toys, it will be heaven for the kids.
• There are no railings at the edge of the cliff facing Lake Ontario along the **Waterfront Trail**.
• There are changing rooms and a snack bar on the premises.
• There are similar football field sized pools in **Bronte Creek** (p. 308) and **Earl Rowe** (p. 313) **Provincial Parks**.
• I have not visited them but you'll find two more of these huge pools under the Grand River Authority, both including **campgrounds**. **Byng Island Conservation Area** is located near Dunnville. Its pool is deep enough in the middle for diving; (905) 774-5755. **Brant Conservation Area** is in Brantford; (519) 752-2040.

Petticoat Creek Conservation Area	C-4 East of Toronto 35-min.

· Pickering
(416) 661-6600, ext 5203
or (905) 509-1534 (weather)
www.trca.on.ca.

Schedule: Park is open from mid-May to Labour Day, 9 am to dusk. Pool opens early June to Labour Day, 10 am to 7 pm.
Admission: $5/adults, $4/seniors, FREE 15 years and under with their family; pool use is $3.50/visitors 5 years and over.
Directions: From Hwy 401 East, take exit #394/Whites Rd. southbound.

NEARBY ATTRACTIONS
Toronto Zoo (5-min.) .... p. 57
Rouge Park (5-min.) .... p. 326

THE WAVE POOL

Photo: Courtesy of The Wave Pool

Surf's up!

I had often heard of the Richmond Hill Wave Pool: a huge indoor pool with 4-foot-high waves. I was in no hurry to go there with my son. Every time I thought of it, I imagined a heavy swell filled with excited kids who would menace my little tadpole.

How far I was from the truth! Not only is this aquatic complex very secure and exciting for little ones, it's as much fun for older kids.

The spacious Wave Pool aquatic complex forms a harmonious whole,

bathed by natural light. Funny fish decorate the ceiling.

A few tables under umbrellas and lined with palm trees are aligned near the bay window. The centre supplies toys and life jackets.

With the irregular shape, the wave pool looks like a shallow bay you go into gradually, just like at the beach. Over a large 5,000 sq. ft. area, the water doesn't go higher than our knees. In this shallow section, the waves are calm, and have the perfect level of turbulence to entertain young children.

The big waves sweep across the rest of the pool. The 160-foot-long waterslide is reserved for users at least 48 inches high. What a surprise! Beside the wave pool is a superb whirlpool delighting young and old alike. It is 70 cms deep and it is kept at a temperature of 96 degrees F.

TIPS (fun for all ages)

• Services offered at the pool include a sauna, one changing room for families and lockers for 25¢ and $1.

• There's no snack bar. You can eat your own lunch upstairs in the gallery with tables and vending machines.

• There's another indoor wave pool in the **Mississauga Valley Community Centre** (1275 Mississauga Valley Blvd., 905-615-4670, **www.mississauga.ca**) in Terry Fox Aquatics. It features 2-ft. waves during the Fun Wave swims in the 25-metre pool. Along with toys and basketball nets, they have a tarzan rope!

NEARBY ATTRACTIONS
Putting Edge (5-min.) .... p. 47

The Wave Pool • Richmond Hill (905) 508-9283 http:// wave.sites.toronto.com	C-3 **North** **of Toronto** **40-min.**

Schedule: Wave Swim is open year-round Fridays, 4:30 to 7 pm, and on weekends, 1:30 to 4 pm and 4:30 to 7 pm. From July to Labour Day, it is also open Monday to Thursday, 1:30 to 4 pm. (extended hours during Christmas and March Break). Closed in September for maintenance. Better call to doublecheck.

Admission: $6.50/16-54 years, $4/3-15 years and seniors, FREE for children 2 years and under (price for one period, those who want to go swimming twice in the same day need to repay their admission fee).

Directions: 5 Hopkins St., Richmond Hill. From Yonge St., turn west on Major Mackenzie Dr., south on Arnold Cr., then east on Hopkins St.

KIDSTOWN WATER PLAYGROUND

A real bargain!

When you accompany young children, you can't expect much more for your money than what you get at Kidstown Water Playground in Scarborough.

With water spurting whales, a water slide that ends in a wading pool, a large pirate boat armed with water pistols and corridor of spraying rings to navigate, this waterpark will thrill children 8 years old and younger. The older ones will be excited too, if they don't have high expectations from previous visits to larger commercial waterparks.

The overall site covers approximately 2,000 sq. feet and is surrounded by a grassy area with benches and picnic tables. Beyond the fence, there is a colourful playground and a lovely grassy hill down which my little stuntman and his new pals happily rolled.

Kidstown is part of **L'Amoreaux Park** but privately managed. At the time of print, I could not reach anyone to find out if they have made any changes. I recommend you call closer to the summer months to see for yourself.

A 15-minute walk across McNicoll Avenue will bring you to the large pond of **L'Amoreaux Park** where I have frequently seen cranes. Nearby, a small forest and many trails prove nice for family exploration. Since my last visit, they've added one of those structures with a large bucket of water periodically spilling on happy kids' heads. The sand box was taken away and they have traded the spurting bicycles with rocking whales.

Kidstown Water Playground • Scarborough (416) 396-8325 (seasonal)	D-3 N-E of downtown 35-min.

Schedule: Open daily, usually from end of June to Labour Day, 10:30 am to 7:30 pm, weather permitting (might close earlier in August when colder). Call to confirm.

Admission: $1 per child.

Directions: 3159 Birchmount Rd., Scarborough. From Hwy 401 East, take exit # 379/Kennedy Rd. northbound. Turn west on Finch Ave. and north on Birchmount Rd.

TIPS (fun for 8 years & under)

• There are change rooms and the park is entirely framed by a fence. However, the entrance gate is always opened by incoming and outgoing visitors. It is therefore safer to keep a watchful eye on children.

• There is a food vendor on the site.

NEARBY ATTRACTIONS

CORONATION PARK

Water fun by the lake

The water sprays spurting out of the ground and out of posts planted in the pavement, wet the children playing on spring-mounted miniature horses and on the seesaw. Facing them, there's a pebble beach with Lake Ontario in the background, as far as the eye can see. No wonder a wise Mom had recommended this Oakville park to me!

I was seduced by the site's setup and by the choice of things to do. The spray pad was enclosed inside a fence, and surrounded by a lawn and beautiful, tall trees with peculiar knots.

The children spent as much time refreshing themselves under the water sprays as they did inventing games with the thousands of plump pebbles in the shade of wide trees.

The large toy truck we brought along worked well. A stone skipping contest kept us busy and I'm still congratulating myself for the pebble I threw that skipped five times.

A paved trail leads to the pebble beach and a very nice playground is located on the premises. It includes two stimulating structures, one of them wooden with a hanging bridge and a tunnel-shaped slide, and three small climbing walls, perfect for small kids.

Note that since my last visit (when these pictures were taken) the park was completely renovated. They still offer the same kind of activities, in a different layout. The splash pad offers a castle theme.

TIPS (fun for 2 years +)

• More about the **Oakville Waterfront Festival** in June on p. 29.

• A funny tradition in Coronation Park is the annual **New Year's Day Polar Bear Dip** involving over 400 dippers and some 5,000 spectators to raise money for World Vision. For details, see **www.polarbeardip.ca** or call 1-800-268-7243.

• Read about nearby **Fire Hall** restaurant under **Riverview Park** on p. 359.

Coronation Park	**D-2**
• Oakville	**West**
(905) 845-6601	**of Toronto**
www.oakville.ca	**30-min.**

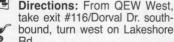

Schedule: Open year-round.
Admission: FREE.
Directions: From QEW West, take exit #116/Dorval Dr. southbound, turn west on Lakeshore Rd.

OTHER SPLASH PADS

**Bayview Village Park
(Bayview Subway Station)** p. 446

Sherwood, Park Ravine, p. 322

Toronto Islands (Centre Island) p. 398

Cobourg Beach, p. 415

Toronto Zoo, p. 57

Hendon Park (Finch Subway Station) p. 447

Woodbine Park, p. 285

ELORA GORGE C. A.

For your inner child

For years I have noticed people floating down the river on innertubes as I watched from the trail above at Elora Gorge. I always thought they were just random people, looking for adventure and braving the natural elements on their own. I was wrong... There is actually a whole crowd of them, seeking thrills, with the full consent of the conservation authority's administration.

Which explained the sign "Tubing Sold Out" at the gate when we got to Elora Gorge at 1 pm on a Saturday, planning to try out tubing ourselves. (As I found out later on, there was a way out of this disappointing situation.)

First, let's say that tubing down this river is not as adventurous as it seems from above. My 9-year-old thought the one-hour long descent did not offer enough action as real whirlpools formed only in three spots (maybe earlier in the season). Still, it beats floating down the lazy river in any waterpark.

Adults really enjoy the relaxing sight-seeing, offering a totally different view of the cliffs.

Children must be at least 42 inches tall and accompanied by a legal guardian who can sign a waiver in order to be allowed to ride. I have seen parents on their tube with a child on their lap.

The equipment consists of a helmet (hockey style), a vest and a tube. You can bring your own, but it can be rented at the

beach house. Unfortunately, the activity is quite popular on hot summer weekends when tubes can be sold out by 9 am!

We waited over an hour before some tubes became available. My patient husband spent the time in the line-up, a good book in one hand and a sandwich in the other, while we swam in the small lake by the beach house.

water is cold but the current is really slow at this point so it offers a great spot to swim for those who are just accompanying... Unless they want to rush back to the trail to take a picture when their friends' tubes pass under the bridge where the cliffs reach a height of 70 feet.

Once you have your equipment, you can catch the school bus serving as a shuttle from the beach house to the launching area. Instead, we chose to drive following the tubing signs along the park's road. We easily found a parking spot and the opening through the bush to the trail leading down the river (also indicated by a little sign). It was hilarious to follow the line of gigantic black tubes through the woods.

The section of the river where everyone gets in the water is simply gorgeous! High walls of rocks with splashes of greenery closely frame the river. The

TIPS (fun for 5 years +)
• BEWARE! During periods of high water flow, water tubing could be cancelled. Call for the "current" conditions.
• Some farms in the vicinity announce tubes for sale, knowing about the limited number of tubes for rent at the park. Tubes generally sell for $15, with $5 back if you return them. When we were visiting, the beach house allowed people to use their air pump to put air into their own tubes.
• The tubes are huge! Kids under 9 will hardly fit on top of them. We could only fit one in our trunk and I had to wear the other one around my waist inside our 4 X 4. Bring bungee cords to creatively tie them on to the roof.
• Wear shoes while tubing, to prevent your feet from scratching against the rocks. The segment of trail leading to the river is lined with slippery rocks. Flip-flops beware!
• Bring a waterproof camera for some amazing pictures as you go down.
• This conservation area includes 550 campsites, some nicely secluded.
• There's a snack bar at the beach house.

NEARBY ATTRACTIONS
Halton Museum (20-min.) .... p. 226

Elora Gorge Conservation Area	D-1
• Elora	West
(519) 846-9742	of Toronto
	65-min.

1-866-668-2267 (camp reservation)
www.grandriver.ca

Schedule: The park is open year-round. The registration shop is open weekends only in May, June and September and daily from last week of June to Labour Day, from 8 am to dusk. Shuttle service on weekends only during the summer.

Admission: $4/adults, $2.50/5-14 years, FREE 5 years and under. Tubing wristband is $2. Full equipment rental is $20 (or $13/tube, $8/helmet, $8/life jacket), plus deposit.

Directions: From Hwy 401 West, take exit #295/Hwy 6 northbound, then follow County Rd. 7 to Elora. Turn left at the first light on County Rd. 21. Elora Gorge is on the right.

ONTARIO PLACE

Photo: Courtesy of Ontario Place

Ride, which spans 873 feet (42"+), or the Pink Twister (48"+) and the Purple Pipeline waterslides (42"+), plunging them into the darkness with their enclosed flumes.

There is also the 50 kmph ride down a gigantic funnel in Hydrofuge (48"+), ending with a 12-foot drop into the water. I passed on that one!

Biggest spray pad!

It used to be impossible for an adult to stay dry while accompanying a child to the Waterplay section of Ontario Place. Grown-ups were the kids favourite targets to aim at with the fortress' water guns. These are gone, but you still can get really soaked... voluntarily.

Ontario Place has recently opted for a "zero depth" waterplay area. They've dried up the small basins but have added lots of spray.

I have not visited the revamped section but they say that it involves 100,000 litres of active water with geysers and spouts shooting water. They've also added one of those tipping buckets dumping a massive amount of water on anticipating visitors.

The site is well adapted for young children due to its shallow depth. It's also very entertaining for older kids, thanks to its numerous activities.

Older kids will go for more intense water games such as the Rush River Raft

TIPS (fun for 2 years +)

• More on **Ontario Place** on page 18.
• The zero depth waterplay area is included with the ground admission. You need a pass if you want to ride the slides.
• You can rent a locker for a loonie in the waterpark.
• Eating is forbidden in the waterplay area. Those exiting the area can get their hand stamped and return after eating. The snack bar by the lake offers a few tables with a view under the shade of umbrellas.

Ontario Place
(416) 314-9900
www.ontarioplace.com

D-3
Downtown
Toronto
10-min.

Consult **Ontario Place** information box on p. 18 for schedule, costs, directions and nearby attractions.

WILD WATER KINGDOM

Wild indeed!

Waist-deep in water, hordes of swimmers dance away with the encouragement of the weekend DJ and his music. My 6-year-old couldn't resist the invitation and jumps in (chest-deep), dancing the Macarena with his friends. There's no lack of ambience at the Carribbean Cove Pool.

Wild Water Kingdom, Canada's largest waterpark, may actually include less slides than the water games section of Canada's Wonderland, but it is still almost half the price. If you plan to play in the water all day, this is certainly your best bet, especially with children 48" and over!

Thirteen body and tube slides, two

7-storey speed slides along with a wave pool, a lazy river and the entertaining pool, are enough to satisfy the legions of teenagers invading the site daily.

All slides have a 48" minimum height requirement, except the Cork Screw, Side Winder and Little Twister, which are accessible to children from 42" in height. Younger children will thoroughly enjoy the large Dolphin Bay water playground. It offers beach-like access, small water slides passing through a mushroom, a fish and a frog, a splashing structure with sprays and a tube slide plus wading spots link it all. Then there's the Big Tipper with large buckets emptying tons of water over the willing visitors.

Next to the waterpark are a mini-golf course and batting cages, with a rock climbing wall under a waterfall that used to be pay-as-you-play but are now included in the admission price. Even better!

TIPS (fun for 2 years +)
• Managed by Toronto Region Conservation Authority, **Indian Line Campground** offers 240 sites and is located along the Claireville Reservoir, right next to the waterpark. Call 1-800-304-9728 or check **www.trca.on.ca**.
• No coolers are allowed on the site (exception is made for parents with babies). We had to take our cooler back to our car. You will find on-site lockers, many food stands, snack bars and a shop.

NEARBY ATTRACTIONS
Swaminarayan Mandir (5-min.) .... p. 101
Pearson Airport (10-min.) .... p. 206

Wild Water Kingdom
• Brampton
(416) 369-9453
www.wildwaterkingdom.com

D-2
N-W
of Toronto
40-min.

Schedule: Open first weekend in June, then daily from end of June to Labour Day, from 10 am to 6 pm (closes at 7 pm from end of June to Labour Day). Call to confirm dates.

Admission: (tax not included) Around $30/10 years and up, $22/seniors and children 4-9 years, FREE 3 years and under, $18/after 4 pm, Parking is around $6.

Directions: 7855 Finch Ave., Brampton. Take Hwy 427 North, turn west on Finch Ave., follow the signs.

WILD WATERWORKS

Go out with a splash!

You can observe children in almost all directions from the ground by the wave pool which sits in the heart of the action.

From the bounty of water activities offered and the new huge slides accessible to children of all ages, to the immense wave pool, you will find Wild Waterworks leaves nothing to be desired.

The Eazy River (a sinuous water path on which you can flow down atop an inner tube), is the only one I know of that comes equipped with side showers, fountains and nooks and crannies. My son and his father chose a double ring to float on and bump me!

Little Squirt Works, the large wading pool for young bathers is quite fun with its unusual shape framed by stairs. The water doesn't go higher than the knees. It is full of small fountains that squirt intermittently and little roofs streaming with water.

The Corkscrew and Kamikaze body slides are some six storeys high, much to the delight of swimmers (min. 42" tall). I tried them both and found them surprisingly smooth, a little like a gentle toboggan ride. The giant tubeslides Night Rider and Blue Demon offer a 480-foot-long drop, solo or with a friend (minimum height requirement of 47").

Good news, they are adding two new tube slides for summer 2008!

TIPS (fun for 2 years +)

• We visited on a warm but cloudy Saturday afternoon and found the place enjoyably quiet. We never waited more than 5 minutes for a ride on the slides.
• There's one colourful playground within **Confederation Park**.
• There are two snack bars on site.
• A few minutes from the waterpark, North Service Road becomes Van Wagner's Beach Road along the waterfront. At 280 Van Wagner's Beach Rd., there's **Hutch's**, a greasy-spoon restaurant from the 50's with large booths by the bay windows, jukebox, great fries, burgers, shakes, etc. (**www.hutchsonthebeach. com**). You must check **Baranga's on the Beach** at 380 Van Wagner's Beach Rd. It offers the best waterfront patio around Toronto and a wide choice on their menu (**www.barangas.com**). See photos on p. 409.
• There is a campground in **Confederation Park** (905-547-6141, ext. 5201 or **campconf@conservationhamilton.ca**).

NEARBY ATTRACTIONS

Wild Waterworks	E-2
• Hamilton	S-W
1-800-555-8775	of Toronto
or (905) 561-2292	50-min.

www.conservationhamilton.ca

Schedule: Open daily from early June to Labour Day. Check website for June schedule. From July to mid-August, 10 am to 8 pm. Mid-August to Labour Day (weather permitting), 10 am to 6 pm (earlier on final days).

Admission: Around $16/adults, $11/ seniors and 4-10 years, FREE 3 years and under, $9/visitor after 4 pm. Vehicle entrance to Confederation Park is $8. (extra fee to rent tube for wave pool).

Directions : From QEW West, take exit #88/Centennial Pkwy.-Hwy 20. Turn north towards the Lake, follow signs to Confederation Park.

CANADA'S WONDERLAND

Splash!

It was not with a light heart that I watched my assertive little boy drag his huge tire for the first time, way up to the launching board of the Whirl Winds. He was so thrilled with his ride that he could not wait to get back in line to do it again! If your child is tall enough and already shows some daredevil inclinations at the local pool, you might want to let her try it too.

Splash Works includes 16 water slides, some of which are 8 storeys tall. They all require a minimum height of 48", except for the Whirl Winds in which adventurers measuring 40-48" can go if they're wearing a life jacket. The Barracuda Blaster ends up with a twist around the vertical walls of a giant bowl before being flushed into the Lazy River.

All the kids like the Pumphouse located at the heart of Splash Works. It features a large coloured structure full of surprising water sprays. It is topped by

a gigantic pail that gradually fills with 1,000 litres of water. Every five minutes, the pail's contents flow forcefully on the heads of delighted children.

The waterpark also boasts a wide and long Lazy River (40"+) on which an adult and child can float on the same tube and a large wave pool equipped with lounge chairs.

For the little ones, there's Splash Island Waterways, an entertaining wading pool and mini water slides.

TIPS (fun for 2 years +)
• More on **Canada's Wonderland** on page 18.
• Kids under 48" tall must now wear a life jacket while swimming in the White Water Bay, the Splash Island Pool Area and the Lazy River. Children's life jackets are available for free. Lockers, beach shop and snack bar are found within the waterpark as well.

Canada's Wonderland	C-3 North of Toronto 40-min.
• Vaughan (905) 832-7000 www.canadaswonderland.com	

Consult **Canada's Wonderland** information box on p.18 for schedule, costs, directions and nearby attractions. Splash Works is open on weekends from mid-May to mid-June, 11 am to 6 pm; then daily until Labour Day, 11 am to 8 pm (closes at 7 pm after mid-August).

FALLSVIEW WATERPARK

Action!

As soon as they smell a hint of chlorine, my four companions run wildly through the glassed sky-pass and instantly split into two age-related teams. It will take me 20 minutes to find them in order to put their wristbands on.

The place is quite a sight! Tropical climate, palm trees, blue dome simulating the sky and, down below, tons of kids screaming with delight.

This impressive waterpark includes 16 slides, some 6 storeys high, some fit for the younger crowd hanging around the Beach House section with the 1,000 gallon tipping bucket.

After a few hours of action, the gang is ready for lunch at the **Planet Hollywood** snack bar by the pool. As we eat, the friends are retelling their best exploits. The yellow slide is unanimously declared the scariest. I wouldn't know. Didn't get near the things!

After the meal, they launch into a hide-and-seek game. Not a bad place for such a game!

Later in the day, we took our ice cream to the mezzanine to lay on the lounge chairs while taking in the overall view of the waterpark. We were also able to admire the falls from the large bay windows in the south-west corner. A must!

The waterpark comes with an out-door heated all-season pool with basketball nets of varying heights.

We stayed at the **Skyline Inn**, the one with the elevated walkway offering a more dramatic access to the waterpark. Its rooms all open into pretty indoor courtyards where kids can run free.

Brock Plaza Hotel and **Sheraton on the Falls**, two other hotels offering the package, are fancier and include indoor swimming pools. Both have indoor access to the waterpark.

TIPS (fun for 2 years +)

- More about **Niagara Falls** on p. 269.
- The waterpark was created as an incentive to stay at one of the Fallsview hotels. It would cost you $45 to spend the day at the waterpark. A hotel package for a family of four will roughly cost you as much as four waterpark admissions. Might as well stay!
- You may enter anytime on the day your waterpark package begins, until 3 pm the day it ends. We checked out early, left our luggage in the car and stayed at the waterpark to the last minute. Then, we drove straight to **Marineland**, which closed at 8 pm.
- Rental lockers are available. Towels are provided at the waterpark.
- There's a **Planet Hollywood** snack bar by the pool, but you might want to snack on slushies and ice cream and wait for dinner time to eat at the big **Planet Hollywood** for the full experience.
- Breakfast was not included in our package. Kids were happy with nearby affordable all-you-can-eat **Tony's Place** (5467 Victoria Avenue, 5-min. walk north on Bender Street, then east on Victoria).
- There are two other waterpark-hotel combos offered in Niagara Falls. Gorgeous 100,000 sq. foot **Great Wolf Lodge** offers 13 slides, 4 pools and a 4-storey-high tree-house fort (4 km north of the Falls, **www.greatwolf.com**). **Americana** is four times smaller and on the US side (5 kms from the Falls, **www.americananiagara.com**). Wondering how the **Fallsview** packages compare? In December 2007, when I checked the rates for the cheapest package including one night stay for a family of four with waterpark passes, it was: $119/**Americana**, $139/**Skyline Inn**, $149 **Hampton Inn**, $159/**Brock Plaza**, $189/**Sheraton by the Falls** and $199/ **Great Wolf Lodge**.

NEARBY ATTRACTIONS

Fallsview Waterpark | E-4 Niagara Region 90-min.
- Niagara Falls
1-888-234-8408
www.fallsviewwaterpark.com

Schedule: Open year-round, from 10 am to 8 pm minimum.
Admission: Including one hotel night and 4 passes for a family of 4: Between $160 and $200 depending on the hotel. Additional fee for extra child is $20, extra adult is $40. Parking is $6/day.
Directions: Falls Ave., Niagara Falls. The complex is located between Victoria and Falls Avenues, east of Clifton Hill.

CEDAR PARK RESORT

Refreshing combo

Being the only place with water games in the Bowmanville area, Cedar Park is a great complement to a visit to one of the local attractions, for a full-day outing in the region.

There are three giant water slides (48"+), a good playground on a large patch of sand, a pretty wading pool with small water slides, a huge pool and even a minigolf.

The waterpark is attached to a trailer park.

NEARBY ATTRACTIONS
Bowmanville Zoo (10-min.) .... p. 63
Jungle Cat World (15-min.) .... p. 64

Cedar Park Resort · Hampton (905) 263-8109	C-4 East of Toronto 60-min.

  Schedule: Open 7 days, mid-June to Labour Day, 10 am to 7 pm.
Admission: (cash only) Ground admission and pool access is $5.50/adults, $4/3-12 years, FREE 2 and under. Minigolf is an extra $4, water slides are an extra $6.50 per visitor.
Directions: 6296 Cedar Park Rd., Bowmanville. From Hwy 401 East, take exit #431/Regional Rd. 57 northbound. Turn east on 6th Concession, then north on Cedar Park Rd.

WILD WATER & WHEELS

Curious?

Water is for the 210-foot-long double spiral flume (42" min.) and the bumper boat ride (48"). Wheels is for the go-kart circuit.

When we visited, there was also a merry-go-round, a giant carpet slide, 145 feet long and 35 feet high, with five huge bumps, which was equally fun for the whole family, batting cages and a mini-

golf. The real surprise was the Pipeline Express Coaster! It is a metal toboggan rolling on tracks on a structure five storeys high and 850 feet long. The view from the top is amazing... and the drop at the beginning of the ride is breathtaking!

NEARBY ATTRACTIONS
Riverview Park & Zoo (15-min.) .... p. 77

Wild Water & Wheels · Peterborough (705) 876-9292 (seasonal)	B-5 N-E of Toronto 2 hrs

 Schedule: Open early April until last Sunday in September, 10 am to 9 pm (end of June to Labour Day) and at least from 12 noon to 6 pm before and after that. Call to confirm.
Admission: Approximately $6 for each ride and $15 for the water slides.
Directions: 1650 Chemong Rd., Peterborough. From Hwy 401 East, take exit #436 (Hwy 35/115) northbound. Follow Hwy 115 to Hwy 28 northbound. At Fowlers Corners, turn eastbound (right), then right again on Chemong.

WHAT'S AROUND THE
SUBWAY STATIONS

Carless Outings!

In this chapter, you'll find the description of anything interesting (for an adult with kids) within a 10-minute walk of every TTC Subway Station!

General tips about subways:

- To estimate the duration of a ride, count two minutes per stop.
- Not all stations have elevators and the escalators are often one way only. Expect to carry your stroller. Dare to ask for help. You'll be surprised!
- Not all entrances to one station are staffed. You might need the exact change.
- There could be 0.2 km between two exits from one station. Read the exit signs carefully to exit to the street closest to your destination.
- Streetcars and buses don't sell the TTC day pass. It's sold at the stations.

(1) Kipling

(2) Islington

(3) Islington

(4) Islington

(5) Islington

GREEN LINE (BLOOR-DANFORTH)

KIPLING

Go up Aukland Rd. to reach Dundas West, past the high-rise buildings surrounding this station. You'll find many restaurants at this intersection.

You'll just need to walk a few minutes westbound on Dundas Street West to get to a **Bowlerama** (1) (5429 Dundas, www.bowlerama.com) and **The Daily Planet**, a greasy spoon next door (416-231-3411). Across the street, visit **Wild Birds Unlimited** offering the biggest selection of bird feeders (5468 Dundas, www.wbu.com/toronto).

Check **McCall's**, biggest cake supply store ever, less than 10 minutes from Aukland (3810 Bloor St. W., walk east on Dundas to Kipling, go north to Bloor (www.mccalls-cakes.com).

ISLINGTON

The **Clarica Shopping Centre** at this station offers a fancy food court.

Go west on Bloor, past the intriguing underpass (2) and take the stairs up to the new playground and impressive gazebo of **Michael Power Place** (3).

Go east of Islington and you'll find the Bloor entrance to gorgeous **Thomas Riley Park** (4) with playground and a river (see p. 324).

Walk north through the park for 15 minutes to reach the exit off Islington. Northbound is Dundas West. If you want to walk a few extra minutes east on Dundas, you'll reach **Montgomery Inn** (see p. 384); west on Dundas, you'll find the pretty indoor playground **Bona Party Place** (4945 Dundas East, www.bonapartyplace.com).

On the 10-minute walk southbound, back to the station from the park, check out the white horse sculpture (5) on Cordova Avenue east of Islington.

ROYAL YORK

This is a pretty stretch of Bloor. The station in front of a big **Swiss Chalet**. Go west on Bloor and north to 8 Brentwood to reach **All Fired Up** (6) ceramic studio (www.afu-ceramics.com, 416-233-5512). East on Bloor, there's **Mary's Playland** (see p. 193).

OLD MILL

Take Old Mill Trail north and turn east on Old Mill Rd. to reach (what else?) **Old Mill Inn**, a fabulous place for brunch buffets (www.oldmilltoronto.ca).

Across the bridge is the entrance to **Étienne Brûlé Park** (7) with paved trail along the **Humber River** (see p. 328).

JANE

Nothing special for kids.

RUNNYMEDE

The Bloor section east and west of this station is pretty. It includes the lovely **Runnymede Public Library** (see p. 90) and **Melonhead** kids' haircuts place (2100 Bloor, www.melonhead.ca).

HIGH PARK

Across the street is the Bloor entrance to **High Park** (see p. 286), leading to the smaller playground and wading pool.

KEELE

This station is a brisk 15-minute walk from **High Park**'s amazing castle playground (off Parkdale, south of Bloor) but it is really worth walking the extra distance!

Lithuania Park offers a pretty playground and wading pool, north on Keele.

DUNDAS WEST

With little adventurers, try the pathway going over the train tracks (8) on the east side of Dundas, a few minutes north of the station. Check the giant boxing gloves south-west of Bloor and Dundas.

LANSDOWNE

Nothing special for kids.

DUFFERIN

A few minutes south of Bloor on Dufferin, you'll find Toronto's biggest sandpit in the playground of groovy **Dufferin Grove Park** (9) (see p. 288). It is located across from **Dufferin Mall** (including **Toys "R" Us**, **Winners** and **Wal-Mart** under the same roof).

OSSINGTON

Offers a mix of multicultural businesses of no interest for kids.

CHRISTIE

Christie Park across from the station offers a great outdoor pool with twisting slide (10) in addition to a good playground with wading pool and more.

A few minutes south of Bloor on Christie, you'll reach funky **Linux Café** (11) serving yummy food (including individual French toast and hot chocolate (very handy if you come during the winter to go tobogganing down **Bickford Park**'s good slopes across from the café).

The park includes a nice playground, south of Harbord Street.

Bloor, east of Christie up to Bathurst, is **Koreatown** (12) with Korean signs and Korean food. Perfect time to try a bubble tea.

(6) Royal York

(7) Old Mill

(8) Dundas West

(9) Dufferin

(10) Christie

(11) Christie

(12) Christie or Bathurst

(13) Bathurst

(14) Bathurst

(15) Bathurst

(16) Spadina or Bathurst

(17) Spadina

BATHURST

You can't miss Toronto's landmark **Honest Eds** (13) near the station. This huge store, filled with funny old signs to read, sold cheap stuff way before the dollar stores started popping up.

Mirvish Village (14), on Markham Street just west of the store, is worth the visit. The street is bursting with affordable restaurants and colourful shops selling comic books, vintage videos, clothes, cinema books, art books, beads and rocks. See www.mirvishvillagebia.com for information on all the stores in the area.

At the corner of **Mirvish Village** and Bloor, the restaurant **Rocco's Plum Tomato** (15) offers wild decor with plenty of details to observe and tons of items on the menu (585 Bloor, 416-539-9009).

On the west side of Bathurst, south of Bloor, the old-fashioned **Kidstuff Toy Store** (738 Bathurst, 416-535-2212) sits next to **Yesterday's Heroes**, selling comic books (416-539-9009).

Just south of these, the **Bathurst Street Theatre** often presents affordable musicals (go to www.ticketmaster.ca, and enter the name of the theatre to find out the current production).

The excellent **Parentbooks** specializing in books relevant to parents is located two blocks south, on Harbord St. east of Bathurst, (201 Harbord, www.parentbooks.ca).

East of Bathurst, you will find the **Bloor** repertoire cinema (506 Bloor, www.bloorcinema.com) and many second-hand stores for DVDs, CDs or books.

SPADINA
(interchange to YELLOW)

Beware! This one can be confusing. There are actually two physical Spadina Stations. The attractions I'm listing are accessible from the Spadina Station on the GREEN Line along Bloor. There used to be an indoor moving walkway linking it to the Spadina Station on the YELLOW Line a few blocks north along Spadina. It was removed but the corridor is still there. It is less trouble to change lines at St. George Station.

The really cool neighbourhood of **The Annex** (16) runs between Bathurst and Spadina.

On the south-west corner of Bloor and Spadina is the **Miles Nadal Jewish Community Centre** where you can buy a day pass to access their Fitness Centre and salt water public pool (www.milesnadaljcc.ca).

West of Spadina along Bloor Street is a charming cluster of restaurants, food stores and shops of all kinds, bursting with the energy of university students. One of the favourites is the large **Future Bakery** (17) with vast patio, serving copious all-day breakfast, cakes and pastries (483 Bloor, 416-922-5875). It is located across from colourful **Tutti Fruitti** candy store. I also love to grab yummy bread and pastries at one of the few **COBS Bread** outlets in Ontario (370 Bloor, www.cobsbread.ca).

Check out the small gift shop **Outer Layers** for cool gadgets (430 Bloor, www.outerlayer.com).

Almost every month, the Baroque **Tafelmusik** (www.tafelmusik.org) is performing at **Trinity-St. Paul's** (427 Bloor).

ST. GEORGE
(interchange to YELLOW)

Cross to the south side of Bloor and you're at the great **Bata Shoe Museum** (18) (see p. 243).

BAY

There's an exit right next to **Cumberland** cinema (19), in the heart of trendy Yorkville (see www.cinema-clock.com for listings).

Yorkville Park (20) offers a patchwork of small gardens along Cumberland Street, starting with a 650-ton mound of granite any child will want to conquer.

There are no less than four toy stores on Cumberland. **Retro Fun** (21) is filled with gadgets from television series and movies (130 Cumberland, www.retrofun.ca).

Kidding Awound (22) is my favourite. Small, yet it was packed with enough gift ideas to cover my whole Christmas shopping list (91 Cumberland, www.kiddingawound.com).

To access the fancy shopping centre **Hazelton Lanes**, go to Yorkville Avenue, one street north of Cumberland (use the alleyway across from Cumberland Cinema) then go up Hazelton Avenue (23). This art gallery district is lined with sculptures that should interest kids. The centre has no interest for them but I noticed **Teatro Verde**, the great gift store by the entrance.

The old **Yorkville Fire Station 312** (24) is adjacent to the **Yorkville Public Library** (34 Yorkville Avenue, see p. 213 about fire stations).

There's a **Winners** nearby, on Bloor Street, next to a big **Starbucks**. The **ROM** (see p. 244) and the **Gardiner Museum** (see p. 88) are only five minutes away.

Varsity Cineplex is just south of Bloor on Bay (www.cinemaclock.com). It sits next to an **Indigo** bookstore where my family always likes to browse before attending a movie.

(18) St. George

(19) Bay

(21) Bay

(20) Bay

(22) Bay

(23) Bay

(24) Bay

(25) Sherbourne

(26) Sherbourne

(27) Sherbourne

(28) Sherbourne

(29) Sherbourne

BLOOR/YONGE
(interchange to YELLOW)
From Yonge to Avenue Road along Bloor are many expensive stores mixed with big name chains. Going south on Yonge leads to a series of fast food restaurants and shops of no special interest to kids.

You can access **Varsity Cineplex** (www.cinema-clock.com) by going west on Bloor, then south on Balmuto to the Manulife Centre. Don't miss the **Felix and Norton** scrumptious cookies on the way, just east of Yonge (15 Bloor E., www.felixandnorton.com).

SHERBOURNE
There's lots of surprises around this one, starting with the passageway lined with murals (25) going under Bloor (exit at Glen Road to see it).

The tunnel leads to a bridge running over Rosedale Valley Road and the impressive houses of Rosedale neighbourhood.

At the time of print, many of the once charming houses on Glen were abandoned.

Turn west on Howard St. and you'll see **St. James Town West Park** (26) including an unexpected playground.

Walk southbound on Sherbourne for another intriguing sight: the **Shrine of Our Lady of Lourdes Church** (27) with its bronze statue of Mary's apparition to a girl. So many people have touched this statue, it is shinier on certain spots. Enter into the church; it is gorgeous and bigger than it looks from outside.

Back on the north side of Bloor, go west, past Mt. Pleasant Rd. and down the stairs leading to Rosedale Valley Road (28), for a different perspective of the area!

West of Jarvis is the recently renovated **St. Paul's Church** (29), where the old and the new were beautifully integrated. (Don't miss the vintage stained-glass windows in the washrooms!)

Across the street is the whimsical sculpture *Community* (29) featuring twenty people of different ages in action. In the background, on the grounds of **Manulife Towers**, is a cute paved trail leading to St. Paul's Square.

Finish the tour by going underneath the monoliths (30) at the northeast corner of Bloor and Church.

CASTLE FRANK
Kids won't appreciate the amazing houses north of the station but you will! Go up Castle Frank Rd. to reach the discrete entrance of **Graigleigh Gardens** (31).

The main interest of this vast park is that an opening in the middle of its northern side will give you access to the **Milkman Lane** (32) going down into the majestic ravine. It's the best outing for young explorers but not for strollers!

At the fork of the trails, one can follow the signs for **Moore Park** (see p. 320) passing by the **Don Valley Brickworks Park** (see p. 302) or **David A. Balfour Park** (see p. 319), both roughly 2 km away.

BROADVIEW
It is quite impressive to walk over the Don Valley Parkway (33) on the Prince Edward Viaduct. The panorama is spectacular and below are the speeding cars and the lazy river. You'll find a telescope aiming at the **CN Tower**, halfway along the viaduct, which you can use for free.

South of Danforth off Montcrest Blvd. is outdoor **Riverdale Pool** with twisting slide (34). **Riverdale Park** includes a playground and the best panorama of Toronto (especially at sunset) from the top of its hill. It is also a most ambitious tobogganing slope (see p. 367).

A few blocks east on Danforth is the **Music Hall** venue (147 Danforth, www.themusichall.ca) where you may sometimes catch a family show.

Another important address for parents is the **Children's After Hours Clinic**, east of the **Music Hall**. It is one of the few drop-in clinics especially for children (235 Danforth, 416-461-3000).

CHESTER

You are in the middle of posh Riverdale. Turn west to access **The Big Carrot**, the large natural food market (358 Danforth, www.thebigcarrot.ca).

From Chester to Pape, Danforth is filled with restaurants and good shops, with a focus on home decor stores, shoes and greek food.

A favourite with kids is the colourful candy store **Sucker's** (35) (450 Danforth) and **It's My Party**, across the street, next to **Wimpy's Diner**, straight from the 50's (443 Danforth).

PAPE

Try a bag of delicious honey balls at **Athens Pastry** (509 Danforth), then go west on Danforth to reach Logan, for a real feel of **Greektown** (36).

On the way, check **Treasure Island Toy Store** (581 Danforth).

South on Logan, there are two great playgrounds and one large wading pool in the beautiful **Withrow Park**.

(30) Sherbourne or Yonge/Bloor

(31) Castle Frank

(32) Castle Frank

(33) Broadview

(35) Chester or Pape

(34) Broadview

(36) Pape

(37) Greenwood

(38) Greenwood

(39) Greenwood

(40) Woodbine

(41) Victoria Park

DONLANDS

There are no attractions around this station, but west of Donlands Avenue I noticed the **Candy Depot** (907 Danforth, 416-462-2633, and an off the beaten track funky café cleverly named **The Only Café** (972 Danforth, www.theonly-cafe.com).

GREENWOOD

Monarch Park is a real treat awaiting you near this station if you walk south on Greenwood or Lamb until you reach Felstead.

This luscious park is far from the flat grassy patch we often see in small parks. It goes up and down and is filled with mature trees.

Its playground (37) is great but the park's best feature is the outdoor pool with a twisting slide (38).

As a bonus for little adventurers, you'll find a tunnel (39) at the south-east end of the park. This is a very good opportunity to test for echo.

If you walk down Woodfield to Walpole on the other side of this short tunnel, you'll find a variety store in the middle of the residential area, the perfect place to buy some drinks and snacks before heading back for more water fun.

COXWELL

The indoor playground **It's Playtime** is located on the south side of Danforth, east of Monarch Park Avenue (1425 Danforth, see p. 191).

WOODBINE

West of Woodbine is a great art supply store part of the chain **DeSerres** (2056 Danforth, www.deserres.ca). Browsing through their online catalogue will show you what's in the store.

Further west, on the south side of Danforth, lies **East Lynn Park** with a wading pool down the slope and gorgeous little playground **Rusty's Reach** (40).

For the amateurs of miniature trains (die-cast or in wood) and other kinds of models, there's the great **John's Hobbies** east of Woodbine (2188 Danforth, www.johnshobbies.ca).

I have noticed many thrift shops between Woodbine and Main.

MAIN STREET

The Danforth section east of Main contains mainly bargain furniture stores of no real interest for kids.

VICTORIA PARK

Wow! Minigolfs are a rarity in Toronto but you'll find a very pretty one in the **Beach Fairway Golf Range** (41) (see p. 44).

It sits on the east side of Victoria Park, just north of a McDonald's, like a little green oasis.

WARDEN

I certainly didn't expect to find a river amidst the concrete high-rises and six-lane wide avenues Warden and St. Clair! But there it is, at the bottom of the ravine in **Warden Woods Park** (42) (see p. 325).

The setting is simply beautiful. It will take you 20 minutes to reach the other end of the park.

Watch carefully on the eastern side of the trail. You'll eventually notice wooden stairs buried in the soil and laced with roots. Take a hike up those stairs for a bit of adventure. You'll discover benches with a view (43) and a cute playground by the forest, further up the ravine.

KENNEDY
(interchange to BLUE)
See p. 445.

(12) Warden

(43) Warden

(44) Kennedy

(45) Scarborough

BLUE LINE
(SCARBOROUGH RT)

KENNEDY
(interchange to YELLOW)
The only thing worth mentioning is the superb mural (44) on the exterior wall of the exit closest to Eglinton. Impressive!

LAWRENCE EAST
Between Lawrence and Ellesmere, Kennedy is lined with large stores selling furniture, appliances, etc. Useful to know.

ELLESMERE
West Birkdale Park offers a playground down Great West Dr.

MIDLAND
This station is lost amidst an industrial district but it is next to **Hamilton's Theatrical Supply**, a huge costume rental store catering to adults but also selling accessories, make-up and a small selection of costumes for kids (2065 Midland, www.hamiltonstheatrical. com).

SCARBOROUGH
This station serves **Scarborough Town Centre** (www. scarboroughtowncentre. com). The mall includes a **Famous Players Coliseum** (www.cinemaclock.com).
This mall offers a special feature: **Kornelia's Korner**, an indoor playground offering drop-in and drop-off service with qualified staff. It is located in section R near The Bay (416-296-0901).
Don't miss the colourful air balloons in front of The Bay (45).

McCOWAN
This station is actually really close to the previous station. There's nothing special for kids around.

(46) Leslie

(47) Leslie

(50) Bayview

(48) Bayview

(49) Bayview

(51) Finch

(52) North York

PURPLE LINE
(SHEPPARD)

DON MILLS
When I visited **Fairview Mall** served by this station, it was under major tasteful renovations (www.fairviewmall.ca). A lovely reflecting pool was built by The Bay and the Food Garden was already elegant and different from standard food courts. By Fall 2008, the mall will include a **SilverCity Theatre** (www.cinemaclock.com) near the Shoppers Drug Mart.

Fairview Library Theatre, north of the mall, hosts a theatre company which produces affordable plays and musicals (www.stage-centreproductions.com).

LESLIE
If you miss the shuttle, **Ikea** is only a 10-minute walk away. Go west on Sheppard and down Provost and check the murals (46) on the way! For young scouters, there's **East Don Park** (47), on the north-west corner of Sheppard and Leslie (boots recommended to explore the **Don River**'s banks).

BESSARION
Nothing special for kids.

BAYVIEW
This is at the door of posh **Bayview Village** centre (www.bayviewvillage-shops.com) with great stores and restaurants, and a **Chapters**.

Go north on Bayview to reach superb **Bayview Village Park** featuring a playground (48) with spray pads and paved paths (49) where you'll notice a huge tree that must have hosted many little monkeys (50).

SHEPPARD/YONGE
(interchange to YELLOW)
See p. 447.

YELLOW LINE
(YONGE-UNIVERSITY-SPADINA)

(53) North York

FINCH

Less than 10 minutes north of the station, you'll find action at the **Bowlerama** (5837 Yonge, www.bowlerama.com) in the Newtonbrook Plaza (also home to a **Scholar's Choice** store (www.scholarschoice.ca).

Closer to the station is the prettiest spray pad in **Hendon Park** (51), off Hendon, west of Yonge. Beware, you'll first have to go through an ugly non-residential section to deserve it!

NORTH YORK

This station offers quite the jackpot. It opens into **Mel Lastman Square** (52), impressive with its majestic public library, fountains and outdoor stage. The great **Douglas Snow Aquatic Centre** (53) with twisting slide is located west of it (see p. 422), not too far from the **Toronto Centre for the Arts** venue (www.tocentre.com).

Across from the square is the futuristic cinema **Empire Empress Walk 10** (54) (5095 Yonge, www.cinemaclock.com).

Those who sew or do crafts will appreciate knowing there's a **Fabricland** adjacent to the cinema (www.fabricland.ca).

North of the station, you'll find the pretty **North York Rose Garden** leading to the **Gibson House** (see p. 381) and the **Gibson Park**, featuring the sculpture of a horse at its west end.

SHEPPARD/YONGE
(interchange to PURPLE)

North of Sheppard, Yonge offers plenty of little restaurants (55) to chose from before or after you've gone to Cineplex **Sheppard Cen-** tre Grande (4861 Yonge, www.cinemaclock.com) to see a movie.

If you want to show a crazy building to your kids, go to the **Claude Watson School for the Arts** (130 Doris Avenue) by walking northbound on Yonge, then turn east on Hollywood Avenue, then south on Doris. You can't miss the giant honeycombs plastered on the building on the west side of Doris Avenue.

(54) North York

As a bonus, **Willowdale Park**'s nice playground (56) awaits on the east side of the street.

The small theatre for younger kids **Solar Stage** is located in the **Madison Centre**, on the west side of Yonge a few blocks north of Sheppard (4950 Yonge, www.solarstage.on.ca, see p. 109).

YORK MILLS

First explore the graffiti adorning the wall of the pathway running under Yonge, using the outdoor stairs adjacent to the station. Then, walk down the paved trail in the park just east of the station. It reaches Mill Street.

(55) Sheppard/Yonge

I suggest you turn west on Mill to access the southern part of **York Mills Valley Park** (see p. 290). This way, you'll get the best view of the most lovely path along the river (57) and you'll reach the playground.

Further, you'll see the little bridge on Donino Avenue. Near that bridge, you'll be able to get closer to the stream but make sure you don't let the kids go right under the bridge, where the water falls into a lower stream.

(56) Sheppard/Yonge

(57) York Mills

(58) Lawrence

(59) Lawrence

(60) Lawrence

(61) Eglinton

(62) Eglinton

LAWRENCE

North of Lawrence, along Yonge and up to Melrose Avenue, is a roster of restaurants and shops, many of them catering to parents: different children clothing stores, children shoe store and hairdresser.

My favourite destination is colourful **Mastermind Toys** (58), a 10-minute walk from the station (3350 Yonge, www.mastermindtoys.com).

South of it is the indoor playground **Just Ducky Yonge Kids**, catering to the 0-5 year-old (3300 Yonge, www.justduckyyongekids.com).

Nearby is a **PJ's Pets** with small animals (3291 Yonge, www.pjspet.com).

Just north of the station, on Yonge's west side, a **Golden Griddle** caught my attention, located at the end of a pretty courtyard (3080 Yonge, 647-436-2047).

On the east side of Yonge is **Fire Station 131** (3135 Yonge, see p. 213).

Next to the public library on the east side of Yonge is a lovely playground down the hill of **Lawrence Park Ravine** (59). It continues south of Lympstone, offering a great slope for tobogganing (60).

Further south, past St. Edmund Drive, there's more: **Alexander Muir Memorial Garden**, itself leading to **Blythwood Ravine Park** (toward Mt. Pleasant Rd.) and, eventually, **Sherwood Park** (see p. 322).

Across from the garden is the entrance to **Duplex Parquette**, which will take you to **Chatsworth Ravine** (see p. 321). These are not stroller accessible.

EGLINTON

A few minutes west of Yonge on Eglinton is the great art supplier **DeSerres** (124 Eglinton W., www.deserres.ca). A bit farther is the superb **North Toronto Memorial Community Centre** (61) with indoor and outdoor pools including big slides (200 Eglinton W., 416-392-6590).

If you follow the trail in the back of the centre, you'll reach **Tommy Flynn Playground** (62).

Cineplex **Silvercity Yonge & Eglinton** is just north of the station, near the **Indigo**. It is fun to combine with dinner at the renovated **Pickle Barrel** (www.picklebarrel.ca) also in the **Yonge-Eglinton Centre**, along with **Toys R Us**. Another great combo is to eat at the **Mandarin** buffet (2200 Yonge, south of Eglinton) then go to Cineplex **Canada Square**, up the stairs. (See listings at www.cinemaclock.com.)

A few minutes further south on Yonge is the **Mysteriously Yours** theatre (2026 Yonge, www.mysteriouslyyours.com, see p. 84).

North of Eglinton, Yonge is filled with nice stores and restaurants (63) with nice facades (64).

DAVISVILLE

I didn't expect to find a playground so close to this station. To get to pretty **Oriole Park** (65), walk a few minutes west on Chaplin Drive and take the small passageway through the houses (across from Colin Avenue). It includes a wading pool and an intriguing dead tree, still standing.

ST. CLAIR

From St. Clair Avenue, east of the station, turn south on Avoca Avenue. It becomes Rosehill Avenue and that's where you'll see the **Rosehill Reservoir** and reflecting pools like you've never seen! Huge, asymmetrical, with tiny bridges. Quite a sight! There's a playground hidden in the south-east side of this park, not too far from a wading pool.

You can access the majestic ravine of **David A. Balfour Park** (66) from the eastern side of the reservoir (see p. 319).

A few minutes north of St. Clair is the entrance to the **Mount Pleasant Cemetery** (see p. 277).

SUMMERHILL
South of the station, on the east side of Yonge, you'll walk under a viaduct that seems straight from the 19th century (67). If you sit by the windows in the adjacent **Timothy's**, you'll get a great view.

The building sits in the modern **Scrivener Square** (68) near an original fountain with water streams that are sure to catch your kids' attention. Across the street, you'll notice the giant rose adorning the **Rosedale Diner** (1164 Yonge, www. rosedalediner.com). It is not cheap but they have a very charming and rustic back patio.

ROSEDALE
Between this station and **Summerhill**, you'll find high-end home decor stores alternating with restaurants and cafés.

Just across the street is **Ramsdel Park**. You can't see it from Yonge but this park includes a playground (69) and wading pool in a very nice setting.

I enjoyed sitting by the open windows by the terrace and tall trees of **Café Doria** to catch the summer breeze... with a dessert (1094 Yonge, 416-920-5315).

The real French bakery **Patachou** is not to be missed. So many delicious treats to try! It also has a patio in the summer (1120 Yonge, 416-927-1105).

(63) Eglinton

(64) Eglinton

(65) Davisville

(66) St. Clair

(67) Summerhill

(68) Summerhill

(69) Hosedale

(70) Wellesley

(71) College

(72) Dundas

(73) Dundas

(74) Dundas

YONGE/BLOOR
(interchange to GREEN)
See p. 442.

WELLESLEY
The groovy indoor skate-park **Shred Central** (70) is a few minutes from this station. Go west on Wellesley and north into the first back alley (19 St. Nicholas, www.shredcentral.com, see p. 353).

COLLEGE
The **Toronto Police Museum** is just west of Yonge on College (40 College, www.torontopolice.on.ca, see p. 241).

If you walk south, around the large building at the south-west corner of Yonge and College (which includes a **Winners**), you'll reach **College Park** (officially know as **Barbara Ann Scott Park** (71). It features one of the biggest fountains with reflecting pool in the city and turns into an artificial ice rink in the winter!

There's a **Tutti Fruitti** candy store at the corner of Yonge and College (Carlton) and **Carlton** Cineplex, a bit farther (20 Carlton, www.cinemaclock.com). If you push a bit further, east of Jarvis, there's **Allan Gardens** (see p. 276).

DUNDAS
For a full account of all you can find around Dundas and Queen stations, read **Hidden Treasure Stroll** on p. 473.

Yonge-Dundas Square (72) is our own little Time Square. Last time I looked up, there were four screens, three electronic boards and twelve billboards competing for my attention on the buildings framing the square. Music was pumping from **Hard Rock Café**'s speakers.

Following all this action, it is amazing to find Zen **Devonian Square**, also a rink during the winter (73) on Gould, one street north of Dundas, east of Yonge.

Enter the **Eaton Centre** and exit on the west side to discover another oasis, **Trinity Square** (74).

QUEEN
This station also exits into the **Eaton Centre** (see p. 166 and 168).

The **Elgin Theatre** is across the street (see p. 174), and **Canon Theatre** and **Massey Hall** are nearby (www.ticketmaster.ca). **Eggspectation** all-day breakfast is very popular with families (220 Yonge, www.eggspectation.ca).

Check out the gigantic metal sculpture (75) hanging from the ceiling inside the building at the south-east corner of Queen and Yonge.

KING
Go west on King, then walk to the end of Jourdan, the first street to your left to reach **Commerce Court** (76) where there are... elephants to be seen!

Further west on King is the **Toronto Dominion Centre**. Walk inside the round metal walls and tap your feet to hear the special sound effect. Then proceed to the park to meet the cows (77)!

At the risk of making male readers roll their eyes, let's mention there's a **Winners** on Adelaide, one street north of King, west of Yonge.

Walk south on Yonge to **Brookfield Place** (formally named **BCE Place**) to admire the architecture. Even kids will react to the wild arches (78). This is the home of **Richtree Market** restaurant, one of the best places to go with a family.

Kids can stroll around the sixteen food stations without annoying anyone and there's something for every taste (www.richtree.ca).

You will find the **Hockey Hall of Fame** (79) in the lower level of the building (see p. 346).

It will take you the same time to walk to **Brookfield Place** from **Union Station**.

There's more about the attractions east on Front Street (80) in **European Flair Stroll** on p. 476.

UNION

There's an indoor corridor linking Union Station to **Air Canada Centre**, south of the station (see p. 337). Around the building, you'll see many scenes carved into the walls (81). Walk through the centre to its western exit and you'll see poles adorned with stars pointing to the sky.

The **Sony Centre**, formerly **Hummingbird**, is located on the south-east corner of Yonge and Front (www.sonycentre.ca), and the **St. Lawrence Centre** is further east on Front (www. stlc.com).

Read **Stroll around Harbourfront Centre** on p. 26 to see what awaits you by the lake.

In the lower level of the Fairmount Royal York, I noticed **Game Trek**, a great toy store for adults and kids (100 Front West, www. gametrek.ca).

The **CN Tower** (see p. 116) is a 15-minute walk west on Front (or the underground PATH inside of **Union Station**).

Note that you can catch an underground streetcar to **Queens Quay** (follow the signs to Harbourfront). Only the first stop is underground. The streetcar goes to **Harbourfront** and the **CNE** (p. 32).

(75) Queen

(76) King

(77) King

(78) King

(79) King or Union

(80) King or Union

(81) Union

(82) St. Andrews

(83) Osgoode

(84) Osgoode

(85) Osgoode

(86) Osgoode

ST. ANDREWS

If you happen to be around on Wednesday, Thursday or maybe Friday if you're lucky, you'll be able to visit the **48th Highlanders Museum** (82) in the basement of **St. Andrew's Church** (entrance on King, east of Simcoe, www.48thhighlanders. com). This small museum has plenty to offer and volunteers with an encyclopedic memory to walk you through the war memorabilia. The kids will be allowed to try the Highland Regiment's ceremony hat topped with black ostrich feathers. Bring the camera!

To find out what lies beyond the **Roy Thomson Hall** (www.roythomson. com), read **Think Big! Stroll** on p. 466).

OSGOODE

I have walked by the gorgeous iron fences of **Osgoode Hall** (83) for years without realizing it is open to the public!

You've got to see this place (130 Queen West, at the north-east corner of University and Queen, www.osgoodehall.com). The architectural details are breathtaking (84). Kids will fancy the imposing judges' chairs scattered all over.

When you look up, at the north-west corner of the Queen-University intersection, you see the **Canada Life** weather beacon (85). Depending on the weather, its light will either be white, red or green, running up if the temperature is getting warmer, or down if colder. If you go inside the building (330 University), you'll be able to get a card summarizing the codes of the beacon and see a miniature model of the tower (86).

The **Nathan Phillips Square** (87) is just a few minutes east of the station.

ST. PATRICK

The **Textile Museum** is but a few minutes from this station and one of the best little museums in Toronto. Go east on Dundas and turn south on Centre Ave. (55 Centre, www.textilemuseum.ca, see p. 242).

Walk a few minutes west on Dundas and you'll see the funky shape of the **OCAD** on McCaul. Walk around it and you'll discover the great playground of **Grange Park** (88) with large wading pool overlooked by the **Art Gallery of Ontario** (see p. 86).

There are many art supply stores around the OCAD but my favourite is **Aboveground** (74 McCaul, www.abovegroundartsupplies.com).

The food court across the street from the OCAD offers many options. It is lit with skylights and includes inviting marble tables with chairs.

QUEEN'S PARK

This station is just south of the large **Queen's Park** hosting yearly **Word on the Street** book fair (89), among other events (see p. 91).

MUSEUM

This is the station to get to the **Gardiner Museum** (90) (111 Queen's Park, www. gardinermuseum.on.ca, see p. 88) and the **Royal Ontario Museum** (91), its entrance is now on Bloor (www.rom.on.ca, see p. 244).

I like to explore the **University of Toronto** courtyards, entering though the arch of the **Institute of Medieval Studies** south of the **Gardiner** (59 Queen's Park). The layout of the stone buildings gives them the intimate feeling of a European village (92) and many courtyards are enriched with sculptures.

ST. GEORGE
(interchange to GREEN)
See p. 440.

SPADINA
(interchange to GREEN)
Beware! This one can be confusing. There are actually two physical Spadina Stations. Better use St. George if you want to change lines.

There are no attractions of interest to kids north of this station. For a description of the attractions a few minutes south if it, see the GREEN Line **Spadina** Station on p. 440.

DUPONT
It will take you less than 10 minutes to reach **Casa Loma** (93) and enjoy one of their fun special events and shows (www.casaloma. org, see p. 120). Go north on Spadina, then west on Davenport to access the staircase leading to the castle's entrance on Austin Terrace. The **Spadina Museum** is just east of it (285 Spadina, 416-392-6910, see p. 380).

ST. CLAIR WEST
Walk 10 minutes west on St. Clair (going north on Vaughan Rd.) and you reach whimsical year-round ice cream place **Dutch Dream** (94) (78 Vaughan, 416-656-6959).

Stroll 10 minutes east of the station and you get to **Sir Winston Churchill Park** (see p. 369).

If you go east on St. Clair and north on Spadina, it will take you 10 minutes to get to pretty **Suydam Park**. For a feel of upscale Forest Hill, take a few steps down Strathearn by the park to admire the statue of kids (95).

Suydam Park leads to **Relmar Gardens** and a cosy playground. From there, you can access **Cedarvale Park** trails (see p. 340).

(87) Osgoode or Queen

(88) St. Patrick

(89) Queen's Park or Museum

(90) Museum

(91) Museum

(92) Museum

(93) Dupont

(94) St. Clair West

(95) St. Clair West

(96) Eglinton West

(97) Yorkdale

(98) Yorkdale

(99) Yorkdale

(100) Yorkdale

EGLINTON WEST

Walk 10 minutes south of Eglinton on the west side of Strathearn Road and you'll meet the huge **Cedarvale Park** (96) (see p. 340).

GLENCAIRN

There's a nice playground in **Viewmount Park**. Just go east and follow the path southbound.

LAWRENCE WEST

Lawrence Square mall is across from this station (www.lawrencesquare.ca). Walk 10 minutes west on Lawrence to reach one of the **Party Packagers** outlets (770 Lawrence, www.party-packagers.com).

YORKDALE

This station serves **Yorkdale** mall (www.yorkdale.com). Animal lovers will go crazy for the themed-restaurant **Rainforest Café** (97) with automated animals, fish tank and rain storm simulation (www.rainforestcafe.com) and they will enjoy the puppies and kitties at **PJ's Pets** (98) near the food court (www.pjspet.com).

Across Dufferin (facing the Sears, you'll notice the giant telescope on the roof of the cool science store **Efton's** (99), which includes a full floor of toys (3350 Dufferin, www.escience.ca).

Surprisingly, there's a nice playground by Highway 401! Simply follow the paved path east of the station to access **Baycrest Park** (100).

WILSON

Big box stores all over, of no interest to kids.

DOWNSVIEW

The **Downsview Park** (see p. 293) and the **Toronto Aerospace Museum** (see p. 209) located in this area are unfortunately more than 2 km away from this station.

ALPHABETICAL INDEX

LOCATION INDEX (TORONTO)

LOCATION INDEX (OTHER CITIES)

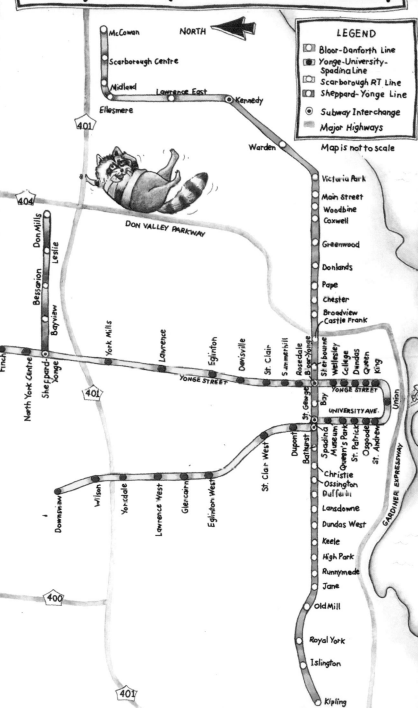

(1) Roy Thomson Hall

(2) Metro Hall

(3) CBC building

(4) Along Front Street

(5) Rogers Centre

THINK BIG!

I mean it!

Whether you have a child enthralled with anything huge or visitors who want to feel how big and bold Toronto really is, this stroll is for you.

I've always loved the fact that from almost every corner of the city, we see the **CN Tower** pointing above the skyline. But as we get closer, there's way more than our trademark tower (and the huge dome of the **Rogers Centre**) to remind us that we are indeed in the biggest city in Canada.

The adventure starts at the edge of the round and shiny structure of the **Roy Thomson Hall** (at the corner of King and Simcoe near St. Andrew Subway Station). At the underground level, you'll discover the large pond (1) simulating a Canadian lake with evergreens and rocks.

Then, walk through the vast paved courtyard between **Roy Thomson Hall** and **Metro Hall** to admire the buildings' architecture and water flowing from a modern sculpture (2). Check the giant arrow and broken pillar inside the building by King.

Across Wellington, on the east side of **CBC** (easy to recognize with the red window frames), you'll see a 25-foot-high aluminum structure shaped like the Scarborough Bluffs. Make sure you enter both **Metro Hall** and the **CBC** building and look up. Their glassed ceilings are quite impressive (3).

On the south facade of **CBC**, along Front Street, you'll notice a very long slab of granite (4). The first time my then 10-year-old boy saw this monument,

commemorating the workers of Ontario who died in the workplace, he read all the engraved "say-it-as-it-is" descriptions of fatal workplace accidents. Here, Joseph Côté died, pinned between tractor scoop and ramp. There, Surinder Mann, was crushed by a 600 lb. slab that shot out of a large press... There's one such plate for each year between 1901 and 1999.

A bit closer to John Street, you can sit by a life-size Glenn Gould on a bronzed bench.

At the foot of John, walk south over the eight train tracks, for a better view of the gigantic sculptures of joyful fans east (5) and west of the **Rogers Centre** (formerly the Sky-Dome). Looking up from the base of the **CN Tower** (6) right next to it will make you dizzy! Take a moment to enjoy the gardens lining the tower.

Further, down the stairs or the ramp adjacent to the **CN Tower**, you'll reach a beautiful fountain filled with a school of sculpted salmon swimming upstream (7).

Take a short walk to the east, on Bremner, for a view of the giant woodpeckers (8) by the south building of the **Metro Convention Centre**.

Nowadays, it seems a prerequisite for any condo project to commission some memorable piece of artwork. If you walk back past the **Rogers Centre**, you'll come across an amazing 40-foot-high stylized boat (9), at the corner of Bremner and Wharf Crescent. There's another one that you can see across Spadina Avenue from the end of Bremner.

If you keep walking

towards the lake, a few minutes down Spadina, read **Stroll around Harbourfront Centre** on p. 26.

Spot is a trendy coffee shop on the south-east corner of Bremner and Wharf serving light meals, pastries and good coffee.

Finally, check the intriguing monument up Wharf Crescent. It is a memorial (10) to commemorate the 17,000 Chinese railroad workers who helped construct the Canadian Pacific Railway. You have to stand at its foot a few steps down to realize how big it is.

Two restaurants my kids love in this area are both located on the same street. There's **Chez Cora**, an all-day breakfast place famous for its huge fruit plates (11) and pancakes (277 Wellington, entrance on Blue Jays Way, www.chezcora.com). Note they also serve lunch but are closed for dinner.

Wayne Gretzky's restaurant, just north of Wellington, does a very good job with the hockey theme, starting with the giant hockey player on the roof and the skates' blades for door handles (99 Blue Jays Way, www.gretzkys.com).

I loved the cozy booths with winter mural. Some walls were covered with Gretzky's interesting memorabilia.

There was food for every taste. Beverages came with miniature hockey sticks we used to improvise a table game. The number 99 was burned on my daughter's burger bun.

For dessert, the kids had a blast sharing a spectacular piece of 12-layer chocolate cake (12). It was the perfect choice to end the **Think Big!** stroll.

This stroll is roughly 1.5 km long.

(6) CN Tower

(7) South of the CN Tower

(8) Metro Convention Centre

(9) Along Bremner Boulevard

(10) Near Wharf Crescent

(11) Chez Cora

(12) Wayne Gretzky's restaurant

(1) On Spadina

(2) On Spadina

(3) Bellevue Square Park

(4) Roach Rama

(5) Shai's

(6) Kensingtons

(7) Kensington Avenue

FUNKY BLOCKS

Streets are for people

That's the name of an organization led by merchants and residents of Kensington which succeeded in reclaiming their streets (regularly and officially) for pedestrians and street celebrations.

The people who live and work around **Kensington Market** are responsible for the funky feel of this neighbourhood (1) (2).

Kensington Market is located west of Spadina. East and west, it is framed by Spadina and Augusta Avenues; north and south, by College and Dundas Streets.

I find it hard to put a label on a place where an **Urban Herbivore** sits next to a **Fat Burrito**, a sushi bar stands by an expresso bar, not too far from a **Hungary Thaï** (go figure) and **Jumbo Empanadas** (all located on Augusta).

You'll find a playground (3) in **Bellevue Square Park** by Augusta Avenue, between Baldwin and Denison Square.

On Baldwin Street, **Roach Rama** braggs they've served potheads since ah... they forget (4). It is located near the **Chocolate Addict**, where you can read the sign "I could give up chocolate but I'm not a quitter". There's a theme right here, isn't there?

Across the street awaits **Shai's** funky restaurant (5). Nearby, **Kensingtons** cute café comes with a couple of swings (seats on ropes) (6) (on the southeast corner of Baldwin and Kensington Avenue).

Most of the stretch on Kensington Avenue, south of St. Andrews, is chock-full of funky vintage stores which young adults really dig (7). If you were a teen in the 70's, chances are you'll recognize some of the stuff in these shops.

Even if you're not a fan of vintage clothes, it's hard not to be charmed by the candy-colour facades of these shops (8).

(8) Kensington Avenue

The best of the rest includes bakeries, cheese store(9), nut importer (10), fruit and vegetable stalls, bargain stores and other choices to discover as you stroll around.

Make sure you check the masks and costumes on display in the windows of the **Red Pepper Spectacle Arts Studio** (160 Baldwin). They are the people responsible for the great **Festival of Lights** taking place every December 21 (see p. 178) when the street is given back to the people.

Street celebrations are really this neighbourhood's forte. Check the calendar of events (and the Patio guide) on their website www.kensington-market.ca.

For more information on the **Pedestrian Sundays** happening on the last sunday of the month from May to October, check www.pskensington.ca. More neighbourhoods are starting to do the same.

There's a municipal parking lot west of Spadina on the south side of Baldwin Street.

Chinatown is at the edge of **Kensington Market** (11), along Spadina and Dundas (see p. 99). The restaurants, stalls (12) (13) and stores (14) are of a different nature and offer a nice complement to the **Funky Blocks** stroll.

This stroll is roughly 2 km long.

(9) On Baldwin

(10) On Augusta

(11) Chinatown on Dundas

(12) Chinatown

(13) Chinatown

(14) Chinatown

COOL FACTOR

Street smart

To get the pulse of the hip Toronto for the young, you must start with Much Music at the corner of John and Queen West, then walk down the lane (literally) to the graffiti "gallery" between Spadina and Portland, enjoying a few cool surprises on the way.

The real utility vehicle popping off the east wall of **Much Music's** building (1) would have logged half a million kilometres since the institution's creation, had its wheels run on the road instead of in the air.

It is not rare to catch a host standing in front of a camera interviewing someone on the sidewalk by the huge bay windows of **Much Music** (2) at the corner of Queen Street West and John.

This corner is buzzing with activity. People coming in and out of the cafés, fashion stores, specialty shops and restaurants crammed around the intersection.

You get a great view of the action from the Thaï restaurant **East** (240 Queen). We had lunch there and were impressed by the fancy presentation of the affordable entrées.

Kids usually love crêpe restaurants so they should love **Café Crêpe**, across the street from **Much Music**. It really has the look of a French bistro, with the large booths and wood. They offer a wide choice of crepes, sweet and salty (246 Queen).

West of John, the independent bookstore **Page Books & Magazines** offers the coolest selection of books of all kinds (256 Queen).

North of Queen, on John, you can't miss the 2-storey-high shocking pink wall of home accessories store **Umbra**, nor the large luminous cube of the **Scotiabank Theatre** (3), south of Queen, facing the **NFB Mediatheque** (see p. 95). Avoid the ludicrous prices of treats at the cinema by visiting **Sugar Mountain** (4) across the street from the cinema. You'll get a little bit more for your money and lots of choice.

Further west on Queen, I always stop by **Fashion Crimes** (322 Queen) to gorge on the glittering decor, filled with exquisite ball gowns and fancy accessories for women and girls. Lace, mousseline, organza, satin, feathers and velvet mixed with glass cabinets and embossed silver high ceiling are all spectacular.

Steve's Music Store, the famous supplier of instruments and music scores, is a favourite stop for musicians (415 Queen).

Across the street is a **Curry's** art supply outlet (344 Queen). You'll also find a **Loomis Art Store** on Spadina, south of Queen (130 Spadina).

At the corner of Spadina and Queen, you've reached the **Fashion District** which used to host factories but still has enough specialized sewing supply shops lined up along Queen (from Spadina to Portland Street) to deserve the name.

There's nothing like adding new buttons from **Fabric & Buttons** (461 Queen) or trims from **Sussman's Glitter Trimmings** (420 Queen) to embellish an outfit. **Sussman's** also sells cheap feather boas and a good choice of appliqués.

(1) Much Music's building

(2) Much Music's host

(3) Scotiabank Theatre

(4) Sugar Mountain

(5) Arton Beads

Looking for beads for a special project? Check **The Beadery** (446 Queen), **Golden Beads** (469 Queen), **Arton Beads** (5) (523 Queen) or **Bling Bling** on Queen (448 Queen).

Even if you don't need ribbons, I suggest you go to **Mokuba** (6) (575 Queen) to admire the art work made out of ribbons displayed on their walls.

Among the many fabric stores, my two favourite for decoration purposes are **Eurofab** (432 Queen) and **Mac Fab** (600 Queen).

There are more businesses with cool facades to discover along the way (7). But the real show is along the back alley just south of Queen Street, from Portland Street to Spadina (8).

This is where you can admire all kinds of graffiti (9) (10) (11). Not often in Toronto can you see this unique urban panorama (12). Beware of its effect on kids! My teenager ended up drawing large graffiti on his bedroom walls (with my permission, I must add).

Note that you'll find an oddity in this urban setting at the western end of the alley, east off Portland: the small green patch of shrubbery of the **Alex Wilson Community Garden** (13).

If you walk down Portland, you'll reach **Sadie's Diner**, north-west of Adelaide (504 Adelaide). This is a quaint place with eclectic furniture that is bigger than it looks, with a cute booth by the window reminiscent ot the 50's. Kids will like the large display of Pez candy dispensers on a wall. I had one of their tasty all-day breakfasts and found it very good (14).

You can get a cheaper bite at the all-day breakfast funky **Java House** (15) (537 Queen at Augusta), where

(6) Mokuba on Queen West

(7) Along Queen West

(8) Just south of Queen West

(9) South of Queen

(10) South of Queen

(11) South of Queen

(12) South of Queen

(13) Community garden

(14) Sadie's Diner

(15) Java House by Augusta

(16) Murmur concept

(17) Fashion District

(18) Around Adelaide and Brant

(19) Brasssai Bistro's courtyard

the kids will find lots of things to look at. They sell the cheapest cup of coffee.

To continue this stroll on a real cool note, arm yourself with a mobile phone and look for the green-ear signs of **Murmur** (16) on certain poles on Spadina, just south of Queen. **Murmur** is a brilliant self-described "documentary oral history project". You can access taped anecdotes told by residents by dialing the phone number and access code on the signs. You'll find them all along Spadina.

Check www.murmurtoronto.ca for more details on the Spadina circuit and the others they've added since the project started in 2003.

On Spadina, south of Queen and past **Le Gourmand Grocer Café** (serving good croissants and pains au chocolat), don't miss the giant measuring tape and thimble (17) by Richmond Street.

If you walk one street south, going west on Adelaide, you'll pass by **Retail Bag Company** (430 Adelaide), a great place for boxes and bags of all kinds and sizes. They even sell cute chinese takeout boxes of different sizes.

There's a playground nearby, at the north-west corner of Adelaide and Brant (18).

Finally, go south on Brant to reach King Street, where shops and restaurants are fancier. See hardware store **Lee Valley** specializing in gardening and woodworking (590 King), or the eye-catching sculpture (19) one can explore from within, in the courtyard of **Brassaii Bistro** (461 King, east of Brant) to see what I mean. Totally cool!

This stroll is roughly 2.5 km long.

Hidden Treasures

Just around the corner

Most people visiting the Eaton Centre are unaware of the hidden treasures surrounding it.

The first time I took my nephews from Montreal to **Yonge-Dundas Square**, they thought they had arrived in New York! There's indeed a buzz to the place, with the line-up of activities at the square (multicultural markets, evening movies, free shows, etc.), the numerous animated billboards and the huge crowd gathering at the crosswalk of Yonge and Dundas.

On a winter night, when more lights are up, it gets even better (1). In the summer, when there's room left by the market's stands (2), you can see water sprays raising from the ground, which kids find very hard to resist.

The square also hosts the **T.O. Tix** box office where you can buy discounted tickets at 12 noon for same-day shows. See www.totix.ca.

You'll find information about the various events taking place at Yonge-Dundas Square on www.ydsquare.ca.

We visited the **Hard Rock Café** (3) just south of the square (couldn't miss that giant guitar!).

It features a large electric guitar collection on the ceiling by the entrance, and showcases genuine rock stars' clothing or instruments, framed on every wall. There was so much to look at and so much read-

(1) Yonge Street

(2) Yonge-Dundas Square

(3) Hard Rock Café

(4) Near Ryerson University

(5) Along Yonge Street

(6) Inside the Eaton Centre

(7) Inside the Eaton Centre

(8) West of the Eaton Centre

(9) West of the Eaton Centre

(10) West of the Eaton Centre

(11) Labyrinth circuit

(12) The Café on the Square

(13) By Nathan Phillips Square

(14) City Hall

ing to do that we decided to stay for a bite. Their menu has something for everyone.

If you have no business around **Ryerson University**, chances are you don't know about the large boulders on the reflecting pond in **Devonian Square** (4). To access it from Yonge Street, you need to turn east on Gould, the first street north of Dundas. This gorgeous pond, lovely in the fall, turns into a skating rink in the winter, where leisure skating alternates with hockey games.

If you like vegetarian food, you'll find the **Commensal** on Elm Street (www.commensal.ca), two streets north of Dundas, west off Yonge. It is the best vegetarian restaurant to go to with kids because of its buffet counter. Customers get two hours of free underground parking at 38 Elm Street when visiting on weekends or holidays.

On our way back, we admired the work of a street artist (5) on Yonge by the **Eaton Centre**.

My favourite way to enjoy the **Eaton Centre** with kids is by taking them for a ride on the glass elevator on the south end of the centre, for a view of the sixty geese art installation suspended from the ceiling (6). Then, midway into the lower floor, we stop by the fountain to see it spraying 20 metres high (7).

When exiting the **Eaton Centre** from the west door by the **Sears** store, you enter another world!

Just turn right and you'll discover a paved courtyard with an old fountain surrounded by stone buildings (8) which are muffling the noise from the street. You'll feel like you're in the public place of a small European village.

The **Trinity Square Café** you'll notice on the back of the church is managed by a non-profit community mental health agency providing opportunity for people to develop work skills. Their food is homemade, tasty and affordable, and is served on weekdays from 9:30 am to 2:30 pm.

It is attached to the pretty **Church of the Holy Trinity** where you can hear music concerts in the summer and the popular **Christmas Story** in the winter (see p. 173).

Straight ahead is the loveliest fountain simulating a stream running towards Bay Street (9) (10), and to the left is a unique labyrinth kids will love to run through (11).

Walking south through the buildings, you will meet Albert Street. Turn west to cross Bay Street in order to reach **Nathan Phillips Square** and the still futuristic **Toronto City Hall** (12).

The **Café On the Square** inside City Hall, with outdoor patio, is open to the public (12) but you might be tempted by the trademark chip trucks parked along Queen (13)!

City Hall still looks as futuristic now as it did when it was built in 1965 (14). No wonder we see it from time to time in science fiction movies.

Don't miss the model of the city with miniature CN Tower (15) inside **City Hall**. There's also a mural made of thousands of nails to look at by the entrance, sure to inspire young artists.

The square's fountain and impressive reflecting pool are decorated with plants in the summer (16) and turned into a rink in the winter (see p. 358).

Two ambitious winter events are hosted at **Nathan Phillips Square**: **Cavalcade of Lights** (see p. 172), when the tall evergreen is lit for the first time of the season, and **WinterCity** (see p. 31), which invariably features a pyrotechnic choreography taking full advantage of the setting.

For a listing of activities taking place at this square, check www.toronto.ca/special_events.

Another great event I like to attend is the huge **Toronto Outdoor Art Exhibition** in July (17) (www.torontooutdoorart.org). The playground (18) west of **City Hall** is open to the public, normally from 12 noon to 3 pm and anytime during daylight hours when not in use by the Hester How Day Care).

The underground parking lot on Queen Street, west of Bay, costs $13 max. on weekdays, $5 in the evenings and $6 on the weekends or holidays.

If you really want to go off the beaten track, try the **Cloud Forest Conservatory** behind The Bay department store on Richmond. It's supposed to feature a small greenhouse but it never was open the many times I visited.

The real attraction is the five-storey outdoor waterfall where 1,800 gallons of water are pouring every minute! There are interconnected stairs and ramps to see it from different points of view.

It also features the *Monument to Construction Workers*: a red steel grid holding a quilt of ornate squares made by the different workers' unions (19). When you look at it, facing south, with the buildings in the background, you get a picture perfect urban landscape.

(15) Inside City Hall

(16) Nathan Phillips Square

(17) Outdoor Art Exhibition

(18) Playground by City Hall

(19) Cloud Forest Conservation

EUROPEAN FLAIR

"Ze reel ting!"

(1) Woofstock

(2) Fountain by Front Street

(3) Solferino on Wellington

(4) Flatiron Building

(5) Flatiron's gift shop on Front

If you've been to a European city, you know the feeling: when everywhere you lay your eyes, everything is man-made and beautiful.

This is the exact feeling I get when I sit by the large fountain in the middle of the public place nestled in the V at the intersection of Front and Wellington. During the **Woofstock** event (see p. 54), this gorgeous fountain is a real dog magnet (1).

From my view point, the 4-storey brick buildings on Front are elegantly framed by the trees of the park (2). Dogs are barking at pigeons.

The kids and I are enjoying a gelato from **Solferino** (3) (38 Wellington St. East), where we always make a point of each choosing differently so we can taste a maximum number of flavours!

On the east part of the park is painted an amazing trompe-l'oeil (4) of windows, on a 5-storey wall. Which ones are real?

This wall is part of the **Gooderham "Flatiron Building"** (which used to belong to the owners of **The Distillery**). It was built in its trademark triangular shape in 1892, ten years prior to the one with the same name in New York!

Hernando's Hideaway (52 Wellington St. E., by the Flatiron building) offers a great colourful decor and mexican food the whole family will enjoy.

Across Front Street, kids will have a blast exploring **Flatiron**'s (5) unique gift shop (51 Front East). (Note that a **Winners** store now sits where the **Timbuktu** store used to be

on Front.)

East of Church Street, on the north side, you'll see a great view of **St. James Cathedral** (6) at the foot of the paved path by the **Dominion** on Front Street.

I often go to this grocery store to get a picnic to eat by the fountain. It includes a huge section of food-to-go (pre-packaged fruit, salads or sandwiches, warm counter, etc.).

The paved path leads to the **Sculpture Garden** and its waterfall, by King Street.

You never know what installation awaits you in this garden! Once, we saw a spectacular web stretched over our head (7). I've seen a Ford painted into a Porshe, a weird sculpture which turned out to be the replica of the tip of the **CN Tower** buried as it could be, hundreds of years from now. Whatever the artwork, make sure you read the artist's rationale. It always adds to the fun.

St. James Cathedral, with the best stained-glass windows (8) in the city (see p. 119), and the adjacent gardens (9) are not to be missed, right across King Street.

The strip along King Street between Church and Berkeley abounds with home decor stores (not any kids' favourite part, but make a mental note to come back with girlfriends!).

I really like **Le petit déjeuner** offering original all-day breakfasts in funky decor with booths (191 King St. E., across from George Brown College). My kids prefer **The George Street Diner**, straight out of the 50's (129 George St., at the corner of Richmond, north of King).